Environment and Ecology

Biodiversity, Climate Change and Disaster Management

For Civil Services Examinations

Sixth Edition

Majid Husain
Former Head, Department of Geography
Jamia Millia Islamia, New Delhi

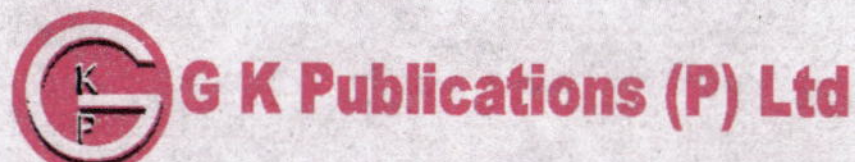

Title : Environment & Ecology for Civil Services Examination (6ed)

Language : English

Author's Name : Majid Husain

Typeset & Published by :

Career Launcher Infrastructure (P) Ltd.

A-45, Mohan Cooperative Industrial Area, Near Mohan Estate Metro Station, New Delhi - 110044

Marketed by :

G.K. Publications (P) Ltd.

Plot No. 9A, Sector-27A, Mathura Road, Faridabad, Haryana-121003

ISBN : 978-93-5681-100-3

Printer's Details : Printed in India, New Delhi.

For product information :
Visit *www.gkpublications.com* or email to *gkp@gkpublications.com*

Preface to the Sixth Edition

To our Esteemed Readers

The sixth, revised and updated edition of this popular and widely read book is before you.

Topics related to Environment & Ecology are urgently discussed and interpreted by various countries and organisations all over the world. This is because environmentalists have been repeatedly warning that a global catastrophe is imminent if we do not address the core issues like global warming, deforestation, population explosion, loss of marine and land habitat etc on a wartime basis.

This comprehensive book on environment and ecology addresses the basic concepts as well the latest developments in a structured and organic manner. Since geography is closely interlinked with ecology, the book also covers the fundamentals of geography, albeit the focus is on ecological issues and developments.

Since its first appearance in 2013, the book has been a valuable resource for students preparing for various competitive examinations especially the UPSC and State Civil Services examinations, Indian Forest Service Examination, etc. The book has undergone repeated revisions and has thus become a trusted, academic resource for students and aspirants of competitive examinations.

This edition has been updated with the latest developments over the past two years through a separate chapter at the end. Also, the data inside the existing book has been updated wherever relevant.

Some of the key topics/updates in this book are:

- National Tiger Conservation Authority (NTCA) Meeting Highlights
- South Asian Consultation on Post-2020 Global Biodiversity Framework
- Water Bird Status Survey 2022
- World Wetlands day 2022
- National Adaptation Fund for Climate Change (NAFCC)
- INCOIS prepares Coastal Vulnerability Index (CVI)
- Multi-Hazard Vulnerability Mapping (MHVM)
- Extended Producers Responsibility (EPR) on Plastic Packaging

- Disaster Management Plan of Ministry of Panchayati Raj
- Rejuvenation of 13 Major Rivers through Forestry
- Programme on Seagrasses
- IPCC Sixth Assessment Report (AR6) on Climate Change
- National Tiger Conservation Authority (NTCA) Meeting
- United Nations Convention to Combat Desertification 23 (UNCCD)
- Purple Revolution
- Steps to promote renewable energy in the country
- Project Cheetah to re-establish the species in its 27 historical range in India
- African Cheetah Introduction Project in India
- 75 Ramsar Sites in 75th Year of Independence
- New Ramsar Sites (added in 2022)
- India's New Climate Action Goals
- India's GHG Emission Sixth Assessment Report (AR6)
- International Solar Alliance (ISA)
- World Heritage Sites in India
- Special Rhino Protection Force (SRPF)
- Forest survey Report (FSR) 2021
- 14th Rhino Census 2022
- Dolphin Census 2022
- Crocodile Census
- Dam Safety Act
- Blue Flag Beaches in India
- Khangchendzonga Biosphere Reserve
- Paris Agreement
- Conference of the Parties (COP26) 2021
- COP26 Goals
- Living Planet Report 2020
- UNFCCC COP 27
- About Mission LiFE 52
- Mangrove Alliance for Climate (MAC)

- Middle East Green Initiative Summit 2022
- Vikramshila Gangetic Dolphin Sanctuary

This revised and updated edition will provide a comprehensive, one-stop resource for aspirants and general readers on this vital topic. Nearly 30% of questions in the UPSC preliminary examination are from the topic of ecology, geography and environment. In the main examination also, there is huge emphasis on the topic.

We wish all aspirants the best in their endeavours.

The Publishers

Preface to the Fifth Edition

To our Esteemed Readers

The **fifth, revised and updated edition** of **Environment & Ecology** by Majid Husain is in your hands.

This book has been thoroughly updated with all the recent developments in the field of ecology and environment.

With each passing day the topic of environment and ecology is gaining importance due to global climatic changes, carbon emissions, deforestation, Arctic and Antarctic melting, heat waves, erratic monsoons etc.

Hence it is imperative that aspirants of UPSC and state public service commission examinations have a holistic understanding of the issues involved.

Moreover, topics of traditional geography like earthquakes, volcanoes, natural resources, mining, energy cycles etc are also closely linked to the present issues of environment, ecology and biodiversity and hence require a conceptual understanding.

Some of the key features of this edition are also follows

- A vastly improved two colour format for better reading and visualisation
- Maps, tables, figures updated wherever relevant
- Updated legislations related to environment and ecology
- Updated list of biosphere reserves and wildlife sanctuaries
- Updated list of World Heritage Sites in India
- India State of Forest Report (ISFR)
- Latest IPCC Report

This revised and updated fifth edition will hopefully provide a complete one-stop resource for aspirants preparing for various competitive examinations. UPSC has given high importance to this topic in the Preliminary Examination. Nearly 30% of questions in the Preliminary Examination (Paper I) come from this topic. In the General Studies Paper III of the main examination, there is huge emphasis on this topic.

Hence we are hopeful and confident that this updated manual would be of immense help in meeting the needs of aspirants.

We wish the readers and all aspirants the best in their endeavours.

The Publishers

Contents

4. BIODIVERSITY 4.1-4.90

CHAPTER

Basic Concepts of Environment and Ecology

ENVIRONMENT

Definition and Types

Environment stands for surroundings. Environment has been defined as **'the sum total of all conditions and influences that affect the development of organisms'** This definition stresses on the totality of environment, implying that every organism including human beings, has its own environment. A number of terms have often been used as synonyms of geographical environment. These synonyms include habitat, ecology, population-ecology, ecosystem, nutrient cycle, biodiversity, geosphere (zone of life) and ecosphere. In other words, environment is an inseparable whole, consisting of mutually interacting systems of physical and biological elements. The physical elements include space, landforms, water-bodies, climate, drainage, rocks, soils, mineral wealth, etc., while the biological elements include man, fauna and flora, including micro-organisms.

Experts recognise the following broad categories of environment:

Categories of Environment

1. **Physical Environment:** The non-living components of environment include landforms, climate, water-bodies, temperature, humidity, air, etc.
2. **Cultural Environment:** The creations of man on the earth's surface are known as cultural environment or man-made environment.
3. **Biological Environment:** The biological environment consists of human beings, fauna, flora and micro-organisms.

4. **Cognitive Environment or Subjective Environment (Mental Map):** The perceived environment is known as cognitive or subjective environment. It differs from person to person. For example, a field has different meanings for a sheepkeeper, vegetable grower, grain farmer, rubber planter, industrialist, and builder of colonies.

Salient Features of Environment

The salient features of environment are given below:

(i) At any given point of time, environment is the sum of biotic and abiotic elements.
(ii) Biodiversity, habitat and energy constitute the three basic components of the structure of an environment.
(iii) Environment changes in space and time.
(iv) It is based on the interactive and functional relationship between biotic and abiotic components.
(v) The working of an environment and its dependent systems are governed by the flow of energy.
(vi) Environment generates its own organic matter which differs in space, from region to region and climate to climate.
(vii) Environment tends to maintain an ecological balance.

Operational Environment

The operational environment includes all those elements, (both cognitive and non-cognitive) which influence the life of an organism. For example, viruses cannot be perceived without the help of precision instruments, yet these do influence human life by causing diseases.

As stated above, the physical environment includes the nature of the living space (land, air, water, natural-vegetation soil, etc.), the chemical constituents and physical properties of the living space, the climate, and the assortment of other organisms present. The cultural environment or the man-made (phenomenal) environment, includes changes and modifications of the natural environment made by man.

The main concern of the study of environment is the spatio-temporal analysis of environment in its totality and in the context of aggregate nature of place. It is basically a systematic study of biotic and abiotic attributes of ecosystems in the context of space and their mutual relationships as well as the spatial implications of such inter-relationships. The fundamental unit of study of environmental geography is the biosphere.

MAN AND ENVIRONMENT

Geography often been defined as the study of man's relationship with the environment. According to Miss Semple—a leading American geographer of the early 20th century, ' *Man is the product of earth or his environment*'. In 1859, Charles Darwin showed that life developed under the selective action of natural forces. It determines scientifically the position of man as a creature adapted to his environment. This approach, for the first time was applied by the German geographer—F. Ratzel in anthropology (Human) and political geography. This scientific position of man resulted into the '*Deterministic School of Thought*'. The point of view of the followers of determinism is that the environment controls the course of human action. In other words, it is the belief that variations in human behaviour around the world can be explained by differences in physical environment and geographical settings.

Deterministic School of Thought

The essence of the deterministic school of thought is that history, culture, customs, traditions, lifestyle, and stage, of economic development of a community or social group are exclusively or largely governed by the natural factors (terrain, topography, climate, drainage, soils, minerals, fauna and flora). The determinists generally consider man as a passive agent on whom the environmental factors are acting and determining his attitude, decision making processes, cultural values, and his approach to life. In other words, the determinists focussed their study on the effects of the physical environment on man, in which nature was taken as active, determining the destiny of man. The lifestyle of man is moulded by natural forces, and the geographer's task is the identification and formulation of the scientific laws which governed the relationship of man and environment.

The deterministic approach was however, criticised for two main reasons. First, it is clear that similar physical environment do not produce same responses. In fact, the Mediterranean civilisation of Greece and Rome did not develop in similar Mediterranean climatic conditions in Australia, South Africa, Chile and California. Similarly, the cultural development of the Thar Desert is different from that of Sahara and Saudi Arabia. Secondly, although environment influences man, but man also influences the environment, and the cause–effect relationship of determinism is too simple to explain.

Looking at these criticisms, the deterministic approach (man is controlled by nature) was rejected. The French geographers under the leadership of Vidal de Lablache stressed that man is a free agent and he is free to choose. Nevertheless, this choice must be made within the limits set by nature. **The approach, in which the emphasis is firmly placed on man rather than on nature, and in which man is seen as an active force, rather than a passive agent, is known as *possibilism*.**

Possibilism as a School of Thought

Possibilism is the philosophy which attempts to explain man and environment relationship in a different way, taking man as an active agent in ecology and environment. This is a belief which asserts that natural environment provides options, the number of which increases as the knowledge and technology of a cultural group develop. The French historian, Febvre, was the first who coined the term possibilism. According to Febvre, the true and only geographical problem is that of utilisation of possibilities. *There are no necessities, but everywhere are possibilities.* Thus the possibilists saw in the natural environment a series of possibilities for human development, but argued that the actual ways in which development took place were related to the culture of the people concerned, except perhaps in regions of extremes, like equatorial regions, deserts, tundra, and the high mountains.

In brief, Possibilism is a view of the environment as a range of opportunities from which the individual may choose. The choice is based on the individual's needs and norms. It grants that the range of choice may be limited by the environment, but allows choices to be made, rather than thinking on deterministic lines. According to possibilists, nature is never more than an advisor.

The real preacher of possibilism was Vidal de Lablache who advocated the philosophy of possibilism. Vidal in his studies minimised the influence of environment on the activities of man. The central idea of Vidal de Lablache's work was the lifestyles (*genres de vie*) that develop in different geographical environments. In his opinion, lifestyles are the products and reflections of culture and civilisation, representing the integrated results of physical, historical and social influences surrounding man's relation to the milieu in a particular place. He tried to explain that the differences between groups are not due to dictates of physical environment, but are the outcomes of variations in attitudes, habits, values, customs, traditions, and ways of life. Variations in attitude and habits create numerous possibilities for human communities. It is this concept which became the basic philosophy of school of possibilism.

This approach of possibilism was also not accepted by many of the geographers. It has been criticised on the ground that 'men can never entirely rid themselves whatever they do, of the hold of their environment'. Taking this into consideration, they utilise their resources more or less according to their culture and traditions. In marginal environments such as the equatorial regions and the tundra regions, man's choices are extremely restricted. In brief, despite numerous possibilities in a given physical setting, man cannot go against the directions laid by the physical environment.

A third approach about man and environment was developed in the form of cultural determinism. **Cultural determinism emphasises the human element, i.e. 'our culture determines the previous nature of the world'.** It has been stressed that human interests, desires, attitudes, prejudices, likes and dislikes aesthetics, and values of the people vary across space and time. The utilisation of resources and modification of environment largely depends on our perceptions and ideas. Advocated mainly by American geographers like Carl Saur and his disciples, this philosophical approach can be summed up as the principle according to which the 'significance to man of the physical and biotic features of his habitat is a function of aspirations, attitude, objectives and technical skill of man himself.' For example, a country richly endowed from the point of view of the hunters, might appear poor to an agricultural people; the importance of coal is not identical for those who can and cannot make use of it. All these truths are self-evident. What is also true, is that technology develops the importance of environment (resources). With the passage of time, technology develops and become more precise and sophisticated.

All the above approaches are considered as the conventional approaches towards the man and environment relationship. These approaches were however inadequate to explain the man and environment relationship. Consequently, after the Second World War, a number of new approaches came in Human Geography to explain the man and environment relationship scientifically. These approaches include, positivism, quantification, radicalism, behaviouralism, humanism, etc.

The objective evaluation of environment is however, a difficult proposition. The technique of trial and error is in progress, and more serious efforts are being made to explain correctly the man and environment (resource) relationship.

Influence of Environment on Man

Men, living both in the rural and urban settings all over the world, are directly and indirectly influenced by the factors of natural environment. Out of these factors, climate is one of the most important factors which has a close bearing on man's economic activities, decision making process about the use of resources and ultimately the culture and lifestyle of people. The direct impact of climate on different races can be seen on the colour of skin, hairs, nose, cheeks, shape of head, stature, physical constitution of body and overall physical appearance. Aristotle believed that peoples of cold climates were brave but deficient in thought, while the peoples of warm climates were thoughtful but without courage. Arab historian, Ibn-Khaldun compared the solidity and lack of vivacity (lively manner) among peoples of cold climates with the passionate nature and ready abandonment to physical pleasures of people in warm zones. This view, that there is some climatically ideal zones, has been developed more recently by Ellsworth Huntington. According to his theory, the climates of areas in moderately cool zones with frequent cyclonic activity and rapid changes of weather, (such as North-Western Europe, New England (USA), and Japan, stimulate individuals to mental activity and nations to world leadership. Some human geographers established a close relationship with the weather conditions and crimes like suicide, rape and murder. Some scholars have also attempted to measure the suitability of an environment of human activity, and his level of comfort and discomfort.

Man can modify the effect of weather and climate by creating artificial conditions. However, despite advancements in science and technology, man is still closely dependent on the physical environment for all his material needs (food, clothing and shelter). The nature of this dependence, however, varies from people to people and region to region. The source of food and raw materials, however, remains the same for all groups. In fact, more than 50 per cent of the labour force of the world is engaged in the primary economic activities (agriculture, fishing, forestry, and mining), upon which the physical environment has great influence.

Impact of Man on the Environment

Environmental change is a continual process. It has been in operation since the Earth came into existence about 4.6 billion years ago. Since the origin of the Earth, the dynamic systems of energy and material have operated on a global scale to bring about gradual and sometimes catastrophic transformations in the atmosphere, hydrosphere, lithosphere, and biosphere. For most of the Earth's history, the agents of change have been the natural forces, like plate tectonics, volcanoes, earthquakes, cyclones, climatic change, and natural elements of wind, ice, water, plants and animals. All these forces have interacted to produce dynamic ecosystems that both control and are controlled by each other. About four or five million years ago, however, a new agent of change emerged in the form of*hominids* (ancestor of ape) culminating in the evolution of Homo sapiens or modern man. Man, in fact, is considered by many to be the most powerful agent of environmental change.

Man is no longer the product of his physical environment, he is also its transformer and creator of his surroundings. In fact, human beings have been an ecological dominant since their emergence on the Earth. Man in other words, has been interacting with his environment right from the primeval stage of human development and continues to do so with even greater vigour in this age of space technology. With the advancement in science and technology, the frontiers of knowledge have expanded beyond the cosmic space and the environment of the Earth has been transformed beyond recognition. People in their increasing numbers and technological skills have placed their imprints upon the natural landscape thereby 'transforming the natural surroundings to conform to their needs. In some instances, such as that of mega-cities, conurbations, and modern towns on land and seas, the human imprints may be so complete that the original landscape of nature has been totally wiped away and replaced by man-made artificial and cultural environment.

The effect of the environment on man is modified, in part, by the way the environment is perceived, and human geographers distinguish this – the subjective environment – from the objective environment (the real world as it is). The objective environment is of less importance to the individual than his or her perceived image of it. A division may also be made between the built environment and the social environment which is made up of the various fields of economic, social, and political interactions. In many ways the distinction of environment into physical and cultural environment is false, since the activities take place within the physical environment, and the physical environment is considerably affected by these activities.

Modern environmental problems call for geographers to examine relations among Earth (environment/resources), society, and cultures throughout space and time.

Critical environmental concerns that are integral to contemporary Physical Geography include:

(i) Human induced global warming.

(ii) Global warming and climatic change.

(iii) Global ozone depletion in the upper atmosphere that allows increasing amounts of ultraviolet radiation to reach Earth's surface.

(iv) Worsening of air pollution, particularly in metropolitan areas.

(v) Identification of natural hazards that threaten society, such as earthquakes, tsunamis, volcanoes, hurricanes, typhoons, surge, landslides, drought, and floods.

(vi) Deliberate destruction of Earth's forests.

(vii) Increasing losses of plant and animal diversity as their habitats disappear.

(viii) Spatial analysis of disasters such as the 1986 Chernobyl nuclear disaster and the Tohoku earthquake and Fukushima Daiichi nuclear disaster of Japan (March 11, 2011).

(ix) Reduction in biodiversity and its conservation.

(x) Judicious utilisation of resources and sustainable development.

(xi) Accounting for natural resources as environmental assets on national economic balance sheets.

(xii) Equitable benefits from biodiversity to all sections of the society.

All these contemporary issues have been covered in this book.

ATMOSPHERE

The atmosphere is the lower layer surrounding the Earth, with an average composition, by volume of 78% nitrogen, 21% oxygen, 0.934% argon, 0.03% carbon dioxide, and traces of rare gases *(Fig.1.1)*. This surprisingly uniform composition is achieved by convection in the troposphere and by diffusion above it, especially above 100 km, where diffusion is rapid in the thin atmosphere, and stirring is weak. Also present are atmospheric moisture, ammonia, ozone, and salts and solid particles. The atmosphere is commonly divided into the troposphere, the stratosphere, the mesosphere, ionosphere, and thermosphere.

Dirunion of Atmosphere

The modern atmosphere is a gaseous mixture of ancient origin (Precambrian Period). The principal substance of this atmosphere is air, the medium of life as well as a major industrial and chemical raw material. Air is a simple additive mixture of gases that is naturally odourless, colourless, tasteless, and formless, blended so thoroughly that it behaves as if were a single gas.

On the basis of composition of gases the atmosphere may be divided into:

(i) Heterosphere: The term heterosphere indicates that the gases in this part of the atmosphere are not evenly mixed, a condition quite different from the blended gases that we breathe closer to Earth in the atmosphere. Gases in the heterosphere are distributed in distinct layers, sorted by gravity, with the lightest elements (hydrogen and helium) at the margin of outer space, and heavier elements (oxygen, nitrogen) towards the Earth.

The heterosphere begins at around 80 km altitude and extends outward some 10,000 km. However, for practical pursoses, most of the meteorologists consider the top of the atmosphere at around 480 km, the same altitude we use for measuring the solar constant. Above 480 km, the atmosphere is rarified (nearly a vacuum) and is called the exosphere, which means 'outer sphere'. Exosphere contains individual atoms of the light gases, viz. hydrogen and helium, weakly bonded by gravity.

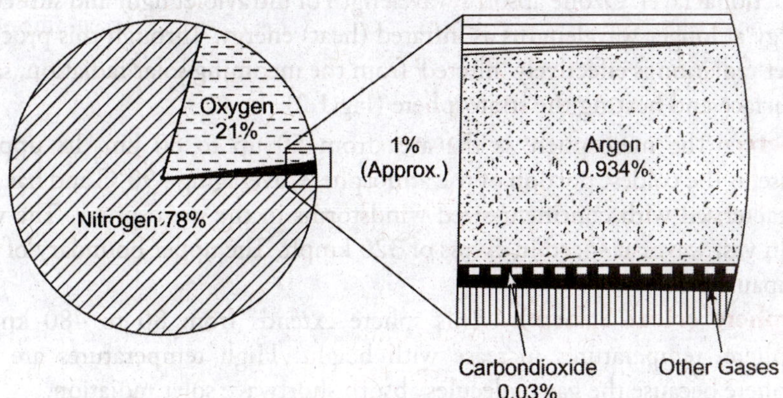

Fig. 1.1 Components of Lower Atmosphere

(ii) Homosphere: Below the heterosphere is the second compositional region of the atmosphere, which extends from the sea-level up to an altitude of 80 km. Even though the atmosphere rapidly decreases in density with increasing altitude, the blend of gases is nearly uniform throughout the homosphere. The only exceptions are the concentration of ozone (O_3) in the ozone layer from 19–50 km, and the variations in water vapour and pollutants in the lowest portion of the atmosphere near the Earth's surface.

The stable mixture of gases throughout the homosphere has evolved slowly. The present proportion of gases in the homosphere was attained approximately 600 million years ago.

Structure of the Atmosphere

For the purpose of systematic study, on the basis of temperature and lapse rate, the atmosphere may be classified under the following layers:

(i) Troposphere, (ii) Stratosphere, (iii) Mesosphere, (iv) Exosphere

1. **Troposphere:** The lowest layer of the atmosphere is known as troposphere. It is the home of biospheric layer that supports life on Earth. Approximately 90% of the total mass of the atmosphere and the bulk of all water vapour, clouds, weather, and air pollution are contained within the troposphere. The tropopause is the upper limit which is defined by an average temperature of –57°C, but its exact elevation varies with the season, latitude, surface temperatures and pressure. Near the equator, because of intense heating from below, the tropopause (upper limit of troposphere) occurs at 18 km; in the middle latitudes, it occurs at 13 km and at the North and South Poles it is only 8 km or less above Earth's surface. In the troposphere, temperatures

decrease with increasing altitude at an average rate of 6.4°C per km which is known as the normal lapse rate. In terms of temperature the upper limit of troposphere is –57°C*(Fig.1.2)* .

2. **Stratosphere and Ozonosphere:** A layer of the Earth's atmosphere, above the troposphere, extends from about 20 to 50 kms above the sea level. Temperature increases throughout the layer of stratosphere. The heat source is the other functional layer, called the ozonosphere, or ozone layer. Ozone is a highly reactive oxygen molecule made up of three oxygen atoms (O3) instead of the usual two (O2) that make up most of oxygen gas. The ozonosphere is also known as the lower functional layer. Ozone absorbs wavelength of ultraviolet light and subsequently eradicates that energy at longer wavelengths as infrared (heat) energy. Through this process, most harmful ultraviolet radiation is effectively 'filtered' from the incoming solar radiation, safeguarding life at Earth's surface and heating the stratosphere (Fig.1.2).
3. **Mesosphere:** The mesosphere is the area from 50 up to 80 km. Its upper boundary, the mesopause, is the coldest portion of the atmosphere, averaging –90°C and has very low pressure. It is characterised with continent-sized windstorms in the mesosphere. The very rarefied air is moving in vast waves at speed in excess of 320 kmph. The upper boundary of this layer is called the mesopause.
4. **Thermosphere (Heat Sphere):** This sphere extends from 80 to 480 kms in altitude. In thermosphere, temperatures increase with height. High temperatures are generated in the thermosphere because the gas molecules absorb shortwave solar radiation.

The temperature curve in*Fig. 1.2* shows that temperature rises sharply in the thermosphere, up to 1200°C and higher. Despite such high temperatures, the thermosphere is not 'hot' in the way one might expect. Temperature and heat are two different things. The intense solar radiation in this portion of the atmosphere excites individual molecules and atoms (principally nitrogen and oxygen). This kinetic energy, the energy of motion, is the vibrational energy that we measure, stated as temperature. However, the density of the molecules is so low that little actual heat is produced (heat is the quantity of thermal energy). Moreover, the air pressure is extremely low. Heating in the lower atmosphere near Earth's surface is different because the greater number of molecules in the denser atmosphere transmit their kinetic energy as sensible heat, meaning that can sense it.

Ionosphere Ionosphere is the lower part of the thermosphere. The atmosphere has two functional layers, so called because both function to filter harmful wavelengths of solar radiation, protecting Earth's surface from bombardment in any significant quantity. The upper functional layer, the Ionosphere lies above 50 km which coincides with the thermosphere. It is composed of atoms that acquired electrical charges when they absorbed cosmic rays, gamma rays, X-rays, and shorter wavelengths of ultraviolet radiation. These charged atoms are called ions, giving the ionosphere its name. Radiation bombards the ionosphere constantly, producing a constant flux (flow) of electrons and charged atoms.

THE FOUR SPHERES OF THE EARTH

Earth's surface is where four open systems interface and interact*(Fig.1.3)* . It may be seen from*Fig. 1.3* that the three abiotic (non-living) systems are overlapping to form the realm of biotic (living) system. The abiotic spheres are the**atmosphere** ,**hydrosphere** , and**lithosphere** . The biotic sphere is called the biosphere. Because these four spheres are not independent units in nature, their boundaries must be understood as transitional rather than sharp delimitations.

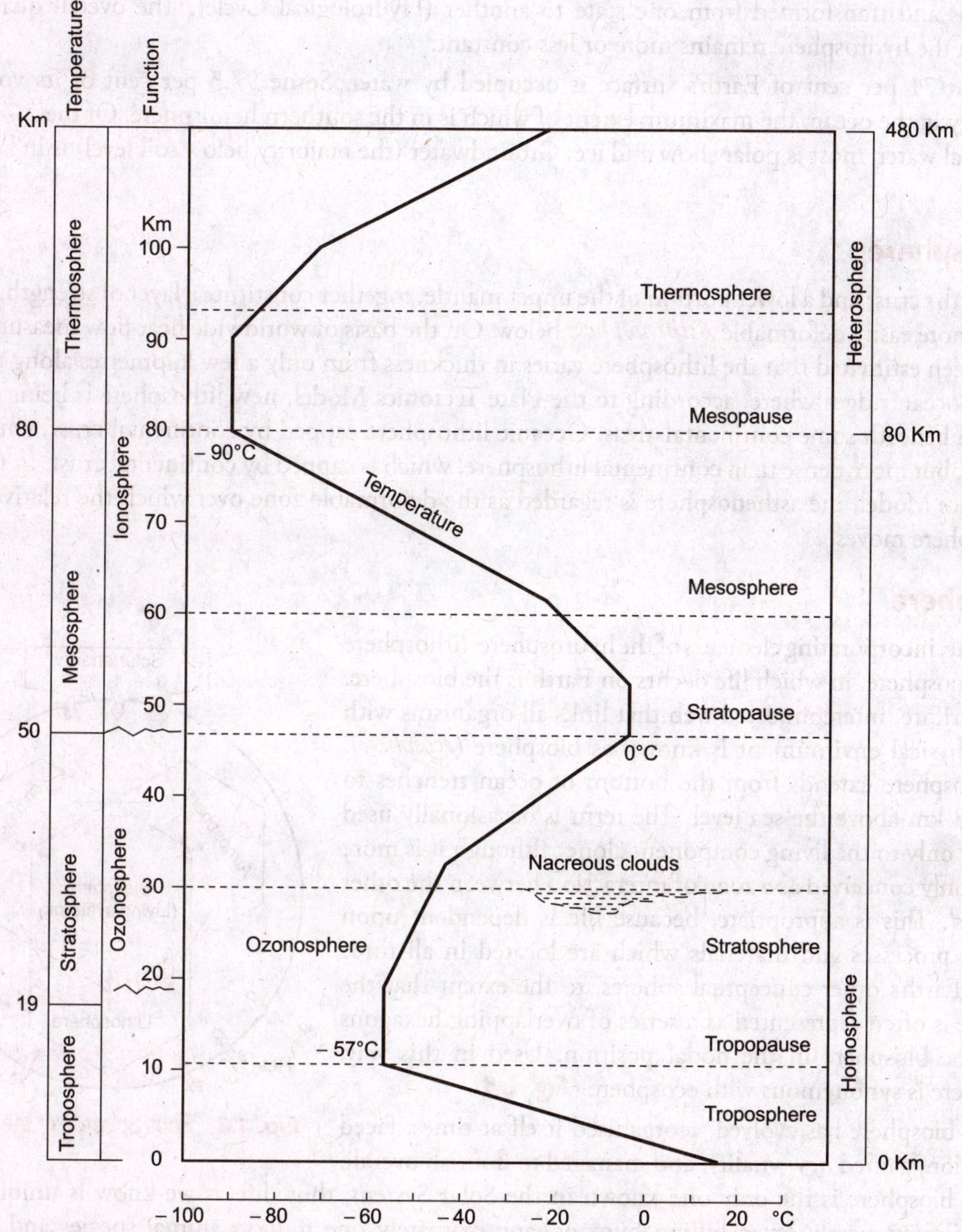

Fig. 1.2 Vertical Structure of the Atmosphere

Atmosphere (discussed above)

Hydrosphere

The Earth's water, which exists in both fresh and saline form and may occur in a liquid, solid or gaseous state. Land, sea and air each contribute to the total volume of water, which is conveyed between various locations and transformed from one state to another (Hydrological Cycle). The overall quantity of water in the hydrosphere remains more or less constant.

About 71 per cent of Earth's surface is occupied by water. Some 97.3 per cent of its volume is currently in the ocean, the maximum extent of which is in the southern hemisphere. Of the 2.7 percent terrestrial water, most is polar snow and ice. Groundwater (the majority below soil level) is in lakes and rivers.

Lithosphere

The Earth's crust and a lower portion of the upper mantle, together constitute a layer of strength, relative to the more easily deformable *Asthenosphere* below. On the basis of worldwide heat flow measurements, it has been estimated that the lithosphere varies in thickness from only a few kilometres along the crest of mid-ocean ridges where, according to the Plate Tectonics Model, new lithosphere is being created, 300 km beneath some continental areas. Oceanic lithosphere capped by continental crust, tends to be thinner, but more dense than continental lithosphere, which is capped by continental crust. In the Plate Tectonics Model, the asthenosphere is regarded as the deformable zone over which the relatively rigid Lithosphere moves.

Biosphere

The zone, incorporating elements of the hydrosphere, lithosphere and atmosphere, in which life occurs on Earth is the biosphere. The intricate, interconnected web that links all organisms with their physical environment is known as biosphere (*ecosphere*). The biosphere extends from the bottom of ocean trenches to about 8 km above the sea level. The term is occasionally used to refer only to the living component alone, although it is more commonly conceived as a zone of interaction between the other 'spheres'. This is appropriate, because life is dependent upon energy, processes and materials which are located in all three of the Earth's other conceptual spheres, to the extent that the scheme is often represented as a series of overlapping hexagons with the biosphere in the nodal position. Used in this way, biosphere is synonymous with ecosphere ***(Fig. 1.3)***.

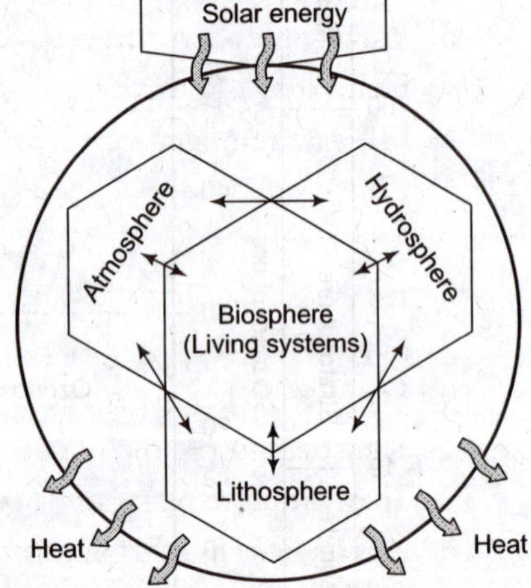

Fig. 1.3 Four Spheres of the Earth

The biosphere has evolved, reorganised itself at times, faced extinction, gained new vitality, and managed to flourish overall. Earth's biosphere is the only one known in the Solar System; thus, life as we know is unique to the Earth. Today, nearly seven billion humans, approximately one million animal species and 355,000 known plant species, depend on the air, water and land of the planet Earth.

ECOLOGY AND ECOSYSTEM

Ecology

The scientific study of the interactions between organisms and their environment is known as ecology.

Ecology examines the relationships between organisms belonging to both the same and different taxonomic groups, and between those organisms and their physical environment. The word was first used by Ernst Haeckel in 1869, but many of its concepts are much more recent. The ecosystem concept is central to an understanding of the nature of ecological relationships and dates from the 1935s works of Arthur Tansley. Still other associated concepts, such as those developed in relation to population ecology, came much later, so that ecology can be considered as a relatively new scientific discipline.

Ecosystem

A self-regulating association of living world such as plants, animals, and microorganisms, with their non-living world such as physical and chemical environment is known as ecosystem. This term was introduced by A.G. Tansley in 1935. In 1969, Odum defined ecology as '*the study of structure and function of nature*'.

Social Relevance of Ecosystems Ecosystems have great social relevance. The resilience characteristics of ecosystems are imperative for the survival of mankind and sustainability of ecology and environment.

The direct and indirect benefits to the society from the ecosystems are given below:

1. Ecosystems provide food, fodder, dry fruits, honey, fiber, fuel-wood, pulp, timber and manure.
2. Ecosystems provide raw material to agro-based and forest based industries.
3. Provide herbal medicinal plants.
4. Helps in the controlling of floods.
5. Mitigate temperature extremes and droughts.
6. Check soil erosion.
7. Add humus content in the soil and enhance soil fertility.
8. Healthy ecosystems help in the purification of water, soils and air.
9. Ecosystems help in the control of pests and diseases.
10. Ecosystems help in maintaining the resilience characteristics of the ecosystems.
11. They help in the maintenance of genetic resources.
12. They promote recreation and eco-tourism.
13. Forests have educational and research values.
14. Forests have cultural and religious values.
15. Conserve natural beauty, cultural diversity and aesthetic.

BASIC ECOLOGICAL TERMS

Habitat

The overall environment, but more often specifically the physical environment in which organisms live.

Ecological Transition

This concept was developed by Bennett in 1976, which concerns the reduction in a farmer's dependence on his land that often accompanies his incorporation into the cash economy. The economic opportunities of industry or urban life gradually provide viable social alternatives to rural life, and individual farmers can afford to be less concerned about the possibility of long-term decline in the productivity of their land. Over-cultivation may result from this reduced ecological sensitivity in rural population.

Ecological Explosion

Ecological events marked by an enormous increase in number of some kind or kinds or organism. The term was defined by Elton in 1958 and was employed to indicate the bursting out from control of populations that were previously held in restraint by other forces. Classic examples of such explosions are found in the epidemics of infectious viruses and bacteria, such as influenza and bubonic plague, etc.

Many organisms subject to such population outbursts are serious agricultural pests, such as the desert locust (*Schistoverca gregaria*). The causes of the devastating plagues appear to be related to weather conditions, particularly to moisture, operating in and through the process of phase transformation, in which the locusts exhibit polymorphism, changing from solitary (*solitaria*) forms to gregarious or swarming forms (*gregaria*). The causes of many ecological explosions remain far from clear, and it is interesting to observe that many species which are rare in their normal habitat, experience such bursts of population when spread by man to new areas and environment.

Niche

(French *nicher*, to nest) : Niche refers to the function, or occupation, of a life form within a given community. It is the way an organism obtains and sustains the physical, chemical, and biological factors it needs to survive. An individual species must satisfy several aspects in its niche. Among these are a habitat niche, a trophic (food) niche, and a reproductive niche. For example, *Goraiya* bird occurs throughout India in habitats of pastures, meadows and marsh where they nest. Their trophic niche is weed seeds and cultivated seed crops throughout the year, adding insects to their diet during the nesting season.

Some species have symbiotic relationships, an arrangement that mutually benefits and sustains each organism. For example, lichen (pronounced "liken") is made up of algae and fungi living together. The algae is the producer and food source, and the fungus provides structure and physical support. Their mutually beneficial relationship (mutualism) allows the two to occupy a niche in which neither could survive alone. *An ecological niche consists of*:

(i) Habitat– where the species live.
(ii) Food niche – what a species eats and decomposes and what species it competes with.
(iii) Reproductive niche – how and when it reproduces.
(iv) Physical and chemical niche – temperature, moisture, and landform.
(v) Geo-ecological niche– topography, terrain, slope, and soils etc.

Ecotone

Ecotone is a boundary transition zone between adjoining ecosystems that may vary in width and represent areas of tension, as similar species of plants and animals compete for resources. In other words, ecotone is the transition on the ground between two plant communities. It may be a broad zone and reflect a gradual blending of two communities, or it may be approximated by sharp boundary line. It may coincide with changes in physical environmental conditions or be dependent on plant interactions, especially competition, which can produce sharp community boundaries even where environmental gradients are gentle. It is also used to denote a mosaic or inter-digitting zone between two more homogeneous vegetation units. They have special significance for mobile animals through edge effects (such as the availability of more than one set of *habitat* within a short distance). The plants and animals that occur in the ecotone are known as edge species. In a terrestrial ecosystem, edge effect is significant in birds. For example, the density of birds is greater in the mixed habitat of the ecotone between the forest and the desert.

Ecotope

The physical environment of a biotic community (biocoenosis). It includes those aspects of the physical environment that are influences on, or are influenced by a biocoenosis. Together with its biocoenosis, the ecotope forms an integral part of biogeoecoenosis. There are two major component parts of the ecotope: the effective atmospheric environment (climatop) and the soil (edaphotope).

Biostasy

A term that was applied by Erhart in 1956 to periods of soil formation, with rhexistasy referring to phases of denudation. In periods of biostasy, there is normal vegetation, while in phases of rhexistasy there is dying out or lack of vegetation, as a result of soil erosion resulting from climatic changes, tectonic displacement, etc.

Biota

The entire complement of species of organisms, plants and animals, found within a given region are known as biota.

Biotope

The habitat of a community, or a micro-habitat with a biocoenosis. In the first sense the word as synonymous with ecotope, the effective physical environment of a biocenosis or biotic community. In the second sense, it refers to a small, relatively uniform habitat within the more complex community, e.g. although a forest community occupies its own habitat, each layer of stratum within the forest may be regarded as a separate biotope (see also niche).

Community

A convenient biotic subdivision within an ecosystem in known as a community. It is formed by interactions among population of living animals and plants.

ECOLOGICAL PRINCIPLES

The main objective of the study of ecology is to examine the utilisation of ecological resources and to keep them in a healthy condition for the future generations. There are certain principles which govern the evolution and distribution of plants and animals, extinction of species, biological succession, consumption and transfer of energy in different components of biological communities, cycling and recycling of organic and inorganic substances through various bio-geo-chemical cycles, life cycle of organisms, interactions and inter-relationships among the organisms and between organisms and physical environment, etc.

The basic ecological principles may be summarised as under:

1. Ecosystem is the fundamental unit of ecological study. Ecosystem consists of both biotic and abiotic components. Ecosystems are well structured and organised units through biotic and abiotic components.
2. Physical and biological processes follow the principles of uniformatism. It is the theory that geologic and ecological events are caused by natural processes, many of which are operating in the present time.
3. All living organisms and physical environment are mutually reactive.
4. Ecosystem functions through the input of energy, mainly solar radiation which is trapped by green plants (primary producers). Thus, the solar radiation is the main driving force of an ecosystem. The energy flow and pattern are governed by the following first and second laws of thermodynamics:

   Law I: In any system of constant mass, energy is neither created nor destroyed but it can be transformed from one type to another type. In other words, the energy inflow or input in a system is balanced by energy outflow.

   Law II: When work is done, energy is dissipated and the work is done when one form of energy is transformed into another form.
5. The circulation of energy in the biosphere is unidirectional. There is increase in the relative loss of energy through respiration with increasing trophic levels.
6. Circulation of matter in the biosphere is accomplished through cyclic pathways, e.g. through geo-biological cycles. The materials are cycled in such a way that their total mass remains almost constant.
7. Ecosystem productivity refers to the rate of growth of organic matter per unit time per unit area by autotrophs (primary producers—plants).
8. There is inbuilt self-regulatory mechanism known as homeostatic mechanism in natural ecosystem. Any change brought in the natural ecosystem is counterbalanced by this mechanism and ecosystem and ecological stability is re-established.
9. If the changes brought by external factors are so immense that they exceed the resilience of ecosystem stability, adjustment of ecosystem becomes unstable and several environmental problems are created.
10. There is successional development of plant community in a habitat of given environmental conditions. There is a positive correlation between solar radiation and primary ecological productivity.
11. The transitional stages of sequential changes from one vegetation community to an other vegetation community are called *sere* which is complete when the succession of vegetation community after passing through different phases culminates into equilibrium condition. The vegetation community developed at the end of succession is called *climax vegetation, climax community or climatic climax.*

12. Man being an active agent of environment, modifies the ecosystem.
13. Increase in the diversity of food-webs promotes ecosystem stability and ecological balance.
14. The ultimate goal of ecological study is to preserve ecological resources by maintaining the ecological diversity and ecosystem stability.
15. Biodiversity conservation is possible by judicious utilisation of resources.

PHOTOSYNTHESIS

The process of joining of carbon dioxide and oxygen in plants, under the influence of certain wavelengths of visible light, releases oxygen and produces energy–rich organic material (sugars and starches). The process uses carbon dioxide and water as raw materials and yields glucose and oxygen.

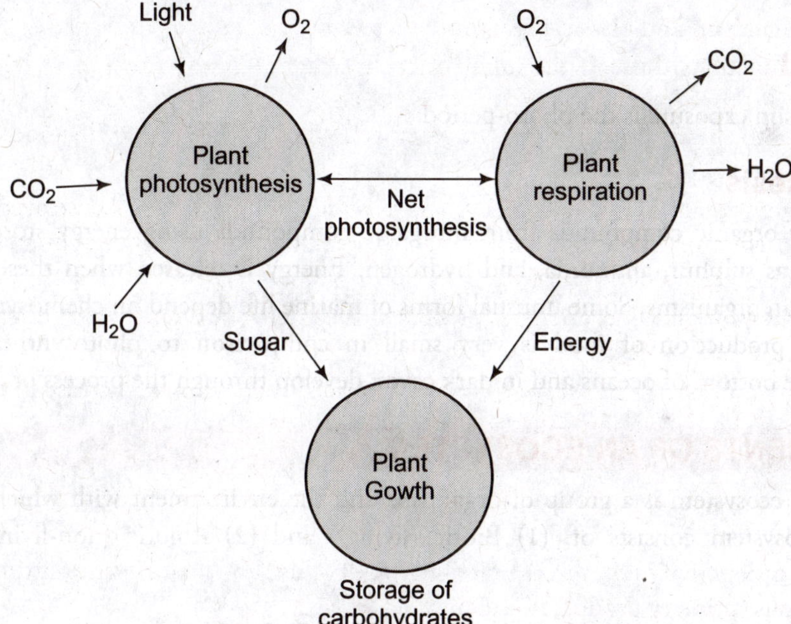

Fig. 1.4 The Balance between Photosynthesis and Respiration Determines Plant Growth (after R.W. Christopherson, p.486).

Photosynthesis and Respiration

Under the influence of certain wavelengths of visible light, photosynthesis unite carbon dioxide and oxygen (derived from water in the plant). The process releases oxygen and produces energy-rich organic material. The term is descriptive: *photo* refers to sunlight, and *synthesis* describes the reaction of materials within plant leaves.

The largest concentration of light responsive, photosynthetic cells rests below the upper layers of the leaf. These are *chloroplasts*, and within each resides a green, light sensitive pigment called *chlorophyll*. Within this pigment, light stimulates photochemistry. Competition for light is a dominant factor in the formation of plant communities. This competition is expressed in their height, orientation, and structure.

Sun is the ultimate source of energy. Sun produces enormous quantities of energy – some in the form of visible light, a tiny portion of which strikes the Earth. Only about one part in 2000 of the light that reaches the Earth's surface is captured by organisms, but that '*small*' input of energy powers all the growth of living things. Light energy from the Sun is trapped by chlorophyll, in organisms called producers (certain bacteria, algae, and green plants) and changed into chemical energy. The chemical energy is used to build simple carbohydrates and other organic molecular-food which are then used by the plant itself or are eaten by animals (or other organisms) called consumers. Because light energy is used to synthesise molecule-rich stored energy, the process, called photosynthesis is used for growth, repair, movement, reproduction, and the other functions of organisms. The metabolism of food eventually produces waste heat, which flows away from the Earth into the coldness of space (***Fig. 1.4***).

Photo-period

The duration of sun exposure is the photo-period.

Chemosynthesis

The synthesis of organic compounds from inorganic compounds using energy stored in inorganic substances such as sulphur, ammonia, and hydrogen. Energy is released when these substances are oxidised by certain organisms. Some unusual forms of marine life depend on chemosynthesis. Overall, chemosynthetic production of food is very small in comparison to photosynthetic production. Organisms at the bottom of oceans and in dark caves, develop through the process of chemosynthesis.

COMPONENTS OF AN ECOSYSTEM

As stated above, ecosystem is a group of organisms and the environment with which the organisms interact. An ecosystem consists of: (1) Biotic (living), and (2) Abiotic (non-living) components (***Fig. 1.5***).

1. Biotic (Living) Components

These include living organisms such as plants, animals, and microorganisms. The biotic components of an ecosystem consist of:

(a) **Producers (Plants) or autotrophs:** Usually plants that are capable of photosynthesis are known as the producers or autotrophs. Producers also include microorganisms such as bacteria near ocean vents that are capable of chemosynthesis (***Fig. 1.5***).

(b) **Consumers or heterotrophs:** These include animals which can be primary consumers (herbivores) or secondary or tertiary consumers (carnivores and omnivores).

(c) **Decomposers or detritus:** Bacteria, fungi and insects which degrade and decompose organic matter of all types and restore nutrients to the environment are known as decomposers or detritus. The producers will then consume the nutrients, thus completing the organic cycle ***(Fig. 1.5).***

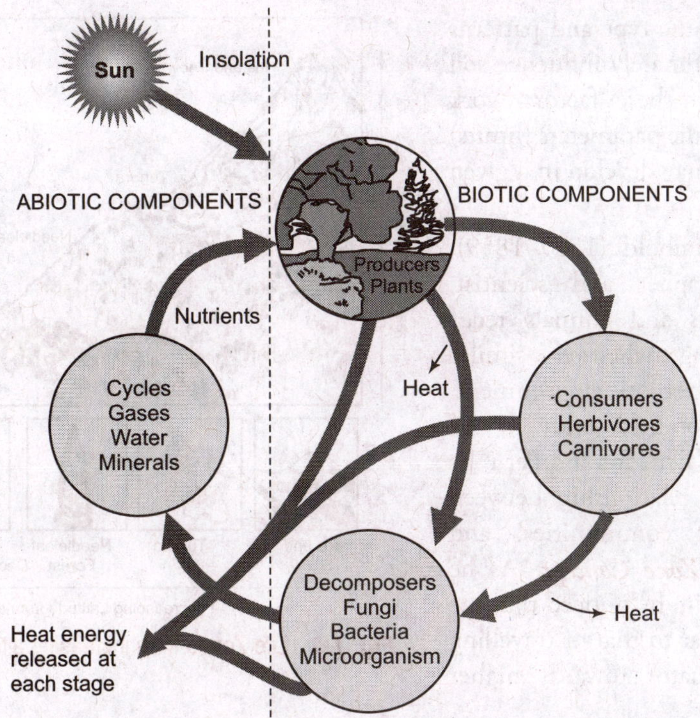

Fig. 1.5 Abiotic and Biotic Components of Ecosystem

2. Abiotic (Non-living) Components

Abiotic components include climate (such as temperature, light, humidity, precipitation, gases, wind, etc.) water, sea-waves, soil, pH, salinity, substratum, minerals, topography, and habitat. Critical in each ecosystem is the flow of energy and the cycling of nutrients and water. Non-living (abiotic) components set the stage for ecosystem operation ***(Fig. 1.5)***.

Light, Temperature, Water and Climate The pattern of solar energy reception is crucial in both terrestrial and aquatic ecosystems. Solar energy enters an ecosystem by way of photosynthesis, with heat dissipated from the system at many points. The duration of sun exposure is the photoperiod. Along the equator, days are almost 12 hours in length throughout the year; however, with increasing distance from the equator, seasonal effects become pronounced on the duration of daylight. Plants have adapted their flowering and seed formation and germination to seasonal changes in insolation (solar incoming radiation).

Temperatures determine the rates at which chemical reactions proceed. Significant temperature factors are seasonal variation, duration and pattern of minimum and maximum temperatures and average temperature.

Operation of hydrological cycle and water availability depend on precipitation/evaporation rates and their seasonal distribution. Water quality is essential with regard to its mineral content, salinity, and levels of pollution and toxicity. Also, daily weather patterns over time create regional climates, which in turn affect the type and patterns of vegetation and ultimately influence soil development. All of these factors work together to establish the parameters (limits) for ecosystems that may develop in a given location.

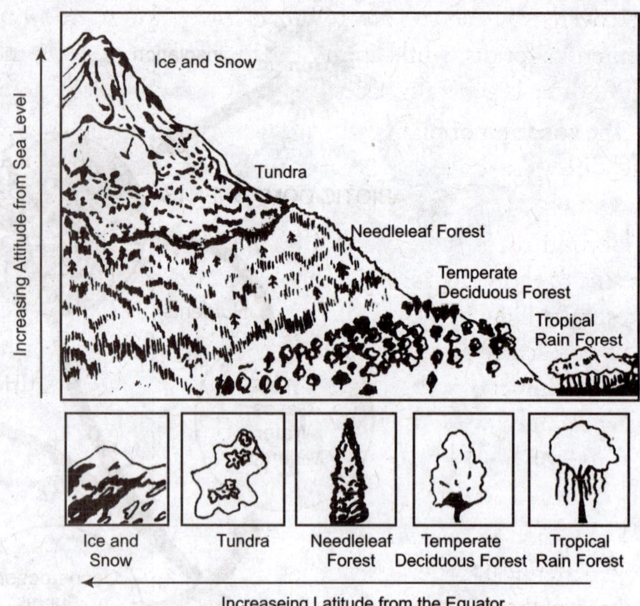

Fig. 1.6 **Life Zones with increasing altitude and latitude**

Alexander von Humboldt (1769–1859), an explorer, geographer and scientist, deduced that plants and animals recur in related grouping wherever similar conditions occur in the biotic environment. After several years of field study in the Andes Mountains of Ecuador and Peru, he described a distinct relationship between latitude and plant communities, and developed the ***Life Zone Concept***. As he climbed the mountain, he noticed that the experience was similar to that of travelling away from the equator towards higher latitudes ***(Fig. 1.6)***.

The vertical zonation of the Himalayas has been given in ***Fig. 1.7***. It may be observed from ***Fig. 1.7*** that at the foothills of Siwaliks, are the subtropical mixed deciduous forest, the Lesser Himalayas

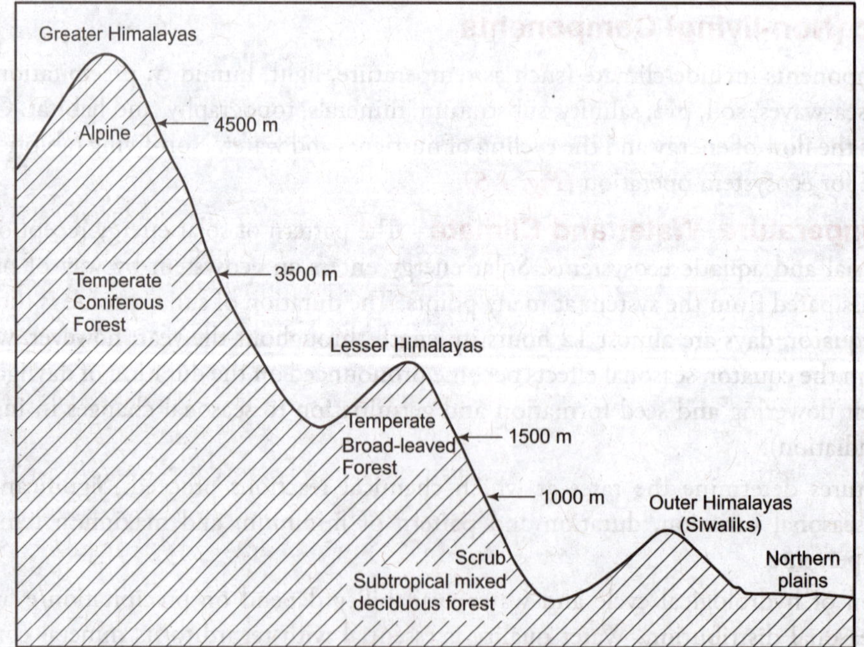

Fig. 1.7 **Tropical Forests' Vertical Zonation in the Himalayas**

are covered by the temperate broad-leaved forest, at around 3500 metre elevation are the temperate coniferous forests, while at high altitudes of about 4500 metres are the alpine pastures (*Margs*). Beyond 4500, there is generally absence of soil and vegetation generally does not grow.

The zonation of plants with altitude is noticeable on any trip from lower valleys to higher elevations. Each life zone processes its own insolation, temperature, and precipitation relationships, and therefore, its own biotic communities.

Beyond these general conditions, each ecosystem further produces its own microclimate, which is specific to individual sites. For example, in forests the insolation reaching the ground is reduced. A pine forest cuts light by 20–40 per cent, whereas a birch-beech forest reduces it by as much as 50–75 per cent. Forests are also five per cent more humid than non-forested landscapes, have warmer winters and cooler summers, and experience reduced winds. Such highly localised micro-ecosystems are evident along the mountain trail where changes in exposure can be seen easily.

BIOGEOCHEMICAL CYCLES

The cycling, at various scales, of minerals and compounds through the ecosystem is known as biogeochemical cycle. The cycles (carbon cycle and nitrogen cycle) involve phases of weathering of rocks, uptake and storage by organisms and return to the pool of the soil, the atmosphere or ocean sediments. The biogeochemistry of carbon has attracted particular attention because of the concern of *global warming and greenhouse effects*.

A brief description of some of the abiotic cycles is given below:

Carbon and Oxygen Cycles

The most abundant natural elements in living matter are hydrogen (H), oxygen (O), and carbon (C). Together these elements constitute more than 99 per cent of the biomass of the Earth. In fact, all life (organic molecules) contains hydrogen and carbon. In addition, nitrogen (N), calcium (Ca), potassium (K), magnesium (Mg), sulphur (S), and phosphate (P) are the significant nutrients—elements necessarily required for the growth and development of living organisms.

Several key chemical cycles function in nature. Oxygen, carbon, and nitrogen each have gaseous cycles, part of which are in the atmosphere. Other elements have sedimentary cycles which principally involve the mineral and solid phases (major ones include phosphorous, calcium, and sulphur). Some of the elements combine gaseous and sedimentary cycles. These recycling processes are called biochemical cycles because they involve chemical reactions in both living and non-living systems.

These two cycles have been considered together as they are closely intertwined through photosynthesis and respiration (*Fig. 1.8*). The atmosphere is the principal reserve of available oxygen. Large reserves of oxygen exist in Earth's crust, but they are unavailable as it is chemically bound to other elements.

As for carbon, the greatest pool is in the ocean—about 39,000 billion tons, or about 93 per cent of Earth's total carbon. However, all of this carbon is bound chemically in carbon dioxide. The ocean absorbs carbon dioxide through photosynthesis by small planktons. Carbon is stored in certain carbonate minerals, such as limestone.

The atmosphere, which is integrating link in the cycle, contains only about 700 billion tons of carbon (as carbon dioxide) at any moment. This is far less than in fossil fuels and oil- shales (12,000 billion tons as hydrocarbon molecules) or living and dead organic matter (2275 billion tons, as carbohydrate molecules). Carbon dioxide in the atmosphere is produced by volcanic activity, respiration of plants and animals, and fossil fuel combustion by industries and transportation.

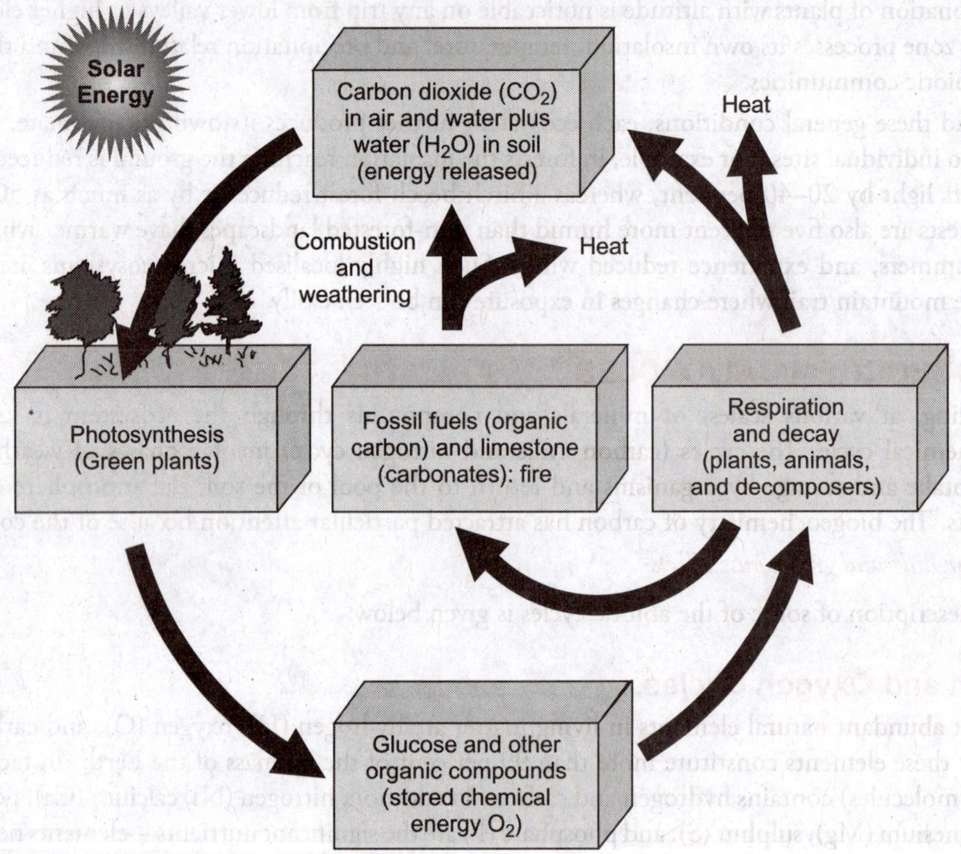

Fig. 1.8 **The Carbon and Oxygen Cycles simplified**

The Nitrogen Cycle

The nitrogen cycle involves the major constituent of the atmosphere, (78.084 per cent of each breath we take). Nitrogen is also an important element in the formation of organic molecules, especially proteins, and therefore is essential to living processes. A simplified view of the nitrogen cycle is portrayed in ***Fig. 1.9***.

The vast atmospheric reservoir is however inaccessible directly to most organisms. The key link to life is provided by nitrogen-fixing bacteria, which live principally in the soil and are associated with the roots of certain plants. For example, the legumes such as *alfalfa*, beans, clover, pulses, peas, soybeans, green-manuring crops and peanuts. Bacteria colonies reside in nodules on the legume-roots and chemically combine the nitrogen from the air in the form of nitrates (NO_3) and ammonia (NH_3). Plants use these chemically bound organic matter. Anyone or anything feeding on the plants thus ingest the nitrogen. Finally, the nitrogen is the organic wastes of the consuming organisms is freed by denitrifying bacteria, which recycle it back to the atmosphere.

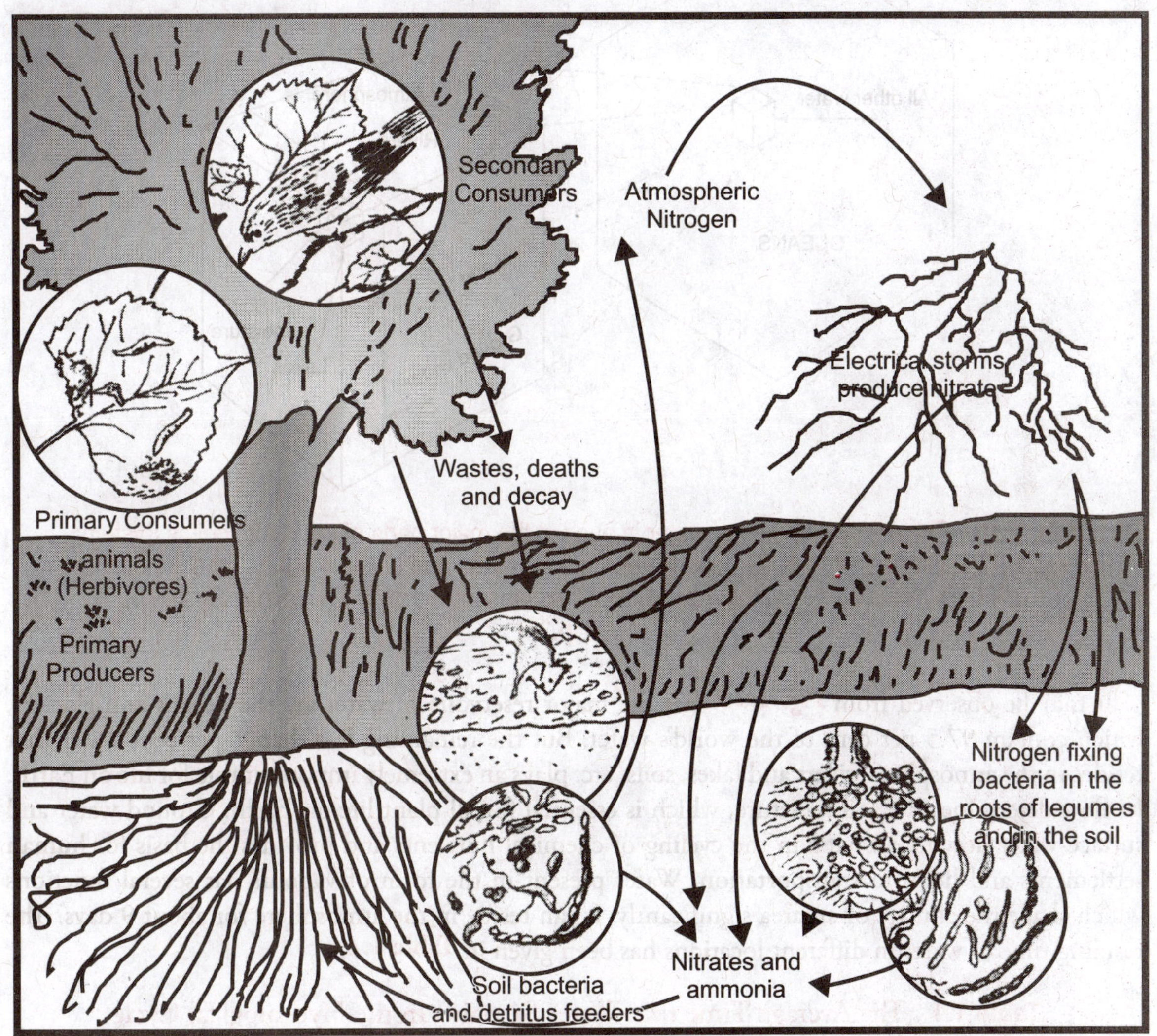

Fig. 1.9 The Nitrogen Cycle

HYDROLOGICAL SYSTEM OF THE EARTH

The total water of the Earth planet is distributed in various systems, i.e. water in the air, on the land, and in the ocean, and in the three states (gas, liquid, and solid). Compared to the total mass of the Earth, the total mass of water in the hydrosphere is extremely small, only one part in 4500. Yet water covers 71 per cent of the surface of the Earth and is extremely mobile, constantly moving from one place to another, often at remarkable speed. The relative amount of water in each of the major hydrological systems has been shown in *Fig. 1.10*.

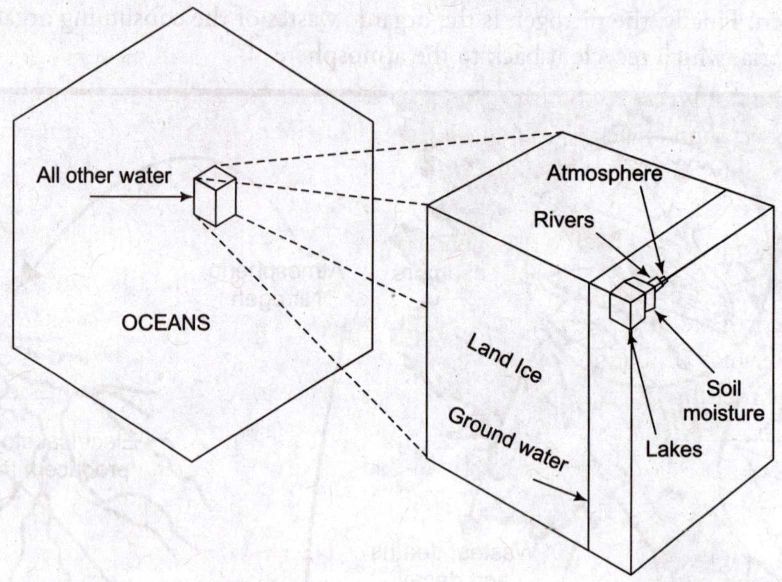

Fig. 1.10 The relative amount of water in each of the major parts of the Hydrological System: Oceans > 97%, Glaciers = 1.9%, Ground water = 0.5%, Rivers and Lakes = 0.02%, and atmosphere = 0.0001% (After W. K. Hamblim and E. H. Christiansen: *Earth's Dynamic System*, 1995, p.37)

It may be observed from ***Fig. 1.10*** that the major reservoirs of water are the oceans and glaciers, which contain 97.5 per cent of the world's water. But the remaining less than 1 per cent water that resides in the atmosphere, rivers and lakes, soils, etc. plays an extremely important role for life on Earth. Its flow determines the soil moisture, which is essential for all plant life on Earth. Ground water and surface water flow that is vital in the cycling of chemical nutrients and provides the basis for human settlements and helps in transportation. Water present in the form of vapours has several functions which shape the climate of an area significantly. It can reside in the atmosphere for about 9 days. The residing time of water in different locations has been given in **Table 1.1**.

Table 1.1 The Average Time that Water Remains in the Hydrological Cycle

Location	Residence Time
Atmosphere	9 days
Rivers (typical speed, 1 m/sec)	1 week
Soil moisture	2 weeks to one year
Largest lakes	10 years
Shallow groundwater	10 to 100s of years
Mixed layer of oceans (Ist 150 metres)	120 years
World Oceans	3 000 years
Deep ground-water and ice-sheets	Up to 10,000 years
Antarctic ice cap	10,000 years

Source: *Ecoscience*, Paul, R., Ehrlich, et al. p.30

The Oceans

About 97.5 per cent of the total liquid water, ice and water vapour is in the vast reservoir of the oceans. The residence time of water in the oceans is about three thousand years. The water near the surface, however, may have a much shorter residence time than the deep water, which may be stored for very long periods, possibly hundreds of thousands of years **(Table 1.1)**.

Ice

Water in the form of ice constitutes about 80 per cent of the water that is not in the oceans, or about 2 per cent of the Earth's total. Most of this is located in the great glaciers and ice-sheets of Antarctica and Greenland. Water may reside in the glaciers for thousands or even millions of years. Present estimates, based on rates of melting, suggest that water reside in glaciers, on an average for about 10,000 years. If the existing glaciers melted completely, the volume of water in the oceans would increase by about 2 per cent and the sea level would rise about 100 metres.

Groundwater

The water contained in the pore spaces of rock and soil is known as groundwater. About 20 per cent of water not in the oceans, occurs as groundwater.

Soil moisture accounts for about 0.005 per cent of the Earth's water, or about 0.5 per cent of the water not contained in the oceans. Even at this low percentage, there is more water in the soil than is contained in river channels. There are two components of the groundwater: (i) water that is migrating down to the water table, and (ii) water that is retained in the soil. Water in the soil is drawn out by evaporation from the soil surface and by plants. Residence time for water in the soil varies between about two weeks to one year **(Table 1.1)**. Soil moisture is important because it migrates into rivers and groundwater systems. Soil moisture is also of supreme biologic importance, because it is the essential foundation of plant and animal life.

Lakes

Lakes contain approximately 0.017 per cent of the Earth's water, or about 0.7 per cent of that not contained in the oceans. Slightly more than half is held in freshwater lakes (lakes with outlets); the rest is saline lakes (lakes without outlets). About 75 per cent of total volume of freshwater lakes occurs in the large lakes of North America, Lake Baikal in Russia, and the large lakes of East Africa. The residence time of water in the big lakes is about ten years, except the Caspian Sea in which the residence time is about 200 years.

Atmospheric Water

The amount of water in the atmosphere is surprisingly small being 0.0001 per cent when compared with other parts of the hydrological system. This volume of water is roughly equivalent to the volume of water carried by the world's rivers. The daily rate of exchange between the water in the atmosphere and that on Earth includes approximately 2.5 mm that falls as precipitation and 2.5 mm that evaporates from the surface. The average residence time of water in the atmosphere is about 9 days, and there is a complete exchange of atmospheric moisture forty times a year.

Rivers

The rivers contain only about 0.0001 per cent of the total water of the Earth, or 0.005 per cent of the water not in the oceans. As water moves in rivers, it erodes and transports huge volumes of rock and soil debris. No other system is so universally important in shaping Earth's surface as running water. The residence time of water in rivers is about one week.

Water stored in Living Organisms

The total amount of water stored in living organisms is extremely small when compared with amounts stored in other parts of the hydrological system. In any given period of time, plants may well release as much water into atmosphere as is discharged by all of the world's rivers combined. It is a significant amount. Its importance is further emphasised when we consider that the residence time of water in organisms is very short, ranging from a few hours, in warm-blooded animals, to a season, for most plants. Thus plants and animals constitute an important segment in the hydrological system. If we continue to destroy the forests, the effect on the hydrological system may be devastating.

HYDROLOGICAL CYCLE.

The hydrological cycle describes the continuous movement of all forms of water (vapour, liquid and solid) on, in and above the Earth's surface and it is the central concept of Hydrology. The processes involved in the hydrological cycle are: evaporation (liquid to gas), condensation (gas to liquid), freezing (liquid to solid), melting or fusion (solid to liquid) and sublimation (solid to gas or reverse).

The hydrological cycle includes the condensation and freezing of water vapour in the atmosphere to form liquid or solid precipitation, the movement of water from precipitation through one or more of a range of conceptual stores, including surface storage, soil moisture storage, groundwater storage, stream channels and the oceans, until at some stage the water returns to the atmosphere as water vapour through the process of evaporation and transpiration *(Fig. 1.11)*.

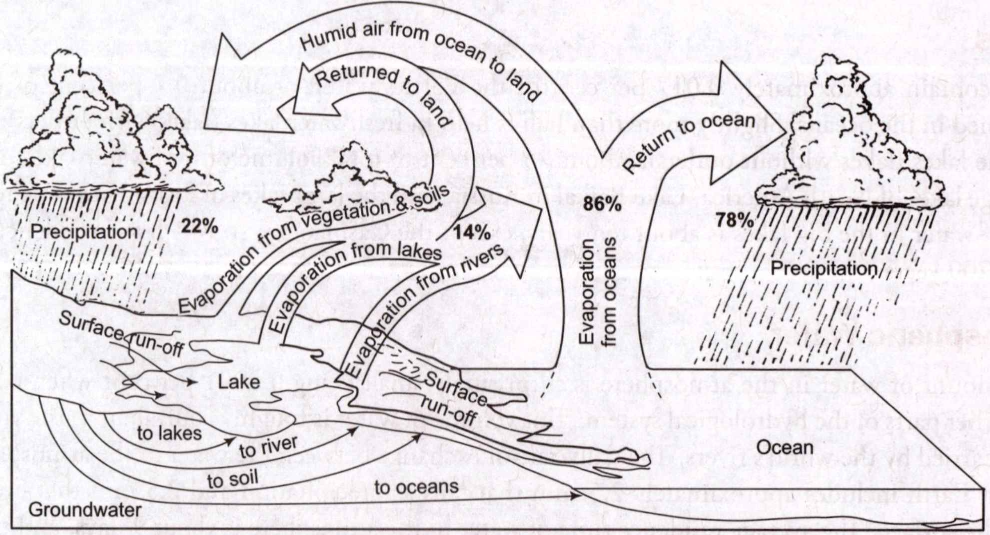

Fig. 1.11 Hydrological Cycle (after A. Strahler, 1997, p.362)

The hydrological cycle is an intricate combination of evaporation, transpiration, air-mass movements, condensation, precipitation, run off, percolation, and groundwater movements. The greater part of atmospheric moisture, which eventually falls to the Earth as precipitation (rains), comes from the oceans. Some water takes a short cut in the water cycle and enters air (atmosphere) directly through evaporation and transpiration (from soil and vegetation) without returning to the oceans. The process of evaporation, condensation and precipitation are essentially climatic and their functions in the water cycle would be quite simple if it were not for the constant motion in the atmosphere. This requires heat as well as moisture. Where heat and moisture are abundant (e.g. in rainy, tropical countries), the water cycle is very active. In dry climates, however, an essential part of cycle, viz., moisture, is lacking. In very cold climates, on the other hand, the energy (i.e. heat) to operate the water cycle is limited. The practical value of an understanding of the water cycle comes from the fact that it is this cycle that makes water available to us on land for its various uses.

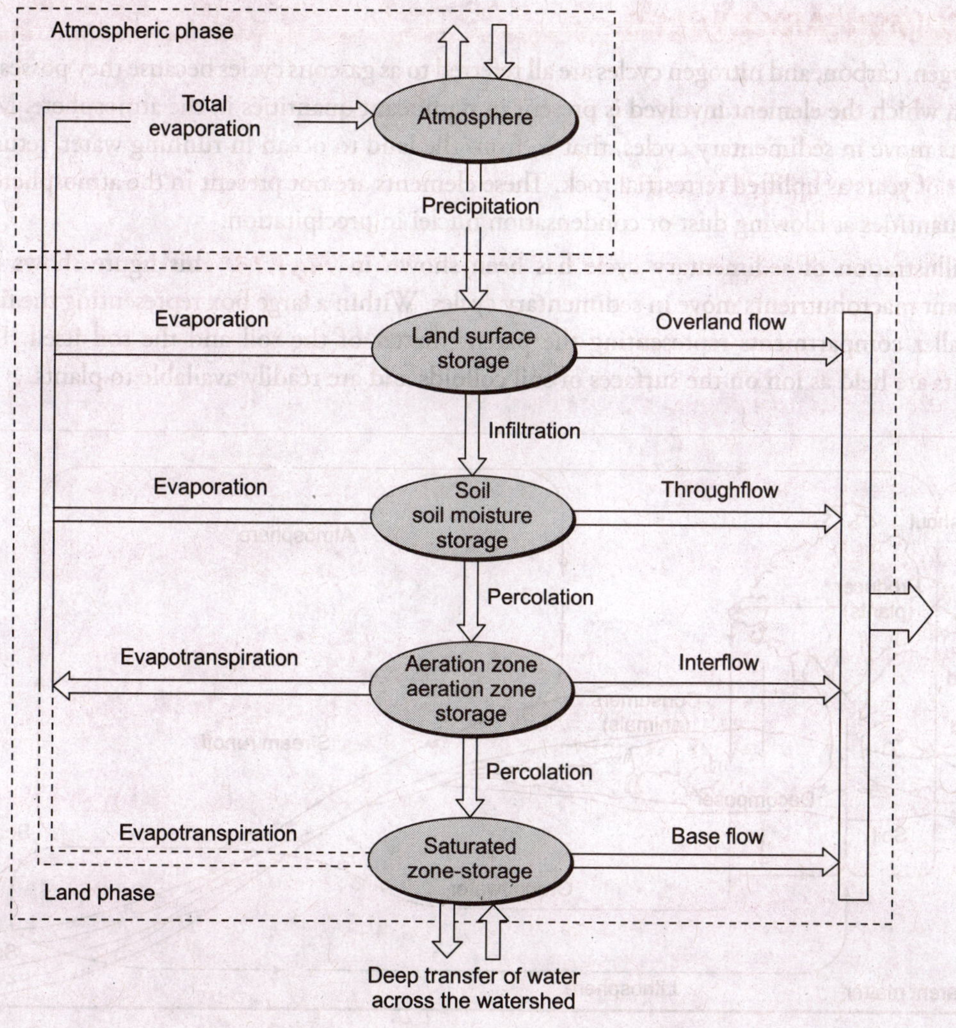

Fig. 1.12 **Hydrological Cycle – Drainage Basin**

The drainage basin cycle has been shown in *Fig. 1.12*. It shows the possible routes that water may follow within a drainage basin to form part of stream discharge at the basin outlet or to be lost to the basin through evaporation. The time taken for water to pass to and from a store, the capacity of storage at a particular time, will strongly influence the discharge response of the drainage basin to a rainfall event. *Figure 1.12* summarises the way in which the different contributions to run-off might be generated in a drainage basin in response to a storm.

Figure 1.12 illustrates, first, that more inaccessible stores will respond more slowly to rainfall, if they generate a measurable response. For example, water must infiltrate the soil and percolate to the water-table before groundwater storage can be increased and so produce increased base flow to the stream. All these processes may take a long time, and so introduces a long lag before the peak of base flow passes the gauging station on the stream at the catchment outlet *(Fig. 1.12)*.

SEDIMENTARY CYCLES.

The oxygen, carbon, and nitrogen cycles are all referred to as gaseous cycles because they possess a gaseous phase in which the element involved is present in significant quantities in the atmosphere. Many other elements move in sedimentary cycles, that is, from the land to ocean in running water, returning after millions of years as uplifted terrestrial rock. These elements are not present in the atmosphere except in small quantities as blowing dust or condensation nuclei in precipitation.

An illustration of sedimentary cycle has been shown in *Fig.1.13*. This figure shows how some important macronutrients move in sedimentary cycles. Within a large box representing the lithosphere, are smaller compartments representing the parent matter of the soil and the soil itself. In the soil, nutrients are held as ion on the surfaces of soil colloids and are readily available to plants.

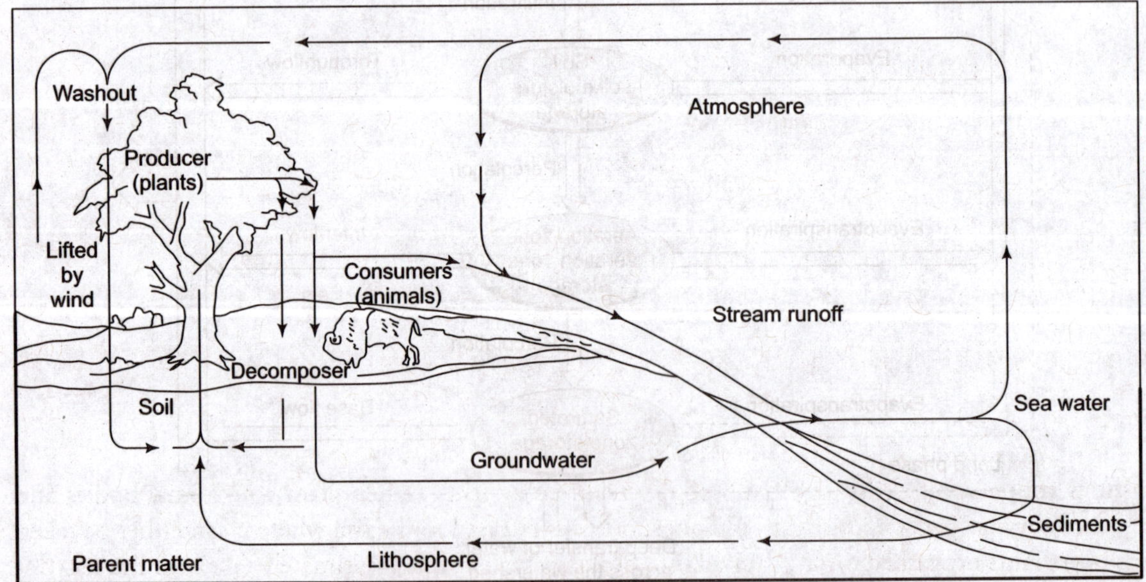

Fig. 1.13 Sedimentary Cycle (after A. Strahler, 1997, p.536)

The nutrient elements are also held in enormous storage pools, where they are unavailable to organisms. These storage pools include sea water (unavailable to land organisms), sediments on the sea-floor, and enormous accumulation of sedimentary rocks beneath both land and oceans. Eventually, elements held in the geologic storage pools are released into the soil by weathering. Soil particles are lifted into the atmosphere by winds and fall back to earth or are washed down by precipitation. Chlorine and sulphur are shown as passing from the ocean into the atmosphere and entering the soil by the same mechanism of fallout and washout.

The organic realm, or biosphere, is shown in three compartments: *producers, consumers,* and *decomposers.* Considerable element recycling occurs between organisms of these three classes and the soil. The elements used in the biosphere, however, are continually escaping to the sea as ions dissolved in stream runoff and groundwater flow.

Phosphorus Cycle

The phosphorus cycle is an example of sedimentary cycle *(Fig. 1.14).* Phosphorus is relatively rare in nature but is essential for plant and animal growth. The exchange pool involves cycling between organisms, soil and shallow marine sediments. Phosphates in the soil are taken into plants for protein

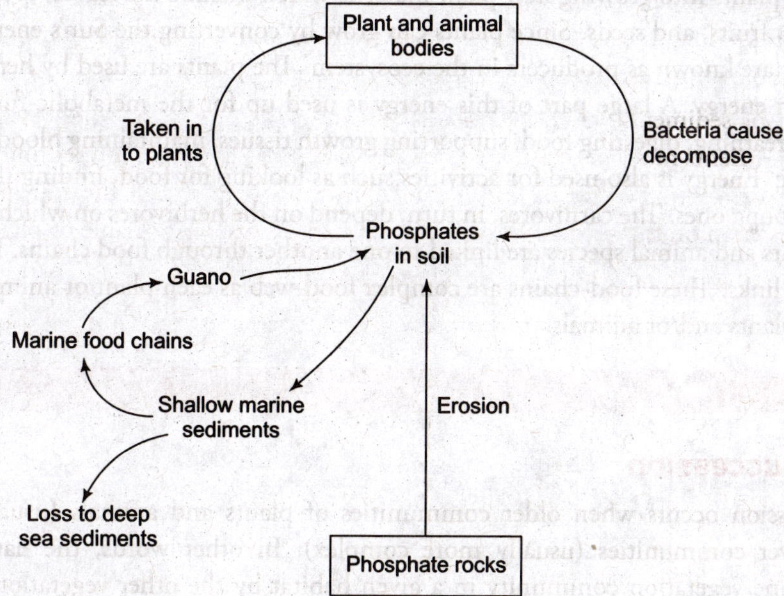

Fig.1.14 The Phosphorus Cycle

synthesis and are passed through the food chains of ecosystems. When plant and animal bodies and their excretory products decompose, the phosphorus is released to the soil where it can either be taken back into plants or washed out by rainfall into drainage system which ultimately take it to the sea. If it happens, it will be incorporated in marine sediments and so lost from the exchange pool. One important route for the rapid return of phosphorus from these sediments occurs where there are upwelling ocean currents. These bring phosphorus to the surface water, where it is taken into marine food chains. Sea-birds feeding on fish in such areas have phosphorus rich droppings called *guano* which can be used as fertilizers. However, the return of phosphorus in this way tends to be localised, occurring, for example, on the islands of the Peruvian coasts, and it is estimated that it accounts for less than three per cent of the total amount lost from the land.

The depletion of phosphorus from exchange pool is compensated very slowly by the release of the element from the phosphate rocks of the reservoir pool. This occurs by the process of erosion and weathering.

The phosphorus cycle can be easily disrupted by the use of phosphate fertilizers in modern agriculture. Most of the manufactured phosphate fertilizers are produced from phosphate rocks, but are rapidly lost from the exchange pool to marine deposits as they are easily leached from the soil. This could lead to serious deficiencies in available phosphorus for agriculture in the future.

ENERGY CYCLE.

The cycle of energy is based on the flow of energy through the ecosystem. The energy from sunlight is converted by the plants into growing new plant material which include the leaves, roots, stems, twigs, branches, flowers, fruits, and seeds. Since plants can grow by converting the Sun's energy directly into their tissues, they are known as producers in the ecosystem. The plants are used by herbivores as food, which gives them energy. A large part of this energy is used up for the metabolic functions of these animals such as breathing, digesting food, supporting growth tissues, maintaining blood circulation and body temperature. Energy is also used for activities such as looking for food, finding shelter, breeding, and rearing the young ones. The carnivores, in turn, depend on the herbivores on which they feed. Thus the different plants and animal species are linked to one another through food chains. Each food chain has three or four links. These food-chains are complex food-web as each plant or animal can be linked to several other plants and/or animals.

SUCCESSION.

Ecological Succession

Ecological succession occurs when older communities of plants and animals (usually simpler) are replaced by newer communities (usually more complex). In other words, the natural process of replacement of one vegetation community in a given habitat by the other vegetation community, is called succession. Each successive community of species modifies the physical environment in a manner suitable for the establishment of a later community of species. Changes apparently move toward a more stable and mature condition, to an optimum for a specific environment. This end product in an area is traditionally called the *ecological climax*, with plants and animals forming a climax community—a stable, self-sustaining, and symbiotically functioning community with balanced birth, growth, and death.

Ecological succession often requires an initiating disturbance, for instance, a volcanic eruption, strong winds, or a practice such as prolonged over-grazing. When existing organisms are disturbed or removed, new communities can emerge. At such times of transition, the interrelationships among species produce elements of chance, and species having an adaptive edge will succeed in the competitive struggle for light, water and nutrients, space, time, reproduction and survival. Thus, the succession of plant and animal communities, is an intricate process with many interactive variables.

The development of vegetation community in any ecosystem or habitat is affected closely by the: (i) climate, (ii) physiography and landforms, (iii) soils, (iv) plants animals and microorganisms, (v) anthropogenic, and (vi) fire.

Terrestrial Succession

An area of bare rock and soil without any vestige of former community can be a site for *primary succession*. The initial community is called a pioneer *community*. It may occur in sites such as a new surface created by mass movements of land, in areas exposed by a retreating glacier, on cooled volcanic lava flows, or on lands disturbed by surface mining, clear-cut logging, and land development. However, terrestrial succession from a previously functioning community is more common. An area whose natural community has been destroyed or disturbed, but still has the underlying soil intact, may experience secondary succession or secondary ecosystem.

In terrestrial ecosystems, secondary succession begins with pioneer species and further soil development. As succession progresses, a difficult set of plants and animals with different niche requirements may adapt.

Secondary succession begins on an abandoned farm of formerly ploughed fields. Crabgrass and ragweed quickly take hold and do well in direct sunlight. Those slowly give way to grasses and shrubs that invade and stabilise the soil, adding nutrients and organic matter. In temperate latitudes, pines eventually dominate the land from year 25 through the first century. The shade created by the pine forest produces conditions in which seed germination becomes more difficult. Shade-tolerant, slow-growing oak and hickory hardwoods, readily take root beneath the pines. As these hardwoods grow, they eventually shade the pine forest, which slowly dies back in reduced light conditions. A fairly stable climax forest of oak and hickory is in place between 150–200 years. But despite the convenient categorisation shown in **Fig. 1.15**, one should not think of succession and disruptions in it as continuous, with succeeding communities overlapping in time and space.

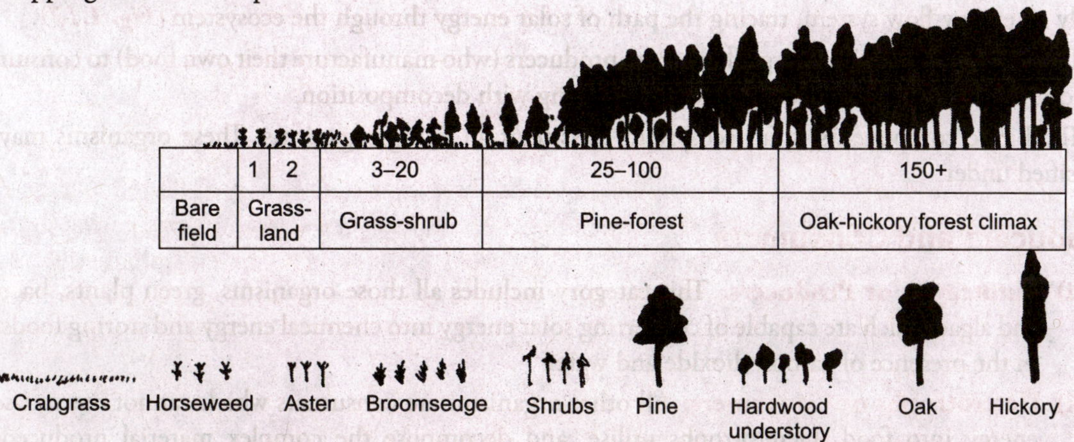

Fig. 1.15 Typical Secondary Succession of Plants

Role of fire in terrestrial succession

In ecology, fire has been recognised as a dynamic ingredient in community succession. Controlled fire secures plant reproduction and prevents the accumulation of forest litter and brush; widely regarded as a wise forest management. In terrestrial succession, successional stages may be interrupted by fire. Earth's land area experiences fire each year. Today, fire is recognised as a natural component of most ecosystems and not the enemy of nature it once was popularly considered. In fact, in many forests, undergrowth is purposely burned in controlled *'cool-fires'* to remove fuel that could enable a catastrophic and destructive *'hot fire'*. In contrast, when fire prevention strategies are rigidly followed, they can lead to abundant undergrowth accumulation, which allows total destruction of forest by a major fire.

Aquatic Succession

Lakes and ponds exhibit another form of ecological succession. A lake experiences successional stages as it fills with nutrients and sediment, and as aquatic plants take root and grow, it captures more sediment and adds organic debris to the system. This gradual enrichment of water bodies is known as eutrophication. For example, in moist climates, a floating mat of vegetation grows outward from the shore to form a bog. Cattails and other plants become established, and partially decomposed organic material accumulates in the basin, with additional vegetation bordering the remaining lake surface. A meadow may form, as water is displaced by peat bog; willow trees follow, and perhaps cottonwood trees; and eventually the lake may evolve into a forest community.

FOOD CHAIN

A food chain is the sequence of energy transfer from the lower levels to the upper or higher trophic levels through complex network of interconnected food chains. It is the way an organism obtains and sustain physical, chemical and biological factors it needs to survive. Basically, as stated above, all animals depend on plants for their food. For instance, foxes may eat rabbits, but rabbits feed on grass. Similarly, a hawk eats a lizard, the lizard had just eaten a grasshopper and the grasshopper was feeding on grass-blades. This relationship is called food-chain. Another example of a food chain is that a caterpillar eats the leaf, the blue-tit eats the caterpillar, but may fall prey to the kestrel. In other words, the food-web is really an energy flow system, tracing the path of solar energy through the ecosystem ***(Fig. 1.17)***.

The circuit along which energy flows from producers (who manufacture their own food) to consumers is a one-directional flow of chemical energy, ending with decomposition.

The biotic components of an ecosystem consist of all living organisms. These organisms may be classified under:

Producers and Consumers

(i) **Autotrophs or Producers:** This category includes all those organisms, green plants, bacteria and algae which are capable of converting solar energy into chemical energy and storing foodstuff in the presence of carbon dioxide and water.

(ii) **Heterotrophs or Consumers:** All other organisms are consumers which cannot convert solar energy into food. Heterotrophs utilise, and decompose the complex material produced by autotrophs. *Depending upon the feeding habits, the heterotrophs are classified as follows*:

(a) ***Primary Consumers:*** Organisms or animals which feed on green plants (autotrophs) to obtain energy for survival are the primary consumers. They are also known as herbivores. Cows, buffaloes, goats, horses, rabbits, insects and grasshoppers are some of the examples of primary consumers *(Fig. 1.16)*.

(b) ***Secondary Consumers:*** Animals which feed on herbivores are known as secondary consumers. For example, frogs, lizards, which eat grasshoppers and other insects *(Fig. 1.16)*.

(c) ***Tertiary Consumers:*** Tertiary consumers are those that eat the flesh of secondary consumers. For example tiger, lion, leopard, vultures. Since they are not killed and eaten by other animals, they are known as top carnivores *(Fig. 1.16)*.

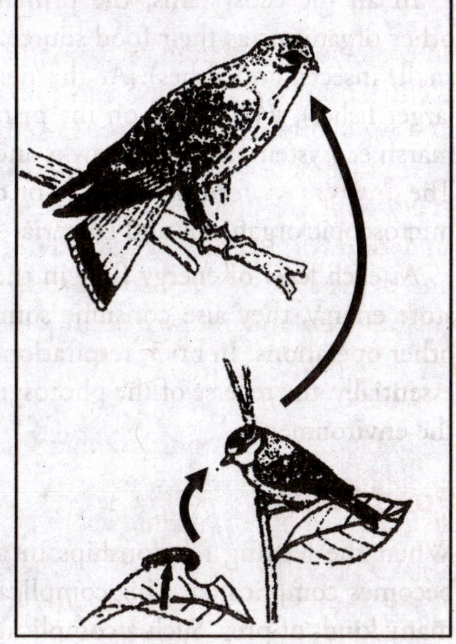

Fig.1.16 A Food-Chain
The caterpillar eats the leaf; The blue tit eats the caterpillar but may fall prey to the kestrel

The trophic level in a grassland may be shown as under:
Plant Æ Insect Æ Frog Æ Snake Æ Eagle
Autotroph Herbivore (Primary) Secondary Top Carnivore
(Producer) (Plants) (Consume) Consumer

Decomposers or Saprophytes

The dead bodies of the producers and consumers are eaten and broken down into simple inorganic substance by certain microbes (bacteria and fungi). They are known as decomposers or saprophytes. The decomposers play a vital role of releasing essential materials from the dead matter and thus maintain a continuous cycle of energy flow and of materials. Water, carbon dioxide, phosphates, nitrogen, sulphates and a number of organic compounds are the by-products of decomposers.

In all the ecosystems of nature, energy passes from one living organism to another. For example, in a salt marsh a variety of organisms are present – algae and aquatic plants, microorganisms, insects, snails, and small-fish, as well as such larger organisms as big-fishes, birds, shrews, mice, and rats. Inorganic components such as water, air, clay-particles and organic sediments, inorganic nutrients, trace elements, and light energy are also present. Energy transformation in the ecosystem occurs by means of a series of steps or levels which is referred to as food chain or food web.

In brief, the plants and algae in the food chain are the primary producers. They use light energy to convert carbon dioxide and water into carbohydrates (long chains of sugar molecules) and eventually into other biochemical molecules needed for the support of life. This process of energy conversion is called photosynthesis. Organisms engaged in photosynthesis form the base of the food web.

In all the ecosystems, the primary producers support the consumers — organisms that ingest other organisms as their food source. At the lowest level of consumers are the *primary consumers* (the snail, insects, and fishes). At the next level are the secondary consumers (the mammals, birds, and larger fishes), which feed on the primary consumers. A still higher level of feeding occurs in the salt marsh ecosystem, as marsh hawks and owls consume the smaller animals below them in the food web. The *decomposers* feed on *detritus*, or decaying organic matter, derived from all levels. They are largely microscopic organisms and bacteria.

At each level of energy flow in the food web, energy is lost to respiration. In fact, plants not only store energy, they also consume some of this energy by converting carbohydrates to derive for their other operations. In brief, respiration is the process by which plants derive energy for their operations; essentially, the reverse of the photosynthetic process which releases carbon dioxide, water and heat into the environment.

Food Web

When the feeding relationships in a natural ecosystem become more complicated, the food chain becomes complicated. This complicated situation develops when greater number of species feed on many kinds of prey. Such a complicated food chain is known as food web.

ECOLOGICAL PYRAMID

The study of food chains and food webs explains who eats what, and where? The ecological pyramid deals with the relationship between the number of primary producers and consumers (herbivores and carnivores) of different orders. Depending on the nature of food chain, in the present ecosystem, the pyramid of numbers may be upright or inverted. For example, in a grassland ecosystem, the amount of grass (producers) is always high, followed by primary consumers (herbivores like rabbits and grasshoppers) that are less, the secondary consumers (carnivores like snakes and lizards) that are lesser and finally the top carnivore, in this case hawks, which are the least in number. So the pyramid in this case is as shown in ***Fig. 1.17***.

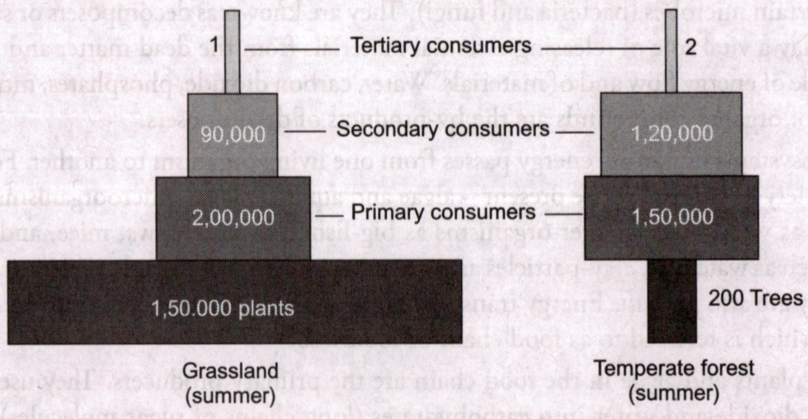

Fig. 1.17 Ecological Pyramids for 0.1 hectares (0.25 acre) of grassland and forest in summer. Number of consumers are shown.

On the other hand, in a forest ecosystem, the producers are big trees on the fruits of which birds and other primary herbivores depend. Thus the number of primary consumers (birds and monkeys) is always greater than the number of producers (big fruit bearing trees). Again, the number of secondary consumers (carnivores) is less than the primary consumers, and obviously the number at the top carnivores (lions and tigers) is least.

Another example of ecological pyramid may be illustrated from the distribution of population in: (i) temperate grasslands, and (ii) temperate forest (*Fig. 1.17*).

It may be observed from *Fig. 1.17* that there is a decreasing number of organisms at each successive higher trophic level. The base of the temperate forest pyramid is narrower. In the temperate forests, most of the producers are large, highly productive trees and shrubs which are outnumbered by the consumers they can support in the food chain. In opposition to this, the base of grassland ecosystems is larger which tapers towards the primary, secondary and tertiary consumers, giving the pyramid a conical shape (*Figs. 1.17* and *1.18*).

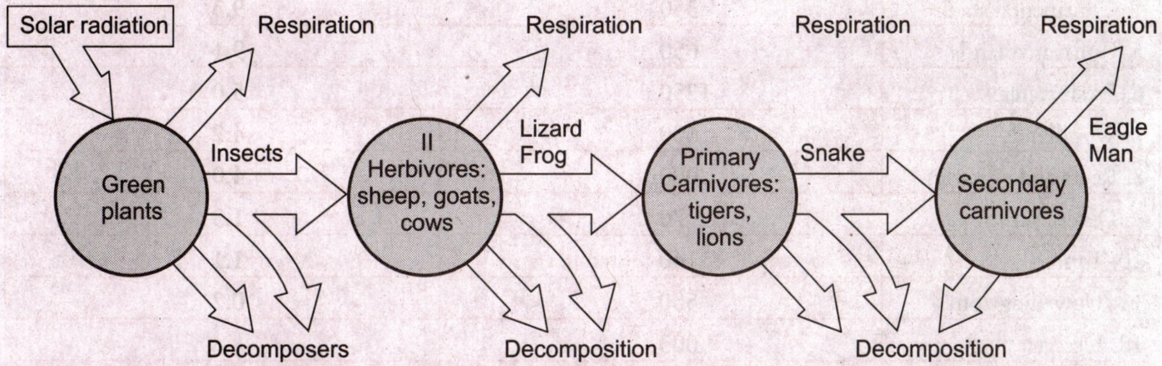

Fig. 1.18 A Simple Linear Food Chain and Energy Flow

ECOLOGICAL PRODUCTIVITY.

Biomass refers to the quantity or weight of living matter per unit area per unit time and is represented in terms of dry weight. Biomass is comprised of plants and animals and therefore it is referred to as plant biomass or animal biomass. Total plant biomass including both above and subsurface plants is called standing crop.

The total accumulated amount of energy stored by the autotrophic (primary producers) per unit area per unit time is called ecological productivity. The productivity of the ecosystem depends on (i) the availability of amount of solar radiation to the autotrophic primary producers, and (ii) the efficiency of the plants to convert solar energy (light energy) into chemical energy (food energy) which is used by green plants to build up their tissues.

Primary production is measured in two ways: (i) gross primary production (GPP), and (ii) net primary production (NPP). Gross primary production is the total amount of energy produced by the autotrophic primary producers at trophic level one. In other words, gross primary production refers to total amount of energy assimilated by autotrophic primary producer i.e. green plants. While net primary production (NPP) represents the amount of energy or organic matter fixed or stored at trophic level one. Thus net primary production excludes the amount of energy which is lost through respiration by autotrophic primary producer plants. Net primary production represents the usable amount of energy at trophic levels. The ecosystem productivity whether, gross or net, is generally measured in gram/m^2/day or year.

Table 1.2 Estimated Net Primary Productivity of the Major Biomes of the World

Vegetation Unit	Mean Productivity (g/m^2/year)	Total of net productivity (10^9 tonnes/year)
1. Forests	1290	64.5
2. Open Ocean	125	41.5
3. Grasslands (Savanna)	600	15.0
4. Continental shelf	350	9.3
5. Cultivated land	650	9.1
6. Fresh water	1250	5.0
7. Woodlands	600	4.2
8. Reefs and estuaries	2000	4.0
9. Desert Scrub	70	1.3
10. Tundra	140	1.1
11. Upwelling zones	500	0.2
12. Desert	003	-
Total continental	669	100.2
Total oceanic	155	55.0
World Total	303	155.2

Source: I.G. Simmons, 1974, Ecology of Natural Resources, London, Edward Arnold.

There is a positive correlation between the primary productivity and solar radiation, there is a marked decrease in the primary productivity from the equator towards the poles.

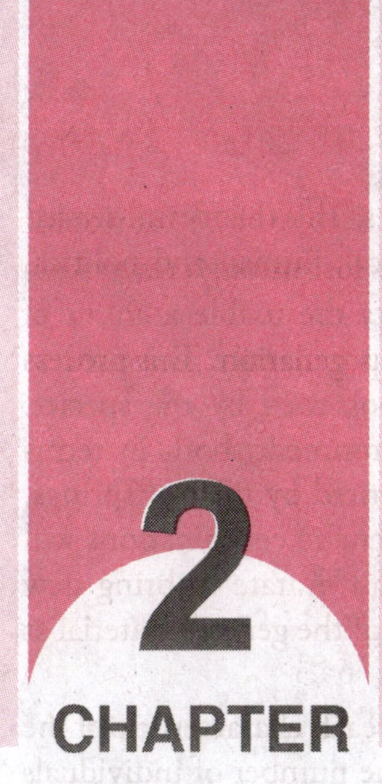

Plant and Animal Kingdoms

EVOLUTION OF SPECIES

Convergent Evolution and Convolution

Cumulative development in the characteristics of species over time is known as evolution. Classically, evolution is regarded as the progressive change in the features of populations, occurring through the course of sequential generations brought about by the process of natural selection. In fact, evolution also explains the diversification of organisms of the presumed common ancestry through geological time and must, therefore, account for speciation and extinction, as well as progressive change as a result of natural selection. Convergent evolution is the process by which unrelated or distinctly related groups evolve similar morphologies or adaptation traits, e.g. the reduced limbs of whales and penguins. Convolution is the contemporaneous evolution of two ecologically linked taxonomic groups, such as flowering plants and their pollinators.

The Contribution of Charles Darwin

Charles Darwin, who published '*On the Origin of Species by Natural Selection*' in 1859, is considered as the *Father* of Evolutionary Theory. Darwin's famous voyage, as the naturalist aboard the British ship, *HMS Beagle*, undertaken between 1831 and 1836, was to be instrumental in formulating his ideas about evolution. His short visit to Galapagos Islands (Ecuador), 800 km off the west coast of South America, appears to have been especially influential. It was here that Darwin observed and reported on morphological variations between individuals belonging to same species. In the process, he was also struck by the degree of adaptation to the environment displayed by several apparently closely related different species of '*finch*', all confined to different habitat or to completely different islands. These ideas were to prove crucial in the development of his idea of modification between generations, and of common ancestry – in short, of evolution.

It transpires that Darwin and a contemporary British zoologist, Alfred Russel Wallace, developed the idea of evolution by natural selection independently. Both Charles Darwin and Alfred Wallace advocated the theory of common ancestry, namely man descended from the apes. This theory influenced the development of thoughts on a number of other subjects including physical, human and political geography.

According to Darwin, the natural habitat exerts a selective pressure on the population. This process of natural selection may lead to persistence of favourable characteristics possessed by the species. The surviving organisms will have genetic combinations suited to the environment, both in terms of environmental and competitive ability. Their genetic material will be inherited by their offsprings, whereas unsuccessful individuals will be eliminated and their unfavourable genetic combinations will be lost from the population. Moreover, genetic material is not static but can mutate to bring new variation to the population. Natural selection, is thus, not limited to a sorting of the genetic material at any one time, but is a continuing process as new variety emerges.

The total genetic material contained in a population is called a *gene pool.* For each characteristic of the population which exhibits continuous variation, such as height or leaf size, the number of individuals at each height or with each size of leaf tend to follow a particular pattern.

Natural Selection

Natural selection also occurs in characteristics which do not vary continuously but exit as alternative forms. For example, different colours, or light or dark bodies. In these cases, selection operates for definite alternatives and can be seen as a change in the relative numbers of the different types. The essential mechanism of natural selection may be summarised as follows:

1. **Higher Ratio of Young ones in a Community:** In most species, far more young are produced than can possibly survive to reproductive age.
2. **Organisms vary:** Individuals in a population differ from each other in numerous morphological and behavioural ways. Some of these variations are heritable and may be passed on to the succeeding generation.
3. **Struggle for Survival:** There is a 'struggle' for existence, competition between organisms, in which those better suited to the prevailing environment are more likely to survive to reproductive age.
4. **Adaptation:** Individuals with characteristics best suited to survival are more likely to reproduce successfully and will, ultimately, predominate in a population. Adaptive change is therefore a result of natural selection operating over long periods, based on the gradual accumulation of small, favourable variations present in population.

Acceptance of Darwin's ideas was slow because the mid-nineteenth century scientific understanding of the processes of '*heritability*' was incomplete. More recently, Darwin and Wallace's ideas have come under scrutiny, especially in regard to the pace of evolutionary change. The fossil record, reveals no such gradual change in morphology of species over time, but rather a history of relative stability interrupted by relatively rapid change. According to American biologists, Stephen Jay Gould and Niles Eldredge, evolution is not a gradual process, but is instead characterised by relatively long periods of negligible or limited change punctuated by short, intense periods of rapid development based on speciation events.

MIGRATION AND ADAPTATION.

Migration can be defined as the spread of species into a new area, and usually implies movement over long distances through time. Both plants and animals can migrate, although in the case of animals, it may be of temporary nature for breeding or to avoid adverse climatic conditions at one season of the year. The ability to migrate, whether on a permanent or temporary basis, is an important aspect for the survival of species because it follows adjustment of the locations inhabited if climates change and also facilitates the extension of the area occupied if population pressure or severe competition from other species builds up.

Barriers to Migration

Although plants and animals may possess the capacity for migration, it may not always be possible for them to do so. They may encounter barriers. These could take the form of competition from the fauna and flora already occupying the area. But the success of the migrating species in comparison with the resident species will depend on their relative tolerance ranges and demands from the environment. Alternatively, the barriers to migration may be due to abiotic environmental factors. This will be apparent if the climates are not changing. A species may migrate to the limits of its tolerance range and then no further, without adaptation. In addition, there may be actual physical barriers that impede dispersal – for example, oceans, seas or lakes. The effect of these as barriers, will of course vary with their size. Time can be considered as a barrier to migration as well, because slow spreading species may be overcome by changing conditions. The length of time a species faces a barrier is very important. This is because the natural selection may take place in response to the stress imposed by the barrier, leading to evolutionary changes which might enable the species to continue to migrate.

PROCESS OF EVOLUTION

The evolution of plants means the origin, growth, development of plant communities through time. The evolution of plants, thus, varies in space and time. There is great variation among all plant species. Within a species, the height, size, shape, and leaves, colour and structure of flowers differ from region to region. Even there is variation among the offsprings of the same parents. Every plant inherits the qualities of its parents and these inherited qualities help in the growth and development of plants. These inherited qualities further get modified by the environmental conditions during the growth phase.

According to biologists, there are two major processes of evolution of species, namely: (i) the process of *selection*, and (ii) the process of *isolation*.

Process of Selection

(i) **Natural Selection:** It was Charles Darwin (1859) who postulated the principle and mechanism of evolution of species by the process of *'natural selection'* wherein the heritable variations form the basis of evolution of species.

The principle of natural selection simply means, that a few of the advantageous qualities inherited from the parents of species by a few populations of that species, are such that these qualities enable a few individual members of that species to survive in their environment and to become adapted to the environmental conditions. On the other hand, some individual members of this species lack in the advantageous qualities, because these could not be inherited by them from their parents. In such cases the individuals, which possess the advantageous qualities, are able to adapt in their environment, while the others get eliminated or disappear from the habitat.

(ii) **Artificial Selection:** Artificial selection occurs through human activities, when man creates a new environment. For instance, man develops new seeds to increase the yield of crops through artificial measures such as cross-pollination and hybridisation. Such newly created hybrid seeds are disease and pest resistant and are capable for their adaptation to various types of soils and climatic conditions. This process may be beneficial for mankind at present, because it may solve the problem of shortage of food-grains through increased production. But it may prove disastrous in near future, when all natural plants of food crops will disappear from the surface of the Earth.

(iii) **Isolation:** Isolation also plays an important role in the evolution of morphologically differentiated populations of species of plants. This process is termed as reproductive isolation. The process of isolation stops the exchange of genes between different members of species. This reproductive isolation is caused by a variety of barriers which may be grouped under two categories, e.g. (a) external barriers, and (b) internal barriers. The external factors (barriers) include geographical isolation, (large mountains, deserts, oceans), ecological isolation, seasonal isolation and mechanical isolation.

The internal factors operate from within the tissues of the plants. These internal factors prevent hybridisation even after cross-pollination of species. Thus the isolation caused by internal factors prevents inbreeding among the members of one species and consequently several sub-species of the main species are evolved and developed.

Dispersal of Plants in Migration

Migration requires a change in the location of individuals that make up the species. For plants this will obviously only be possible at the reproductive stages, the position of the off-springs being different from that of parents. Therefore the speed of migration and hence the ability of a plant species to keep pace with climatic change will be closely linked to life cycles and methods of reproduction. In brief, the dispersal of plants becomes effective through external factors mainly through the dispersal of seeds. *The following factors determine and control the nature of seed dispersal of plants and therefore, dispersal and migration of plants:*

(i) Properties of seeds
(ii) Agents of seeds transportation
(iii) Speed and distance of dispersal
(iv) Geographical barriers
(v) Tolerance factors
(vi) Continental Drift.
(vii) Anthropogenic factor (Man as a medium of dispersal of seeds)

Plants which reproduce vegetatively by asexual means, such as rhizomes, corms and bulbs, will have an extremely limited capacity for migration as the offspring will be immediately adjacent to the parents and so will hardly be dispersed at all from the previous generation. In contrast, plants which reproduce by spores or seeds, will have faster rates of migration as they will be dispersed further between generations.

The seed plants are by far the most efficient at dispersal and exhibit a vast range of adaptation to aid movement away from the parent plant. Most of these species rely on external agents, although there are a few which have exploding or twisting seed cases that expel the seeds. In other species the seeds may not have any structural modification, but may be light enough to be blown about by wind; a good example of this can be seen in the dust seeds of the orchids, which are minute but are produced in vast numbers. Many seeds have special adaptations such as wings or plumes of hairs to help them to become dispersed by wind, whereas others may rely on water or even ice, for transport. There are also many examples of seed dispersal by animals. Hooked or sticky seeds may adhere extremely to fur, and others may be carried in mud clinging to feet. In addition, seeds may be dispersed by being eaten, particularly by birds, and then passed out with the faeces of animals. Humans have also contributed to seed dispersal. Many agricultural pests are the results of unwitting transport of seeds by humans travelling from one area to another.

Agents of seed transportation

The main agents of transportation of seeds are wind, birds, animals, running water, ocean currents, and human beings. These agents transport seeds of various types in varying amounts, in different ways to different parts of the world.

Out of the above, wind, water and human beings, are the most important agents of dispersal of plants. Wind transport seeds mainly in suspension from one place to another. Smaller and lighter seeds are more efficiently transported by wind, but such seeds are susceptible to high rate of mortality. Birds can transport seeds to very long distances and they carry such seeds which stick to different parts of their bodies. Water transports seeds and disperses them through its various types of movements, e.g. sea-waves, tidal and ocean currents. Other animals transport seeds through their bodies, when seeds are stuck to the different parts of their bodies. Man has now emerged as the most important and effective carrier of seeds because he is capable of increasing the speed and range of seed dispersal from one continent to another, separated by huge ocean bodies, mountains and deserts. The pace of migration of man to different parts of the world during the last four or five hundred years has increased significantly. It could become possible because of the fast means of transportation. The international trade and commerce has also accelerated the rate of human migration and the consequent dispersal of plants and their seeds. Because of these factors, rubber and cinchona has been diffused from South America to the countries of south-east Asia; potato, tomato and water-nut from South America to different parts of the world; wheat, barley, oats, flax, lentil from south west Asia to North and South America, and Europe; rice and sugarcane from south-east Asia to different parts of the world.

Constraints and limitations in seed dispersal

The dispersal of plants is however, constrained by the following geographical factors:

(i) In general, smaller and lighter seeds are more efficiently transported to greater distances but they are susceptible to high rate of mortality.

(ii) Larger seeds are difficult to be dispersed, but these have low rate of mortality.

(iii) The size and number of seeds produced by different plants also affect the dispersal of seeds. For example, annual plants produce large quantities of small seeds which can be transported to greater distances, while many perennial plants produce few seeds but of large size. Such seeds are transported and dispersed slowly.

(iv) Ocean and sea are the most formidable limiting factors of seed dispersal. The size of oceans is so large that that becomes a serious physical barrier in the dispersal of seeds. The ocean currents however, may carry the seeds for long distances. Similarly, large and high and young folded mountains, large deserts are effective formidable barriers in the dispersal of seeds.

PLANT KINGDOMS

Traditionally, biologists are divide the living organisms into plants and animals. In plant kingdom, a systematic study of plant development, floral characteristics, dispersal, distribution, plants association, diseases, sustainability and vulnerability are examined.

The distribution of plants in the world is closely controlled by the topography, terrain, climate, soils, bio-diversity, tectonic activities and land-use practices. In general, the vegetation varies from equator towards poles, and from sea-level to altitudes.

On the basis of floral characteristics, the flora of the world may be divided into the following six floral kingdoms. According to ecologists and bio-geographers, there are six major plant kingdoms in the world, namely, 1. Australian Kingdom, 2. Cape Kingdom (South Africa), 3. Antarctic Kingdom, 4. Palaeo-tropical Kingdom, 5. Neo-tropical Kingdom, 6. Boreal Kingdom. Their distribution has been shown in *Fig. 2.1*.

1. Australian Kingdom

The Australian floristic kingdom is in Australia and its neighbouring islands and surrounding seas and oceans. The dominant species of trees in this kingdom are eucalyptus. According to one study, there are 600 species of eucalyptus in the world, out of which 75% are found in this region. The eucalyptus varies in characteristics and height from region to region. Eucalyptus has been dispersed in Australia by the Europeans from South America *(Fig. 2.1)*.

2. Cape Kingdom

The Cape floral Kingdom stretches over the southern province of South Africa. The plants of this kingdom belong to the category of cryptophytes, which bear buds in the form of bulbs and tubers which are buried in the soils. These bulbs and tubers give birth to other plants, as new shoots come out from these bulbs and tubers and are developed as plants *(Fig. 2.1)*.

3. Antarctic Kingdom

The Antarctic floral kingdom stretches in the higher latitudes of the Southern Hemisphere including the Desert of Patagonia, southern parts of South Chile and New Zealand. The dominant plant of this zone is *Southern Beech* (Nothofagus). Its important grasses include *Tussock Grasses* and a few *sedges* (plants which grow in water).

4. Palaeotropical Kingdom

This plant kingdom stretches over the greater parts of Africa, West Asia, South Asia, China and the countries of south Asia and south east Asia *(Fig. 2.1)*. There is great variation in floral species in the different parts of this zone. There are however, a few plants common to all the parts of this floral kingdom.

5. Neo-Tropical Kingdom

This plant kingdom covers the continent of South America excluding the desert of Patagonia and southern parts of Chile *(Fig. 2.1)*. The trees of this zone developed mainly during the Cretaceous Period – about 130 million years back. The original flowering plants were developed in South America.

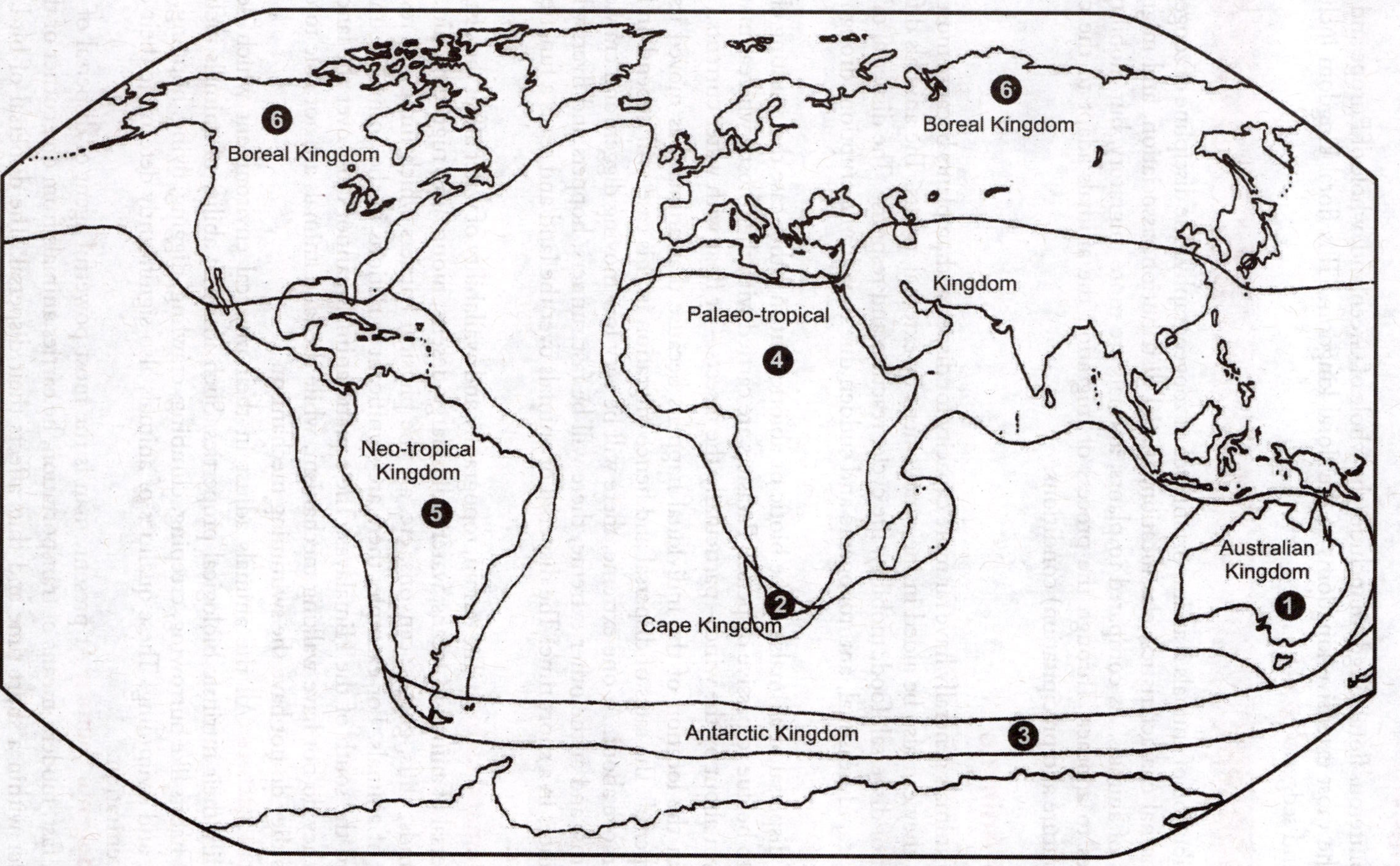

Fig. 2.1 **Present Distribution of Land Plants**

6. Boreal Kingdom

The Boreal or coniferous floral kingdom includes the whole of Greenland, whole of Europe and Eurasia. This is one of the most extensive kingdoms of the floral kingdom. This floral kingdom includes the mosses, lichen and sedges.*(Fig. 2.1)*.

ZOOGEOGRAPHY

The spatial distribution of animals is an important area of zoogeography. The discipline of zoogeography deals with the faunal characteristics, classification, spatial distribution, association, and migration of different species of animals. As compared to plants, animals are more migratory, but mobility ranges from one species to another. Through the process of migration the animals adapt to the changing weather (temperature and precipitation) conditions.

Dispersal of Animals

As stated above, animals generally have far more capacity for dispersal than plants because most of them are mobile, and they can also be aided in their movement by external agents. The animals differ from plants in respect of dispersal, food, mobility, life cycle, reaction and response. The dispersal of animals may be gradual, rapid, seasonal, anthropogenic and sudden due to volcanic eruption, drought, floods and sea surges.

The agent of dispersal of animals can be biotic or abiotic, but in either case the resulting change in location is said to be due to passive dispersal. Parasites are carried with their hosts, whereas many other animals are blown about by the wind – particularly the insects – or float with water currents.

If a change in the location of the individual happens because that animal has moved itself, it is called active dispersal. The rates of dispersal and hence migration in this case, will depend on how fast the animal can move about. At one extreme, there will be very low moving diggers and crawlers, such as the earthworms, and at the other extreme, there will be fast runners, hoppers and flyers which can move long distances in a short time. The dispersal of animals over the land and sea is a function of the following factors:

(i) **Environmental factors:** The terrain, topography and availability of water affect the distribution and dispersal of animals. Oceans, waterbodies, large-deserts, mountains, rugged terrain, ravines, barren lands, cliffs, gorges, canyons, etc. are the physical barriers which limit and restrict the dispersal of animals. For example, there are significant variations in the animals found to the north and the south of the Himalayas. The aquatic animals cannot cross over the land surface because they do not have walking mechanism, while the land animals are not able to cross the oceans as they do not have the swimming mechanism.

(ii) **Biological Factors:** All the animals adjust in their physical environment which determine and modify their intrinsic biological properties. Such intrinsic ability of animals includes the ability of habits like burrowing, creeping, climbing, crawling, digging, flying. hopping, leaping, running, and swimming. These qualities of animals also significantly determine their dispersal and concentration.

(iii) **Anthropogenic Factors:** At present, man is the most powerful agent of dispersal of animals. Through fast, modern means of transportation, he carries animals from one corner of the world to another within a short time and thus affects their dispersal. The dispersal of bird, rabbits, deer, rats, lions, cows, buffaloes, goats, sheep, horses, camels, donkeys, dogs, cats, mules, etc are affected by man. It has been observed that while the natural dispersal of animals is slow and gradual, man can disperse the animals through modern means of transportation from one continent to another in a short period of time.

Distribution of Fauna

The distribution of fauna in world is quite complex. It is closely influenced by the geo-climatic, and ecological conditions. The controlling factors of animals\ distribution may be examined under: (i) Physical factors, and (ii) Biological factors.

1. **Physical Factors:** Each animal irrespective of its size lives in a particular habitat. The landforms, temperature and precipitation have a direct bearing on the distribution of animals. The animals living in a desert cannot survive in a humid climatic condition. It is because of this factor that camels habitat is arid region, while rhinos and buffaloes live in hot and moist region.
2. **Biological Factors:** The distribution of animals is also influenced by the number of a particular animal community, its density, concentration, birth, death, longevity, migration pattern, reproduction and survival rates. In addition to these, the competition for food, food habits (herbivores, carnivores) and the food chain also affect the distribution and concentration of animals. The centre of evolution and dispersal routes of animals since the Mesozoic Era (about 245 million years) has been shown in *Fig. 2.2.*

It may be seen from *Fig. 2.2* that deer, sheep, oxen, bison, saiga (Asian antelope), mammoth, etc. migrated from Asia to North America and through the Central American countries descended to South America. In opposition to this cats, horses, racoons, etc. migrated from North America to Asia. Butterflies, bugs, moths, locusts, grasshoppers, etc. migrated from Africa to Europe and Asia and from Europe were taken to North and South America by ships *(Fig. 2.2).*

FAUNAL REGIONS OF THE WORLD

The leading ecologist and environmentalist A.R. Wallace attempted to classify the world animals into fauna regions in 1876. Since then a number of attempts have been made by ecologists to delineate the faunal regions of the world. The experts divide the world into the following faunal regions *(Fig. 2.3)*.

1. Palaearctic Region

This faunal region stretches over the greater parts of Europe and Eurasia, north of Himalayas. This faunal region includes 136 families of vertebrates, 100 genera of mammals, 174 genera of birds.

The important animals of this region are Russian desmans, arctic-fox, arctic-hare, caribou, reindeer, polar bear; Mediterranean moles, rats, saiga and chiru antelope, ancestors of crocodiles, lizards, moose, mole, deer, lemming, musk-fox, lynx, wild-ass, horse, camel, hamster, jackal, etc., red-fox, black bear, hedge-hog, jerboa, cotton-tail, etc. *(Fig. 2.3)*.

2. Nearctic Region

This faunal region sprawls over North America, Greenland and the Canadian Islands west of Greenland. This is also known as the Arctic Fauna Region. The main animals of this region include deer, lynx, mouse, mules, wolf; bison, jack-rabbit, prairie-dog, gopher, fox; lizards, snakes, kangaroo, jerboa, hamster, hedgehog, cotton-tail, etc *(Fig. 2.3)*.

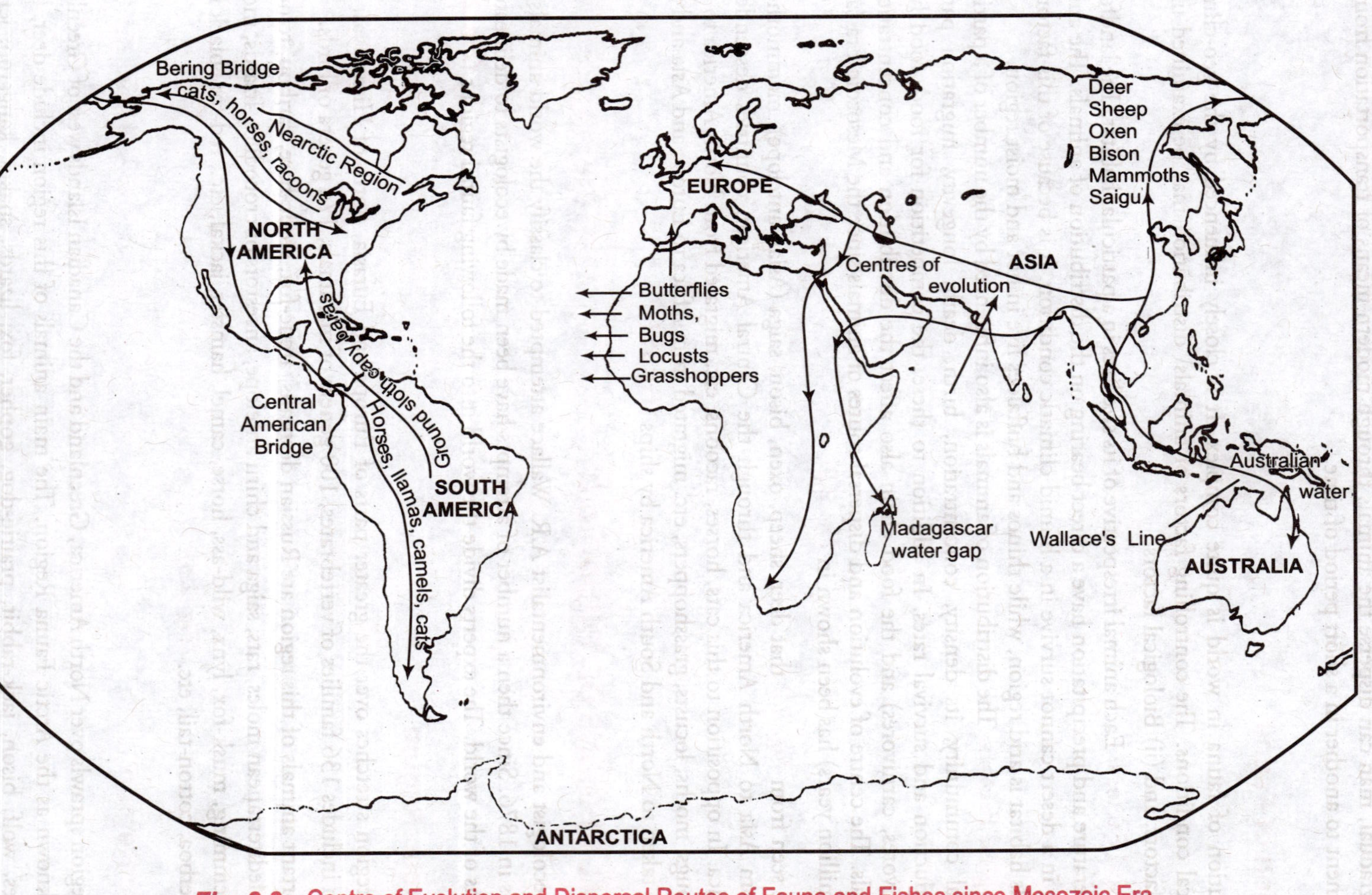

Fig. 2.2 Centre of Evolution and Dispersal Routes of Fauna and Fishes since Mesozoic Era

(**Source:** After G. de Beer, 1964)

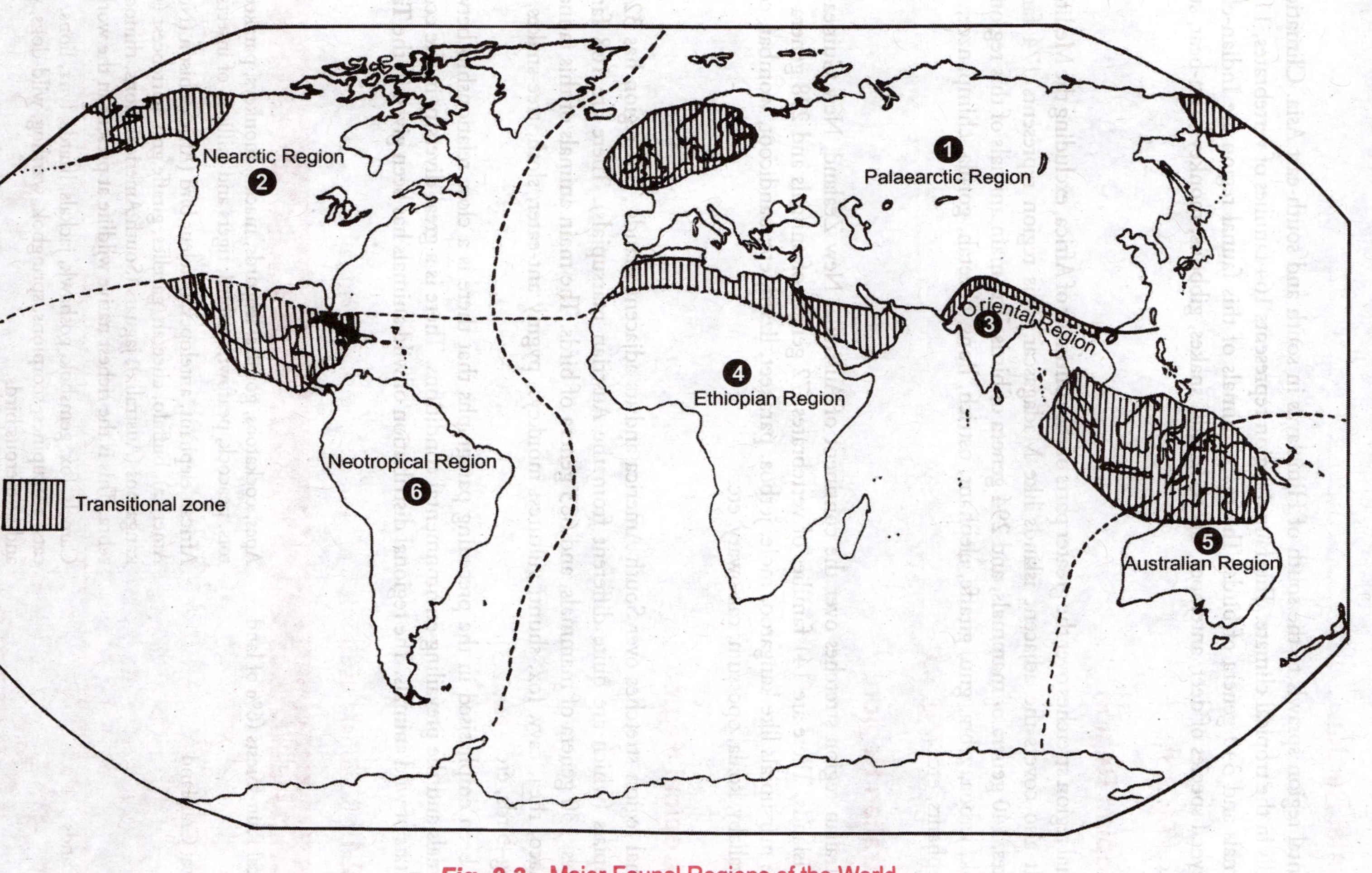

Fig. 2.3 Major Faunal Regions of the World

3. Oriental Region

The oriental region sprawls to the south of Himalayas in south and south-east Asia. Climatically this region falls in the tropical climate. This faunal region represents 164 families of vertebrates, 118 genera of mammals and 340 genera of birds. The main animals of this faunal region are Indian-elephants, rhino, several species of deer, antelopes, tigers, lizards, snakes, gibbons, monkeys, sun-bear, stag, tree-shrew, etc. *(Fig. 2.3)*.

4. Ethiopian Region

This faunal region stretches over the greater parts of the continent of Africa, excluding the Mediterranean region. It also covers the adjacent islands like Madagascar. This region represents 174 families of vertebrates, 140 genera of mammals, and 294 genera of birds. The main animals of this region include springbok, jerboa, zebra, gnu, giraffe, elephant, ostrich, lions, cheetah, gorilla, chimpanzee, monkey, forest elephants, etc. *(Fig. 2.3)*.

5. Australian Region

The Australian region stretches over the continent of Australia, New Zealand, New Guinea and the adjacent islands. There are 141 families of vertebrates, 72 genera of animals and 298 genera of birds. There are marsupials like kangaroo, mole, jerboa, parakeet, lizard, etc; bandicoot, wombat, cockatoo, parrot; wallaby, koala, opossum, cassowary, etc.

6. Neotropical Region

This faunal region stretches over South America and its adjacent islands. This region has 32 families of marsupials (which are quite different from the Austrian marsupials). There are 168 families of vertebrates, 130 genera of mammals, and 683 genera of birds. The main animals of this faunal region are guanaco, rhea, cavy, fox, shunt; vultures; monkeys, pygmy ant-eater, sloth, tree-snakes, parrots, humming–birds, etc. *(Fig. 2.3)*.

It has been emphasised in the preceding paragraphs that there is a close relationship between the wild animals and the prevailing environmental conditions. There is a great diversity in the ecosystems and habitats of wild animals. The regional distribution of wild animals has been given in the **Table 2.1**.

Table 2.1 Regional Distribution of Some of the Wild Animals

Region	Wildlife
1. Tropical Rain-forests (6% of land area)	Apes, cockatoos, gorillas, leopards, macaw, monkeys, parakeet, parrots, peacock, peafowl, sunbird, tigers and millions of insects.
2. Tropical Grassland	African elephant, antelopes, bateleur bird (Africa), bison (North America), buffalo, cheetah, gazelles, giraffe,gnu, hartebeest (Africa), kangaroos (Australia), jaguars (South America), lions, rhinoceros, zebra. This is the richest native wildlife at present in the world.
3. Arid Lands	Camels, fox, gemsbok, goshawk, jackals, lizards, lynx, lions, meercats, porcupines, scorpions, springbok, warthog, wild-dogs, wolf, and numerous birds.

(*Contd.*)

Table 2.1 (*Contd.*)

Region	Wildlife
4. Temperate Forests/Grasslands	Badger, eagle, hoopoe, Koala, raccoon, red-deer, red-fox, sapsucker, stag-beetle, woodpacker and numerous birds.
5. Boreal Forests	Beever, black-gouse, Canadian-horned-owl,Canadian-lynx, coyotes, moose, pole-cat, mule-deer, nut-cracker, red-squirrel, timber-wolf, wolverine,
6. Polar Regions	Arctic-fox, blue-whale, eagles, elephant-seals. Killer-whale, krill, musk-ox, polar-bear, (world's heaviest terrestrial carnivores), penguins, pigeons/pentads-petrels, seals, snow-geese, spotted-seal, trumpeter-swan, walrus,
7. Folded Mountains	Andean candor (the largest bird of the world with wing-span of 3.7 metres), Andean-geese, dall-sheep, golden-eagle, lammergeyer or bearded-vulture, mountain-goat, mountain-gorilla, mountain-lion, pandas, snow-leopard, yaks,
8. Islands	Dodo-bird (Mauritius), frigate-bird, ground-iguana, king-penguins, komodo-dragon, lemurs and tenrees (madagascar), marine-iguana, moa-bird (New Zealand) solenodous (Caribbeans),southern-sea-lion, tomato-red-frog (Madagascar), tortoise (Galapagos Islands-Ecuador-South America), tuatara-lizard (New Zealand).
9. Oceans	Angler, dolphins, fishes, killer-whale, mollusks, reptiles,seal, sea-lion (California), spotted-eal, tortoise, whales, insects,
10. Freshwaters (2% of the planet's total area)	Amphibians, birds, cormorants, eagles, fishing-owl, flamingo, hippopotamus, jacana, pelican, king-fisher, planktons, piranhas (Amazon Basin), mammals, snake-bird, swan, water-buffalo, etc.
11. Wildlife in India	Antelopes, black-bear, black-buck, bustard (the second heaviest terrestrial bird in the world), cobra, elephant, gazelles, gibbon, goat, hyaenas, Kashmiri-stag, leopard, lions, snakes, tiger, vultures, wolf,

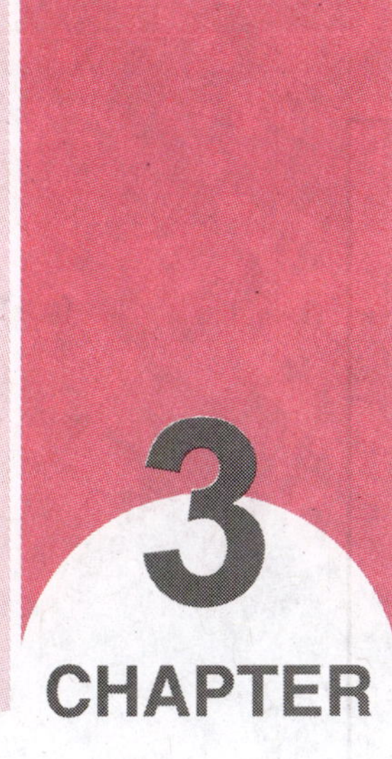

Major Biomes

DEFINITION OF A BIOME

A large terrestrial or aquatic ecosystem characterised by specific plant communities and formations, usually named after the dominant vegetation in a region is known as a biome. The earth's surface, except ice-sheets and the most barren of deserts are covered by some sort of plant cover or biome. No two biomes are alike. In general, the geo-ecological and climate determine the boundaries of a biome. These biomes are important because humans depend on them for food, clothing, shelter, fuel, herbal-medicine, recreation, eco-tourism, natural resources and aesthetics. A biome includes all plants, animals and soils where all the biota have minimum common characteristics and the areas of a biome are characterised by more or less uniform environmental conditions. In brief, biome is a large natural ecosystem wherein we study the total assemblage of plants and animal communities. The biomes of the world may be divided under two categories, namely: (i) Terrestrial Biomes (Forests, Grasslands and deserts), and (ii) Aquatic Biomes (Fresh-waters, saline waters, and marine waters).

Terrestrial Biomes

Terrestrial biome is a self regulating association, characterised by specific plant formations; usually named for the predominant vegetation and known as biome when large and stable. The ecologists recognise the following major terrestrial biomes of the world *(Fig. 3.1)*:

1. Tropical Evergreen Rainforest Biome
2. Monsoon Deciduous Forest Biome
3. Tropical Savannah Biome
4. Subtropical Deciduous Biome
5. Temperate Rainforest Biome
6. Mediterranean Biome
7. Temperate Grassland Biome

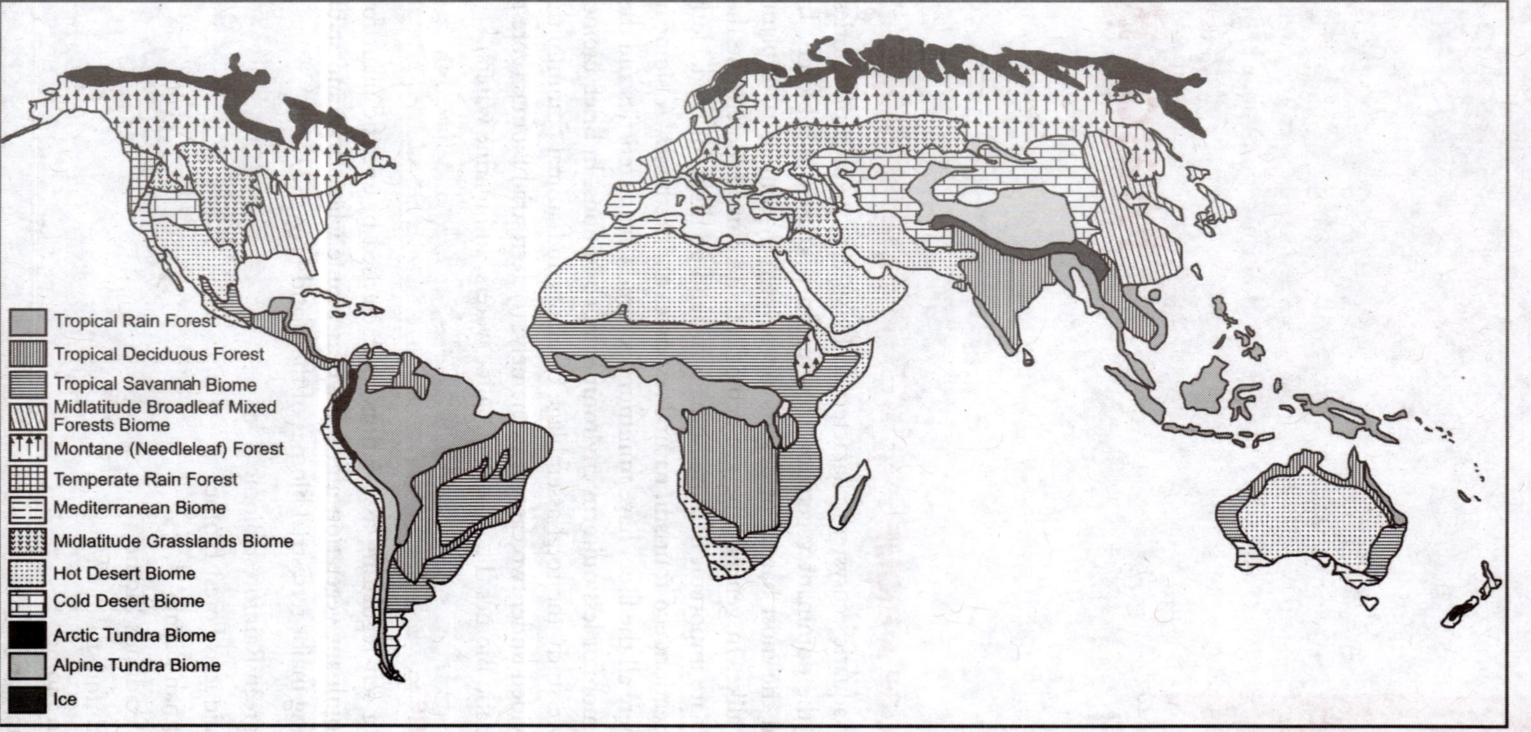

Fig. 3.1 **Major Terrestrial Biomes of the World**

8. Taiga Biome (Coniferous Forest) Biome
9. Desert Biome
10. Tundra and Alpine Biome

1. Tropical Evergreen Rainforest Biome

The Tropical Evergreen Rainforest Biome is a narrow fluctuating belt of unsteady, light, variable winds, low atmospheric pressure, and frequent small scale disturbances. It is located near the equator (10° North and South) between the trade wind belts of the two hemispheres. However, its position, breadth, and intensity are constantly changing. The tropical evergreen rainforest biome provides the optimum environmental conditions for the growth and development of plant and animals as it has high temperature and high precipitation throughout the year. This biome is also called '*optimum biome*' because it has the hot and humid climate and consequent, enormous species of plants and animals ***(Fig. 3.2).***

The largest area of this biome is found in Amazon Basin (South America), Congo Basin (Africa) and the countries of South-East Asia. The Amazon basin is the largest tract of tropical rainforest which is called as *selvas*. In addition, tropical rainforests cover the equatorial regions of Africa, Indonesia, Malabar coast, hilly tracts of north east India, the Madagascar and low-lying areas of south-east Asian countries, the Pacific coast of Ecuador, Peru, Colombia, and the eastern coast of Central America. The '*cloud forest*' at high elevation in the Andes Mountain, which remain perpetuated by high humidity and cloud cover are also the part of the tropical rainforest biome **(Fig. 3.2)**.

Tree is the most significant member of the tropical evergreen rain-forest biome, constituting about 70% of the total plant species. Creepers (climbers) are the second important floral members of the rainforests, followed by epiphytes, which do not have their roots on the ground surface.

The trees in this biome are tall and their density is significantly high. Crowns of trees form a continuous canopy of foliage and provide dense shade for the ground and lower layers. The trees are characteristically smooth barked and without branches in the lower two-thirds. Tree leaves are large and evergreen – thus, the equatorial rainforests are often described as '*broadleaf evergreen forest*.'

A particularly important characteristic of the low-latitude rainforest is the large number of species of trees that coexist. In the equatorial evergreen rainforest biome, as many as 3000 species may be found in a few square kilometres. The ground surface is generally covered only by a thin litter of leaves. Dead plant matter (leaves, etc.) rapidly decomposes, because the warm temperatures and abundant moisture promote its breakdown by bacteria. Nutrients released by decay are quickly absorbed by roots. As a result, the soil is low in organic matter (humus). Many species of plants and animals in this very diverse ecosystem still have not been identified or named by ecologists.

In the equatorial rainforest, because of the competition for light, ecological niches are distributed vertically rather than horizontally. The canopy is filled with a rich variety of plants and animals. *Lianas* (vines or climbers) stretch from tree to tree, entwining them with cords that can reach 20 cm in diameter. About 90 per cent of the climbing communities of the world are found in the equatorial evergreen forest biome.

Epiphytes are also numerous in this biome. Epiphytes are the plants which do not have their roots on the ground surface. The epiphytes live in almost all the layers of the forests of this biome. Plants such as orchids, bromeliads and fern that live entirely above ground, supported physically but not

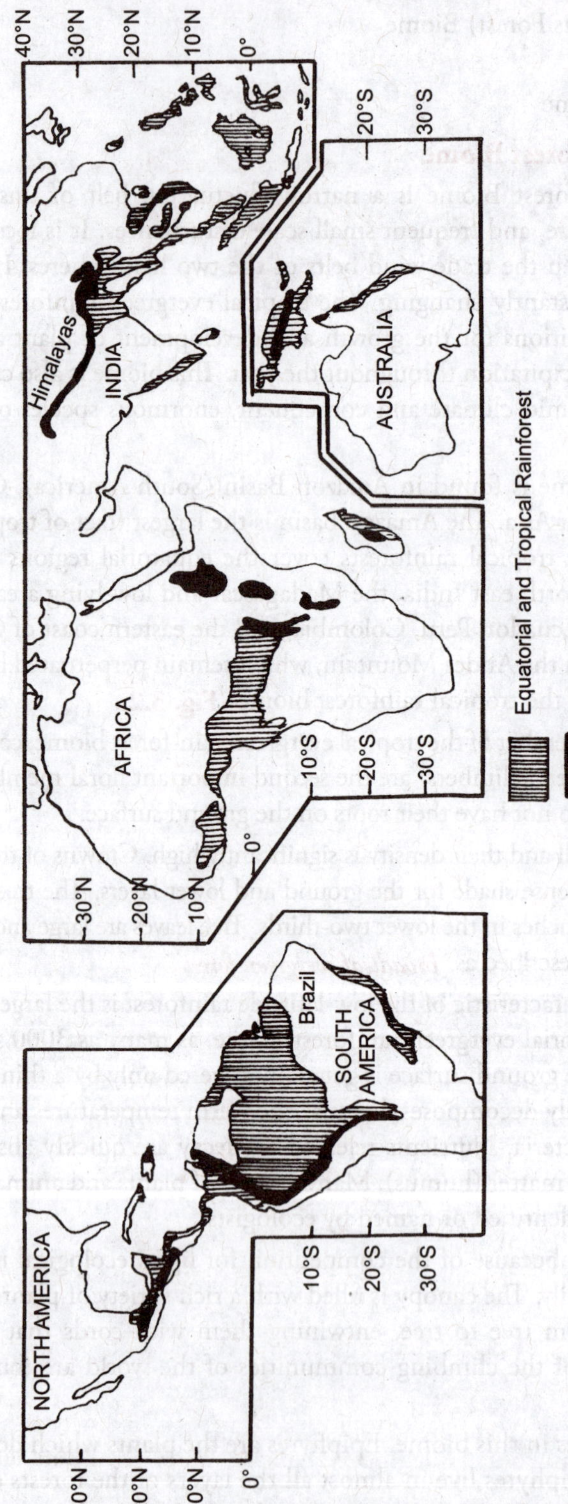

Fig. 3.2 Tropical Evergreen Rainforest Biome

nutritionally by the structures of other plants are epiphytes. Epiphytes plants attach themselves to the trunk, branches or foliage of trees and lianas. Their '*host*' is used solely as a means of physical support. Epiphytes include plants of many different types – ferns, orchids, mosses, and lichens. Undergrowth is restricted in many areas by the shortage of sunlight at ground level. These epiphytes provide certain habitats to microorganisms, such as snails, centipedes, termites, earthworms, lizards, tree-frogs, ants, tse-tse flies, mosquitos, and numerous insects. The main animals include numerous birds, bats, falconet, swifts, parakeets, barbets, monkeys, squirrels, peacocks, bill-bird and fowls. The number of large sized animals is less. Interestingly enough, the elephants of this biome are much smaller in size.

The vertical structure of the forest has three layers. The top layer represents the uppermost canopy of the tallest trees of the forests. The upper level is not continuous but features tall trees whose high crowns rise above the middle canopy. This layer receives the maximum amount of sunlight. The height of the top layer varies between 30 to 60 metres. The second or the middle layer, is the most continuous, with its broad leaves blocking much of the light and creating darkened forest floor. The height of trees of this layer varies from 25 to 30 metres. The lower level is composed of seedlings, ferns, bamboo etc leaving the litter strewn ground level in deep shade. The trees of this layer have broad leaves. The broad-leaf of this layer trap more sunlight which is very low in this layer ***(Fig. 3.3)***.

In the equatorial rainforest biome, the smooth, slender trunks are covered with thin and buttressed by large, wall-like flanks that grow out from the trees to brace the trunk. There buttresses form angular open enclosures, a ready habitat for various animals.

The animals of the tropical rainforests are least mobile because of the abundance of food supply. Most of the animals are arboreals (tree-living) and thus they have been provided additional features by the nature to climb the trees like claws, adhesive-pads, fingers and toes. The ground animals have to pass through the dense and thick covers of trees, shrubs and climbers and thus they have aquired special qualities to make their way through the forests viz. (i) Mammals have generally larger and sturdy bodies so that they can move by pushing thickets of plants away. Such animals include chimpanzee, gorilla, bison, African-elephant, leopard, pigs, etc. Some ground animals are very small in size who can pass through dense vegetation. Some animals are cryptozoic animals. These animals live beneath stones, logs, dead branches of trees, litters and leaves, etc. At the tree tops are the habitats of fast flying species, such as Asian falconet, and swifts etc. Moreover, the forest is full of animal activities throughout the 24 hours of a day. Some animals are active during the daytime while the others are active in the night-time. Consequently, there is always activity in this biome both in day and night, making it as this biome most alive.

2. Monsoon Deciduous Biome

Monsoon forest biome is mainly deciduous, adapted to a long dry season in the wet-dry tropical climate. The trees lose their leaves before the commencement of dry season. Monsoon forests develop in wet-dry tropical climate in which a long rainy season alternates with a dry, rather cool season. The teakwood of monsoon forest is widely used for making furniture, panelling and decking.

These forests are found on the margins of tropical rainforests. The main areas of deciduous forest include the monsoon regions of India, Myanmar, Thailand, parts of Indonesia, Malaysia, Vietnam, Laos, Cambodia, Philippines, Angola, Zambia, Zimbabwe, Tanzania, Nigeria, Central America,

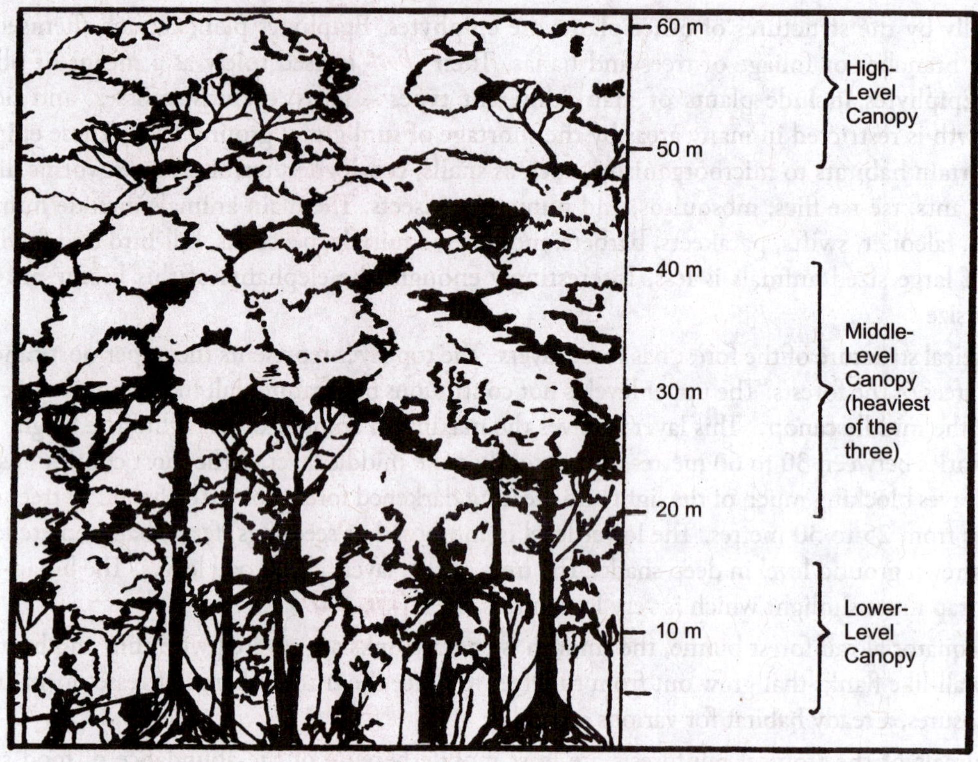

Fig. 3.3 The Tropical Evergreen Rainforest and its three canopies (after Wolfgang Koehler in *Elemental Geosystems*, p.510)

West Indies, parts of Brazil, Guyana, and Venezuela. The tropical deciduous biome is confined to the monsoon regions where the average annual rainfall is generally between 100 and 200 cm. The rainfall occurs mainly during the rainy season. The average height of these forests is about 15 to 25 metres with no continuous canopy of leaves. Locally, they are known as ***caatinga*** in the Bahai State of north-east Brazil, the ***chaco*** area of Paraguay and Argentina, the ***brigalow*** scrub of Australia, and the ***dornveld*** of South Africa ***(Fig. 3.4)***.

The deciduous monsoon forest is typically open. It grades into woodland, with open areas occupied by shrubs and grasses. Because of its open nature, light easily reaches the lower layers of the monsoon forest. As a result, these lower layers are better developed than in the rainforest. Tree trunks are massive, often with thick, rough bark. Branching starts at a comparatively low level and produces large, round crowns.

The trees of this biome are good for lumber, valuable for cabinetry. Most of the trees are deciduous, but the shrubs are evergreen. The trees are characterised by thick girth of stems, thick and coarse bark and large hydromorphic or small and hard xeromorphic leaves. There are numerous climbers, lianas and epiphytes also, but their numbers are far less in the monsoon deciduous biome as compared to the tropical evergreen rainforest biome.

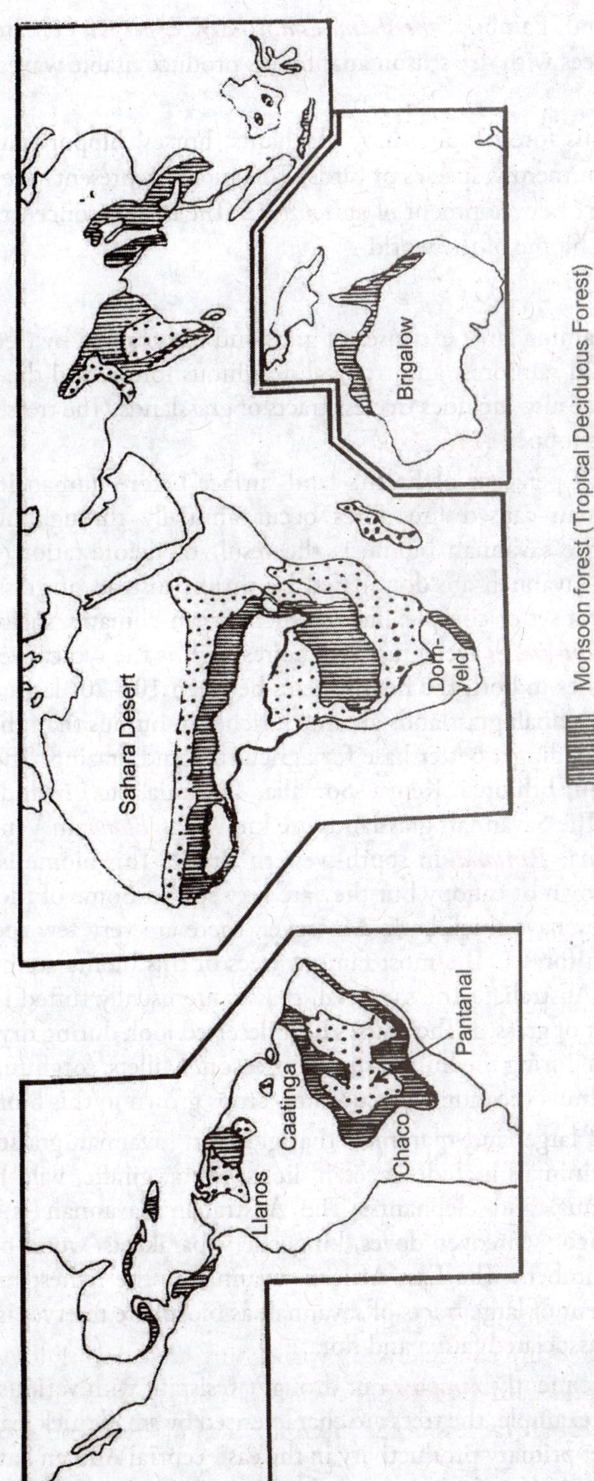

Fig. 3.4 **Monsoon Deciduous Forests and Savannah Biomes**

Teak (*sagon*), sal (Shorea robusta), bamboo, *sheesham, khair, bargad, peepal*, etc. are the important trees of this biome. Some of the trees with dry season adaptation produce usable waxes and gum, such as carnauba, and palm-hard waxes.

The tropical monsoon deciduous forest biome have elephants, horses, hippopotamus, rhinoceros (rhinos), lions, wild-buffalo, and numerous species of birds. This biome represents the largest number of domesticated mammals because of development of agriculture. The largest concentration of human population is also in the monsoon biome of the world.

3. Tropical Savannah Biome

It is one of the major biomes containing large expanses of grassland interrupted by trees and shrubs; a transitional area between the humid rainforest and tropical deciduous forests and the drier, semi-arid tropical deserts. The savannah biome also includes treeless tracts of grasslands. The trees of the savannah grasslands are characteristically flat-topped ***(Fig. 3.4)***.

Savannah covered more than 40 per cent of Earth's land surface before human intervention but were especially modified by human–caused fire. Fires occur annually throughout the savannah biome. According to ecologists, the savannah biome is the result of deforestation, frequent forest fires and overgrazing. The Indian savannah are dominated by shrubs instead of grasses. In fact, the savannah biome is the outcome of a set of complex factors such as geo-climatic, socio-economic and anthropogenic interactions. *Elephant-grasses* averaging five metres high is the typical vegetation of this biome. The savannah biome stretches in both the hemispheres between 10°–20° latitudes. The largest area of this biome lies in Sudan. Savannah grasslands are much richer in humus than the wetter tropics and are better drained, thereby providing a better base for agriculture and grazing. The largest area of savannah biome is in Africa (Sudan, Ethiopia, Kenya, Somalia, Tanzania, etc.) including the famous Serengeti Plain and *Sahel* region. The Savannah grasslands are known as *Llanos* in Venezuela, *Campo-Cerrado* in north Brazil and Guiana, *Pantanal* in south-western Brazil. This biome is dominated by grasses. The trees form flattened crown or canopy but they are very sparse. Some of the savannah trees are fire resistant (*pyrophytic*) as they have thick bark. Moreover, there are very few species of trees as compared to the tropical monsoon forests. The most famous trees of this biome are baobab (Sudan), palm, eucalyptus, and calophylla (Australia). The savannah grasses are usually tufted in structure and form. There is not contiguous cover of grasses. The grasses bear deserted look during dry warm summer season, but they become lush-green during the humid summer season. Millets, sorghum, wheat, maize, fodder, pulses, oilseeds and groundnuts (peanuts) are common crops grown in this biome.

Savannah biome is the home of large land-mammals that graze on savannah grasses or feed upon the grazers themselves. The main animals include cheetah, lions, zebra, giraffe, wild-buffalo, gazelle, antelope, rhinoceros, hippopotamus, and elephants. The Australian Savannah is dominated by marsupials (kangaroo), deer, guanaco. Moreover, doves, kingfishers, parakeets, wood-peckers, parrots, toucans are also found in large numbers. The East African savannah is the richest in terms of total population of animals. Establishment of large tracts of savannah as biosphere reserves is critical for the preservation of this biome and its associated fauna and flora.

Savannah shrubs and trees are frequently *xerophytic* or drought-resistant with various adaptations to protect them from the dryness. For example, the trees are characterised by small thick leaves, rough bark or waxy leaf surface. The average net primary productivity in the east central African Savannah is about 900 dry gram per day sq meter. The African Savannah are the richest in terms of primary productivity.

4. Subtropical Evergreen Biome

The mid-latitude broadleaf and mixed deciduous biome is also known as subtropical humid climate. It occurs in the eastern parts of USA, Great Lakes region (North America), northern China, North Korea, South Korea, and Japan. On the eastern side of this biome are found the warm water currents, e.g. Gulf Stream off the coast of USA, Kuro-Shio along the east coast of China and Japan, Brazil current along the east coast of South America, East Australian Current off the coast of Australia, and Mozambique Current along the south-east coast of Africa. The main species include red-pines, hemlock (evergreen), mixed and deciduous varieties of oak, beech, hickory, maple, elm, chestnut, etc. ***(Fig. 3.5)***.

This biome is characterised by dense forests of evergreen nature in more humid areas, and deciduous in less rainfall recording areas. Normally, mixed forests of coniferous trees and broadleaf trees are found. The broad-leaved forests are both evergreen and deciduous, depending on the distribution of annual rainfall. These forests contain valuable timber but their distribution has been greatly altered by human activities. In northern China, these forests have almost disappeared as a result of centuries of occupation. This deforestation, as elsewhere, was principally for agricultural purposes as well as for the construction materials and fuel-wood.

5. Mediterranean or Sclerophyllous Biome

The Mediterranean Biome lies between 30° and 40° (in some areas upto 45°) latitudes in both the hemispheres. This biome is found mainly around the Mediterranean Sea in Europe, Africa and Asia Minor (coastal Turkey), central California, central Chile, southern parts of South Africa, Tasmania and south-eastern and south-western coastal Australia ***(Fig. 3.6)***.

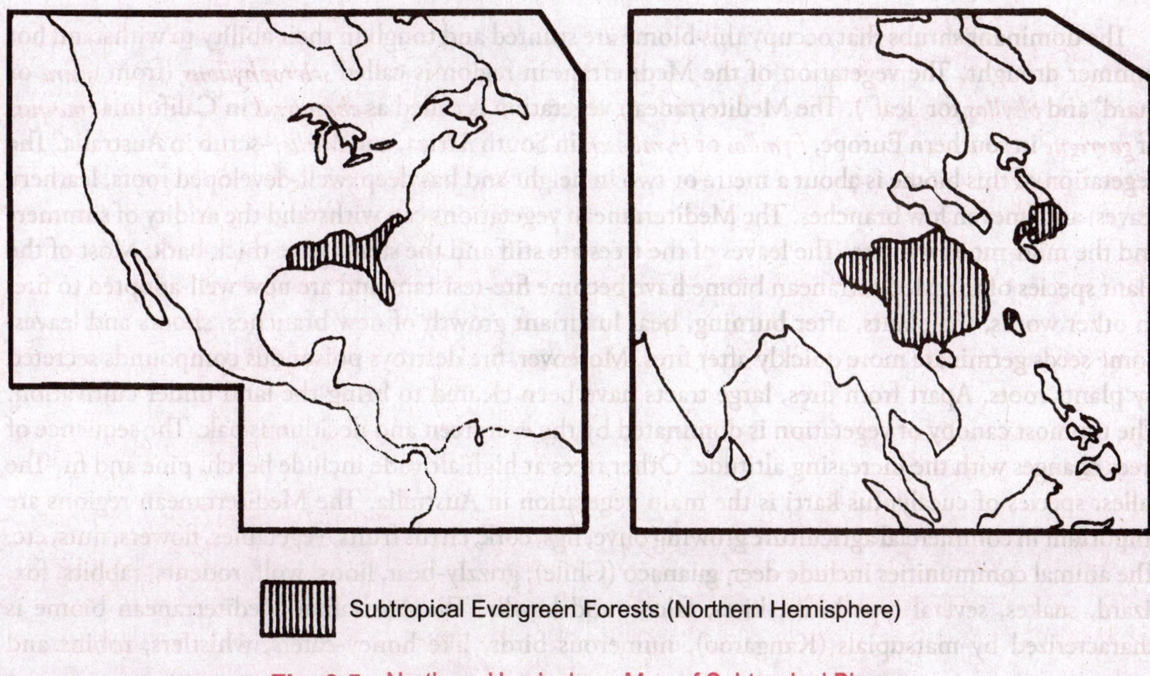

Fig. 3.5 Northern Hemisphere Map of Subtropical Biome

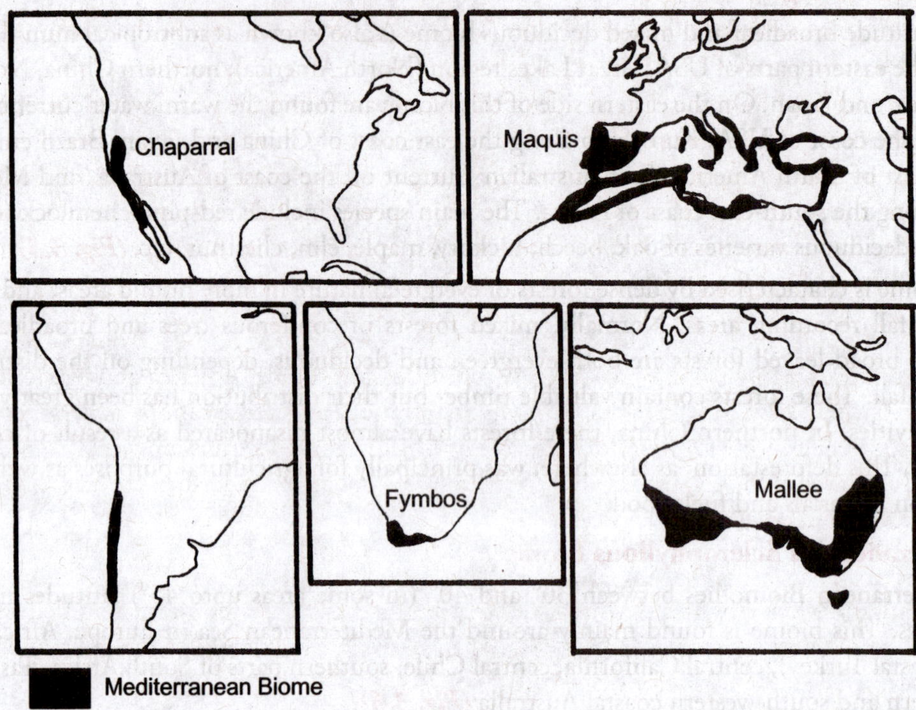

Fig. 3.6 **Mediterranean or Sclerophyllous Biome**

The dominant shrubs that occupy this biome are stunted and tough in their ability to withstand hot summer drought. The vegetation of the Mediterranean region is called *sclerophyllous* (from *sclera* or 'hard' and *phyllos* for 'leaf'). The Mediterranean vegetation is called as *chaparral* in California, *maquis* or *garrigue* in southern Europe, *Fymbos* or *Fymbosch* in South Africa, and *Mallee*-scrub in Australia. The vegetation of this biome is about a metre or two in height and has deep, well-developed roots, leathery leaves, and uneven low branches. The Mediterranean vegetations can withstand the aridity of summers and the mild-moist winters. The leaves of the trees are stiff and the stems have thick bark. Most of the plant species of the Mediterranean biome have become fire-resistant and are now well-adopted to fire. In other words, the plants, after burning, bear luxuriant growth of new branches, shoots and leaves. Some seeds germinate more quickly after fires. Moreover, fire destroys poisonous compounds secreted by plants roots. Apart from fires, large tracts have been cleared to bring the land under cultivation. The topmost canopy of vegetation is dominated by the evergreen and deciduous oak. The sequence of trees changes with the increasing altitude. Other trees at high altitude include beech, pine and fir. The tallest species of eucalyptus karri is the main vegetation in Australia. The Mediterranean regions are important in commercial agriculture growing olive, figs, cork, citrus fruits, vegetables, flowers, nuts, etc. The animal communities include deer, guanaco (Chile), grizzly-bear, lions, wolf, rodents, rabbits, fox, lizard, snakes, several type birds, kites, falcon and hawks. The Australian Mediterranean biome is characterized by marsupials (Kangaroo), numerous birds, like honey-eaters, whistlers, robins and quil.

6. Temperate Rainforest Biome

Known for lush green middle and high latitudes, the biome occurs only along the narrow margins of the Pacific coast in north-west USA.

This biome has few species of trees. The tallest trees in the world are found in this biome. The main species of tallest trees are red-woods (Sequoia sempervirens). These trees can exceed 1500 years of age and in height from 60 to 90 metres, with some exceeding 100 metres. Virgin tracts of other representative trees – Douglas fir, spruce, cedar, and hemlock have been reduced to a few remaining valleys in Oregon and Washington states of USA, occupying less than 10 per cent of the original forest *(Fig. 3.7)*.

7. Temperate Deciduous Biome

Mid-latitude deciduous forest is the native forest type of eastern North America and Western Europe. It is dominated by tall, broadleaf trees that provide a continuous and dense canopy in summer but shed their leaves completely in the winter. Lower layers of small trees and shrubs are weakly developed. In the spring, a lush layer of lowermost shrub quickly develops, but soon fade after the trees have reached full foliage and shaded the ground *(Fig. 3.7)*.

8. Temperate Grasslands Biome

Of all the natural biomes, the mid-latitude (temperate) grasslands are the most modified by human activity. It lies in the interior parts of continents. This biome is also known for the grain and livestock production or '*bread-basket*' region of the world *(Fig. 3.8)*.

In these regions, the only naturally occurring trees were deciduous broad-leaf along streams and other limited sites. These regions are called grasslands because of original predominance of grass-like plants. The history of these plains is the history grasslands. These grasslands are known as *Prairies* in North America, *Steppe* in Eurasia, *Pampas* in Argentina and Uruguay, *Veld* in South Africa and *Downs* in Australia.

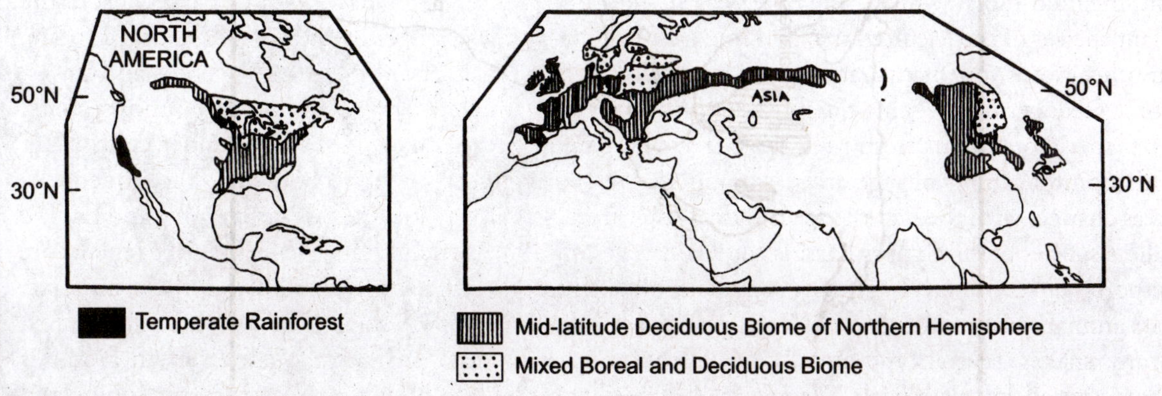

Fig. 3.7 Temperate Deciduous and Mixed Boreal Biomes

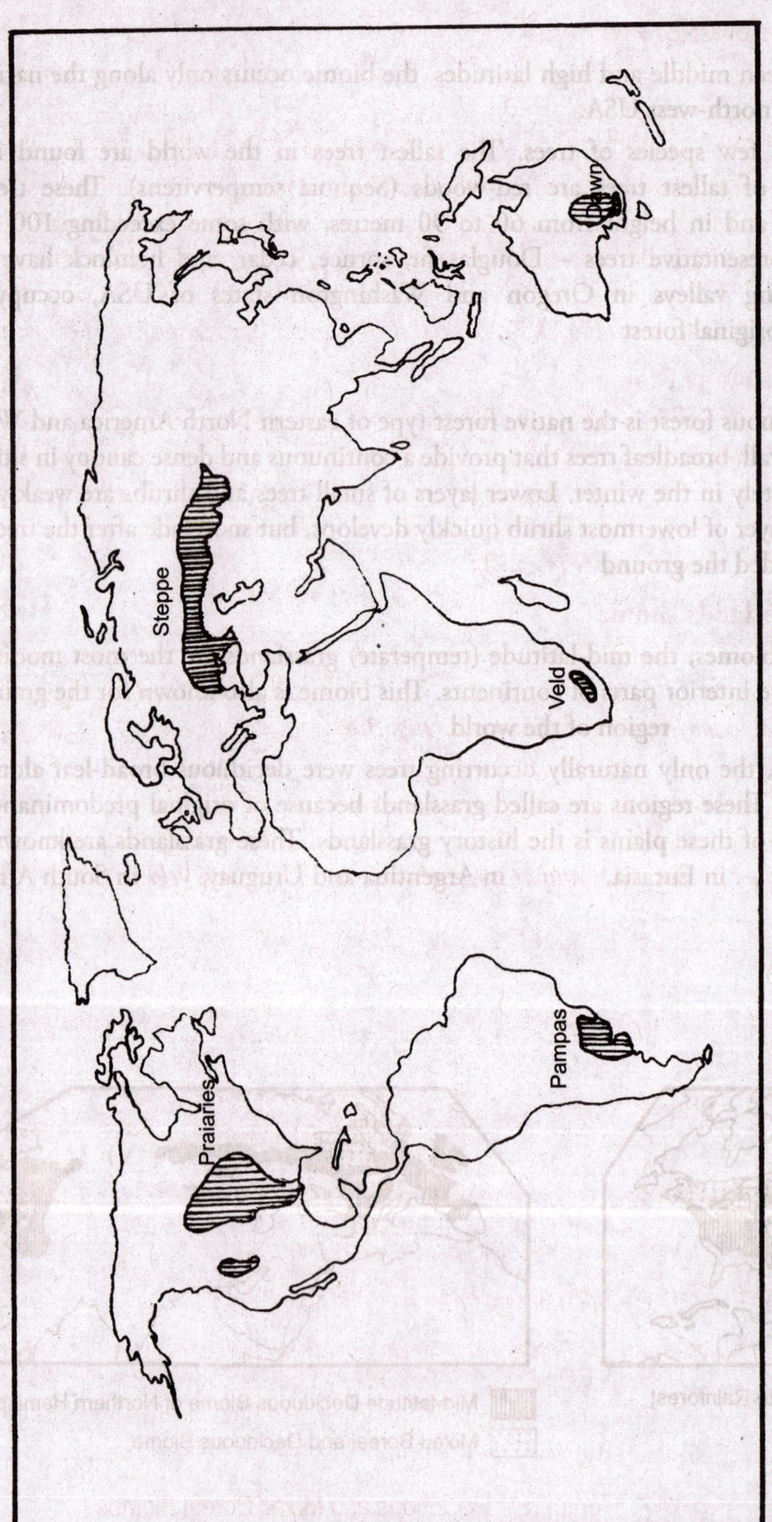

Fig. 3.8 Temperate Grassland Biome

9. Taiga (Boreal) Biome or Coniferous Forest Biome

The taiga biome stretches from Alaska to the eastern coast Canada, Scandinavian countries and the entire extent of Eurasia from the Europian Russia to Siberia. It is confined mainly to the northern Hemisphere. The high altitudes of Himalayas, Andes, Rockies, Alps, etc. are also covered with the trees of this biome. However, montane forests of needle-leaf trees exist worldwide at high elevation. This biome is characterised by extreme continentality. The highest annual range of temperature in the northern Hemisphere is recorded in this biome. Verkhoya-nsk of Siberia records the lowest temperature of –69°C in the northern Hemisphere. There is permafrost of soil from 5 to 7 months. The mean anuual precipitation varies from 35 to 60 cm. The rainfall is however, uniformly distributed throughout the year. Moscow with temperatures of –12°C in Jan and 20°C in July lies in this biome. The main trees of this biome include pines, spruce, fir and larch. Some temperate deciduous trees, e.g. alder, birch, and poplar are also found in this biome. Leaves of the conifer trees are small, thick, leathery and needle-shaped so that they may control excessive transpiration during winter season. Economically, these forests are important for lumbering, furniture and paper making ***(Fig. 3.9)***.

10. Desert Biomes

The desert biome covers more than one-third of the total land area of the world (**Fig. 3.10**). The deserts stand out as unique regions, fascinating for survival techniques. The seeds of some desert plants, called *ephemerals*, wait years for rainfall event for germination. At the occurrence of rainfall, the seeds of ephemeral plants germinate, and the plants develop, flower and produce new seeds, which then rest again until the next rainfall event. The seeds of some *xerophytic* species open only when fractured by tumbling, churning action of flash floods, cascading down a desert arroyo, and of course such an event produces the moisture that germinating seeds need.

Perennial desert plants employ other adaptive features to cope with the desert, such as long, deep tap-roots (e.g. the *chaparral* and *maquis*), succulence (i.e. thick, fleshy, water-holding tissue such as that of cacti and *saguaro-cactus* in the desert of Arizona (USA), spreading root-systems to maximise water availability, waxy-coatings and fine hairs on leaves to retard water loss, leafless conditions during dry periods, reflective surfaces to reduce leaf temperatures, and tissues that taste bad to discourage herbivores. The deserts of the world are classified into (i) hot-deserts, principally tropical and sub-tropical, and (ii) cold deserts, principally in mid-latitudes ***(Fig. 3.10)***.

Hot Desert Biome

The hot deserts of the world are caused by the presence of dry air and low precipitation from subtropical high pressure cells. The true deserts are under the influence of the descending drying, and stable air of high pressure system from 8 to 12 months of the year. These areas are very dry, like the Atacama Desert of northern Chile, where only a minute amount of rain has ever been recorded (a 30-year annual average of only 0.05 cm). A few of the subtropical deserts like Atacama (Chile), Western Sahara, Namibia (Africa), Arizona (USA) and Great Victoria Desert (Australia) are along the sea coast and are influenced by cold offshore ocean currents. These deserts experience summer fog and mist, needed by the plant and animal population. The perennial plant species like cactus, creosote-bush, fetrocactus and acacia are scattered throughout the desert biomes. In salt deposits areas, seepwood, geesewood, sarcobatus and salt grasses are common. In deserts only plants and animals having special adaptations are able to establish themselves. ***(Fig. 3.10)***.

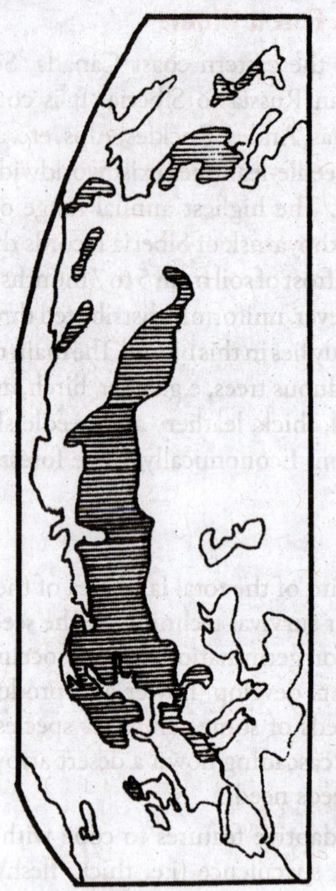

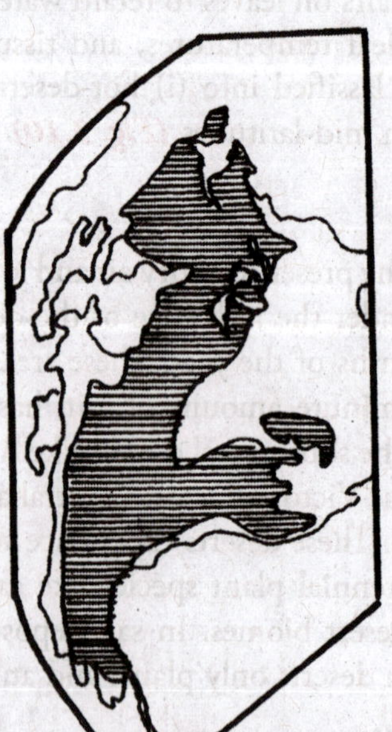

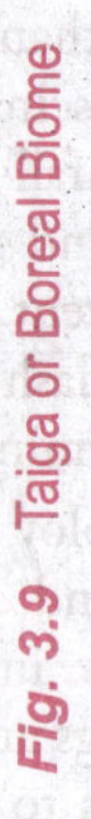

Fig. 3.9 Taiga or Boreal Biome

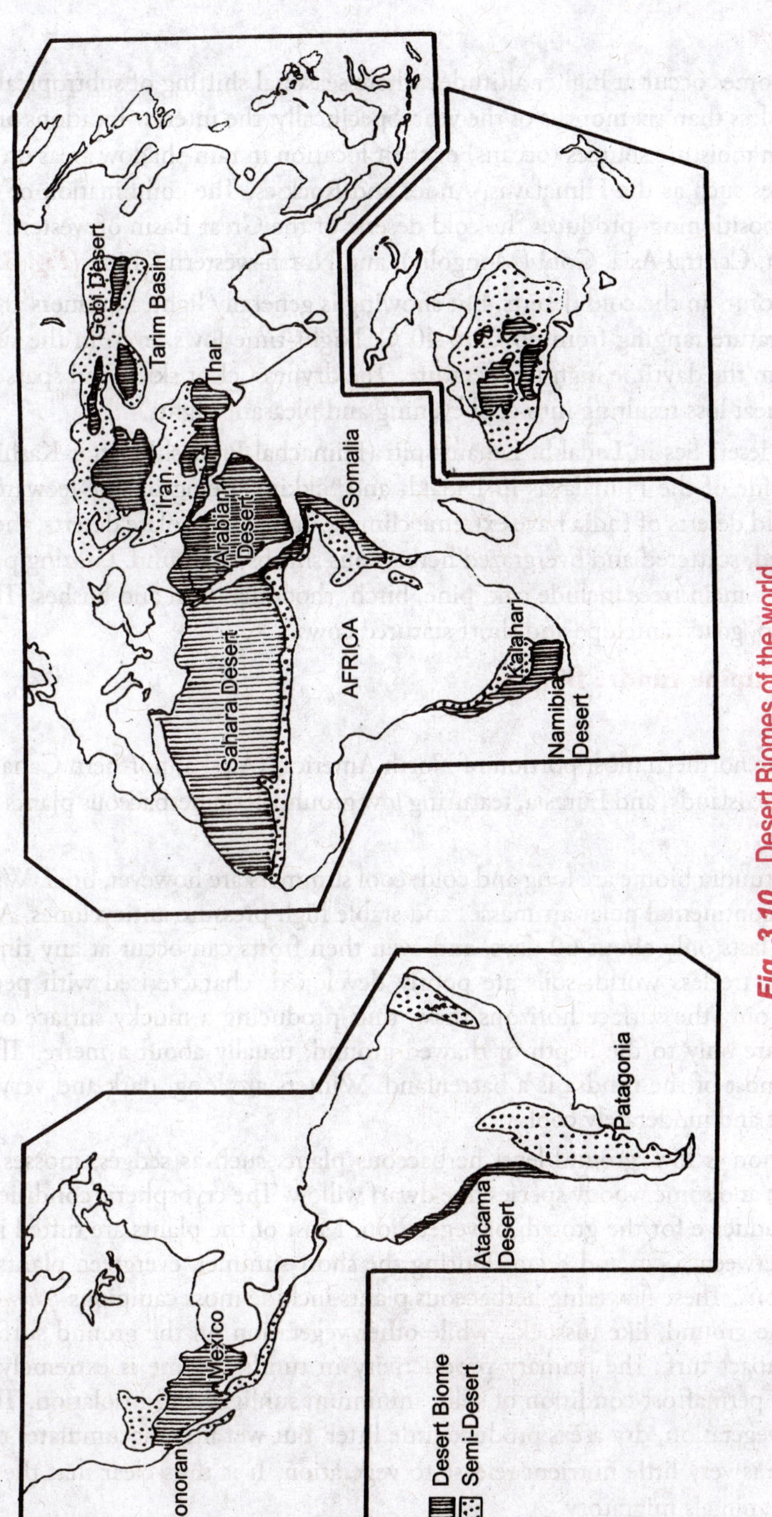

Fig. 3.10 Desert Biomes of the world

Cold Desert Biome

The cold desert biomes occur at higher altitudes where seasonal shifting of subtropical high pressure is of some influence less than six months of the year. Specifically, the interior locations are dry because of their distance from moisture sources (oceans) or their location in rain-shadow areas on the leeward side of mountain ranges such as the Himalayas, Andes and Rockies. The combination of interior location and rain-shadow positioning, produces the cold deserts of the Great Basin of western North America, Patagonia, Ladakh, Central Asia, Gobi (Mongolia), and North-western China *(Fig. 3.10)*.

Winter snow occurs in the cold deserts, but snowing is generally light. Summers are hot with mean maximum temperature ranging from 30°C to 40°C. Night-time lows, even in the summer, can cool 10°C to 15°C from the daytime high temperature. The dryness, clear skies, and sparse vegetation lead to high radiative heat loss resulting into cool evening and pleasant nights.

In India, cold desert lies in Ladakh, Lahaul-spiti (Himachal Pradesh), Uttar-Kashi (Uttarakhand), and the leeward side of the Himalayas in Ladakh and Sikkim. Being on the leeward of the Greater Himalayas, the cold deserts of India have extreme climate. In these desolate deserts, the flora and fauna are unique, isolated, scattered and overgrazed herbaceous shrubs are found. Grazing period is less than 3 to 4 months. The main trees include oak, pine, birch, rhododendron and bushes. The main animals include yaks, sheep, goats, antelope and short statured cows.

11. Tundra and Alpine Tundra Biomes

Tudra biome

The biome is in the northern most portion of North America, (Alaska, northern Canada), coastal strip of Greenland, arctic islands, and Eurasia, featuring low ground-level herbaceous plants as well as woody plants *(Fig. 3.11)*.

Winters in the tundra biome are long and cold; cool summers are however, brief. Winter is governed by intensely cold continental polar air masses and stable high pressure anticyclones. A growing season of short duration lasts only about 60 days, and even then frosts can occur at any time. Vegetation is fragile in this flat, treeless world; soils are poorly developed, characterised with permafrost. In the summer months, only the surface horizons thaw, thus producing a mucky surface of poor drainage. Roots can penetrate only to the depth of thawed ground, usually about a metre. There is total lack of trees. In fact, most of the tundra is a barrenland. Winters are long, dark and very severe, whereas summers are short and moderately cool.

Tundra vegetation is low, ground-level herbaceous plants such as sedges, mosses, arctic meadow grass, snow lichen, and some woody species like dwarf willow. The cryospheric conditions of the tundra region are not conducive for the growth of vegetation. Most of the plants are tufted in the form, and range in height between 5 cm and 8 cm. During the short summer, evergreen plants develop on the ground like cushions. These flowering herbaceous plants include moss campions *(silence acaulis)*. Some plants grow on the ground, like tussocks, while other vegetation on the ground surface horizontally, like mats, or compact turf. The primary productivity in tundra biome is extremely low because of low temperatures, permafrost condition of soils, minimum sunlight and insolation. The harsh climate results into poor vegetation, dry areas produce little litter, but wet litter accumulates to form peat and swamps and there is very little nutrient release to vegetation. It is thus clear that the scarcity of food makes the tundra animals migratory.

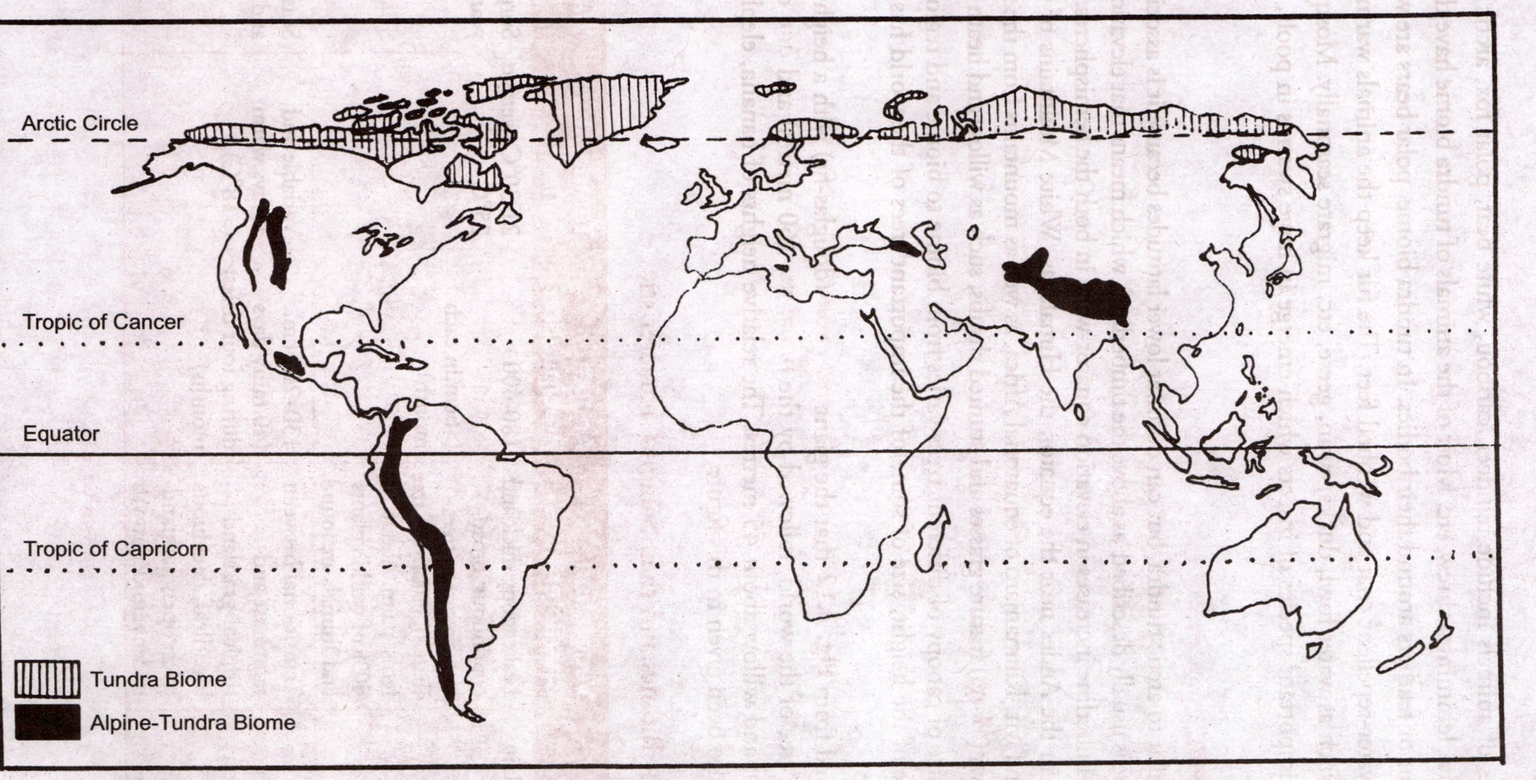

Fig. 3.11 Tundra Alpine Biomes

The main species of animals include reindeer, caribou, white-bear, polar fox, arctic fox, musk-ox, stoat, wolves, rodents, lemmings, shrew, etc. Most of the animals of tundra biome have thick and dense insulating coat of fur or feathers around their bodies. In tundra biome, polar bears are well-adapted to swimming with a water-repellent coat and webbed feet. The fur keep the animals warm during severe winters. The birds such as water fowl, ducks, swan, geese, etc. migrate seasonally. Mosquitoes, midges and blacky are the important species of insects which emerge in huge swarms in pools, lakes, swamps during summer.

Alpine Tundra Biome

Alpine tundra is similar to arctic tundra, but can occur at lower latitudes because it is associated with high elevation. This biome is usually described 'as above the timberline', which means that elevation above which trees cannot grow. Timberline increases in elevation equator-ward in both the hemispheres. Alpine tundra communities occur in the Andes near the equator, the Himalayas, White Mountains of California, the Rockies, the Alps, and Mt. Kilimanjaro of equatorial Africa, as well as mountains from the Middle East to Asia. Alpine meadows (*Margs*) feature grasses and stunted shrubs, such as willow and heath ***(Fig. 3.11)***.

The height and size of canopy of different trees varies from biome to biome and region to region. A comparative picture of the height, size of some of the important trees of the world has been given in ***Fig. 3.12.***

It may be observed from **Fig. 3.12** that the giant *red-wood* (douglas-fir) with a height of 90 to 100 metres is the tallest tree of the world, followed by the *Brazil-nut* (60 metres) and *Elm* of North-West Europe (50 metres), and willow about 45 metres. The relative heights of banana, elephant-grass and other grasses have also been given in this figure.

Table 3.1 Major Biomes and their Salient Characteristics

S. No.	Biome	Vegetation Characteristics	Annual Precipitation	Temperature Pattern	Water Balance
1.	Tropical Rain Forests	Leaf canopy thick and continuous; broad-leaf, evergreen trees (lianas), epiphytes, tree ferns, palm. About 40% of world's plants and animals are found.	180-400 (>6cm,in each month)	21-30°C average 25°C	Surplus all the year
2.	Tropical Deciduous or Monsoon Biome	Transitional between rainforest and tropical-grasslands; broadleaf, deciduous trees; open parkland to dense undergrowth	130–200 cm, (40 rainy days during four driest months)	Variable and always warm (>18°C)	Seasonal surplus and deficits

(*Contd.*)

Table 3.1 (*Contd.*)

S. No.	Biome	Vegetation Characteristics	Annual Precipitation	Temperature Pattern	Water Balance
3.	Savannah Biome	Transitional between deciduous rain-forests, and semi-arid tropical steppes and deserts; trees with flat crowns, great diversity of grazers, antelopes, buffaloes, zebras, elephants, rhinoceros, lions, cheetah, hyena, mon-goose and rodents.	90–150 cm, seasonal	No cold weather limitations	Tend to moisture deficit, therefore fire and drought susceptible
4.	Subtropical mixed Ev-ergreen and Deciduous Biome	Mixed broadleaf and needle-leaf trees; deciduous broad-leaf, losing leaves in winter, southern and eastern evergreen pines demonstrate fire association	75–150 cm	Temperate, with cold season	Seasonal pattern with summer and maximum precipitation
5.	Temperate Rainforest	Narrow margin of lush evergreen and deciduous trees on windward slopes: red-wood, douglus-fir (tallest trees of the world-height about 100 meters)	150–500	Mild summer and mild winter	Large surplus and run-off
6.	Mediterranean-Biome	Short shrubs, drought adapted, tending to grassy woodlands; chapar-ral, maquis, etc	25–65 (summer season dry)	Hot, dry sum-mer, cool winter	Summer deficit, winter surplus
7.	Mid-latitude Deciduous Biome	Broad leaf forest maple, etc. Beach, oak, maple, mul-berry, willow, and cherry. Most animals are vertebrates and invertebrates	75–150 cm	More rains in winter	Adequate in all months

(*Contd.*)

Table 3.1 (*Contd.*)

S. No.	Biome	Vegetation Characteristics	Annual Precipitation	Temperature Pattern	Water Balance
8.	Temperate Grasslands	Highly modified by human activity; major areas of commercial grain farming. Bison, antelope, rodents, dog, wolves and ground-resting birds.	25–75 cm	Temperate continental climate	Soil moisture utilisation and recharge balanced; irrigation and dry farming in drier areas
9.	Taiga Biome	Coniferous, needle-leaf Biome spruce, fir and pine are the main trees, small seed eating birds, hawks, fur bearing-carnivores, little mink, elks, puma, siberian tiger, fox and wolves are the main wild animals.	25–60 cm	Continental climate, high annual range of temperature	Water surplus throughout the year
10-A	Hot deserts and semi-deserts	Bare ground, graduating into xerophytic plains including succulents, cacti, saquaro, sagebrush and dry shrubs, reptiles, mammals and birds	<20 cm	Average annual temperature around 18°C	Chronic deficit, irregular precipitation; more evaporation than precipitation
10-B	Cold desert and semi-desert	Short grass, and dry shrubs	10–20 cm	Average annual temperature less than 18°C	More evaporation than precipitation
11.	Arctic and Alpine Tundra	Treeless, dwarf shrubs, stunted sedges, mosses, lichen and short grasses, alpine pastures, grass-meadows (*Margs*) snowy owl, lemming, arctic hare, white fox, white bear. Reptiles and amphibians are almost absent.	25cm	Warmest month 10°C, only 2 or 3 months are above freezing temperature	Not applicable most of the year, poor drainage in summer

Source: Christopherson, R.W., 1995, *Elemental Geo-systems: A Foundation in Physical Geography*, New Jersey, Prentice Hall, pp.508–9.

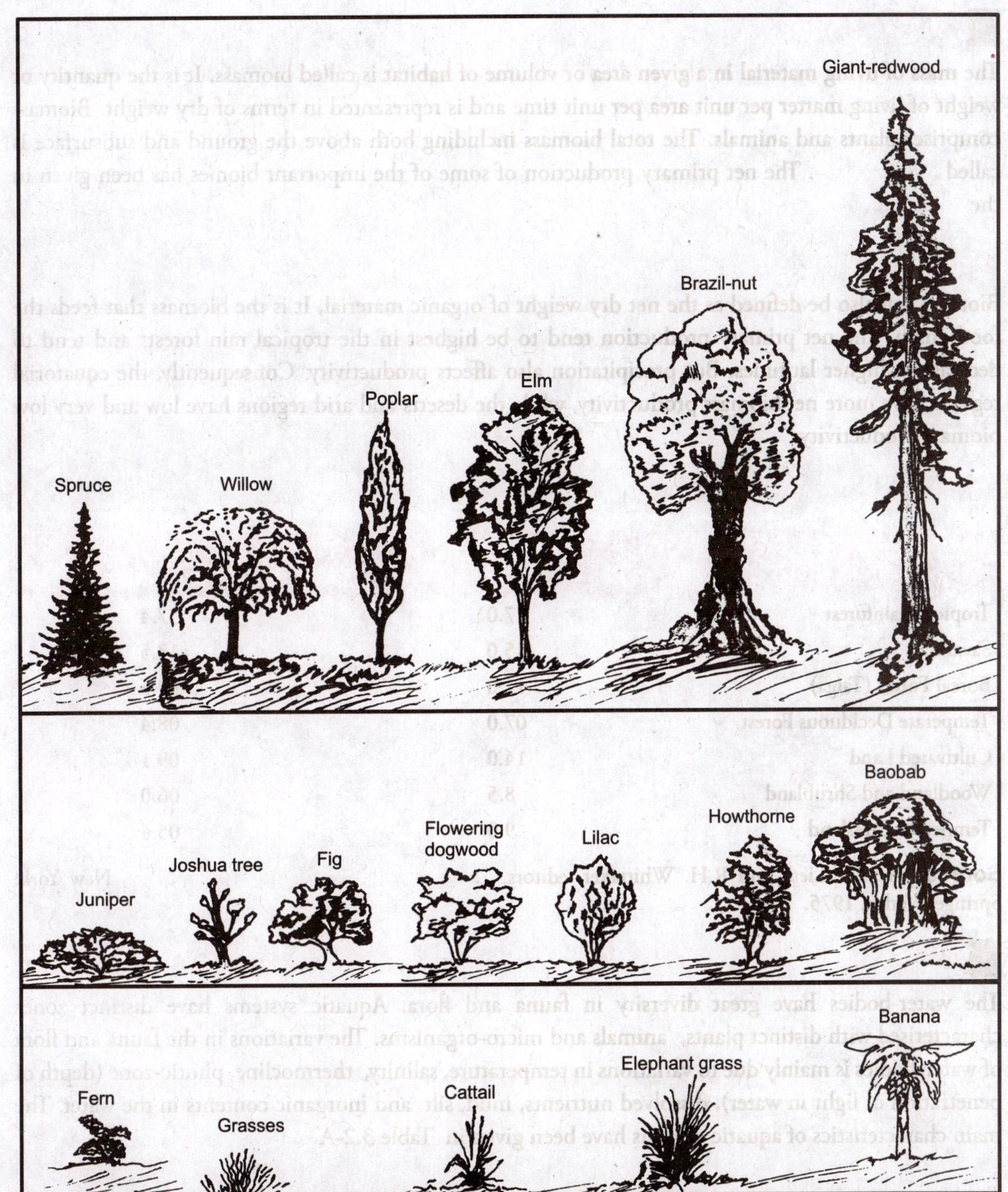

Fig. 3.12 Forms of Plants (after W. M. Marsh and J. Dozier, Landscape: *An Introduction to Physical Geography*, 1981, p.273)

BIOMASS

The mass of living material in a given area or volume of habitat is called biomass. It is the quantity or weight of living matter per unit area per unit time and is represented in terms of dry weight. Biomass comprises plants and animals. The total biomass including both above the ground and subsurface is called *standing crop*. The net primary production of some of the important biomes has been given in the Table 3.2.

Biomass Pyramid

Biomass can also be defined as the net dry weight of organic material, It is the biomass that feeds the food chain. The net primary production tend to be highest in the tropical rain-forests and tend to decrease in higher latitudes. But precipitation also affects productivity. Consequently, the equatorial regions have more net biomass productivity, while the deserts and arid regions have low and very low biomass productivity.

Table 3.2 Biomass and their Net Primary Production

Biome/Ecosystem	Area (106 sq km)	World Net Primary Production
Tropical Rainforest	17.0	37.4
Savanna	15.0	13.5
Boreal Forest (Taiga)	12.0	09.6
Temperate Deciduous Forest	07.0	08.4
Cultivated Land	14.0	09.1
Woodland and Shrubland	8.5	06.0
Temperate Grassland	9.0	05.4

Source: Helmut Lieth and R.H. Whittaker, editors, *The Primary Production of the Biosphere*, New York: Springer-Verlag, 1975.

AQUATIC ECOSYSTEMS

The water-bodies have great diversity in fauna and flora. Aquatic systems have distinct zones characterised with distinct plants, animals and micro-organisms. The variations in the fauna and flora of water-bodies is mainly due to variations in temperature, salinity, thermocline, photic-zone (depth of penetration of light in water), dissolved nutrients, mud, silt and inorganic contents in the water. The main characteristics of aquatic systems have been given in Table 3.2-A.

Table 3.2 Characteristics of Aquatic Ecosystems

Aquatic Ecosystem	Salient Characteristics
Fresh Water Ecosystem	Fresh water may be: (i) running water (lotic) or stagnant water (lentic). Lotic water system includes freshwater streams, springs, rivulets, brooks, rivers, water-falls, cataracts rapids and waterfalls. Lentic water bodies include ponds, swamps, bogs and lakes. They vary considerably in their physical, chemical and biological characteristics.
Marine Ecosystem	About 71 per cent of the Earth's surface is covered by ocean with an average depth of 3750 m and with an average salinity of 35 per thousand.
Estuaries	Coastal bays, river mouths, deltas, tidal marshes. In estuaries, fresh water from rivers meet oceanic saline water and the two are mixed by tidal action. Estuaries are highly productive as compared to the adjacent river, sea or ocean.

The ecosystems of lakes, ponds, bogs, swamps, rivers, deltas, estuaries, brackish water, seas and oceans are known as the aquatic ecosystems. In other words, the plants and animals in water and their abiotic setting constitute the aquatic ecosystems. The aquatic ecosystems provide human beings with a wealth of natural resources. The fauna and flora of aquatic ecosystems may be classified as (i) stagnant ecosystems, and (ii) running water ecosystems

Table 3.3 Classification of Aquatic Ecosystems

Fresh-water ecosystem	Marine-ecosystem
Running water, Rivers, Stagnant water, Ponds, lakes and wet-lands	Brackish water, Deltas and estuaries, Saline-water, Shallow seas (continental-shelf) and deep oceans

Types and characteristics of the major aquatic ecosystems have been described briefly in the following:

Pond Ecosystem

Ponds are generally found in almost all the villages of India. These ponds may be temporary ponds that have water in the monsoon season and a large tank (lake) that has aquatic ecosystem throughout the year. When a pond begins to fill during the rains, its fauna and flora come out of the floor of the pond where they have remained dormant during the dry season. Gradually, crabs, frogs and fish return to the pond. The vegetation in the water consists of floating weeds and rooted vegetation on the periphery, whose roots are in the muddy floor under the water and whose foliage emerges out of the surface of the water. These are in turn eaten by birds such as kingfishers, herons and birds of prey. Aquatic insects, worms and snails feed on the waste materials excreted by animals and the dead plant and animal matter. They act on the detritus, which is broken down into nutrients which aquatic plants can absorb, thus completing the nutrient cycle in the pond. The temporary ponds begin to dry up after the rains and the surrounding grasses and terrestrial plants spread into the moist mud that is exposed. Animals like frogs, snails, and worms remain dormant in the mud, awaiting the next monsoon.

Lake Ecosystem

Lake is a terrestrial body of standing water surrounded by land or glacial ice. A lake ecosystem functions like a huge permanent pond. Lakes are generally more than three meters in depth. A large amount of its plants consist of algae, which drives energy from the Sun. This energy is transferred to the microscopic animals, which feed on algae. There are fish that are herbivores and are dependent on algae and aquatic weeds. The small animals such as snails are eaten by small carnivorous fish, which in turn are preyed upon by larger carnivorous fish. Some fish, like catfish, feed upon detritus on the muddy bed of the lake. Such fish (catfish) are called as '*bottom feeders*'.

Energy moves through the lake ecosystem from the sunlight that penetrates the water surface to the plants. From the plants, the energy is transferred to herbivorous animals and carnivores. Animals excrete waste products, which settle on the bottom of the lake, which is decomposed by the microorganisms that live in the mud of the lake. In this process, plants use carbon from CO_2 for their growth and in the process release oxygen. This oxygen is then used by aquatic animals, which filter water through their respiratory system.

In India, most of lakes lie in the Himalayas and the Satluj-Ganga-Brahmaputra Plains. There are many artificial or man made lakes in India. Out of these the 'Sudarshan Lake' of Girnar (Gujarat) made in 300 B.C. is perhaps the oldest artificial lake of the country.

The lakes may be (i) freshwater lake (Dal, Wular etc.), and (ii) brackish or saline lake (Chilka, Asthamudi, Vembanad, etc.). On the basis of nutrient contents, the lakes may be categorized as: (i) oligotrophic (very low nutrients), (ii) eutrophic (highly nutrient rich) like Dal Lake. Most of the Indian lakes are eutrophic.

Lakes irrespective of their size, are generally more than three meters in depth. The ecology of lakes is different from that of rivers, estuaries, wetlands, seas and oceans. The lakes generally receive their water from the surface runoff. In the long run the lakes receives enormous quantities of nutrients (phosphate and nitrate) from the adjacent areas and human activities. These nutrients promote the growth of algae, aquatic plants and different types of fauna. This process of growth of weeds and plants in water-bodies is known as eutrophication.

Eutrophication

Eutrophication is a natural process in which lakes receive nutrients and sediment and become enriched; the gradual filling and natural aging of water bodies. In other words, it is a natural process associated with a progressive increase in lake's primary productivity as lakes are ineffective at removing accumulated nutrients. Eutrophication is also known as 'ageing' of a lake. In eutrophication, as stated above, the accumulation of nutrients stimulates plant growth, producing a large supply of dead organic matter in the lake. Microorganisms break down this organic matter, but require oxygen in the process. However, oxygen dissolves only slightly in water, and so it is normally present only in low concentrations. The added burden of oxygen use by the decomposers, reduce the oxygen level to the point where other organisms such as desirable types of fish, cannot survive. After a few years of nutrient pollution, the lake can take on the characteristics of shallow lakes/ponds that result when a lake is slowly filled with sediment and organic matter over thousands of years by natural 'ageing' processes.

Consequences of Eutrophication: The main consequences of eutrophication are: (i) change in ecosystem, (ii) decrease in biodiversity, (iii) invasion of new species, (iv) algal boom, (v) depletion of dissolved oxygen level, (vi) loss of coral reefs, (vii) increased biomass, (viii) obnoxious smell (ix) decrease in recreation utility, (x) decrease in aesthetic value.

Red Tide

It is a common name for such a phenomenon where certain phytoplankton species contain pigments and 'bloom' such that the human eye perceives the water to be discoloured. Bloom can appear greenish, brown or even reddish orange depending on the type of organism, the type of water, and the concentration of organism. Blooms can be due to rich nutrients and warm water.

The term 'red-tide' is thus a misnomer because blooms are not always red, they are not associated with tides, they are usually not harmful. Some of the species however, may be harmful or dangerous at low cell concentrations that do not discolour the water.

Wetland Ecosystem

Land areas of poor surface drainage, such as marshes and swamps are known as wetlands. The wetland ecosystems experience periodic flooding from the adjacent deepwater habitat, and therefore supports plants and animals specifically adapted to such shallow flooding or water logging. Wetlands are shallow lakes, generally less than three meters in depth.

Wetlands include lake littorals (marginal areas between the highest and the lowest water level of the lakes), floodplains, bogs, fens, peat-land, marshy and swampy areas.

Classification of Wetlands

The wetlands may be classified into (i)inland wetland, (ii) coastal wetland. The inland wetland may be natural or man made. The natural inland wetlands include lakes, ponds, ox-bow lakes, bogs, swamps and marsh, while the man made wetlands include reservoirs, tanks and waterlogged tracts.

The coastal wetlands include bays, backwaters, creek, estuaries, lagoons, mangroves, salt-marsh, tidal-flats. There may be man-made wetlands also along the coasts like salt-pans and aquaculture tracts.

Social Relevance of Wetlands

Wetlands have great significance for humanity and ecology. Some of the important benefits from the wetlands are: (i) they are the habitats of aquatic plants, animals, birds including the migratory species, (ii) areas where sediments and nutrients are filtered from the surface water, (iii) they help in the purification of water, (iv) they mitigate floods, (v) help in the recharge of underground water-table, (vi) provide drinking water, fish, fodder and fuel, (vii) help in maintaining biodiversity, and (viii) promote tourism and ecotourism.

The wetlands are however, depleting at a faster pace. The main causes of depletion of wetlands are: (i) rapid growth of population, (ii) encroachment of agriculture on wetlands, (iii) over-grazing, (iv) aquaculture, (v) reclamation, (vi) water-pollution, (vii) dumping grounds for industrial and domestic waste.

Estuary Ecosystem

Estuary is the point at which the mouth of a river enters the sea and freshwater and seawater are mixed. Moreover, it is place where tides ebb and flow. In other words, it is the bay of river that receives fresh water from a river mouth and saline water from the sea/ocean.

Estuaries are the most productive water bodies in the world. They are daily washed once or twice by the seawater.

Salient Features of Estuary Ecosystem

Following are the salient features of an estuary ecosystem.

(i) there is free mixing of sea and river water.

(ii) it is relatively calm from the sea waves and provides shelter for numerous type of fauna and flora.

(iii) it is the most productive region, as it receives high amount of nutrients from both fresh and marine water.

(iv) estuaries are the most densely populated areas in the world. About 50 per cent of the world population live along the estuaries and the coasts.

(v) estuaries act as a filter for some dissolved constituents in river water. These precipitate in the zone where river water meets seawater.

(vi) it detoxifies pollutants, working as a natural water filter.

(vii) estuaries support diverse habitats such as mangroves, salt-marshes, sea-weeds, sea-grasses, micro-organisms and mudflats.

(viii) they are the habitat of all kinds of terrestrial plants and animals, such as turtles, catfish, sea-lions, eelgrass, sea-grass, sedge, bulrush.

(ix) they have immense recreational and aesthetic values.

(x) they provide a good ground for teaching and research.

(xi) they protect soil erosion.

(xii) the suspended mud and sand carried by the rivers is deposited in the mouth of rivers, which results in the formation of a delta.

Streams and River Water Ecosystems

A long, narrow body of flowing water occupying a stream channel, and moving to lower levels under the force of gravity, is known as a stream. The enlarged form of a stream is known as river. Streams and rivers are flowing water systems. Some plants and animals, such as snails and other borrowing animals, can withstand the rapid flow of the hill streams. Other species of plants and animals, like water beetles and skaters, can live only in slower moving water. Some species of fish, like the *Mahseer*, go upstream from rivers to hill streams for breeding. They need crystal clear water to be able to breed. The fauna and flora of rivers depend on purity, flow and oxygen content, as well as the geometry of their bed, and banks. The sandy, muddy and hard rock bed, each has its own species of plants and animals.

Marine (Sea/Ocean) Ecosystem

The basic functional mechanisms common to all ecosystems apply as much to the sea as to the land. But major differences exist between the environmental conditions and life forms in the marine ecosystem and those of the terrestrial types. Oceans are the great body of saline water that covers 70.78 per cent of the surface area of the world. They support a total biomass, probably as much as ten times that on land. In many ways the marine environment is much more favourable to life than land areas; it is more equable, and the two most essential gases for life (oxygen and carbon dioxide) are readily available in water, provided it is not polluted. In addition, many of the nutrient minerals found in the Earth's crust are dissolved in the sea in varying amounts.

The marine ecosystem is, however, much larger and more complicated version of the freshwater pond system. The ecosystems in the oceans are influenced by the following: temperature, salinity, and light intensity.

(i) ***Temperature:*** Temperature variations in the sea are much less than those on land. The difference between the surface temperature of the warmest seas like Red Sea (32°C) and the coldest like Arctic Ocean (–2°C) gives a range far less than that of land (about 90°C).

(ii) ***Salinity:*** There is great variation in the salinity of the oceans. The most saline conditions occur where temperatures, and hence evaporation, are highest. For example, the Red Sea has an average value of 40 grams of salt per thousand of sea water (40 %). The lowest values of salinity occur near melting ice or near river mouths. The Baltic Sea has a salinity in summer months of barely 31%o. In open water of the major oceans, the range is much less, from 37% in the tropics to 33%o in the polar seas. Many marine organisms have very narrow tolerance ranges to particular salinity concentration, which may therefore localise them considerably in terms of area and depth.

(iii) ***Light:*** The availability of light exercises as much fundamental control on the basic process of photosynthesis in the sea, as it does on the land. The amount of light reaching the surface varies with latitude and with seasons; much is lost by reflection from the water surface in high latitudes and when the sea is rough. Absorption by the water increases very rapidly with depth; this rate is also affected by the amount of turbulence and suspended matter in the sea. The depth at which the compensation point occurs, i.e. the point at which the light is not sufficient to allow photosynthesis to proceed at a rate which compensates for the rate of respiration, varies considerably; it may be as little as ten metres in inshore water, as much as hundred metres in open sea. The latter figure approximately separates the ***euphotic*** zone, in which there is enough light for photosynthesis, from the deeper ***disphotic*** zone lying between one and two hundred metres below the surface. Light penetrates into the water zone, but it is too dim for photosynthesis. It is noteworthy that the maximum depth of ***euphotic*** zone roughly coincides with the average depth of the continental shelf.

Plant Life in a marine ecosystem

Marine plants are confined to the euphotic zone by light factor. They are far less diverse than land plants, being dominated by algae. The most obvious and visible types of marine algae are seaweeds, but about 99 per cent of marine vegetation is made up of microscopic floating algae (phytoplankton). The phytoplankton are responsible for all but a minute fraction of primary productivity of the marine ecosystem. At this level, total productivity is probably less than on land, mainly because of the relative lack of nutrients in the euphotic zone. Production varies with time and place in the ocean; this is related to light, temperature and particularly to the availability of nitrate and phosphate nutrients. Nutrients absorbed by phytoplankton sink to deeper layers of the sea when the plants, or more usually the animals which feed on them, die. The return of the nutrients for reuse is dependent on upward-moving sea-water. Thus maximum phytoplankton production occurs in areas of upwelling sea-water, as off the coast of Peru or where turbulence and mixing of water is initiated by waves, as on continental shelves *(Fig. 3.13)*. Near-shore areas additionally receive nutrients from rivers. Coastal and estuarine areas, therefore, have a high productivity and great diversity of plant life, making them among the most fertile parts of the marine ecosystem.

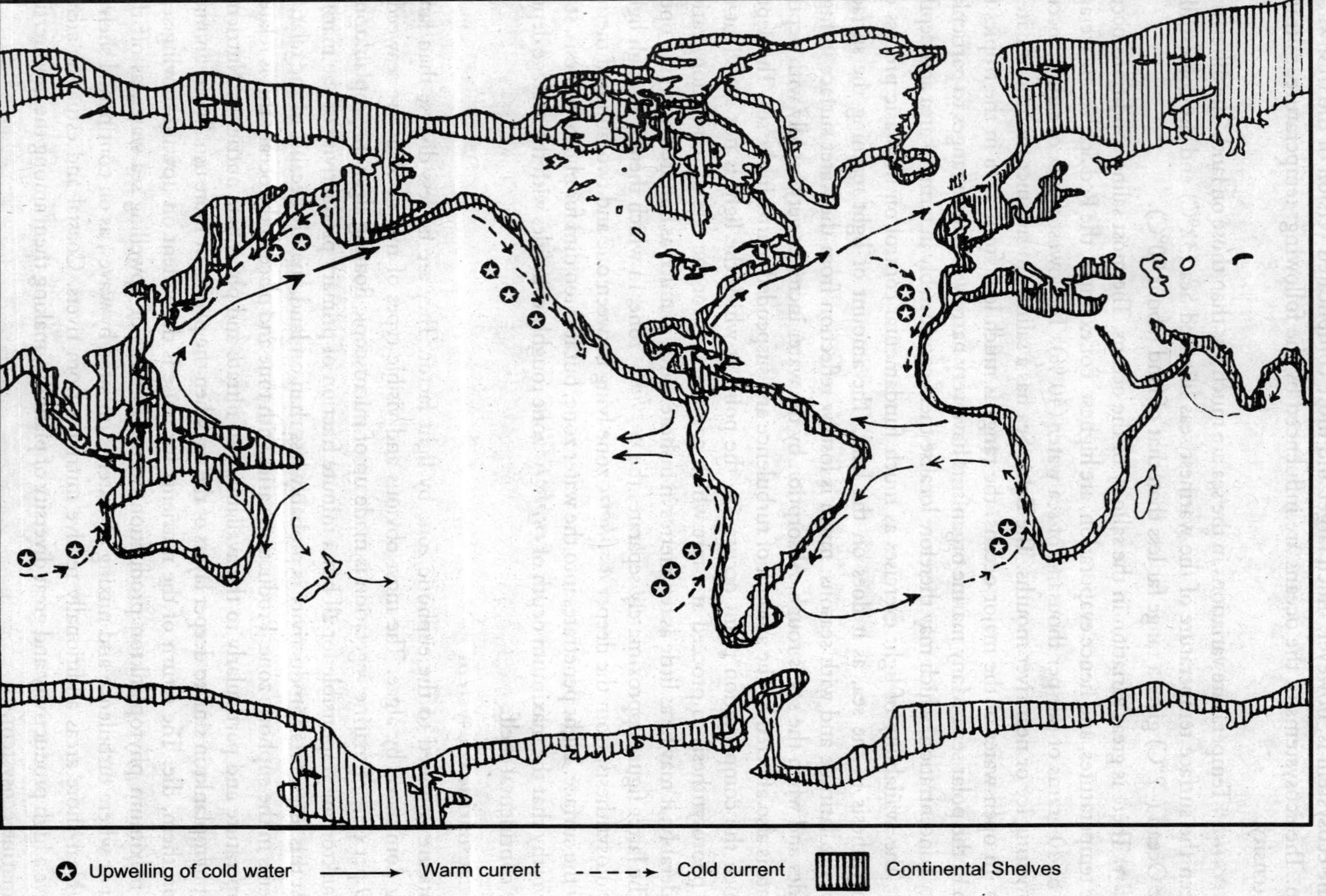

Fig. 3.13 Oceanic Circulation

Classification of marine ecosystems

Numerous types of habitats and ecosystems are found in the oceanic environment at different depths. On the basis of sunlight penetration, depth, sediments, nutrients, and salinity the marine ecosystems may be classified under the categories of (i) pelagic, and benthic *(Fig. 3.14)*.

(i) *Pelagic Biome:* The coasts and sea-shores are characterised with different types of rocks, landforms, temperature and salinity. The pelagic biome is found up to a depth of about 200 metres, mainly on the continental shelves. Pelagic organisms include planktons (phytoplankton-plant-planktons and zooplanktons-animal planktons). There are numerous nektons (swimming organism). Most of the animals of nekton group are vertebrates (fishes). These are found in all oceanic depths. At different landforms of the seashore, there develop numerous types of fauna and flora. Crabs, crustaceans are important in the seashore, who make holes in the sea-sand. A large number of birds feed on their prey by probing into the sand or mud on the seashore. Several species of fish and grasses are also found in the coastal ecosystems.

The numerous fauna and flora species are confined and concentrated along the photic zone. The communities include planktons, phytoplanktons and diatoms. Algae and diatoms are the most important species of phytoplankton communities. Numerous types of bacteria are also found in the pelagic biome.

(ii) *Benthic Biome:* It is the zone of the ocean bottom. It is the realm of open water. The depth of this marine biome, generally, varies between 200 metres to more than 10,000 metres in the abyssal plains and bottom of the ocean trenches. The benthos marine communities live

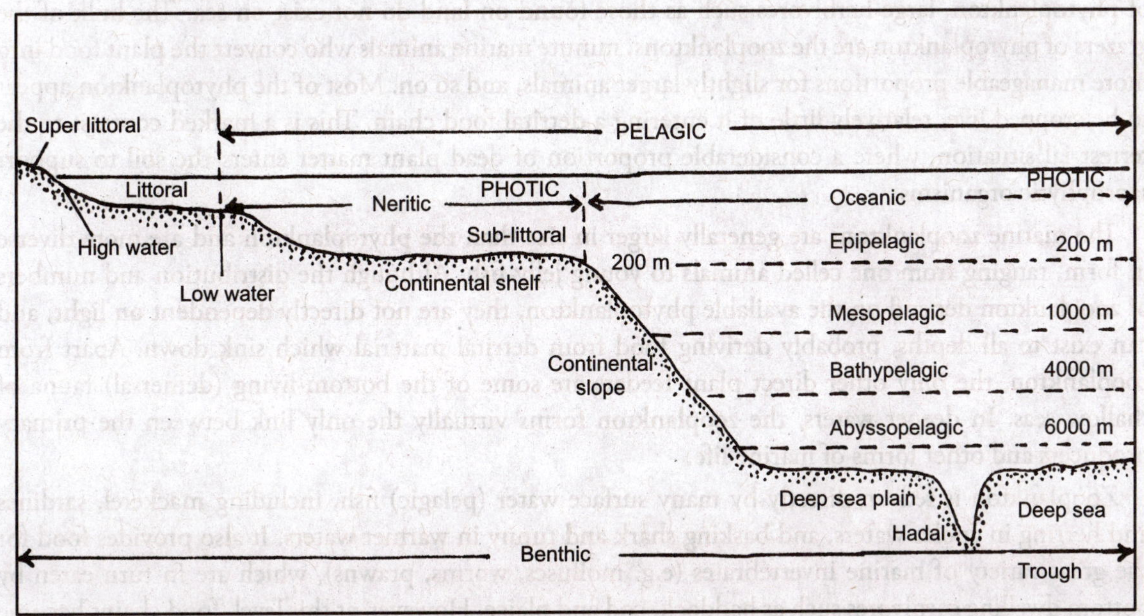

Fig. 3.14 Ocean Classification of Marine Biome Zones

(*Source:* P. Furley and W. Nesey, 1984. *The Geography of the Biosphere*, London, Butterworth; Fig. 13.1)

at the bottom of the seas and oceans. The main fauna and flora of this marine biome include seaweeds, large algae, eel-grass, and turtle-grass. The benthos animals include numerous species of mollusca (bivalve mussels, oysters and cockles) worms, jellyfish, prawns, fish, squids, star-fish, sea-cucumber, comb jellies, brittle stars, sea-spiders, and several bacteria. These animals live in hard outer shells.

The average net primary productivity of different marine biomes is about 350 dry grams per square metre per year. With the increase in depth of the marine biome, the net primary productivity declines steadily.

The peninsular India is surrounded by the Indian Ocean (Bay of Bengal and the Arabian Sea). In the coastal areas (continental-shelf), the sea is shallow, while farther away, it is deep. Both these ecosystems are different from each other.

The shallow seas near Lakshadweep, Gulf of Mannar, Palk Strait, and Gulf of Kachchh are characterised with coral formations. Fish, crustacean, starfish, jellyfish and polyps form the coral ecosystems in the shallow seas.

In the shallow water, mangroves are also an important ecosystem. These ecosystems are dependent on saline water and tides. The marine ecosystem is mainly used by coastal fishermen for fishing. In the past fishing used to be done at a sustainable level and the marine ecosystems were able to replenish and maintain their resilience. At present, with pressure of population and more demand of fish, fishermen are using mechanised boats. Consequently, the population of fish is depleting at a faster pace.

Animal Life in a marine ecosystem

Marine fauna is very diverse, and food chains tend to be long and complex. Because of the tiny size of phytoplankton, large herbivores such as those found on land do not exist on sea. The bulk of the grazers of phytoplankton are the zooplanktons, minute marine animals who convert the plant food into more manageable proportions for slightly larger animals, and so on. Most of the phytoplankton appear to be cropped live, relatively little of it entering a detrital food chain. This is a marked contrast to the terrestrial situation, where a considerable proportion of dead plant matter enters the soil to support saprophytic organisms.

The marine zooplanktons are generally larger in size than the phytoplankton and are more diverse in form, ranging from one celled animals to young jelly-fish. Although the distribution and numbers of zooplankton depend on the available phytoplankton, they are not directly dependent on light, and can exist to all depths, probably deriving food from detrital material which sink down. Apart from zooplankton, the only other direct plant feeders are some of the bottom-living (demersal) fauna of shallow seas. In deeper waters, the zooplankton forms virtually the only link between the primary producers and other forms of marine life.

Zooplankton is fed on directly by many surface water (pelagic) fish, including mackerel, sardines and herring in cooler waters, and basking shark and tunny in warmer waters. It also provides food for the great variety of marine invertebrates (e.g. molluscs, worms, prawns), which are in turn eaten by bottom dwelling carnivores such as haddock, cod and plaice. However, at this level, food chains become complicated; there are numerous invertebrate predators or scavengers which may prey on or compete with demersal fish for food. In addition, certain demersals and pelagic fish prey on each other. At the top of marine food chain, the fish themselves are eaten by sea-birds, seals and man.

Food Chains in Marine Biomes

The food chains in the ocean water are much more complex than that of the terrestrial biomes as there is no effective barrier in the oceans and seas which can restrict fauna and flora to certain fixed localities. The phytoplanktons are the primary producers in the photic zone (up to a depth of 200 m from the sea surface). The primary producers (planktons) provide directly or indirectly, food to all the plant and animal communities of the oceans. Zooplanktons are the heterotrophic primary consumer animals and form trophic level two of the food chain because these feed on phytoplanktons. Phytoplanktons manufacture food through the process of photosynthesis because of the availability of sunlight during daytime. These zooplanktons come upward during the night time to graze phytoplanktons. Most of the nekton fishes and many benthos animals like carnivorous crustaceans also come upward during nights to catch their preys. These carnivorous nekton and benthos animals again return to their respective places during daytime. The above description reveal that the maritime food chain is very complex.

Man's activities in the marine ecosystem have been confined largely to the uppermost trophic level. Exploitation of marine life by man, has been almost solely concerned with animals large enough in size and numbers to make them worth catching. Because of the complexity of the marine ecosystem, the visible affects of pollution are often only seen at a late stage, when it has already affected all trophic levels.

THREAT TO AQUATIC ECOSYSTEMS

Water Pollution

The aquatic ecosystems are facing serious threats both in the developing and the developed countries. The main threat to aquatic ecosystems are from water-pollution, resulting mainly from sewage, disposal, dumping of garbage, and poorly managed solid and liquid waste. The sewage disposal in aquatic ecosystems results into eutrophication. Eutrophication is the excessive growth of algae and other related organisms in a water-body as a result of the input of large amounts of nutrient *ions*, especially phosphate and nitrate. The eutrophication destroys life in water, as oxygen content is severely reduced. Fish and crustaceans cannot breathe and get killed. Moreover, a foul odour is produced which destroy the flora and the fauna of the aquatic ecosystems.

Excessive Use of Chemical Fertilisers

In the wet agricultural ecosystems, the excessive use of chemical fertilisers results into increase in nutrients which ultimately results into eutrophication. The Dal, Wular and Manasbal Lakes of Kashmir, wetlands of Assam, Loktak (Manipur), Nainital, Bhimtal (Uttarakhand), Bhoj Lake of Madhya Pradesh and most of the ponds in the country are facing this problem.

CONSERVATION OF AQUATIC ECOSYSTEMS

The misuse and overuse of aquatic ecosystems may adversely affect the resilience characteristics of biodiversity and ecosystems. For instance, when dams are constructed across the rivers the continuous supply of water is hampered downstream. Similarly, when wetlands are drained, their connected rivers lead to floods in the surrounding areas. As stated above, the most important threat to the aquatic ecosystems is the eutrophication due to sewage and solid waste disposal. Water pollution should get top priority to make the aquatic ecosystems in a sustainable condition. Aquatic ecosystems, especially wetlands, can be protected by including them in sanctuaries and national parks.

Table 3.4 Wildlife in Major Biomes of the World

Natural Environment (Biome)	Wildlife
1. Tropical Evergreen Forests (Biome)	Anthropoid apes, butterflies, gorillas, leopards, macaw, monkeys, parakeet, peafowl (peacock), sunbirds (cockatoos),
2. Deserts and semi-deserts (Biome)	Camels, Goshawk, fox, Indian-lions, jackals, lynx, meer-cat, porcupines, scorpions, springbok, warthog,
3. Temperate Forests (Biome)	Badger, eagle, hoopoe, koala, red-deer, red-fox, sapsucker, stag-beetle, woodpecker,
4. Grasslands (Biome)	Antelopes, bateleur, buffalo, cheetah, elephants, gazelles, gnu (African), jag-uars, kangaroo, lions, zebra,
5. Boreal Forests (Biome)	Black-grouse, Canadian lynx, Canadian owl, Coyotes beaver, mule-deer, moose, nut-cracker, polecat, red-deer, red-squirrel, timer-wolf, wolverine.
6. Polar regions (Biome)	Arctic-hare, Blue-whale, eagles, elephant seal, musk-ox, penguins, polar bear, Krill, seals, snow-geese, snow-owl, pigeons (pentads-petrels), trumpeter, walrus, Weddle-seal,
7. Mountains (Biome)	Andean candor, the largest bird of the world (with a wingspan of 10.6 feet), Andean-geese (dall-sheep, golden-eagle, Lammergeir (bearded-vulture), mountain-goat, Mountain-gorilla, mountain-lion, panda, snow-leopard, yak
8. Wildlife of Islands (Biome)	Dodo-bird (Mauritius), frigate-bird, ground-iguana, iguana, king-penguins, komodo-dragon, Lemurs, tenrees (Madagascar), moa-bird (New Zealand) Solenodous (Caribbeans), sea-lion, tomato-frog/red-frog (Madagascar), Tuatara.
9. Fresh-water (Biome)	Brown-bear, cormorants (fish-eating bird), fishing-owl, hippopota-mus, Jacana, kingfisher, piranhas (Amazon-Basin), Planktons, pelican, piranhas, snake-bird, swan, water-buffalo,
10. Oceans	Angler, dolphin, killer-whale (California), reptile-turtles, seals, sea-lions,

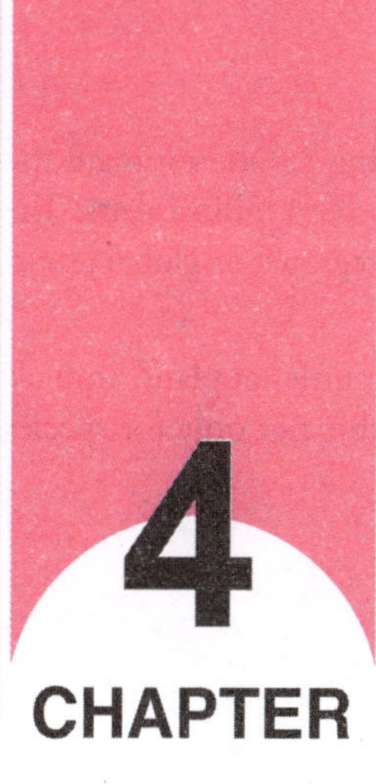

Biodiversity

INTRODUCTION

The term 'biodiversity' was coined by R.F. Dasmann in 1968. Biodiversity is the abbreviation of '*biological diversity*'. It refers to the variety and abundance of living organisms living in a particular region. In other words, biodiversity is the variability among living and non-living organisms and ecological complexes of which they are part, including diversity within and between species and ecosystems. Biodiversity has significance for the survival of human beings and the existence of flora and fauna. Biodiversity provides a large number of direct and indirect benefits to humanity. For example, biodiversity provides food, fuelwood, raw-materials for industries and materials for the construction of houses and shelter. The production of oxygen, reduction of carbon-dioxide, maintaining the water cycle, and protecting soil are some important services. The loss of biodiversity contribute to global climate changes. The loss of forest cover, contributes to 'greenhouse effect'. Biodiversity loss is also causing major atmospheric changes, leading to increase in temperature, serious drought in some areas and unexpected floods in other areas.

Biological diversity is also essential for preserving ecological processes, such as fixing of nutrients, soil formation, circulation and cleansing of air and water, maintaining river flows throughout the year and local flood reduction. Biodiversity, apart from food, clothing and energy provides medicines. This is most obvious in the case of tribal communities. Moreover, biodiversity has great aesthetic, recreational and eco-tourism significance. Biotechnologists use bio-rich areas for the purpose of teaching and research and for the development of better varieties of crops for use in farming and plantation and to develop better livestock. Biodiversity has great ethical and moral values. All the religions and secular creeds believe that all forms of life have the right to exist on earth. Indians have a large number of sacred groves or '*deorais*' preserved by the tribal people in several states. These sacred groves around ancient sacred sites and temples act as gene-banks for wild plants.

The total number of species on the Earth is still not known fully. According to one estimate the number may vary from 10 to 100 million. These species are the products of about 4 billion years. The variety and richness of plant and animal species may be examined at the local, regional or global levels. *Biodiversity has the following five aspects:*

1. The distribution of different kinds of ecosystems, which comprise communities of plant, animals and microorganisms and the surrounding environment which are valuable not only for species they contain, but also in their own right.
2. The total number of species in a region or area.
3. The number of endemic species in a region or area.
4. The genetic diversity of an individual species.
5. The sub-populations of an individual species which embrace the genetic diversity.

In recent years, especially after the concern of global warming and greenhouse gases, the biogeographers are focusing their efforts towards biodiversity, hotspots, environmental pollution, threatened species, and biodiversity management.

BIODIVERSITY HOTSPOTS

The concept of biodiversity hotspots was developed by the British ecologist Norman Myers. The term 'hotspot' is used to define regions of high conservation priority with their biodiversity richness and high endemism and a high threat. Biodiversity hotspots are the areas with a large percentage of endemic species. *The biodiversity hotspots are demarcated on the basis of the following two criteria:*

1. Contains least 0.5 per cent or 1500 of the world's 300,000 species of plants.
2. The region has lost 70 or more than 70 per cent of its primary vegetation.
3. In the case of marine hotspots, coral reefs, snails, lobsters and fish are taken into consideration.

Most of the hotspots are found in the tropical and subtropical areas where the temperature and humidity remain high throughout the year. Species and ecosystems diversity also varies with altitudes above the sea level and depth of oceans.

On the basis of Myers' definition of hotspot, the ecologists have identified the following hotspots in the world *(Fig. 4.1)*.

North and Central America

1. **California Floristic Province** North America has great diversity in topography and climate. The California region of USA has a Mediterranean type of climate in which most of the rainfall occurs during the winter season. This biodiversity hotspot stretches over the state of California and adjacent mountainous areas. In the northern parts of this hotspot, are the tallest trees of the world like the Douglas -fir and oak. In the Mediterranean biome, are found the numerous plants and animals which may adapt to hot summer and cool winters (*Fig. 4.1*).
2. **Caribbean Islands Hotspot** The West Indies Islands support exceptionally diverse ecosystems, ranging from montane–cloud–forest to cactus shrub-lands which have been devastated by deforestation to bring the land under agriculture, grazing and other uses.

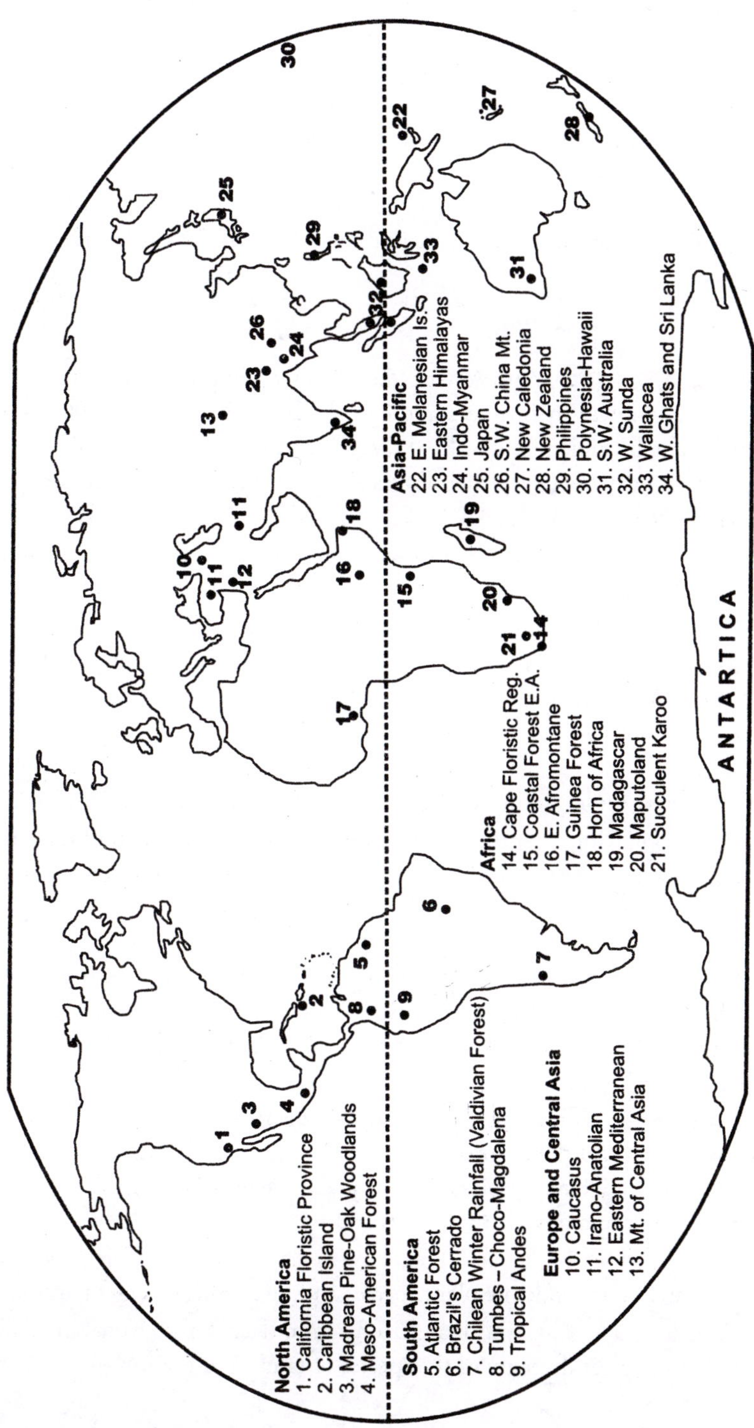

Fig. 4.1 Hotspots of the World

3. **Madrean Pine-Oak Woodlands of the USA and Mexico Border** Along the Mexico border, the summers are hot and dry. The daily range of temperature is significantly high, but the nights are generally pleasant. This biodiversity hotspot stretches over the mountains of Mexico, Baja Peninsula (Mexico) and southern states of USA. It is an area of rugged terrain, deep gorges and canyons.
4. **The Meso-American Forests** Stretching over Central America, it is the third largest hotspot in the world. The endemic species of this region include quetzals, howler monkeys and 17,000 species of plants.

South America

5. **Atlantic Forests of Brazil** South America has distinct physical and cultural personality. This is one of the richest biodiversity hotspots in the world. It contains over 20,000 plant species, out of which 40 per cent are endemic. Locally the vegetation of this region is called as selvas. These are the evergreen forests which keep their leaves all the year round. Each leaf lasts for years, and usually dark and waxy green (**Fig. 4.1**).
6. **Brazil's Cerrado** The Cerrado region of Brazil consists of 21 per cent of the country. It covers the greater parts of savannah biome of South America. It contains a large number of endemic species of plants and animals.
7. **Chilean Winter Rainfall (Valdivian) Forests** This biodiversity hotspot stretches over the Andes mountains. Atacama Desert and low level areas of Chile along the coast of Pacific Ocean. It contains rich endemic species of fauna and flora.
8. **Tumbes-Choco-Magdalena** It is bordered by two other hotspots, i.e. Meso-America to the north and the tropical Andes to the east. It has great diversity in fauna and flora.
9. **Tropical Andes** Sprawling over the equatorial Andes Ecuador, Peru and Brazil, it is one of the smallest biodiversity hotspots of the world, but has rich endemic plants and animals.

Europe and Central Asia

10. **Caucasus Region** Stretching over the mountainous regions of Armenia, Georgia and Azerbaijan, the Caucasus Biodiversity Hotspot contains a large number of endemic plant species. The over-interference of man in this region has threatened the endemic species of fauna and flora.
11. **Iran-Anatolia Region** Sprawling over the plateau of Anatolia (Turkey), Kurdistan (northern Iraq) Elburz Mountain and the central parts of *Dasht-e-Kavir* (desert of Iran), this biodiversity hotspot has numerous endemic species of plants and animals. Many of these plants and animals of this region are not found anywhere in the world.
12. **The Mediterranean Basin and its Eastern Coastal Region** This biodiversity hotspot contains more than 22,500 endemic plant species and numerous species of animals.
13. **Mountains of Central Asia** The Plateau of Pamir, Tien Shan, Kun-Lun and Hindukush mountains region has great diversity of the species of fauna and flora.

Africa

14. **South Africa's Cape Floristic Hotspot** Essentially, it is a shrub-land along the southern parts of South Africa. It has great diversity in endemic plants and animals. Many of these plants and animals are not found anywhere in the world.
15. **Coastal Forests of Eastern Africa** This is a small tract along the eastern coast of Africa. It is rich in endemic plants.
16. **Eastern Afro-Montane** The Eastern African-montane hotspot is scattered along the eastern mountains of Africa. It extends from Saudi Arabia and Yemen in the north to Ethiopia, Kenya, Tanzania and Zimbabwe in the south. The climatic and altitudinal diversity has resulted into a number of species of plants and animals (***Fig. 4.1***).
17. **The Guinean Forests of Western Africa** The lowland forests of West Africa are the home of more than a quarter of African mammals, including more than 20 species of primates.
18. **Horn of Africa** Rich in endemic plants and animals, the arid Horn of Africa (Somalia) has been a renowned source of biological resources for thousands of years.
19. **Madagascar and the Indian Ocean Islands** Madagascar and its neighbouring island groups have an astonishing total of eight plant families, four bird families, and five primate families that live nowhere else in the world (***Fig. 4.1***).
20. **Maputoland-Podoland-Albany Hotspot** This biodiversity hotspot stretches along the east coast of southern Africa, below the Great Escarpment, and is an important centre of plant endemism.
21. **Succulent Karoo** Stretching in Namibia and south Africa, the Karoo Desert has great diversity in endemic plants and animals.
22. **East Melanesian Islands** Stretching to the north of New Guinea in South-East Asia, the Melanesian Biodiversity Hotspot consists of over 16,000 islands. These islands are rich in endemic plants and animals.

Himalayas and East and South East Asia

23. **Himalayan Hotspot (Formerly Eastern Himalayan Hotspot)** This Himalayan Hotspot stretches over the Himalayas, covering Pakistan, India, Nepal, Bhutan and the eastern states of India. Most of the highest peaks of the world are located in this region. In the Himalayas, there is altitudinal zonation of ecosystems. The growing population, deforestation, industrialisation, urbanisation and agricultural encroachment have transformed the ecosystems of the Himalayas substantially. Several species of plants and animals of this hotspot are in the list of endangered or threatened species (***Fig. 4.1***).
24. **The Eastern Himalayas** Identified in 2005, this hotspot spreads over the hill state of north-east India including Sikkim, Bhutan, western Myanmar and the Yunnan province of south-west China. The eastern Himalayas have greater variety of oaks, rhododendron because of higher rainfall and relatively warmer conditions than that of the Western Himalayas. Surrounding more than two million square km of tropical Asia, the Eastern Himalayan Hotspot is still revealing biological treasures. A wide diversity of ecosystems is found in this hotspot including mixed wet evergreen, dry-evergreen, deciduous and montane forests. There are also tracts of shrub-lands and woodlands on limestone outcrops and in some coastal areas, scattered heath forests. It is also characterised by swamps, mangroves and seasonally inundated

grasslands. This hotspot covers about 2,373,000 sq km. The discovery of a new large mammal Muntiacus gongshanensis and four new genera of flowering plants in the region have confirmed that it is a region of active centre of organic evolution. This hotspot is also the home of 163 globally threatened species including Asian-elephant (*Elephas Maximus*), the Great one-horned Rhinoceros (*Rhinocero Unicorn*), wild water buffalo (*Bubalus Bubalis*). The first ever mapping of birds in the Eastern Himalayan region of India has confirmed that it is the home to more than 360 different songbirds species, most of which are to be found nowhere else on the earth *(Times of India 30.5.14, p.23)* The over-interference of man in this region has threatened the ecosystem of this region. *(Fig. 4.1)*.

25. **Japan Biodiversity Hotspot** The islands that comprise the Japanese Archipelago stretch from the humid subtropics in the south to the boreal zone in the north, resulting in a wide variety of climates and bio-diversity in ecosystems.
26. **Mountains of South-West China** The province of Yunnan (China) and surrounding mountainous areas have great diversity in endemic plants and animals.
27. **New Caledonia** A group of islands in the South Pacific Ocean, New Caledonia is the home of more than five endemic plant families.
28. **New Zealand Biodiversity Hotspot** It is a mountainous archipelago once dominated by temperate rainforests. New Zealand has great biodiversity in endemic plants and animals.
29. **Philippine Biodiversity Hotspot** This biodiversity hotspot is spread over 7000 islands of Philippines. It is identified as one of the richest biodiversity hotspots of the world.
30. **Polynesia and Micronesian Islands Complex including Hawaii** Based on 4500 islands, this biodiversity hotspot is the epicentre of current global extinction crisis.
31. **South-Western Australia** The forests, woodlands, shrub-lands and heath of this hotspot are characterised by high endemism among plants and reptiles.
32. **Western Sunda (Indonesia, Malay and Brunei)** Stretching over Indonesia, Borneo, Brunei, Celebes, and Malaysia, this biodiversity hotspot is quite rich in endemic plants and animals.
33. **Wallace (Eastern Indonesia)** The fauna and flora of Wallace are varied that every island in this hotspot needs secure protected areas to preserve endemic plants and animals, and the biodiversity of the region.
34. **The Western Ghats of India and the Islands of Sri Lanka** This biodiversity hotspot sprawls over the Western Ghats in India and the islands of Sri Lanka. The two main centres of diversity are Agasthymalai Hills, and the Silent Valley of Kerala. In this region, there is a great diversity in terrain, topography, climate, drainage, soils, and natural vegetation. Its natural vegetation varies from the tropical evergreen forests to deciduous and thorny bushes. It is the home of 1100 animal species out of which 20 are endemic including the Lion-tailed Macaque and Asian Elephants. Moreover, out of the 450 bird species, 35 are endemic. This hotspot also contains 6000 vascular plant species out of which more than 3000 (52%) are endemic to the area. Moreover, it has 15,000 flowering plants, and a large number of endemic amphibians, freshwater fish and invertebrates. The forests of the Western Ghats are adversely affected by the rapid growth of population, industrialisation, urbanisation and agricultural encroachments. Deforestation in Sri Lanka for the purpose of timber has threatened the biodiversity of the hotspot *(Fig. 4.1)*.

EXTINCTION OF WILDLIFE

Evolution not only creates new species, but also eliminates some old ones. Extinction or elimination implies complete disappearance of a species from the Earth. Complete disappearance means when the last surviving member of a species dies. Of all the species existing on Earth, man is considered to be the most powerful.

Types of Extinction

There are three types of extinction of species: (a) Natural extinction, includes glaciation, climate change, volcanic eruption, disease, epidemics, increase of competitions, predators, shortage of food supply, and invasion of species. (b) Mass extinction which occurs in million of years, e.g. dinosaurs, mammoth, etc. (c) Anthropogenic extinction such as hunting, or capture and persecution. This is due to unlimited needs of man which deplete biodiversity severely in short period of time.

Natural Extinction: The natural extinction of species is due to (i) Continental Drift and Plate Tectonics, (ii) climatic change, (iii) volcanic eruptions, (iv) increased frequency of earthquakes, and high frequency of drought, floods and (v) epidemics.

Extinction in vascular plants has been more gradual compared with the loss of animals. It is believed that extinction among this group was due to more competitive displacement by more advanced plant forms, or due to a gradual climate change than due to any sudden and catastrophic event.

Artificial Extinction: Extinction of species is a natural process. The role of man in the extinction of fauna and flora cannot be underestimated. The extinction of flora and fauna by human interaction with nature is known as artificial extinction. The species of fauna and flora are threatened with extinction by the intervention of humans due to:

(i) Direct causes: such as hunting, poaching, capture and persecution.

(ii) Indirect causes: Such as habitat loss, modification and fragmentation and the introduction of invasive species.

The main anthropogenic factors include: (i) rapid growth of human population (ii) changes in cropping patterns (iii) unscientific rotation of crops (iv) increase in the population of livestock (v) degradation of habitat (vi) growing interest in tourism and eco-tourism (vii) global warming and climatic change and (viii) stochastic factors like fire.

Strategies to prevent artificial extinction

Preventive Strategies: (i) construction of artificial barriers (physical and biological) (ii) alternative livestock husbandry (iii) resettlement of human habitations and settlement of population (iv) garbage and waste management which restricts wildlife access to refuse.

Mitigatory Strategies: The following steps can mitigate the adverse situation: (i) insurance programmes (ii) community based natural resource management (iii) regulated harvest (iv) increase alternate crops, forests and water points (v) education and awareness of the local population and (vi) sharing of information at different levels.

The main characteristics of species susceptible to extinction are:

(i) Large body size viz. Bengal-tiger, lion and Indian elephant.

(ii) Small size of population and low reproductive rate, blue-whale, giant-panda.
(iii) Feeding at high trophic levels in food-chain, Bengal-tiger, White-bellied-eagle, etc.
(iv) Fixed migratory routes and habitat: blue-whale, whooping-crane.
(v) Localised and narrow range of distribution, e.g. woodland-caribou and many island species.

Man has been responsible for the extinction of many biological species, due to overexploitation of resources and the consequent environmental degradation. It is estimated that since 1900, on an average, one species of mammals has been disappearing from the Earth every year. Apart from this, numerous species of plants and other animals have also been disappearing from the Earth every year.

The extinction may be caused by numerous factors which may include: (i) destruction of natural habitat; (ii) hunting of wild animals for food, sport or recreation; (iii) forest fire; (iv) induction of exotic species; (v) ignorance or lack of education, and (vi) apathy of the law enforcing agencies.

The rapid growth of population, industrialisation, urbanisation, higher standard of living, modernism, and consumerism are the main factors responsible for the destruction of natural habitat of many of the plants and animals. For instance, deforestation is done for the development of grazing grounds, agricultural land, infrastructure for industries and transport for socio-economic development. But the process of clearing of forests may have deprived many wild species their natural habitat. Interestingly enough, even the improving hygiene ethics and cleanliness, may deprive some scavenger species like the crows, vultures, kites, etc. of their food.

During the period of stone age (Paleolithic Period) hunting was done by hunters and food gatherers to get food, but at present, killing of wild animals, facilitated by availability of firearms, is being carried on for games, sports, recreation, trade of animal products (like hides, skins, ivory, fur, feathers, horns, meats, etc.). Hunting thus has endangered the existence of many species ever since the appearance of man on the Earth's surface. Similarly, forest fires, whether accidental or for clearing of forests for agricultural purposes, alter the natural habitat altogether depriving the wildlife of their natural habitat.

IUCN and its Red Data Book

Established in 1964, the International Union for Conservation of Nature's Red List of Threatened Species has evolved to become the world's most comprehensive information source on the global conservation status of animal, fungi and plant species.

The IUCN Red List is a critical indicator of the health of the world's biodiversity.Far more than a list of species and their status, it is a powerful tool to inform and catalyze action for biodiversity conservation and policy change, critical to protecting the natural resources we need to survive. It provides information about range, population size, habitat and ecology, use and/or trade, threats, and conservation actions that will help inform necessary conservation decisions.

The Red Data Book is the state document established for documenting rare and endangered species of plants, animals, and fungi, that exist within the berritory of the state or country.

Currently there are more than 105,700 species on The IUCN Red List, with more than 28,000 species threatened with extinction, including 40% of amphibians, 34% of conifers, 33% of reef building corals, 25% of mammals and 14% of birds.

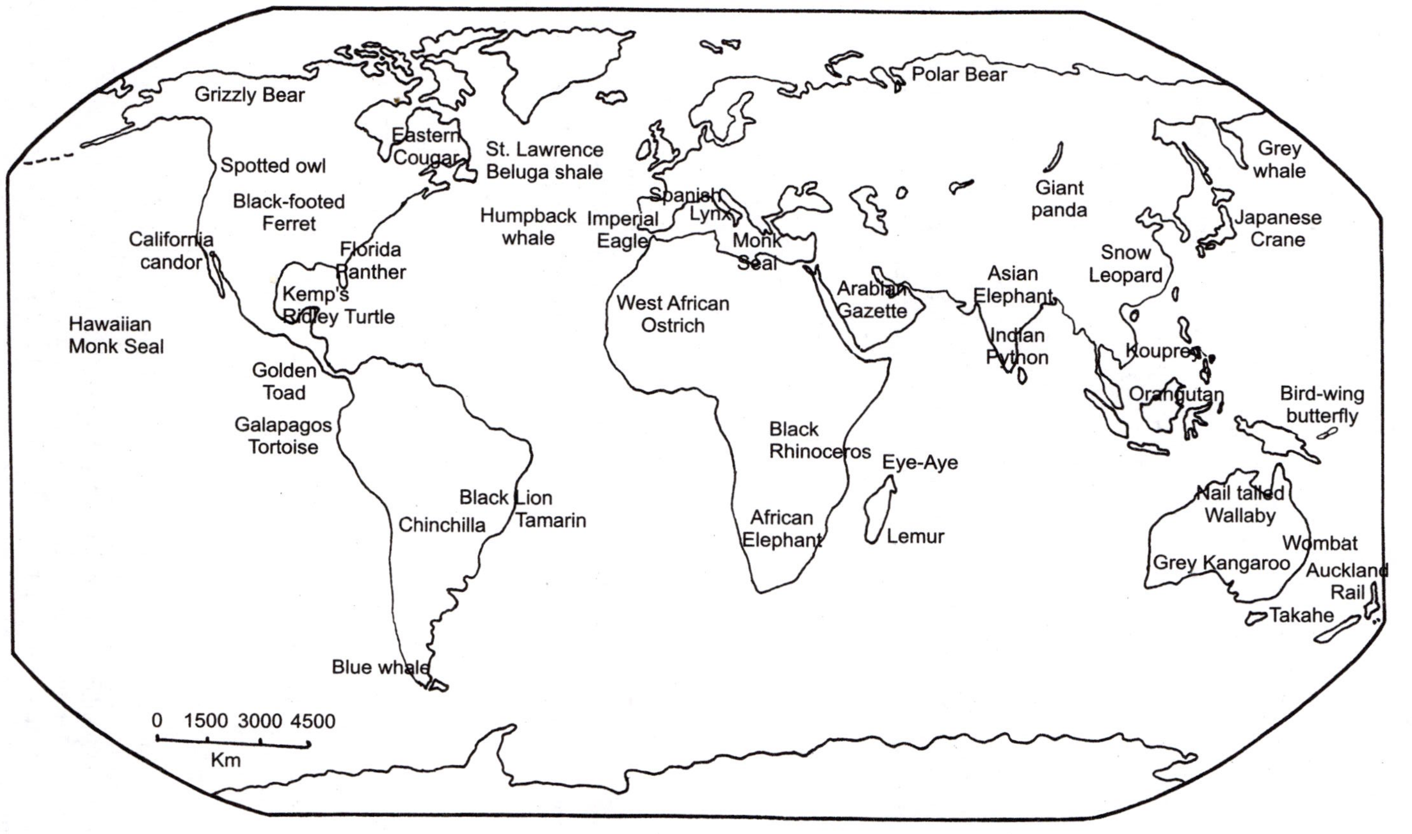

Fig. 4.2 Endangered Species of the World

CATEGORISATION OF SPECIES

The International Union for Conservation of Nature (IUCN) which publishes the Red Data Book has categorised the species under the following:

(i) Extinct Species,
(ii) Normal Species
(iii) Rare Species,
(iv) Critically Endangered Species,
(v) Endangered Species,
(vi) Vulnerable Species,
(vii) Near Threatened,
(viii) Data Deficient and
(ix) Not Evaluated.

Extinction of Species

According to Charles Darwin, the appearance (speciation) and disappearance (extinction) of species are natural processes. There are numerous factors responsible for the extinction of species. Apart from natural factors, there are human induced factors which are responsible for the extinction of species of fauna and flora. For example, (i) climatic change or sudden change in temperature and precipitation, (ii) sudden outbreak of diseases, (iii) forest fire, (iv) hunting and over-killing.

The criteria of the various categories of species has been given below:

(i) Extinct Species

These are the species which are not found after exhaustive survey and search of known or likely areas, where they occur. A species may be extinct from a local area, region, country, continent or the entire world. In other words, a species is extinct when there is no reasonable doubt that the last individual has died. A species is presumed as extinct, when exhaustive survey have failed to record an individual species. Examples of such species are the Asian Cheetah, Pink Head Duck, Mammoth, Dinosaurs etc.

(ii) Normal Species

Species whose population levels are considered to be normal for their survival, such as cattle, goats, sheep, rodents, Neem *(Azadirachta-Indica)*, mango, babul *(Acacia)*, peepal, banyan, teak, pines etc.

(iii) Rare Species

Rare Species are those species whose population is small and the location is confined to limited areas. The rare species, in times to come may become vulnerable and finally may be endangered. These species need to be provided special care and attention in conservation programmes.

(iv) Critically Endangered (CR)

The Critically Endangered Species have been given in Tables 4.1 and 4.2. A species a considered as critically endangered, when the best available evidence fulfill the following:

(i) reduction in population (more than 90 % over the last 10 years),
(ii) population size (number less than 50 mature individuals), and
(iii) quantitative analysis showing the probability of extinction in wild is at least 50 per cent in ten years time.

(v) Endangered (EN)

A species is Endangered when the best available evidence indicates that it meets any of the following criteria.

(i) reduction in population size (70 per cent over the last 120 years)

(ii) population size estimated to number fewer than 250 mature individuals.

(iii) quantitative analysis showing the probability of extinction in wild is at least 20 per cent within the last 20 years.

(vi) Vulnerable (VU)

A species is vulnerable when the best available evidence indicates that it meets any of the criteria:

(i) reduction in population (more than 50 per cent over the last 10 years)

(ii) population size estimated to number fewer than 10,000 mature individuals.

(iii) probability of extinction in wild is at least 10 per cent within the last 100 years.

(vii) Near Threatened (NT)

A species is near threatened when it has been evaluated against the criteria but does not qualify for Critically Endangered or Vulnerable now, but is close to qualifying for or is likely to qualify, for a threatened category in the near future.

(viii) Least Concern (LC)

A species is Least Concern when it has been evaluated against the criteria and does not qualify for Critically Endangered, Endangered, Vulnerable or Near Threatened. Widespread and abundant species are included in this category.

(ix) Data Deficient (DD)

A species is Data Deficient when there is inadequate information to make a direct or indirect assessment of its risk of extinction based on its distribution and/or population status. Data Deficient is therefore, not a category of threat.

(x) Not Evaluated (NE)

A species is Not Evaluated when it has not yet been evaluated against the given criteria.

Table 4.1 Some of the important Endangered Species of the world

Endangered Species	Continent/Country/Ocean
1. Africa	African Elephant, Aye-Aye (Madagascar), Black Rhinoceros, Lemur, West African Ostrich
2. Asia	Arabian-Gazelle, Asian Elephant, Giant-Panda, India-Python, Snow-Leopard
3. Australia	Grey-Kangaroo, Nail-Tailed Wallaby, Wombat
4. Europe	Imperial Eagle, Spanish-Lynx
5. North America	Black-footed Ferret, California-Candor, Florida-Panther, Grizzly-Bear, Spotted-Owl
6. South America	Black-Lion, Chinchilla, Tamarin
7. Atlantic Ocean	Blue-Whale, Humpblack-Whale, Kemp's Ridley-Turtle
8. Pacific Ocean	Blue-Whale, Galapagos-Tortoise, Grey-Whale, Hawaiian- Monk-Seal

The main endangered species of India has been shown in Fig. 4.3, while their names have been given in Table 4.2 and Table 4.3.

Table 4.2 Endangered Species of India

Endangered Species	Region/State/Union Territory
1. (i) Andamane and Nicobari Shrew, (ii) Asian Elephant	(i) South Andaman and Nicobar (ii) Peninsular India
2. Bara-Singha (swamp-deer)	Marshy lands and swamps
3. (i) Black-Baza (ii)Brown Bear	(i) Kerala, (ii) Himalayas: Himachal Pradesh, Jammu and Kashmir, Sikkim and Uttarakhand
4. Clouded leopard	Himalayan Foot-hills, Arunachal Pradesh, Assam, Manipur, Meghalaya, Mizoram, Nagaland, Sikkim, Tripura
5. Dhole (Asiatic/Indian Wild-Dog)	Different parts of India
6. Eld's Deer	Keibul-Lamjo (Manipur)
7. Ganges River Dolphin	Ganga River (India)
8. (i) Golden Langur, (ii)Great Teal	(i) Assam, North Eastern States of Indian (ii) Andaman Islands
9. Hangal (Kashmiri-Stag)	Jammu & Kashmir
10. Himalyan–Wolf	Jammu & Kashmir, Himachal Pradesh, Uttarakhand and Sikkim
11. Hog Deer	Northern India
12. Indian–wolf	South of Himalayas, Tarai Region of Northern Plains of India
13. Kondana Rat	Sinhagarh Plateau near Pune (Maharashtra)
14. Large Rock Rat (Elvira Rat)	Eastern Ghats (Tamil Nadu)
15. Lion-Tailed Macaque (Wondru)	Western Ghats (Karnataka and Kerala)
16. Malabar Civet	Kerala
17. Marbled Cat	Northern India
18. (i) Markhor, (ii) Marsh Mongoose	(i) Jammu & Kashmir (ii) Peninsular India, Rann of Kachchh
19. Namdhapa Flying Squirrel	Arunachal Pradesh
20. Nilgiri Langur	Kerala and Karnataka
21. Nilgiri Martin	Western Ghats (Karnataka and Kerala)
22. Oriental Small Clawed Otter	Karnataka, Kerala, Tamil Nadu
23. Pygmy-Hog	Terai Region
24. Red–Panda	Sikkim, Darjeeling, Eastern Himalayas
25. Rhinoceros	Assam
26. Swamp Deer	Rann of Kachchh (Gujarat), Sundarban (W.Bengal)
27. Wild–Ass (Khur)	Rann of Kachchh (Gujarat)
28. Wild Buffalo	Assam
29. White Bellied Musk-Deer	Jammu & Kashmir, Himachal Pradesh, Uttrakhand, Sikim
Endangered Birds	
30. Bengal Florican	West Bengal

(*Contd.*)

Table 4.2 (*Contd.*)

31. Forest Owlet	Southern Madhya Pradesh and Maharashtra
32. Himalayan quil	Jammu & Kashmir, Himachal Pradesh and Uttrakahand
33. Jerdon's Courser	Northern parts of Andhra Pradesh
34. Pink Headed Duck	States of North East India
35. Siberian Crane (Winter migrant to India)	Keoladeo (Bharatpur-Rajasthan)
36. Sociable Lapwing (Winter migrant to India)	North-West India
37. Tiger (i) White Bellied Heron, (ii)Wild Buffalo	Peninsular India and the Great Plains of India (i)Assam, Andhra Pradesh, West Bengal (ii) Assam
Critically Endangered Reptiles	
38. Four Toed River Terrapin turtle or River Terrapin turtle	Fresh water rivers and lakes
39. Gharial	Clean rivers with sand banks
40. Hawkbill-turtle	Andaman and Nicobar Islands, Odisha and Tamil Nadu
41. Red Crowned Roofed Turtle or Bengal Roofed Turtle	Ganga River Basin
42. Sispara Day Gecko	Western Ghats, Nilgiri, and Kavali Sispara,Cochin
Critically Endangered Fish	
43. Ganges Shark	Ganga River
44. Knife -tooth Sawfish	Coastal Indian Ocean
45. Large –tooth Sawfish	Western Parts of the Arabian Sea
46. Long-comb Sawfish	Indo-Pacific Ocean

Table 4.2-A Vulnerable Species of India

Species	Region/State/Union Territory
1. Asian Black Bear (white- chested bear)	Himalayas
2. Barasingha (Swamp Deer)	Northern and Central India
3. Black-Buck	Thar Desert
4. Clouded Leopard	Himalayan Foot-Hills
5. Chiru (Tibetan Antelope)	Cold Desert (Himachal Pradesh and Ladakh)
6. Four Horned Antelope (Chausingha)	Swampy areas
7. Gaur/Mithun (Indian Bison)	Assam, States of North East India
8. Himalayan Tahr	Himalayas

(*Contd.*)

Table 4.2-A (*Contd.*)

9. Indian Wolf	Foot-Hills of Himalayas- extends to the south of the Himalayas
10. Marbled Cat	Northern India and North-East India
11. Nilgiri Marten	Western Ghats (Kerala and Karnataka)
12. Red Panda	Temperate Forests of the Himalayas
Marine Mammals	
13. Dugong (Sea Cow)	Indian Ocean
14. Fresh Water Dolphin (River Dolphin)	Ganga and its tributaries
15. Ganga River Dolphin	Ganga and Brahmaputra
List of Marsupials (pouched mammals of Australia)	Bandicoot, Dasyure, Kangaroo, Koala, Marsupial Mole,Opossum, Phalangers, Tasmanian Devils, Tasmanian Wolf, Wallaby, Wombats
Extinct Marsupials (Australia)	Marsupial Wolf and Quagga

Table 4.2-B Main Diseases of Wildlife

Disease	Animals Affected
1. Anthrax (Plague)	Braking Deer, Cheetal, Gaur, Wild Pig
2. Foot and Mouth Disease	Cheetal, Gaur, Nilgai, Methun, Sambar, Yak
3. Rabies	Bear, Lion, Mongoose, Squarrel, Tiger
4. Reindeer-pest	Deer, Wild Buffalo, Wild Pig
5. Taxoplasomosis	Civet-cat, Macaque, Rhesus
6. Trypanosomia	Elephant, Macaque, Sambar, and Tiger
7. Tuberculosis	Cat, Deer, Elephant, and Primates

MIGRATION OF BIRDS

Migration of birds takes place throughout the year all over the world. Migration refers to the regular, recurrent and cyclical seasonal movement of birds from one place to another. The distance of migration ranged from short distance to thousands of kilometers. But at the end of the period, birds eventually return to the original place.

Causes and Classification of Migration

The main causes of migration are: (i) to avoid extreme climate, (ii) in search of food and water, (iii) to have a better breeding condition, (iv) to avoid competition for food and to find safe nesting place.

The migratory birds of India may be classified under the following two categories:

Winter Birds

Black-Tailed Godwit, Blue-Throat, Common-Teal, Greater Eurasian Pigeon, Flamingo, Long Billed Pipit, Northern Shoveler, Rosy Pelican, Siberian Cranes, Spotted Redshank, Starling, Wood Sandpiper, Yellow Wagtail.

Summer Birds

Asian Koel, Black-Crowned Night Heron, Blue Cheeked Bee-Eater, Comb Duck, Cuckoos, Eurasian Golden Oriole.

THREAT TO WILD ANIMALS

The rapid growth of human population, industrialization and urbanization have put great stress on the habitat of wild animals. The changing patterns of land and agrarian practices are significantly reducing the habitats and corridors of wildlife. The habitat of wild animals in fact, is shrinking at a faster pace. Tourism and eco-tourism as well as forest fires have damaged and reduced the habitat of wild animals.

These changes in land use are causing damage to life and property, injuries to wildlife, animals death and injuries to people. In order to overcome these problems the following steps may be effective:

(i) Create artificial barriers (physical and biological),
(ii) guarding.
(iii) relocation of human settlements, and
(iv) waste management system that restrict wild animals access to refuse and garbage.

Table 4.3 Major National Parks of India and their Endangered Species

National Park	State	Endangered Species
Annamalai	Tamil Nadu	Porcupine
Bandavgarh	Madhya Pradesh	White Tiger
Bandipur	Karnataka	Asian elephant
Bannerghata	Karnataka	Sambhar
Bhitarkanika	Odisha	Olive Ridley Turtle
Climere	Tamil Nadu	Flamingo
Dachigam	Jammu & Kashmir	Hangul
Desert	Rajasthan	Black-Buck
Dudhwa	Uttar Pradesh	Tiger
Hemis	Jammu & Kashmir	Snow Leopard
Kaziranga	Assam	One-horned Rhino
Keibul Lam Jao	Manipur	Brown-antlered Deer
Keoladeo-Ghana	Rajasthan	Siberian Crane
Namdhapa	Arunachal Pradesh	Clouded leopard
Nelaputta	Andhra Pradesh	Pelican
Neyyar	Kerala	Crocodile
Rajmala	Kerala	Nilgiri Tahr
Rann of Kachchh	Gujarat	Wild Ass
Silent Valley	Kerala	Lion-Tailed Macaque
Wayanad	Kerala	Indian Muntjac

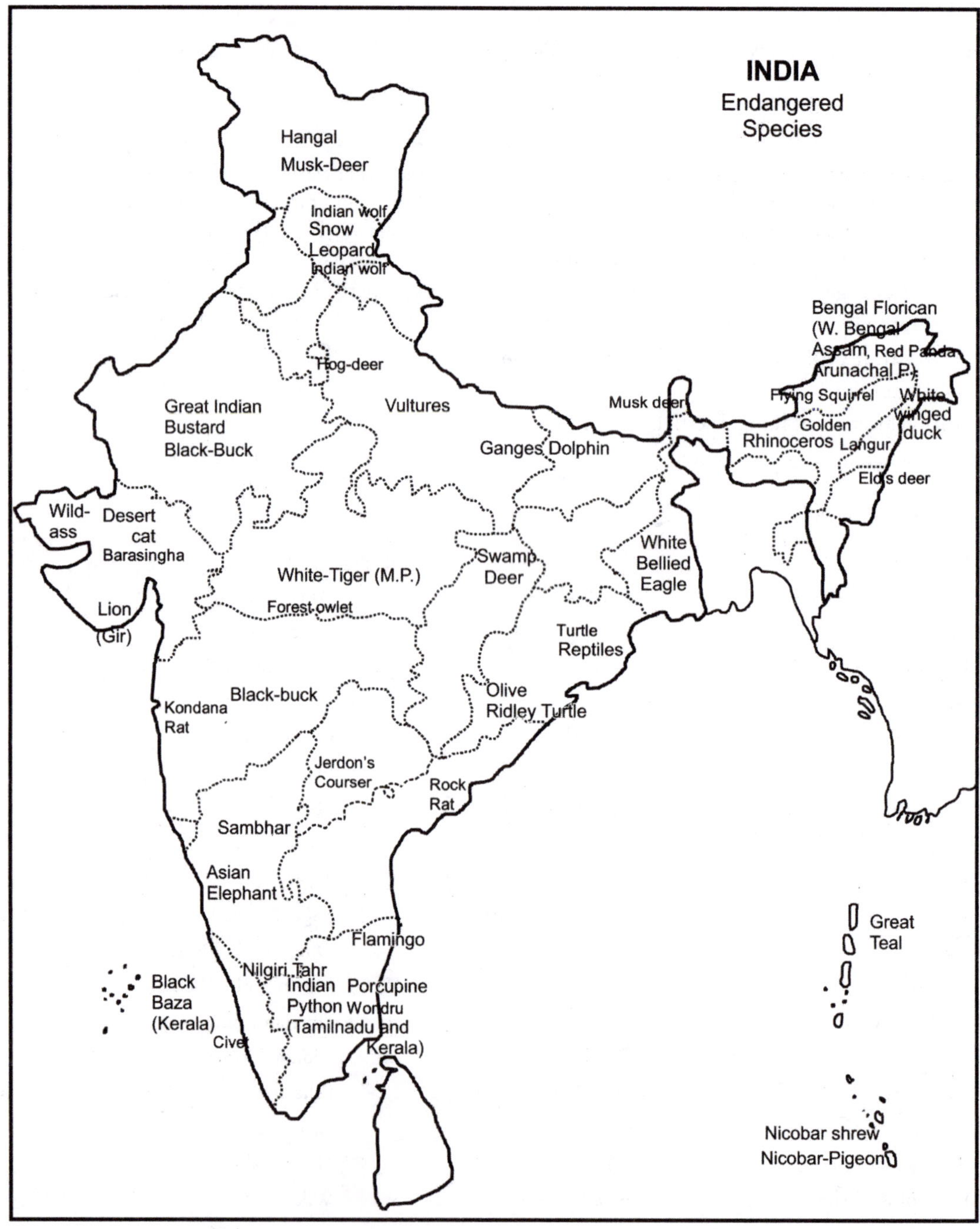

Fig. 4.3 Main Endangered Species of India

Endemic Species

These are the species which are found only in some specific areas, usually isolated by natural or geographical barriers. Examples of such species are the Andaman-Teal, Nicobari-Pigeon, and Mithun of Arunachal Pradesh.

NATURAL VEGETATION AND FORESTS

Natural Vegetation

Vegetation that has been unaffected by humans and their activities. It seems like that of true natural vegetation, in perfect equilibrium with existing climatic (climatic climax vegetation) and edaphic condition is rare or non-existent, certainly in areas such as the Great Plains of India or W. Europe that have been occupied and utilized by humans for thousands of years. A particularly good example of what appears to be natural vegetation, but in fact, much altered, is Savannah.

Social Relevance of Forests

Natural vegetation and forests provide numerous direct and indirect benefits to humanity. Some of the important benefits from the forests to mankind have been given below:

(i) Forests provide timber, bamboo, canes, leaves, grasses, oils, resins, gums, shellac, *katha*, tanning materials, dyes, honey, bee-wax, ivory, hides, horns, fur, vegetables, fruits, nuts, roots, and tubers.

(ii) Forests are the grazing grounds for domesticated animals and habitat for numerous species of plants, animals and micro-organisms.

(iii) Forests provide raw material to forest based industries.

(iv) Forest provide medicinal herbs.

(v) Forests directly and indirectly affect climate (temperature, precipitation, moisture, run-off, underground water-table, micro-climate, etc). It is said that larger the area under forests, greater is the amount of precipitation and vice versa.

(vi) Forests prevent floods and soil erosion.

(vii) Forest cover affects biota, soil erosion, land degradation, pollution and quality of air and water.

(viii) Forests help in purifying air, water and soil pollution.

(ix) Forests help in keeping the natural balance.

(x) Forest helps in maintaining the resilience characteristics of ecosystems and make environment and ecology sustainable.

According to the Food and Agricultural Organization (FAO 2012), India ranks among the top ten countries in terms of area of forest cover. India has 1.6 per cent of global forest area with per capita forest of 0.06 hectare.

Table 4.4 India's Ranking in World Species

Organism	Number of Species	World Ranking
1. Amphibians	182	15
2. Angiosperms	14,500	15–20
3. Birds	1200	8
4. Mammals	350	8
5. Reptiles	453	5

Table 4.5 Bio-geographic Zones of India

Sl. No.	Biogeographic Zone	No. of Biotic Provinces in the Zone	Area percent of India
1	Peninsular India	5	42
2	Semi-arid	2	16.6
3	Gangetic Plain	2	10.8
4	Thar Desert	2	6.6
5	Himalaya	4	6.4
6	Trans-Himalayas	2	5.6
7	North-East India	2	5.2
8	Coastal Plains	2	2.5
9	Islands	2	3.0
10	Coasts	2	2.5

Table 4.5-A Types of Indian Forests

	Types of Forest	States/Union Territories	Species of vegetation
1.	Tropical Wet-evergreen Forests	Andaman & Nicobar Islands and Western Ghats	Betel-nut-palm, fern, hillock, jack-fruit, rubber, cincona, rose-wood, iron-wood, orchids, etc.
2.	Tropical Semi-evergreen Forests	Andaman and Nicobar, Eastern Himalayas and Western Ghats	Mixture of wet and dry evergreen trees
3.	Tropical Moist Deciduous Forests	Western Ghats, Eastern Ghats, North Eastern Hills of India,	Tall trees, thick trunks, thick bark, long branches with butts, trees drop their leaves in dry season, teak, sal, shisum, bamboo, etc.
4.	Tropical Dry Deciduous Forest	Andhra Pradesh, Chhattisgarh, Gujarat, Jharkhand, Karnataka, Madhya Pradesh, Northeast Hilly States	Acacia, bamboo, Mahuva, sal, teak, etc.
5.	Tropical Thorn Forests	Black earth region, North-west and Peninsular India	Caper, cactus, spurge, stunted flat topped trees (less than ten meters in height)

(*Contd.*)

Table 4.5-A (*Contd.*)

6.	Tropical Dry Evergreen Forests	Karnataka, Andhra Pradesh, Tamil Nadu, Telangana	Hard leaved evergreen trees with fragrant flowers mixed with a few deciduous trees
7.	Subtropical Broad-leaved Forest	Eastern Himalayas, Western Ghats, Silent Valley	Cinnamon, fragrant grasses, poonspar, rhodo-dendron. In Eastern Hi-malayas the main species include alder, bamboo, chestnut, birch, cherry, oak, and a large variety of orchids.
8.	Subtropical Pine Forests	Shiwaliks, Western Himalayas, Garo, Khasi, Jaintia (Meghalaya), Mizoram, Nagaland, Tripura	Amla, chir, laburnum, oak, pine, rhododendron, sal.
9.	Sub-tropical Dry Evergreen Forests	Shiwaliks and foothills of Himalayas. These forests are found up to height of 1000 meters.	Evergreen trees with shin ing leaves with varnished look.
10.	Montane Wet Temperate Forests	Arunachal Pradesh and Himalayas with over 200 cm of rainfall, Nilgiri Mountain, and higher reaches of the Western Ghats.	Champa, oak, rhododen–dron. Numerous ground flora and herbs.
11.	Himalayan Moist Deciduous Forests	Shiwaliks, and the Lesser Himalayas	Broad-leaved oak trees, brown oak bamboo, coniferous trees, fern, oak, rhododendron, walnut
12.	Himalayan Dry Temperate Forests	Lahaul-Spiti, Kinnaur (Himachal Pradesh), Sikkim, etc.	Predominantly coniferous trees, broad leavedash, maple (chinar) oak, at higher altitudes *chilgoza*, deodar, fir, juniper.
16.	Sub-alpine Forest	Arunachal Pradesh and Jammu and Kashmir state	Birch, black-juniper, red-fir, larch, many species of rhododendron.
17.	Moist Alpine Scrub	Himalayas and higher hills of North East India	Birch, scrub, dense ever green forest, rhododen-dron, mosses and ferns
18.	Dry Alpine Scrub	Himalayas between 3000 to 4900 metres	Dwarf plants, black juniper, drooping juniper, honeysuckle and willow
19.	Littoral and Swamps	Andaman and Nicobar Islands, Brahmaputra Valley, Sundarban Delta,	Mangrove, roots, with soft tissues so that plants can breathe in water.

INDIA — A MEGA-BIODIVERSITY NATION

India has great diversity in its geo-climatic conditions. The diversity in terrain, topography, climate and soils are able to sustain diverse forms of life. Thus, there is great diversity in India's forests, wetlands, mangroves wildlife and marine areas. The richness in fauna and flora makes it as one of the 12 mega-biodiversity countries of the world.

The great diversity of India's wildlife owes its origin to the country's location and the subcontinent size. In fact, India constitutes the confluence zone of world's three major bio-systems, i.e. African, European and South-East Asian biological systems. Thus, India possesses a bio-matrix of all the systems encompassing some vital components of each of the three continents. For example, one can find in India the hyenas and the gazelles of the African system; the wolf, the wild-goat and Kashmir–stag of the European system; the gibbon and elephant of the South-East Asian system. The fauna peculiar to India, however, includes the south-bear, black-bear, four-horned antelope, and many species of snakes. The list of birds of India would, among others, include our national bird the peacock, the saurus-crane, the great Indian bustard, etc.

Of the 2,50,000 known species of plants in the world, about 45,000 have their occurrence in India. Similarly, out of 1.5 million known animal species in the world, India can claim as many as 75,000. Thus, although India accounts for about 2.4 per cent of the total area of the world, it supports over 5.7 per cent of the total fauna and 11 per cent of the total flora of the world. India has 350 different mammals, 1200 species of birds, 453 species of reptiles and 45,000 plant species. India has 50,000 known species of insects, including 13,000 butterflies and moths. It is estimated that the number of unknown species could be several times higher.

According to one estimate, 18 per cent of Indian plants are endemic to the country which are found nowhere else in the world. Among the plant species, the flowering plants have a much higher degree of endemism, one third of these are not found anywhere in the world. Among amphibians found in India, about 62 per cent are unique to the country. Among lizards, of the 153 species recorded, 50 per cent are endemic. High endemism has also been recorded in various groups of insects, marine worms, centipedes, mayflies, and freshwater sponges.

In addition to the high biodiversity in fauna and flora, there is also a great diversity in cultivated crops and breeds of domestic animals. The traditional cultivated crops include 30,000 to 50,000 varieties of cereals, fodder, vegetables, flowers, fruits and nuts. The highest diversity in cultivated plants is found in the states of the Himalayas, North-East India, Western Ghats, and Eastern Ghats.

India has 27 indigenous breeds of cattle, 40 breeds of sheep, 22 breeds of goats, and 8 breeds of buffaloes. Many of these have died out or dying out due to our misguided adoption of all foreign things like Jersey and Holstein cows have largely replaced Indian cattle like the Brahma-bull, cash-crops have replaced the tradition food crops, eucalyptus and wattle plantations have replaced the mixed shoal forest. Unfortunately, the Indian ecosystems are losing their traditional endemic species. India's air-borne wildlife diversity is perhaps unrivalled by any other part of the world, except Latin America.

Biogeographic Zones of India

As stated above, India has great diversity in its fauna and flora. On the basis of natural vegetation and wildlife India has been divided by the ecologists into ten bio-geographic regions and 25 bio-geographic provinces. The biogeographic regions have been delineated to utilise the ecosystems judiciously and to conserve the biodiversity. The biogeographic regions have been shown in Fig. 4.4 (Table 4.5). A brief description of these regions have been given in the following:

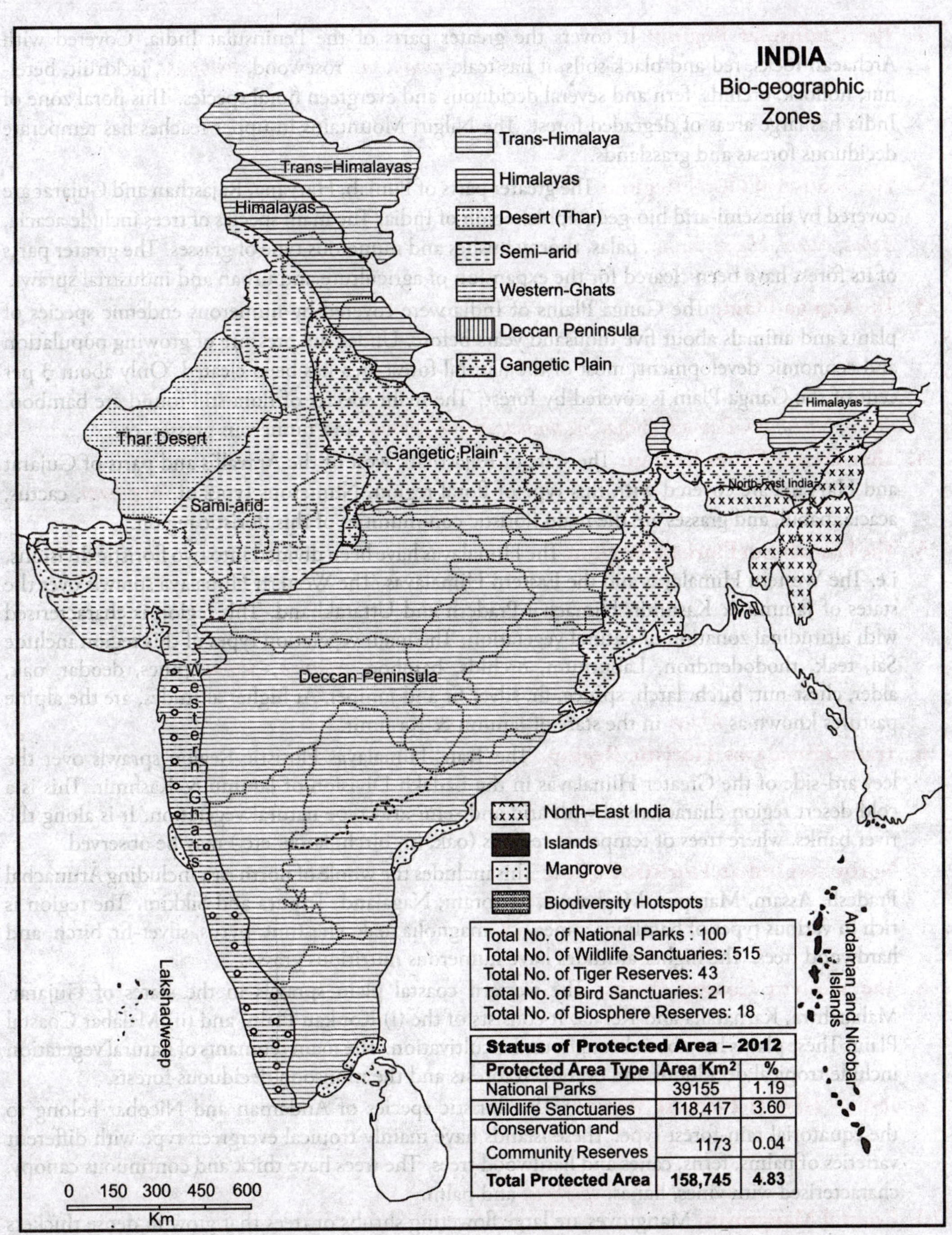

Status of Protected Area – 2012

Protected Area Type	Area Km²	%
National Parks	39155	1.19
Wildlife Sanctuaries	118,417	3.60
Conservation and Community Reserves	1173	0.04
Total Protected Area	**158,745**	**4.83**

Fig. 4.4 India – Biogeographic Zones

1. **The Peninsular Region:** It covers the greater parts of the Peninsular India. Covered with Archaean rocks, red and black soils, it has teak, *tendu*, *sal*, rosewood, *mahuwa*, jackfruit, betel-nut, hollock, orchids, fern and several deciduous and evergreen floral species. This floral zone of India has large areas of degraded forest. The Nilgiri Mountains in upper reaches has temperate deciduous forests and grasslands.
2. **The Semi-arid Floral Region:** The greater parts of Punjab, Haryana, Rajasthan and Gujarat are covered by the semi-arid bio-geographic region of India. The main species of trees include acacia, *Babul*, *Neem*, *khejra, kanju*, palas, thorny bushes and numerous type of grasses. The greater parts of its forest have been cleared for the expansion of agriculture and urban and industrial sprawl.
3. **The Ganga Plain:** The Ganga Plains of India were covered by numerous endemic species of plants and animals about five thousand years before. Under the pressure of growing population and economic development, most of the natural forest area has been cleared. Only about 3 per cent of the Ganga Plain is covered by forest. The main species of flora still found are bamboo, *Arjun*, *Sheesham, Bargad, Peepal, Mahuwa, Neem, Jamun,* and numerous grasses, etc.
4. **Thar Desert Floral Region:** The state of Rajasthan, west of the Aravallis and parts of Gujarat and Haryana are covered with this type of floral region. Numerous types of *Nagphani*, cactus, acacia, babul, and grasses are the main floristic communities of this floristic region.
5. **The Himalayan Floristic Region:** The Himalayas have been divided into two floristic divisions, i.e. The Western Himalayas and the Eastern Himalayas. The Western Himalaya sprawls over the states of Jammu & Kashmir, Himachal Pradesh and Uttarakhand. This region is characterised with altitudinal zonation of natural vegetation. The main vegetation types of this region include Sal, teak, rhododendron, Laburnum, orchids, bamboo, *champa*, *Semul*, pines, deodar, oak, alder, chest-nut, birch, larch, spruce, fir, silver fir and juniper. At higher altitudes, are the alpine pastures known as *Margs* in the state of Jammu & Kashmir.
6. **Trans-Himalayas Floristic Region:** The Trans-Himalayas Floristic Region sprawls over the leeward-side of the Greater Himalayas in the Ladakh Division of Jammu & Kashmir. This is a cold desert region characterised with arid and semi-arid type natural vegetation. It is along the river banks, where trees of temperate regions (oak, fir, birch, larch, etc.) may be observed.
7. **North East Indian Floristic Region:** This includes the whole of north east including Arunachal Pradesh, Assam, Manipur, Meghalaya, Mizoram, Nagaland, Tripura and Sikkim. The region is rich in various types of bamboos, pines, *sal*, magnolia, oak, chestnut, pyrus, silver-fir, birch, and hardwood trees. The higher altitudes have numerous nutritious grasses.
8. **The Western Coastal Plains:** The western coastal plain sprawls in the states of Gujarat, Maharshtra, Karnataka and Kerala. It consists of the (i) Konkan Plain, and (ii) Malabar Coastal Plain. These plains have been brought under cultivation. The main remnants of natural vegetation include tropical deciduous and evergreen forests and the monsoon deciduous forests.
9. **Indian Islands Floristic Region:** The floristic species of Andaman and Nicobar belong to the equatorial rain-forest type. These islands have mainly tropical evergreen type with different varieties of palms, ferns, canes and hardwood trees. The trees have thick and continuous canopy, characterised with vines, lianas, *epiphytes* and palm.
10. **Coastal Mangroves:** Mangroves are large flowering shrubs or trees that grow in dense thickets along muddy or silty tropical coasts. Along the coastal areas, especially along the Eastern Coastal shallow seas, are the highly productive ecosystems which are capable of exporting energy and

material to adjacent communities. They support a diverse heterotrophic food-chain. At present, like many types of wetland, they are under severe anthropogenic pressure.

Table 4.6 Forest Communities of India

Type of Forest	Plants/ Tree Species	Common Fauna	Rare Animals
1. Tropical Evergreen Forest	Ficus, *Jamun*, Rubber, Rosewood	Tiger, chital, barking-deer, hornbill, tree-frogs, etc.	Pigmy-hog, rhino, lion-tailed macaque
2. Moist Deciduous Forest	*Sal, Tun, Haldu, teak*	Black-bear, fox, hyena, jackal, lion, tiger, etc.	Tiger
3. Dry-deciduous forest	Teak, *Ain*, Terminalia	Tiger, Chital, Barking-deer, Hornbill	
4. Himalayan Broad-leaved	Maple, Oak		
5. Himalayan-conifers	Pine, Deodar	Wild-goat and wild sheep, Himalayan-black-bear	Snow-leopard, Hangul, Himalayan brown-bear, Musk-deer, Himalayan-wolf.
6. Thorn and scrub – semi-arid forest	Xerophytes, acacia, *babul*, Neem	Black-buck, Chinkara, Four-horned antelope, partridge, lizard	Bustard, Florican
7. Mangrove	Avicenia, sundri	Crocodiles, Shore bird, sandpipers plovers, fish, crustacean	Water-monitored-lizard

Table 4.6-A Flora and Fauna of India

Region	Geographical Sprawl	Flora	Fauna
1.Himalayan Foothills	Jammu & Kashmir, Himachal Pradesh and Uttarakhand	Dwarf-hill-bamboo, birch, giant-bamboo, rhododendrons, sal, tall grassy meadows, silk cotton tree	barking-deer, black-bear, cheetal, elephant, Gangetic-gharial, golden langur, Great Indian one horned rhinoceros, hog-deer, hyena, porcupine, sambar, sloth-bear, swamp-deer, tiger, wild-boar, wild buffalo, wild-dogs,
2.Western Himalayas-High Altitude Region	Jammu & Kashmir, Himachal Pradesh and Uttarakhand	Alpine-pastures, birch, dwarf hill bamboo, rhododendrons	Antelope (chiru and Tibetan-gazelle), deers, brown-bears, (hangal or Kashmiri stag, musk-deer), golden eagle, marmots, pikas or mouse hare, wild ass, wild goats (ibex, markhor, tahr),wild sheep (bharal, blue-sheep, marcopolo-sheep, nayan-sheep), snow-cats, snow cocks, snow-fox, snow partridges, snow-leopard, wolf. Birds (choughs, griffon-vultures, Himalayan-monal pheasant, koklas, lammergiers, ravens,

(*Contd.*)

Table 4.6-A (*Contd.*)

3.Eastern Himalayas	Arunachal Pradesh, Sikkim	Birch, dwarf-bamboos fern, epiphytes, junipers, laurels, lichen, magnolia, oak, orchids, pine, yew,	Hog-badgers, crestless porcupines, goat-antelopes (goral, scrow, takins) red-panda,
4. Peninsular India	Peninsular India excluding Eastern and Western Ghats and the Coastal plains (Coromanadel-coast, Konkan, Malabar).	Acacia, sal, teak, thorny bushes and scrubs, savannah grasses	Antelope (black-buck, chinkara, four-horned-antelope, gazelle, nilgai, deers (cheetal or axis deer), cheetah, elephant, hog-deer, gaur, jackal, leopard, lion, monkey, stripped hyena, swamp-deer or barasingha, wild-boar, wild-dog or dhole, wild-pig,
5.Indian Desert	Thar Desert	Acacia, cacti, thorny trees with reduced leaves, numerous grasses	Black-buck, caracal, desert-cat, desert lizards (geckos), Great Indian-bustard, lacertides red-fox, reptiles (lizards, snakes, tortoise, etc), rodents, wild ass,
6.Tropical Rain Forest	Anaimalai Hills, Nilgiri, southern parts of Western Ghats,	Ebony, epiphytes, fern, herbs, lianas, mosses, orchids, sandalwood, shrubs, vines,	Assam macaque, capped langur or leaf-monkey, bats, civets, elephant, flying squirrels, gaur, lion-tailed macaque, Nilgiri-langur, Nilgiri mongoose, pig-tailed macaque, golden langur, hoolock-gibbon, spiny mouse. squirrel,
7.Andaman & Nicobar Islands	Andaman & Nicobar Islands	giant-dipterocarpus, lagerstoemia, mangroves, terminalia,	Bats, crab-eating macaque, coconut-crab, dolphin, dugong, deer, mega-pode, false killer-whale, lizards, Nicobar-pigeon, palm-civet, rats, pig, salt-water crocodile,python, sambar, sea-eagle, sea-snake, white-breasted swiftlet, viper,
8.Mangrove Swamps	Sundarban and Coastal Areas	Avicennia, bruguiria, excaecaria, neepa-palm, rhizophora, sonneratia, sundari,	dorippe, fish, monitor-lizard, monkeys, Royal-Bengal Tiger, small-crabs, pigs, spotted-deer, weaver ants,

Conservation of Biodiversity

Biodiversity has great social relevance. The main factors which necessitate the conservation of biodiversity are given below:

1. **Ecological necessity:** It is a well-known fact of bio-science that all organisms have their own place in the food-chain and interact with their abiotic environment in a way that the ecosystem becomes a self-sustaining unit. Obviously, disappearance of any link in the food chain is bound to upset the nature's ecological balance and hence create problems. For instance, excessive killing of snakes may explode the population of rats, which in turn may destroy the food chains. Thus, in order to maintain the ecological balance in nature, it is necessary to conserve the wildlife in its native form.
2. **Biological necessity:** The growing human population has its own demands on crop yields and animal products. In order to increase continuously the produce from crops and animals, the plant

varieties and the animal breeds have to be improved upon continuously. This is possible by useful selection of genes by screening a wide range of their wild relatives. Such genetic modification can yield improved varieties of plants and useful animals. In order to continue with this biological process of improvement through breeding programmes, it is absolutely necessary to protect and preserve as large a variety of native wildlife as possible.

3. **Economic necessity:** All the three basic forms of wildlife, the plants, the animals and the micro-organisms have distinctive economic value. Plants provide timber, paper, pulp, rubber, drugs, fibres, charcoal, gum, resins, etc.; animals provide nutritious food, fur, silk, wool, leather, honey, acetone, vinegar, methane, antibiotics, vitamins, etc., all of which have great economic value. The economic implications of wildlife extinction could also be serious. It also necessitates the conservation of wildlife.
4. **Scientific necessity:** Biodiversity needs to be conserved for education and scientific research. For instance, Guinea-pigs, rabbits, monkeys, dogs, frogs and fish have been used by the scientific community for promoting the cause of science both biological and pharmaceutical. This is itself a sacred factor necessitating conservation of wildlife.
5. **Cultural necessity:** Conservation of biodiversity is also necessary for cultural diversity. Wildlife can contribute in its own way to the cultural growth of a nation. Literature and religion in most parts of the world rely heavily upon nature. Certain plants and animals have sacred place in certain religious groups as the case with *Tulsi* (tree) and cow in Hinduism, yak among Tibetans, etc. turkey among the Christians, while, pig is a prohibition in Islam. Thus, from the cultural and religious point of view also, it is essential to conserve the wildlife.
6. **Ethical necessity:** Biodiversity conservation is essential for ethical values. The wide variety of organisms existing today have evolved through billions of years. Any species lost due to any factor may be lost for ever. It would be unethical to permit such permanent disappearance of any species. Hence, we must strive for the conservation of entire wildlife.
7. **Aesthetic necessity:** Biodiversity, environment and ecology have great aesthetic value. The natural landscapes, mountains, sea-beaches, lush-green forests etc. are the source of great pleasure and enjoyment. Monuments of nature and natural areas, therefore, should be protected and guarded from being ruined. In brief, the use of biodiversity for recreation, eco-tourism is very vital in the promotion of tourism, ecotourism and '*leisure industry*'. People in white collar-jobs prefer to visit a biosphere reserve, national park, sanctuaries and enjoy nature based activities such as hiking, trekking, rafting, birds and wildlife watching, fishing, and photography. The aesthetic value of our ecosystem contributes to the emotional and spiritual well-being of highly urbanised and industrialised societies.
8. **Miscellaneous:** At the top, if we have not discovered any valuable use of some of the species of plants, animals and microorganisms, may be that the coming generations succeed in discovering an exceptionally valuable use of species. For such miscellaneous reasons also, it is imperative to conserve biodiversity. All the factors listed above, among many more, signify the importance of wildlife and the need for its conservation.

Habit Degradation as a Threat to Biodiversity

As stated above, the physical location in which an organism is biologically suited to live is known as habitat. Most of the plants and animal species have specific habitat parameters or limits. Loss of habitat is considered as the greatest threat to the world. Because of anthropogenic causes, the habitats, of numerous plants and animals have been transformed significantly. Because of degradation and modification of habitat, many of the species are threatened or facing extinction.

According to one estimate by the ecologists, at least 120 out of the 620 living primate species (apes, monkeys, lemurs, etc.) will become extinct in the next 20 years. Large animals like tigers, mountain gorilla, pandas, Indian lions, tropical orchids and spotted owls are also threatened/highly vulnerable because they need large areas for survival.

According to an estimate by the IUCN (2000), 89 per cent of all threatened birds, 83 per cent of all threatened mammals, and 91 per cent of all threatened plants, have already been affected adversely by loss of degradation in habitat. This loses of habitat may be caused by natural disasters (floods, fire, cyclones, erosion, shifting cultivation, over-grazing, water pollution, soil pollution, mining, construction of dams, etc.).

Causes of Biodiversity Loss

The biodiversity loss takes place when the habitat of a particular species is destroyed. The destruction of habitat may be either by natural or anthropogenic causes.

1. **Natural Causes:** (i) volcanic eruptions, (ii)earthquakes, (iii) landslides, (iv) floods and droughts, (v) tsunami, (vi) lack of pollination, (vii) epidemics in plants and animals.
2. **Anthropogenic Causes:** (i) habitat destruction because of developmental activities, (ii) uncontrolled commercial exploitation, (iii) hunting and poaching, (iv) extension of agriculture and grazing lands, (v) urbanization and urban sprawl, (vi) land, soil and water pollution, (vii) reclamation of wetlands, and (viii) damage and destruction of the coastal areas.

STRATEGIES FOR CONSERVATION OF BIODIVERSITY

The term biodiversity conservation is primarily associated with the judicious utilisation of natural resources with an approach of sustainable development. Biodiversity conservation is required for ecological, biological, scientific, economic, cultural, and ethical necessities. The main objectives of biodiversity conservation are the protection, preservation, management and restoration of natural resources, especially fauna, flora, water-bodies, natural sites, landforms and the culture and traditions of the respective societies. Biodiversity conservation is essential for the survival of mankind.

The experts of ecology and environment have formulated a World Conservation Strategy for a judicious and un-exploitative use of biodiversity and the sustenance of life on the Earth's surface. The strategy for the conservation of biodiversity as designed by the ecologists may be summarised as under:

Key Strategies

(i) The natural habitat of the wildlife must be preserved to provide an unaltered environment for the preservation of all species of old and new flora, fauna and microbes.

(ii) The basic life-supporting system of soil, water, air and energy must be conserved through its proper management and optimal use. As far as possible, the species of fauna and flora should be protected in their natural environment or at the most in the man-created conducive environment in zoological parks and botanical gardens. Protection and preservation of critical habitats and unique ecosystems.

(iii) While all species of plants and animals should be protected, special care should be made to conserve the threatened and vulnerable species.

(iv) Protected areas should be demarcated where the natural habitat of wild relatives of useful plants and animals could be preserved.

(v) The critical habitats, such as nesting sites, feeding areas, and breeding grounds of wild animals need special attention.

(vi) The ecosystem as a whole, rather than a single species need to be preserved.

(vii) Over-exploitation of the various ecosystems should not be done.

(viii) International trade in endangered species should be regulated.

(ix) Regulation of international trade in wildlife. Bilateral and multilateral agreements need to be reached to regulate the production and preservation of natural habitats of migratory animals and birds. Reduction in pollution.

(x) Biosphere reserves, national parks, sanctuaries, zoological parks, etc. should be set up in all countries in order to protect the species of plants and animals.

(xi) Hunting of threatened species should be completely banned, and in case of other species, it should be regulated through grant of licences.

(xii) The government must initiate an environmental awareness programme at the national, regional and local levels.

Sooner the above steps taken, the better for the conservation of biodiversity.

In-situ and *Ex-situ* Conservation

Experts of ecology and environment have suggested the strategy of *in-situ* and *ex-situ* biodiversity conservation. A brief description of these strategies has been given in the following:

In-situ Conservation

In *in-situ* biodiversity conservation, the natural habitats of different species of plants and animals are protected. The establishment of biosphere reserves, national parks and sanctuaries are some of the examples of *in-situ* conservation. In this type of biodiversity conservation, not only the endangered species and vulnerable species are benefitted, but also the constituent present in the ecosystem are protected. It is a cheap and natural way of conservation. The species are allowed to grow in their own natural habitat. As the species grow in their natural habitat, they face inclement weather such as extremes of temperature, scorching heat, precipitation, rainfall, snowfall, sleet, hails, permafrost, floods and droughts, and thereby evolve into better adapted forms. For this reason, the wild species are more sturdy and resistant to the prevailing environmental conditions than the domesticated and hybrid species.

The main advantage of *in-situ* conservation is that it requires a large area for the complete protection and conservation of biodiversity. This implies the restriction of human activity and a greater overlap or interaction of wildlife with local residents near a reserved area. At present, there are more than 7000 protected areas, parks, sanctuaries and natural reserves in the world. It has been stressed that species cannot be protected individually as they are interdependent on each other and therefore, the whole ecosystem is to be protected. With the passage of time, new biosphere reserves and national parks are being delineated for the *in-situ* conservation of bio-diversity.

Ex-situ conservation

In case the natural habitat is degraded substantially, numerous species are in the category of endangered species and *in-situ* conservation is not possible In such cases, conservation need to be done away from the natural habitat and should be under total human supervision in places such as zoological parks (zoo), botanical gardens, and seed banks. Such efforts are known as *ex-situ* conservation. Sprawling over 2212 hectares, the Sri Venkateshwara in Tirupati (Andhra Pradesh) is the largest zoological park in the country. For the purpose of *ex-situ* conservation of endangered species of wild animals, certain rehabilitation centres have been established in India under the government sponsored National Wildlife Action Plan (NWAP) of 1983. The main functions of such rehabilitation centres are as under:

(i) Identification of the species to be conserved. The species which are at maximum risk of extinction are generally chosen for conservation.

(ii) To capture some individuals of the concerned highly endangered species of animals from their natural habitat and keep the same as captives at these centres.

(iii) To study thoroughly the feeding, breeding and other habits as well as patterns of their pathology (nature of diseases).

(iv) To provide all facilities for captive breeding of all such animals as well as for their healthy multiplication.

(v) To release young ones of these animals into the natural habitat after these have attained the safe age for the purpose.

(vi) Use of artificial insemination, embryo transfer and cryo-preservation of gametes embryos to maintain the genetic diversity in *ex-situ* conservation.

(vii) Creation of zoological parks, botanical gardens, seed banks and rehabilitation centres.

BIODIVERSITY CONSERVATION IN INDIA

The Government of India has taken several important steps including enactments of laws for the *in-situ* and *ex-situ* conservation of endangered and vulnerable plants and animals. Creation of biosphere reserves, national parks, sanctuaries, world heritage sites, zoological parks, etc. are some of the important steps in this direction which have been described briefly as below:

Biosphere Reserves

The term 'Biosphere Reserve' was introduced by the UNESCO in 1971 for the 'natural areas'. It was refined by the Task Force of UNESCO's 'Man and Biosphere (MAB) in 1974, and the programme was formerly launched in 1976. The Biosphere Reserves are rich in biological and cultural diversity and encompass unique physical and cultural features.

"Biosphere Reserve is an International designation by the UNESCO for the representative parts of natural and cultural landscape, extending over large area of terrestrial or coastal/marine ecosystems or a combination of both'.

The main objectives for the delineation of Biosphere Reserves are:

1. to conserve the diversity and integrity of plants and animals within the ecosystem and to conserve the cultural diversity,
2. to promote research on ecological conservation and other environmental aspects,
3. to provide facilities for education, training, and awareness about issues related to biodiversity and environment.
4. to develop a symbiotic relationship between society and biodiversity and ecology.

5. to ensure sustainable use of natural resources through appropriate technology,
6. to integrate the biological, socio-economic and cultural dimensions in ecosystems.

Criteria for selection of Biosphere Reserves

1. Minimally disturbed core area with unique fauna and flora, and additional land and water suitable for teaching, training and research.
2. The core area should be characterized with typical fauna and flora.
3. Areas having rare and endangered species.
4. Areas having typical geo-ecological and pedological conditions.
5. Areas characterized with tribal culture and traditions.

The Indian National Man and Biosphere Committee constituted by the Central Government identifies new sites of Biosphere Reserves. It also advises on policies, programmes and reviews and evaluates the Biosphere Reserves.

The management of Biosphere Reserves is the responsibility of the concerned State/Union Territory with necessary financial assistance and technical expertise provided by the Central Government.

Biospheres are designated for inclusion in the Network by the International Coordinating Council (ICC) of the MAB Programme according to the prescribed procedure.

The distinction between Biosphere Reserves and Protected Areas (National Parks, Sanctuaries and Tiger Reserves) have been given in Table 4.6-A:

Table 4.6-A Distinction between biosphere reserves and Protected Areas

Biosphere Reserves	Protected Areas (National Parks, Sanctuaries and Tiger Reserves)
1. Biosphere Reserves are created by UNESCO.	1. Protected areas are created mainly by the State Governments or by the Central Government according to the norms of the Indian National Man and Biosphere Committee.
2. Conservation of all the fauna, flora and landscape of the Biosphere Reserve.	2. Fauna and flora of ecosystems may be partly modified.
3. Biosphere Reserve conserves the natural and cultural diversity	3. Protected areas (National Parks, Sanctuaries and Tiger Reserves) may become a part of the Biosphere Reserve
4. Research education and training facilities are provided	4. Research, education and training facilities are not available.
5. Biosphere Reserves are internationally recognized	5. The protected areas are identified and demarcated according to the Wildlife Protection Act 1972.
6. Human interaction in the core zone is completely prohibited	6. Grazing and limited hunting in the sanctuaries are permitted after prior permission of the competent authority.

Table 4.6-B Distinction between National Parks and Sanctuaries

National Parks	Sanctuaries
1. National Parks enjoy greater degree of protection than sanctuaries	1. Human interaction is allowed up to some extent in sanctuaries.
2. National parks have more than one ecosystem	2. Sanctuaries generally have one ecosystem.
3. Grazing of livestock is prohibited	3. Grazing of livestock and limited hunting of birds etc. is allowed in sanctuaries after taking permission from the competent authority.
4. National Parks are not focused on a particular species.	4. Wildlife Sanctuaries may be created for a particular species like the turtles sanctuary at Bhitarkanika (Odisha)
5. National Parks are created by the State Government and in some cases by the Central Government	5. Wildlife Sanctuaries are created by the State Governments.

Conservation and Community Reserves

The Wildlife Protection Act (1972) was amended in 2003. As a result of this amendment, the Conservation Reserves and Community Reserves were created.

Conservation Reserve

Conservation Reserve is an area owned by the State Government adjacent to National Parks and Sanctuaries for protecting landscape, sea-capes and habitat of fauna and flora. It is managed by Conservation Reserve Management Committee.

Community Reserve

It provides a mechanism to provide recognition and legal backing to the community initiated efforts in wild-life protection. Moreover, it provides a flexible system wherein wildlife conservation is achieved without compromising the community needs.

Marine Protected Area

Marine Protected Area (MPA) is 'any area of intertidal or sub-tidal terrain, together with its overlying water and associated flora, fauna, historical and cultural features, which have been reserved by law or other effective means to protect part or all of the enclosed environment'.

Marine protected area ensures sustainable productivity of fish, helps in the conservation of coral reefs, lagoons, estuaries, fauna and flora along the coast.

There are 31 Marine Protected Areas in India consisting of 33 National Parks and Wildlife Sanctuaries. Marine National Parks and Marine Sanctuaries consist of the Gulf of Kachchh, Bhitarkanika National Park, and Bhitarkanika Sanctuary. Marine Protected Areas cover about 4 per cent of all the protected areas of the country.

Sacred Groves of India

Sacred groves consist of tracts and patches of small forests varying from a few trees to forests of several acres that are dedicated to local folk deities. There forests are protected by the local communities because of their religious belief and traditional rituals. People believe that any kind of disturbance will offend the local deity, causing diseases, natural calamities, failure of crops and causing poverty and unemployment.

The important Sacred Groves of India have been given Table 4.6-C:

Table 4.6-C India: List of Sacred Groves

State/ Union Territories	Local Terms of Sacred Groves	No. of Sacred
1.Andhra Pradesh	Pavithravana	580
2.Arunachal Pradesh	Gumpa Forests	101
3.Goa	Deorai and Pann	55
4.Jharkhand	Sarana	29
5. Karnataka	Devara Kadu	1531
6.Kerala	Kavu, Sara	299
7.Maharashtra	Devrai, Devrahati, and Dev-Gudi	2820
8.Manipur	Gamkhap, Mauhak (sacred bamboo reserves)	166
9.Meghalaya	Ki Law Lyngdoh, Ki Law Kyntang, and Ki Law Niam	101
10.Odisha	Jahera, Thakuramma	169
11.Puducherry	Kovil-Kadu	108
12.Rajasthan	Kenkris, Jogmaya and Orans	560
13.Tamil Nadu	Koilkadu and Swami-Shola	752
14.Uttarakhand	Deo-Bhumi, Bugyal (sacred alpine meadows)	22
15.West Bengal	Garamthan, Harithan, Jhera, Sabitrithan and Santalburithan	39

The following items are prohibited and are not permitted to be exported from the sacred groves:

(i) All wild animals,
(ii) beef of cows, oxen and calf,
(iii) meat of buffalo,
(iv) peacock tail feathers and its handicraft articles,
(v) sea shell,
(vi) wood and wood products,
(vii) fuel-wood,
(viii) sandalwood in any form,
(ix) mechanical, chemical and semi-chemical wood-pulp.

Zoning of Biosphere Reserves

'Conservation of Resources of the Biosphere' conference was organized by the Man and Biosphere (MAB) committee in 1968. One of the recommendations of this conference was related to the 'utilisation and preservation of genetic resources'.

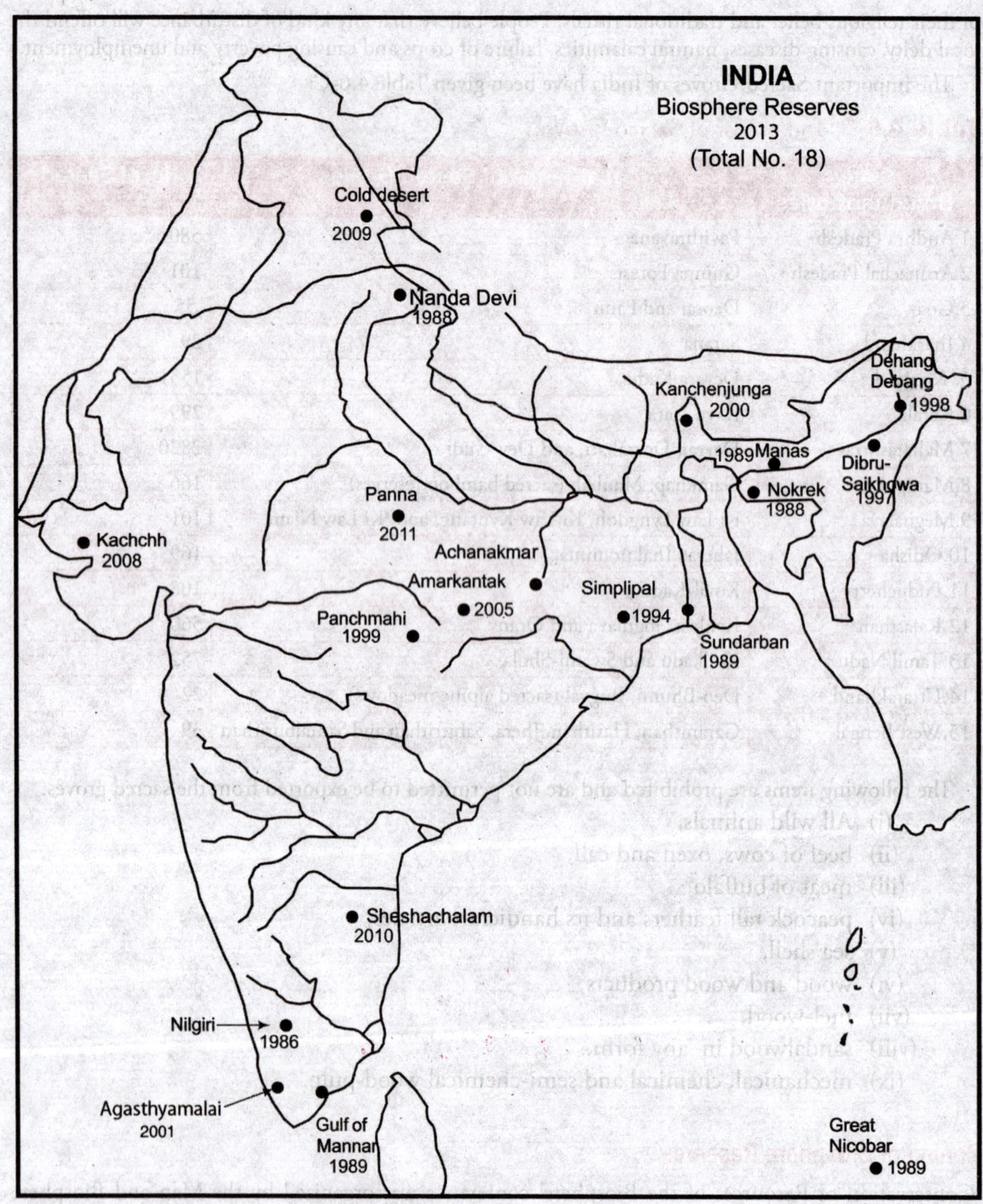

Fig. 4.5 India: Biosphere Reserves

The Man and Biosphere in 1976, proposed a simple zoning pattern for biosphere reserves which comprised the following three zones (**Fig. 4.5-A**):

1. **Core Zone:** The core zone should be kept absolutely undisturbed. Strictly protected, and no interference from man for economic or cultural activity. Each biosphere reserve includes one or several core areas, that are strictly protected according to well-defined conservation objectives. It is the least disturbed ecosystem of the biosphere reserve. The core areas may be much larger in sparsely populated areas and relatively small in densely populated areas. Core areas exclude the presence of significant human settlements. The core area/areas of the biosphere reserve are generally surrounded by a delineated buffer zone. The core zone is to be kept free from all human pressures, external to the ecosystem.
2. **Buffer Zone:** The area surrounding the core zone is known as the buffer zone (**Fig. 4.5-A**). It has environmental research, education, and training places and buildings. The future needs for research, education, training, fishing, grazing are extended in the buffer zone.
3. **Transitional Area:** The transitional area surrounds the buffer zone. It covers large open area. The tourist infrastructure is developed in the transitional area. The local population is allowed to enter in this zone to assist the researchers, managers, tourists and eco-tourists. This area is managed by different authorities with understanding and co-operation for the management and development programme. Since this zone is managed by different authorities, hence proper co-operation and coordination are required for the management and development programmes.

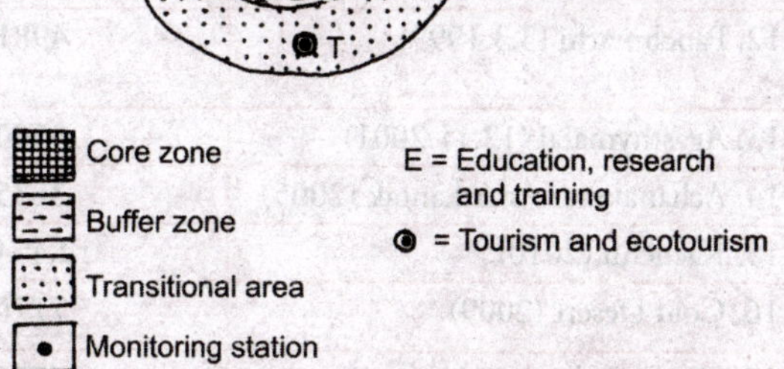

Fig. 4.5-A Zonation of Biosphere Reserve

The Biosphere Reserves Programme was initiated in India in 1986 and till date, 18 sites have been designated as biosphere reserves (BR) in different parts of the country. The names of the biosphere reserves in India have been given in **Table 4.7**.

Table 4.7 Biosphere Reserves of India

Biosphere Reserve and the Year of notification	Geographical Area in sq km	State/States (species)
1. Nilgiri (1.8.1986)	5520	Tamil Nadu, Kerala and Karnataka (Nilgiri-Tahr, Lion-tailed macaque)
2. Nanda Devi (18.1.1988)	6407	Uttarakhand (snow leopard)
3. Nokrek (1.9.1988)	820	Meghalaya (Garo Hills) (Red-Panda)
4. Manas (14.3.1989)	2837	Assam (Golden Langur, Red Panda)

(*Contd.*)

Table 4.7 *(Contd.)*

Biosphere Reserve and the Year of notification	Geographical Area in sq km	State/States (species)
5. Sundarban (29.3.1989)	9630	West Bengal (Royal Bengal Tiger)
6. Gulf of Mannar (18.2.1989)	10,500	Tamil Nadu Coast between India and Sri Lanka (Dugong)
7. Great Nicobar (6.1.1989)	0885	Andaman and Nicobar Islands, (Saltwater-Crocodile)
8. Simlipal (21.6.1994)	5569	Odisha (Gaur, Royal Bengal Tiger, Wild-elephant)
9. Dibru-Saikhowa (28.7.1997)	0765	Assam (Dibrugarh and Tinsukhia distt.), (Golden Langur)
10. Dehang-Debang (2.9.1998)	5112	Arunachal Pradesh (Dibang Valley)
11. Khangchendzonga (7.2.2000)	2931	Sikkim (Kanchenjunga), snow leopard, Red panda
12. Panchmarhi (3.3.1999)	4981	Panther, Barking deer, Madhya Pradesh (Giant squirrel, Flying squirrel)
13. Agasthymalai (12.11.2001)	3500	Kerala Nilgiri Tahr, Elephant
14. Achanakmar Amarkantak (2005)	3835	Madhya Pradesh and Chhattisgarh
15. Kachchh (2010)	12,454	Gujarat (Indian wild Ass)
16. Cold Desert (2009)	7770	Lahaul-Spiti and Ladakh (snow leopard)
17. Sheshachalam (2010)	4755	Andhra Pradesh/Seemandhra (Indian-elephant) Red *Chandan*
18. Panna (2011)	2999	Madhya Pradesh (Tiger, Chital, Sambhar and Sloth bear).

Total Area = 1,19,712

Out of the 18 biosphere reserves, 11 biosphere reserves have been included in the World Network of Biosphere Reserves so far. The seven biosphere reserves in the list of World Network of Biosphere Reserves include 1. Sundarban, 2. Gulf of Mannar, 3. Nilgiri, 4. Nanda Devi, 5. Panchmarhi, 6. Simlipal, and 7. Nokrek 8. Great Nicobar 9. Achanakmar (Amarkantak), 10. Agasthyamalai, 11. Khangchendzonga (**Table 4.8**).

BIOSPHERE RESERVES OF INDIA

1. **Nilgiri Biosphere Reserve (NGBR):** Location: states of Kerala, Tamil Nadu and Kerala.

   Date of Notification: 1 August, 1986.

   Altitudinal Range: 300 m to 2635 m.

   Total Area: 5520 sq km, Core area: 1240 sq km

   Buffer Area: 3574 sq km

   Transitional Area: 3574 sq km

Biogeographic Province: Western Ghats

Core zone: Silent Valley National Park, Bandipur National Park, Mudumalai National Park, Nagarahole National Park, Mukkuruthi National Park.

Main Rivers: Bhavani, Chaliyar, Kabini, Noyil, Suvarnavati.

Main Tribes: Cholanaikans Kurichians (hunters, staying in caves), Toda, Badagas, Kothas, Kurumbas, Irulas.

Important Fauna: Tiger, common leopard, wild dog, elephant, gaur, sambar, chital, four horned antelope, Nilgiri Tahar, lion-tailed macaque, Nilgiri langur.

2. **Nanda Devi Biosphere Reserve (Uttarakhand):**

Location: Uttarakhand State

Date of Notification: 18 January, 1988

Total Area : 6407 sq km

Buffer Area: 5149 sq km

Transition Area: 546 sq km

Altitudinal range:1800 to 7816 m.

Main Rivers: Rishi-Ganga a tributary of the Dhauli-Ganga which feeds a major tributary of the Ganga-Alaknanda.

World Heritage Site by UNESCO

Biogeographic Province: West Himalayan Highlands

Core Zone: Nanda Devi National Park, and Valley of Flower National Park.

Important Fauna: Snow leopard, Common leopard, Himalayan black bear, Bharal, Musk deer, Himalayan Tahr, Goral.

3. **Nokrek Biosphere Reserves (Garo Hills -Meghalaya):**

Location: Assam State

Date of Notification :1st September, 1988

Biogeographic Province : North East India, Meghalaya Hills -9B.

Altitudinal range: 55m to 1412 m.

Core Zone: Nokrek National Park

Buffer Area: 228 sq km

Transition Area: 545 sq km

Special Feature of Flora: abundant natural occurrence of *Citrus inica Tanaka* (a progenitor of citrus or ancestors of oranges).

Main Tribe: Garo

Important Fauna: Tiger, leopard (clouded and common), golden cat, leopard cat, stumped tailed macaque, Assamese macaque, slow loris, golden langur, caped monkey, hollock-gibb.

4. **Sunderban Biosphere Reserve (SBBR)**

   Location: 29th March, 1989

   Date of Notification: 29th March, 1989

   Total area: 9630 sq km

   Core Zone: Sunderban National Park

   Buffer Area: 2233 sq km

   Transition Area: 5705 sq km

   Altitudinal range : 6m to 9 m.

   Biogeographic Province East Coasts- 8B

   Main Rivers: Baratala, Bidya, Gosaba, Herobhanga, Ichamati, Matla, Raimangal, Saptmukhi, Thakuran.

   Tribes: No tribal population.

   Important fauna: Tiger, common leopard, salt water crocodile, chital, fishing cat, leopard cat, Gangetic dolphin.

5. **Manas Biosphere Reserve (Brahmaputra Valley, Assam)**

   Location: Assam State

   Date of Notification: 14th March. 1989

   Altitudinal range: 61m 110 m

   Total Area: 2837 sq km

   Core Area: 1692 sq km

   Buffer Area: 2233 sq km

   Transition Area: 5705 sq km

   Biogeographic Province: Brahmaputa Valley-9A

   Core Zone-Manas National Park

   Main Rivers: Aie, Beki, Champamati, Dhansiri, Hel, Manas,Pagladia, Phumara, Saralbhanga, Sankosh.

   Tribes: Adivasi, Bodo, Rahha-Hasang, Koch-Rajbongis, Bengalis and Nepalis.

   Important Fauna: Tiger, Leopard (Clouded and Common), Indian one horned rhino, Elephant, Hollock-gibbon, Golden Langur, and Pigmy-hog.

6. **Simlipal Biosphere Reserve (SPBR)**

   Location: Orissa State

   Date of Notification: 21st June, 1994

   Location: Orissa State

   Total Area: 5569 sq km

   Core Area: 1195 sq km

Buffer Area: 1336 sq km

Transition Area: 3038 sq km

Main Rivers: Bhandan, Budhabalanga, Khadkei, Khairi, Palpala, Sanjo West Deo.

Main Tribes: Bathudi, Bhumija, Kolho, Santhal, Ho, Munda, Gonds, Pauri-Bhuyans, ***Khadias***, and ***Mankadias*** (food gatherers).

7. **Dibru-Saikhowa Biosphere**

Location: Assam State

Date of Notification: 28th July, 1997

Altitudinal range: 110-to 126 m

Total area: 765 sq km

Core Area: 340 sq km

Buffer Area: 425 sq km

Transition Area: Not defined

Main Rivers: Brahmaputra and channels, namely, Ananta-nala, Chabru-nadi, Dadhia-nala, Dimoruhola Hatigulinala, Kolomi, Laikajan, Naya-nadi,Salbeel-nala and Lohit River.

Main Tribes: Ashing, Bokar, Boti, Idu, Karko, Khamba, Memba, Minyong, Tangam.

Main Tribes: Minshingh.

Biogeographic Province: Brahmaputra Valley-9

Core Zone: Dibru Saikhowa Wildlife Sanctuary

Waterfalls: Joranda (150m) and Barehipani (400 m).

Important Fauna: Tiger, Elephant, Hollock-gibbon, Gangetic Dolphin, and Feral horses.

8. **Dehang-Dibang Biosphere Reserve (DDBR)**

Location: Arunachal Pradesh

Date of notification : 2nd September, 1998

Altitudinal zone: 500m to 5000 m

Total area: 5,111 sq km

Core Area: 4094 sq km

Buffer Area: 1017 sq km

Transition Area: Not defined

Biogeographic Province: East Himalayas-2D.

Main Rivers: Siang River

Core Zone : Mouling National Park and Debang Wildlife Sanctuary.

Important Fauna : Snow leopard, Common leopard, Mechuka giant flying squirrel, Red panda, Asian golden cat, Marbled cat, Red Goral, Takin, Gaur.

9. **Great Nicobar Biosphere Reserve (GNBR)**

Location: Andaman and Nicobar Islands

Date of Notification : 6th January, 1989

Total Area: 885 sq km

Core Area: 705 sq km

Transition Area: 159 sq km

Altitudinal range Sea: level to 642 m

Biogeographic Province Islands :10B

Main Rivers: Alexandra River, Galathea River.

Main Tribes: Shompen (Mongoloid)

Core Zone: Cambell Bay National Park and Galathea National Park

Important Fauna : Crabeating Macaque, Nicobar tree shrew, Dugong, Saltwater-crocodile Marine turtle and Reticulated Python.

10. **Gulf of Mannar Biosphere Reserve (GMBR)**

Location: Pamban Islands southern coastline includes Rameshwaram and Kanyakumari to mainland coast.

Date of notification: 18th Feb. 1989

Altitudinal range: Sea level

Total area: 10,500 sq km

Core Area: 21 Islands

Buffer Area: 20x160 sq km aquatic Area

Biogeographic Province : East Coast - 8B

Core zone: Biosphere Reserve cluster.

Main Tribes: Marakaeyars (fisherman)

Important range: Sponges, Corals, Sea-fan Polychaetes, Prawns, Crabs, Lobsters, Cephalopods, Echinoderms.

11. **Panchmarhi Biosphere Reserve (PMBR)**

Location: Madhya Pradesh

Date of Notification: 3rd March, 1999.

Altitudinal range: 320 m- 1352 m

Total area: 3981 sq km

Core Area: 1555 sq km

Buffer Area: 1786 sq km

Transition Area: 1641 sq km

Biogeographic Province: Deccan Peninsula Central Highlands-6A.

Core zone: Satpura National Park

Main Rivers: Denwa, Dudhi, and Tawa

Main Tribes: Bharia which is one of the most primitive tribes.

Important Fauna: Tiger, gaur, common leopard, Indian giant squirrel, and flying squirrel.

12. Khangchendzonga Biosphere Reserve (KBR)

Location : Sikkim State

Date of Notification : 7th February, 2000

& re-notification: 24th May, 2010

Total area : 2931 sq km

Core Area: 1784 sq km

Buffer Area: 836 sq km

Transition Area: 311 sq km

Altitudinal range : 1220-8586 m

Main Rivers: Lhonak River, Tista, Tholung Valley.

Main Tribes: Bhutias, Lepchas (most primitive), Limboos and Sikkimi.

Biogeographic Province: Central Himalayan Highland -2C and Sikkim-Himalaya-1C

Core zone: Khangchendzonga National Park

Important Fauna: Snow leopard, Leopard (Clouded & Common), Tibetan wolf, Himalayan black bear, Musk deer, Himalayan Thar, Blue sheep.

13. Kachchh Biosphere Reserve (KBR)

Location: Gujarat State

Date of Notification : 29th January, 2008

Altitudinal range 5m: 15 m

Total area: 12,454 sq km

Core Area: 4455 sq km

Buffer Area: 7999 sq km

Transition Area: Fringe area of the width of 5 km (proposed)

Biogeographic Province: Desert Kachchh-3-B

Main Rivers: Luni, Kara Rivers.

Main Tribes: Bhil, Koli, Parachi, Charan, Meghwal.

Core zone: Kachchh Desert Wildlife Ass Sanctuary

Important Fauna: Wild Ass, Stripped hyena, Indian gazelle, Jackal, Desert fox, Desert-cat,

14. Agasthyamala Biosphere Reserve (AMBR)

Location: States of Tamil Nadu and Kerala

Date of Notification: 12th November 2000

Altitudinal range: 100 to 1800 m

Total area: 3,500 sq km

Core Area: 1135 sq km

Buffer Area: 1445 sq km

Transition Area: 920 sq km

Biogeographic Provinces: Western Ghat-5B

Core Zone: Neyyar Wildlife Sanctuary and Shendurney Wildlife Sanctuary

Main River: Tamiraparani

Main Tribe: Kanikar/ Kani.

Important Fauna: Tiger, Common leopard, Elephant, Gaur, Flying squirrels.

15. Achnakmar-Amarkantak Biosphere Reserve (AABR)

Location: Chhattisgarh and Madhya Pradesh

Date of Notification: 30th March, 2005

Altitudinal range: 280 m to 1102 m

Total area: 3835 sq km

Core Area: 552 sq km

Buffer Area: 1956 sq km

Biogeographic Province: Deccan Peninsula Central Highlands -6A.

Main Rivers: Johilla, Maniari and Sone.

Main Tribes: Baiga, Gond, Kol, Kanwar, Pradhan, Panka.

Waterfalls: Durgadhara, Kapildhara, and Shambhudhara.

Important Fauna: Tiger, Common leopard, Gaur, Chital, Sambar, Wild boar, Flying squirrels.

Core zone: Achanakmar Wildlife Sanctuary.

16. Cold Desert Biosphere Reserve (CDBR)

Location: Himachal Pradesh State

Date of Notification: 28th August, 2009

Altitudinal range: 3300 m- to 6600 m

Total area: 7770 sq km

Core Area: 2665 sq km

Buffer Area: 3977 sq km

Biogeographic Province: trans-Himalaya-Tibetan Plateau - 1 A

Main Rivers: Pin, Spiti, Sutlej.

Main Tribes: Bhutias and pahadis.

Salient Fetaures: 'Fossil Park of the World'

Core zone: Pin Valley, Chandratal Wildlife Sanctuary

Important Fauna: Snow leopard, Himalayan brown bear, musk deer, Himalayan Thar, Himalayan Ibex.

17. Seshachalam Biosphere Reserve (SCBR)

Location: Andhra Pradesh

Date of Notification 20th September, 2010
Total area : 4756 sq km.
Core Area: 751 sq km
Buffer Area: 1865 sq km
Transition Area: within 5 km radius of outer boundary of buffer zone
Altitudinal range: 400 to 1370 m
Biogeographic Province: Eastern Ghats, 6E
Main Rivers: Nandyal (Kunderu) River
Waterfalls: Gundalakona, Gunjana, and Talakona,
Main Tribes: NA
Core zone : Sri Venkateshwara National park
Important Fauna: Slender loris, Indian giant squirrel, Mouse deer, Golden gecko

18. Panna Biosphere Reserves (PBR)

Location: Madhya Pradesh State
Date of Notification : 25th August 2011
Total area: 9630 sq km
Altitudinal range: 200-550 m
Biogeographic Province: Deccan Peninsula Central Highland
Main Rivers: Ken
Main Tribes: Gond, Rajgond, Nandgond, Khairuas, Dauvas, Yadvas.
Important fauna: Tiger, Wolf, Chital, Sloth Bear, Chinkara, Sambar, Leopard,

Table 4.8 Biosphere Reserves of India on the World Network of Biosphere Reserves

Biosphere Reserve	Year	State/States
1. Nilgiri Biosphere Reserves	1986	Tamil Nadu, Kerala, Karnataka
2. Gulf of Mannar	1989	Tamil Nadu
3. Sundarban	1989	West Bengal
4. Nanda Devi	1988	Uttarakhand
5. Nokrek	1988	Meghalaya (Garo Hills)
6. Panchmarhi	1999	Madhya Pradesh
7. Simlipal	1994	Odisha
8. Great Nicobar	1989	Andaman & Nicobar Islands
9. Achnakmar (Amarkantak)	2005	Chhattisgarh and Madhya Pradesh
10. Agasthyamalai	2016	Kerala & T.N.
11. Khangchendzonga National Park	2018	Sikkim

WORLD HERITAGE SITES

The World Heritage Site as an institution was established in November 1972 at the 17th General Conference of UNESCO under the terms of the convention concerning the protection of world culture and natural heritage. The main responsibility of the World Heritage Committee was to provide technical co-operation under the World Heritage Fund to safeguard the selected sites of great biodiversity importance. The World Heritage Sites of India have been given in **Table 4.9**.

Table 4.9 India: World Heritage Sites

Name of Site	State
1. Kaziranga National Park	Assam
2. Manas Wildlife Sanctuary	Assam
3. Keoladeo National Park	Rajasthan
4. Sundarban National Park	West Bengal
5. Nanda Devi National park	Uttarakhand
6. Western Ghats	Maharashtra, Goa, Karnataka, Kerala and Tamil Nadu

NATIONAL PARKS

The National Parks in India are created by the respective State Governments under the provisions of Wildlife (Protection) Act 1972. National Parks are declared in areas that are considered to have adequate ecological, geomorphological, edephic, cultural and natural significance. A national park is a relatively large area of one or several ecosystems that are not being materially altered by human exploitation and occupation. Here, plant and animal species, geomorphic sites and habitats are reserved for education and research.

NATIONAL PARKS AND TIGER RESERVES

1. Anshi National Park (1987): Located near the city of Dandeli in the Uttara Kannada District of Karnataka along the border of Goa, it is a habitat of Bengal tigers, black panthers and elephants. It has moist deciduous forests. The species of flora include true cinnamon, bamboo, bauhinia, eucalyptus, silver oak, teak and jamba.

2. Balpakhran (1988): Located near Tura-the Headquarters of the Garo Hills (Meghalaya), Balpakhran is a National Park. The highest peak Balpakhran is often referred as the *'abode of perpetual winds'* as well as the *'land of spirits'*.

The main fauna of this National Park includes wild water- buffalo, red panda, elephant, several species of cats, monkeys, baboons and barking deer. It is also famous for pitcher plant and many medicinal herbs. The National Park is full of sprawling vegetation consisting of sub-tropical and deciduous trees.

3. Bandhavgarh National Park (1968): Located in the Umaria District of Madhya Pradesh, it sprawls over an area of 105 km^2. It has the highest density of Bengal - tigers in India. The park has a large breeding population of leopards and various species of deer. It also had white tigers a longtime back. The last white tiger, *Mohan*, is now stuffed and on display in the palace of the Maharaja of Rewa. Rising mining activities around the park are putting the tigers at risk. Among other species are sambar, barking-deer, nilgai, gaur etc.

4. Bandipur National Park (1974): Located about 80 km from the city of Mysore in Chamarajanagar district of Karnataka, it was once a private hunting reserve of the Maharaja of Mysore. At present, it is upgraded as Bandipur Tiger Reserve.

Bandipur supports a wide range of timber trees including teak, rosewood, sandalwood, Indian laurel, Indian kino tree, giant clumping bamboo and Grewia- tiliaefolia. In addition to these, there are kadam tree, Indian gooseberry, axelwood, golden shower tree, satinwood, black cutch, etc.

The fauna of the National Park includes tigers, leopards, Indian elephant, gaur, chital, sambhar, sloth bear, four-horned antelope, gray-langur, wild-boar and muntjac. The main birds include buzzards, red-headed vultures, Indian vultures, flower-peckers, hoppoes, Indian rollers, brown fish-owl, crested serpent eagle, bee-eaters and kingfisher. The main reptiles are cobra, python, rat-snake, muggers, monitor lizards, Indian chameleon and flying lizards.

5. Bannerghatta National Park (1974): Located near the city of Banglore (Karnataka), it is a popular tourist destination with a zoo, a pet corner, an animal rescue centre and a butterfly enclosure. The main flora includes sandalwood, neem, arjun, tamarind, bamboo and Eucalyptus. Fauna Elephants, gaur, leopard, jackal, wild boar, sloth bear, sambar, chital, hippopotamus spotted deer, common langur, procupine, hare, monitor-lizard, cobras, krait and zebra.

6. Betla National Park (1989): Located in the Latehar District (Jharkhand) of the Chota Nagpur Plateau, the Betal National Park has vast areas of vegetation of tropical wet evergreen forests in the lower reaches, (moist and dry) deciduous forests in the middle, and temperate alpine forests in the upper reaches. The main species include sal, mahua, bamboo and grasses.

It is famous for bison, elephants, tigers and leopards. Among other wild animals hyena, panther, sloth bear and wolf are common. Other animals include deer, sambhar, four-horned antelope, nilgai, kakar, civet, porcupine and mongoose.

7. Bhadra Tiger Reserve (1974): Located in the Western Ghats in the state of Goa, it is famous for the tropical evergreen forests and moist deciduous forests. The main fauna of the sanctuary includes Bengal-tiger, black panther, leopard, barking deer, macaque, langur, civet, flying squirrel, giant squirrel, gaur, mouse deer, porcupine, slender loris, sambar, spotted deer and wild dog. In addition to these, there are emerald dove, blue-bird, great Indian hornbill, black woodpecker, grey-headed myna, jungle fowl, yellow bulbul and kingfisher. The Dudhsagar waterfall is a tiered waterfall located on the Mandvi River at the Karnataka border in the south western part of the park. Drango, emerald dove, fairy blue-bird, hornbill woodpacker, grey-headed myna jungle fowl, and bulbul are important.

8. Bhagwan Mahavir Sanctuary and Mollem National Park (1978): Situated near the town of Mollem, it is a sanctuary and National Park in Goa. It has several important temples of the Kadamba Dynasty and also the Dudhsagar Waterfalls. It is the home of nomadic buffalo herders known as Dhangar tribe.

This National Park contains deciduous and moist deciduous forests. The predominant species are *Terminalia* and *Dalbergia*. The forest canopy is almost closed and the availability of grass is very limited. Wild mammals include: black panther, barking deer, gaur, Malabar giant squirrel, mouse deer, pangolin, porcupine, slender loris, sambar, spotted deer, wild boar and wild dog.

9. Bhitarkanika (1975): Located in the Kendrapara District of Odisha, it is surrounded by the Bhitarkanika Wildlife Sanctuary and the Gahirmatha Beach and Marine Sanctuary. The park is a home of the endangered Saltwater Crocodile, White Crocodile, Indian Python, King Cobra and Black Ibis. The vegetation species include mangroves (Sundari, thespia, grasses and indigo-bush). Every year about 80,000 migratory birds arrive in this park for nesting during monsoon season.

10. Bori National Park (1977): Located in the Hoshingabad District of Madhya Pradesh, Bori Wildlife Sanctuary was established in 1977. It is a part of the Pachmarhi Biosphere Reserve. The Tawa River lies to the west of the sanctuary. The sanctuary is mostly covered by mixed deciduous and bamboo forests. The dominant species include teak dhaora, tendu etc.

11. Buxa Tiger Reserve (1983): Located in the Alipurduar District of West Bengal, to the south of Bhutan, it is National Park and a Tiger Reserve. It has the species of Eastern Bhabhar and Tarai-Sal, Eastern Himalayan Moist Deciduous Forest, Moist Sal, Northern Dry Deciduous, Sub-Himalayan Mixed Deciduous, and Northern Tropical Evergreen Forests. The main trees are sal, champa, gamar, simul and chikrasi. The fauna include rhino, Asian elephant, tiger, gaur, wild-boar, sambhar.

12. Chandoli National Park (2004): The Chandoli National Park is located in the Sangli District of Maharshtra State. Chandoli National Park is notable as the southern portion of the Sahyadri Tiger Reserve, with Koyna Wildlife Sanctuary forming the northern part of the reserve.

The main flora of this National Park includes moist deciduous forest and the dwarf evergreen forests. Its fauna consists of iron-wood, jamun, pisa, fig, olea, katak, kanjal, kokum, indian laural, amla, umber and grasses. The main fauna includes tigers, leopards, gaur, barking deer, mouse-deer, sloth-bears and black-buck.

13. Dachigam (1981): Located about 22 km from the city of Srinagar (J & K), it sprawls over an area of about 141 km^2. It is located in the Zabarwan Range of the Western Himalayas. Its altitudinal variation is between 1700 to 4300 meters above the sea level.

The mountain sides below tree line are heavily wooded. Most of the coniferous forests consists of broad leaf species. Interspersed between these are alpine pastures and meadows.

The main animal species in the Dachigam National park are musk-deer, leopard, Himalayan sparrow, Himalayan grey-langur, leopard-cat, Himalayan brown bear, jackal, hill-fox, Himalayan weasel, Yellow-throated marten, jungle-cat, otter and long--tailed marmot. The main birds include cinnamon sparrow, black bulbul pygmy owlet, woodpecker, babbler, Himalayan vultures, bearded vultures, wall-creeper and chough.

14. Dampa Tiger Reserve (1985): Situated in the western part of Mizoram at the international border of Bangladesh about 127 km from Aizawl, it covers an area of 550 sq km. It is the natural home of leopards, Indian bison, barking deer, sloth bear, gibbons, langurs, slow loris, Indian python, wild boar, and a variety of birds. Tiger population is insignificant in this sanctuary.

15. Desert National Park (1992): Located near the city of Jaisalmer, it is one of the largest National Parks of India. It is a typical example of the ecosystem of Thar Desert. About 20 per cent of its area is covered by sand-dunes.

The National Park is a heaven for the migratory birds. Many eagles, harriers, falcons, buzzards, kestrels and vultures can be seen in this National Park. The endangered great Indian bustard is a magnificent bird found in relatively fair numbers. The Indian bustard migrates locally in different seasons. The Desert National Park has a collection of fossils of animals and plants of 180 million years old. Some fossils of dinosaurs of about 6 million years old, have been found in the area.

16. Dudhwa National Park (1977): This National Park is located in the Kheri-Lakhimpur District of Uttar Pradesh. The main species of vegetation include moist deciduous, tropical seasonal swamp forests and tropical dry deciduous forests. The main flora includes sal, asna, shisham, jamun, gular, sehore bahera and numerous grasses. The major attraction of the Dudhwa National Park are the tigers and swamp deer. In 1980, Indian rhinoceros was introduced into Dudhwa from Assam and Nepal.

17. Fossil National Park (Mandla-M.P.): Located in the Mandla District of Madhya Pradesh, it has the fossils of plants existed in India between 40 million and 150 million years back. These fossils are spread over seven villages (Barbaspur, Chanti-Hills, Chargaon, Deorakhurd, Deori-Kohani, Ghuguwa, and Umaria). The National Park is spread over agricultural fields in the seven above given villages. The fossils look like ordinary rocks and are either removed from the field unwittingly by the farmers or are damaged by the tourists and other unscrupulous people.

18. Gir or Gasan Gir National Park (1965): This National park and Wildlife Sanctuary is located in the state of Gujarat. It is the sole home of Asiatic lions. It is traversed by the seven major perennial rivers of Gir region. These rivers are Hiran, Shetrunji, Datardi, Shingoda, Machhundri, Godavari and Raval. The Kamleshwar Dam is a located in the Gir National Park.

Teak occurs mixed with dry deciduous species. The savannah of this National Park are known as *'vidis'*. It is the largest deciduous forest in Western India.

The main fauna include Asiatic lion, Indian leopard, Indian cobras, jungle cat, stripped hyena, golden jackal, Indian mongoose, India palm-civet. Moreover there are chital, nilgai, sambar, four horned antelopes, chinkara, blackbuck, wild-boa and python.

19. Guindy (1977): Located in Chennai (Tamil Nadu), it is one of the smallest National Parks, situated in a city. It is an extension of the Raj Bhavan. The park has a role in both *ex-situ* and *in-situ* conservation and is the home of over 400 blackbucks, 2000 spotted deers and a wide variety of snakes.

The Guindy National Park has a dry evergreen scrub and thorn forest, grasslands, shrubs, climbers and herbs. Its vegetation also consists of sugar-apple, wood-apple and *Neem* trees.

There are 14 species of mammals including blackbuck, chital, or spotted deer, jackal, small Indian civet, palm civet, macaque, hyena, hedgehog, common mongoose and stripped palm squirrel. Guindy snake park is famous for king cobra, python, vipers and other reptiles.

20. Hamis National Park (1981): Located in the Leh District of the Jammu and Kashmir State, it is a high altitude and the largest National Park of India. It is world famous for the highest density of snow-leopards. The *Rumbak* stream flows through the National Park. It also has a small population of Asiatic Ibex, Bharal (Blue sheep) and Argali (Tibetan-sheep). The endangered Tibetan wolf and the Eurasian brown bear are also found in the National Park. The Rumbak Valley offers good opportunities for bird-watching. The main vegetation includes juniper, sub-alpine dry birch and fir.

21. Indian Wild Ass Sanctuary (1972): The Indian Wild Ass Sanctuary is located in the Little Rann of Kachchh in Gujarat. In Gujarati, 'Rann' stands for desert. The Rann gets flooded for a period of about one month during monsoon and is spotted with about 74 elevated islands (plateaus) locally called 'bets'. These bets are covered with grasses and feed the population of animals. It has the world's last population of Khur sub-species of wild ass.

22. Indira Gandhi National Park and Wildlife Sanctuary (1974): Located in the Anaimalai Hills (Coimbatore District) of Tamil Nadu it is a wildlife sanctuary and National Park. It has the unique Karian Shola vegetation. The National Park and Sanctuary are under consideration by the UNESCO as part of the Western Ghats World Heritage site.

The wild animals of the sanctuary include the threatened species of Bengal Tiger, Indian elephant, *dhole*, and lion-tailed macaque. In addition to these, there are jackals, leopards, spotted deer, barking deer, mouse deer, wild boar, common langur, Asian Palm civet, sambhar, giant squirrel, Indian porcupine and stripped squirrel.

23. Indravati National Park (1982): Located along the bank of Indravati River in the Bijaipur District of Chhattisgarh, it is home to one of the last populations of rare wild buffalo. It derives its name from the Indravati River which flows from west to east.

The flora in the Indravati National Park consists mainly of tropical moist deciduous type with predominance of sal, teak, bamboo, mahua, tendu, semal, haldu, jamun, ber, salai, and trees. There are also rich patches of excellent grasslands providing much required fodder to buffalos, chital, barking deer, nilgai, gaur (Indian bison) and other herbivores of the park.

It is one of the last habitats for the endangered wild buffalo. Moreover, there are nilgai, black buck, chausingha (four-horned antelope), sambar, chital, wild boar, tigers, leopards, sloth bear, dhole (wil-dog) and stripped hyena. Fresh water crocodiles, lizards, Indian chameleon, common krait, Indian rock-python, cobra are also found. The park also gives shelter to a large variety of birds of which hill -myna is the most important.

24. Kalakkad Mundanthurai Tiger Reserve (1988): Located in the southern-western Ghats in Tirunelveli and Kanniyakumari districts of Tamil Nadu, the Kalakad Mundanthurai Tiger Reserve was established in 1988. It has 150 endemic plants, 33 fish, 37 amphibians, 81 reptiles and 273 birds. It has tigers, leopards, wild-cat, Nilgiri- tahr, wild pig, mouse deer sloth bear, lion-tailed macaque, langur slender loris, giant squirrel and crocodiles.

25 Kanger Ghati (Valley) National Park (1982): Located in the Jagdalpur district of Chhattisgarh, it is also called as the Kanger Valley National Park. The flora of the park consists of mixed moist deciduous type of forest with predominance of sal, teak and bamboo trees. In addition to these, the National Park is also known for medicinal plants, grasses, climbers, wild sugarcane, canes, ferns and epiphytes.

The main fauna of the Kanger Valley National Park include tigers, leopards, mouse-deer, wild-cat, chital, sambar, barking deer, jackals, langurs, sloth bear, flying squirrel, wild-boar, striped hyena, rabbits, pythons, cobra and crocodiles.

26. Kanha National Park and Tiger Reserve (1955): It is the largest National Park of Madhya Pradesh. The park has a significant population of Royal Bengal Tiger, leopards, sloth bear, swamp deer, Indian-gaur, *barasingha* and Indian wild dog. Kanha National park is rich in sal, and other mixed forest trees interspersed with meadows. The highland forests are tropical moist dry deciduous type. It has many open grasslands. Moreover, there are climbers, shrubs and numerous flowering plants.

27. Kasu Brahmanand Reddy National Park (1998): Famous for peacocks, the Kasu Brahmanand Reddy National Park is located in the Jubilee Hills in Hyderabad (Teangana). Sprawling over 400 acres, this National Park houses the famous *Chiran Palace* complex. It is often described as a jungle amidst the concrete jungle. The park has Indian civet, peacock, jungle cat, more than 600 species of plants, 140 species of birds and 30 varieties of butterflies.

28. Kaziranga National Park (1905): Located in the Golaghat and Nagaon districts of Assam, the Kaziranga National Park is a World Heritage Site. There are more than two-thirds of world's great one-horned rhinocerous. According to the census of 2015, the current population of rhinocerous in Kaziranga is 2401 as published by the Forest Department, Govt. of India. Moreover, it has the highest density of tigers among protected areas in the world. It is the home to large breeding populations of elephants, wild water buffalo and swamp deer. Kaziranga National Park has a vast expanse of tall elephant grass, marshland and dense moist deciduous forests.

29. Keibul Lamjo National Park (1977): Located in the Bishanpur District of Manipur, this National Park was created in 1977. It is an integral part of Loktak Lake and the only *floating park in the world.* The park is characterised by many floating decomposed plant materials locally called *phumdis.*

The park, primarily composed of moist semi-evergreen forests, has a rich amalgam of aquatic and terrestrial ecosystems. The grassland structure of the park is aquatic flora recorded in the park which includes wild rice., reeds and grasses. The main fauna includes brown-antlered deer which is the flagship species of the park. In addition to this, hog-deer, wild boar, large Indian civet, common otter, fox, golden cat, and sambar are important. The main birds include kingfisher, black kite, lesser sky-lark, northern hill myna, crow, cranes. and woodpecker.

30. Jim Corbett National Park (1936): Located in the Nainital District of Uttarakhand, it is the oldest National Park of India. The Ramnagar River passes through the Jim Corbett National Park. Its flora consists of dense moist deciduous forests mainly sal, haldu, peepal, rohini, and mango trees. Among the fauna, Bengal Tiger, leopard, elephants, small cats, black bears, mongoose, sambar, hog-deer, langur, macaques, chital and owls are important.

31. Manas National Park (1990): Located in the foothills of the Himalayas, it is a national park is a UNESCO Natural World Heritage site, a Project Tiger Reserve, an Elephant Reserve and a biosphere reserve in Assam. This National Park is known for its rare and endangered endemic wildlife such as Assam roofed turtle, hispid hare, golden langur, wild water buffalo, Indian tigers, rhinoceros, gaurs, clouded leopards, golden cat, macaques, gibbons, otters, barking deer, panthers sambar and pygmy hog.

The main vegetation types include Sub-Himalayan semi-evergreen forests, moist deciduous and dry deciduous forests. It also has low alluvial savanna woodlands and numerous types of grasses.

32. Marine National Park (1982): Located on the southern shore of the Gulf of Kachchh in the Jamnagar District of Gujarat, it was declared a National Park in 1982. There are 42 islands on the Jamnagar coast in the Marine National Park. Most of these islands are surrounded by coral reefs. The best known island is Pirotan. The main fauna includes, 52 species of corals, jellyfish, crabs, lobsters, shrimps, prawns, oysters octopus, starfish, sea-cucumbers, sea-urchins, sea horse (dugongs), sharks, endangered sea turtles.

33. Melgat National Park (1973-74): Located in the Amravati District of Maharashtra, its boundaries are formed by the Tapi River and Satpura Range. The Tapi River flows through the northern end. The main fauna found are tiger, leopard, sloth bear, wild dog, sambar, gaur, barking deer, nilgai, chital, chausingha, flying squirrel, langur, monkeys, porcupines python, otter and hare.

34. Nagarhole National Park (1999): Located in the Brahmagiri Hills of Karnataka, it is located to the north-west of Bandipur National Park. The main flora includes teak and rosewood, sandalwood, silver oak and golden shower trees. The fauna of this National Park include tiger, leopard, wild dog (Dhole), gaur, wild boar, elephant and langurs.

35. Nagarjunsagar National Park (1967): Nagarjunsagar Srisailam Tiger Reserve is the largest Tiger Reserve spread over the districts of Nalgonda, Mahboobnagar and Kurnool districts in Andhra Pradesh. The total area of the tiger reserve is 3568 km^2.

The main types of flora consists of tropical dry mixed deciduous forest and thorn scrub forest. Important plant species are axlewood, terminalia. The main mammals in the reserve are: Bengal Tiger, Indian leopard, sloth bear, *dhole*, Indian pangolian, chital, sambar deer, blackbuck, chinkara, and chowsingha. Crocodiles, Indian pythons, king cobra and India pea-fowl are also found in this National Park.

36. Namdapha National Park (1974): Located in Arunachal Pradesh, it is the largest National Park in the Eastern Himalayas and the third largest in India. It is known for the evergreen forests and for extensive Dipterocarp forests. Moreover, the National Park has extensive bamboo forests. The park is the home of a great diversity of mammal species. It is known for snow leopard, clouded leopards, and tigers. Other large predators are *dhole*, wolves, and Asiatic black bears. Smaller carnivores include red panda, red fox, yellow-throated marten, Eurasian Otter and common palm civet, fishing cat, Asiatic golden cat, and two species of mongoose.

Large herbivores are represented by elephants, wild-boar, musk-deer, hog-deer, sambhar, gaur, serow and bharal.

37. Nameri National Park (1978): Nameri is a National Park at the foothills of the Eastern Himalayas in Sonitpur District of Assam about 35 km from Tezpur. The main flora includes semi-evergreen, moist deciduous forests with cane and bamboo brakes and narrow strips of open grasslands along the rivers. Elephants, tigers, leopards, sambhar, dhole, pygmy hog, gaur, wild boar, sloth bear, capped langur and Indian giant squirrel are the main fauna.

38. Neora Valley National Park (1986): This National Park is located in the Kalimpong Subdivision under the District of Darjeeling. The Neora River is the major river of the National Park. It is the land of the elegant panda. It has virgin natural forests, dense bamboo groves, rhododendron trees, lush green valleys. The park reaches up to an elevation of over 3500 meters above the sea level. It is characterised with tropical subtropical, temperate and alpine vegetation. The forest consists of rhododendron, bamboo, oak, ferns, sal, etc. The valley also has numerous species of orchids.

39. Neyyar Wildlife Sanctuary (1958): Lying in the south-east corner of the Western Ghats, the Neyyar Wildlife Sanctuary is located in Thiruvananthapuram District of Kerala. The Neyyar River traverses this sanctuary. The towering peak of Agasthyamalai (1868 m) is the very prominent landmark.

This sanctaury has a substantial natural vegetation cover. The diversity of its flora makes the sanctuary an ideal gene pool preserve. The main fauna of this sanctuary consists of Elephant, Sambar, Barking Deer, Bonnet Macaque, Nilgiri Langur and Nilgiri Tahr. A crocodile farm at Neyyar has 20 snout crocodiles.

40. Pakhui Tiger Reserve (1966): Located in the East Kameng District of Arunachal Pradesh, the Pakhui Tiger Reserve sprawls over 862 sq km. The elevation of the reserve varies from 100 m to 2000 meters above the sea level. The sanctuary slopes southwards towards the river valley of the Brahmaputra River.

The habitat types are lowland semi-evergreen, evergreen forests and broad-leaf deciduous forest. It is characterised by tigers, leopards, clouded leopards, wild dog, and jackal. In addition to these, there are elephants, barking deer, gaur, sambhar, bison, monkeys and capped langurs.

41. Palamau Tiger Reserve (1974): The Palamau protected area was designated as the Tiger Reserve in 1974. The North Koel River runs through the reserve. The initial count in 1874 when the tiger reserve was created was only 50 tigers. In 1989, there were 65 elephants in the reserve. Apart from tigers and elephants, leopard, gaur, sambhar and wild dogs are also found in the reserve. Increased pressure from human activities including illegal settlements and poaching have reduced the number of tigers.

42. Pench Tiger Reserve (1977): This Tiger Reserve gets its name from the Pench River, that flows from north to south about 74 km through the reserve. The Reserve lies in the southern lower reaches of the Satpura Range along the southern border of Madhya Pradesh.

Ecologically it has tropical moist deciduous forests and the dry deciduous forests. Teak is a ubiquitous species in the region. The main fauna includes tigers, leopards, *dhole*, wild-cat, small India civet, wolves,, stripped hyena, sloth bear, jackal, common palm-civet, chital, sambhar, nilgai and wild pigs.

43. Peppara Wildlife Santuary (1983): This sanctuary lies in the basin of Peppara Dam and the Karamana River near Thiruvananthpuram. The elevation of the sanctuary varies between 100 m to 1717 m.

The forest types include West coast tropical evergreen, Southern hill-top tropical evergreen, West coast semi-evergreen, Southern moist mixed deciduous and sub-montane hill valley swamp forests. The common animals found tiger, leopard, sloth bear, elephant, sambar (deer), bonnet macaque, nilgiri langur and Nilgiri-Tahr.

44. Pin Valley National Park (1987): Located in the Lahaul and Spiti districts, in the state of Himachal Pradesh, it is apart of the Cold Desert Biosphere Reserve. The elevation of the park ranges from about 3500 m to more than 6000 m at its highest point.

With its snow laden unexplored higher reaches and slopes, the park forms a natural habitat for a number of endangered animals including the Snow-leopard and Siberian Ibex. Because of the parks high altitude and extreme temperatures, the vegetation density is sparse, consisting mostly of alpine trees and groves of cedar. Himalayan snow-cock, chukar- partridges and snow-finch flourish in the park.

45. Ranthambore (1980): Situated in the Sawai- Madhopur District of south-eastern Rajasthan, Ranthanbore is one of the largest National Parks in northern India. The park is bounded by the Banas River in the north and by the Chambal River in the south.

The Sawai Madhopur National park is known for its tigers. Tigers can be easily spotted even in the day time. Other major animals include leopard, nilgai, sambar, sloth bear, wild-boar, gray langur, macaque and chital. The park has deciduous forests. The park has more than 500 flowering species.

46. Sariska Tiger Reserve(1955): Located in the district of Alwar in the Aravallis of Rajasthan State, it is known for the Bengal Tigers. It is the tiger reserve in the world to have successfully relocated tigers.

The other wild animals include leopard, jungle cat, striped hyena, golden jackal, chital, sambhar, nilgai, chinkara, four horned antilope, wild boar, hare, langur and monkeys.

The dominant tree in the forest are dhak, salar, kadaya, gol, ber, kair, bargad, arjun, gugal, bamboo, shrubs and jhar-ber.

47. Satkosia Tiger Reserve (1976): Located in the Angul District of Odisha, the Satkosia Sanctuary was created in 1976 and was designated as Tiger Reserve in 2007. It is along the 22 km gorge of Mahanadi River. The major plant communities are mixed deciduous forests including sal and riverine forests.

48. Shendurney Wildlife Sanctuary (1984): Located in the Kollam District of Kerala, it lies in the Agasthamalai Biosphere Reserve. The sanctuary surrounds the reservoir of the Thenmala Dam.

It is characterised by the tropical evergreen and semi-evergreen forests. Its main fauna include Lion-tailed Macaque- a highly endangered species.

49. Silent Valley National Park (1980): Located in the Palakkad district of Kerala, it is one of the last undisturbed tracts of the Western Ghats. The majority of the plants of this National Park are endemic. It is characterised with tropical moist evergreen forests on India. It is the core of the Niligiri International Biosphere Reserve and a part of the Western Ghats World Heritage Site, recognized by the UNESCO in 2007. The Kunthipuzha River drains the entire 15 km length of the park.

The Silent Valley has a rich diversity of fauna and flora. The threatened lion-tailed macaque, Nilgiri langur, Nilgiri tahr, bats, and hairy winged bat, Malabar giant squirrel, spotted deer, barking deer, mouse deer, elephant and gaur. Moreover, tiger, leopard (panther), leopard cat, jungle cat, fishing cat, common palm civet, small Indian civet, clawless otter, sloth bear, porcupine, wild boar, sambar, spotted deer, barking deer, mouse deer, elephant and gaur.

50. Simlipal National Park and Biosphere Reserve (1994): Simlipal National Park/ Biosphere Reserve is located in Mayurbhanj District of Odisha. It represents moist deciduous forests including tropical evergreen and dry deciduous forests. Simlipal lies almost on the Tropic of Cancer. It is a high plateau with steep slopes overlooking the plain surfaces. Simlipal is a predominantly tribal landscape with a heavy dependence on forest resource for their livelihood. The major tribes include Bathudi, Bhumija, Kolho, Santhal, Ho, Munda, Gonda and Bhuyans. Among mammals , Simlipal is known for its population of rare tigers and elephants. It also enjoys the staus of a tiger and elephant reserve.

51. Sanjay National Park (1881): Located in the Singrauli and Sidhi districts of Madhya Pradesh, it is a national park and tiger reserve. The main flora consists of deciduous especially sal and teak. The main animals consists of tiger, leopard, nilgai, spotted deer, chinkara, civet, lizards and more than 300 birds.

52. Sirohi National Park (1982): Located in the state of Manipur, the Sirohi National Park is famous for tigers and leopards. The main peak of this National Park (Shirui Kashong) near Ukhrul abounds with flowers during the monsoon season.

53. Satpura National Park (1981): Located in the Hoshingabad District of Madhya Pradesh, it sprawls over 424 sq km. It has the Dhupgarh Peak (1350 m). The Satpura National Park is very rich in biodiversity. The flora consists of dry deciduous forests. The fauna includes tiger, leopard, sambhar, chital, four-horned antelope (Chausingha), chinkara, gaur, wild dog, black-buck, fox, flying squirrel, mouse deer and numerous birds.

54. Tadoba Andhari National Park (1955): Located in Chandrapur, it is the oldest and the largest National Park of Maharashtra. It has been named after the Andhari River which meanders through the National Park. In 1995 it was declared as the Tiger Reserve. There are 43 tigers in the reserve, one of the highest in the country. The elevation of the hill ranges from 200 m to 350 m. The lake Tadoba which acts as a buffer between the park's forest and the extensive farmland extends up to the Irai Water Reservoir.

This National Park has predominantly tropical dry deciduous forest. Teak is the main tree species. Other deciduous trees include Ain (crocodile bark), bija, dhauda, hald, salai, tendu, behta, hirda, karaya, mahua, and madhuca. Apart from Bengal tiger, Tadoba Tiger Reserve is home to Indian leopard, sloth bear, gaur, nilgai, dhole (wild dog), striped hyena, small Indian civet, jungle cats, sambar, spotted deer, barking deer, chital, chausingha and honey badgar.

55. Valmiki: Located in the West Champaran District in the north-west corner of Bihar, Valmiki Tiger Reserve is one of the natural virgin lands. The Gandak River forms the western boundary of Valmiki National Park. The other rivers passing through or along the borders of the national park are Burhi Gandak, Pandai, Pachnad, Sohna. The main vegetation include champa trees, sheesham, bhabhar and terai grasses.

The main fauna of the Valmiki National Park includes tiger, rhinocerous, leopard, black deer, wild dog, wild buffalo, wild boar, barking deer, spotted deer, hog deer, sambhar, neel-gai, hyena, leopard cat, wild cat, fishing cat, langur, monkeys, flying fox (a type of bat) and flying squirrel. Among the reptiles, python, king cobra, krait, *do-muha* snake are important.

The National Parks are gateway to conservation ethics. National Parks are the areas that have been reserved strictly for the welfare of wildlife, plants, and where such activities as forestry, grazing, cultivation, etc. are banned. The following activities are strictly prohibited in the National parks:

(i) Hunting, killing or capturing of animals.
(ii) Deprivation of any wild animal of its habitat.
(iii) Destruction and collection of plants.
(iv) Use of weapons
(v) Grazing by any livestock other than wild animals of the national park.
(vi) Alteration of boundaries of national parks.

The total number of national parks in India in 2012 was 100. Some of the important national parks of India have been plotted in **Fig. 4.6** and their characteristics have been given in **Table 4.10**.

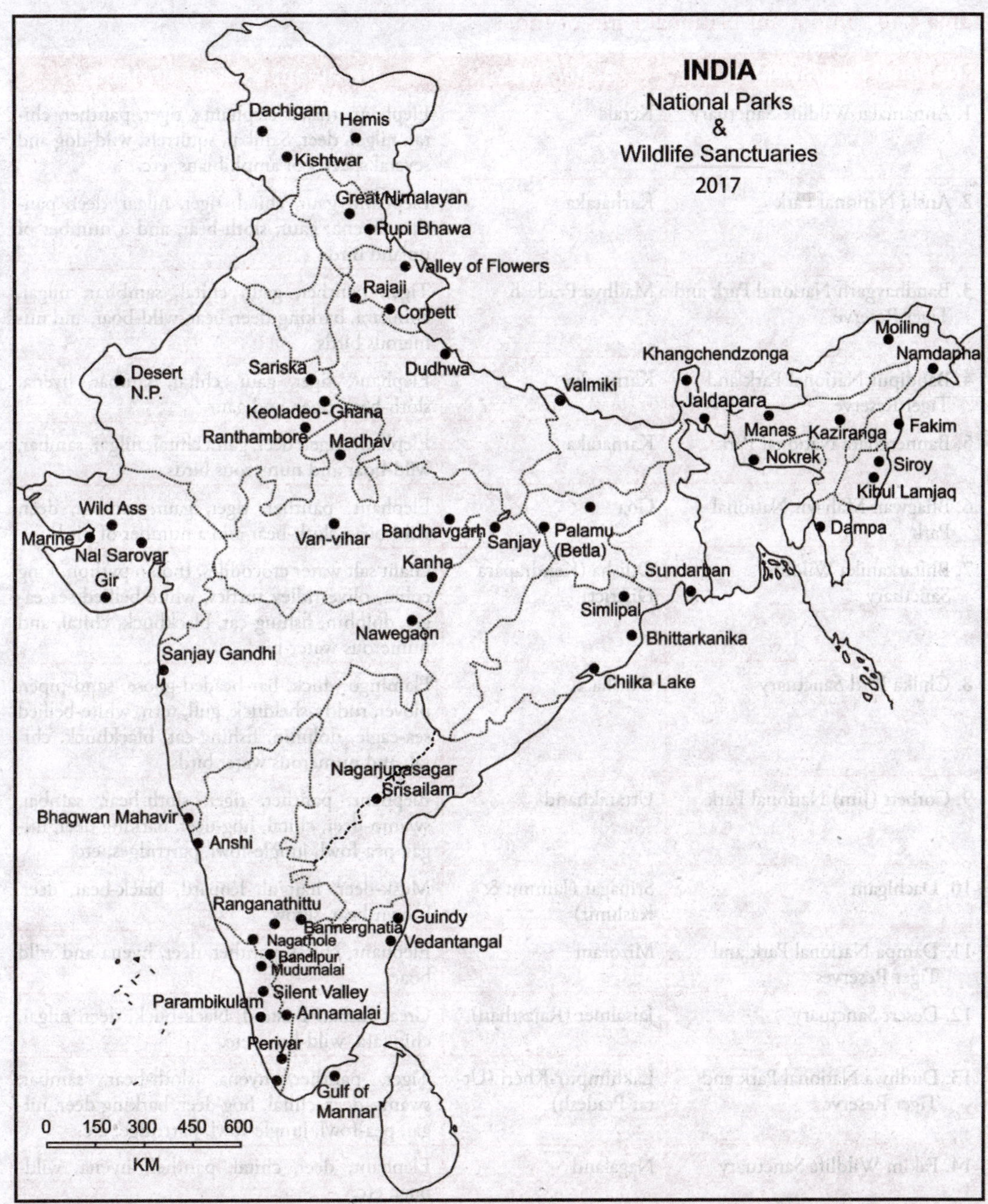

Fig. 4.6 India: National Parks and Wildlife Sanctuaries

Table 4.10 Important National Parks of India

National Park/Sanctuaries	State/States	Dominant Species Protected
1. Annamalai Wildlife Sanctuary	Kerala	Elephant, tusker-elephants, tiger, panther, chital, nilgai, deer, Sambar, squirrels, wild-dog and several species of amphibians, etc.
2. Anshi National Park	Karnataka	Elephant, gaur, chital, tiger, nilgai, deer, panther, hyena, gaur, sloth-bear, and a number of upland birds.
3. Bandhavgarh National Park and Tiger Reserve	Madhya Pradesh	Tiger, panther, gaur, chital, sambhar, nilgai, chinkara, barking-deer, bear, wild-boar, and numerous birds
4. Bandipur National Park and Tiger Reserve	Karnataka	Elephant, tiger, gaur, chital, sambar, hyena, sloth-bear, tiger, and gaur
5. Bannerghata National Park	Karnataka	Elephant, tiger, deer, gaur, chital, nilgai, sambar, wild-boar and numerous birds
6. Bhagwan Mahavir National Park	Goa	Elephant, panther, tiger, gaur, sambar, deer, wild-boar, sloth-bear and a number of birds
7. Bhitarkanika Wildlife Sanctuary	Odisha (Kendrapara District)	Giant salt water crocodiles, Indian python, king cobra, olive-ridley turtles, white-bellied-sea-eagle, dolphin, fishing-cat, blackbuck, chital, and numerous water-birds
8. Chilka Bird Sanctuary	Odisha	Flamingo, duck, bar-headed-goose, sand-piper, plover, ruddy-shelduck, gull, tern, white-bellied sea-eagle, dolphin, fishing-cat, blackbuck, chital, and numerous water birds
9. Corbett (Jim) National Park	Uttarakhand	Elephant, panther, tiger, sloth-bear, sambar, swamp-deer, chital, hog-deer, barking deer, nilgai, pea-fowl, jungle-fowl, partridges, etc.
10. Dachigam	Srinagar (Jammu & Kashmir)	Musk-deer, hangul, leopard, black-bear, deer, brown-bear, serow
11. Dampa National Park and Tiger Reserves	Mizoram	Elephant, chital, panther, deer, hyena and wild boar
12. Desert Sanctuary	Jaisalmer (Rajasthan)	Great Indian Bustard, black-buck, deer, nilgai, chinkara, wild-boar, etc.
13. Dudhwa National Park and Tiger Reserve	Lakhimpur-Kheri (Uttar Pradesh)	Tiger, panther, hyena, sloth-bear, sambar, swamp-deer, chital, hog-deer, barking deer, nilgai, pea-fowl, jungle-fowl, partridge, etc.
14. Fakim Wildlife Sanctuary	Nagaland	Elephant, deer, chital, panther, hyena, wild-boar, etc.
15. Gir National Park	Gujarat	Asiatic-lion, panther, stripped-hyena, sambar, nilgai, chital, deer, chousingha, chinkara, wild-boar, crocodile, etc.

(*Contd.*)

Table 4.10 (*Contd.*)

National Park/Sanctuaries	State/States	Dominant Species Protected
16. Guindy National Park	Chennai (Tamil Nadu)	Elephant, panther, hyena, wondru, antilope and birds
17. Gulf of Mannar National Park and Biosphere Reserve	Tamil Nadu	Dugong (sea cow), Mangrove, corals, fishes, molluscs, marine plants and marine life, etc.
18. Hemis National Park	Leh/Ladakh (J&K)	Musk-deer, yak, hangal, chausingha, brown-bear, wild-cat, etc.
19. Jaldapara Wildlife Sanctuary	West Bengal	One horned-rhino, tigers, wild-elepants, deer, swamp-deer, hog-deer, wild-pig, birds and pea-fowl, etc.
20. Kanha National Park	Madhya Pradesh	Tiger, panther, hyena, deer, hog-deer, wild-boar, birds, etc.
21. Khangchendzonga (Kanchenjunga) National Park and Biosphere Reserve	Sikkim	Snow-bear, white-fox, panda, bear, jackal, birds, etc.
22. Kaziranga National Park	Jorhat (Assam)	One horned rhino, tiger, panther, elephant, wild-buffalo, deer, etc.
23. Keibul Lamjao Wildlife Sanctuary	Manipur	Elephant, brown-antlered-deer, Eld's deer, wild-boar, hog, fox, jackal and water-birds.
24. Keoladeo-Ghana National Park and Bird Sanctuary	Bharatpur (Rajasthan)	Siberian-crane, stork, spoon-bill, quil, coot, heron, teal, tern, sambar, chital, black-buck, civet, wild-boar, hog, fox, jackal, etc.
25. Madhav National Park	Madhya Pradesh	Elephant, panther, hyena, deer, nilgai, sambar, birds, etc.
26. Manas National Park and Tiger Reserve	Barpeta (Assam)	Golden Langur, Red Panda, Tiger, elephant, panther, gaur, wild-buffalo, rhino, golden langur, civet-cat, otter, swamp-deer, hog-deer, sambar, pygmy-hog, wild-boar, great-pied hornbill, florican, etc.
27. Marine National Park	Gujarat	Turtles, fishes, corals, molluscs, marine –fauna and flora
28. Moiling National Park	Arunachal Pradesh	Snow-bear, white-leopard, white-fox, brown-bear, yak, etc.
29. Mudumalai Sanctuary	Nilgiris (Tamil-Nadu)	Elephant, gaur, chital, sambar, tiger, panther, sloth-bear, wild-hog, etc.
30. Nagarhole National Park	Coorg (Karnataka)	Elephant, tiger, panther, chital, sambar, hyena, sloth-bear, jungle-fowl, partridges, etc.
31. Nagarjunasagar–Srisailam Sanctuary	Andhra Pradesh	Tiger, panther, sloth-bear,chital, Jerdon's courser, sambar, nilgai, black-buck, jackal, fox, rock rat, wolf, hyena, mugarmuchh (crocodile)

(*Contd.*)

Table 4.10 (*Contd.*)

National Park/Sanctuaries	State/States	Dominant Species Protected
32. Namdhapa National Park	Arunachal Pradesh	Tiger, leopard, clouded-leopard, gaur, goral, hyena, gibbon, musk-deer, red-panda, macaque, horn-bill, jungle-fowl, pheasants, etc.
33. Nawegaon National Park	Maharashtra	Elephant, panther, hyena, deer, nilgai, wild-boar, fox, jackal, wolf, birds, etc.
34. Nokrek National Park and Biosphere Reserves	Garo Hills (Meghalaya)	Red Panda, Elephant, panther, hyena, wild-boar, barking-deer, gaur, chital, sambar, nilgai, pea-fowl, etc.
35. Palamau (Betla) Tiger Reserve and Sanctuary	Daltenganj (Jharkhand)	Elephant, panther, hyena, wild-boar, barking-deer, gaur, chital, sambar, nilgai, peafowl, etc.
36. Parambikulam National Park	Kerala	Elephant, civet, panther, hyena, gaur, chital, fox, wild-cat, wild-dog, deer, wild-boar, hog, numerous birds, etc.
37. Periyar National Park	Idukki (Kerala)	Elephant, tiger, panther, wild-hog, gaur, sloth-bear, nilgai, wild-boar, sambar, and barking-deer
38. Ranganathittu National Park	Karnataka	Elephant, panther, hyena, deer, nilgai, sambar, wild-boar, hog, wolf, fox, jackal, birds, etc.
39. Rajaji National Park	Haridwar (Uttarakhand)	Elephant, panther, hyena, deer, nilgai, sambar, wild-boar
40. Ranthambore National Park and Tiger Reserve	Sawai-Madhopur (Rajasthan)	Tiger, panther, hyena, jungle-cat, civet, sambar, chital, nilgai, wild-boar, partridges, green-pigeon, red-spur-fowl, etc.
41. Rupi-Bhawa Wildlife Sanctuary	Himachal Pradesh	White-bear, white-fox, yak, panda, brown-bear, jackal, birds, etc.
42. Sariska National Park and Tiger Reserve	Alwar (Rajasthan)	Tiger, panther, hyena, jungle-cat, civet, sambar, nilgai, chowsingha, monkeys, wolf, fox, partridge, green-pigeon, and spurfowl
43. Sanjay National Park	Chhattisgarh	Elephant, panther, hyena, wolf, fox, jackal, deer, nilgai, chital, birds, etc.
44. Sanjay Gandhi National Park	Maharashtra	Elephant, panther, hyena, chital, deer, Kondane-rat, wild-boar, reptiles, birds, etc.
45. Silent Valley National Park	Kerala	Elephant, panther, hyena, chital, deer, wild-boar, reptiles, etc.
46. Simlipal National Park and Tiger Reserve	Mayurbhanj (Odisha)	Gaur, Royal Bengal Tiger, Wild-elephant, gaur, chital, hyena, sambar, nilgai, chital, chausingha, chinkara, wild-boar, crocodile, etc.
47. Sirohi National Park	Manipur	Elephant, leopard, hyena, fox, jackal, deer, wild-boar, hog, chital, birds, etc.

(*Contd.*)

Table 4.10 (*Contd.*)

National Park/Sanctuaries	State/States	Dominant Species Protected
48. Sundarban National Park and Tiger Reserve	West Bengal	Royal Bengal, Tiger, leopard, hyena, elephant, rhino, deer, wild-boar, esturian crocodile, dolphin, numerous birds, etc.
49. Valley of Flowers National Park	Uttarakhand	White-bear, panda, yak, deer, white-fox, a large variety of flowers, etc.
50. Vedanthangal Water-birds Sanctuary	Tamil Nadu	Different species of water-birds
51. Wild-Ass Sanctuary	Rann of Kachchh (Gujarat)	Wild-ass, nilgai, wolf, chinkara, deer, wolf, fox, jackal, birds, etc.

Table 4.10-A National Parks/ Sanctuaries and Rivers

National Park, Sanctuary	State	River
1. Bandipur National Park	Karnataka	Kabini, Moyar and Nugu rivers
2. Bhadra wildlife Sanctuary	Karnataka	Bhadra River
3. Bori Wildlife Sanctuary	Madhya Pradesh	Tawa River
4. Chandoli (Sahyadri Tiger Reserve) National Park	Maharashtra	Warna River
5. Dudhwa National park	Uttar Pradesh	Kali/Sarda river
6. Gir national Park	Gujarat	Hiran, Shetrunji, Datardi, Shingoda and machhundri
7. Hemis National Park	Jammu & Kashmir	Indus River
8. Indira Gandhi Wildlife Sanctuary and National Park	Tamil Nadu	Manjampatti River
9. Jim Corbett National Park	Uttarakhand	Ramnagar River
10. Kalakkad Mundanthurai Tiger Reserve	Tamil Nadu	The Thamirabarani, Ramanadi, Karaiyar, Servalar, Manimuthar, Pachayar, Kodaiyar, Gadananathi and Kallar rivers.
11. Kangar Ghati National Park	Chhattisgarh	Kangar River and Kolab River and Tirathgarh Waterfalls.
12. Melghat Tiger Reserve	Maharashtra	Tapi River
13. Nagarhole National Park	Karnataka	Kabini River
14. Nagarjunsagar-Srisailam Tiger Reserve	Telangana	Krishna River
15. Neora Valley National Park	West Bengal	Neora River
16. Neyyar Wildlife Sanctuary	Kerala	Neyyar River and its tributaries : Mullayar and kallar

(*Contd.*)

Table 4.10-A (*Contd.*)

National Park, Sanctuary	State	River
17. Natangki National Park	Nagaland	Natangki-Dhansiri rivers.
18. Pakhui Tiger Reserve	Arunachal Pradesh	Bhareli or Kameng River
19. Pench Tiger Reserve	Madhya Pradesh	Pench River
20. Karamana Wildlife Sanctuary	Kerala	Karamana River
21. Ranthambore National Park	Rajasthan	Banas River and Chambal River
22. Satkosia Tiger Reserve	Odisha	Mahanadi
23. Silent Valey	Kerala	Kuntipuzha and Bharathapuzha rivers
24. Sirohi National Park	Manipur	Shirui River
25. Tadoba Andhari Tiger Reserve	Maharashtra	Andhari River
26. Valmiki National Park	Bihar	Gandak, Sonha, Pachnad and Burhi-Gandak

SANCTUARIES

The state government may, by notification, declare any area other than an area comprised within any reserve forest or the territorial waters, as a sanctuary, if it considers that such an area is of adequate ecological, faunal, floral, geomorphological, natural or zoological significance, for the purpose of protecting, propagating, or developing wildlife or its environment. Such a notification shall specify, as nearly as possible, the situation and limits of such areas. The Central Government may also declare a sanctuary under certain conditions. The chief objective of declaring an area as sanctuary is to protect the forest and wildlife. The responsibility of managing such sanctuaries rests with the Chief Wildlife Warden. No person can enter the sanctuaries without proper permission. No person can carry any weapon inside the sanctuaries. Teasing of animals or molesting of animals, causing any damage to the habitat inside a sanctuary is a punishable offence. The total number wildlife sanctuaries in India in 2012 were 515, out of which 44 were tiger reserves, 21 bird-sanctuaries and the remaining national parks.

The total number of sanctuaries in India, covering an area of more than 3.7 per cent of country's area (2012) was 515. Some of the important sanctuaries of India have been given in Table 4.11.

Table 4.11 Major Sanctuaries of India

State	Sanctuaries
Andhra Pradesh	Nagarjunasagar Sanctuary
Haryana	Sultanpur Bird Sanctuary
Himachal Pradesh	Shikari Devi Sanctuary
Jammu & Kashmir	Dachigam Sanctuary
Kerala	Periyar Sanctuary
Punjab	Harike Pattan Wildlife Sanctuary, Motigarh Sanctuary
Odisha	Chilka Lake Bird Sanctuary
Rajasthan	Keoladev Ghana Bird Sanctuary

Table 4.11-A Differences between National Park, Sanctuary and Biosphere reserve

	National Park	Sanctuary	Biosphere reserve
1.	Hitched to the habitat for particular wild animal species like tiger, lion, hangul, rhino etc.	Generally species-oriented as citrus, pitcher plant, Great Indian Bustard.	Not hitched to anyone, two or more species, but to the whole ecosystem i.e. totality of all forms of life i.e. ecosystem-oriented.
2.	In India, the size range is 0.04 to 3162 sq. km. Most common (in about 40%) is 100 to 500 sq. km. In 15% is 500 to 1000 sq. km.	Size range is 0.61 to 7818 sq. km. Most common (in about 40%) is 100 to 500 sq. km. In 25% is 500 to 1000 sq. km.	Size range over 5670 sq. km.
3.	Boundaries circumscribed by legislation	Boundaries sacrosant	Boundaries circumscribed by legislation
4.	Expect the buffer zone, no biotic interference	Limited biotic interference	Except the buffer zone, no biotic interference.
5.	Tourism permissible	Tourism permissible	Tourism normally not permissible
6.	Research and scientific management lacking	Researce and scientific management lacking	Managed
7.	So far no attention to genepools and conservation	So far no attention	Attention given

Source: Ecology & Environment by P.D. Sharma

ANIMAL CONSERVATION PROJECTS

Project Tiger (Panthera tigris)

Project Tiger was launched in India on April 1, 1973 by the then Prime Minister, Indira Gandhi. In 2014, there were 44 tiger reserves. Of these 27 tiger reserves, Manas National Park of Assam has been declared a World Heritage Site by UNESCO. Project Tiger recognised the fact that tigers cannot be protected in isolation, and that to protect tigers, its habitat needed to be protected. According to one estimate, there were 40,000 tigers in 1900 which declined to about 1700 in 2011 and increased to 2226 in 2014. The main objectives of Project Tiger are: (i) to ensure maintenance of the available population of tigers in India for scientific, economic, cultural and aesthetic values. (ii) to preserve, for all times, the areas of such biological importance as a national heritage for the benefit of education and enjoyment of the people. (iii) conservation of the endangered species. (iv) to protect the rights of the tribals and local people around the tiger reserves. The tiger reserves of India have been given in Table 4.12 and their locations have been shown in Fig. 4.7.

Table 4.12 Tiger Reserves of India

Tiger Reserve	Year	Area in sq km
1. Achnakmar (Chhattisgarh)	2009	557.55
2. Anaimalai (Tamil Nadu)	2008-09	958.00
3. Bandhavgrah (M.P.)	1993-94	717.00
4. Bandipur (Karnataka)	1973-74	872.24
5. Bhadra (Karnataka)	1998-99	257.26
6. B.R.Hills (Karnataka)	1999-2000	185.00
7. Buxa (W.Bengal)	1982-83	390.58
8. Corbett, J. (Uttarakhand)	1973-74	821.99
9. Dampa (Mizoram)	1994-95	492.46
10.Dandeli-Anshi (Karnataka)	2007-08	340.00
11.Dudhwa (U.P.)	1987-88	1093.79
12. Indravati(Chhattisgarh)	1982-83	1258.37
13. Kalakad-Mundanthurai (Tamil Nadu)	1988-89	895.00
14. Kanha (Madhya Pradesh)	1973-74	917.43
15. Kawal (Andhra Pradesh)	1989-90	351.00
16. Kaziranga (Assam)	2008-09	625.58
17. Manas (Assam)	1973-74	840.04
18. Melghat (Mahanashtra)	1973-74	1500.00
19. Mundamalai (Tamil Nadu)	2008-09	321.00
20. Mukanda Hill (Rajasthan)	2004-05	625.00
21. Namdhapa(Arunachal–Pradesh)	1982-83	1807.82
21. Nagarhole (Karnataka)	2008-09	643.35
22. Nagarjunsagar (Andhra Pradesh) & (Telangana)	1982-83	2527.00
23. Nameri (Tezpur-Assam)	1985	200.00
24. Pakhui/Pakke (Arunachal Pradesh)	1999-2000	683.45
25. Palamau-Betla(Jharkhand)	1973-74	414.08
26. Panna (M.P.)	1994-95	576.14
27. Parambikulam (Kerala)	2008-09	390.89
28. Pench (Maharashtra)	1992-93	411.33

(*Contd.*)

Table 4.12 (*Contd.*)

Tiger Reserve	Year	Area in sq km
29. Pench (Maharashtra)	1992-93	257.26
30. Periyar (Kerala)	1978-79	881.00
31. Ranthambore (Rajasthan)	1973-74	1113.36
32. Sanjay-Dubri (M.P.)	2008-09	831.25
33. Sariska (Alwar-Raj,)	1978-79	681.11
34. Satkosia (Angul-Odisha)	2008-09	523.61
35. Satpura-Bori (M.P.)	1999-2000	1339.26
36. Sahydari/Chandoli (Maharashtra)	2007	317.67
37. Simlipal (Odisha)	1973-74	1194.74
38. Sathyamangalam(Tamil-Nadu)	2008-09	1411.06
39. Satkosia (Angul-Odisha)	2008-09	796.00
40. Sundarban (W.Bengal)	1973-74	1699.62
41. Tadoba-Andharai (Maharashtra)	1993-94	625.82
42. Udanti-Sitandi (Chhattisgarh)	1994-95	437.00
43. Valmiki (Bihar)	1989-90	840.00
44. Nawegaon-Nagzira (Maharashtra)	2013-14	1894.94
45. Amrabad (Telangana)	2015	2611.39
46. Pilbhit & (Uttar Pradesh)	2014	730.24
47. Bor (Maharashtra)	2012	816.27
48. Rajaji (Uttarakhand)	2015	1075.17
49. Orang & (Assam)	2016	492.46
50. Kamlang & (Arunachal Pradesh)	2017	783.00
51. Srivilliputhur Megamalai (TamilNadu)	2021	1061.57
52. Ramgarh Vishdhari (Rajasthan)	2022	1501.89
53. Guru Ghasidas National park & Tamor Pingla Wildlife Sanctuary (Chattisgarh)	2022	466.7

Project Elephant

The Project Elephant was launched by the Government of India in February, 1992. The main objectives of the project is (i) to assist the states to protect the existing population of elephants, and to ensure long term survival of identified viable populations of elephants in their natural habitat. (ii) to protect their habitat and corridors, (iii) to address issues of man-elephant conflict, and (iv) welfare of the domesticated elephants and their breeding, and (v) to protect elephants from poaching.

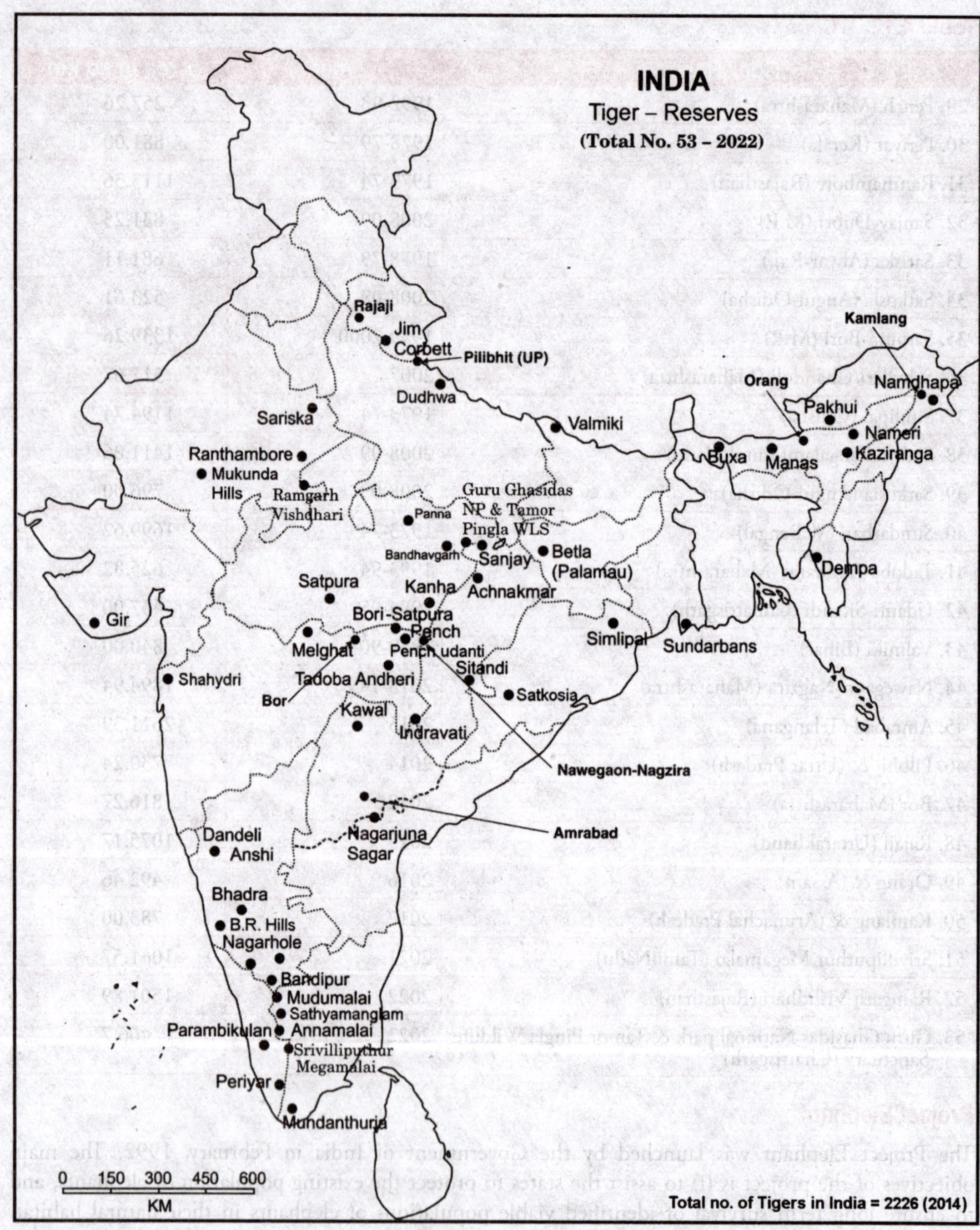

Fig. 4.7 India Tiger Reserves—2022

The project is being implemented in 17 states namely, (i) Andhra Pradesh, (ii) Arunachal Pradesh, (iii) Assam, (iv) Chhattisgarh, (v) Jharkhand, (vi) Karnataka, (vii) Kerala, (viii) Manipur, (ix) Maharashtra, (x) Meghalaya, (xi) Nagaland, (xii) Odisha, (xiii) Tamil Nadu, (xiv) Tripura, (xv) Uttarakhand, (xvi) Uttar Pradesh, and (xvii) West Bengal.

At present, there are 26 Elephant Reserves (ERs) in India, stretching over an area of about 60,000 sq km. The enumeration of elephants is done after every five years. It is encouraging to note that the population of elephants in India is increasing every year. The estimated population of elephants has gone up by more than two thousand, as compared to the base year of 2002. India is also closely monitoring the illegal poaching and killing of this huge mammal.

Rhinoceros Project

The Indian rhinoceros known as the Great One-Horned Rhino, is mostly found in Assam. In the beginning of the 20th century, it was considered as one of the endangered species, mainly due to poaching and encroachment of its habitat. The Government of India launched a conservation programme of rhino after independence. At present, there are more than 1800 rhinos in Assam. The Kaziranga National Park, Dibru-Saikhowa and the Manas Reserves are the main areas of their concentration. Rhinos are also found in the Sundarban Biosphere Reserve.

India- Rhino Vision 2020

The India rhino vision 2020 was implemented by the Department of Environment and Forests, Assam with the Bodo Autonomous Council. The programme is to be financed by the WWF, Asia Rhino and Elephant Action Strategy India, and the International Rhino Foundation.

The main objective of the Vision 2020 is to increase the population of rhinos from 2000 to 3000 in 2020. Another objective is to distribute the rhinos in seven protected areas. The seven protected areas in which the Rhinos are to be distributed for protection are: (i) Dibru Saikhowa Wildlife Sanctuary, (ii) Kaziranga National Park, (iii) Laokhowa-Bura Chapori Wildlife Sanctuary, (iv) Manas Biosphere Reserve, (v) Probitira Wildlife Sanctuary, (vi) Sonai Rupai and (vii) Sundarban Biosphere Reserves.

The Manas National Park/Biosphere Reserve was selected as the first site for the translocation of rhino. Translocation of rhino will help to create a viable population of this threatened species.

Gharial Project

Gharial, a unique species of crocodile, characterised by its long, thin snout and the bulbous growth at the end of its snout, is the last remaining species of this ancient reptile and the last surviving species of the family—Gvialidae. Crocodile skin is used for making leather articles. The main objectives of the project were: (i) to protect the population of crocodiles, (ii) to increase the population of crocodiles, (iii) to promote captive breeding, (iv) to promote, research about the management of crocodiles, and (v) to train staff for the breeding and management of crocodiles. In the 1970s, the gharial was at the brink of extinction. Since then, various measures have been taken to conserve the gharial species and the conservation programme for gharial is considered as one of the most successful among all the conservation efforts initiated for various endangered species in India. Beginning in 1981, the population of gharial has increased to more than 3000.

Project Vulture

The Government of India, initiated preventive steps to curb further decline in the population of vultures. In order to protect vultures the use of diclofenac was banned in veterinary sector. Vulture is known as the scavenger. It feeds on the dead animals. There are nine important species of vultures in India. They are: (i) Oriental white-backed vulture, (ii) slender billed vultures, (iii) Long billed vulture, (iv) Indian Griffon vulture, (v) Egyptian vulture, (vi) Red Headed vulture, (vii) Himalayan Griffon vulture, (viii) Beareded vulture, and (ix) cinereous vulture. Out of the above, the population of three (white-backed vultures, slender billed vultures and long-billed vultures) is declining. These three species are included in the list of '*critically endangered species*'. The main cause of decline of vultures is Diclofenac sodium which affect the kidney adversely. Looking at the declining trend of vultures population, the Government of India started the Vulture Recovery Programme in 2004.

The Great Indian Bustard

Indian bustard is found in the short grass desert plains of west Rajasthan and northern parts of Gujarat. This bird is on the red list of IUCN, due to its small and declining population. Indian bustard is one of the most endangered member of the bustard family in the world. The total population of bustards in wild may not be more than 700.

Snow Leopard

The high altitudes of Himalayas, above the tree line (3000m) in the habitat of snow leopards. They are found in the states of Jammu and Kashmir, Himachal Pradesh, Uttarakhand, Sikkim and Arunachal Pradesh. Project Snow Leopard was launched in 2009 with the set objective to conserve the species and their habitat. It was also one of the objectives to promote awarness among the local communities about the significance of snow leopard in northern India are the home to about 200 to 600 snow leopards. The 'Project Snow Leopard' has been launched by the Government in January 2009 for conversion of snow leopard and its habitat. It aims to promote a knowledge-based and adaptive conservation framework that fully involves the local communities who share the snow leopard's range.

Ganges Dolphin

The Ministry of Environment and Forests notified the Ganges River Dolphin as the National Aquatic Animal. Dolphin in India is found in the Ganga and Brahmaputra rivers. The Ganges Dolphin is among the four 'obligate' freshwater dolphins found in the world. The other three fresh water dolphin are (i) Baiji (Yangtze Kiang), (ii) the 'Bhulan' of the Indus (Pakistan), and the 'Boto' of the Amazon River. These four species live either in rivers or in lakes.

The Ganga River Dolphin is threatened by river water pollution, accidental trapping in fishing nets and poaching for their oil. Moreover, construction of barrages and dams are also responsible for the depletion of dolphin population. The Government of India has initiated programmes for the conservation of dolphin in Uttar Pradesh.

Project Hangul (Kashmiri-stag)

Hangul or Kashmiri stag is a critically endangered species found mainly in the Dachigam National Park (Srinagar) and adjoining areas in the state of Jammu & Kashmir. The government of Jammu and Kashmir launched a special programme to conserve the species of hangul.

Project Red Panda (Cat- Bear)

Red Panda is found in Arunachal Pradesh, Sikkim and the Himalayas around Darjeeling. Its habitat is between 1500 and 4000 metres above the sea level. The project was started in 1966 at Padmaja Naidu Himalayan Wildlife Park.

Project Manipur Thamin

The Thamin deer is found in the south-eastern parts of Loktak Lake of Manipur. It is enlisted among the rarest species of mammals. To increase the population of the deer, the Thamin Project was launched in 1977.

The Ramsar Convention

The Ramsar Convention on Wetlands (waterfowl convention) was held at Ramsar (Iran) in 1971. It is an inter-governmental treaty that embodies the commitments of its members to maintain the ecological character of their wetlands of international importance and to plan for the 'wise use' or sustainable uses, of all the wetlands in their territories. Unlike the other global environmental conventions, Ramsar is not affiliated with the United Nations System of Multilateral Environmental Agreements (MEAs), but it works very closely with the other MEAs and is a full partner among the 'biodiversity-related cluster' of treaties and agreements.

Any wetland to be declared a wetland of international importance should support vulnerable endangered or threatened species and attract more than 20,000 or more water birds. The declaration would provide an opportunity to seek international technical support for conservation and sustainable use of wetland through participatory mechanism. It would also ensure international co-operation and financial assistance for wetland conservation. World Wetland Day, 2nd February every year. The number of contracting parties is 163.

The total number of Ramsar wetlands in India is 75 situated in different parts of the country. Ramsar wetlands of India have been shown in Fig. 4.8.

Table 4.13 Year wise designation of 75 Ramsar sites

S. No.	Year of Designation	No. of site designated (As per date of designation)	Sites of designated upto 2013 and after 2014 to till date	Area covered in Ha
1	1981	2	26 (1981 to 2013)	633871
2	1990	4		
3	2002	13		
4	2005	6		
5	2012	1		
6	2019	11	49 (2014 to 2022)	692807
7	2020	5		
8	2021	14		
9	2022	19		
	Total	75	75	1326678

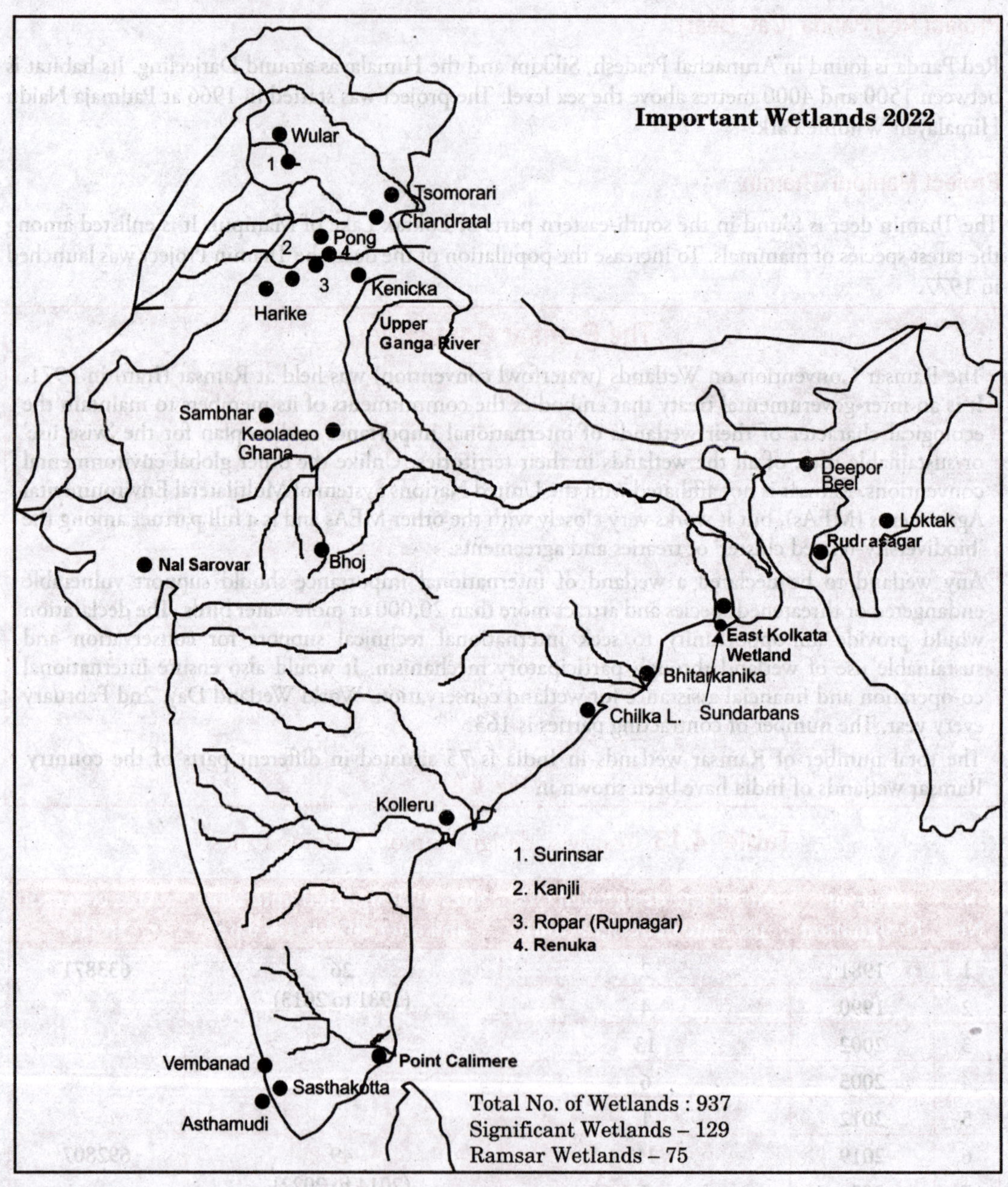

Fig. 4.8 Major Wetlands of India

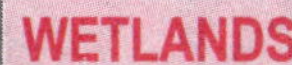

WETLANDS

Impact of Climate Change on Wetlands

Wetlands, estimated to cover about 6% of the Earth's terrestrial area provide invaluable services and benefits human populations including regulation of climate. Climate change would threaten wetlands in a number of ways. Increased temperatures would adversely affect temperature sensitive plant and animal species. Decreased precipitation in wetland areas would result in shrinkage of wetlands that will release more carbon into atmosphere due to decay of organic matter. Climate change may also lead to shift in the geographical distribution of wetlands. Moreover, wetlands are highly dependent on water levels, so change in climate conditions affecting water availability will influence the nature and function of specific wetlands including the type of plant and animal species. Climate change, therefore, is an important issue for wetland management. Conservation and use of wetlands can no longer be achieved without taking climate change into account.

Indian Scenario

In the opinion of experts, in India there will be a general increase in precipitation. Initially, there may be increased frequency and magnitude of freshwater floods due to melting of glaciers. The impacts could be loss of property and lives, water pollution by way of overflow of sewage systems and damage to agricultural areas. Wetlands can reduce peak flood flows by delaying and storing floodwaters and also can detain polluted floodwaters and improve their quality. Subsequently, due to rising temperatures and less rainfall there may be increased frequency and magnitude of droughts. The impacts could be decreased food production, loss of ecosystems and biodiversity and thereby decline in migratory birds. Wetlands can play a role in maintaining river base flow-releasing wet-season flows slowly during drought periods, recharging groundwater aquifers.

Any increase in additional pressure on wetlands due to human activity is likely to increase the impact and limit the adaptation options.

Mitigation Measures

1. Reduce the effects of climate change by restricting further emissions of carbon dioxide to the atmosphere.
2. Impound carbon entering or already in atmosphere, or
3. Facilitate adaptation to change in climate that are already taking place.
4. The developing countries should reduce the growth of their population.
5. The developed countries should reduce consumption and there should be judicious use of available resources.

A brief description of the Ramsar wetlands of India has been given in the following:

RAMSAR Wetlands of Indian

1. Ashtamudi Wetland, Kerala :

- Designated - 18 August 2002
- Area (km^2) - 61.4
- About - A natural backwater in Kollam district, Kerala. The rivers Kallada and Pallichal drain into it. It forms an estuary with the sea at Neendakara which is a famous fishing harbour. National Waterway 3 passes through it. The tastiest backwater fish in Kerala, the karimeen of Kanjiracode Kayal is from Ashtamudi Lake.

2. Beas Conservation Reserve, Punjab :

- Designated - 26 September 2019
- Area (km^2) -64
- About - A 185-kilometre stretch of the Beas River located primarily in the north-west of Punjab. The river meanders down from the Himalayan foothills to the Harike Headworks, where its course is diverted into a number of channels. The river is dotted with islands, sand bars, and braided channels creating a complex environment supporting substantial biodiversity. The reserve hosts the only known population in India of the endangered Indus river dolphin (Platanista gangetica minor). In 2017, a programme was initiated to re-introduce the critically endangered gharial (Gavialis gangeticus) with 47 individuals released into the river 30 years after their disappearance.

3. Bhitarkanika Mangroves , Odisha :

- Designated – 19 August 2002
- Area (km^2) – 650
- About - In 1975, an area of 672 km^2 was declared the Bhitarkanika Wildlife Sanctuary. The core area of the sanctuary, with an area of 145 km^2, was declared Bhitarkanika National Park in September 1998. Gahirmatha Marine Wildlife Sanctuary, which bounds the Bhitarkanika Wildlife Sanctuary to the east, was created in September 1997, and encompasses Gahirmatha Beach and an adjacent portion of the Bay of Bengal. Bhitarkanika Mangroves were designated a Ramsar wetland of international importance in 2002. It is also famous for its saltwater crocodiles and olive ridley sea turtle.

4. Bhoj Wetland, Madhya Pradesh :

- Designated – 19 August 2002
- Area (km^2) – 32
- About - It consists of two lakes located in the city of Bhopal, the capital of Madhya Pradesh. The two lakes are the Bhojtal (Upper Lake) and the Lower Lake, which lie to the west of the city centre. It is a man-made reservoir.

5. Chandra Taal - Himachal Pradesh :

- Designated – 8 November 2005
- Area (km^2) – 0.49

- About - A high altitude lake on the upper Chandra valley flowing to the Chenab River of the Western Himalayas (4,337 m asl) near the Kunzam pass joining the Himalayan and Pir Panjal ranges. It supports the CITES and IUCN Red Listed snow leopard and is a refuge for many species like the snowcock, chukor, black ring stilt, kestrel, golden eagle, chough, red fox, Himalayan ibex, and blue sheep. These species have developed adaptations to the cold arid climate, intense radiation, and oxygen deficiency.

6. Chilika Lake, Odisha :

- Designated – 1 October 1981
- Area (km^2) – 1165
- About - A brackish water lagoon, spread over the districts of Puri, Khordha and Ganjam on the east coast of India, at the mouth of the Daya River, flowing into the Bay of Bengal, covering an area of over 1,100 km^2. It is the largest coastal lagoon in India and the second largest lagoon in the world. Nalbana Island is the core area of the Ramsar designated wetlands of Chilika Lake. Nalbana was notified in 1987 and declared a bird sanctuary in 1973 under the Wildlife Protection Act. The Irrawaddy dolphin (Orcaella brevirostris) is the flagship species of Chilika lake. Chilka is home to the only known population of Irrawaddy dolphins in India and one of only two lagoons in the world that are home to this species. It is classified as critically endangered in five of the seven places it is known to live.

7. Deepor Beel, Assam :

- Designated – 19 August 2002
- Area (km^2) – 40
- About - A permanent freshwater lake in a former channel of the Brahmaputra River. It is of great biological importance and also essential as the only major stormwater storage basin for the city of Guwahati.

8. East Kolkata Wetlands , West Bengal :

- Designated – 19 August 2002
- Area (km^2) – 125
- About - World-renowned as a model of a multiple-use wetland, the site's resource recovery systems, developed by local people through the ages, have saved the city of Kolkata from the costs of constructing and maintaining waste water treatment plants. It is described as "one of the rare examples of environmental protection and development management where a complex ecological process has been adopted by the local farmers for mastering the resource recovery activities.

9. Harike Wetland, Punjab :

- Designated – 23 March 1990
- Area (km^2) – 41
- About - A shallow water reservoir with thirteen islands, at the confluence of two rivers.

10. Hokera Wetland, Jammu and Kashmir :

- Designated – 8 November 2005
- Area (km^2) – 13.75
- About - Located in the northwest Himalayan biogeographic province of Kashmir, on the back of the snow-draped Pir Panjal

11. Kanjli Wetland, Punjab :

- Designated – 22 January 2002
- Area (km^2) – 1.83
- About - A permanent stream, the Kali Bein, converted by construction of a small barrage in 1870 into a water storage area for irrigation purposes.

12. Keoladeo National Park, Rajasthan :

- Designated – 1 October 1981
- Area (km^2) – 28.73
- About - A complex of ten artificial, seasonal lagoons, varying in size, situated in a densely populated region. Vegetation is a mosaic of scrub and open grassland that provides a habitat for breeding, wintering, and staging migratory birds.

13. Keshopur-Miani Community Reserve, Punjab :

Designated – 26 September 2019

Area (km^2) – 3.44

About - The reserve is a mosaic of natural marshes, aquaculture ponds, and agricultural wetlands maintained by rainfall runoff.

14. Kolleru Lake, Andhra Pradesh :

Designated – 19 August 2002

Area (km^2) – 901

About - A natural eutrophic lake, situated between the two major river basins of the Godavari and the Krishna, fed by two seasonal rivers and a number of drains and channels, which functions as a natural flood balancing reservoir between the deltas of the two rivers.

15. Loktak Lake, Manipur :

Designated – 23 March 1990

Area (km^2) – 266

About - The largest freshwater lake in the north-eastern region of the country, which is famous for the phumdis (heterogeneous mass of vegetation, soil, and organic matters at various stages of decomposition) floating over it. Keibul Lamjao, the only floating national park in the world, floats over it. The Keibul Lamjao National Park, which is the last natural refuge of the endangered sangai or Manipur brow-antlered deer is situated in the southeastern shores of this lake and is the largest of all the phumdis in the lake.

16. Nalsarovar Bird Sanctuary, Gujarat :

Designated – 24 September 2012

Area (km^2) – 120

About - A natural freshwater lake (a relict sea) that is the largest natural wetland in the Thar Desert Biogeographic Province and represents a dynamic environment with salinity and depth varying depending on rainfall.

17. Nandur Madhameshwar, Maharashtra :

Designated – 21 June 2019

Area (km^2) – 14

About - The site is a mosaic of lakes, marshes and riparian forest on the Deccan Plateau. Construction of the Nandur Madhameshwar Weir at the confluence of the Godavari and Kadva rivers helped create a thriving wetland

18. Nangal Wildlife Sanctuary, Punjab :

Designated – 26 September 2019

Area (km^2) – 1.16

About - Located in the Sivalik Hills of Punjab, the sanctuary supports abundant flora and fauna including threatened species, such as the endangered Indian pangolin and Egyptian vulture and the vulnerable leopard . It occupies a human-made reservoir constructed as part of the Bhakra-Nangal Project in 1961.

19. Nawabganj Bird Sanctuary, Uttar Pradesh :

Designated – 19 September 2019

Area (km^2) – 2.25

About - A shallow marshland 45 kilometres from Lucknow in Uttar Pradesh.

20. Parvati Arga Bird Sanctuary, Uttar Pradesh

Designated – 2 December 2019

Area (km^2) – 7.33

About - A permanent freshwater environment consisting of two oxbow lakes.

21. Point Calimere Wildlife and Bird Sanctuary, Tamil Nadu :

Designated – 19 August 2002

Area (km^2) – 385

About - A coastal area consisting of shallow waters, shores, long sand bars, intertidal flats, and intertidal forests, chiefly mangrove, and seasonal, often-saline lagoons, as well as human-made salt exploitation sites.

22. Pong Dam Lake, Himachal Pradesh :

Designated – 19 August 2002

Area (km^2) – 156.62

About - A water storage reservoir created in 1975 on the Beas River in the low foothills of the Himalayas in the northern edge of the Indo-Gangetic Plain.

23. Renuka Lake, Himachal Pradesh :

Designated – 8 November 2005

Area (km^2) – 0.2

About - A natural wetland with freshwater springs and inland subterranean karst formations, fed by a small stream flowing from the lower Himalayas out to the Giri river.

24. Ropar Wetland, Punjab :

Designated – 22 January 2002

Area (km^2) – 13.65

About - A humanmade wetland of lake and river formed by the 1952 construction of a barrage for diversion of water from the Sutlej River for drinking and irrigation.

25. Rudrasagar Lake, Tripura :

- Designated – 8 November 2005
- Area (km2) – 2.4
- About - A lowland sedimentation reservoir in the northeast hills, fed by three perennial streams discharging to the Gomti River.

26. Saman Bird Sanctuary, Uttar Pradesh :

Designated – 2 December 2019

Area (km^2) – 5.26

About - A seasonal oxbow lake on the Ganges floodplain. It is heavily reliant on the arrival of the south-westerly monsoon in July and August, which provides the vast majority of annual rainfall.

27. Samaspur Bird Sanctuary Uttar Pradesh :

Designated – 3 October 2019

Area (km^2) – 8

About - A perennial lowland marsh typical of the Indo-Gangetic Plain in Raebareli district.

28. Sambhar Lake Rajasthan :

Designated – 23 March 1990

Area (km^2) – 240

About - India's largest inland salt lake, it is a key wintering area for tens of thousands of flamingos and other birds that migrate from northern Asia. The specialized algae and bacteria growing in the lake provide striking water colours and support the lake ecology that, in turn, sustains the migrating waterfowl.

29. Sandi Bird Sanctuary Uttar Pradesh :

Designated – 26 September 2019

Area (km^2) – 3

About - A freshwater marsh in the Hardoi district, the wetland is typical of the Indo-Gangetic Plain and receives most of its water from monsoon rains.

30. Sarsai Nawar Jheel Uttar Pradesh :

Designated – 19 September 2019

Area (km^2) – 1.61

About - A permanent marsh in the Etawah district, this typical wetland of the Indo-Gangetic Plain is fed by the southwest monsoon rains. It is an example of co-habitation of humans and wildlife. The site's name is derived from this large non-migratory crane. It is recognized by BirdLife International as an Important Bird Area.

31. Sasthamkotta Lake Kerala :

- Designated – 19 August 2002
- Area (km^2) – 3.73
- About - Situated in Kollam district, it is the largest freshwater lake in Kerala. The Kallada River had a unique replenishing system through a bar of paddy field which has now disappeared due to indiscriminate clay and sand mining. The lake is now depleting due to the destruction of its replenishing mechanism.

32. Haiderpur Wetland Uttar Pradesh :

Designated – 13 April 2021

Area (km^2) – 69.08

About - This human-made wetland was formed in 1984 by the construction of the Madhya Ganga Barrage on a floodplain of the River Ganga. It is located within the boundaries of Hastinapur Wildlife Sanctuary.

33. Sundarban Wetland West Bengal :

Designated – 30 January 2019

Area (km^2) – 4230

About - Located within the largest mangrove forest in the world, it encompasses hundreds of islands and a maze of rivers, rivulets and creeks in the delta of the rivers Ganges and Brahmaputra on the Bay of Bengal. The Indian Sundarban, covering the south-westernmost part of the delta, constitutes over 60% of the country's total mangrove forest and includes 90% of Indian mangrove species. The mangrove forests protect the hinterland from storms, cyclones, tidal surges, and the seepage and intrusion of saltwater inland and into waterways. They serve as nurseries to shellfish and finfish and sustain the fisheries of the entire eastern coast.

34. Surinsar-Mansar Lakes Jammu and Kashmir :

Designated – 8 November 2005

Area (km^2) – 3.5

About - A freshwater composite lake in semi-arid Jammu Region, adjoining the Jhelum Basin with the catchment of sandy conglomeratic soil, boulders, and pebbles.

35. Tsomoriri Ladakh :

Designated – 19 August 2002

Area (km^2) – 120

About - A freshwater to brackish lake lying at 4,595 m above sea level, with wet meadows and borax-laden wetlands along the shores. The site is said to represent the only breeding ground outside of China for one of the most endangered cranes, the black-necked crane and the only breeding ground for bar-headed geese in India.

36. Upper Ganga River (Brijghat to Narora Stretch) Uttar Pradesh :

Designated – 8 November 2005

Area (km^2) – 265.9

About - A shallow river stretch of the great Ganges with intermittent small stretches of deep-water pools and reservoirs upstream from barrages. The river provides habitat for the IUCN Red Listed Ganges river dolphin, gharial, crocodile, six species of turtles, otters, 82 species of fish, and more than a hundred species of birds.

37. Vembanad-Kol Wetland Kerala :

- Designated – 19 August 2002
- Area (km^2) – 1512.5
- About - It is the largest lake of Kerala

38. Wular Lake Jammu and Kashmir :

- Designated – 23 March 1990
- Area (km^2) –189
- About - The largest freshwater lake in India with extensive marshes of emergent and floating vegetation, particularly water chestnut, that provide an important source of revenue for the state government and fodder for domestic livestock.

39. Asan Barrage Uttarakhand :

- Designated – 21 July 2020
- Area (km^2) – 4.44
- About - The Asan Conservation Reserve is a 444-hectare stretch of the Asan River running down to its confluence with the Yamuna River in Dehradun district.

40. Kanwar Taal or Kabar Taal Lake Bihar :

- Designated – 21 July 2020
- Area (km2) –26.2
- About - It covers 2,620 hectares of the Indo-Gangetic Plain. The site is one of 18 wetlands within an extensive floodplain complex; it floods during the monsoon season to a depth of 1.5 metres. This absorption of floodwaters is a vital service in Bihar where 70% of the land is vulnerable to inundation.

41. Sur Sarovar Uttar Pradesh :

- Designated – 21 August 2020
- Area (km^2) –4.31
- About - Also known as Keetham Lake, it was originally created to supply water to the city of Agra in the summer, the wetland soon became an important and rich ecosystem.

42. Lonar Lake Maharashtra :

- Designated – 22 July 2020
- Area (km^2) –4.27

- About - An endorheic or closed basin, almost circular in shape, formed by a meteorite impact some 50,000 years ago, onto the basalt bedrock. It is one of the four known, hyper-velocity, impact craters in basaltic rock anywhere on Earth. It is high in salinity and alkalinity, as the lack of an outflow leads to a concentration of minerals as the lake water evaporates. It is a National Geological Monument recognized by the Geological Survey of India (GSI). It is the only crater lake in the country formed by the meteorite impact. Recently, the color of Lonar lake water had turned pink due to a large presence of the salt-loving "haloarchaea" microbes. Haloarchaea or halophilic archaea is a bacteria culture that produces pink pigment and is found in water saturated with salt.

43. Tso Kar Ladakh :

- Designated – 17 November 2020
- Area (km^2) –95.77
- About - It is a high-altitude wetland complex, found at more than 4,500 metres above sea level in the Changthang region of Ladakh. It includes two connected lakes, the freshwater Startsapuk Tso and the larger hypersaline Tso Kar.

44. Sultanpur National Park Haryana :

- Designated – 25 May 2021
- Area (km^2) – 1.43
- About - It is located in the Gurgaon district of Haryana, 46 km. from Delhi and 15 km. from Gurgaon on the Gurgaon - Farukh Nagar Road.

45. Bhindawas Wildlife Sanctuary Haryana :

- Designated – 25 May 2021
- Area (km^2) –4.11
- About - It is a human-made freshwater wetland, located in Jhajjar district, Haryana. It is the largest wetland in Haryana.

46. Thol Lake Gujarat :

- Designated – 05 April 2021
- Area (km^2) – 6.99
- About - It is located in Mehsana district of Gujarat. It is a shallow freshwater reservoir and a predominantly open water area. It is a man-made wetland, that was originally constructed for irrigation in 1912.

47. Wadhvana Wetland Gujarat :

- Designated – 05 April 2021
- Area (km^2) – 6.30
- About - It is located in Dabhoi Tehsil (Taluka), Vadodara district, Gujarat. This reservoir was created in 1910 by the former Baroda State (King Gaikwad). It is located in a semi-arid agricultural landscape and it is surrounded by wheat and paddy fields and villages.

48. Bakhira Sanctuary Uttar Pradesh :

- Designated – 29 June 2021
- Area (km^2) – 28.94
- About - It is the largest natural flood plain wetland of India in Sant Kabir Nagar district of Eastern Uttar Pradesh. The sanctuary was established in 1980.

49. Khijadiya Bird Sanctuary Gujarat :

- Designated – 13 April 2021
- Area (km^2) – 5.12
- About - It is a bird sanctuary located in Jamnagar district. About 300 species of migratory birds have been recorded here. The sanctuary is unique having both fresh water lakes, and salt and freshwater marshlands. [19]

50. Karikili Bird Sanctuary Tamil Nadu :

- Designated – 8 April 2022
- Area (km^2) – 0.58
- About - Karikili Bird Sanctuary is a 58 hectare protected area located in the Kancheepuram district of Tamil Nadu. The sanctuary is about 75 km from Chennai, south of Chengalpattu.

51. Pallikaranai Marsh Reserve Forest Tamil Nadu :

- Designated – 8 April 2022
- Area (km^2) –12.48
- About - Pallikaranai wetland is a freshwater marsh located in Chennai, Tamil Nadu. It is the only surviving wetland ecosystem of the city and among the few and last remaining natural wetlands of South India.

52. Pichavaram Mangrove Forest Tamil Nadu :

- Designated – 8 April 2022
- Area (km^2) – 14.79
- About - Pichavaram mangrove is located in a village near Chidambaram in Cuddalore district of Tamil Nadu. The mangrove is one of the largest mangrove forests in India, covering 1,100 hectares.

53. Pala Wetland Mizoram :

- Designated – 31 August 2021
- Area (km^2) –18.50
- About - The Pala wetland is the largest natural wetland in Mizoram. The renowned landmark is surrounded by green woodlands and is home to a rich diversity of animal species including a range of animals and birds.

54. Sakhya Sagar Madhya Pradesh :

- Designated – 7 January 2022
- Area (km^2) – 2.48
- About - Sakhya Sagar Lake is an integral part of the beautiful ecology of the Madhav National Park in Shivpuri, Madhya Pradesh.

55. Satkosia Gorge Odisha :

- Designated – 12 October 2021
- Area (km^2) – 982
- About - Satkosia Gorge is located in Angul district of Odisha carved out of Mahanadi river. The gorge is located within the Satkosia Tiger Reserve which is a United nations Protected area

56. Nanda LakeGoa :

- Designated – 8 June 2022
- Area (km^2) –0.42
- About - Nanda Lake is located in Curchorem district of Goa. Nanda Lake comprises intermittent freshwater marshes that lie adjacent to one of the major tributaries of the Zuari river.

57. Gulf of Mannar Marine Biosphere Reserve Tamil Nadu :

- Designated – 8 April 2022
- Area (km^2) – 527
- About - Gulf of Mannar is located at the south-eastern tip of India in the state of Tamil Nadu

58. Ranganathittu Bird Sanctuary Karnataka :

- Designated – 15 February 2022
- Area (km^2) – 5.18
- About - Ranganathittu is located in Mandya district of Karnataka.

59. Vembannur Wetland Complex Tamil Nadu :

- Designated – 8 April 2022
- Area (km^2) – 0,20
- About - Vembannur Wetland Complex is a man-made inland tank which forms the southernmost tip of peninsular India. It is located 4 km from Rajakkamangalam in Tamil Nadu. it provides suitable habitat to several species of waterbirds.

60. Vellode Bird Sanctuary Tamil Nadu :

- Designated – 8 April 2022
- Area (km^2) – 0.77
- About - Vellode Bird Sanctuary is located in Erode district of Tamil Nadu. It is a man-made tank which is an ideal habitat for birds.

61. Udhayamarthandapuram Bird Sanctuary Tamil Nadu :

- Designated – 8 April 2022
- Area (km^2) – 0.44
- About - Udhayamarthandapuram is located in Thiruvarur district of Tamil Nadu. The site consists of man-made irrigation tanks and serves as an important staging and breeding ground for several species of waterbirds.

62. Vedanthangal Bird Sanctuary Tamil Nadu :

- Designated – 8 April 2022
- Area (km^2) – 0.40
- About - Vedanthangal is located in Chengalpattu district of Tamil Nadu.It is the oldest water bird sanctuary in the country.

63. Sirpur Wetland Madhya Pradesh :

- Designated – 7 January 2022
- Area (km^2) – 1.61
- About - The site is located in Indore district of Madhya Pradesh. It is a man-made wetland that supports terrestrial plants species, macrophytes, fish, reptiles, amphibians and waterbirds.

64. Koonthankulam Bird Sanctuary Tamil Nadu :

- Designated – 8 November 2021
- Area (km^2) – 0.72
- About -Koonthankulam is located in Thirunelveli district of Tamil Nadu. The Site consists of irrigation tanks interconnected by a network of canals.

65.Tampara Lake Odisha (Ganjam district) :

- Designated – 15 August 2022
- Area (km^2) – 3
- About - Freshwater lakes , The wetland supports at least 60 species of birds, 46 species of fishes, at least 48 species of phytoplanktons

66. Hirakud Reservoir Odisha

- Designated – 15 August 2022
- Area (km^2) – 654
- About - largest earthen dam in Odisha and support a range of floral and faunal species. The reservoir is a source of water for producing around 300 MW of hydropower and irrigating 436,000 ha of cultural command area.The wetland also provides important hydrological services by moderating floods in the Mahanadi delta

67. Ansupa Lake Odisha

- Designated – 15 August 2022
- Area (km^2) – 2.31
- About - largest freshwater lake of Odisha (Cuttack district). The wetland is an oxbow lake formed by River Mahanadi and is spread over an area of 231 ha.

68. Yashwant Sagar Madhya Pradesh

- Designated – 15 August 2022
- Area (km^2) – 8.229
- About - Yashwant Sagar is one of the two Important Bird Areas (IBA) in the Indore region as well as one of the most important birding sites in Malwa region of Madhya Pradesh. Presently it is mainly used for water supply to the city of Indore. Yashwant Sagar is considered to be a stronghold of the vulnerable Sarus Crane in central India.

69. Chitrangudi Bird Sanctuary. Tamil Nadu

- Designated – 15 August 2022
- Area (km^2) – 2.6047
- About -Located in Ramanathapuram district in Tamil Nadu. The wetland is a protected area since 1989 and declared as Bird Sanctuary. Chitrangudi Bird Sanctuary is an ideal habitat for winter migratory birds.

70. Suchindram Theroor Wetland Complex Tamil Nadu :

- Designated – 15 August 2022
- Area (km^2) – 0.9423
- About - It is part of the Suchindrum-Theroor Manakudi Conservation Reserve. It is declared an Important Bird Area and lies at the southern tip of the Central Asian flyway of migratory birds. It was formed for birds' nesting purposes and it attracts thousands of birds every year.

71. Vaduvur Bird Sanctuary Tamil Nadu :

- Designated – 15 August 2022
- Area (km^2) – 1.1264
- About - It is a large human-made irrigation tank and shelter for migratory birds as it provides a suitable environment for food, shelter, and breeding ground.

72. Kanjirankulam Bird Sanctuary Tamil Nadu :

- Designated – 15 August 2022
- Area (km^2) – 0.9689
- About - It is a Protected area near Mudukulathur Ramanathapuram District, Tamil Nadu. It is notable as a nesting site for several migratory heron species that roost in the prominent growth of babul trees there. The site qualifies as an IBA as the threatened Spot-billed Pelican Pelecanus philippensis breeds here.

73. Thane Creek Maharashtra :

- Designated – 15 August 2022
- Area (km^2) – 65.2108
- About - Thane Creek is located in Maharashtra, India. There are several sources of fresh water to the creek, of which Ulhas River is the largest. It has been declared as Thane Creek Flamingo Sanctuary. Thane creek is fringed by mangroves on both banks & comprises around 20% of the total Indian mangrove species. The mangrove forest acts as a natural shelter belt & protects the land from cyclones, tidal surges, seawater seepage & intrusions.

74. Hygam Wetland Conservation Reserve, Jammu and Kashmir :

- Designated – 15 August 2022
- Area (km^2) – 8.0182
- About - Hygam Wetland falls within the River Jhelum basin. The wetland is located in the Baramulla district. It serves as an abode to many residents and migratory bird species. It is also recognized as an Important Bird Area (IBA).

75. Shallbugh Wetland Conservation Reserve, Jammu and Kashmir :

- Designated – 15 August 2022
- Area (km^2) – 16.75
- About -Shallabug Wetland Conservation Reserve is located in the District Srinagar, UT of J&K.The area has extensive reedbeds of Phragmites communis and Typha angustata, and rich growth of Nymphaea candida and N. stellata on open water. It serves as an abode to more than four lakh resident and migratory birds of at least 21 species.

State wise RAMSAR WETLANDS OF INDIA

State/UT	No. of sites	Names of sites
1. Andhra Pradesh	1	Kolleru Lake
2. Assam	1	Deepor Beel
3. Bihar	1	Kanwar Lake
4. Goa	1	Nanda Lake
5. Gujarat	4	Khijadiya, Nalsarovar, Thol Lake, Wadhvana Wetland
6. Haryana	2	Sultanpur National Park, Bhindawas Wildlife Sanctuary
7. Himachal Pradesh	3	Chandra Taal, Pong Dam Lake, Renuka Lake
8. Jammu and Kashmir	5	Hokersar Wetland, Hygam Wetland Conservation Reserve, Shallbugh Wetland Conservation Reserve, Surinsar-Mansar Lakes,Wular Lake,
9. Karnataka	1	Ranganathittu Bird Sanctuary
10. Kerala	3	Ashtamudi Wetland, Sasthamkotta Lake, Vembanad-Kol Wetland

11. Ladakh	2	Tso Kar, Tsomoriri Lake
12. Madhya Pradesh	4	Bhoj Wetland, Sakhya Sagar,Sirpur Lake, Yashwant Sagar
13. Maharashtra	3	Lonar Lake, Nandur Madhameshwar, Thane Creek
14. Manipur	1	Loktak Lake
15. Mizoram	1	Pala Wetland
16. Odisha	6	Ansupa Lake, Bhitarkanika Mangroves, Chilika Lake, Hirakud Reservoir, Satkosia Gorge, Tampara Lake
17. Punjab	6	Beas Conservation Reserve, Harike Wetland, Kanjli Wetland, Keshopur-Miani Community Reserve, Nangal Wildlife Sanctuary, Ropar Wetland
18. Rajasthan	2	Keoladeo National Park, Sambhar Lake,
19. Tamil Nadu	14	Chitrangudi Bird Sanctuary, Gulf of Mannar Marine Biosphere Reserve, Kanjirankulam Bird Sanctuary, Karikili Bird Sanctuary, Koonthankulam Bird Sanctuary, Pallikarnai Marsh Reserve Forest, Pichavaram Mangrove, Point Calimere Wildlife and Bird Sanctuary, Suchindram Theroor Wetland Complex, Udhayamarthandapuram Bird Sanctuary, Vadavur Bird Sanctuary, Vedanthangal Bird Sanctuary, Vellode Bird Sanctuary, Vembannur Wetland Complex
20. Tripura	1	Rudrasagar Lake
21. Uttar Pradesh	10	Bakhira Sanctuary, Haiderpur Wetland, Nawabganj Bird Sanctuary, Parvati Arga Bird Sanctuary, Saman Bird Sanctuary, Samaspur Bird Sanctuary, Sandi Bird Sanctuary, Sarsai Nawar Jheel, Sur Sarovar, Upper Ganga River
22. Uttarakhand	1	Asan Barrage
23. West Bengal	2	East Kolkata Wetlands, Sundarban Wetland

MANGROVE (FORESTS)

Mangroves are the distinctive ecosystems found along the shallow coasts 30° N or S and the equator. Mangroves are found in tidal flats, estuaries and muddy coasts in tropical and subtropical areas. Communities of mangroves, termed *mangals*, play an important role on many tropical coasts. They are highly productive ecosystems which are capable of exporting energy and materials to adjacent communities. They support a diverse heterotrophic food chain, act as nurseries in the life cycle of some organisms, and offer some protection against coastal erosion and storm surge attack. At present, like many types of wetland, they are under severe anthropogenic pressures.

The sediment in which mangrove trees live must be covered with brackish or salt-water for part or all of the day. Many mangroves avoid taking up salt-ion from seawater or selectively remove salt from sap with salt excreting cells. The fine coastal mud they colonise does not provide firm footing for these substantial plants; so an intricate network of arching prop roots is required for support. The strut-like-roots are supplemented by many smaller roots equipped with breathing pores and air passages.

Atmospheric air is conducted by these passages to the portions of the plant submerged in oxygen deficient mud. The root system also traps and holds sediment around the plant by interfering with the transport of suspended particles by currents. The root complex forms an impenetrable barrier and safe haven for organisms around the base of the tree. Mangroves exhibit viviparity mode of reproduction, i.e. sheeds germinate in the tree itself (before falling to the ground). This is an adaptive mechanism to overcome the problem of germination in saline water.

The low muddy coasts of tropical and sub-tropical regions are often home to tangled masses of evergreen thick leaves trees and bushes (mangroves). These large flowering plants are never completely submerged, but because of their intimate association with ocean they are considered marine plants. They thrive in sediment rich lagoons, bays, and estuaries of the Indo-Pacific, tropical Africa and tropical Americas. The distribution of mangrove largely depends on temperature, precipitation, sediments, salinity of the water, and ocean currents. The regional distribution of mangroves in the world has been shown in **Fig. 4.9.**

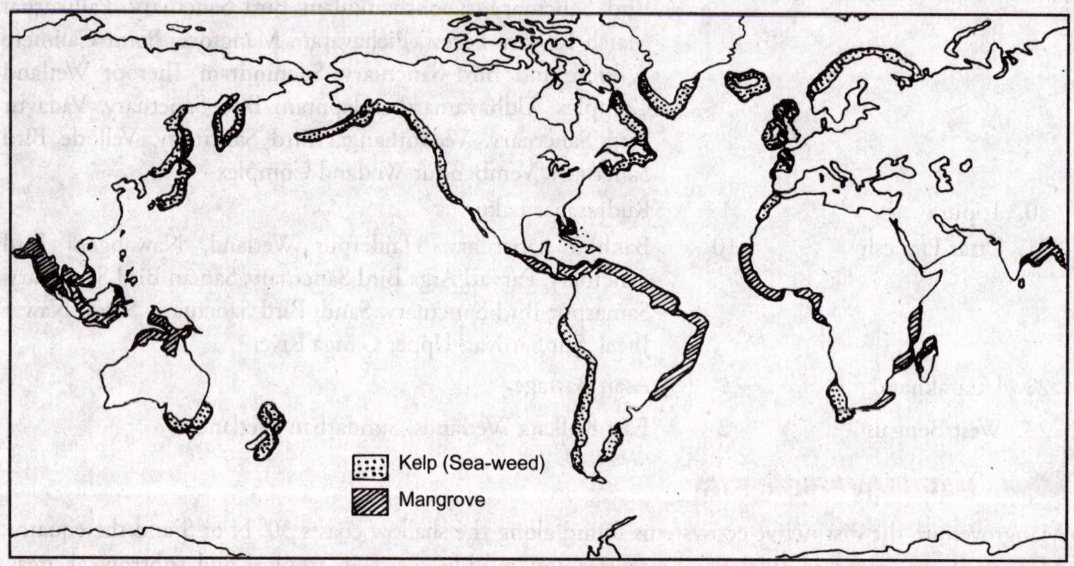

Fig. 4.9 Distribution of Kelp-beds and Mangroves

An examination of **Fig. 4.9** shows that mangroves concentration is significantly high in the islands of south-east Asia, tropical and sub-tropical African coasts, Caribbean Sea and the eastern tropical and sub-tropical coasts of South America and Central America. They are rarely found in the areas of cold water currents even in the subtropical regions.

Major Mangroves of India

Mangroves in India are found in all the coastal states and islands of India. According to one estimate, mangroves cover 4921 sq km area, which is about 0.15% per cent of the total area of the country. There are, however, 12 important mangroves in India given in Table 4.14.

The Sundarban mangrove is one of the largest single mangroves in the world. The major floral species of this dense mangrove forest include Herritiera-fames, Rhizophora spp., Bruguiera spp., Ceriops decandra, Sonneratia spp, and Avicennia spp., Avicennia spp., and Nypa fructican. This mangrove is famous for the Royal Bengal Tiger and crocodiles. Several parts of this mangrove have been cleared for paddy cultivation.

Bhitarkanika along the coast of Odisha is the second largest mangrove of India, followed by the Godavari-Krishna mangrove. The other important mangroves of India are Coondapur (Karnataka), Point Calimere and Pichavaram (Tamil Nadu), Loringa (Andhra Pradesh).

Table 4.14 Major Mangroves of India

Mangrove	State
1. Bhitarkanika	Odisha
2. Coondapur	Karnataka
3. Goa	Goa
4. Godavari Delta	Andhra Pradesh
5. Gulf of Kachchh	Gujarat
6. Krishna Delta	Andhra Pradesh
7. Loringa	Andhra Pradesh
8. Mahanadi Delta	Odisha
9. North Andaman and Nicobar	Andaman & Nicobar Islands
10. Pichavaram	Tamil Nadu
11. Point Calimere	Tamil Nadu
12. Sundarban Delta	West Bengal

Table 4.14-A Medicinal Plants of India

Medicinal Plant	Region/State/Union Territory	Use
1.Beddomes Cycad/Perita/Kondaitha	Himachal Pradesh and Uttarakhand	Cure for rheumatoid-arthritis and muscle pain
2.Blue-venda	Arunachal Pradesh, Assam, Manipur, Meghalaya, Nagaland, Tripura, West Bengal, etc.	Its blue flowers are used for medicines.
3.Cycads (known as living fossil)	Western Ghats, Eastern Ghats, Andaman and Nicobar Islands	Source of starch, neurological diseases and parkinson
4.Kuth/Kustha	Jammu & Kashmir, Himachal Pradesh and Uttar Pradesh	Anti-inflammatory drugs. Roots are used for oil and perfumes, used for insecticides
5.Ladies Slipper Orchids	Uttarakhand and Himachal Pradesh	Used to treat anxiety,/insomnia. Also used as plaster for muscular plain

6.Red-venda	Arunachal Pradesh, Andhra Pradesh, Assam, Manipur, Meghalaya, Mizoram, Nagaland, etc.	Used for orchids fanciers.
7.Sarpagandha	Sub-Himalayan Tract, Sikkim, North-eastern States of India	Used for treating central nervous system disorder, sedation, hypertension, brodyeardia, myosis, ptosis, tremors, etc.
8. Tree Fern	Lower elevations of the Himalayas and Tarai region	

Table 4.14-B State/UT wise mangrove cover assessment 2017 as per Forest Survey of India (km^2)

Sl No.	State/Union Territory	Total Mangrove Cover in Sq/km
1.	West Bengal*	2,114
2.	Gujarat	1140
3.	Andaman Nicobar	617
4.	Andhra Pradesh & Telangana	404
5.	Odisha	243
6.	Maharashtra	304
7.	Tamil Nadu	49
8.	Goa	26
9.	Kerala	9
10.	Karnataka	10
11.	Daman & Diu	3
12.	Puducherry	2
	Total-All India	**4921**

*As per the West Bengal Forest Department, mangrove area in Sundarban is approximately 4200 km^2 which is almost double the area estimated by Forest Survey of India (FSI). This mainly because of the fact that the West Bengal Forest Department includes the areas of waterbody also along with the mangrove vegetation.

Social and Ecological Significance of Mangroves

Mangroves have great social and ecological significance. Some of the important benefits of mangroves are as under:

1. Reduce the danger of floods, cyclones, sea surge and tsunami.
2. They prevent coastal and soil erosion.
3. They promote recycling of nutrients.
4. Mangrove supports numerous flora and fauna.
5. Provide food, fodder, fuel-wood, medicinal herbs.
6. Provide employment and job opportunities to the local people.
7. Mangroves have great recreational, eco-tourism and aesthetic values.

Reasons for Increase in Mangrove Cover

- **Andhra Pradesh:** The positive change of 37 sq km in Andhra Pradesh is mainly due to plantation and regeneration.
- **Gujarat:** The positive changed of 33 sq km in the mangrove is mainly due to conservational effort such as planation and regeneration particularly in Bhavnagar, Jamnagar, Kuchch and junagarh.
- **Maharashtra:** The positive change of B2 sq km in Maharashtra is mainly due to plantation and regeneration of mangroves.
- **Odisha:** The positive change of total 12 sq km is reflected in the Mangroves in Balasore, Bhadrak & Kendrapara districts. The change is mainly due to mangrove plantation, natural regeneration and growing of mangroves in some newly formed island.
- **West Bengal:** The positive change of 8 sq km is reflected in the mangroves of Purba Medinipur and South 24 Pargana districts. The change is mainly due to mangrove plantation in some island and along the river creeks and natural regeneration at few places.

Mangroves and Climate Change

Mangrove forests are the buffer zones of the coasts and destruction of mangroves leads to tremendous coastal erosion, coastal siltation and terrible losses to human life that are due to destructive hurricanes, storm surges and tsunamis. Due to the degradation of mangroves in Bangladesh, repeated floodings are taking place. Today, there is urgency to recognise the importance of conserving and restoring protective mangrove greenbelts. Due to change in climate systems it is expected that the cyclones will hit the coast lines more frequently than ever before. Under this condition, mangroves can buffer against the fury of such destructions, protecting those settlements located behind.

Nearly half of the urban population of the world today lives in big cities and urban places located along the vulnerable coasts. In this context, global warming and consequent sea level rise cannot be ignored. Already, evacuation of low-lying islands have begun in South Asia (Maldives) and South Pacific Islands. It is expected that mass evacuation of millions of coastal residents will occur within the next 50 years as sea level continues to rise as a result of greenhouse effect. The productive mangrove wetlands are often the first line of defence, to secure the coast against erosion and storms. Not only that, the mangrove ecosystem is the potential system to control the global warming because of their high capacity for sequestering carbon from atmosphere and storing in their wetland substrate.

Moreover, mangroves are one of the nature's best ways to combat global warming because of their greater capacity of sequestering carbon and storing in their wetland substrates. According to the latest study by the UN's Food and Agriculture Organization (FAO), the current rate of mangrove loss is around 1 per cent per annum. This is a serious problem which needs to be addressed at a priority basis.

Deforestation: The complete or partial removal of forest by cutting or burning is known as deforestation. The growing pressure of population, industrialization, urbanization, mining, and development of infrastructure are the main causes of deforestation. In India. The main factors responsible for deforestation may be given as under:

(i) shifting cultivation, (ii) collection of fuel-wood and fodder, (iii) obtaining raw-material for forest based industries, (iv) development of dams and multi-purpose projects, (v) construction of roads, railways, airports, and sea-ports, (vi) mining, over-grazing agricultural encroachment, fire, pests, diseases and defense are also responsible for deforestation.

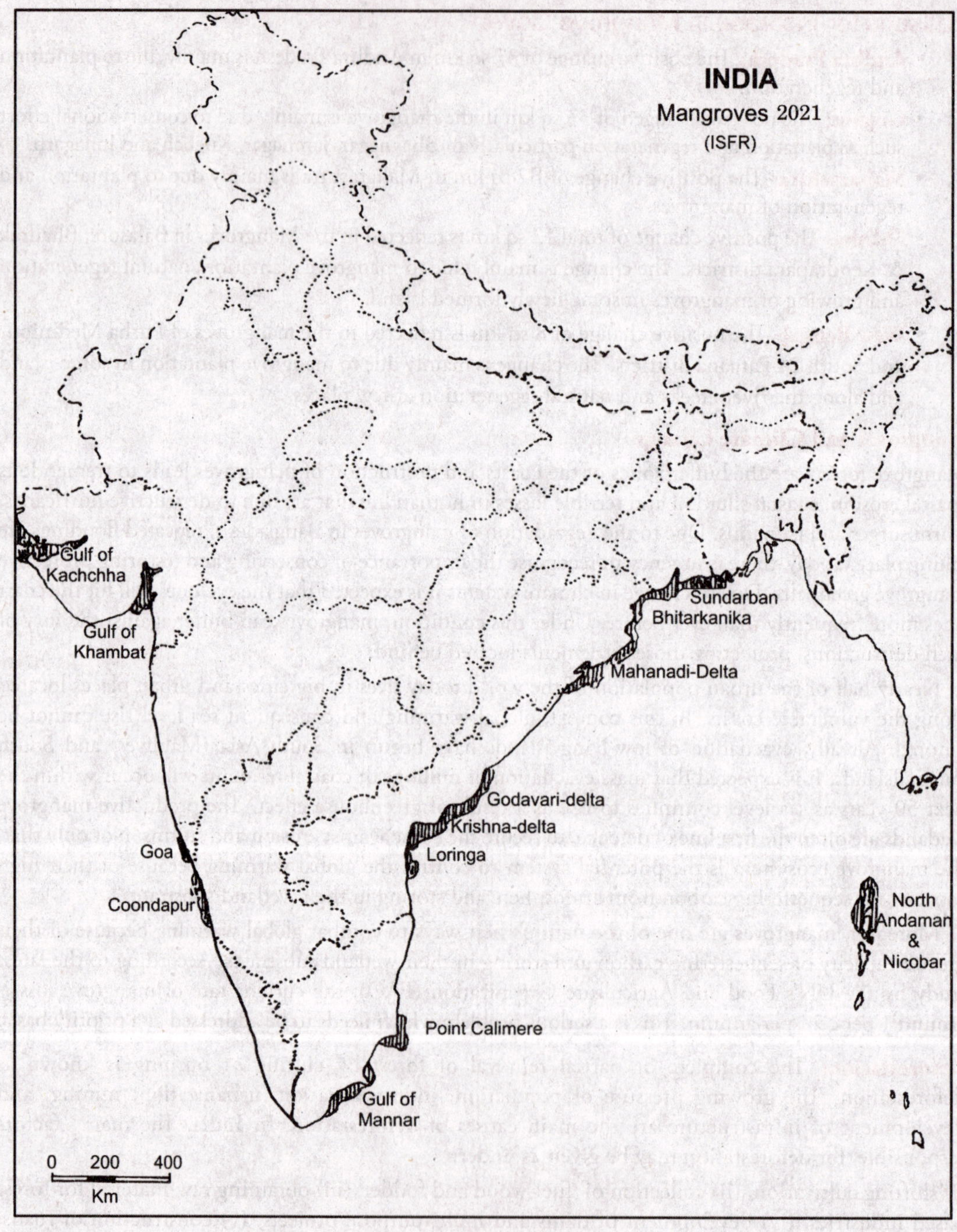

Fig. 4.10 Major Mangroves of India

CORAL REEFS

Coral reef is a linear mass of calcium carbonate (aragonite and calcite) assembled from coral organisms, algae, molluscs, worms, etc. In India, there are four coral reef areas which have been identified for intensive conservation and management. The coral reefs are the natural protective barriers against sea-surge and coastal erosion. They provide a large variety of animals and plants. Moreover, they produce biogenic calcium carbonate. The distribution of coral reefs and coral formations are controlled by environmental factors, notably water temperature, purity of water, and salinity. Most of reef-forming corals prefer sea temperatures between 18°C to 32°C, salinity between 30 and 38 parts per thousand, and clear water. Light is also important, and coral growth is usually restricted to the upper 25 or 30 metres of the sea surface. Because of these factors, coral reefs are mainly found between latitudes 30° N and S on mud free coastlines, particularly in western parts of Pacific, Indian and Atlantic Oceans. The corals live in symbiotic association with unicellular algae, and are colonial organisms with the ability to reproduce sexually or asexually. According to the U.N. Environment Reports, there are more cold-water coral reefs worldwide than tropical reefs. The largest cold water reef is the Rost Reef along the coast of Norway. Reef ecosystems are vulnerable to catastrophic events, such as hurricanes, marine pollution and bleaching epidemics, which may cause mass mortality of corals. Human stress such as pollution and increase in sediment load, have damaged reefs in many areas. Recently, there has been much speculation over the future impact of global warming and climatic change on coral reefs.

The main coral reefs of India about 19,000 sq km are: (i) Gulf of Mannar, (ii) Lakshadweep Islands (iii) Rann of Kachchh, and (iv) Andaman and Nicobar Islands. The National Coral Reef Research Centre has been established at Port Blair (Andaman and Nicobar Islands).

Coral Bleaching

This baffling disease in coral reefs was identified by marine scientists in 1983, in Pacific Ocean. This disease causes coral animals to expel their brownish zooxanthellae and turn an uncharacteristic creamy colour. Without zooxanthellae, the coral can not secrete calcium carbonate and generate a skeleton or reef. After one bout of bleaching, corals usually recover, but while they are bleached, they stop growing, leaving the reef vulnerable to erosion.

As stated above, the disease was first discovered in the Pacific Ocean in 1983. In 1987 it was indentified in the Caribbean Sea and Gulf of Mexico. At present, most of the coral formations of the tropical oceans are affected by this disease.

The cause of coral bleaching is unknown. The initial suspicion centred on global warming and marine pollution. The important causes of coral bleaching may be summarized as under:

1. **Global Warming:** The coral reefs thrive well in a range of temperatures between 18°C to 30°C. Bleaching is more frequently reported from the elevated sea-water where temperature is relatively more (Caribbean Sea, Persian Gulf, Java Sea, Coral Sea and Solomon Islands).

2. **Marine Pollution:** The introduction by humans of substances or energy into the ocean that change the quality of the water or affect the physical and biological environment, is also considered as one of the main causes of coral bleaching.
3. **Exposure to sun:** Many of the zooxanthellae in shallow water develop disease, if they are directly exposed to the sunlight.
4. **Sedimentation:** In some cases, sedimentation in the vicinity of coral formation is considered as the main cause of coral bleaching.
5. **Inorganic nutrients:** An increase of ammonia and nitrate in the water increases the process of eutrophication. The excessive europhication damage the corals and their formations.

WORLD HERITAGE SITES

World Heritage Sites mean 'sites any of various areas inscribed on the list of United Nations Educational, Scientific and Cultural Organisation (UNESCO).

The heritage sites are designated as having outstanding universal value under the Convention on Protection of World Cultural and Natural Heritage, 1972 (enforced 1975).

Criteria for being selected as a Cultural World Heritage Site:

1. Should represent a masterpiece of human creative genius, e.g. Taj Mahal.
2. Should exhibit an important interchange of human values in architecture, monumental arts, town-planning or landscape design.
3. Should be an outstanding example of cultural tradition.
4. Should be an outstanding example of building or landscape which illustrates a significant stage of human history.
5. Should be an outstanding example of traditional human settlement, land use or sea use which is representative of a culture.
6. Should be areas of exceptional natural beauty or aesthetic importance.
7. Should be outstanding examples representing major stages of human history.
8. Should be outstanding areas of biological diversity.

Western Ghats as a World Heritage Site

Western Ghats has been included in the UNESCO World Heritage List in the meeting of the World Heritage Committee held at St. Petersburg in Russia on 1st July, 2012.

The Western Ghats has 'outstanding examples representing significant ongoing ecological and biological processes in the evolution and development of terrestrial, freshwater, coastal and marine ecosystems and communities of plants and animals. It is also the most significant natural habitat for *in-situ* conservation of biological diversity, including those containing threatened species of outstanding universal value from the point of view of science and conservation. Apart from being designated as a World Heritage Site, it is one of the eight hottest hot-spots of biological diversity in the world.

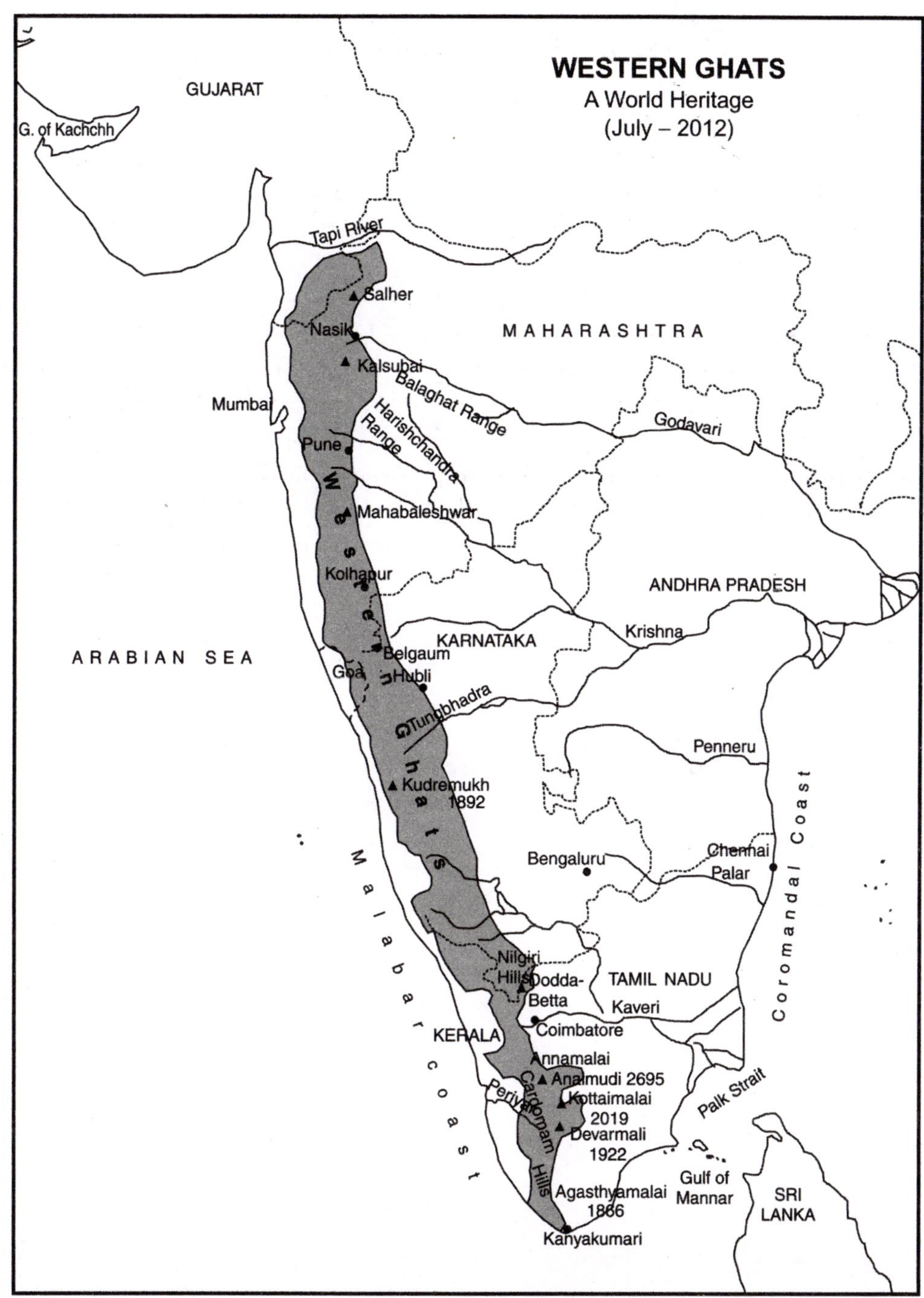

Fig. 4.11 Western Ghats : A World Heritage Site (UNESCO)

The Western Ghats and the *Sahyadri Mountain Range* separates the Deccan Plateau from the narrow coastal plain along the Arabian Sea. It starts south of the Tapi River in Gujarat and runs about 1600 km through the states of Maharashtra, Goa, Karnataka, Kerala and Tamil Nadu, ending at Kanyakumari, the southern tip of the Peninsular India (**Fig. 4.11**).

The main peaks of the Western Ghats are: Asthamudi (2695 m), Doddabetta (2636 m), Mukurthi (2554 m) and Kodaikanal (2133 m). There are 5000 species of flowering plants, 139 mammal species, 508 bird species and 179 amphibian species. According to one estimate, 325 globally threatened species are found in the Western Ghats.

Western Ghats are covered with tropical and subtropical forests that provide food and natural habitat for the native tribal people. The region is ecologically sensitive to development. The Government of India and the state governments have established many protected areas including two biosphere reserves, 13 national parks and several wildlife sanctuaries to protect the endangered species of the region.

The Nilgiri Biosphere Reserve (5500 sq km) of the evergreen forests of Nagarhole, the Bandipur National Park covered with deciduous forest, the Tamil Nadu National Park and Mukurthi National Park in the states of Tamil Nadu and Kerala are the important protected areas. A judicious use of resources and conservation practices can improve the resilience characteristics of the ecosystem of such important world heritage sites.

Chapter 5 Biodiversity and Legislations

INTRODUCTION

Human beings are entitled to a healthy and productive life in harmony with nature. Thus, to keep the biodiversity and environment in a healthy condition is the need of the hour. Efforts are being made at the international and national levels to maintain the equilibrium and resilience characteristics of the ecosystems with the objective to make them sustainable. In fact, conventions and conferences on environment have now assumed an important place in international diplomacy. The two most important milestones in this direction have been (i) the Stockholm Conference, 1972, and (ii) The Rio-de-Janeiro or Earth Summit, 1992. Out of these, the Earth Summit or Rio Conference (Brazil) was a big success, as virtually all the participating countries agreed to cooperate more closely in tackling the global environmental issues and problems. A brief description of some of the important national and international legislations related to the ecology, environment and sustainable development are discussed in this chapter has been given in the following.

Treaty: A treaty is an agreement under international law entered into by sovereign states and international organisations. A treaty may also be known as an (international) agreement, protocol, convention, pact or exchange of letters. Regardless of terminology, all of these forms of agreements are, under international law, equally considered treaties and rules are the same.

Protocol: A protocol is generally a treaty or international agreement that supplements a previous treaty or international agreement. A protocol can amend the previous treaty or international agreement or add additional provisions. Parties to the earlier agreement are not required to adopt the protocol. Sometimes this is made clearer calling it an 'optional protocol', especially where many parties to the first agreement do not support the protocol.

Conventions: It is an agreement between states, especially one less formal than a treaty.

EARTH SUMMIT

The United Nations sponsored Earth Summit was held in Rio de Janeiro in 1992 from 3rd to 14th June. In this summit, leaders of 100 nations, over 10,000 delegates from over 160 countries, are nearly 9000 journalists participated. The focus of the conference was the *Agenda 21*, the problems of 21st Century and the treaties, biodiversity and climatic change. The summit ended with the declaration of 27 principles which came to be known as Agenda 21 (the Agenda for 21st century). Maurice F. Strong, a Canadian and Secretary General of the UNCED, summarised in his conference address.

The people of our planet, especially our youth and the generation which follow them, will hold us accountable for what we do or fail to do at the Earth Summit in Rio. Earth is the only home we have, its fate is literally in our hands …. The most important ground we must arrive at Rio is the understanding that we are all in this together.

The Five Earth Summit Agreements

Five key agreements that emerged from the Earth Summit conference are summarised below.

1. **Climate Change Framework:** This legally binding agreement is a first-ever attempt to evaluate and address global warming on an International scale. This was signed in 1992 by 154 nations including Canada and USA.
2. **Biological Diversity:** This legally binding agreement is the first international attempt to protect the Earth's biodiversity. It provides more equitable rights among nations in biotechnology and genetic wealth of tropical ecosystems in particular.

   Out of 161 signatories, the United States, Vietnam, Singapore and Kribati (a Pacific Island nation) refused to sign the original treaty.
3. **Management, Conservation, and Sustainable Development of all Types of Forests:** This non-binding agreement guides world forestry practices toward a more sustainable future of forest yields and diversity.
4. **The Earth Charter:** This is a non-binding statement of 27 environmental and economic principles. They establish an ethical basis for a sustainable human–earth relationship. An important emphasis is inclusion of *environmental costs* in economic assessments. Improvisation and utilization of air, soil, water and ecosystems sometimes is mistaken for progress. The environment is not an inexhaustible mine of resources to be tapped indefinitely. In terms of *natural capital—air, water, timber, fisheries, petroleum*—Earth is indeed a finite physical system.
5. **Agenda 21 (Sustainable Development):** This non-binding action programme is an 800–page guide for all nations into the 21st Century. The idea of '*sustainable development*' as proposed in a business proposal of 'sustainable growth' is examined in Agenda 21.

Agenda 21 covers many key topics: energy conservation and efficiency to reduce consumption and related pollution, climate change, stratospheric ozone depletion, trans-boundary air-pollution, ocean and water resource protection; soil losses, and increasing desertification; deforestation, regulations for safely handling radioactive waste and disposal; hazardous chemicals exports for disposal in developing countries, and disparities of wealth and the plague of poverty.

Agenda 21 also discusses the difficult question of financing sustainable development. Developing countries are asking the developed nations to spend 0.7% of their gross domestic product – about $125 billion per year – to assist them in implementing the Earth Charter and Agenda 21.

Towards a Sustainable Future

From the Earth Summit, emerged a new organisation – The U.N. Commission on Sustainable Development – to oversee the promises made in the above five documents and agreements. Most of the participating countries completed Statement of the Environment Reports (SERs) and gathered environmental statistics for publication. These reports are an invaluable resource that will direct further research efforts in many countries. Considering these environmental problems and the possible world actions, these are challenging times for humanity, as we ponder our relationship with our home planet. Over the long term, we no longer can sustain human activity through old patterns.

THE MONTREAL PROTOCOL

The Montreal Protocol was about the substances that deplete the ozone layer of the stratosphere. It is an international treaty, designed to protect the ozone layer, by phasing out the production of numerous substances believed to be responsible for ozone depletion. The Treaty was opened for signature on 16th September, 1987 and entered into force on 1st January, 1989. Its first meeting was held at Helsinki in May, 1989. Since then, it has undergone seven revisions in London (1990), Nairobi (1991), Copenhagen (1992), Bangkok (1993), Vienna (1995), Montreal (1997), and Beijing (1999). It was believed that if this international agreement is adhered to, the ozone layer would recover by 2005. Initially, the target was set to remove harmful chemicals like the CFCs by 50 per cent by 1998. The target was further revised so as to curtail the production of these chemicals at the earliest. It has been ratified by 196 states.

KYOTO PROTOCOL ON CLIMATIC CHANGE

This is a protocol to the 1992 UN Framework Convention on Climatic Change (UNFCCC). It was adopted in the conference at Kyoto (Japan) in 1997.

Kyoto Protocol is a voluntary treaty signed by 141 countries including the European Union, Japan, and Canada. According to this Protocol, the developed industrialised countries are required to reduce emission of greenhouse gases by an average of 5.2 per cent below 1990 levels by 2012. The Intergovernmental Panel on Climatic Change (IPCC) has predicted an average global rise in temperature of Earth from 1.4°C to 5.8°C between 1990 and 2100. If successfully implemented, the Kyoto Protocol will reduce that increase by somewhere 0.02°C and 0.28°C by the year 2050 (*Nature*, October 2003).

The six greenhouse gases included under Kyoto Protocol are: (i) Carbon-dioxide, (ii) Methane (CH_4), (iii) Nitrous-oxide (N_2O), (iv) Per-Fluorocarbons (PFCs), (v) Hydro-Fluorocarbons (HFCs), and (vi) Sulphur Hexafluoride (SF_6).

There were two main flaws in the Kyoto Protocol:

(i) The largest polluters of the world, i.e. USA which accounts for one third of the total CHG emission boycotted it.

(ii) Although India and China (two emerging Asian economic powers) signed it, they were not required to cut their share of emissions by 2012. The argument being that they should not pay the penalty for being late industrialisers (India and China account for 14 per cent of CHG emissions). Russia ratified the treaty, it accounted for 17 per cent of the emissions. The Kyoto Protocol had to be ratified by countries accounting for at least 55 per cent of the global emissions in 1990, to go into effect. Hence, Russia's decision on the treaty was very crucial.

THE MONTREAL ACTION PLAN

The Montreal Action Plan was one of the greatest intergovernmental conference on climatic change ever held. It took place at Montreal (Canada) in December 2005. The event marked the entry into force of the Kyoto Protocol. The Monreal Action Plan is an agreement hammered out at the end of the Conference to extend the life of the Kyoto Protocol beyond 2012 expiration date, and to negotiate deeper cuts in greenhouse gas emission.

BALI SUMMIT

The Bali Summit was held on 1st December 2007 at Nausa Dua (Bali, Indonesia). Agreement on a timeline and structured negotiation on the post-2012 framework was achieved with adoption of the Bali Action plan. Under the Convention, was established as a new subsidiary to conduct the negotiation aimed at urgently enhancing the implementation of the Convention up and beyond 2012.

POZNAN SUMMIT

The Poznan Summit (Poland) was held in December 2008 In this summit the delegates agreed on principles for financing of a fund to help the poorest nations to cope up with the effects of climate change. They approved a mechanism to incorporate forest protection into the efforts of the international community to combat climatic change.

COPENHAGEN SUMMIT

The convention on climatic change was held at the Bella Centre of Copenhagen in December 2009. This conference was attended by 150 global leaders, ministers and officials from 192 countries. The overall goal of the Summit was to establish an ambitious global climate agreement from 2012 when the first commitment period under the Kyoto Protocol expires. The conference did not achieve a binding agreement for long-term action. In this Summit, a 'political accord' was negotiated by approximately 25 parties including USA and China, but it was only noted by a 'COP' as it is considered an external document, not negotiated within the UNFCCC process. The accord was notable in that it referred to a collective commitment by developed countries for a few additional resources including forestry. The Summit emphasised on mobilisation of financial resources for supporting reforestation efforts of the developing countries.

CANCUN SUMMIT

The 2010 United Nations Climate Change Conference was held at Cancun (Mexico) in December 2010. The conference is officially referred to as the 16th Session of the Conference of the Parties to the United Nations Framework on Climate Change (UNFCCC).

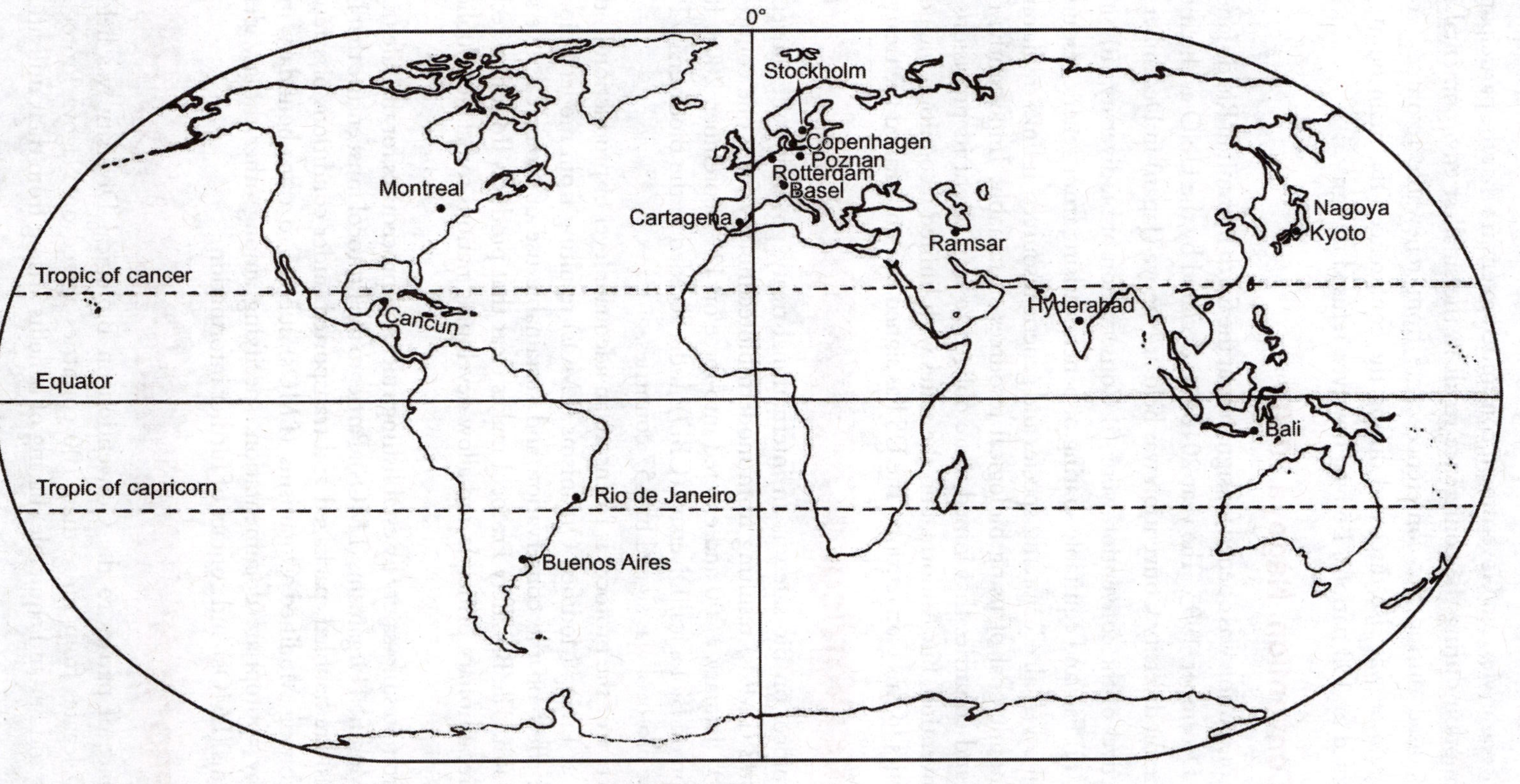

Fig. 5.1 Venue-cities of International Conventions and Protocols

In this conference, the Mexican Government committed to ensure that the participants mobilisation and energy consumption during the conference result in the smallest environmental impact. A large amount of energy used during the conference came from renewable resources. A residual waste management programme was also discussed during the conference. The main points of the Cancun Agreement was signed by 193 nations. Bolivia, however, refused to sign.

Biodiversity Convention, Nagoya 2010

The Biodiversity Convention was opened for signature at the Earth Summit in Rio de Janeiro and entered into force on 29th December, 1993. The year 2010 was declared by the UNO as the International Year of Biodiversity. The Biodiversity Convention was held at Nagoya (Japan) in December 2010.

The main objectives of the convention were: (i) Conservation of biodiversity, (ii) Sustainable use of components, and (iii) Fair and equitable sharing of benefits arising from genetic resources.

The Convention covers all ecosystems, species and genetic resources. It links traditional conservation efforts to the economic goal of using biological resources sustainably. Importantly, the Convention is legally binding and countries that joined it are obliged to implement its provisions. There are 193 parties of this Convention, but Andorra, and the states with limited recognition including the United States are non-parties to this Convention. The US has signed but not ratified the treaty.

CARTAGENA PROTOCOL

The Cartagena Protocol on Bio-safety is an international treaty, governing the movements of Living Modified Organisms (LMOs) resulting from modern biotechnology from one country to another. It was adopted on 29th January, 2000 and entered into force on 11th September, 2003. It was under the aegis of Convention on Biological Diversity (CBD). India acceded to the Biodiversity Protocol on 17th January, 2003. The protocol was signed by 157 countries.

The main objective of the protocol is to ensure an adequate level of production in the field of safer transfer, handling of Living Modified Organisms (LMOs) resulting from modern biotechnology that may have adverse effect on the conservation and sustainable use of biological diversity taking into account risk to health. The Biosafety Protocol makes clear that products from new technologies must be based on the precautionary principle and allow developing nations to balance public health against economic benefits.

The Protocol promotes bio-safety by establishing rules and procedures for the safe transfer, handling and use of Living Modified Organisms (LMOs). Parties to the Protocol must ensure that Living Modified Organisms (LMOs) are handled, packaged and transported under conditions of safety. Furthermore, the shipment of Living Modified Organisms (LMOs) subject to trans-boundary movement must be accompanied by appropriate documentation, specifying among other things, identity of Living Modified Organisms (LMOs) and contact of further information.

NAGOYA PROTOCOL

The 10th Conference of parties to the Convention on Biological Diversity was held at Nagoya in October, 2010. Delegates from more than 100 countries agreed on Nagoya Protocol on Access to Genetic Resources and fair and equitable sharing of benefits arising from their utilisation.

ROTTERDAM CONVENTION

This Convention was signed on 10th September, 1998 at Rotterdam. It is a multilateral treaty on Hazardous Chemicals and Pesticides in International trade. The Convention promotes open exchange of information and calls on exporters of hazardous chemicals to use proper labelling and directions on safe handling and inform purchasers of any known restrictions or bans. There are 73 signatories of this convention.

STOCKHOLM CONVENTION

This Convention was about the persistent organic pollutants. This treaty was signed on 23rd May, 2001 at Stockholm. The main objective of the Convention was to restrict the production and use of persistent organic pollutants. Parties to this convention have agreed to a process by which persistent toxic compounds can be reviewed and added to the Convention, if they meet certain criteria for persistence and trans-boundary threat.

Initially, there were 12 distinct chemicals listed in three categories. But subsequently, the use of DDT to control malaria and curtail inadvertent production of dioxins and furans—Adrin, Chlordane, Dieldring, Heptachlor, Hexachlora, Mirex, etc. were also added.

BASEL CONVENTION

The Basel Convention was held to control the trans-boundary movement of hazardous wastes. It mainly focused on the transfer of hazardous wastes from the developing countries. The Convention was opened for signature on 22nd March, 1989 and it entered 175 parties to the Convention.

INTERNATIONAL TREATY ON PLANT GENETIC RESOURCES FOR FOOD AND AGRICULTURE, 2004

This treaty covers all plant genetic resources for food and agriculture. It specifically covers 64 crops. The main objectives of the treaty are the conservation and sustainable use of plant genetic resources for food and agriculture, and the fair and equitable sharing of benefits arising out of their use, in harmony with the Convention on Biological Diversity.

Table 5.1 International Protocols and Treaties

MEAs	Year	Entry into Force	Date of Ratification	Issues covered
1. Ramsar Convention on Wetlands	1971	21.12.1975	11.02.1982	Conservation and wise use of wetlands, primarily as habitats for water birds.
2. Biodiversity Conservation	1972	17.12.1975	4.11.1977	Protection and conservation of natural and cultural heritage.
3. Convention on International Trade of Wild animals	1973	1.7.1975	20.7.1976	International Trade in Endangered Species of wild-fauna and flora
4. Bonn Convention on Migratory Species of Wild animals	1979	1.11.1983	1.11.1983	Conservation, management and wise use of migratory species of wild animals and their habitat

(Contd.)

Table 5.1 *(Contd.)*

MEAs	Year	Entry into Force	Date of Ratification	Issues covered
5. Vienna Convention for the protection of Ozone Layer	1985	22.9.1988	18.3.1991	Protection of ozone layer.
6. Montreal Protocol	1987	1.1.1989	19.6.1992	Protection of atmospheric ozone
7. Basel Convention	1989	5.5.1992	24.6.1992	Regulation of trans-boundary movements of hazardous waste and their disposal.
8. UN Framework Convention on Climatic Change (UNFCCC)	1992	21.3.1994	1.11.1993	Change in Earth Climate System due to anthropogenic interference.
9. Kyoto Protocol (UNFCCC)	1997	16.2.2005	26.8.2002	Quantified emission limitation and reduction commitments for Annex parties.
10. Convention on Biological Diversity (CBD)	1992	29.12.1993	18.2.1994	Biological Diversity and biological resources.
11. Cartegena Protocol Bio-safety to the CBD	2000	11.9.2003	11.9.2003	Regulation of trans-boundary movement, transit, handling and use of LMOs.
12. United Nations Convention to Combat Desertification	1994	26.12.1996	17.12.1996	Combating desertification and to mitigate the effects of droughts, particularly in Africa.
13. Rotterdam Convention	1998	24.2.2004	24.5.2005	To promote shared responsibility among the parties in the co-operative efforts among international trade of certain hazardous chemicals in order to protect human health and the environment.
14. Stockholm Convention	2001	17.5.2004	13.1.2006	Protect human health and environment from persistent organic pollutants.
15. Hyderabad Convention on Persistent Organic Pollutant	2001	17.5.2004	13.1.2006	To conserve marine coastal ecosystems

ANTARCTIC TREATY

The Antarctic Treaty and related agreement, collectively called Antarctic Treaty System (ATS) regulate international relations with respect to Antarctica, the earth's only continent without a native population. For the purpose of treaty system, Antarctica is defined as all of land and ice-shelves south of 60°S latitude. The Treaty entering into force in 1961 and eventually signed by 45 countries, set aside Antarctica as a scientific reserve, establishes freedom of scientific investigation and bans military activity on that continent. The treaty was the first arms control agreement established during the Cold War. The Antarctic Treaty Secretariat Headquarters is located in Buenos Aires (Argentina).

ENVIRONMENTAL LAWS IN INDIA

India has significant provisions in its constitution for having enacted over 200 laws for the protection of environment. Some of the important environmental laws of India have been described briefly below:

1. The Wildlife (Protection) Act of 1972.
2. The Water (Prevention and Control of Pollution) Act of 1974.
3. The Forest (Conservation) Act of 1980.
4. The Air (Prevention and Control of Pollution) Act of 1981.
5. The Environment (Protection) Act of 1986.
6. The National Environmental Tribunal Act of 1995.

The Wildlife Act, 1972

The Wildlife (Protection) Act, 1972 provides the following:

(i) Protection of specified plants.
(ii) Prohibition of hunting of wild animals.
(iii) Declaration of sanctuaries, national parks, and closed areas.
(iv) Management of sanctuaries, national parks, and closed areas.
(v) Constitution of Central Zoo Authority.
(vi) Granting licence for hunting of animals for the purpose of education, scientific research, and scientific management.
(vii) Granting of licence (permits) for picking, uprooting, etc. of specified plants for the purpose of education, and scientific research.
(viii) Granting of licence (permit) for trade and commerce in wild animals, and animal products.
(ix) Granting of licence (permits) for cultivation of specified but otherwise prohibited plants.
(x) Protecting the rights of Scheduled Tribes Population.
(xi) Penalties for violation of various provisions of the Act.

Violation of various sections of the Act do attract penalties of varying degree. For instance, if a person violates any conditions laid down in his licence (permit) granted to him under Section 38J, he/she is liable to: (i) imprisonment up to three months and/or a fine up to Rs. 25,000; (ii) cancellation of his/her licence granted for the purpose; and (iii) cancellation of his/her Arms licence. The penalties in the violation of some the clauses of the Act may give a punishment of six months and cash punishment up to Rs. 10,000.

The Wildlife Protection Act 1972 consists of six scheduled list with varying degree of protection to wild animals. The species of wild animals, the degree of protection and the prescribed penalties for the violeters are given in the Table 6.1-A:

Schedule	Species	Level of Protection and penalties
I	Black-Buck, Great Indian Bustard, Lion-tailed Macaque. Narcondam Hornbill, Nicobar Megapode Rhinoceros, etc.	Poaching, smuggling and illegal trade prohibited. Maximum penalties
II	Bengal Porcupine, Dhole, Flying Squirrel, Himalayan Brown Bear, King Cobra, Rhesus Macaque,	Poaching, smuggling and illegal trade prohibited Maximum penalties
III	Barking Deer, Goral, Hyaena, Hogdeer, Nilgai, Sponges, etc.	Protected but relatively less penalties
IV	Mangoose, Vultures, etc.	Protected but penalties are relatively low
V	for example, Common Crow, Flying Fox, and Mice, Rats,	These species are 'vermin' which can be hunted,
VI	Beddomes cycad, Blue Vanda, Kuth, Ladies Slipper Pitcher PlantRed Vanda, etc.	Cultivation, collection, extraction, trade, etc. of plants and their derivatives are prohibited.

Water (Prevention and Control of Pollution) Act, 1974

The main objectives of the Water Act 1974 is to make judicious use of water resources and to control water pollution. The Act also empowers the Central Government to establish Central Water Pollution Control Board and the State Governments to constitute their own Water Pollution Control Boards in their respective states.

The main functions and powers of these pollution control boards are:

(i) To promote cleanliness of streams and wells.
(ii) To advise central or state governments on matters relating to water pollution.
(iii) To promote and sponsor research with a view to controlling water pollution.
(iv) To train personnel for such purposes.
(v) To conduct survey of any area with a view to obtaining any information regarding water pollution.
(vi) To take samples of effluents.
(vii) To enter into any premises for the purposes of inspecting any documents, register, records of any plant/unit suspected to be source of pollution.
(viii) To prohibit the use of any stream or well for disposing the effluents.
(ix) To grant permission to new outlets for discharge.
(x) To execute any work which the polluter may not have implemented and to charge the cost of the same from the polluter.
(xi) To undertake the emergency measures in case of any accidental pollution of water.
(xii) To approach the courts, if necessary, to prevent wells and from apprehensive pollution; and
(xiii) To order: (a) closure of any industry, and (b) stop supply of electricity to the polluting industry.

Violation of the above clauses of the Act the violator may be punished for six years of rigorous imprisonment and a punishment up to six months.

Forest (Conservation) Act, 1980

Under this Act, it is obligatory for the State governments to obtain prior permission for: (i) any de-reservation of forests, and (ii) use of any forest land for non-forest purposes.

The violation attracts an imprisonment up to 15 days. The responsibility in case of government department lies with the Head of the Department.

Air (Prevention and Control of Pollution) Act, 1981

The Air Act was enacted on 29th March 1981. The main objective of this Act was the prevention, control and abatement of air pollution through the Air Pollution Control Boards, constituted at the National Level. The powers and functions of the Board are given below:

(i) To declare any area as air pollution control area.
(ii) To fix up of the emission levels from automobiles.
(iii) Location of industry from the point of view of pollution.
(iv) To approach to the court against any polluter.
(v) To inspect any factory premises to assess pollution being caused by it.
(vi) To obtain any information from industry with regard to pollution.
(vii) To take samples from the concerned unit.

Violation of various Sections of the Act attract punishment of varying degree which may be imprisonment up to three months and/or a fine up to Rs. 10,000.

Environmental Protection Act, 1982

The main objectives of the Environmental Protect Act, 1982 are to provide for protection and improvement of environment. The Act empowers the Central Government to take all such measures as to deem necessary or expedient for achieving the chief objectives of the Act. The main points of the Act are given below:

(i) To plan and execute a nation-wide programme for prevention and control of environmental pollution.
(ii) To lay down standards for the quality of environment in its various aspects.
(iii) To lay down standards for emission and discharge of pollutants.
(iv) To restrict the areas in which industrial process could be carried out.
(v) To lay down procedures and safeguards for the prevention of accidents that may cause environmental pollution and to take effective remedial measures expeditiously.
(vi) To lay down procedures and safeguards for handling of hazardous substance.
(vii) To examine all such manufacturing processes, materials and substances that are likely to cause pollution.
(viii) To carry out research and sponsor research laboratories for understanding all problems relating to environmental pollution.

(ix) To inspect any premises, industrial plant, equipment, machinery, etc. and to issue directions necessary for controlling environmental pollution.

(x) To prepare manuals, codes, guidelines relating to prevention and control of environmental pollution.

The Act also empowers the Central Government: (a) to appoint officers for performing various functions, (b) to issue directions and to order closure of any industry, if necessary and to stop the supply of electricity and water or any other service to the defaulting unit, (c) to prohibit emission of pollutants beyond the prescribed limits, (d) to ensure that the hazardous materials are handled in accordance with the prescribed safeguards, (e) To take samples of pollutants for examination in the duly certified research laboratories, (f) to frame rules regarding all matters concerning environmental pollution.

Radiation Laws

(i) The Atomic Energy Act, 1962.
(ii) Radiation Protection Rules, 1971.
(iii) The Environmental Protection Act, 1982.
(iv) The Environment Impact Assessment Notification, 1994, as further amended in 1994.

Violation of the Environmental Protection Act, 1982 attract imprisonment up to five years and/or fine up to one lakh.

The National Environment Tribunal Act, 1995

In pursuance to the recommendations of the United Nations sponsored second Earth Summit at Rio-de-Janeiro, the National Environment Tribunal was established in 1995. The main objectives of the Act to provide effective and expeditious relief and compensation for damages to human health, property and environment caused by industrial accidents and disasters.

Under the Act, one could claim the damages for the following:

(i) Death
(ii) Permanent, temporary, total/partial disability or other injury or sickness.
(iii) Loss of wages due to disability.
(iv) Medical expenses incurred for treatment.
(v) Damage to property.
(vi) Expenses incurred by the government in providing relief, aid, and rehabilitation to the affected persons.
(vii) Expenses incurred by the government for any administrative or legal action or to cope with any harm or damage, including environmental degradation and its restoration.
(viii) Loss to government.
(ix) Harm to fauna including milch, draught animals and aquatic fauna.
(x) Harm to flora including aquatic flora, crops, vegetables, trees and orchards.
(xi) Cost of any damage to environment including pollution of soil, air, water, land and ecosystem.
(xii) loss and destruction of any property other than private property.
(xiii) Loss of business or employment or both.
(xiv) Any other claim arising out of, or connected with, any activity of handling hazardous substance.

Any one who fails to comply with any order made by the Tribunal, is liable to punishment with an imprisonment up to 3 years and/or a fine up to Rs. ten lakh.

BIODIVERSITY ACT, 2002

Biodiversity Act, 2002 provides for setting up of a National Biodiversity Authority (NBA), State Biodiversity Board (SBB), and Biodiversity Management Committees (BMCs). The National Biodiversity Authority was established in Chennai in 2003.

According to this Act, all foreign nationals/organisations require prior approval of NBA for obtaining biological resources and/or associated knowledge for any use. Indian individuals require approval of NBA for transferring results of research, with respect to any biological resources, to foreign nationals/organisations for commercial purposes.

Indian industry is required to give prior intimation to the concerned SBBs about obtaining any biological resources for commercial use, and SBB may restrict the activity if it is found to violate the objectives of conservation, sustainable use and benefit sharing.

However, Indian citizens including (*Hakims* and *Vaids*) would have a free access to use biological resources within the country for their own use.

The monetary benefits, fees or royalties accruing as a result of approvals by the National Biodiversity Authority are to be deposited in the NBA Funds, which will be used for the conservation of biodiversity.

CHAPTER 6 Environmental Degradation and Management

INTRODUCTION

Environmental change is a continuous process that has been in operation since the Earth came into existence about 4.6 billion years ago. Since then, dynamic systems of energy and material transfers have been operated at the global scale to bring about gradual and sometimes catastrophic transformation in the atmosphere, hydrosphere, lithosphere and biosphere. For most of the history of the Earth the agents of change have been the natural forces, like earthquakes, volcanoes, landslides, subsidence, seas-surges, tsunamis, hurricanes, tornadoes, floods, droughts and epidemics. All the phenomena have interacted to produce dynamic ecosystems. Environment, however, is an integrated system in which all elements act and react is such a way that the balance is always maintained. Undoubtedly, the physical elements (relief, structure, climate, natural vegetation, soils, water-bodies, etc.) are the determining factors of environment but man has always disrupted the natural environment and created background for accelerated environmental degradation. In fact, at present, man is bringing radical changes in ecology and ecosystems, thereby degrading the environment.

Human beings have an ecological dominance since their appearance on the Earth. In fact, man has diverted and manipulated drainage systems, altered the quality and flow of water, both in the surface and subsurface, changed the atmosphere, modified the oceanic water, altered the soil chemistry, and significantly transformed the forests ecosystems through exotic varieties and social forestry. Though these changes were intended to produce improvements in the society, but the results are quite opposite at the national, international, local and regional levels. Consequently, there are atmospheric changes which further accelerated the processes of greenhouse effect, global warming, acidification, ozone depletion, desertification, soil-erosion, deforestation, waste-disposal, biodiversity degradation and ecological imbalances.

A brief account of these processes and their impact on environment and society is given below.

Greenhouse Effect and Global Warming

The process whereby radiatively active gases absorb and delay the loss of heat to space, thus keeping the lower troposphere moderately warmed through the radiation and eradication of infrared wavelengths. In other words, the greenhouse effect is a natural phenomenon that occurs when short-wave solar radiation from the Sun passes largely through the Earth's atmosphere, is absorbed at the planetary surface, is reradiated upward as long-wavelength thermal radiation, and is absorbed by various atmospheric constituents and again reradiated. Since some of this latter radiation flux is directed downward, it results in a surface warming that would not occur in the absence of an atmosphere. And this extra warming is what is commonly called the greenhouse effect.

The most important 'greenhouse gases' are water vapour and carbon dioxide. Their presence in the atmosphere allows the Earth to maintain an average temperature of approximately 15°C. Without them, the surface temperature of the planet would be about –19°C, and the Earth could not support life. Consequently, it is clear that we owe our very existence to the greenhouse effect. With the onset of the Industrial Revolution, however, the CO_2 content of the air began to rise, and people began to worry that this phenomenon might have a 'dark side' we had not anticipated. The greenhouse effect has become a topic of both scientific and political debate, and will probably remain so for years to come.

The effect of greenhouses and the manner in which progressive global warming may affect Earth's ecosystems in the future is difficult to predict. However, recent studies showing how higher CO_2 levels and slightly warmer global temperatures have affected the biosphere. Some of the studies have demonstrated that, since 1960s, warmer average temperatures have brought an earlier spring and later winter over the temperate and higher latitudes of the Northern Hemisphere, advancing the growing season by about seven days in the spring and extending it by about two to four days in the autumn. This extended growing season, along with elevated level of CO_2, has spurred greater plant growth over a wide swath of territory, including Alaska, Canada, Norway, Sweden, Finland, Siberia (Russia), northern-China and Mongolia.

According to the experts, about 10 per cent reduction in snow cover is associated with warmer temperatures in higher latitudes, which probably translates to quicker warming of the soil and a faster start to spring growth. The increased CO_2 available, probably also adds to photosynthesis rates as 10 per cent in the affected regions that provides some of the best direct evidence so far of a large scale ecosystem response to climate change. This response, however, is not likely to be universal. Higher temperatures and less rainfall in some areas may decrease soil moisture levels and actually suppress growth and agricultural yields.

In addition to these, the ecologists and bio-geographers have predicted that as global temperature increases, the animal and plant species will shift towards the poles and to higher elevations to maintain their preferred temperature conditions.

Acidification

Acidification is yet another major factor responsible for biodiversity depletion and environmental degradation. Acid precipitation is rain or snowfall with a pH of less than 5.65. The term acid rain was coined by a British chemist, Angus Smith, in 1858. It refers to precipitation with a pH of less than 5.6. When precipitation has a pH of less than 5.6, it is usually due to the injection of sulphur compounds or nitrogen oxides into the atmosphere. Coal burning in thermal power plants, industrial furnaces, and motor vehicles inject large amounts of these chemicals into the atmosphere. In the atmosphere, the chemicals combine with water to form sulphuric acid and nitric acid. These droplets may be transported at great distances by wind before they precipitate to the ground (Fig. 6.1).

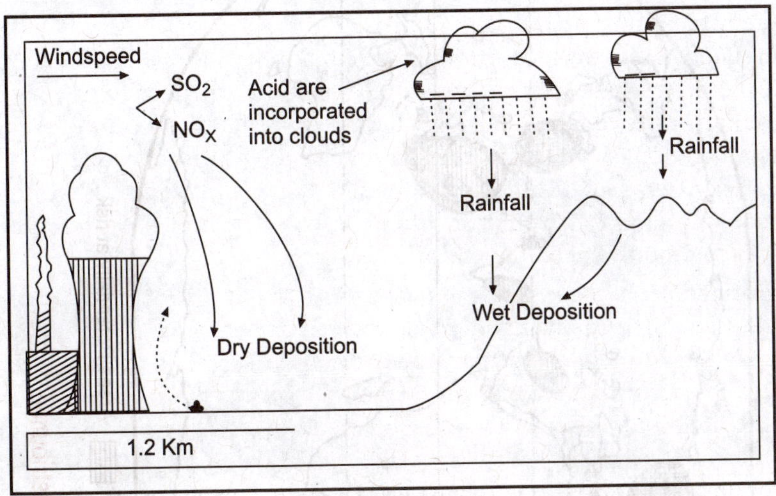

Fig. 6.1 Acidification

The main gases involved in the production of acid rains are nitrogen oxides—sulphur dioxide (SO_2), nitrogen dioxide (NO_2) and nitrous oxide (NO). The major sources of these gases is due to burning of fossil fuel and industrial processes.

Acid rain is a phrase that applies to a process that results in deposition of acid on the surface of the Earth. All precipitation is slightly acidic in nature. One index of measuring acidity is the concentration of hydrogen ions (pH). A neutral solution has a pH of 7.0. The lower the pH, the more acidic the water. For each unit the pH drops, the acidity increases by a multiple of 10. Thus, a pH of 6 represents an acidic element 10 times that of pH of 7. A pH 5 represents 100 times the acidity of water with a pH of 7.

World Distribution of Acid Rain

Acid rain has become a worldwide problem. In Europe, Norway, Sweden, Denmark, Finland, Poland, Germany, Britain, Belgium, Netherlands, and France all have problems with acid rain. Great Britain is accused by the continental nations as being the main source of the pollution. Great Britain has admitted to being a source of sulphur dioxides and nitrogen oxides. The main source of the sulphuric acid and nitric acid particles is believed to be automobile traffic on the continent. This incident was worse than the incident at Pitlochry, Scotland, in 1974. The Pitlochry acid mist had a pH level of 2.4 – stronger than vinegar.

The other parts of the world adversely affected by acid rains have been shown in Fig. 6.2. It may be seen from Fig. 6.2 that the eastern industrial regions of China, especially the Guiyang has the serious problem of acid rain. Moreover, the industrial regions of Thailand, Malaysia, Indonesia, India, Nigeria, West Indies, Argentina and Uruguay are also the areas of potentially at risk because of acid rain. In addition to these, the entire North East of North America from the New Foundland up to the Gulf of Mexico is recording high degree of acidic rain. In fact, the acidity of precipitation has increased over North America to the level where pH is less than 4.6 over most of the continent east of the line from Houston, Texas, to the southern tip of Hudson Bay (Fig. 6.2).

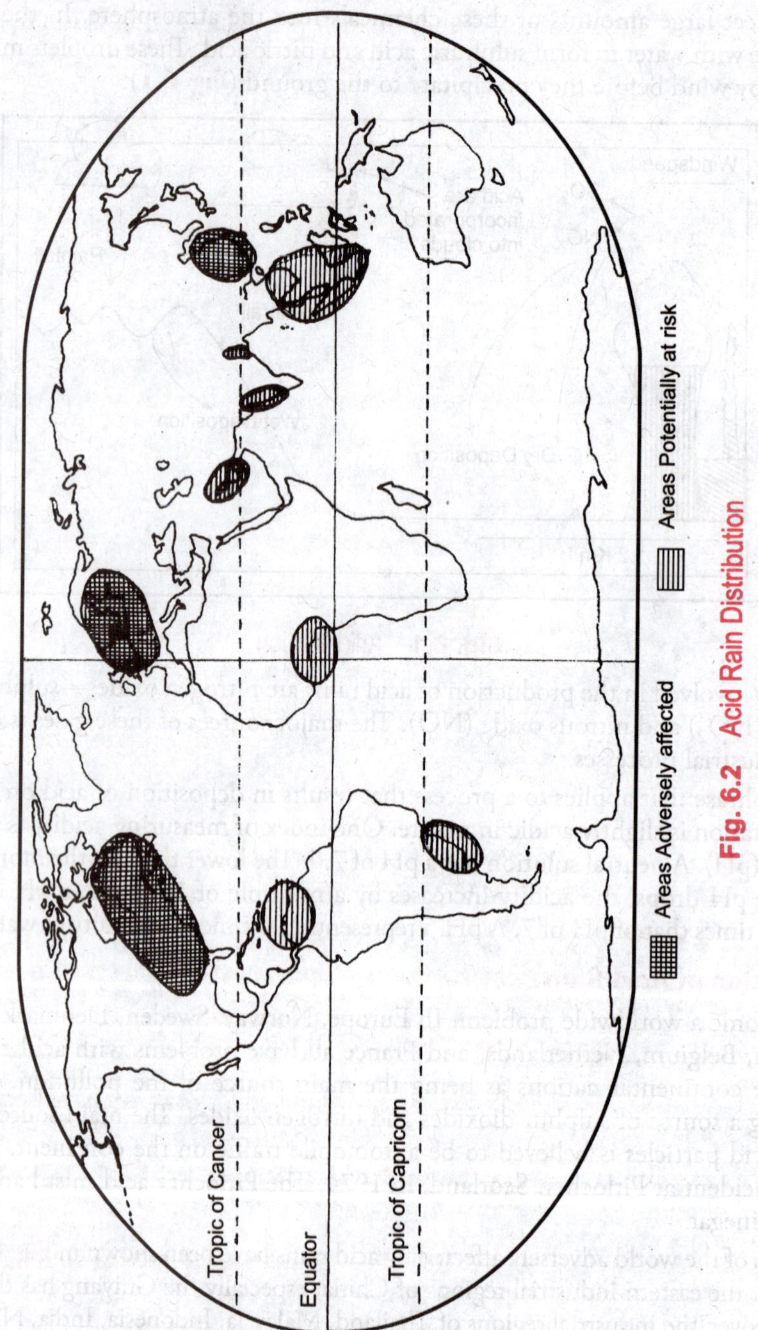

Fig. 6.2 Acid Rain Distribution

Impact of Acid Rain on Precipitation

The impact of acid rain on aquatic environments, particularly fresh water lakes, has been clearly established. Aquatic systems, especially fish are very susceptible to acidification. Fish become endangered when pH drops to about 5.5. Most species of fish stop reproducing at pH levels between 5.3 and 5.6.

The sensitivity of lakes to acidification depends on their natural ability to neutralize the acidic runoff into the lake. Lakes located in the areas where the parent rock is igneous and metamorphic, containing lots of silicates are most sensitive to acid deposition. The dissolved minerals from these rocks result in acidic runoff. In regions where the parent rock is high in mineral salts such as calcium, magnesium, and phosphorus, lakes can better tolerate the acid runoff. The reason is that the soil solution tends more toward alkaline and the salts neutralize the acid.

All over the world, there are more than 1000 lakes that have become too acidic to support aquatic life. The worst affected lakes of Northern Europe (Scandinavian countries) have been shown in **Fig. 6.3**.

The impact of acidic rain on terrestrial ecosystem is less than clear as compared to aquatic ecosystem. According to the experts, there is widespread forest damage in North-east, North America, North-West Europe, Germany, East China, and the Western Ghats of India.

It may be that the damage is done through acidification of the soil. When soils become more acidic, there are more dissolved metals in the soil water taken in by the tree roots and there is less decomposition of organic matter in the soil. In fact, the acid rain may result in leaching of potassium, calcium, magnesium and other chemical elements from the soil which may result into the death of trees and forests.

In addition to these, the buildings made of marble and limestone are also adversely affected. The famous structure suffering from solution by acidic precipitation is the Taj Mahal in India. Many of the historical monuments in Athens have also been damaged by acidic precipitation. From the human health point of view, the cases of asthma, pneumonia and respiratory problems are frequent in regions of acidic rain.

The acid-rain-water reach rivers, lakes, and wetlands which adversely affect plant and animal life adversely. Acid rain and dry acid deposition damage marble structures like Taj Mahal in India and the Parthanon in Greece.

Acid, along with other chemicals in the air, produces urban smog which causes respiratory problems.

Measures to Check Effects of Acidic Precipitation

Both in the developed and developing countries various remedial measures have been taken to reduce the adverse affect of acidic precipitation. Some of the remedial steps are:

(i) Curtailing the emission of harmful gases and substances from the thermal and other chemical plants.

(ii) Compelling the industries to use better quality of coal which has low emission level of sulphur and other harmful substances.

(iii) Using alternate technologies for efficient use of fossil fuels.

(iv) Implementation of the environmental pollution laws more effectively.

(v) Environmental Impact Assessment on plants, animals, humanity and ecology before the establishment of any major or minor industry.

(vi) Public awareness about acidic rain and its impact on economy, society and ecology.

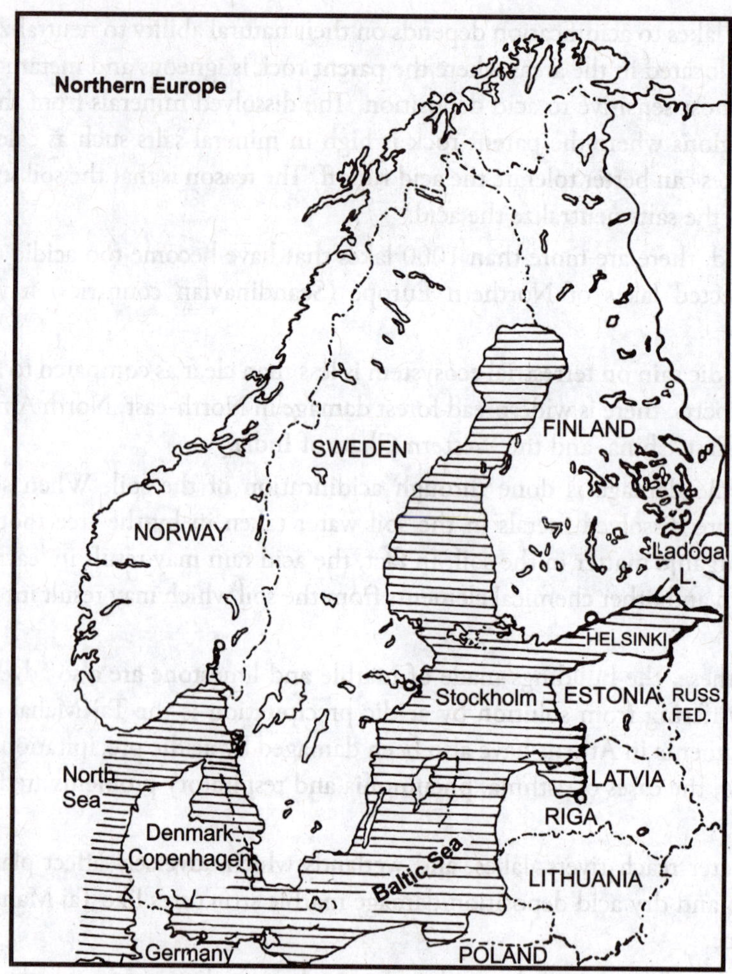

Fig. 6.3 Acid Rain and adversely affected lakes of Scandinavia

Ozone Depletion

Ozone is a form of oxygen in which three atoms of oxygen combine to form a single molecule of ozone. Ozone normally is not abundant in the lower atmosphere under natural conditions. It does, however, form in smog by the action of sunlight on oxides of nitrogen and organic compounds. This ozone does not stay in the air for very long. It reacts with other gases in the atmosphere and changes to normal oxygen molecules.

Ozone exists in the stratosphere, though the total amount is small. It is concentrated in a layer between 20 and 50 kilometres. The ozone is continually formed and then removed. The process that forms ozone is the absorption of ultraviolet radiation in the range from 0.1 to 0.3 microns in length. The position of ozone in the stratosphere and the processes of its depletion have been shown in Fig. 6.4.

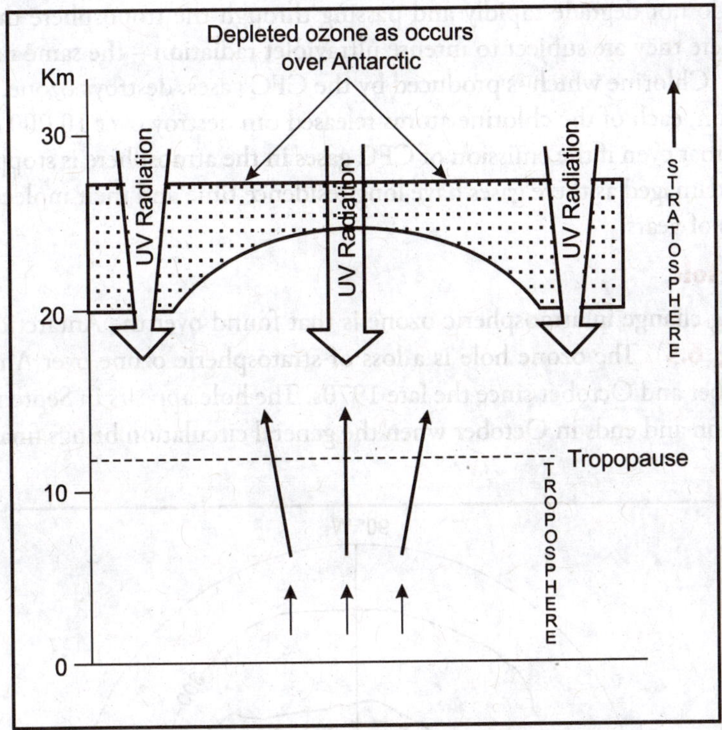

Fig. 6.4 Ozone Depletion

The presence of ozone in the atmosphere is particularly important because it filters out incoming ultraviolet (UV) radiation and thus acts as a screen against ultraviolet B (UV-B) radiation that can increase the occurrence of skin cancer, cataracts and other diseases of eyes. The UV-B rays also suppress the body defence mechanism which increases vulnerability to a variety of infectious diseases.

The problem of ozone depletion was first identified in 1970s due to the advent of supersonic aircraft which fly in the lower stratosphere and which emit nitrogen oxides. Subsequently, it was established that the major cause of ozone depletion is the CFC gases. The compounds of CFC gases are non-toxic, non-flammable and chemically inert gases. These properties make them useful for a wide range of applications including refrigerants, foaming agents, plastic manufacturing, fire extinguishing agents, solvents for freezing food, cleaners for electronic components fine retardant, solvents, aerosol propellants, and the production of foamed plastics.

CFCs is widely used because of its properties like non-corrosiveness, non-inflammability, low toxicity and chemical stability.

CFCs cannot be eliminated from the atmosphere by the usual scavenging processes like photodissociation, oxidation and rain out. The residence time of CFCs in the atmosphere is estimated to be between 40 to 150 years. During this period, the CFCs move upwards by random diffusion, from the troposphere to stratosphere.

The CFC gases do not degrade rapidly and passing through the troposphere they eventually enter into stratosphere, here they are subject to intense ultraviolet radiation – the same radiation is absorbed by ozone (**Fig. 6.4**). Chlorine which is produced by the CFC gases, destroys ozone. In a chain reaction of oxygen destruction, each of the chlorine atoms released can destroy over 10,000 ozone molecules. It has been estimated that even if the emission of CFC gases in the atmosphere is stopped, the ozone layer will continue to be damaged as these gases have long residence time and their molecules do not dissolve even after hundreds of years.

Antarctic Ozone Hole

The most disturbing change in atmospheric ozone is that found over the Antarctica Continent called the *'ozone hole'* (**Fig. 6.5**). The ozone hole is a loss of stratospheric ozone over Antarctica, which has occurred in September and October since the late 1970s. The hole appears in September when sunlight first reaches the region and ends in October when the general circulation brings final summer warming over Antarctica.

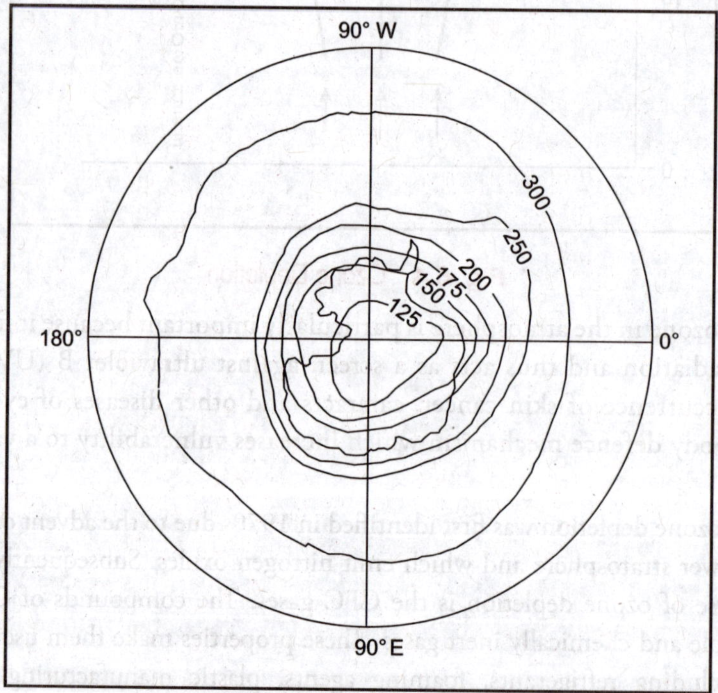

The Antarctic ozone hole over the Southern Hemisphere on September 28 1992 as measured by the total ozone Mapping Spectrum (TOMS) aboard the Nimbus – 7 Source : Hiddore, J.J, *Global Environmental Change,* 1996, Printice Hall (N. J.)

Fig. 6.5 The Antarctic Ozone-hole

In August and September 1996, the amount of ozone over the Antarctica reached the lowest level recorded to this date. In this year, the ozone hole, covered nearly half of the Antarctic Continent (**Fig. 6.5**).

In the winter over Antarctica, a very large mass of extremely cold, dry air keeps out the relatively warmer air surrounding the continent. This cold air gets even colder during the winter months when there is no sunlight. Temperature in Antarctica falls as low as –84°C. In the extreme cold, moisture condenses into ice-crystals and nitric acid crystals also form. These crystals form very high thin clouds called as 'mother of pearl' on *polar stratospheric clouds* (PSCs). The cloud crystals play a very important role in the chemistry of the CFCs and ozone depletion. The nitrogen oxide crystals drop out of the stratosphere leaving behind the chlorine and bromine compounds and the ice crystals. The chemical processes are more rapid where there is a surface on which the reaction can take place. Ice particles are good surfaces and are some 10 times as efficient as the surface of water droplets. This partially explains the speed with which the process takes place in the Antarctic spring. It also explains why the process is less effective in low latitudes.

The chemical process begins when sunlight appears in the spring. The warming increases the rate of chemical reactions, and chlorine destroys ozone at a rapid rate. The depletion actually first begins near the Antarctic Circle, where sunlight begins to penetrate the stratosphere. It may begin here by mid-August. Spring over the South Pole occurs in September and October. During this time, the ozone level drops until there is no more ozone left or the clouds evaporate. There may be a total loss of up to 60 per cent of the ozone in the centre of the Antarctic hole. At some altitudes it is 90 per cent. Eventually, air from the surrounding regions flows into the area and ozone levels recover. Polar stratosphere clouds disappear with the spring warm up. The same process takes place elsewhere in the atmosphere, but at higher altitudes and at slower rates.

In the spring of 1991, record depletion of ozone occurred in the Antarctica. Record lows in ozone occurred in September. By mid-November, the system broke up and ozone levels recovered. The depletion usually takes place at altitude of 12 to 22 kilometres. This is the range where most of the polar stratosphere clouds form.

There are serious consequences of ozone depletion. Some of the important adverse consequences of ozone depletion are given below:

1. Plants and animals vary in their tolerance of ultraviolet rays. The ultraviolet rays damage DNA (the genetic code in every living cell). Crops like soybean are the worst affected.
2. Animals and humans also have adapted to the UVB radiation. In case of depletion of ozone layer, there is danger of melanoma (one type of skin cancer). The disease is now almost epidemic in the United States.

Some Basic Facts about Ozone Depletion

- Antarctic scientists experience the equivalent of 'standing under an ultraviolet lamp 24 hours a day'. Exposed skin quickly burns and swells, and certain protective clothing deteriorates rapidly.
- During the months of Antarctic spring, ozone concentrations approach almost total depletion in the stratosphere over an area twice the size of Antarctic continent. The protective ozone layer is being depleted over southern South America, southern Africa, southern parts of Australia, and New Zealand.

- Antarctic researchers have recorded steady losses in the ozone layer since 1970, noting a huge temporary decrease every September–October. Each year, the '*ozone hole*' widens and deepens. In addition to ground based measurements, NOAA satellites also recorded this alarming situation.
- At Earth's opposite pole, a similar ozone depletion over the Arctic exceeded 35 per cent in 1989. Losses have increased in each subsequent year. Since 1992, the Canadian Government regularly reports an 'ultraviolet index'.
- Environment Canada measured an 8 per cent loss in normal ozone levels in 1993, with greatest thinning between January and April when it dropped to 14 per cent below normal. Extreme lows of 22 per cent below normal were achieved in March 1993 over Toronto and Edmonton. This produced increases in ultraviolet radiation at the surface.
- In 1994, Environment Canada opened a new scientific observatory to monitor the ozone losses over Canada. This high Arctic facility is at a remote weather station on Ellesmere Island, NWT, about 1000 km from the North Pole.
- Over all losses in the middle latitudes are continuing at 6 to 8 per cent per decade. In North America, related skin cancers are increasing at an alarming 10 per cent per year now totalling more than 8,00,000 cases annually with over 10,000 malignant melanoma deaths. Most affected are light skinned persons who live at higher latitudes and higher elevations and those who work principally outdoor.
- Other potential problems related to increased ultraviolet radiation include eye tissue damage, reduced immunity, crop damage, and injury to some aquatic life-forms. Losses of 6 to 12 per cent now are measured in the primary production of small light-using organisms (phytoplankton) in Antarctic water.

SALINISATION

The process of accumulation of soluble salts in upper soil horizons is known as Salinisation. Though there are many plants that can grow in salt-rich soils, many plants grown as crops cannot do so effectively. In dry-lands, especially, attempts to increase crop production by irrigation can, in a matter of few years, result in salinisation, either because water application exceeds the amount which plant can use, and drainage is poor, or/and because high evapo-transpiration rates cause salt to be precipitated in the soil.

According to Thomas, the seriously affected areas of the world are largely confined to the semi-arid areas of Mesopotamia (Iraq), Nile Valley (Egypt), Indus Valley (Pakistan), San Joaquin Valley (California), The Syr and Amu Valleys in Uzbekistan, Kazakhstan and Turkmenistan, the lower reaches of Huang-He (Hwang-Ho) and Changjiang (Yangtse-Kiang) and the states of Punjab, Haryana, Rajasthan and Uttar Pradesh of India.

In several semi-arid areas, the saline affected soils have been reclaimed for agriculture by the application of gypsum with cow-dung, and by the cultivation of green manuring crops. Though remedial measures may be attempted, including efforts to flush excess salts out of the soil, salinisation may simply be a facet of attempting to increase crop yields in environments generally unsuited to agriculture.

DESERTIFICATION OR DESERTISATION

Desertification is a term coined by the French forester Abbeville in 1949 to describe land degradation. A number of definitions have been given of desertification but the approved definition was given by Thomas and Middleton in 1994. In 1995, the UN Convention to Combat Desertification (CCD) was signed; it has since been ratified by the governments of over 150 countries.

In the Convention to Combat Desertification (CCD), *desertification is defined as land degradation in arid, semi-arid, and dry-sub-humid areas resulting from various factors including climatic variations and human activities*. The problem is therefore confined to the susceptible drylands, with land degradation regarded as soil erosion, internal soil changes, depletion of groundwater reserves and irreversible changes to vegetation communities.

Though the Convention to Combat Desertification (CCD) definition includes possible multiple causes for desertification, it is undoubtedly the case that the principal agent of degradation is human actions.

The regions of severe desertification of arid-lands have been shown in Fig. 6.6. The spatial patterns of desertification show that the tropical and sub-tropical lands are more prone to desertification. According to an estimate made by the United Nations, about 40 per cent of the African continent's non-desert land is in danger of desert. Nearly 33 per cent of Asia's land and about 20 per cent of Latin America's land are similarly endangered. According to the National Environment Policy, 2006, the Indian Desert Ecosystem (arid and semi-arid region) occupy about 38.8 per cent of the total area of India, which spreads over 10 states of the country.

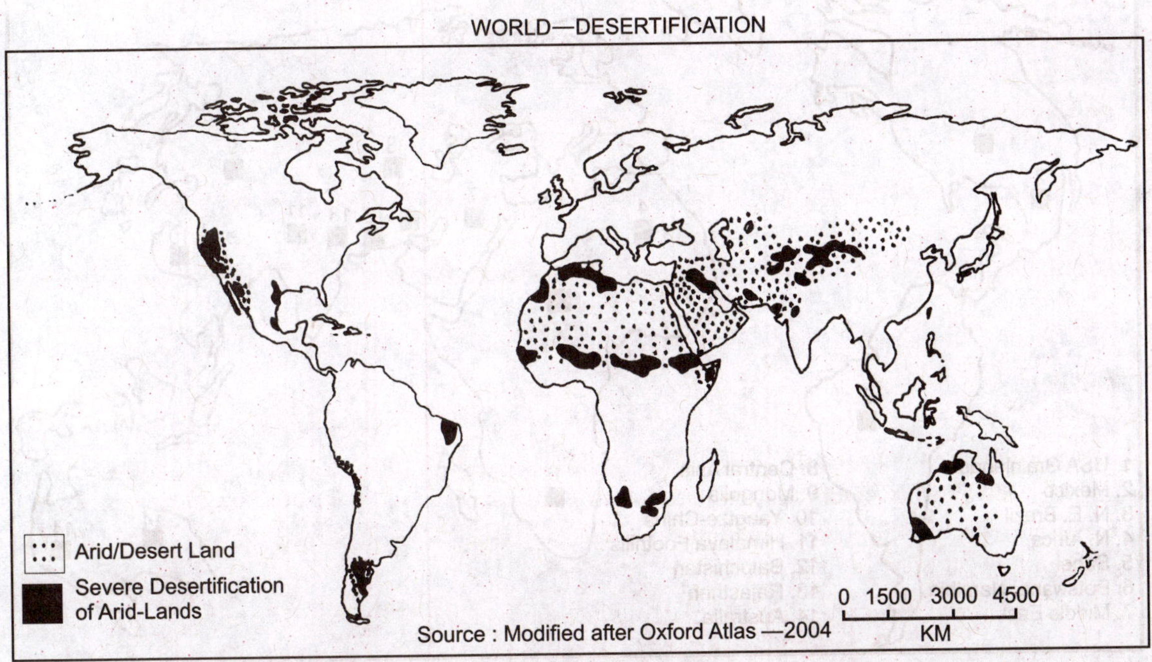

Fig. 6.6 Severe Desertification Regions of the World

In countries where desertification is particularly extensive and severe are Jordan, Lebanon, Somalia, Ethiopia, Southern Sudan, Chad, Mali, Mauritania, and Western Sahara. The Sahel region of Africa suffers severe drought after every two years. In the decade of 1990 it recorded one of the worst drought as a result of which the crop production was minimal and thousands of people died because of starvation. The resulting threat of starvation spurs population of the affected areas to increase their farming and livestock pressure on the denuded land, further contributing to their desertification. It has been suggested that Mali may be the first country in the world rendered uninhabitable by environmental destruction.

SOIL EROSION

The natural process of removal of top soil mainly by water and wind is known as soil erosion. It is a process whose rates may be magnified by humans (accelerated erosion). On a global scale the fastest rates occur in zones with highly seasonal precipitation, as in monsoonal, Mediterranean and semi-arid climates.

The rate of soil erosion in a given region is influenced by: (i) rainfall efficiency to erode, (ii) volume of run off, (iii) wind strength, (iv) relief, (v) slope angle, (vi) slope length, (vii) slope shortening (terrace, ridges), (viii) length of wind fetch, and (ix) shelter belts. The rate of soil erosion also depends on the pressure of population on arable land, cropping patterns, fallowing, crop rotation, land management, tillage practices and application of chemical fertilisers. In brief, at present, the main anthropogenic causes which accelerate soil erosion are deforestation, intensification of agriculture, urbanisation, poverty, fire, war, mining, and tourism.

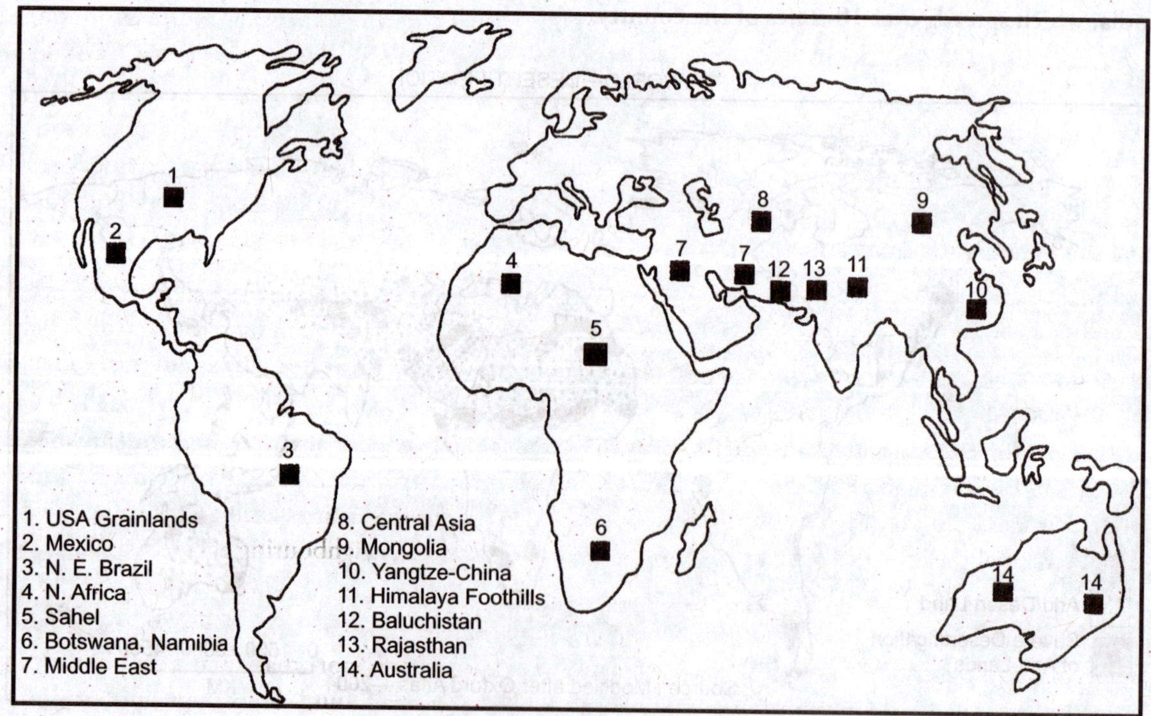

Fig. 6.7 World Areas of Major Soil Erosion

The worst affected areas of soil erosion have been shown in Fig. 6.7. These areas include: 1. USA Grainlands (Prairies), 2. Central Mexico, 3. North-East Brazil, 4. North Africa (Egypt, Libya, Algeria, Tunisia and Morocco), 5. Sahel region of Africa stretching over Somalia, Ethiopia, southern Sudan, Chad, Niger, Mali, Mauritania, and Western Sahara, 6. Botswana and Namibia, 7. Middle-East, 8. Central Asia (Kazakhstan, Turkmenistan, Uzbekistan, etc.), 9. Mongolia, 10. Yangtze-Hwang Ho basins of China, 11. Himalayan region (Siwalik and Lesser Himalayas), 12. Baluchistan, 13. Rajasthan (Thar Desert), and 14. the desert and semi-arid regions of Australia.

Types of Soil Erosion

The experts of soil sciences classify soil erosion into the following three categories, namely: (i) sheet erosion, (ii) rill erosion, and (iii) gully erosion.

(i) **Sheet Erosion:** It refers to sheet washing. It means a uniform removal of soil layers over the entire segment of the sloping area. The unprotected lands are most susceptible to sheet erosion. Sheet erosion gradually and imperceptibly develops into rill erosion.

(ii) **Rill Erosion:** Rills are small ephemeral channels that often form in sub-parallel sets on sloping agricultural land in response to intense run-off. They are also common on steep and unprotected surfaces, lie along the roads and other earth embankments. Rills erosion is more visible than sheet erosion, and does more damage to agricultural and grazing lands. It is more frequent in the soils with more silt content. Rill erosion ultimately take the shape of gully erosion.

(iii) **Gully Erosion:** Gully is a deep sided channel, often several meters deep, that is cult into poorly consolidated bedrock, weathered sediment or soil. Gully erosion is the pronounced erosion, by ephemeral streams, of soils and other poorly consolidated sediments, producing a network of steep-sided channels. The Chambal ravines (catchment area of Chambal River in Rajasthan, Madhya Pradesh, and Uttar Pradesh) are the typical examples of gully erosion. Gully erosion is also pronounced in the Colorado River and along some of the tributaries of the Nile River (Egypt and Sudan), Rio-Grande (North America), Mekong River and Parana rivers (South America).

According to one estimate 75,000 million tones of productive soil is eroded all over the world annually. In India, the problem of soil erosion is quite serious as about 6000 million tons of soil is being eroded annually. In China and India more than 60 per cent of their cultivated land is adversely affected by water and wind erosion.

Soil erosion not only affects the areas from which soil is removed, but also the environment where it is deposited. Such deposits, if take place in lakes and ponds, destroy the aquatic ecosystems by adding more nutrients, notably nitrogen and phosphorus. Since soil erosion is irreversible, it is imperative to adopt remedial measures to combat soil erosion and to protect the neighbouring agro-ecosystems.

SOIL CONSERVATION

Soil is one of the most important resources available to mankind. Still more than 50 per cent of the total population of the world is directly or indirectly dependent on agriculture. Soil is not only providing food, clothing and raw materials for industries, the very survival of humanity depends on it.

Soil conservation has been defined differently by different scholars. In simple words, soil conservation means that the land resource base be used rationally and scientifically. The ultimate objective of soil conservation is to keep the land resource base in a healthy and sustainable condition. Soil conservation can be done effectively by adopting the following measures:

(i) Rotation of Crops

A scientific rotation of crops can help significantly in the reduction of soil erosion. Scientific rotation of crops means the sowing of soil exhaustive crops followed by soil enriching (nitrogen fixing) crops. For example, rice, wheat, maize, etc. are the soil exhaustive crops. After their harvest a leguminous crop like pulses (peas, lentil, gram, etc.) should be sown. Such a rotation of crops helps in maintaining the soil fertility. In monoculture (only rice or only sugarcane cultivation year after year), some of the nutrients of soil are exhausted, consequently, the rate of soil erosion gets accelerated.

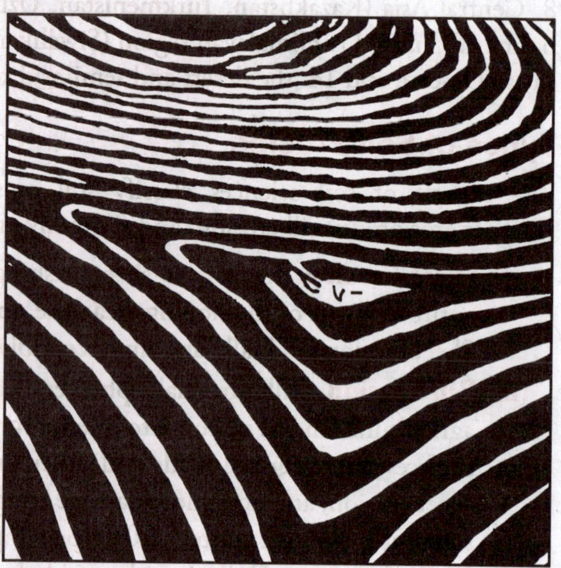

Fig. 6.8 Contour Farming

(ii) Contour Ploughing

In this type of agriculture, crops are planted/ sown in relatively narrow strips across the slope of the land. It is the most effective form of soil conservation, especially in the hilly and sloppy lands. In contour ploughing, the strips are planted on contours at right angle (90°) to the direction of natural slope. The main objective of contour ploughing is to reduce the capacity of run off or wind to erode and carry away the soil (Fig. 6.8)

(iii) Strip Cropping

In strip cropping, crops are grown in alternate strips, parallel to one another. Some strips may be allowed to lie fallow while others are sown to different kinds of crops, e.g. grains, grasses, oilseeds, legumes and vegetable. The various crops ripen at different times of the year and are harvested at intervals. This ensures that at no time will the entire area be left bare or exposed. The tall-growing crops work as wind-breaks and the strips, which are often parallel to the contours, help to increase water absorption by the soil by slowing down run-off (Fig. 6.9).

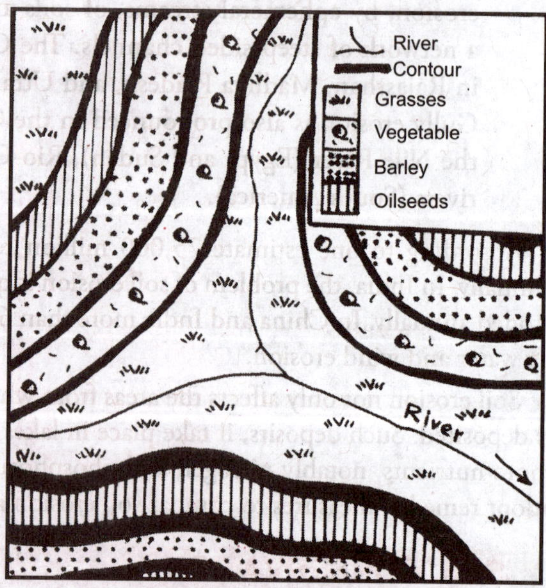

(Modified after Leong, G. C. and Morgan, G. C., 1985 PP.139–140)

Fig. 6.9 Strip Cultivation following Contour Pattern

(iv) Green Manuring

Cultivation of green manuring crops can reduce soil erosion appreciably. Some of the green manuring crops used in India are jute, *sani*, *dhaincha, barseem, rizka,* clover, alfafa, and other green fodder crops.

(v) Use of Organic Manures

Use of organic manures, like cow-dung, straw, mulch, stalks of maize, millets, bulrush millets, wheat barley, potato plants are all good to enhance the fertility of soil and to reduce the rate of soil erosion.

(vi) Terraced Farming

Terraced cultivation is a good technique to control soil erosion especially in the hilly and sloppy areas. Terraced cultivation is generally adopted in case of gentle hill slope (<30°) The Angami tribe of Nagaland has developed some of the most beautiful terraced fields up to the slope of 45° around the town of Kohima, Nagaland (**Fig. 6.10**).

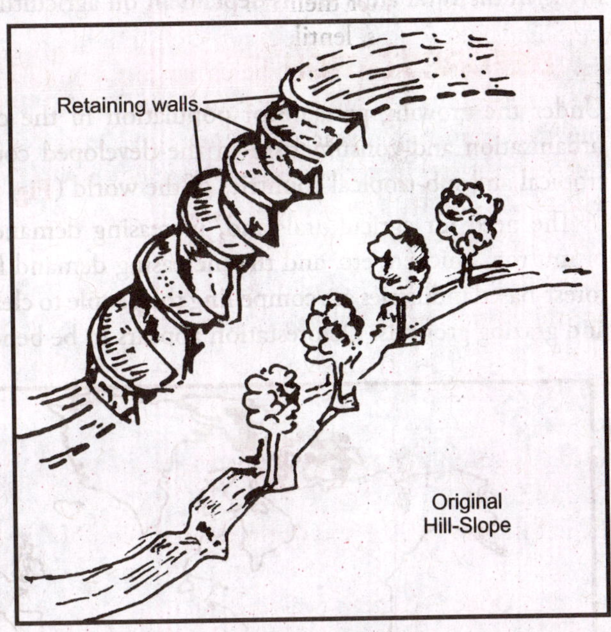

Two Ways of terracing steep hill slopes to check soil erosion (after Leong, G. C. and Morgan G. C. 1985, p.140)

Fig. 6.10 Two ways of terracing steep hill slopes

(vii) Mixed Cropping

In the mixed cropping, different crops are grown in the same field at the same time with varying maturity periods. For example, in India maize and pulses (leguminous crops), wheat and gram, millets and pulses, cotton and gram, etc. are frequently mixed to assure the returns from agriculture and to reduce the rate of soil erosion.

(viii) Crop Diversification

This practice is often like crop rotation in that it helps to maintain soil fertility. While annually harvested crops are grown they can be altered in the field. Crop diversification is better than monoculture. In monoculture (one crop, like rice only year after year) exhaust the soil nutrients, thereby making soil more vulnerable to soil erosion. Crop diversification is a good practice to check the soil erosion.

(ix) Mulching of Fields

After the harvest of the crop the field needs to be covered by mulch which can reduce the rate of soil erosion. In fact, the uncovered fields are more exposed to wind and water erosion.

(x) Development of Wind Breaks

Planting of trees in lines in the arid and semi-arid areas can reduce the wind erosion in the deserts.

(xi) Prevention of Shifting Cultivation

Checking and reducing shifting cultivation by persuading the tribal people to switch over to settled agriculture is a very effective method of soil conservation. This can be done by making arrangements for their resettlement which involves the provision of residential accommodation, agricultural implements, seeds, manures, cattle and reclaimed land.

If the above methods are adopted collectively, the problem of soil erosion can be solved significantly in different parts of the world, especially in India where still about 70 per cent of the population is living in the rural areas and is dependent on agriculture.

DEFORESTATION

Under the growing pressure of population in the developing countries and over industrialisation, urbanisation and consumerism in the developed countries, there is large scale deforestation in the tropical and sub-tropical countries of the world (**Fig. 6.11**).

The need for agricultural land, increasing demand for fuel and commercial wood, consumption of mutton, chicken, etc. and the increasing demand for agricultural raw materials for agro-based and forest-based industries are compelling the people to clear the forests to bring more area under cultivation and grazing grounds. Deforestation appears to be beneficial to a country because it raises GNP (Gross

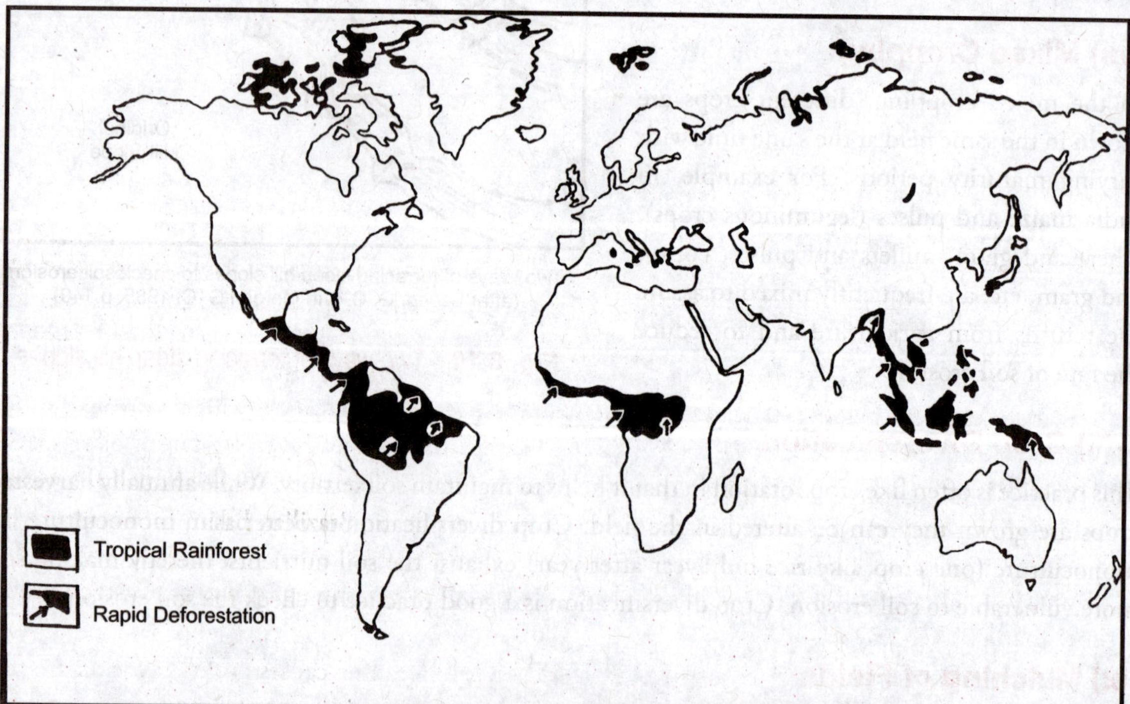

Fig. 6.11 Deforestation in Tropical World

National Product) through the production of pulp, paper, timber, furniture, and charcoal. However, GNP does not measure the negative impacts of deforestation, such as soil erosion, flooding, siltation, salinisation, global warming and climatic change. In the opinion of ecologists, deforestation is being considered as one of the leading causes of environmental degradation.

Factors Responsible for Deforestation

The main factors responsible for the rapid rate of deforestation are:

(i) Rapid growth of population in the developing countries.
(ii) Extension of agriculture and grazing lands.
(iii) Rising demand for lumber, timber, paper, pulp, fuel-wood and charcoal, and other forest products.
(iv) Industrialisation, urbanisation and consumerism in the developed and developing countries.
(v) Demand of raw material for the forest-based and agro-based industries.
(vi) Demand of land for infrastructural (roads, highways, railways, airways, irrigation, electricity and telecommunication services) facilities and civic amenities.
(vii) Construction of multi-purpose dams all over the world.
(viii) Practice of shifting cultivation in the humid-tropical regions of the world.
(ix) Change in food habits—more demand non-vegetarian-food, e.g. chicken, mutton, beef and pork.
(x) High rate of poverty in the third world countries. It is said that poverty directly or indirectly lead to deforestation.
(xi) Forest fires (natural and man made).
(xii) Acid rains.
(xiii) Delayed administrative decisions, and less effective implementation of forest laws, especially in the developing countries.

FAO Assessment of Deforestation

Although, public awareness of the impact of global deforestation has increased in recent years, it has not slowed the rate of deforestation appreciably. A comprehensive assessment of the state of the world's forest, recently released by the Food and Agriculture Organisation (FAO) of the United Nations (2002) indicates that the total forest area continues to decline significantly. According to the FAO analysis, deforestation was mainly concentrated in the developing countries, which lost nearly 200 million hectares between 1980 and 1995. This loss was partially offset by reforestation efforts, raw forest plantations, and the gradual regrowth and expansion of forested areas in the developed countries.

In brief, deforestation rates remain high in many countries. In the Brazilian basin, for example, the annual deforestation rate declined from a peak of more than 20,000 sq. km. in 1988 to just over 11,000 sq km in 1991. However, newly released data from the Brazilian government shows that it redounded to more than 30,000 sq. km. in 2010.

The Food and Agriculture (FAO) analysis concludes that the leading causes of deforestation are the extension of subsistence agriculture (more common in Asia, Africa and Central American countries), and government-backed conversion of forests to other land uses, such as large scale ranching in Australia,

Brazil and other Latin American countries. Poverty, joblessness and inequitable distribution of land also force many landless peasants to invade the forest for lack of other economic means of subsistence. Often, people move into forest areas as logging activity creates roads that open, formerly inaccessible regions.

Consequences of Deforestation

Continued forest loss and degradation is having serious implications at the local, regional, national and global levels. Some of the consequences of deforestation are given below:

(i) Soil erosion, (ii) floods, (iii) desertification, (iv) loss of biodiversity, (v) Decrease in forest products like fruits, nuts, medicinal plants, wood and timber, (vi) drying up of springs in the mountains, (vii) alteration in the rate of albedo, (viii) spread of certain disease because of global warming, (ix) aesthetic loss, (x) climatic change.

WASTE DISPOSAL

The countries of the world are increasingly becoming industrialised and urbanised. The industrial society produces an ever increasing variety and quantity of toxic wastes. Traditionally, people have used fresh water to remove and dilute solid and liquid wastes, and have used the atmosphere to dilute the gaseous waste products of combustion. Until recently, however, people generally have been unaware that a local natural system of waste disposal can become saturated, creating an unhealthy environment.

The waste products are in the Earth's natural systems and will remain in them. The problem is made particularly acute by such business practices as planned obsolescence, use of throw away containers, the hard sell of new models of old products and adoption of throw away culture. In addition, high labour costs often make it uneconomical to repair, reclaim and recycle used items, so the volume of waste grows unnecessarily at a staggering rate. The replacement of products, of course, greatly reduces natural resources. Unfortunately waste is not just a by-product. Eventually, it is a product itself.

Waste disposal has many geologic ramifications. If waste is buried, the quality of groundwater is threatened. If it is dumped into streams and rivers, it accumulates on the beaches deltas and estuaries altering the environment of the ocean. Previous methods of waste elimination have not been '*waste disposal*'; they have been '*waste dispersal*'. Any significant solution of the problem of elimination must consider what kinds of waste disposal and dispersal a given geologic environment can accommodate, without critical alterations in geologic, hydraulic and biological conditions. A brief account of the (i) solid, (ii) liquid, (iii) gaseous, and (iv) nuclear waste disposal has been given in the following:

(i) Solid Wastes

Solid wastes are disposed off in many ways, including land-filling, incinerating, composting, open dumping, animal feeding, fertilising and dumping in the oceans. Solid waste consist of highly heterogeneous mass of discarded materials from the urban and rural communities as well as the more homogeneous accumulation of discarded materials from agricultural and industrial activities. Essentially the solid waste comes from (i) agriculture, (ii) urban waste, (iii) industrial waste, (iv) social/domestic waste – garbage, rubbish and animals as pathological waste.

Efficient collection and transportation are essential parts of the overall solid waste management programme since these two activities account for about 75% of the total cost of solid waste management. In India, many different types of vehicles, e.g. handcarts, tractors and modern mechanised vehicles are used for garbage collection. The collected solid waste is carried to the disposal site.

The Solid waste disposal has several adverse environmental consequences. The geologic consequences include change in environment, especially that of rivers, lakes, ponds and underground-water where the mass of waste is concentrated. The major problems with solid waste disposal involves site's hydrologic characteristics. These include the porosity and permeability of rock in which the fill is located. The altered topography associated with dumps and landfills is also critical because it can change the drainage and groundwater conditions. In fact, the most critical contamination problem is created as water passes through a landfill, dissolve organic and inorganic compounds enter the underground water-table.

(ii) Liquid Waste

Liquid waste mostly produced by industries. It may be (i) hazardous and (ii) non-hazardous. The hazardous industrial waste may be solid or liquid. Traditionally, liquid waste have been discharged into surface drainage systems and diluted. Liquid waste ultimately accumulate in lakes, seas and oceans, where they are stored. As the volume of liquid waste increases, the capacity of the natural water system to dilute it is overwhelmed, and the drainage system becomes a system of moving waste.

One of the subtle type of liquid pollutant is the hot water created by cooling systems in power plants and factories. Although, the water itself is not contaminated, the temperature alone is enough to alter the biological conditions in the streams and lakes into which it flows. Such pollution is called *thermal pollution*.

Oil-Pollution

The oceans, seas, gulfs and bays are increasingly polluted by natural seeps of oil in large quantities (Fig. 6.12). The amount of oil entering the ocean has increased greatly in recent years, because of our growing dependence on marine transportation for crude oil, petroleum and petroleum products, offshore drilling, near-shore refining, and street runoff carrying waste oil from automobiles.

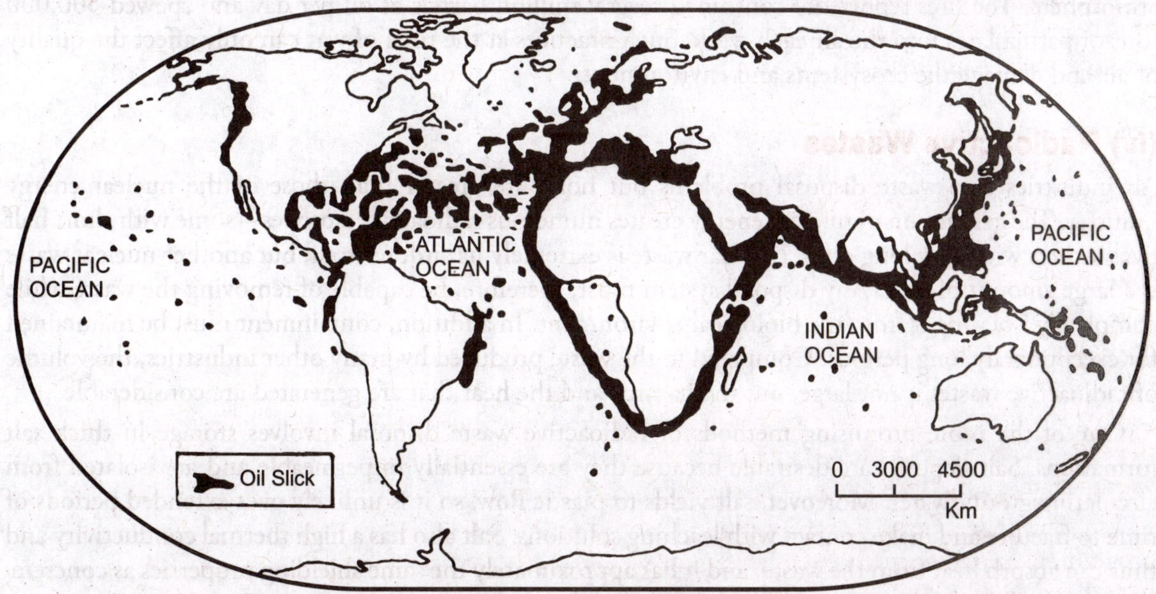

Fig. 6.12 Visible Oil slicks World-wide (after Christopherson, R.W., 1995, p.533)

It is difficult to generalise about the effects that concentrated release of oil and oil spill from a tanker, coastal storage, or will have in the marine environment. The consequences of spill vary with its location and proximity to shore; with the quantity and composition of the oil; with the season of the year, ocean-currents, and weather conditions at the time of release; and with the composition and diversity of affected communities. Intertidal and shallow-water sub-tidal communities are most sensitive to the effects of an oil spill.

Spills of crude oil are generally larger in volume and more frequent than spills of refined oil. Most components of crude oil do not dissolve easily in water, but those that do can harm the delicate juvenile organisms even in minute concentrations. The remaining in soluble components form sticky layers on the surface that prevent free diffusion of gases, clog adult organisms' feeding structures, and decrease the sunlight available for photosynthesis. Spills of refined oil, especially near shore where marine life is abundant, can be more disruptive for longer periods of time.

The best way to deal with oil pollution is to prevent it from happening in the first place. Tanker design is being modified to limit the amount of oil internationally released in transport. International co-operation is required to reduce the oil pollution for which Legislation at the UN level is imperative to limit new tankers construction.

(iii) Gaseous Waste

Heavy industrialisation, urbanisation and consumerism have produced a variety of gaseous waste and pollutants in the form of gases and minute liquid and solid particles that are suspended in the atmosphere. The problem is so severe in some areas that rain is made more acidic than normal by pollutant.

A dramatic example of air pollution is the oilfield fires in Kuwait that resulted from the 1991 Persian Gulf War. In this war 600 wells were ignited, sending clouds of thick, black smoke into the atmosphere. The fires reportedly consumed several million barrels of oil per day and spewed 500,000 tons of particulates into the air each week. Such practices at the time of war can only affect the quality of air and damage the ecosystems and environment.

(iv) Radioactive Wastes

All industries face waste disposal problems but none are greater than those of the nuclear energy industry. The generation of nuclear energy creates numerous radioactive isotopes – some with short half lives, others with very long ones. Nuclear waste is extremely hazardous itself, but another nuclear waste is a large amount of heat. Any disposal system must, therefore, be capable of removing the waste while completely isolating it from the biological environment. In addition, containment must be maintained for exceptionally long periods. Compared to the waste produced by many other industries, the volume of radioactive wastes is not large, but the hazards and the heat that are generated are considerable.

One of the more promising methods of radioactive waste disposal involves storage in thick salt formations. Salt deposits are desirable because they are essentially impermeable and are isolated from circulating groundwater. Moreover, salt yields to plastic flow, so it is unlikely over extended periods of time to fracture and make contact with leaching solutions. Salt also has a high thermal conductivity and thus can absorb heat from the waste, and it has approximately the same shielding properties as concrete. In theory radioactive wastes would be solidified and sealed in containers from 15 to 60 centimetres in diameter and as much as 3 metres in length. The containers would then be shipped to salt mines, in the stable interior of the continent, where seismic activity is minimal. There, they would be placed in holes drilled in a salt formation deep in the mine. When filled with waste, the hole would be packed with crushed salt and close.

ENVIRONMENTAL DEGRADATION AND WATER SCARCITY

The world's thirst for water is likely one of the most pressing issue of the 21st Century. Global water consumption rose six-fold between 1900 and 2000 – more than double the rate of population growth and continues to grow rapidly as agricultural, industrial, and domestic demand increases.

Looming Crisis

Globally, water supplies are abundant, but they are most unevenly distributed among and within continents and countries. In some areas, water withdrawals are so high, relative to supply, that surface water supplies are literally shrinking and groundwater reserves are being depleted faster than they can be replenished by precipitation.

This situation has already caused serious water shortage to develop in some regions, short-changing human water needs damaging aquatic ecosystems. An assessment in 2001 by the United Nations about the freshwater resources found that one-third of the world's population lives in countries experiencing moderate to high water stress.

The UN assessment makes clear that the global water situation will get considerably worse over the next 30 years without major improvements in the way water is allocated and used. In fact, the United Nations projects that the share of the world's population in countries undergoing moderate or high water stress could rise to two-thirds by 2025. Population growth and socio-economic development are currently driving a rapid increase in water demand, especially from the industrial and household sectors. Industrial water use, for instance, is predicted to double by 2025 if current growth trends persist.

Water use in agriculture is slated to increase as world food demand rises. Agriculture already accounts for about 70 per cent of water consumption worldwide, and the United Nations projects a 50 to 100 per cent increase in irrigation water need by 2025. Much of the projected increase in water demand will occur in developing countries in which population growth, industrialisation, urbanisation, and expansion of agriculture will be the greatest. The scarcity of water is accentuated because of the surface and underground water pollution. Eutrophication, heavy metals, acidification, persistent organic pollution have also aggravated the availability of drinking water in the third world countries.

Judicious Management of Water Resources is the Key

Better management of water resources is the key to mitigating water scarcities in the future and avoiding further damage to aquatic ecosystem. In the short term, more efficient use of water could dramatically expand available resources. In developing countries, for example, 60 to 75 per cent of irrigation water never reaches the crop and is lost to evaporation or runoff. Although the use of water efficient drip irrigation has increased 30 folds since the 1970s, it is still employed in less than 1 per cent of the world's irrigated areas.

In the long term, however, the UN assessment makes clear that looming water crisis in many regions must be addressed through hard policy decisions that reallocate water to the most economically and socially beneficial uses. Far greater emphasis on water efficient technologies and pollution control is also essential for the sustainability and conservation of water resources.

The UN study also highlights the potentially desperate situation of developing countries that combine high water stress with low per capita income. The majority of these countries are found in the arid or semi-arid regions of Africa and Asia. Many use most of their available water supplies for crop irrigation and suffer from a lack of pollution controls.

SUSTAINABLE DEVELOPMENT

Definition

In order to overcome the problems of environmental degradation and to reduce adverse consequences of global warming and climatic change, the concept of sustainable development has emerged after the Earth Summit (1992). The concept of sustainable development and its socio-ecological significance has been examined in the following.

Sustainable development has been defined differently by different social scientists. According to Brundtland sustainable development has been defined as *"the development that meets the needs of the present without compromising the ability of future generations to meet their own needs."* Sustainable development, therefore, implies protecting the environmental wealth, human capital stock, land, water and air, ecological biotic and abiotic resources, and socio-cultural and economic resource base. In the Earth Summit (Rio Conference, 1992) Agenda 21, particularly emphasised on biodiversity, water quality, eradication of poverty and role of females and children in sustainable development. *The main characteristics of sustainable development are:*

(i) Sustainability is the ability of development or an activity to continue in the long term without undermining that part of the environment which sustains it.
(ii) Sustainable development is the development that seeks to improve the quality of human life without undermining the quality of our natural resources and physical environment.
(iii) Sustainability implies that human use or enjoyment of world's natural and cultural resources should not, in overall terms, diminish or destroy them.

Sustainable development is the need of the day to make the ecosystems more productive and to maintain the resilience characteristics of biodiversity. In fact, the survival of mankind very much depends on the sustainability of resources and environment. The experts of population and environment are increasingly concerning on the issues of sustainable development. The main objectives of sustainable development is to maximise human well-being or quality of life without jeopardising the life support system. The measures of sustainable development may be different in the developed and developing countries according to their level of technological and economic development.

A Historical Perspective

The concept of sustainable development as quite old. Its importance has however, been significantly realised in the second part of the 20th Century. A brief description of the historical perspective of sustainable development has been given in the following paragraphs.

The United Nations (UNO) Conference on Human Development, commonly known as 'Stockholm Conference' was organised at Stockholm in 1972. In 1974, the famous book *'The Closing Circle'* was published by Barry in which he underscored the following points: (i) Everything is connected with everything, (ii) Everything must go somewhere, (iii) Nature knows best, (iv) There is no such thing as a free lunch.

Subsequently, the World Chapter for Nature was adopted by the United Nations General Assembly in 1982. Later on, the term '*sustainable development*' was incorporated by Brundtland Report '*Our Common Future*' which gave stress on the following:

(i) A political system for effective participation of citizens in decision making.
(ii) An economic system to generate surpluses and technologies on a self reliant and sustained basis.
(iii) A social system to resolve the ecological base for development.
(iv) A production system to preserve the ecological base for development.
(v) A technical system to search new solutions continually.
(vi) An administrative system which is flexible and capable of self correction.
(vii) An international system of faster sustainable patterns of trade and finance.

The Brundtland Report gives emphasis on the formulation of development strategies by all nations so as to achieve sustainable development. According to him sustainability would have to include the following:

1. Sustainable environment.
2. Sustainable world.
3. Sustainable human development.
4. Sustainable peace and development.
5. Sustainable consumption.
6. Sustainable technology.

Between 1980's and 1990's there had been several International Commissions and Conventions relating to sustainable development. The prominent among them were the following:

1. Montreal Protocol on Ozone Depletion, 1987
2. The Basel Convention on Hazardous Wastes, 1989
3. The Convention on Climate Change, 1992
4. The Biodiversity Convention 1992
5. The Earth Summit, 1992
6. The World Summit on Sustainable Development, Johannesburg, 2002

Eco-development

Eco-development is a concept of sustainable development in which all developmental activities are performed in such a way that regional ecological balance can be maintained. This was originally advocated by UNEP for environmental planning and was defined as 'development at regional and local levels consistent with the potentials of the area involved, with attention given to the adequate and rational use of natural resources, and to application of technological styles' (UNEP, 1975).

Basic Aspects of Sustainable Development

The rapid growth of population in the developing countries and consumerism in the developed countries resulted into the question of sustainable development. The main aspects which deserve special attention about sustainable development are: (i) biodiversity), (ii) greenhouse gases, (iii) disposal of hazardous and toxic waste, (iv) disposal of pollution generating industries and food, and (v) ecological security.

It has been increasingly realised by the ecologists that ecological base is deteriorating due to misuse of resources and irrational management of environment. The main causes of environmental degradation have been discussed in the preceding paragraphs.

Prerequisite of Sustainable Development

The basic need for sustainable development is the conservation of natural resources. For conservation the policy of development should be designed and implemented on the following points:

(i) The resilience characteristics of the renewable resources should not be damaged.
(ii) All the technological changes and planning strategy processes, as far as physically possible, must attempt to switch from non-renewable to renewable resource uses.
(iii) Formulate a phase out policy of the use of non-renewable resources.

Principles of Sustainability

The basic principles of sustainable development are as under:

1. Judicious and scientific use of resources: *Providing resources for today, and conserving them for tomorrow.*
2. Conservation of biological diversity.
3. Conservation of biological and cultural diversity.
4. Sustainable income from resources and environment.
5. Use of resources in such a way that social justice is done. The benefit of resources should reach the level of poor of the poorest.
6. Recycling of resources.
7. Qualitative development of human being, through good health, education and high per capita income.
8. Global rather than local, regional or national perspective of environmental issues.
9. Efficient use of resources by all sections of the society.
10. People must change their worldviews and value system. They should recognise that the natural resources are limited.
11. People all over the world should consider the needs of future generations more than we do now.
12. Strong community participation in the policies and practices of sustainable development.

Measurement of Sustainability

The sustainability of environment and resources is measured on the basis resilience characteristics of resources, energy efficiency, maintenance of cultural and biodiversity and human development. The main indicators of sustainability development have been given as under:

The sustainability of an ecosystem can be measured with the help of ecological, economic, social and cultural indicators. These indicators have been briefly described in the following:

1. **Ecological Indicators:** The ecological indicators include the land-use patterns, land-use changes, quality and quantity of biomass, quantity and quality of water, fertility and productivity of soil, and availability of energy and its management.
2. **Changing Patterns of Land Use and Land Cover:** With the help of revenue records, and remote sensing one can ascertain the existing patterns and the changes in the patterns of land use which can be utilise for making future projection.

3. **Biomass Quantity and Quality:** The quantity of biomass and its quality generated from the terrestrial and aquatic ecosystems are also the important indicators of sustainability of ecosystem.
4. **Water Quality and Quantity:** Water is the ultimate source required for the survival of organisms including human beings. Proper monitoring of the water quality and quantity in the fresh water bodies (rivers, lakes, ponds, underground, etc.) are also good indicators of sustainability of ecosystem and environment.
5. **Soil Fertility:** Judicious utilisation of soils and scientific rotation of crops indicate the productivity and sustainability of environment.
6. **Energy:** Energy is one of the most important components of ecosystem and environment. It is vital for the generation as well as sustenance of organic life. It includes both solar, fossil-fuel, geothermal wind, sea-waves and tidal energy. The ultimate source of energy in the ecosystem is the Sun. The availability, transition of energy surplus or deficit, renewable and non-renewable, consumptive and non-consumptive, existing and potential sources of energy in an ecosystem deserve careful examination.
7. **Economic Indicators:** The input output ratio is also a good indicator of sustainability. On a macro-level, the gross national product (GNP) is a unified indicator of the national development level.
8. **Social Indicator:** From the point of view of social indicators, the 'quality of life' is the most important indicator. Higher the standard of living, in general, better the sustainability of ecosystem. Evaluation of quality of life is, however, a complex indicator which demands careful examination of level of satisfaction, social empowerment, status of females and the prevailing socio-cultural values of the people.

   The most appropriate approach to sustainable development is an integrated approach through in-depth understanding of linkages between the ecological and social processes.

Role of Individuals in Sustainable Development

Each of us can make daily decisions that collectively make a difference and directly or indirectly help in maintaining the resilience characteristics of ecosystems and ultimately lead to sustainable development. *Some things we can do for environment protection are listed below:*

A. Energy

(i) Drive few kilometres. Ride your bicycle or walk. Use public transport system.

(ii) Replace lamps with smaller wattage light bulbs. Replace incandescent bulbs with compact fluorescent ones. Turn off lights in rooms not being used.

(iii) Purchase energy-efficient appliances and cars.

(iv) Check insulation and weather stripping around your house, and apartment. Keep thermostats relatively high in summer and low in winter.

(v) Check into alternative energy sources such as solar and wind power units.

(vi) Buy and use rechargeable batteries.

B. Food

(vii) Prefer to obtain food from the areas where cow-dung, compost and green-manures have been used by the farmers, though it is difficult in a country like India where food and vegetable crops are generally grown with the help of chemical fertilisers.

(viii) Consider how your food choices affect the forests, ecology, biodiversity and environment.

(ix) Raise a kitchen garden

(x) Buy bulk or unpackaged goods, or buy food in reusable containers.

C. Water

(xi) Use water-saving showerheads, sink faucet, and toilets.

(xii) Water lawns infrequently but thoroughly. Better yet, replace them with drought tolerant ground covers.

(xiii) Take shorter showers.

(xiv) Run full cloth-washer and dishwasher loads.

D. Toxic Materials and Pollutants

(xv) Check for toxic materials (old cans of paints, pesticides, engines-oil, pool chemicals, etc.) you may have around the house. Take them to an approved toxic waste receiving station/centre.

(xvi) Read labels. Buy the least toxic material available.

(xvii) Buy clothing that does not require dry cleaning. Dry clean only when necessary.

E. Recycling and Waste

(xviii) Recycle newspapers, cans, bottles, glass and plastics.

(xix) Buy products that are refillable and recyclable.

(xx) Volunteer your time in locality, and beach clean-up campaigns.

(xxi) Use cloth rags and diapers instead of paper diapers and paper towels.

(xxii) Take your grocery bags back to the market for another trip home.

F. Preservation of Life and the Environment

(xxiii) Afforestation.

(xxiv) Preserve open space. Establish and involve in parkland and open-space movements.

(xxv) Avoid CFCs. Check air conditioners to see if they leak.

(xxvi) Boycott organisations that violet sound environment practices.

(xxvii) Do not litter. Pack your trash out of campsites.

G. Other Things

(xxviii) Write to your legislators. Better yet, visit them.

(xxix) Get involved in environmental group such as Chipko Movement.

(xxx) Talk to your friend about environmental matters.

(xxxi) Buy quality goods. Purchase a well-built item, maintain it, repair it if possible, keep it forever.

(xxxii) Sit quietly on beach or in the park/ fields at sunset or sunrise.

(xxxiii) Read. Listen.

(xxxiv) Be positive about results. Be encouraged.

ENVIRONMENTAL POLLUTION

Introduction

Pollution has been defined differently by different scientists. Pollution has been defined as the release of substances and energy as waste products of human activities which result in changes, usually harmful within the natural environment. Pollution is a condition which ensues when environmental attributes become inimical to the normal existence of living organism. A contaminant is a substance foreign to an environment and capable of pollution within it. A contaminant has a source from which it is dispersed, usually by means of an atmospheric or aquatic pathway. During this process it may be tendered harmless by transformation. If this does not occur, the contaminant becomes a pollutant which has a target.

According to Mellanby (1972), while there are numerous instances of natural pollution (volcanic emission), the pollution resulting from human activity is more significant. In other words, after the Industrial Revolution, 1779, especially in the 20th Century most of the pollution is anthropogenic. There is no doubt that man has made the earth more productive; has generated a large variety of fauna and flora; has made the parts of the Earth free from epidemics, but at the same time, the human interaction with nature has created threats to human life itself by generating large quantities of pollutants. The over-interaction of man with environment in the form of deforestation, expansion and intensification of agriculture, industrialisation and urbanisation and construction of infrastructure have polluted the atmosphere to the level that the very survival of mankind is at stake.

At present, environmental pollution is a serious problem. Air, water and soil are essential for the survival of life on Earth, but unfortunately pollution is causing them irreparable damage. Beyond certain limits, air pollution may cause illness and even deaths. Polluted water damage the aquatic ecosystems especially fish and microorganisms. Soil pollution reduces the amount of land available for the cultivation of crops, fruits and vegetables. All these factors have led the people to become conscious about and aware of adverse effects of pollution.

Pollutant

A pollution is defined as any form of energy, or matter or action that causes disequilibrium state from equilibrium state in any existing natural ecosystem. Pollutants are divided on different bases into various types as follows:

1. On the basis of source and genesis, pollutants are divided into two types:
   (i) natural pollutants, and
   (ii) man-made pollutants.
2. Pollutants can also be divided on the basis of visibility:
   (i) visible pollutants e.g. smoke, gases, dust, etc.
   (ii) invisible pollutants, e.g. bacteria, toxic chemicals mixed with water and soils etc.
3. Pollutants may also be classified as solid, liquid or gaseous.
4. Pollutants may be:
   (i) physical
   (ii) cultural, and
   (iii) biological

A pollutant causes damage by interfering directly or indirectly with the biochemical processes of an organism. Some pollution-induced changes may be instantly lethal; other changes may weaken an organism over weeks or months, or alter the dynamics of population of which it is part, or gradually unbalance the entire community.

In most cases, an organism's response to a particular pollutant will depend on its sensitivity to the *combination* of quantity and toxicity of that pollutant. Some pollutants are toxic to organisms in tiny concentrations. For example, the photosynthetic ability of some species of diatoms is diminished when chlorinated hydrocarbon compounds are present in parts-per-trillion quantities. Other pollutants seem harmless, as when fertilisers flowing from agricultural land stimulate plant growth in estuaries. Still other pollutants may be hazardous to some organisms but not to others. For example, crude oil interferes with the delicate feeding structure of zooplanktons and coats the feather birds, but it simultaneously serves as a feast for certain bacteria.

Pollutants also vary in their persistence; some reside in the environment for thousands of years, while others last only a few minutes. Some pollutants break down into harmless substances spontaneously or through physical processes (like the shattering of large molecules by sunlight). Sometimes pollutants are removed from the environment through the biological activity. For example, some marine organisms escape permanent damage by metabolising hazardous substances to harmless ones. Indeed many pollutants are ultimately biodegradable, that is, able to be broken down by natural processes into simpler compounds. Most pollutants, however, resist attack by water, air, sunlight, or living organisms because the synthetic compounds of which they are composed resemble nothing in nature.

The ways in which pollutants are changing the atmosphere, lithosphere and hydrosphere are often difficult for researchers to determine. Environmental impact cannot always be predicted or explained. As a result, marine scientists vary widely in their opinion about what pollutants are doing to the atmosphere and ocean, and what to do about it. Environmental issues are frequently emotional, and media reports tend to sensationalise short-term incidents (like oil spill) rather than more serious, long-term problems (like atmospheric changes or the effects of long-lived chlorinated hydrocarbon compounds).

TYPES OF ENVIRONMENTAL POLLUTION

Ground Water Pollution

When surface water is polluted, groundwater also becomes contaminated because it is recharged from surface-water supplies. Ground water migrates slowly compared to surface water. Surface water flows rapidly and flushes pollution downstream, but sluggish groundwater, once contaminated, remains polluted virtually forever. Soil pollution reduces the amount of land available for the cultivation of crops, fruits, and vegetables.

Pollution can enter groundwater from: (i) industrial waste injection wells, (ii) septic tank outflows, (iii) seepage from hazardous – waste disposal sites, (iv) industrial toxic waste dumps, (v) Mining activities, (vi) residues of agricultural toxic-waste dumps, (vii) residues of agricultural pesticides, herbicides, fertilizers, (viii) Overgrazing, (ix) residential and urban waste in landfills, (x) Deforetation. Thus, pollution can come either from a point source (about 35% does so) or from a large general area (a non-point source, 65%) and it can spread over a great distance. The major type of pollutions have been described in the following:

1. Soil Pollution

Decrease in the quality of soils either due to anthropogenic sources or natural sources or by both is called as soil pollution or soil degradation. Soil is a dynamic natural body made up of fine materials covering Earth's surface in which plants grow; composed of both mineral and organic matter. Soil is not only imperative for the growth of plants, the food, raw material for the agro-based industries are obtained from the soils. Thus, the survival of mankind is largely dependent on healthy soils. The resilience characteristics of the soil are however, damaged by the over-interaction and mismanagement of the soil resource.

Decrease in the quality of soil either due to the physical processes or anthropogenic factors is known as soil pollution. The main causes of soil degradation are: (i) deforestation, (ii) over-grazing, (iii) mining, (iv) soil erosion, (v) decrease in soil microorganism, (vi) mining activity, and (vii) excessive use of irrigation, (viii) excessive use of chemical fertilizers, and (ix) the mismanagement of the soil, (x) excess or deficit of moisture, (xi) high fluctuation of temperature, (xii) lack of humus context, (xiii) unscientific rotation of crops, etc.

Soil erosion is the main factor of soil pollution and soil fertility degradation. Soil pollution is caused by the following factors:

1. *Physical processes:* Physical source of soil pollution is related to soil erosion and the consequent soil degradation caused by the natural and anthropogenic factors. The magnitude of soil erosion depends on the amount and intensity of rainfall, temperature, wind, slope, vegetation cover and physical and chemical characteristics of soils. Deforestation is one of the most important causes of soil erosion in the developing countries.
2. *Biological processes:* The biological factors include the presence or absence of micro-organism in soil. The micro-organisms enter the soils from the various sources and degrade them.
3. *Air-borne sources:* Air-borne sources of soil pollutants are, in fact, air-pollutats which are released into the atmosphere by chimneys of factories, automobiles, thermal power plants, and domestic sources. The fallout of these pollutants are deposited in the soils which are polluted due to toxic substances. Sulphur emitted from the factories causes acid rains which lower the pH value of the soils. Thus, acid rains increase the acidity in the soil.
4. *Chemical fertilisers and insecticides:* Application of chemical fertilisers, insecticides and pesticides has become is an essential part of modern agriculture. Excessive use of these inputs change the soil chemistry making them more vulnerable to soil erosion. Insecticides and pesticides not only kill the insects and pests, they also kill some useful bacteria in the soil which are known to enhance the fertility in the soil. Many agricultural tracts in Punjab, Haryana and Uttar Pradesh are adversely affected by saline and alkaline formations.
5. *Urban and industrial wastes:* Improper disposal of industrial and urban wastes and irrigation of agricultural fields from polluted urban sewage water degrade the physical and chemical properties of soil. The toxic chemical substances of industrial effluents and urban sewage enter the soils and pollute them mostly in the vicinity of factories and urban settlements.

Consequences of Soil Pollution

Soil as stated above is essential for the sustainable development and the survival of humanity. Soil pollution has the following adverse consequences on society and ecology:

(i) Decrease in agricultural production.
(ii) Reduced nitrogen fixation.
(iii) Increased soil erosion.
(iv) Increased salinity
(v) The chemical fertilisers, insecticides and pesticides used in the agriculture, reach the human and animal bodies through food-chain which cause numerous diseases and deaths. According to one estimate more than 700,000 persons die every year in the world because of insecticides and pesticides.
(vi) Silting of tanks, lakes and reservoirs.
(vii) Release of pollutant gases.
(viii) Reduction in biodiversity.
(ix) Choking of drains.
(x) Obnoxious smell.

Control of Soil Pollution

Since the very survival of biodiversity and mankind depends on soils, there it is necessary to control soil pollution. The following steps may go a long way in controlling the soil pollution:

(i) Adopt the agricultural practices required to control soil erosion.
(ii) More use of cow-dung and green manure in the cultivation of crops.
(iii) Scientific rotation of crops. The soil exhaustive crops should be followed by soil enriching leguminous crops.
(iv) Proper disposal of industrial and urban solid and liquid wastes.
(v) Education of the farmers about the judicious uses of chemical fertilisers, insecticides and pesticides.
(vi) Afforestation
(vii) Controlled grazing
(viii) Reduce refuse and garbage
(ix) Reuse and recycle of resources

2. Water (Aquatic) Pollution

Water pollution may be defined as alteration in physical, chemical and biological characteristics of water which may cause harmful effects on human and aquatic life. Water pollution include surface, underground, sea and oceans waters. Water is our ultimate resource as life without water is not possible. The distribution of water in the world is, however, most uneven. In many countries precipitation is concentrated in a few months. For instance, in India, more than 80 per cent of precipitation occurs in four months, popularly known *Chaumasa*. Such a pattern of rainfall distribution means a low level of water availability on normal days. It necessitates construction of network of dams and reservoirs and interlinking of rivers.

Availability apart, the quality of water is also not uniform all over the world. The quality of water is evaluated on the basis of colour, odour, taste, temperature, proportion of dissolved salts, pH value, and the suspended organic and inorganic elements. Rain water is considered to be the purest form of water. But as the rain water passes over land surface and percolates through rocks, salts and minerals get dissolved in it. The polluted water is injurious to health.

Water pollution can result from the addition of harmful substances such as acids or hydrocarbons. However, the gradual build-up of essential elements in freshwater subsequent to their application as terrestrial agricultural fertilisers (eutrophication), may also pollute. In the terrestrial environment, the major pollutant by volume is urban-industrial refuse which, if treated, is either stored, or reduced – usually by biodegradation and burning. The main causes of water pollution have been briefly described in the following:

(i) ***Sewage and Sludge:*** The most important cause of water pollution is the sewage and sludge which is being disposed of in the rivers and streams in its most raw form. The sewage contains human and animal excreta, food residues, cleaning agents, detergents and other wastes. The water polluted by sewage and sludge is the source of disease carrying organisms like viruses, parasites and bacteria. Such a polluted water is main cause of water-borne diseases like cholera, gastroenteritis, dysentery, fever, typhoid, and paratyphoid. Moreover, the dissolved organic compounds in sewage and sludge, reduces the amount of dissolved oxygen which may threaten the aquatic ecosystems.

(ii) ***Inorganic Compounds and Minerals:*** Inorganic compounds including acids, mineral fibres, and heavy metals are being discharged by mining and industrial wastes are the other important water pollutants. The heavy metals like arsenic, cobalt, copper, lead, mercury, magnesium, etc. get dissolved into water through the natural process of weathering and anthropogenic factors. These heavy metals get concentrated in higher tropic levels within the food chain and can lead to such serious ailments as brain-damage, liver damage and may be fatal in many cases.

(iii) ***Nitrates:*** Nitrates constitute another serious source of water pollution, which are also considered as the health hazards. The chemical fertilisers applied by the farmers in their crops may flow into water bodies. Nitrates may also get accumulated in high concentrated in certain crops. Nitrates can cause several stomach diseases including stomach cancer. Nitrates in water bodies can cause eutrophication which is injurious to aquatic ecosystems.

(iv) ***Synthetic Organic Compounds:*** A variety of synthetic organic compounds is also an important source of water pollution. The main sources of synthetic pollutants are industrial, agricultural and household garbage. Sometimes such minerals (chlorine, etc.) are deliberately added for treating the water. The excess use of chlorine may be health hazard.

(v) ***Oil and Petroleum:*** Mixing of petroleum oil into water also adversely affects the quality of water. The main causes of pollution of water by oil and petroleum may be tankers' accidents, offshore oil drilling, combustion engine, and deliberate discharge from ship, natural seepage from the coastal areas and sea-floor. The adverse effects of oil pollutants damage the marine ecosystems.

(vi) ***Radioactive Waste:*** The radioactive waste is also an important source of water pollution. Nuclear elements constitute the basic radioactive substances. Such dangerous pollutants get released from the commercial and military applications of nuclear energy or nuclear warheads.

(vii) ***Miscellaneous Water Pollutants:*** Water is also polluted by thermal discharge from power plants, and other industries. Solid wastes accumulated on land in the form of landfills also pollute the surface and underground water tables. All the pollutants described above have a disastrous effect upon human health, ecosystems, and environment and ecology.

Table 6.1 Water Pollution by Industries

Type of Industry	Inorganic Pollutants	Organic Pollutants
1. Chemical Plants	Various acids and alkalies, chlorides, sulphates, nitrates of metals, phosphorous, silica and suspended particles.	Aromatic compounds solvents, organic acids dyes, etc.
2. Food Processing		Highly putrescible organic matter and pathogens
3. Iron & Steel	Suspended solids, iron-cyanide, sulphides, oxides of copper, chromium, cadmium and mercury.	Oil, phenol and neptha
4. Mining	Mine wastes, various metals, ferrous sulphate, sulphuric acid, hydrogen sulphides, surface wash offs, etc.	
5. Paper & Pulp	Sulphides, bleachin liquors	Cellulose fibers, bark, woods sugar organic acids
6. Pharmaceutical		Proteins, carbohydrates, organic solvents products, drugs and antibiotics.
7. Soap & Detergent	Ammonium compounds alkalies	Flats and fatty acids, glycerol, polyphosphates, hydrocarbons, etc.

Consequences of Water Pollution

The adverse effects of water pollution may be summarised as follows:

(i) ***Waterborne Diseases:*** The polluted water is the main cause of waterborne diseases such as cholera, dysentery, diarrhoea, jaundice, paratyphoid, tuberculosis, typhoid, etc.

(ii) ***Stomach Disorder:*** Water polluted with high concentration of certain trace minerals causes stomach disorder and cancer and hardening of tissues.

(iii) ***Lung Cancer:*** Water contaminated by fibres of asbestos, when used by humans, causes asbestosis, a form of lung cancer. The water polluted with mercury causes minamata diseases in humans.

(iv) ***Skin Diseases:*** Higher concentration of arsenic matter causes severe skin diseases. It is increasingly found in the middle and lower parts of the Ganga–Brahmaputra Plains.

(v) ***Damage to Aquatic Ecosystems:*** The acidic water damage the aquatic ecosystem.

(vi) ***Eutrophication:*** Heavy concentration of nitrates in water bodies lead to eutrophication which damages the ecosystems.

(vii) ***Damage to Soil:*** Water having higher concentration of salt content increase alkalinity of soils.

(viii) *Damage to Marine ecosystem:* Sea water polluted with oil slicks causes ecological disasters in the marine littoral ecosystems.

Water Conservation

At present, there is scarcity of water in many parts of the world and the quality of water is depleting, especially in the developing countries. The water requirements of the present billions of people is enormous. The quantity and quality of water can be conserved by adopting the following steps.

(i) ***Environmental Education:*** Individuals and the masses should be educated about the significance of quality of water and its impact on economy, society and ecology.

(ii) ***Accountability of Industrial Units:*** Industrial units should discharge the treated water in the drains and rivers.

(iii) ***Financial Support:*** The government should provide adequate funds to the civic bodies, municipal corporation for water pollution control.

(iv) ***Afforestation:*** Planting of trees can reduce the water pollution to a large scale as they reduce the rate of soils and salt erosion by running water.

(v) ***Soil Conservation:*** Soil erosion adds many inorganic substances in the surface and underground water. Soil conservation, therefore, is a useful technique to reduce the water pollution.

(vi) ***Less Use of Chemical Fertilisers in Agriculture:*** Chemical fertilisers add nitrates in the water bodies. The more use of compost manures can reduce the problems of eutrophication in the water bodies.

(vii) ***Legislation of Strict Environmental Laws:*** Government should legislate and implement strict environmental laws. The violators of such laws should be given rigorous punishment.

(viii) Individuals, communities, officials and owners of factories must be made accountable for the violation of environmental laws and regulations.

3. Air Pollution

Air pollution is defined as limited to situation in which the outdoor ambient atmosphere contains materials in concentration, which are harmful to man and his surrounding environment. Air pollution is one of the most widespread form of pollution all over the world. The main agent of air pollution is wind. Wind gathers and moves pollutants from one area to another, sometimes reducing the concentration of pollution in one location, while increasing it in another. Such air movement makes the atmosphere's condition an international issue. For example, in Europe, the cross boundary drift of pollution is a major issue because of the close proximity of nations and has led to Europe's unification.

As stated above air pollution is caused by natural forces, like volcanic eruptions and forest fire. But human interaction and resource utilisation is perhaps taxing the atmosphere's capacity to absorb the pollutant. Various human activities, particularly industrial and transport activity lead to the emission of a variety of pollutants to the atmosphere which lead to a number of environmental problems. The adverse effect of air pollution appears in the form of poor quality of air, acidic precipitation and deposition, and health hazards. The main pollutants of air the carbon dioxide (CO_2), carbonic acid (H_2SO_3), water (H_2O), nitric acid (HNO_3) sulphuric acid (H_2SO_4).

Consequences of Air Pollution

Atmospheric pollution have serious health implications. When these pollutants occur in higher concentrations in atmosphere, these result into high general morality rate in the concerned region. The children of younger age group and senior citizens are most vulnerable to air pollution. The London smog disaster of 1952 did make a heavy toll of human life. Such disasters apart, even day-to-day exposure to high concentrations of air pollutants is more harmful. It may be pointed out that each of the air pollutant has its own impact upon human health, especially in the big cities and industrial towns. 'The study, Health Impact of Particulate Pollution in Mega City-Delhi', conducted by a team of experts from the IIT Delhi and the Desert Research Institute, Reno, and ARIA Technologies, France, published by Elsevier in 2013, show that the polluted air is blamed for the spurt in respiratory ailments in Delhi and 7350 to 16,200 premature deaths every year. It was also found that the polluted air is responsible for about 6 million asthma attacks in the National Capital (Delhi) every year.

Table 6.0 Air Pollution and Human Health

Name of Pollutant	Source/Sources	Effects on Health
1. Asbestos- dust	Asbestos mining, asbestos-sheet manufacturing	Severe respiratory problem may lead to cancer.
2. Cadmium	Industries	Adversely affects the heart
3. Carbon Dioxide	Burning of fossil fuels	Difficulty in breathing, severe headache, unconsciousness and death.
4. Carbon Monoxide	Vehicular emissions and burning of fossil fuels	Difficulty in breathing, severe headache, irritation to mucous membrane, unconsciousness and death.
5. Chlorofluorocarbons	Refrigerators, emissions from jets, detergents, spays, foam	Depletion of stratospheric ozone layer, global warming.
6. Coal -dust and Particles	Coal mines	Black lung cancer, pulmonary fibrosis which lead to respiratory failure.
7. Cotton dust	Cotton textile factories	Destruction of lung tissues, chronic cough, bronchitis and emphysema.
8. Hydrocarbons	Burning of fossil fuels	Carcinogenic effect on lungs, kidney damage, hypertension, respiratory distress, irritation of eyes, nose and throat, asthma, bronchitis and damage to respiratory system.
9. Lead	Leaded petrol emissions	Damage to brain and central nervous system, kidneys and brains, impaired intelligence.
10. Mercury	Industries	Nervous disorders, insomnia, memory loss, excitability, irritation, tremor, gingivitis and minamata disease.

11. Nitrogen Oxide	Thermal power plants, industries and vehicles	Irritation and inflammation of lungs, breathlessness, impairs enzyme function in respiratory system and causes bronchitis and asthma.
12. Ozone	Automobile emission	Breathlessness, asthma, wheezing, chest pain, emphysema and chronic bronchitis.
13. Radioactive pollutants	Cosmic rays, x-rays, beta-rays, radon and radium	Destroy living tissues and blood cells, affects cell membrane and cell enzyme functions, leukemia, and permanent genetic changes.
14. Silica dust	Silicon quarries	Silcosis affects the lungs.
15. Smog (The term smog was coined by Dr. H .A. Des Voeux in 1905)	Industries and vehicular pollution	Respiratory problems and intense irritation of eyes.
16. Sulphur Oxide	Thermal power plants and industries	Eye and throat irritation, cough, allergies, impairs respiratory system, reduces exchange of gases from lung surface.
17. Suspended Particulate Matter (SOM)	Vehicular emission and burning of fossil fuel	Lung irritation, and causes pulmonary malfunctioning.
18. Tobacco Smoke	Cigarettes, cigars, and tobacco products	Chronic bronchitis, asthma and lung cancer, irritation of eyes, nose and throat.

Management of Atmospheric Pollution

Air pollution control is a cumbersome task. There are numerous difficulties involved in resolving the air pollution. Air pollution can be reduced significantly by: (i) maintenance of vehicles and roads, (ii) efficient public transport system, (iii) reduction in garbage burning, (iv) reduction in shifting cultivation area, (v) increased production of solar and hydro-electric power, (vi) afforestation, and (vii) replacement of old industrial and thermal power machinery.

Some of the main barriers in the control of air pollution are:

1. There are a large number of pollutants involved in air pollution. Some of them are difficult to detect.
2. The pollutants vary greatly in the different parts of the world.
3. The technologies required for monitoring most of the pollutants are also not equally accessible in different parts of the world.
4. The degree of exposure to such pollutants may vary from individual to individual and different persons may respond differently to such exposures.
5. Since a person gets exposed to a variety of pollutants simultaneously, it becomes difficult to ascertain the real pollutant responsible for the damage to human health and ecosystems. In order to make an effective control of air pollution, an international action at the global level is required. Some efforts have already been made in this direction through a series of international conventions, protocols and agreements. Some of the notable examples in this regard are:
   (i) Convention on Long Range Trans-boundary Pollution in 1970.
   (ii) the Stockholm Conference on the Acidification of Environment in 1982.

(iii) The 30 per cent Club Introduced in Ottawa in 1982.
(iv) The Munich Multi-lateral Conference on Environment in 1984.
(v) The Helsinki Meeting of 1985.
(vi) The Amsterdam International Conference on Acidification and its implications, 1986.
(vii) The Sofia Meeting of 1988.

In addition to these conferences and conventions, individual countries at their own level have taken legislative measures to curtail the concentration of harmful pollutants in the atmosphere. India was perhaps the first developing country to adopt legislation on environmental management as early as 1986. Most of the developed countries already have laws to protect their environment. But the legislative measures alone are inadequate, particularly in the less developed countries. Public awareness and mass education of the people and propagation of environmental awareness are very important to control the air pollution and maintain the resilience characteristics of the ecosystems and biodiversity.

4. Noise Pollution

Noise pollution may be defined as the state of discomfort and restlessness caused to humans by unwanted high intensity sound known as noise. Noise pollution is also an important environmental hazard, which is becoming increasingly injurious with the passage of time because of industrialisation and urbanisation. Noise beyond a particular level tends to become a health and environmental hazard. The main causes of noise pollution in India are given below:

1. **Social gatherings:** Marriage and other social parties are a big source of noise pollution, especially in the developing countries like India.
2. **Places of worship:** Use of loudspeakers in religious palces is also an important irritant and a source of noise pollution.
3. **Commercial activities:** Hawkers, weekly and periodic markets and *pheriwalas*, also add to the noise pollution.
4. **Festival days:** Festivals all over the world are celebrated with different pomp and shows. In the developing countries like India, festivals are celebrated with drum beats, crackers and loudspeakers which pollute the air and increase noise pollution.
5. **Industrial activities:** Industrial activities of all kinds from blast-mining to factory industry all generate high intensity sounds. And thus make significant contribution to noise pollution.
6. **Automobiles and Transport System:** Automobiles without adequate provisions for higher quality silencers are also an important source of noise pollution. Heavy vehicles like trucks, buses and continuously generate noise pollution. Railway network too is one such source which generates sound of high intensity. The jet fighters like MIGs and aeroplanes contribute significantly to noise pollution. Construction equipments, manufacturing processes are also the sources of noise pollution.
7. **Power generators:** Use of power generators like thermal power plants and hydro-power generating turbines contribute substantially to noise pollution.
8. **Agricultural equipments:** New agricultural technology like tractors, harvesters, and threshers create enough noise pollution in the rural areas of the country.

9. **Household appliances:** Household appliances like electric grinders, food-blenders and use of heavy machines at construction sites, and roads and railways construction are also an important source of noise pollution.

Impact of Noise Pollution on Society

Noise pollution affects the society in different ways. The adverse affects of noise pollution may be examined under the following categories:

(i) **General impact:** In general noise pollution is a growing threat to human health. High intensity sound, popularly known as noise adversely affects speech, sleep and concentration of individuals, particularly those who are seriously engaged in creative work. The concentration of students, teachers, scientists and mediators are disturbed by noise pollution.

(ii) **Psychological impact:** The experts of psychology believe that frequent exposure to high intensity sound waves may cause behavioural changes among animals as well as in human beings.

(iii) **Physiological impact:** Psychologically, the impact of noise pollution may include: temporary, mild or permanent damage to hearing mechanism; changes in the hormonal content of blood so as to stimulate blood pressure; reproductive problems, miscarriages, etc. High intensity sound increase anxiety, strain, stress, blood-pressure, heart ailment, nervousness, depression, etc. which are injurious to health and efficiency.

(iv) **Nervous system:** It causes pain, ringing in the ears, tiredness, adversely affecting the functioning the human system.

(v) **Damage to material:** The buildings and structures may get damaged.

Ambient Noise Level Monitoring

Noise pollution (Control and Regulation) Rules, 2000 defines ambient noise for various areas as follows:

	Area/Zone*	Limits in dB (A) LeQ Day Time (6 a.m. to 10 p.m.)	Limits in dB(A) Leq Night Time(10 p.m. to 6 a.m.)
1	Industrial Area	75	70
2.	Commercial Area	65	55
3.	Residential Area	55	45
	Silence Zone	4. 50	40

Zone is an area of not less than 100 meters around hospital, educational institution, courts, religious places or any other area declared as such by a competent authority.

The Government of India on March 2011 launched a Real Time Ambient Noise Monitoring Network. Under this network, the following three phases were initiated:

Phase I: In this phase five Remote Noise Monitoring Terminals were installed in different noise zones in seven cities, namely: (i) Bangalore, (ii) Chennai, (iii) Delhi, (iv) Hyderabad, (v) Kolkata, (vi) Lucknow, and (vii) Mumbai.

Phase II: In this phase another 35 monitoring stations were installed in the above seven cities.

Phase III: Phase III will cover 18 more cities in which 90 stations will be installed. These 18 cities include: (i) Ahmadabad, (ii) Amritsar, (iii) Bhopal, (iv) Bhubaneshwar, (v) Dehradun, (vi) Gandhinagar, (vii) Guwahati, (viii) Indore, (ix) Jaipur, (x) Kanpur, (xi) Ludhiana, (xii) Nagpur, (xiii) Patna, (xiv) Pune, (xv) Raipur, (xvi) Ranchi, (xvii) Surat, (xviii) Thiruvananthapuram.

Control of Noise Pollution

According to the World Health Organisation (WHO), of all the environmental problems, noise is the easiest to control. This can be achieved by adopting the following steps:

(i) Public awareness about the need of control of noise pollution.
(ii) Reduction in exposure to noise by application of engineering control techniques such as alteration and modification of design to reduce noise, by construction of sound barriers or the use of sound absorbers.
(iii) Reduction in exposure to noise by making exposed personnel use protective ear plugs and decreasing exposure time.
(iv) Construction of academic institutions and hospitals away from highways, railways, and airports.
(v) By creating vegetation buffer zones through large-scale tree plantation which absorbs noise.
(vi) Improved building designs may also reduce the impact of noise pollution.
(vii) There should be appropriate and effective legislative measure at the Central Government and States level.

In India, the Section 133 Indian Penal Code (IPC) regulates the use of loudspeakers. The noise pollution in India, is covered by the Environmental Act of 1986. Under this Act, noise generation itself is a criminal offence under Section 268 of IPC. Similarly, silence zones around hospitals, educational institutions, courts, etc. have been created. The limits of such silence zones extended to a radius of 100 metres for all the institutions like hospitals, schools, colleges, laboratories, courts and other academic institutions.

If all the above steps are taken together in combination with each other, the problem of noise pollution can be solved significantly.

Solid Waste

Solid waste is a substance which has a definite shape and volume and some fundamental strength. They are the useless abandoned material. Solid waste includes garbage, sludge and refuge. It may be solid, semi-solid, liquid or contained gaseous material resulting from industrial, commercial, mining and agricultural operations. It also include plastic waste.

The main sources of solid waste are: (i) household, (ii) agricultural fields, (iii) industries and mining, (iv) hotels and catering, (v) roads and railways, (vi) hospitals and educational institutions, (vii) cultural centres and places of recreation, and (viii) tourism and ecotourism. Plastic waste is also solid waste.

Land area littered with plastic bags becomes, ugly, unaesthetic and unhygienic and they choke drains Conventional plastics have been associated with reproductive problems both in humans and animals. Plastic bags may contaminate foodstuffs. They deteriorate soil fertility and create health problems.

Solid Wastes from may be classified under the following three categories:

(a) **Municipal waste:** Municipal waste includes garbage from household, construction materials, demolition debris, sanitation residue and waste from streets and lanes.

(b) **Hospital wastes:** Hospital waste is generated during the diagnosis, treatment of human beings and animals. It is also generated in biological research activities or in production or testing of medicines on humans and animals.

(c) **Hazardous waste:** Industrial and hospital is considered hazardous as they contain toxic substances.

The solid waste may be safely disposed off in the following ways:

(i) open dumps, (ii) landfills, (iii) sanitary land fills, (iv) Incineration plants, (v) composting, (vi) vermiculture or earthworms farming, (vii) bioremediation or the use of micro-organisms (bacteria and fungi) to degrade the environmental contaminants into less toxic forms, and (viii) pyrolysis – a process of combustion in the absence of oxygen.

Nuclear Pollution/Radiation Pollution

Radioactive substance releases invisible radiations which cause many deleterious effects on all living organisms directly or indirectly. These radioactive substances are radium, uranium, plutonium, pdonium etc. Low levels of radiations have been enamating from natural resources since evolution but the level of exposure has increased enormously after the advent of nuclear weapons and the development of nuclear energy. Nuclear pollution is a kind of physical of the environment which differes from air, water, and soil pollution. There is no safe dose of radiation.

Effect of Nuclear Pollution

1. The acute radiation exposure cause sudden death after some weeks, loss of hairs and bleeding from gums.
2. High doses of radiation may damage to bone marrow and thus retard body's ability to fight against infection.
3. Brain is highly vulnerable which may result in mental retardation.
4. High doses of radiation cause blood haemorrhage.
5. Nuclear radiation may cause leukaemia, bone cancer, and hereditary diseases.
6. Natural vegetation is damaged.
7. Atomic radiation may melt metals and even vapourise.
8. The areas subjected to radiation have reduced biodiversity in the respective areas.

Control of Nuclear Pollution

1. All the precautions must be adopted in the use of radioactive substances.
2. Manufacturing and use of nuclear weapons must be stopped.
3. Nuclear tests should be suspended.
4. The design of the existing and proposed nuclear power station is so that any radiation cannot spread even in any accident.
5. Ocean dumping of nuclear wastes should be checked strictly.

6. People in industry, research and medicine using radionuclides must be protected from exposure to radiation by more suitable means.
7. There must be proper and safe disposal of nuclear waste.

5. Marine Pollution

About 71 percent of the earth surface is covered with oceans. Oceans are the ultimate sink of natural and man-made pollutants. Rivers discharge their pollutants into the sea. The sewerage and garbage of coastal cities, towns and villages are also dumped into the sea. The oceanic pollution are navigational discharge of oil, detergents, sewage, garbage and radioactive wastes, off shore oil mining, oil spills, and volcanic eruptions. The introduction by humans of substances or energy into the oceans that change the quality of the water or affect the physical and biological environment is known as marine pollution. The utilisation of ocean resources can result in the accidental (or intentional) release of harmful substances. It is not always easy to identify a pollutant; some materials labelled as pollutants are produced in large quantities by natural processes. For example, a volcanic eruption can produce immense quantities of carbon dioxide, methane, sulphur compounds, and oxides of nitrogen. Excess amounts of these substances produced by human activities may also cause global warming and acid rain. While the main causes of marine pollution may be similar to that of general water pollution, there are natural (e.g. volcanoes and seepage of oil in the coastal areas, and anthropogenic pollutants), generated by man accidentally or deliberately.

A pollutant causes damage by interfering directly or indirectly with the bio-chemical processes of an organism. Some pollution-induced changes may be instantly lethal; other changes may weaken an organism over weeks or months, or alter the dynamics of population of which it is a part, or gradually unbalance the entire community.

Sources of Marine Pollution

There are physical and anthropogenic sources of marine pollution. A brief description of the sources of marine pollution has been given in as below:

1. ***Crude oil and petroleum:*** Natural seeps have been leaking large quantities of oil into the sea for millions of years. The amount of oil entering the ocean has increased greatly in recent years. Our growing dependence on marine transportation for petroleum products, offshore drilling, near-shore refining, and street runoff carrying waste oil from the automobiles are the important sources of marine pollution. According to one assessment, natural seeps accounted for about 8 per cent of this annual input.
2. ***Intentional release of petroleum products:*** Some petroleum and petroleum products are released in the oceans intentionally, quietly, and routinely, during the loading, unloading, discharging, and flushing of tanker ships. This oil is particularly harmful to seabirds, zooplanktons, and microorganisms.
3. ***Marine pollution due to organic waste:*** There is great diversity in marine fauna and flora. The amount of oxygen dissolved in the water is vital for the plants and animals living in it. Wastes, which directly or indirectly affect the oxygen concentration, play an important role in determining the quality of water.

4. ***Sewage Disposal into the Seas and Oceans:*** Normally, the greatest volume of waste discharged into the sea is sewage. It is one of the biggest marine pollutant. The sources of oil pollution have been given in Table 6.1.
5. ***Volcanic Eruptions:*** Volcanic eruptions add enormous quantities carbon dioxides, methan, sulphur compounds, etc. into the oceans.
6. ***Cosmic dust:*** Meteors and cosmic dust from the space fall into the oceans known as taktites. This is also an important source of marine pollution.

Table 6.1 Source of pollution and their percentage share

Source of oil pollution	Percentage
1. Use and disposal	34%
2. Transportation operations	32%
3. Accidental spills	13%
4. Natural sources	8%
5. Atmospheric inputs	8%
6. Offshore production and coastal refining	5%

Source: Garrison, T., 1995, *Essentials of Oceanography*, Wadsworth Publishing Company, New York, p. 281.

Duration of Marine Pollutants

Pollutants vary in their persistence. On the basis of persistence the pollutants may be classified in the following categories:

(i) Some reside in environment for thousands of years while others last only a few minutes.

(ii) Some pollutants break down into harmless substances spontaneously or through physical process (like the shattering of large molecules by sunlight).

(iii) Sometimes pollutants are removed from the environment through biological activity. For example, some marine organisms escape permanent damage by metabolising hazardous substances to harmless ones.

(iv) The volatile components of any oil spill eventually evaporate into the air, leaving the heavier tars behind. Wave action causes the tar to form into balls of varying sizes. Some of the tar balls fall to the bottom, where they may be assimilated by bottom organisms or incorporated into sediments. Bacteria will eventually decompose these spheres, but the process may take years to complete, especially in cold polar waters. This oil residue-especially if derived from refined oil – can have long-lasting effects on seafloor communities.

It is interesting to note that most pollutants, resist attack by water, air, sunlight, or living organisms because the synthetic compounds of which they are composed resemble nothing in nature.

Effect of Pollutants on Marine Life

It is difficult to generalise about the effects of pollutants, especially that of a concentrated release of oil – an oil spill from a tanker, coastal storage facility, or well – will have in the marine environment. The consequences of spill vary with its location and proximity to shore; with the quantity and composition of the oil; with the season of the year, ocean currents, and weather conditions at the time of release; and with the composition and diversity of the affected communities. Intertidal and shallow-water sub-tidal communities are most sensitive to the effects of an oil spill. Spills of refined oil, especially near shore where marine life is abundant, can be more disruptive for longer period of time.

In most cases, an organism's response to a particular pollutant will depend on its sensitivity to the combination of quantity and toxicity of that pollutant. Some pollutants are toxic to organisms in tiny concentration. For examplc, the photosynthetic ability of some species of diatoms is diminished when chlorinated hydrocarbon compounds are present in parts-per-trillion quantities. Other pollutants seem harmless, as when fertilisers flowing from agricultural land stimulate plant growth in estuaries. Still other pollutants may be hazardous to some organisms but not to others. For example, crude oil interferes with the delicate feeding structures of zooplanktons and coats the feathers of birds, but it simultaneously serves as a feast for certain bacteria.

In general, polluted water reduces Dissolved Oxygen (DO) content, thereby, eliminates sensitive organisms like planktons, molluscs and fish. There are, however, a few tolerant species like Tubifex (annelid worms) and some insect larvae which may survive even in highly polluted water. Such species are recognised as 'indicator species' for polluted water.

Marine Pollution Control

A number of preventive and technological steps have been suggested by the experts of oceanography and ecology. Some of the important steps are described briefly in the following:

1. ***Treatment of sewage:*** There should be installation of treatment plants along the drains which discharge liquid and solid wastes into the bays and sea.
2. ***Sludge Processing:*** The sludge contains pollutants and harmful bacteria should be treated before it is discharged into the seas, gulfs, and oceans.
3. ***Seepage oil-proof tankers:*** The loading and unloading of crude oil and petroleum in the tankers should be through the '*top load system*'. There should be special arrangements for the washing and cleaning of the tankers. Moreover, there should be dry docking for servicing, repairs, cleaning the hull, etc. In this process, the residual oil should not find its way to the sea.
4. ***Offshore oil production and onshore refineries:*** Efforts should be made to locate the petroleum refineries near the sea coasts.
5. ***Prevention of tankers accidents:*** A large number of oil tanker accidents occur every year. Careful navigation can avert many of these accidents.
6. ***Cleaning responsibility:*** In case of any tanker accident, the responsibility of cleaning the polluted marine area should be of the country the ranker belongs to.
7. ***Effective international law:*** There is a need to legislate more effective laws at the international level with severe financial punishments to those countries who do not abide by the international laws, rules and regulations.

ENVIRONMENTAL IMPACT ASSESSMENT

The concept of Environmental Impact Assessment (EIA) was developed in 1969 with the enactment of National Environmental Policy Act (NEPA) in USA. The natural resources (land, water, forest, minerals) are limited. There is however, an increasing demand of the natural resources to feed the teeming millions and raise the standard of living of the people. The use and misuse of natural resources is rapidly depleting the resource base. The objective of Environmental Impact Assessment is to ascertain the probable effect of anthropogenic activities on environment. In other words, the assessment and evaluation of environmental effects of human actions may be termed as 'environmental impact assessment' (EIA). The broader aspects of the Environmental Impact Assessment (EIA) are:

(i) appraisal of prevailing environmental conditions;
(ii) appraisal of production methods – both existing and proposed;
(iii) methodologies related Environmental Impact Assessment.
(iv) possible impact of projects on environment – both existing and proposed;
(v) development of the techniques of conservation of environment by modifying and improving the existing production technology.

Objectives of Environmental Impact Assessment (EIA)

The major objectives of the Environmental Impact Assessment are:

1. To provide a broad, integrated perspective of a region about to undergo or undergoing developments;
2. To ascertain the cumulative impacts from the multiple developments in the region.
3. To establish priorities for environmental protection.
4. To assess policy option.
5. Identify information gaps and research needs.
6. On the basis of Environmental Impact Assessment to provide a chance to adopt an alternative strategy for the project.
7. To identify the positive and negative aspects of any project.
8. To promote efforts so that damage to the environment can be prevented.
9. To make the developers accountable.

Environmentally Sensitive Places of India

1. Religious and historic places
2. Archaelogical monuments
3. Scenic and aesthetic areas
4. Hill resorts, mountains, hills and plateaus
5. Sea beaches
6. Coastal areas characterized with coral formations
7. Health resorts
8. Estuaries and mangroves
9. Gulfs, bays and creeks
10. Biosphere reserves
11. National parks and sanctuaries

12. Lakes, swamps and wetlands
13. Areas of scientific and geological interest
14. International borders and frontiers
15. Lakes, reservoirs and dams
16. Rivers and streams
17. Railways
18. Areas of aesthetic beauty
19. National and States Highways
20. Urban agglomeration

Environmental Impact Assessment in India

In India, the Environmental Impact Assessment (EIA) was introduced in 1978. At present the Indian EIA includes the following projects:

1. Major Projects like (i) river valley, (ii) thermal power plants, (iii) mining, (iv) industries, (v) nuclear power plants, (vi) railways, national highways, roads, bridges, (vii) ports and harbours, (viii) airports, (ix) new towns, and (x) communication projects.
2. Those projects requiring the approval of the Public Investment Board/Planning Commission/ Central Electricity Authority, etc.
3. Those referred to the Ministry of Environment and Forests by other ministries for any project.
4. Those which are sensitive and located in environmentally hazardous areas.
5. Those projects which cost more than Rs. 50 crores.

A Government of India Notification of January 1994 makes EIA statutory for 29 categories of developmental projects under various sectors such as irrigation, mining, industrial power, transport, tourism, communication, etc.

The EIA Notification was amended in 1984 in order to make public hearing an integral part of the assessment procedure. Environmental clearance is granted by the Impact Assessment Agency in the Ministry of Environment and Forests. This power has been delegated to the state governments in the case of power generation plants of any capacity, gas/naphtha based and coal based power plants with fluidised bed technology of up to 500 MW capacity and conventional coal based power plants of up to 250 MW capacity except when located within a boundary of 25 km of the reserved forests, biosphere reserves and critically polluted areas or within 50 km of interstate boundary.

Depending on the nature of the project, certain safeguards are recommended. For monitoring and timely implementation of safeguards, six regional offices of the Ministry of Environment and Forests have been set up at (i) Bangalore, (ii) Bhopal (iii) Bhubaneswar, (iv) Chandigarh, (v) Lucknow, and (vi) Shillong (Meghalaya).

A National Environmental Appellate Authority has been constituted to hear appeals with respect to rejection of proposals from the environmental angle. The objective is to bring in transparency in the process and accountability, and to ensure the smooth and expeditious implementation schemes and projects.

Environment Action Plan

The Indian government formulated an Environment Action Programme (EAP) in January 1994. The main objective of this programme is to strengthen Environment Impact Assessment (EIA) of various projects through an organised system of natural resource accounting and environmental statistics. The Environment Action Programme focuses on the following areas:

(i) conservation of biodiversity including forests, marine life and mountain ecosystems,
(ii) conservation of soil and moisture and ensuring that water resources do not get polluted,
(iii) control of industrial pollution and waste,
(iv) access to clean technologies,
(v) tackling urban environmental issues,
(vi) strengthening environmental education, training, awareness and resources management,
(vii) alternative energy plan.

The programme envisaged in EAP co-ordinate with the thrust areas identified in the Agenda 21 adopted at the Earth Summit in June 1992.

ENVIRONMENTAL AUDIT

It is an inventory of the 'pollutants' generated by a firm or corporation that are regulated by the state. An audit usually involves tracking quantities of inputs, outputs and geographical disposal.

Eco-auditing

Eco-auditing in fact, is a systematic multidisciplinary method used periodically to assess the environmental performance of the project. Eco-auditing evolved as a management tool in USA in 1980. It has been promoted in Europe by the International Chamber of Commerce and by some multinational corporations as a means of getting effective environmental management. In the developing countries, however, the eco-auditing concept is still a theoretical concept. Although, India has modified its Companies Act to include a requirement for eco-audits. Eco-auditing is an effective tool of EIA and its benefits are as under:

(i) It is a means for ensuring the continual improvement in environmental management.
(ii) It is a good method of monitoring.
(iii) It can assist efforts for sustainable development.
(iv) It helps in involving public in environmental management.
(v) It may reduce the need for government inspections.
(vi) It may help to identify cost recovery through recycling and sale of by-products.
(vii) It may generate valuable data for regional and national environment reports.

GREEN ECONOMICS

Green economics also known as ecological economics is not limited to environmental concerns as its name might imply. It encompasses social, environmental and spiritual concerns, all of which have been historically overlooked in the study of economics, and proposes that we design a new model of economy. This model, according to Brian Milani, the author of '*Designing the Green Economy*' (Brian Milani, 2000) must establish direct democracy, meet everyone's needs and harmonise human activity with nature.

In its simplest form 'green economy' mean an economy with (i) low carbon, (ii) judicious utilisation of resources, and (iii) socially inclusive which provide the benefit of resource utilisation to the weakest section of the society.

Many aspects of our daily lives are excluded from mainstream economics, which measures industrial production and the exchange of money. In general terms, producers and consumers only take into consideration their own direct costs and benefits when making decisions rather than the costs and benefits to society as a whole. Examples of these externalities (costs or benefits that are passed along the society at large) can be positive or negative. A common example of a negative externality is pollution which is produced by one manufacturer but affects many others. This pollution harms factory neighbours and workers, but as it stands at present does not directly affect the bottom line of the manufacturer – which means that the manufacturer does not consider the effects of that pollution. An example of a positive externality is something like a vaccine which not only benefits the recipient but those in society at large by reducing the spread of disease to others. Current economic measures were not designed to consider externalities and leave the job of managing these to governments, which must discourage or encourage them as they see fit.

Green economics assumes that humanity can regenerate community and ecosystems and that there can be positive qualitative change, while environmental economics continues to focus on quantitative control. In brief, green economics is about designing a new economic system that takes more than materials and money into account. Green economics may use the tools of environmental economics to build social and environmental costs into prices but recognises these actions in the long run will not bring about the changes that are needed. While environmental economics asks how the industrial economy can do less damage to the environment and people, green economics asks why the economy needs to be destructive in the first place.

GREEN ELECTRICITY

The solar-energy, wind energy, hydro-power, waves, tidal waves energy, geothermal energy, biomass-gas and landfill gas are known as '*Green Electricity*'. A brief description of the sources of green energy has been given in the following.

(i) Solar Energy or Photovoltaic (PV) Energy

Solar energy is one of the most important sources of green electricity. Solar energy is non-exhaustible, reliable and pollution free. It may be utilised for water heaters, power generation devices, air-conditioning, space heating, development of pisci-culture, multifarious uses of water and refrigeration. This energy is generated by converting sunlight directly into electricity even on cloudy days, using semi-conductor technology. Even in the winter season a useful amount of hot water can be produced from roof top collectors. The buildings are also designed in such a way in which solar energy may be generated and utilised.

The average amount of solar energy received in the Earth's atmosphere is about 1353 KW per sq. metre. It is 1000 times the total consumption of the global energy. Solar energy programme has been implemented in many countries of the world. In India, solar energy is produced at Sagar Island in Sundarban Delta of West Bengal. Similar experiments have been implemented in Jodhpur (Rajasthan), Kalyanpur (Aligarh) and Coimbatore (Tamil Nadu).

(ii) Hydropower

Hydroelectricity is a renewable, cheap, clean and environmentally clean source of energy. River water, if not properly used, will drain into the sea as a waste. Hydroelectricity can meet largely the future requirements of energy both in the developing and developed countries. Water turbines have been used in a big way all over the world for over 100 years for the generation of hydro-power. The water turbines are installed by constructing big or small dams across the perennial or seasonal rivers. Hydroelectricity generation was started in India in 1879 to supply electricity to the city of Darjeeling. Though about 20 per cent of our electricity requirements are met by hydro-power, India has developed only a small percentage of its total water potential available.

(iii) Nuclear Energy

Looking at the increasing demand of energy and the exhaustible nature of fossil fuels, nuclear energy development has become of great significance in most of the big and small countries of the world. It is also a source of green energy. Nuclear energy is produced from uranium and thorium. Although, India is largely dependent on other countries for the supply of uranium, it has 27 nuclear power plants generating about 4 per cent of the energy supply of the country.

(iv) Wind Energy

Wind energy is also a green electricity. It has been developed substantially in the Netherlands, Denmark, France, Germany, USA, China, Spain, the Scandinavian countries. In India wind energy (green energy) is produced in the states of Tamil Nadu and Gujarat, especially along the coastal areas where wind blows regularly at a steady speed.

For the generation of wind energy, a wind speed of more than five km per hour is considered to be suitable. Wind speed above 10 km per hour are prevalent over parts of the coastal regions of Gujarat, Andaman and Nicobar Islands, Andhra Pradesh, Odisha, Karnataka, Kerala, Jammu & Kashmir, Madhya Pradesh, Maharashtra, Rajasthan, Tamil Nadu, Uttarakhand, and the Islands of West Bengal in the Delta of Sundarban. The highest potential of wind energy in India is in the state of Gujarat.

(v) Wave Energy

A number of electricity generating plants have been designed over the years to generate electricity with the help of strong ocean waves. With the proper support, wave power could provide a significant proportion of the electricity. This energy is also green energy.

(vi) Tidal Waves

Tidal energy is generated at the occurrence of spring and neap tides. The turbines are installed in the estuaries of rivers/coastal areas as the tide waves rise, the turbines start the generation of tidal energy. India has a very long coastline, more than 6100 km, but the ocean energy production is limited. The suitable areas for the generation of tidal energy are: (i) Gulf of Khambat, (ii) Gulf of Kachchh, and (iii) Estuary of Hugli. In India, at present, the maximum tidal energy is produced along the coast of Gulf of Khambat.

(vii) Geothermal Energy

Geothermal energy comes from hot rocks deep underground. In some parts of the world steam comes to the surface which can be used to run stream turbines for the generation of geothermal energy. Iceland is the leading geothermal producing country of the world, followed by New Zealand. India, however, has very limited potential of geothermal energy. In India geothermal energy is produced in the Puga Valley of Ladakh (J&K), Manikaran area of Himachal Pradesh, Western Ghats of Maharashtra, Narmada and Son and Damodar River Valley.

(viii) Biomass Energy

Bio-energy is also a clean source of energy which improves sanitation, hygiene and living style of the rural population. In the generation of biomass energy, the agricultural waste or especially grown plants are utilised. There are, however, concerns about the sustainability of sourcing of biomass from countries as forests are being cleared increasingly to bring more land under cultivation, grazing and other uses.

(ix) Landfills

The rubbish dumped in the landfill sites is also being utilised for the generation of landfill gas. This gas can be captured and burnt in a gas turbine to produce electricity. Bio-gas is used for cooking and lighting. According to one estimate, India has a capacity to produce bio-gas to the extent of 25,000 million cubic metres. The left-over slurry serves as manure. Moreover, burning the gas does not give off CO_2.

ECOLOGICAL DEBT

The concept of ecological debt encompasses the social and environmental impacts suffer mainly by the developing countries as well as the intensive exploitation of natural resources to support production and consumption patterns of the rich developed countries.

Although as a concept, 'ecological debt' is relatively new, the phenomenon apparently began in the 17th century and acted as engine to Industrial Revolution. According to the international environmental organisations that are the main proponents of the notion of ecological debt, this is a historical obligation that the developed countries have towards the developing countries, due to the looting and exploitation of their natural goods. Countries have become rich as a result of the continued usurpation of the poor countries' natural resources, of unfair trade and of using the global environment as garbage dump. One of the clearest examples of this is climate change – a phenomenon that has been almost exclusively created by industrialised countries but the consequences of which are suffered by all the world's inhabitants. But there is also deforestation to feed demand for timber or meat products in the developed countries. The governments of the developing countries generally lack the capacity to impose minimum environmental or social restrictions, since they are in such dire need of investments to alleviate their poverty.

The Developing Countries as Creditor

Ecological debt has four components: (i) the carbon debt, owed by industrialised countries as a result of their disproportionate pollution of the atmosphere through greenhouse gas emissions, (ii) biopiracy (the intellectual appropriation of local and indigenous knowledge for trade purposes by laboratories from the developed countries, banned under the Cartagena Protocol), (iii) damage to the natural environment caused by the activities of transnational corporations in the developing countries, and (iv) the dumping of toxic waste of the developed countries in the developing countries (banned the Basel Convention, signed by all the rich countries except the USA).

In addition, however, ecological debt acts as a form of vindication for the developing countries, and aims at counteracting the effects of the unsustainable and unpayable external debt.

BLACK CARBON

Black Carbon (BC) has recently emerged as a major contributor to climate change, possibly second only to CO_2 as the main driver of change. Black Carbon particles strongly absorb sunlight and give soot its black colour. Black Carbon is produced both naturally and by human activities as a result of incomplete combustion of fossil fuels, and biomass. Primary sources include emissions from diesel engines, cook stoves, wood burning and forest fires. Reducing CO_2 emissions is essential to avert the worst impacts of future climate change, but CO_2 concentrations to begin to stabilise after emissions reduction would immediately reduce the rate of warming, particularly in the rapidly changing Arctic. Moreover, reduced exposure to Black Carbon provides public health co-benefits, especially in developing countries. Technologies that can reduce global Black Carbon emissions are available today.

CARBON DEBT

Inequalities in terms of carbon emissions between the developed and the developing countries are huge. For example, the US citizen produces seven tons of carbon gas a year, while an Indian citizen barely reaches 0.5 tons.

Energy consumption in developed countries is almost exclusively based on the burning of fossil fuels, resulting in large emissions of carbon-dioxide (CO_2) – the gas mainly responsible for the greenhouse effect and, therefore, for climate change. Such pollution has global consequences, and is considered responsible for the increased strength and frequency of extreme natural events such as floods and long droughts. These natural disasters mainly affect those countries situated in the tropics and with poor infrastructure, despite their limited contribution to the overall carbon problem.

Extreme natural events entail the loss of human lives and agricultural crops and the destruction of road infrastructure and housing. In order to prevent and repair the damage caused, the developing countries often have to resort to new foreign loans. This is the reason why it is said that the developed countries have a debt towards the developing countries – though it is also necessary to consider all the greenhouse gases currently absorbed by the forests and ocean waters of the developing countries.

CARBON CREDIT

The concept of carbon credit was the outcome of Kyoto Protocol, an International agreement between 169 countries.

A carbon credit is a tradable certificate or permit representing the right to emit one tone of carbon or carbon dioxide equivalent (tCO_2e). One carbon credit is equal to one ton of carbon dioxide, or in some markets, carbon dioxide equivalent gasses.

An organization which produces one tonne less carbon or carbon dioxide equivalent than the standard level of carbon emission is allowed for its outfit or activity, earn a carbon credit. Countries which are signatories to the Kyoto Protocol have laid down gas emission norms for their companies to be met by 2012. In such cases, a company has two ways to reduce emissions.

1. It can reduce the greenhouse gases (GHG) by adopting new technology or improving upon the existing technology to attain the new norms for emission of gases.
2. It can tie up with the developing nations and help them to set up new technology that is eco-friendly, thereby helping developing country or its companies to 'earn' credits. This credit becomes a permit for the company to emit greenhouse gases (GHG) in its own country.

Developing countries like India and China are likely to emerge as the biggest sellers and the European countries as the biggest buyers of the carbon credit. At present China is the largest seller of carbon credit, controlling about 70 per cent of the market share.

Carbon like other commodities, has begun to be traded on India's Multi-Commodity Exchange.

CARBON TAX

Carbon Tax is the potential alternative to the 'cap and trade' method currently used by the protocol. This tax is based on the amount of carbon contained in a fuel such as coal, petroleum and natural gas.

The aim of this tax is to cause less fossil fuel use and hopefully cause an incentive to use other sources of energy. The main reasons why carbon tax could prove more beneficial are given below:

(i) Predictability

The tax could help to predict energy prices which might also help investment in energy efficiency and alternate fuels.

(ii) Implementation

A carbon tax could be put into use much easily compared to the legalities that go alongwith the 'cap trade' method.

(iii) Understandable

The carbon tax is easy to understand.

(iv) Lack of Manipulation

Special interest groups have less of a chance of manipulation a carbon tax because of its simplicity.

(v) Rebates

Like other norms of taxes, the carbon tax could be open for rebates to the public.

Table 6.2 Current Carbon Emissions in Selected Countries

S.No.	Country	Carbon-Dioxide Emission per head, per annum (in metric tons)
1	U.S.A.	20.00
2.	Russia	11.75
3.	Japan	9.90
4.	European Union (EU)	9.50
5.	China	3.60
6.	India	1.00
	World	**4.25**

An examination of Table 6.2 show that the maximum quantity of Carbon dioxide is emitted in U.S.A. where it is 20 metric tonnes per head per annum followed by Russia (11.75 metric tonnes), Japan 9.90 and European Union (9.50 metric tonnes). The per head per annum emission in China is about 3.60 metric tonnes, while in India it is only one metric tonne per head per annum.

GREEN ECONOMY

The term 'Green Economy' is inter-changeable with 'sustainable Development'. Green economy focuses on the fundamental changes that are required to ensure that economic systems are made more productive and sustainable. Green economy reduces the carbon emission and pollution and enhances the efficiency of energy and resources and maintains the ecosystems in a healthy condition.

Thus 'green economy is about sustainable energy, green jobs, low carbon economies, green policies, green-buildings, agriculture, forestry, fisheries, industry, sustainable transport, waste management, water efficiency and eco-tourism.

Green economy tries to make the resource use economically viable, socially acceptable and environmentally sustainable.

ENVIRONMENT EDUCATION, AWARENESS AND TRAINING SCHEME (EEAT)

The Central Government of India launched in the Sixth Five Year Plan in 1983-84. The main objectives of the scheme were as under:

(i) to promote environmental awareness among all the section of the society,

(ii) to spread environmental education, especially in the non-formal system,

(iii) to facilitate development of education/training materials and aids in formal education sector,

(iv) to promote environmental education through existing educational/scientific institutions,

(v) to ensure training and manpower development of Environment Education, Awareness and Training.

(vi) to encourage NGOs, mass media and other concerned organizations for promoting awareness about environmental issues,

(vii) to use different media (audio and visual) for spreading messages concerning environment awareness, and

(viii) to mobilize people's participation for the preservation and conservation of resources and environment.

CARBON FOOTPRINT

It is the mark that we leave on our planet as a result of our daily activities and usage or emissions of carbon dioxide. In more precise terms, it is the measure of impact that human activities have on the environment and this is calculated in proportion to the greenhouse gases produced and measured in units of carbon dioxide.

CARBON SINK

A *carbon sink* is anything that absorbs more carbon than that it releases, while a *carbon source* is anything that releases more carbon than is absorbed. Forests, soils, oceans, water-bodies, and atmosphere all store carbon and this carbon moves between them in a continuous cycle. This constant movement of carbon means that forests act as sources or sinks at different times. In other words, a carbon sink is natural or artificial reservoir that accumulates and stores some carbon-containing chemical compounds for an indefinite period. The artificial sinks are (i) landfills, and (ii) carbon capture and storage proposals.

CARBON TRADING

The idea of carbon trade watch came into force in 2002. The inclusion of pollution trading policy in the Kyoto Protocol signals a historical proliferation of the free market principle into the environmental sphere. With a focus on emerging greenhouse gases, carbon trading watch monitors the impact of pollution trading up on environmental, social and economic justice.

Case Study in Carbon Trading

Powerguda village in the Adilabad District of Andhra Pradesh had sold 147 tonnes equivalent of saved carbon credit to the World Bank for US $ 645. According to villagers of Powerguda and E. D'Silva a farmer, the World Bank staff who are working in the area for creating awareness about their trade have extracted biodiesel from 4500 *Pongamia* trees in their village. By using biodiesel instead of petroleum, they were able to save 147 MT of CO_2 and were also able to enhance the air quality. The World Bank was buying the carbon credits to balance the aviation fuel burnt by aircrafts carrying bank officials. At present, many other villages of India are following Powerguda and making carbon credit sale.

CHAPTER 7 Climate Change

INTRODUCTION

The long-term variability associated with the earth-ocean climate system is known as climate change. The study of climate change has become one of the most important sciences in recent years. In fact, the growth and decline of past human civilisations and other species of plants and animals as well as the formulation of future public policy regarding all elements of human life depend on the climate and climatic change.

What causes climates to change is a fascinating question. Many theories have been postulated, but no single one can totally satisfy all necessary requirements. Although, there is little doubt that changes in Earth-Sun relationships may be a basic cause of long-term climatic change on Earth, it appears that the effects must be considered in conjunction with other factors. The problem of explaining the change is further complicated because human activity is now a major factor in the modification of climate. To explain what is happening, the so-called natural causes must be considered together with the impacts of humans. This is well demonstrated by the extensive surface changes created by human activity and the addition of carbon dioxide to the atmosphere. In cities, the human impact is so great that a new set of climatic condition is created.

The solar energy received at the Earth's surface can change due to the amount of energy given off by the Sun, changes in the transparency of the atmosphere, or changes in the distance between Earth and the Sun, There is little doubt that solar irradiance affects weather. The average temperature of the Sun is near 5438°C, but varies slightly, and hence the energy output varies. There is a close relationship between the irradiance of the Sun and the climate of the Earth. According to experts, a decline of 2 per cent irradiance of the Sun for 50 years would be enough to cause renewed glaciations. A drop of 5 per cent should be adequate to bring about a major glaciation of the Earth.

For the time associated with human civilisations, many historical records, diaries, planting records and even clothing and building materials can supply useful information on climate conditions for a given civilisation.

Global climatic changes, a continuous process, has been great and diverse during the Earth's history of 4.6 billion years. In general, Global climate has undergone more or less cyclic variations. Some periods have seen a warm climate, some cold, and, in many instances, there was an abrupt change from one period to another. The early climatic history of the world is, however, not well understood but it is known that during the last one million years there had been alternating of glacial and inter-glacial episodes.

THEORIES ON CLIMATE CHANGE

A number of theories have been postulated about the change in climate of the Earth. The main theories about climate change are: 1. The Sunspot Theory, 2. Variation in Atmospheric Dust Theory, 3. Human Induced Greenhouse-gases Theory, 4. Sunspot Theory, 5. Earth Orbital Eccentricity Theory, 6. Extraterrestrial Impact Theory and the Passage of Earth through an Interstellar Dust Theory. (For detailed description see Dictionary of Physical Geography, 2000, by S.G. Thomas, et al. 3rd ed. pp. 87–88).

ANTHROPOGENIC CAUSES OF CLIMATE CHANGE

At present, human activities are considered largely responsible for climate change, enhancing the greenhouse effect. The main anthropogenic causes of climate change have been described briefly in the following:

1. Increase in Air Temperature

There is little scientific doubt that air temperatures are the highest since recordings were begun in earnest more than 100 years ago. The rate of warming in the past 50 years exceeded comparable period in the temperature record. Experts of climatology are almost unanimous in the matter of increase in temperature and the consequent climatic change. Most of them agree that the planet Earth is getting hotter. After the Industrial Revolution in Britain in the 18th Century, the global warming is, however, largely the result of emission of carbon dioxide and greenhouse gases from human activity including industrial processes, fossil fuel combustion, deforestation and change in the land-use patterns. According to NASA scientists, the present climatic condition and rise in greenhouse gases have been described as under:

The world is warming. Climatic zones are shifting. Glaciers are melting. Sea-level is rising. These are not hypothetical events from a science fiction movie; these changes and others are already taking place, and we expect them to accelerate over the next years as the amounts of carbon dioxide, methane, and other trace gases accumulated in the atmosphere through human activities increase.

The trend of change in surface temperature for the past 18,000 years has been shown in **Fig. 7.1.** It may be seen from **Fig. 7.1** that in about 18,000 years before present, the air temperature of the Earth was around –5°C, which showed a fluctuating trend, crossing the 0°C around 9000 years before present. Since then, there is a steady increase in the surface temperature of the Earth being around 15°C at present.

The trend of change in surface temperature has been shown in **Fig. 7.2**. It may be observed from **Fig. 7.2** that the increase in the air temperature in the 20th Century has been about 0.5°C. The rate of change in temperature is, however, steadily increasing with the passage of time. In fact, the last five decades of the 20th Century and first decade of the 21st Century (1950–2010) have been the warmest years since the systematic recording of temperature began in 1878. It may also be seen from **Fig. 7.3** that the earth temperature was about 14°C in 1950 which rose to about 15°C in 2000.

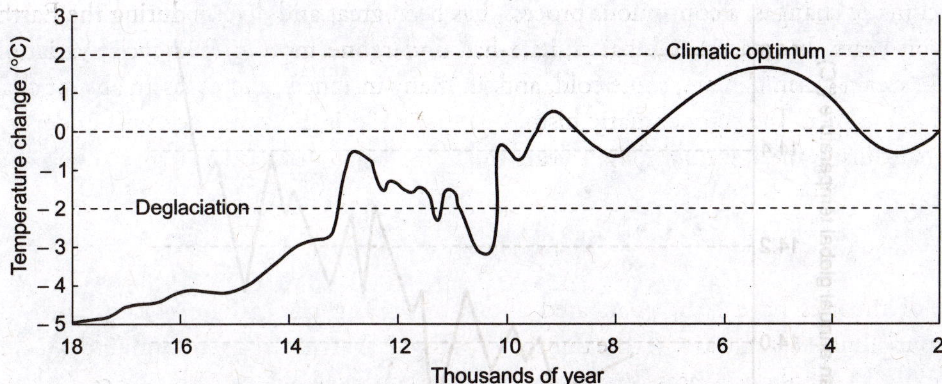

Fig. 7.1 Trend of change in surface temperature for the past 18,000 years (after J.E. Olioer and J.J. Hidore, 2003)

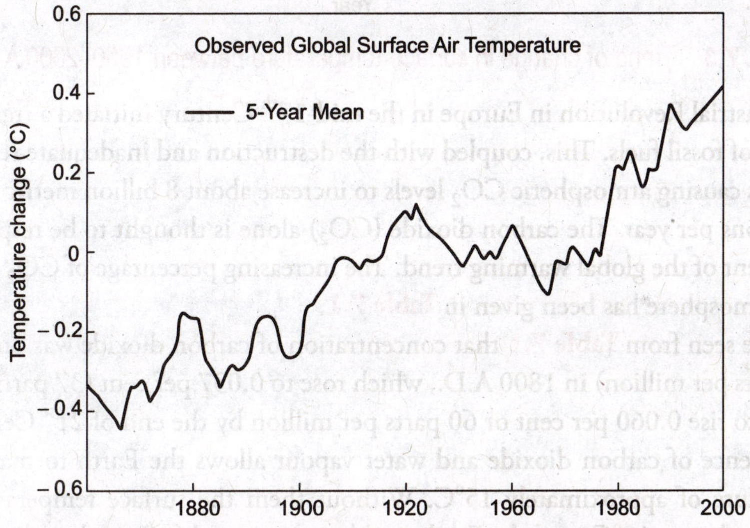

Fig. 7.2 Trend of Change in surface temperature since 1880 (*Source:* H. Wilson and J. Hansen)

2. Greenhouse Gases

The gases which absorb and re-emit infrared radiation are known as greenhouse gases. These gases may be added in the atmosphere either by the natural or by the anthropogenic processes. According to the experts, carbon dioxide (CO_2), methane, chlorofluoro-carbon, etc. are the main gases responsible for the global warming.

(i) **Carbon-Dioxide and Global Warming:** Carbon dioxide and water vapour are the most important greenhouse gases in the atmosphere because they allow short-wave radiation to enter the Earth's atmosphere, but help to stop long-wave radiation from escaping. This traps heat, raising Earth's temperature. An excess of these gases helps to trap more heat, thereby, lead to global warming.

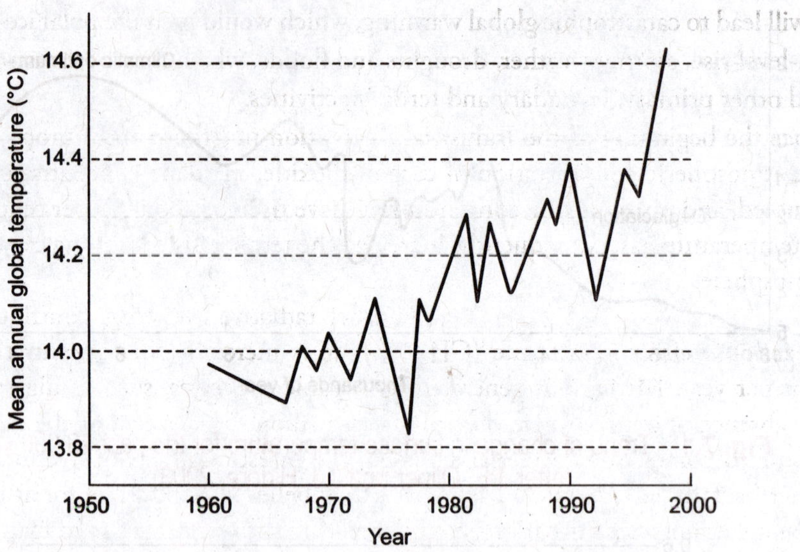

Fig. 7.3 Trend of change in surface temperature between 1950–2000 A.D.

The Industrial Revolution in Europe in the mid-17th Century initiated a tremendous surge in burning of fossil fuels. This, coupled with the destruction and inadequate replacement rate of forests, is causing atmospheric CO_2 levels to increase about 8 billion metric tons to 10 billion metric tons per year. The carbon dioxide (CO_2) alone is thought to be responsible for about 60 per cent of the global warming trend. The increasing percentage of CO_2 in the lower parts of the atmosphere has been given in Table 7.1.

It may be seen from Table 7.1 that concentration of carbon dioxide was only 0.020 per cent (200 parts per million) in 1800 A.D., which rose to 0.037 per cent (37 parts per million) and is likely to rise 0.060 per cent or 60 parts per million by the end of 21st Century.

The presence of carbon dioxide and water vapour allows the Earth to maintain an average temperature of approximately 15°C. Without them the surface temperature of the Earth would be about –19°C, and the Earth could not support life. It is clear that we owe our very existence to the greenhouse gases and their effect. But because of rapid growth of population and consumerism, the carbon dioxide is increasing significantly in the atmosphere. During the last century, it has increased by more than 30 per cent. The doubling of the atmospheric CO_2 concentration will enhance the planet's natural greenhouse effect to such an extent that

Table 7.1 Lower Atmosphere Concentration of Carbon Dioxide (CO_2)

Year	CO_2 Concentration (%)	Parts per million
1800	0.020	200
1950	0.028	280
2000	0.037	370
2050 (estimated)	0.60	600

it will lead to catastrophic global warming, which would melt the polar ice-caps, resulting into sea-level rise, stormy weather, droughts and floods, which may be catastrophic to agriculture and other primary, secondary and tertiary activities.

Since the beginning of the Industrial Revolution in Britain and Europe (1779), apart from the atmospheric concentration of carbon dioxide, methane concentrations have more than doubled, and nitrous oxide concentrations have risen by about 15 per cent. The enhancement in temperature has, consequently, increased the temperature trapping capability of the Earth's atmosphere (Fig. 7.4).

(ii) **Methane and Global Warming:** Another radiative active gas contributing to the overall greenhouse effect is methane (CH_4), which is increasing in concentration at about 1 per cent per year. Methane is generated by organic processes, such as digestion and rotting in the absence of oxygen (anaerobic processes). About 50 per cent of the excess methane being produced comes from bacterial action in the intestinal tracts of livestock and from under-water bacteria in rice fields. Methane is now believed responsible for at least 12 per cent of the total atmospheric warming, complementing the warming caused by the build-up of CO_2 and equaling about one-half the contribution of CFCs.

(iii) **Chlorofluorocarbon (CFCs) and Global Warming:** Chlorofluorocarbon gases are produced by large manufactured molecules (polymers) containing chlorine, fluorine, and carbon. These gases possess remarkable heat properties. After slow transport to the stratosphere ozone layer CFCs react with ultraviolet radiation freeing chlorine atoms that act as a catalyst to produce reactions that destroy ozone.

Chlorofluorocarbon (CFCs) are thought to contribute about 25 per cent of the global warming. As stated above, CFCs absorb infrared in wavelengths missed by carbon dioxide and water vapour in the lower troposphere. As relatively active gases, CFCs enhance the greenhouse effect, and also play a negative role in stratospheric ozone depletion.

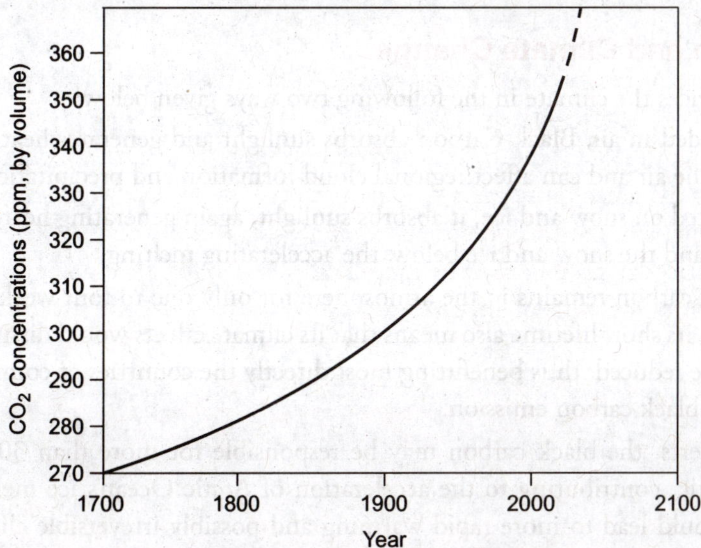

Fig. 7.4 The rise in atmosphere Carbon dioxide since 1700 A.D.

3. Cryogenic/Cryergic Processes and Global Warming

The processes of permafrost, glaciations, defrosting and de-glaciations are known as cryogenic processes. Nearly 20 per cent of the Earth's land surface currently experiences cryogenic or peri-glacial conditions in the form of either intense frost action or presence of ice and permafrost, or both.

The cryogenic processes are also the very important factors of global warming and consequent, climatic change. The period of widespread glaciations is called the *great ice age* which comprises several glacial and interglacial periods. The glacial period denotes onset of cold climate while interglacial periods indicate relatively warmer period when ice sheets retreat and the valley glaciers shrink.

The most pervasive effect of climatic change may be observed in the melting of glaciers and ice-sheets. This will directly affect the area under pastures and agriculture, especially in the higher latitudinal regions of Eurasia and, and Canada (**Figs. 7.5 and 7.6**). The recent evidences have shown that the ice sheets of Antarctica, Greenland, Baffin Island, etc. are breaking, thinning and melting. Moreover, the valley glaciers of folded mountains are also shrinking. According to the experts of glaciology, the Gaumukh Glacier (source of Bhagirathi–Ganga), and Satopanth Glacier (source of Alaknanda) are shrinking at a faster pace. Same is the case with the glaciers of Karakoram, Hindukush, Andes, Rockies, Alps, Carpathian, and Altai, etc. The reduction in the size of glaciers is a clear and conclusive evidence which proves beyond doubt the phenomena of global warming and climate change.

CO_2 can Crack Ice

Atomic level simulation studies by material science of Massachusetts Institute of Technology (MIT) suggest that increased concentrations of carbon dioxide (CO_2) in the atmosphere can cause ice to become more brittle, not unlike the breaking up or cracking of materials due to corrosion. Thus CO_2 can play the role of corroding agent and lead to destabilization of the structure.

4. Black Carbon and Climate Change

Black Carbon influences the climate in the following two ways given below:

(i) When suspended in air, Black Carbon absorbs sunlight and generates heat in the atmosphere, which warm the air and can affect regional cloud formation and precipitation patterns.

(ii) When deposited on snow and ice, it absorbs sunlight, again generating heat, which warms both the air above and the snow and ice below, the accelerating melting.

Because the black carbon remains in the atmosphere for only one to four weeks, its climate effects are strongly regional. Its short lifetime also means that its climate effects would dissipate quickly if black carbon emission were reduced, thus benefitting most directly the countries of communities that invest in policies to reduce black carbon emission.

According to experts, the black carbon may be responsible for more than 30 per cent of recent warming in the Arctic, contributing to the acceleration of Arctic Ocean's ice melting. Loss of ice of the Arctic Ocean would lead to more rapid warming and possibly irreversible climate change. Black Carbon may also be driving some of the observed reduction of the snowpack in the Pacific Northwest of North America.

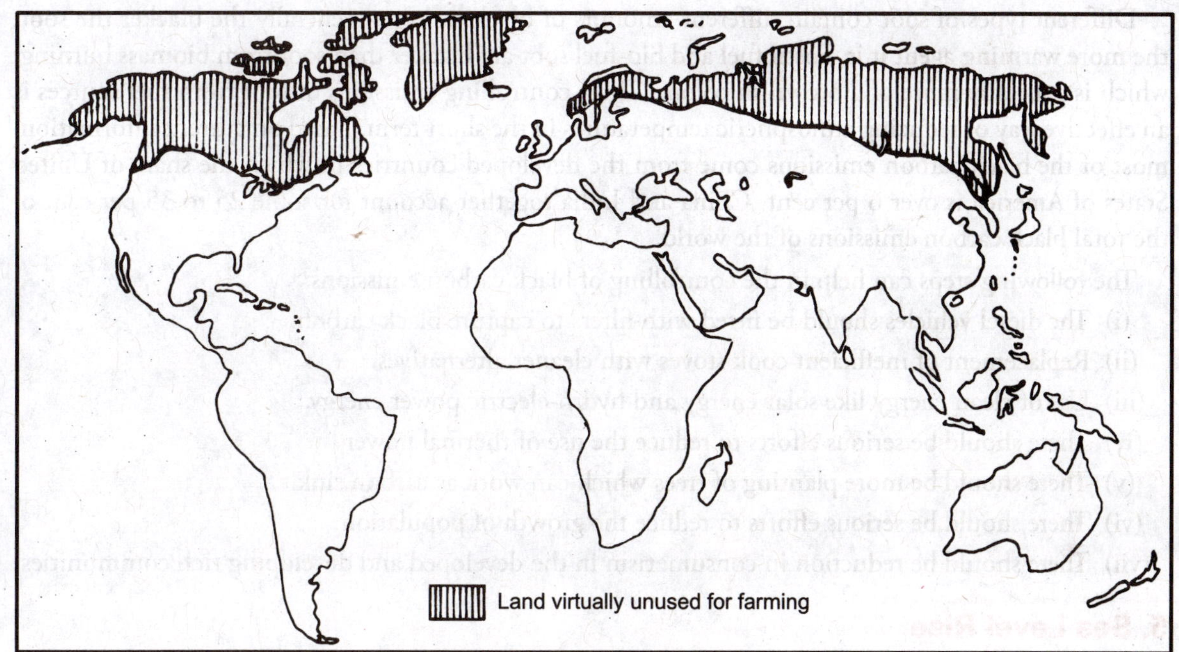

Fig. 7.5 Limits to arable land—2012

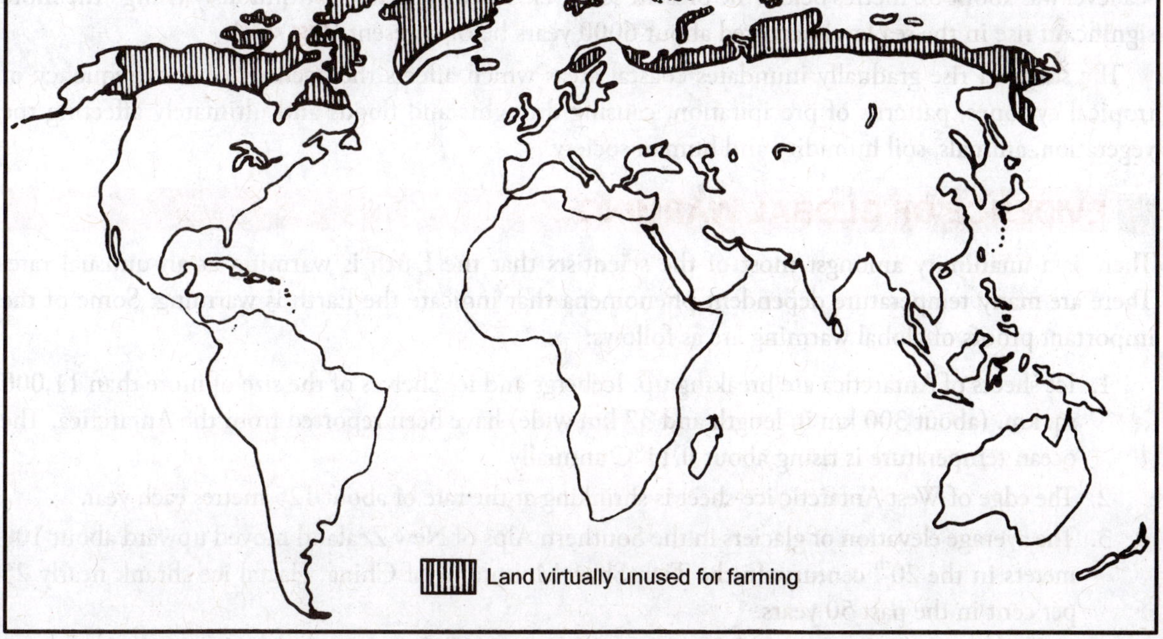

Land virtually unused for farming

Fig. 7.6 Projected limits of arable land—2050

Different types of soot contain different amounts of black carbon—generally the blacker the soot, the more warming agent it is. Fossil fuel and bio-fuel soot are blacker than soot from biomass burning, which is generally more of a brownish colour. Thus, controlling emissions of soot from fuel sources is an effective way of reducing atmospheric temperatures in the short term. Based on current information, most of the black carbon emissions come from the developed countries in which the share of United States of America is over 6 per cent. China and India together account for some 25 to 35 per cent of the total black carbon emissions of the world.

The following steps can help in the controlling of black carbon emissions:

(i) The diesel vehicles should be fitted with filters to capture black carbon.

(ii) Replacement of inefficient cook stoves with cleaner alternatives.

(iii) Use of clean energy like solar energy and hydro-electric power energy.

(iv) There should be serious efforts to reduce the use of thermal power.

(v) There should be more planting of trees which can work as carbon sink.

(vi) There should be serious efforts to reduce the growth of population.

(vii) There should be reduction in consumerism in the developed and developing rich communities.

5. Sea Level Rise

The experts of Oceanography opine that significant changes are taking place in the sea level. In fact, the measurements of sea level exhibit cyclical changes in sea level. The main cause of sea level rise is the melting of ice-sheets and glaciers. The sea level changes during the last 18 thousand years have been shown in **Fig. 7.7**. It may be observed from this figure that about 18 thousand years before present, the sea level was about 82 metres below the present sea level. Since then, it is continuously rising. The more significant rise in the sea level occurred about 6000 years before present (**Fig. 7.7**).

The sea level rise gradually inundates coastal areas which affects the occurrence and frequency of tropical cyclones, patterns of precipitation, causing droughts and floods and ultimately affecting the vegetation, animals, soil humidity and human society.

EVIDENCE OF GLOBAL WARMING

There is a unanimity amongst most of the scientists that the Earth is warming at an unusual rate. There are many temperature dependent phenomena that indicate the Earth is warming. Some of the important proofs of global warming are as follows:

1. Ice sheets of Antarctica are breaking up. Icebergs and ice shelves of the size of more than 11,000 sq. km. (about 300 km in length and 37 km wide) have been reported from the Antarctica. The ocean temperature is rising about 0.11°C annually.
2. The edge of West Antarctic ice-sheet is shrinking at the rate of about 125 metres each year.
3. The average elevation of glaciers in the Southern Alps of New Zealand moved upward about 100 meters in the 20th century. In the Tien Shan Mountains of China, glacial ice shrank nearly 25 per cent in the past 50 years.
4. In the Cuacasus Mountains of Georgia and Russia, half of glacial ice melted away in the past 50 years.

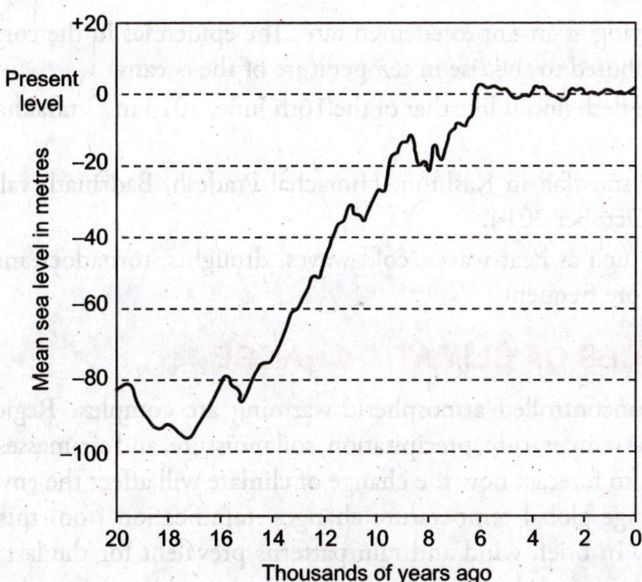

Fig. 7.7 Fluctuations in Sea level (after Fairbridge in H.J. Crichfield, 2002)

5. Garhwal Himalayas (Uttarakhand—India) glaciers are rapidly retreating. For example, the Pindari, Gaumukh, Chorabari, Milam and Satopanth glaciers are retreating at the rate of about 10 metres per year.
6. In the Bering Sea, the area of sea shrunk by about 5 per cent in the last 50 years.
7. The largest glacier of Mount Kenya almost completely melted away in the 20th century.
8. The Bering Glacier in Alaska is retreating.
9. The glaciers in National Park, Montana State (USA), are melting rapidly.
10. Glaciers of Alps Mountains of Europe shrank by about 50 per cent in the 20th century.
11. Sea level is rising.
12. The temperature of global ocean is rising. A global temperature of 15.4°C was reached in 1990.
13. Permafrost is melting in the Northern Hemisphere.
14. Vegetation (mosses and lichen) appearing on the slopes of the mountains of Antarctica.
15. The tree-line in mountain ranges is moving upward.
16. Many tropical diseases (malaria, cholera, yellow-fever, dengue-fever, plague and hantavirus) are spreading towards the higher latitudes and the polar regions.
17. Snowfall was recorded in the desert of Dubai and Abu-Dhabi (Ras-al-Khaima) for the first time in the recorded history in January/February, 2005.
18. The 20th Century was the warmest century of the millennium.
19. The year 1998 was the warmest year of the 20th Century.
20. Seven out of ten warmest years were recorded in the last decade of the 20th Century.
21. The population of Adele-Penguins on Antarctica declined by 40 per cent.
22. The frequency of El-Nino years is increasing.

23. The corals are dying at an unprecedented rate. The epidemics in the corals in the form of coral bleaching is attributed to the rise in temperature of the oceans.
24. Cloudbursts and flesh floods like that of the 16th June, 2013 in Uttarakhand are becoming more frequent.
25. Untimely heavy snowfall in Kashmir, Himachal Pradesh, Badrinath valley (Uttarakhand) and Nepal on 16th October 2014.
26. Extreme events such as heat-wavcs, cold-waves, droughts, tornadoes and western disturbances are becoming more frequent.

CONSEQUENCES OF CLIMATIC CHANGE

The consequences of uncontrolled atmospheric warming are complex. Regional and international responses are expected as temperature, precipitation, soil moisture, and air-masses characteristics change. Although, it is difficult to forecast how the change of climate will affect the environment, ecology and society, but if the average global temperature changes, ramification from this change will have far-reaching consequences. In brief, wind and rain patterns prevalent for the last million of years could change; sea-level would rise and threaten island, sea-beaches and low-lying coastal regions. This might result into droughts, desertification, floods, landslides, avalanches, hurricanes, natural hazards, and disasters which lead to large-scale migration of human population, animals and shift in the vegetation belts.

Some of the effects of climatic change are already being felt. For instance, the Arctic Ice Cap has lost 42 per cent. According to one study, 27 per cent of the coral formations on the tropical oceans may disappear. ***Following are some of the consequences of climate change:***

1. Rise in sea level.
2. Change in pressure belts and atmospheric circulation.
3. Change in the direction of permanent and periodic winds.
4. Change in the directions of warm and cold water currents.
5. The Inter-Tropical Convergence Zone (ITCZ) may mover northward in the Northern Hemisphere.
6. Increase in the frequency of tropical and temperate cyclones, cloud cover, tornadoes and storms.
7. Change in the intensity and patterns of precipitation.
8. Change in the soil-moisture, and humus contents of soils.
9. Alteration in natural vegetation and soil belts.
10. Change in cropping patterns, crop combination, and agricultural productivity.
11. Change in hydrological cycle and water supply.
12. The marine life will be favourably/adversely affected.
13. Warming of temperature of the oceans may endanger the corals worldwide.
14. Fields of the farmers of delta regions may submerge.
15. Expansion of deserts and more desertification within the deserts.
16. The land-based animals will have to adapt to changing patterns of climatic belts.
17. Effect on food supply and international trade of grains.

18. National parks, sanctuaries and biosphere reserves may be altered.
19. Change in the international trade pacts and geo-politics of the world.
20. Countries like Maldives, and greater parts of the Netherlands, etc. may submerge under water.
21. Climatic change is making food crops less nutritious. Rising carbon dioxide emissions lead to iron and zinc deficiencies in food crops.

Consequences of Climate Change in India

The expected general consequences of climatic change have been given concisely in the preceding paragraphs. But the impact of global warming and climate change may be more serious at the national and regional levels. The scientists of the Indian Institute of Tropical Meteorology (IITM) found that temperature would increase by about 5°C in several parts of India, especially in Gujarat (Rann of Kachchh) and Rajasthan, and 3°C to 4°C in Peninsular India by the end of the 21st Century. In addition to this, the incidence of violent and stormy weather and the frequency of tropical cyclones may increase by about 50 per cent. This may lead to heat waves, more torrential rainfall and more prolonged dry spells in the less rainfall recording areas (**Figs. 7.8 and 7.9**).

The extreme events of weather are bound to change, the fauna, flora, ecosystems, biodiversity, economy, society, polity and gamut of life of the people in most of the parts of the country. Thus rising temperature may affect every aspect of ecology and society. ***According to experts of Indian Institute of Tropical Meteorology, New Delhi, following are the expected consequences of global warming and climate change in India:***

1. The discharge of water even in the perennial rivers may decrease by about 20 per cent by 2050.
2. Agricultural production in India may decline by about 15 per cent.
3. The hydrological cycle will be adversely affected.
4. Decrease in fresh water availability.
5. Increase in rate of evaporation. More water vapour will get in the atmosphere and then back to the ocean as rain.
6. Decrease in soil moisture in the northern plains of India and the consequent increase in saline affected areas.
7. The forest cover will change in nature and there will be shift in vegetation belts.
8. In several areas, the total number of rainfall will increase, while in others there will be decrease in the number of rainy days (**Figs. 7.8 and 7.9**).
9. Increase in flood prone area. With a warming climate, flow of water, from the Himalayan glaciers into Indus, Satluj, Ganga and Brahmaputra will increase until at least 2050.
10. The unseasonality of hot and cold spells will not be conducive for good agricultural returns.
11. The areas of Biosphere Reserves and National Parks have to be altered.
12. The attractive sea-beaches may submerge under water.
13. The deltas along coast of Tamil Nadu, Andhra Pradesh, Odisha, and West Bengal may submerge under water.
14. The islands in front of Sundarban Delta and the Lakshadweep may submerge and disappear because of sea-level rise.

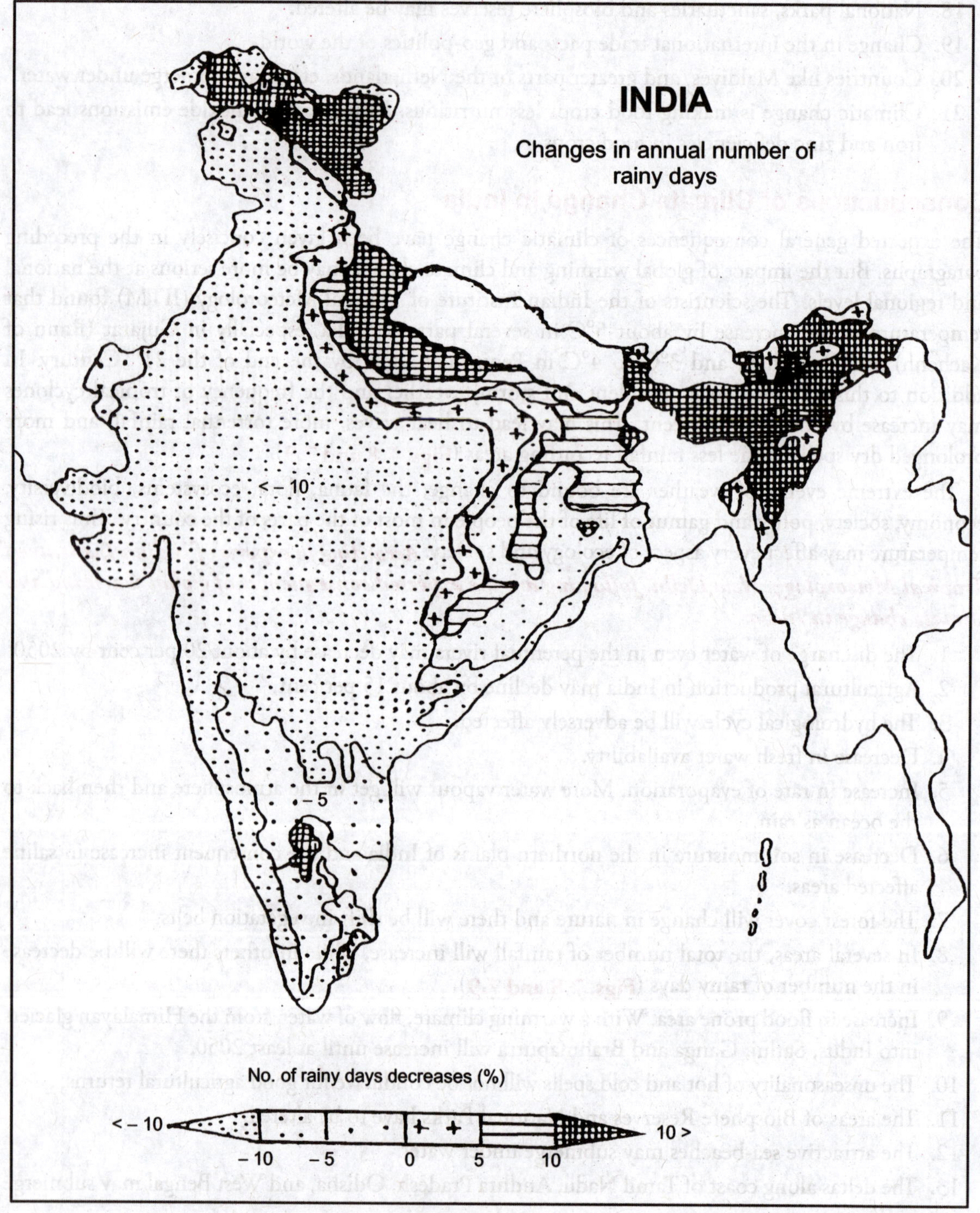

Fig. 7.8 India: Changes in annual number of rainy days
(*Source:* Indian Institute of Tropical Meteorology)

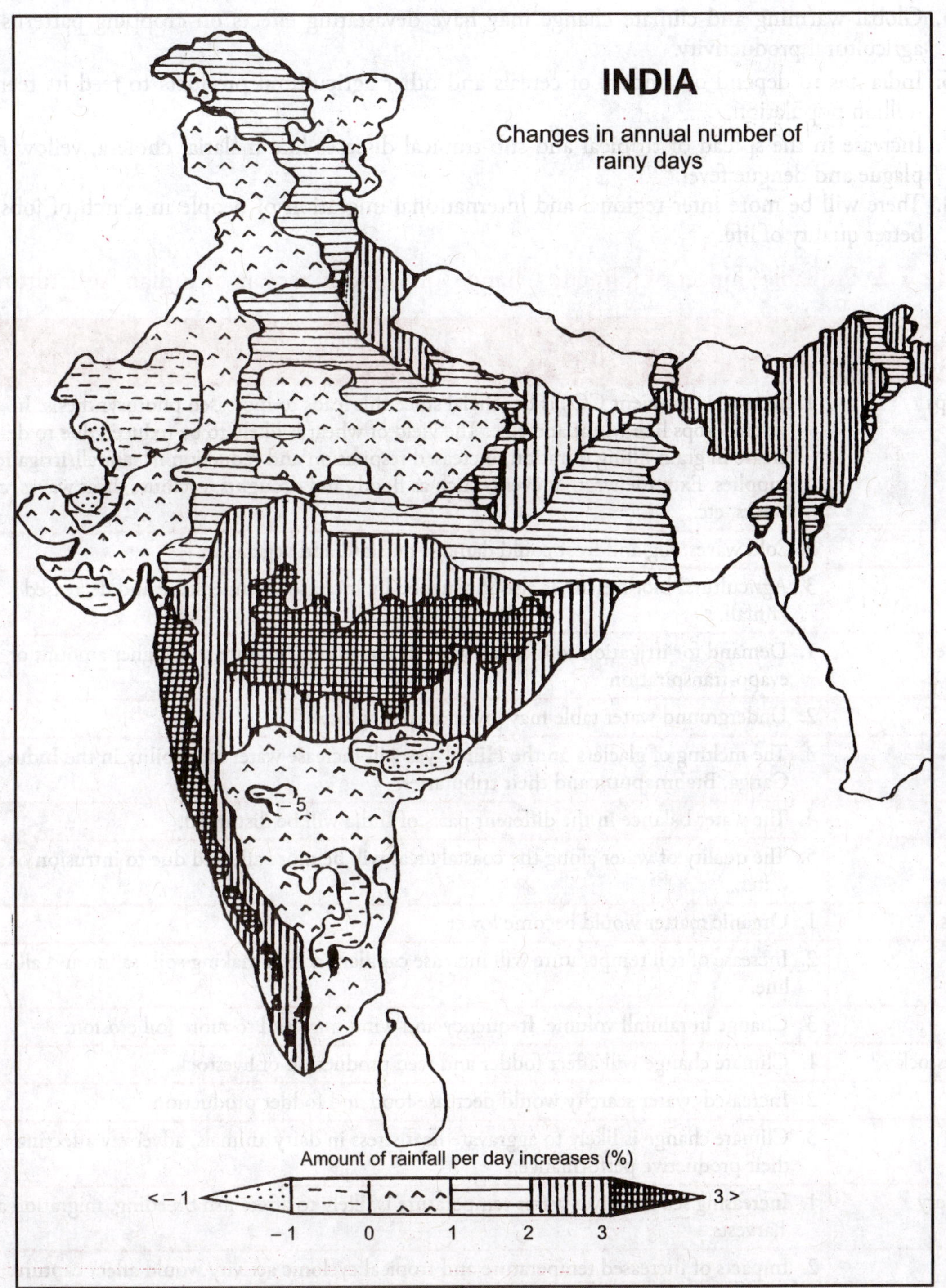

Fig. 7.9 India: Changes in annual number of rainy days
(*Source:* Indian Institute of Tropical Meteorology)

15. Global warming and climate change may have devastating effects on cropping patterns and agricultural productivity.
16. India has to depend on import of cereals and other agricultural products to feed its teeming million population.
17. Increase in the spread of tropical and sub-tropical diseases like malaria, cholera, yellow fever, plague and dengue fever.
18. There will be more inter-regional and international migration of people in search of jobs and better quality of life.

Table 7.2 Probable Impact of Climate Change on Various Sectors of Indian Agriculture

Agricultural Sector	Probable Impact
Crops	1. Increase in ambient CO_2 is beneficial since this leads to increased photosynthesis. In several crops like wheat and rice. The yield of wheat is likely to be reduced due to decrease in grain filling duration, increased respiration and reduction in rainfall/irrigation supplies. Extreme weather events such as floods and droughts, cyclones, heat waves, cold waves, etc.
	2. Cold waves, fog and frost could damage mustard and vegetables.
	3. Agricultural biodiversity is also threatened by increased temperature and decreased rainfall.
Water	1. Demand for irrigation to increase with increased temperature and higher amount of evapo-transpiration.
	2. Underground water table may lower at some places.
	3. The melting of glaciers in the Himalayas will increase water availability in the Indus, Ganga, Brahmaputra and their tributaries.
	4. The water balance in the different parts of India will be disturbed.
	5. The quality of water along the coastal areas will be more affected due to intrusion of sea water.
Soils	1. Organic matter would become lower.
	2. Increase of soil temperature will increase capillary action making soils saline and alkaline.
	3. Change in rainfall volume, frequency and wind may lead to more soil erosion.
Livestock	1. Climate change will affect fodder and feed production of livestock.
	2. Increased water scarcity would decrease food and fodder production
	3. Climate change is likely to aggravate heat stress in dairy animals, adversely affecting their productive performance.
Fishery	1. Increasing sea and river water temperature is likely to affect fish breeding, migration and harvests.
	2. Impacts of increased temperature and tropical cyclonic activity would affect capture, production and marketing cost of marine fish.
	3. Coral bleaching is likely to increase due to higher sea surface temperature.

Source: ICAR, Handbook of Agriculture, 2012, p.69.

ADAPTIVE STRATEGIES FOR CLIMATE CHANGE MITIGATION

Many of the governments opine that society has adapted to many problems and natural hazards in the past. According to them, capital can be raised and technology harnessed to block the flood and guard the coastlines and deltas. Moreover, a cooperative global network of nations, under the United Nations Environment Programme (UNEP), participate in the World Watch System and the Global Change Programme to gather temperature, weather, and climatic information to assist climate modellers and policy maker. Many studies and participants at numerous world conferences have agreed that governmental policies can profoundly alter greenhouse effect, thereby can minimise the impact of climate change.

According to the U.N. Climate Science Panel, the world would have to reduce greenhouse gas emissions by 40-70% below 2010 levels by 2050 in order to have a fair chance to keep the rise in the global temperature below 2 degree celsius. Moreover, to check temperature rise, greenhouse gas concentration to be brought down to 430-480 parts per million (ppm) of carbon dioxide equivalent by 2100. The renewable energy development needs to be ramped up 300-400% frm 2010 levels by 2050. In order to achieve these goals hundreds of billions of dollars to be given annually to developing countries to shift to renewable resources. It is also a fact, that emissions rising in developing countries but more due to exports to developed countries.

Climate change mitigation is an action to decrease the emission and intensity of greenhouse gases in the atmosphere. Some of the important steps which can go a long way in reducing the emissions of greenhouse gases and ultimately in the mitigation of climate change have been given briefly in the following:

Steps to Reduce Emission of Greenhouse Gases

(i) **Alternative sources of energy:** Low carbon renewable energy. Renewable energy currently provides only about 18 per cent of the total electricity generated in the world. There is a need to generate more solar, wind, tidal and thermal energy. Solar water heating, and renewable bio-fuel for transportation are also the effective methods of climate change mitigation.

(ii) **Generation of Nuclear Power:** Nuclear power generation at present accounts for about 14 per cent of the worlds electricity produced and consumed. There is urgent need to double this production.

(iii) **Afforestation:** The forest cover in different parts of the world, especially in the equatorial and subtropical countries is decreasing at an alarming rate. Indiscriminate felling of trees should be stopped and there should be then a movement to plant more trees both in developed and the developing countries.

(iv) **Urban Planning:** There should be less urban encroachment on agricultural land. This can be done by compact community development, multiple transport choices, and by developing green areas and green belts.

(v) **Building designing:** New buildings can be constructed using to use the solar heat and light resources. The existing buildings can be made more efficient through the use of insulation, high efficiency appliances.

(vi) Controlled burning of biomass: The bio-mass should be utilised in biomass fuelled power plants to reduce the emission of greenhouse gases.

(vii) Reduction in the growth of population: There should be strict population policies in the developing countries to control the growth of population. More the population more is the emissions of greenhouse gases.

(viii) Reduction in consumerism: In the developed countries and among the rich people of the developing countries there is a growing trend of use and throw culture. This practice puts more pressure on forest and other resources. There should be serious efforts to control consumerism.

(x) Eradication of poverty: It is the poor and the people who are below the poverty line who depend on forest in the forested areas. Such people need to be elevated above the poverty line to conserve the forests and other renewable and non-renewable resources.

(xi) Mass education about ecology and environment: Use of media, and organisation of conferences and seminars can train the students and masses to realise the significance of the environment. Conservation of resources and environment should be a habit to be developed right from the childhood.

India is committed to reduce the greenhouse gases which are the main cause of climate change, and for this purpose, a number of legislations have been made. There is emphases in Indian Planning to protect the poor and vulnerable sections of the society through an inclusive and sustainable development strategy. India is also developing appropriate technologies for both adaptation and mitigation of greenhouse gases emissions.

BIODIVERSITY AND CLIMATE CHANGE

Introduction

The term biodiversity was coined by R.F. Dasmann in 1968. Biodiversity is an abbreviation of 'biological diversity'. It refers to the variety of abundance of living organisms in a particular region/country. In other words, biodiversity is the variability among living and non-living organisms and ecological complexes of which they are part, including diversity within and between species and ecosystems.

Biodiversity has great significance for survival of human beings and existence of flora, fauna and humanity. Biodiversity provides a large number of direct and indirect benefits to humanity. For example, biodiversity provides food, fodder, fuel-wood, raw-materials for industries and timber for construction of houses and shelters and medicinal herbs. The production of oxygen, reduction of carbon-dioxide, maintaining the water cycle, and protection of soils are some of the important services. The loss of biodiversity contributes to global warming and global climate change. Biodiversity loss is also causing major atmospheric and weather changes, leading to increase in temperature, serious droughts in some areas and unexpected floods in other areas.

Biodiversity is also essential for preserving ecological processes such as fixing soil nutrients, soil formation, circulation and cleaning of air and water, maintaining of river flow throughout the year and local flood reduction. It has great aesthetic, recreational and eco-tourism significance. Biotechnologists use bio-rich areas for the purpose of teaching, training and research and for the development of better varieties of crops for use in farming, plantation and to develop better livestock. Biodiversity has great ethical and moral values. India has a large number of sacred groves or *'deorais'* preserved by tribal people in several states. These sacred groves around ancient sacred sites and temples act as gene-banks for wild plants.

The total number of species on Earth is still not known fully. According to one estimate the number may vary from 10 to 100 million. These species are the products of about four billion years. The largest number of plants, animals and micro-organisms are found in the equatorial biome (tropical rainforests), while the Tundra and Alpine biomes are poor in biodiversity. The variety of richness of plants and animal species may be examined at the local, regional or global level. Biodiversity has the following five aspects:

1. The distribution of different types of ecosystems which comprise community and plants, animals and micro-organisms, and the surrounding environment which are valuable not only for species they contain, but also for their own right.
2. The total number of species in a region/area.
3. The number of endemic species in a region or area.
4. The genetic diversity of an individual species.
5. The sub-population of an individual species.

In recent years ecologists are increasingly concerned with global warming, greenhouse gases and climatic change. It is of great interest and social relevance to examine the climatic change and its direct and indirect effect on biodiversity with especial reference to India.

Change of climate is the law of nature. There have been episodes of climate change throughout the geological history of the Earth, but the current global warming is likely to have significant impact on biodiversity (flora and fauna), and humanity of both the developed and the developing countries. The global warming may lead to sharp increase in species extinctions according to Inter-governmental Panel on Climate Change (ICPP) Report). The impact may be more serious in tropical and sub-tropical countries where the population is increasing at a faster pace and there is tremendous encroachment of forests, grazing lands and wetlands to bring more area under cultivation. We examine the effect of climate change on the biodiversity of the Himalayan Ecosystems, mangroves, on cropping pattern, agricultural production, fresh-water and the coastal urban population with especial reference to India.

Overall Effect of Climate Change

1. Impact of Climate Change on the Biodiversity of the Himalayas: The young folded mountains of the Himalayas are one of the most complex and dynamic systems in the world. The Himalayan region is vulnerable to global climate change mainly due to increased human interaction with ecosystems. This vast mountain system with a geographical area of about 5,91,000 km^2 representing about 18 per cent area of the country, is important part of the global climate system. The protected area network in the Himalayan region comprises of three biosphere reserves, 18 national parks and 71 wildlife sanctuary occupying about 9.2 per cent of the Indian Himalaya *(Manikhuri & Rao-2005)*.

Global warming has and will have serious impact on the biophysical environment and the socio-economic conditions and livelihood of people in Himalayas and the adjacent plain areas. it will also affect species composition and diversity, habitat and occurrence of rare and endangered species as well as invasive species in high altitude areas.

The loss of biodiversity due to global warming has direct and indirect impact on the life and livelihoods of the communities in the high altitudes of the Himalayas. For example, the Nanda Devi Biosphere Reserves has rich alpine meadows/pastures which are utilised by the tribes of Bhotias, Tolchas, Marchas, Nitiwal, Johri, Darmi, etc. The possible impact of rising temperatures on alpine meadows could be an upward migration of woody plants from lower elevations. The moraines exposed, as a result of global retreat, will drive alpine species upward but colonisation may be constrained by erosion and nutrient limitations.

The temperature rise may bring more opportunities particularly of cash crops, especially vegetables like tomato, cabbage, chilly, peas, carrot and medicinal herbs. However, reduction in winter snowfall and spring rainfall and melt-water flows will produce a soil moisture deficit which could limit an increase in yield resulting from temperature increase.

Considering the unprecedented rate of global climate change in recorded human history, it will adversely affect people inhabiting the Himalayan region in general, and the high altitudes people- like Nanda Devi Biosphere Reserves in particular. There is an urgent need to develop adaptation mechanism and coping strategies so as to ensure sustainable growth for reducing vulnerability, especially for the most vulnerable regions and socio-economic groups, as these groups are already under pressure due to population growth and socio-economic inequalities.

2. Effect on Mangroves: Mangroves are large flowering shrubs or trees that grow in dense thickets or forests along the muddy or silty tropical coasts. The mangroves are large and wide along the east coast of India due to the nutrient rich alluvial soil formed by the mighty rivers (Ganga, Brahmaputra, Mahanadi, Krishna and Kaveri) and a perennial supply of fresh water along the deltaic coasts. But, the deltas with alluvial deposits are almost absent on the west coast (Arabian Sea) of India, and their places are taken by the funnel-shaped estuaries or backwaters. Moreover, the east coast has smooth and gradual slope which provides larger area for the development of mangroves, whereas the western coast has a steep and vertical slope not very much suitable for mangroves colonization, growth and development. Mangroves are present in the Andaman and Nicobar Islands, where many tidal estuaries, small rivers, neritic islet, and lagoons support a rich mangrove flora. The distribution of mangroves in some of the states of India have been given in the Table below

Table State and Union Territory wise mangrove cover in 2005 as per Forest Survey of India (km^2).

State /Union Territory	Assessment Year
1. West Bengal (Sundarban)	2118
2. Gujarat	936
3. Andaman and Nicobar	637
4. Andhra Pradesh	329
5. Odisha	203
6. Maharashtra	158
7. Tamil Nadu	35
8. Goa	16
9. Kerala	8
Total	**4440**

Source: Forest Survey of India, 2006.

It may be seen from the above Table that West Bengal has the largest area under mangrove, followed by Gujarat, Andaman & Nicobar, Andhra Pradesh and Odisha. It is interesting to note that most of the mangroves are along the eastern coast of India as compared to the Western Coast (Arabian Sea).

Mangrove forests are the buffer zones of coasts and destruction of mangroves leads to tremendous coastal erosion, coastal siltation and terrible losses to human life from destructive hurricanes, storm surges and tsunamis. Due to the degradation of mangroves in West Bengal, Odisha, Andhra Pradesh and Tamil Nadu, repeated floodings are taking place. Today, there is growing urgency to recognise the importance of conserving and restoring protective mangrove greenbelts. Due to the change in climate systems, it is expected that the cyclones will hit the coast lines more rapidly than ever before. Under this condition, mangroves can buffer against the fury of such destructions, protecting those settlements located behind them.

The productive mangrove wetlands are often the first line of defence, helping to secure the coasts against erosion and storms. In fact, mangrove ecosystem is the potential system to control the global warming because of their high capacity for absorbing carbon from atmosphere and strong wetland substrate.

3. Effect on Agriculture: Climatic change has a direct bearing on the cropping patterns, crop combinations, crop rotation, and productivity of different crops. Climatic change leads to extreme events of weather. The frequency of droughts and floods will increase resulting to severe damage to cereal and cash crops. Thus, global warming will lead to food and water shortage, which shall affect not only humans but also plants, animals and entire ecosystems. There will be more deaths in the developing countries because of malnutrition, disease and heat stress, extinction of species and other related effects. Thus climate change will have disastrous consequences for millions of the developing countries who are largely dependent on agriculture, forestry and fishery for their livelihood. The experts are of the opinion that the poorer sections of the developing countries are more vulnerable to climate change with little capacity to withstand adverse conditions.

4. Effect on the Coastal Urban Population: About 50 per cent of the total urban population or about 25 per cent of the total population of the world is living in big urban cities along the coastal areas. In case of sea level rise because of global warming and sea level change the coastal urban population will be submerged under water and people have to push back to safer elevated areas. It may be catastrophic to economy and society.

5. Climate Change and Water Resources: The climate change will adversely affect the availability and access to water resources in the subtropical countries, especially in countries like India. The Inter-Government Panel on Climate Change (IPCC) Report points out towards the stark reality that the mighty rivers such as Ganga, Brahmaputra and Indus might become seasonal rivers, drying between monsoon rains as Himalayan glaciers will continue their retreat, vanishing entirely by 2035, if not sooner. Water tables will continue to fall and the gross per capita water availability in India will decline by over one-third by 2050. As rivers dry up, water tables fall or grow more saline. Water scarcity will affect the health of vast population, with rise in water borne diseases such as cholera. Other diseases such as dengu-fever, and malaria are also expected to rise.

The Inter-Government Panel on Climate Change (IPCC) Report has predicted a very grim future for humanity and the biosphere if we fail to reduce the greenhouse gas emission. The world needs to adapt to newer and innovative ways towards population growth and a sustainable lifestyle in order to save this self inflicted damage to our ecosystems, ecology and environment. The poor and communities who are the least responsible for the problem, are on the frontline of climate change and the highest price in terms of its impact. They can be protected by controlling the growth of population in the developing countries, by reducing consumerism in the developed countries and by making a judicious use of of the available natural resources.

Climate Change and Ecology of Antarctica

Antarctica is the second smallest continent in area. It is highest, driest, coldest, windiest continent. International boundaries have not been demarcated on this continent. Forty three countries have agreed to co-operate in this region in the interest of peace and science.

Antarctica receives about 7% more radiation. Its atmosphere is thin being at the South Pole. The winter months are May till September, while the summer months are October till April. The lowest temperature of -88.3°C was recorded at Vostok (Russian Observatory) in 1960. About 90% of all the ice on Earth is found in Antarctica.

The main type of soil in Antarctica is ahumic soil. This includes cold desert soil. Soil consist of sand that is frozen . In this soil, bacteria have been found. The other type of soil is organic soil. Some vegetation that is found here is in the form of algae, fungi, mosses and tussock. The algae and lichens grow where there is moisture, and they hid in cracks to be protected from the wind.

Antarctica is the only continent that does not have a land mammal population and no bird resides in Antarctica. During the summer season, a few birds of South America are spotted in Antarctica.

If all the ice of Antarctica melted, it would raise the level of the world oceans by about 60 meters (200 feet). The effect of sea level rise could be devastating - displacing more than 100 million people in low-lying coastal areas around the world. Accompanying this rise in sea level would be increased winter temperatures and warmer hot spells, increased rainfall and flooding, and overall unpredictable shifting of temperature and rainfall patterns that could wreak havoc with agriculture, natural ecosystems, and other daunting effects.

There is every possibility of ozone depletion. The depletion of ozone will lead to skin cancers, a suppression of human immune systems, disruption of plant life including increased susceptibility to pests or disease, reduction in phytoplankton growth, and the eventual decrease in the numbers of aquatic species - all these effects and more are anticipated due to ozone depletion.

The main consequences of climate change in Antarctica according to the Inter-Governmental Panel on Climate Change (IPCC) are likely to be as under:

1. If Antarctica's ice sheets melted, the world oceans would rise by 60 to 65 metres (200-210 ft) everywhere.
2. Poleward migration of existing species and competition from invading species.
3. The Antarctic pearlwort and the Antarctic hair grass currently occur in niche habitats on the Antarctic continent. Climate change is also affecting the vegetation, which is largely composed

of algae, lichens and mosses, and changes are expected in future, as temperature and water and nutrient availability change.

4. There is likely to be an increase in the growth of zooplanktons which ultimately increase the population of fish.
5. The population of krill, Adelie and Emperor penguin are like to decline as a result of climate change.

REFERENCES

Jerath, N., and Ram Boojh, G. Singh, 2010, **Climate Change, Biodversity and Food Security in South Asian Region**, *Macmillan Publishers India.*

Manikhuri, R.K. et.al, 2006, "Impact of Climate Change and Coping Strategy in Nanda Devi Biosphere Reserve, Central Himalayas' India IMBC-Technical Working Group I: Climate **Change Impacts on Biodiversity and Mountain Protected Areas.**

Husain, M., 2015, **Environment and Ecology**, *3rd edition New Delhi, Access Publishing India.*

Ram Boojh, et.al. 2010, 'The Impacts of Climate Change and the Himalayas in the Local

Context: The Case of Nanda Devi Biosphere Reserve' published in **Climate Change, Biodiversity and Food Security in South Asian Region**, *New Delhi, Macmillan Publishers India Ltd. pp.101-121.*

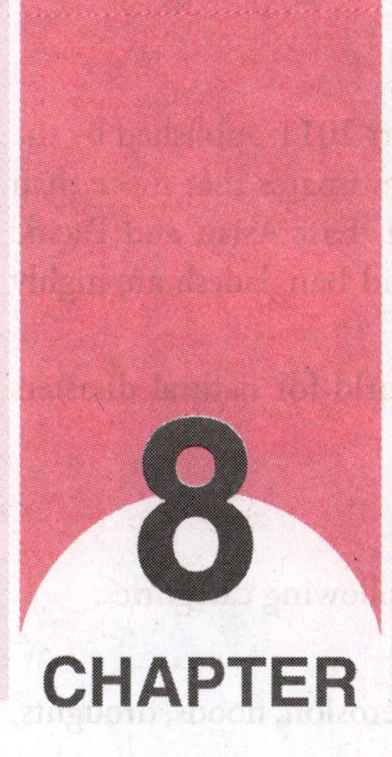

Natural Hazards and Disaster Management

DISASTERS AND NATURAL HAZARDS

Environmental hazards is an important area of physical geography in which the geographers and the geomorphologists are increasingly concentrating and probing. Man has always been subject to natural disasters over which he has little or no control. Most people include volcanic eruptions, earthquakes, tsunami, landslides, cyclones, tornadoes, hurricanes, cyclones, storm surges, floods, droughts, blizzards, epidemics and famines in a list of environmental hazards. In addition to these, many of environmental problems are clearly of man's own making.

Disaster

Disaster in general and natural disasters in particular, are some such changes that are always disliked and feared by mankind. In brief, "disaster is an undesirable occurrence from forces that are largely outside human control, strikes quickly with little or no warning, which causes or threatens serious disruption of life and property including death and injury to a large number of people, and requires therefore, mobilisation of efforts in excess of that which are normally provided by statutory emergency service".

Natural Hazards

Throughout the human history man has been adversely affected by natural hazards. In fact, they have been an integral part of human history right from the dawn of culture and civilisation. Some of the environmental disasters become hazards because man selects to use areas susceptible to these natural phenomena; this applies especially to earthquakes and flood prone areas.

According to the World Disaster Report 2010 published by the International Federation of Red Crescent Societies (IFRC), during the period 2000 to 2009, as many as 85 per cent of people affected by disasters belonged to the Asia Pacific Region. The Global Assessment Report 2011 published by the United Nations International Strategy for Disaster Reduction (UN- ISDR) estimates that more than 90 per cent of the global population exposed to floods lives in South Asian, East Asian and Pacific countries. Among the disaster-prone countries, South Asia, India, Pakistan and Bangladesh are highly vulnerable due to the large size of population exposed to disasters.

According to UNISDR, in the year 2010, India ranked second in the world for natural disasters after China.

TYPES OF DISASTERS

The disasters affecting the humanity and society may be classified under the following categories:

1. Geological: Volcanoes, earthquakes, tsunamis, landslides, avalanches.
2. Climatic: Cyclones, sea-surge, eutrophication, storms associated coastal erosion, floods, droughts, cloudbursts wildfire, etc.
3. Biological: Epidemics and public health crisis.
4. By hostile elements: War, terrorism, extremism, insurgency.
5. By disruption/failure of major infrastructure facilities.
6. By large crowds getting out of control.

The frequency of disasters each year is very high, but since 1948, the following disasters proved to be the most destructive.

Table 8.1 Top Fifteen Natural Disasters since 1948

Year	Location	Type	Deaths
1948	The Soviet Union (Russia)	Earthquakes	110,000
1949	China	Floods	57,000
1954	China	Floods	30,000
1965	East Pakistan (now Bangladesh)	Tropical Cyclone	36,000
1968	Iran	Earthquake	30,000
1970	Peru	Earthquake	66,800
1970	East Pakistan(now Bangladesh)	Tropical Cyclone	500,000
1971	India	Tropical Cyclone	30,000
1976	China	Earthquakes	700,000
1990	Iran	Earthquake	50,000
2001	India (Bhuj-Gujarat)	Earthquake	30,000
2004	Indonesia, India, Sri-Lanka	Earthquake	250,000
2005	Pakistan-India	Earthquake	70,000
2011	Japan (Tohoku)	Earthquake	30,000
2015	Gorkha Distt. (Nepal)	Earthquake	>15,000

Source: United Nations Environmental Programme (UNEP).

GEOLOGICAL DISASTERS.

Volcanoes

Volcano is a landform at the end of a conduit or pipe which rises from below the crust and vents to the surface. Magma rises and collects in the magma chamber deep below, resulting in eruptions that are effusive or explosive forming the mountain landform. According to Holmes (1978), a volcano is essentially a fissure or vent, communicating with the interior from which lava flows. Volcano is usually in the form of a peak which may be cone-shaped or dome-shaped.

The molten rock that issues from the volcano is termed as lava. The ejected material from a volcano is known as lava, gases, ashes, tephra (pulverized rock) pumice, dust, etc. At present over 1300 volcanoes exist on the Earth, out of which about 600 are active. In a year about 50 volcanoes erupt worldwide, varying from modest activity to major explosion.

Causes of Volcanic Eruptions

The volcanic eruptions are closely associated with sea-floor spreading, plate-tectonics and mountain building processes. The main causes of volcanism may be summarised as under:

1. There is a gradual increase in temperature with increasing depth at the rate of 1°C per 32 metres. The main cause of this increase in temperature is the disintegration of radio-active elements deep within the Earth. Consequently at certain depth the heated rocks take the shape of molten lava.
2. Origin of magma because of lowering of melting point inside the Earth caused by reduction in the pressure due to splitting of plates and their movements in opposite directions.
3. Origin of gases and vapour due to heating of water which reaches underground through percolation of rainwater and snow-melt water.
4. The volcanoes also erupt because of the ascent of magma forced by enormous volume of gases and water vapour.
5. Movement and splitting of the major and minor plates of the Earth.

Types of Volcanic Eruptions

On the basis of mode of eruptions, numerous classifications volcanoes have been given. The most commonly used classification of volcanic eruptions was given by Lacroix in 1908. According to Lacroix, there are four principal types of eruptions: (1) Hawaiian, (2) Strambolian, (3) Vulcanian, and (4) Pelean (**Fig. 8.1**).

1. ***Hawaiian Eruption:*** In this type of eruption large quantities of extremely fluid basic lava flow out from a fissure or a central vent to form a typical shield. It is a fissure, caldera and pit-crater eruption characterized with mobile lavas, with some gas. It is a quite to moderately active eruption with occasional rapid emission or gas charged lava produces fire fountain. The explosive activity is almost absent in this type of eruption **(Fig. 8.1).**
2. ***Strombolian (Summit Crater) Eruption:*** In this type of volcanic eruption, the basic lava (basaltic) is less fluid than that of Hawaiian type.The associated lava more viscous. Eruption increase in violence over longer periods of quite until lava crust is broken up, clearing vent, ejecting bombs, pumice and ash. Lava flows from top of flank after main explosive eruption. Explosions are more common and more tephra (solid-material) is ejected. It is named after the volcano on the Island of Stromboli off north Sicily **(Fig. 8.1).**

3. ***Vulcanian:*** In this type of eruption, the lava at the surface solidifies rapidly because of its high viscosity. The solidification of lava results in building up of pressure beneath the lava crust and continuous series of violent explosions during which large quantities of pyroclastic materials are ejected violently from the vent. It is characterised with dark ash-laden clouds, convoluted, cauliflower-shaped, rise to moderate heights more or less vertically, depositing tephra (solid material) along flanks of volcano. The ash coming out of the volcano may be distributed widely by wind (**Fig. 8.1**).
4. ***Pelean Eruption:*** In a Pelean type of eruption, lava is extremely viscous. There is delayed explosiveness; conduit of stratovolcano usually blocked by dome or plug; gas (some lava) escapes from lateral (flank) openings or by destruction of uplift of plug. Gas, ash, and blocks move down-slope in one or more blasts as *nuee ardentes* or glowing clouds, producing directed deposits. It erupts generally in violent form. One of its salient feature is the formation of *nuee ardentes* (glowing clouds). This type of volcanic eruptions are found in the Caribbean Sea. One may observe *nuee ardentes* and violent type of eruptions in the volcanoes of West Indies (**Fig. 8.1**).

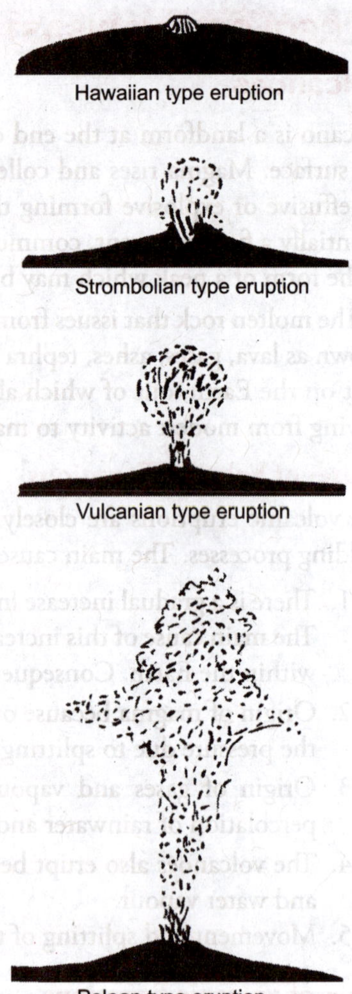

Fig. 8.1 Types of volcanic eruptions

Classification of volcanoes on the basis of period of eruption

On the basis of periodicity, the volcanoes may be divided into the following three categories:

(i) ***Active Volcanoes:*** Volcanoes with constantly ejected lava, gases, ashes, cinder, pumice and tephra (solid material) are known as active volcano. At present, there are about 600 active volcanoes in the world. Most of the active volcanoes are along the '*Ring of Fire*' in the Pacific Ocean. In Andaman and Nicobar Islands (India), the Barren Island has an active volcano (**Table 8.1**).

(ii) ***Dormant Volcanoes:*** A volcano which, although not extinct, has not been known to erupt within the historic time. The Vesuvius volcano (Italy) is one of the best examples of dormant volcano. This volcano erupted first in 79 A.D. It remained dormant for over 1550 years and then suddenly erupted with great force in 1631 A.D. The subsequent eruptions occurred in 1803, 1872, 1906, 1927, 1928, 1929. Kilimanjaro (Tanzania) is also an example of dormant volcano.

(iii) ***Extinct Volcanoes:*** A volcano that was active in distinct geological past and remains of which occur in an area, where there is no longer any volcanic activity is known as an extinct volcano. The crater is filled up with water converting it into a crater-lake. The Aurthur Seat (Edinburg – Scotland), Aconcagua (Andes Mountain), Koh-Sulaiman and Demavand in Elburz Mountain (Iran) are some of the important examples of extinct volcanoes.

Distribution of Volcanoes in the World

Most volcanic activity coincides with the active seismic regions of the world and is clearly associated with plate boundaries. Thus, there is a close relationship between the plate boundaries and the distribution of volcanoes in the world. In fact, the volcanoes are concentrated along the plates margins. The major areas of volcanic eruptions lie in the following belts (**Fig. 8.2**).

1. ***Belts of Convergent boundaries:*** The subduction zones or convergent plate boundaries in the form of '*Ring of Fire*' in the Pacific Ocean are the typical examples of the volcanic belt of the world. Over 70 per cent of the active volcanoes of the world are found along the '*Ring of Fire*' (**Fig. 8.2**).
2. ***The Divergent Plate Boundaries (Oceanic Ridges):*** At divergent plate margins, basaltic magma is generated by compression melting of the upper mantle and is extruded for the most part as fissure eruptions. The mid-oceanic ridges, are the divergent plate boundaries. These divergent Plate Boundaries also constitute the important areas of volcanic eruptions. The volcanic eruption in Iceland (located on the Mid-Atlantic Ridge) fall in this category. The volcanoes of Great Rift Valley of East Africa are also located on the divergent boundaries (**Fig. 8.2**).
3. ***Hot Spots:*** Hot spot is an individual point of upwelling material originating in the asthenosphere. A hot spot tends to remain relaxed relative to migrating plates. According to the experts of volcanoes, at present, there are more than one hundred hotspots in the

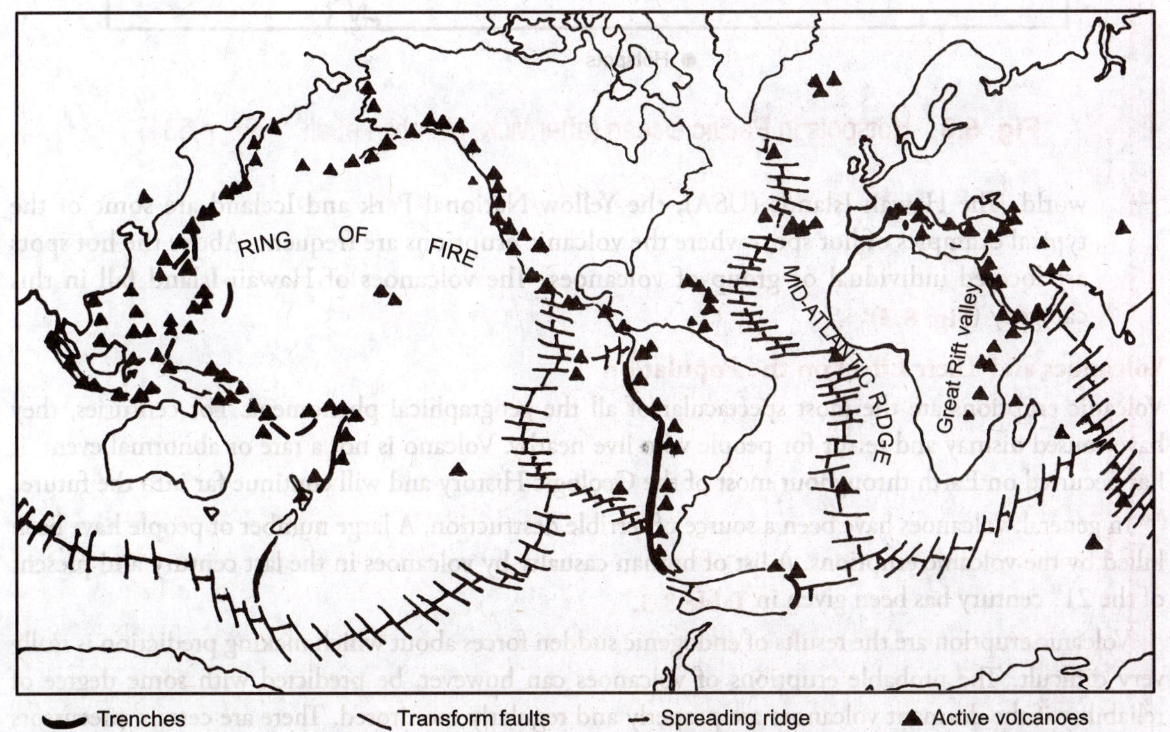

Fig. 8.2 Distribution of active volcanoes

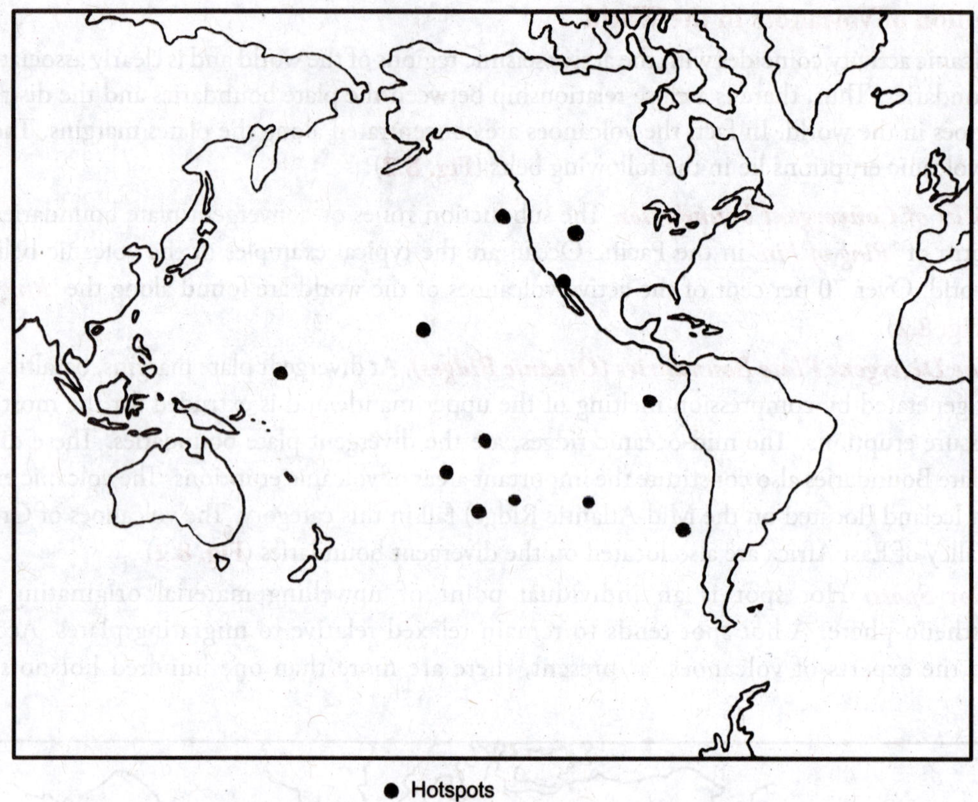

Fig. 8.3 Hotspots in Pacific Ocean (after W.K. Hamblin et al., 1995, p.531)

world. The Hawaii Islands (USA), the Yellow National Park and Iceland are some of the typical examples of hot spots where the volcanic eruptions are frequent. Above the hot spots are located individual or group of volcanoes. The volcanoes of Hawaii-Island fall in this category (**Fig. 8.3**).

Volcanoes and Their Effect on the Population

Volcanic eruptions are the most spectacular of all the geographical phenomena. For centuries, they have caused dismay and terror for people who live nearby. Volcano is not a rare or abnormal event, it has occurred on Earth throughout most of the Geologic History and will continue far into the future.

In general, volcanoes have been a source of terrible destruction. A large number of people have been killed by the volcanic eruptions. A list of human casualty by volcanoes in the last century and present of the 21st century has been given in **Table 8.3.**

Volcanic eruption are the results of endogenic sudden forces about which making prediction is really very difficult. The probable eruptions of volcanoes can however, be predicted with some degree of reliability if the dormant volcanoes are properly and regularly monitored. There are certain precursors events which can help in making prediction about the behaviour of dormant volcanoes:

Table 8.2 Major Active Volcanoes of the World

Volcano	Height in metres	Location	Country	Year of Last Eruption
1. Popocatepeti	5451	Altiplano de Mexico	Mexico	1920
2. Ana	155	Karakotoa	Indonesia	1929
3. Mt. Cameroon	278	Monarch	Cameroon	1959
4. Guallatiri	6060	Andes	Chile	1960
5. Fuego	3836	Sierra Madre	Guatemala	1962
6. Surtsey	173	South-east-Iceland	Iceland	1963
7. Agung	3142	Bali Island	Indonesia	1964
8. Tupungatiti	5640	Andes	Chile	1964
9. Lascar	5641	Andes	Chile	1968
10. Klyuchevskaya	4850	Sredinny – Kherbet	USSR	1974
11. Frebus	3795	Ross Island	Antarctica	1975
12. Sangay	5230	Andes	Colombia	1976
13. Semru	3676	Java	Indonesia	1976
14. Nyiragongo	3470	Virunga	Zaire	1977
15. Purace	4590	Andes	Colombia	1977
16. Mauna Loa	4170	Hawaii	USA	1978
17. Mt. Etna	3308	Sicily	Italy	1979
18. Ojos del Salado	6885	Andes	Argentina – Chile	1981
19. Navado del Ruiz	5400	Andes	Colombia	1985
20. Mt. Unzen	-	Honshu	Japan	1991
21. Mt. Mayon	-	Luzon	Philippines	1991
22. Mt. Mayon	-	Luzon	Philippines	1993
23. Mt. Eyjafjoell	-	Iceland	Iceland	2010

(i) Increase in the frequency of tremors, as recorded by seismographs.

(ii) Deformation of existing craters, as indicated by tilt-meter.

(iii) Rise in the temperature of water of crater lake.

(iv) Emission of gases and smokes from existing craters.

(v) Restlessness of bird, reptiles and animals.

An efficient administration can do the rescue operation by evacuating the people from the volcanic eruption region. It may be mentioned that there is speedy flow of immense volume of hot and liquid lava down the slope of volcanic mountain and all the objects (vegetation, crops, houses, buildings, animals and people, if not evacuated in time) are burnt and destroyed. A timely evacuation can save

Table 8.3 Human Casualties in Major Volcanic Eruptions 1901–2010

Year	Location of Volcano	Deaths
1902	Mt. Pelee, Martinique Island (West Indies)	28,000
1902	La Souffriere, St. Vincent	1665
1919	Kelut, Japan	5500
1951	Mt. Lamington, Papua – New Guinea	3000
1963	Mt. Agung, Bali (Indonesia)	1500
1965	Mt. Taal, Philippines	500
1980	Mt. St. Helen (Washington – USA)	70
1985	Colombia	23,000
1991	Mt. Mayon (Philippines)	1500
1991	Honshu (Japan)	255
2010	Mt.Eyjafjoell (Iceland)	150

precious life and property. If the lava flow is slow, its speed can be minimised by using huge volume of water spray and chemicals. In addition to these, the people should not be allowed to settle down in the vicinity of a dormant volcano.

Volcanoes, however, yielded life sustaining valuable resources like metallic minerals. Among the resources provided by volcanoes are: (i) rich volcanic soils, (ii) metallic mineral ore deposits, like gold, silver, copper, iron-ore, lead, zinc, etc., and precious stones, (iii) geothermal heat, and (iv) air we breathe and the water we drink.

Earthquake Disasters

Earthquake has been defined differently by different geographers and seismologists. In general term, earthquake is a release of energy that produces shaking in Earth's crust at the moment of rupture along a *fault* or in association with volcanic activity. According to Hamblin, earthquakes are vibrations of Earth, caused by the rupture and sudden movement of rocks that have been strained beyond their elastic limits. In the opinion of Strahler, earthquake is a form of energy of wave motion transmitted through the surface layer of the Earth in winding circles from a point of sudden energy release – the *earthquake focus*. Like ripples produced when a pebble is thrown into a quiet pond, these *seismic waves* travel outward in all directions, gradually losing energy.

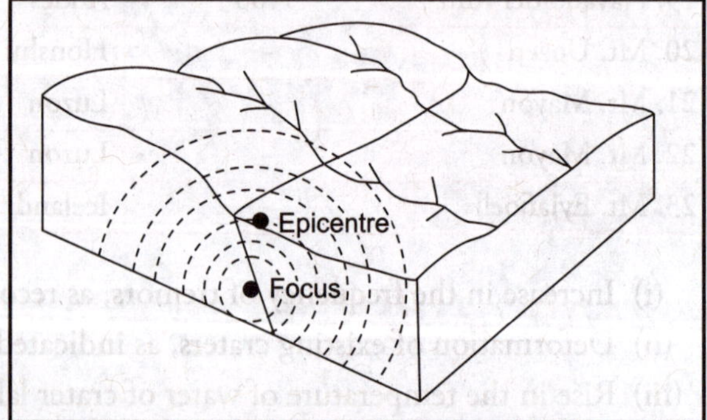

Fig. 8.4 Focus and Epicentre

The quantity of energy released during an earthquake at the place where the fault slipping originates is known as the *focus* of the earthquake; while, the point on the surface directly above the focus is the *epicentre* (**Fig. 8.4**).

Magnitude of Earthquake

The magnitude of an earthquake is a measure of the amount of energy released. Earthquake magnitude are based on direct measurements of size (amplitude) of seismic waves, made with recording instruments (*seismograph*), rather than on objective observation.

In 1935, a leading seismologist, Charles F. Richter, devised a rating scale of the earthquake magnitude. The Richter scale consists of numbers ranging from less than 0 (negative numbers) to more than 8.5. Values are given to the nearest one-tenth, thus: 2.5, 4.9, 6.2, 7.8, 8.5. There is neither a fixed maximum nor a minimum, but the highest magnitude earthquake thus far measured have been 9.1 (Tohoku earthquake – Japan, 11th March, 2011) on the Richter Scale. Earthquakes of magnitude 2.0 are the smallest normally detected by the human sense, but instruments can detect quakes which are very feeble magnitude.

The total quantity of energy released by all earthquakes of the world in a single year is estimated to be 10^{18} to 10^{19} joules. Most of this quantity is from a very few earthquakes of Richter magnitude greater than 7.0. The magnitude of earthquake as developed by Richter has been given in **Table 8.4**.

The approximate number of earthquakes with different magnitudes have been given in **Table 8.5.** It may be observed from **Table 8.4** that 98 per cent of the earthquakes in a year have a magnitude of less than 3 and only 20 have a magnitude of more than 8, while one in a year is more than 8 at the Richter Scale.

Earthquake Intensity Scale or Mercalli Scale

The actual destructiveness of an earthquake depends upon factors other than the energy release given by Richter magnitude – for example, closeness to the epicentre, nature of the subsurface earth materials

Table 8. 4 Richter Magnitude and Energy Release

Magnitude, Richter Scale	Energy Release (Joules)	Comment
2.0	6×10^7	Smallest quake normally detected by humans
2.5–3.0	10^8–10^9	Quake can be felt if it is nearby. About 300,000 shallow quakes of this magnitude per year
4.5	4×10^{11}	Can cause local damage
5.7	2×10^{13}	Energy released by Hiroshima atom bomb.
6.0	6×10^{13}	Destructive in a limited area. About 800 shallow quakes per year of this magnitude
6.7	7×10^{14}	Uttarkashi earthquake (Uttarakhand), 1991
7.0	2×10^{15}	Rated a major earthquake above the magnitude. Quake can be recorded over whole Earth. About 120 per year this great or greater
7.1	3×10^{15}	Sopore Earthquake (Jammu & Kashmir), 1885.
7.25 (7.9)	4.5×10^{16}	Bhuj Earthquake, 2001
8.1	10^{17}	Kangra Earthquake,1905
8.4 (9.2)	4×10^{18}	Arunachal-Assam border earthquake, 1950
8.3 (9.5)	10^{19}	Sumatra Earthquake, 2004

Table 8.5 Magnitude and approximate number of earthquakes per year

Magnitude (Richter Scale)	Approximate Number Per Year
1	700,000
2	300,000
3	300,000
4	50,000
5	6,000
6	800
7	120
8	20
>8	One every few years

and the density of population. An earthquake intensity scale, designed to measure observed earth-shaking, is important in practical engineering aspects of seismology.

An intensity scale used extensively is the *modified Mercalli Scale*. The original Mercalli Scale was prepared by an Italian seismologist of that name in 1902, and was modified in 1935 by Charles Richter to apply the various types of building construction. The modified Mercalli Scale recognises 12 levels of intensity, designated by Roman numerals I through XII representing "barely felt" to catastrophic total destruction." (Table 8.4). Each intensity is described in terms of phenomena that any person might experience. For example, at intensity IV, hanging objects swing, a vibration like that of a passing truck is felt, standing automobiles rock, and windows and dish rattle. Damage to various classes of masonry is used to establish criteria in the higher numbers of the scale. At an intensity of XII, damage to human-made structures is nearly total and large masses of rock are displaced. On the basis of reports gathered after an earthquake, maps can be prepared to show concentric zones of intensity. The numbered lines are known as *isoseismals*.

Causes of Earthquakes

The main causes of earthquakes are:

(i) ***Volcanic eruptions:*** Volcanic eruption is one of the main causes of earthquakes. Volcanic earthquakes are caused by gas explosion or the up-doming and fissuring of volcanic structures. Such earthquakes occur either simultaneously with eruption or more commonly in the period preceding an eruption. They are generally of shallow origin and their area of disturbance is relatively small which rarely exceeds a few hundred square kilometres.

(ii) ***Faulting:*** A fracture in a rock along which there has been an observable amount of displacement is known as *fault*. Earthquakes occur when movement of the earth takes place along a line of fracture or fault. Faults can be found in the rocks of all ages, but the likelihood of movement occurring is minimal unless the fault is located in an active area of the plate motion, i.e. in a zone where one plate moves against another. The San Andreas Fault of California is a typical example which led to earthquakes in 1906. In India, the Bhuj Fault (Gujarat) is also quite active, causing many of the earthquakes of varying magnitudes.

Table 8.6 The Modified Mercalli Scale

Intensity	Description
I	Not felt. Marginal and long period effects of large earthquakes.
II	Felt by persons at rest, on upper floors, or favourably placed.
III	Felt indoors, Hanging objects swing. Vibration like passing of light trucks. Duration estimated. Many not be recognised as an earthquake.
IV	Hanging objects swing. Vibration like passing of heavy truck; or sensation of a jolt like a heavy ball striking the walls. Standing cars rock. Windows, dishes, doors rattle. Glasses clink. Crockery clashes. In the upper range of IV, wooden walls and frames crack.
V	Felt outdoors; direction estimated. Sleepers wakened. Liquids disturbed, some spilled. Small unstable objects displaced or upset. Doors swing, close, open. Shutters, pictures move. Pendulum clocks stop, start, change rate.
VI	Felt by all. Many frightened and run outdoors. Persons walk unsteadily. Windows, dishes, glassware broken. Knick-knack, books, etc., off shelves. Pictures off walls. Furniture moved or overturned. Weak plaster and masonry D cracked. Small bells ring (church, schools). Trees, bushes shaken visibly, or heard to rustle.
VII	Difficult to stand. Noticed by drivers. Hanging objects quiver. Furniture broken. Damage to masonry D, including cracks. Weak chimneys broken at roof-line. Fall of plaster, loose bricks, stones, tiles, cornices, also unbraced parapets and architectural ornaments. Some cracks in masonry C. Waves on ponds, water turbid with mud. Small slides and caving in along sand or gravel banks. Large bells ring. Concrete irrigation ditches damaged.
VIII	Steering of cars affected. Damage to masonry C; parallel collapse. Some damage to masonry B; none to masonry A. Fall of stucco and some masonry. Twisting, fall of chimneys, factory stacks, monuments, towers, elevated tanks. Frame houses moved on foundations if not bolted down; loose panel walls thrown out. Decayed piling broken off. Branches broken from trees. Changes in flow or temperature of springs and wells. Cracks in wet ground and on steep slopes.
IX	General panic. Masonry D destroyed; masonry C heavily damaged, sometimes with complete collapse; masonry B seriously damaged. General damage to foundations. Frame structures, if not bolted, shifted off foundations. Frame cracked. Serious damage to reservoirs. Underground pipes broken. Conspicuous cracks in ground. In alleviated areas sand and mud ejected, earthquake fountains, sand craters.
X	Most masonry and frame structures destroyed with their foundations. Some well-built wooden structures and bridges destroyed. Serious damage to dams, dikes, embankments. Large landslides. Water thrown on banks of canals, rivers, lakes, etc. Sand and mud shifted horizontally on beaches and flat land. Rails bent slightly.
XI	Rail bent greatly. Underground pipelines completely out of service.
XII	Damage nearly total. Large rock masses displaced. Lines of sight and level distorted. Objects thrown into the air.

Table 8.6(a)

Masonry types	The quality of masonry, brick or otherwise, is specified by the following letter code:
Masonry A	Good workmanship, mortar, and design; reinforced, especially laterally, and bound together by using steel.
Masonry B	Good workmanship and mortar; reinforced, but not designed in detail to resist lateral forces.
Masonry C	Ordinary workmanship and mortar; no extreme weakness like failing to tie in at corners, but neither reinforced nor designed against horizontal forces.
Masonry D	Very ordinary material and workmanship

Source: C.F. Richter (1958), *Elementary Seismology,* W.H. Freeman and Company, San Francisco, pp. 136–38. Minor editorial changes, following B.A. Bolt (1978), *Earthquake: A Prime*, W.H. Freeman and Company, San Francisco, Appendix C, pp.204–05.

(iii) ***Plate Tectonics:*** Seismicity is quite significant along the plates margins. In fact, earthquakes are recorded along the divergent, convergent and conservative plate margins. The oceanic ridges are the divergent plate margins on which moderate earthquakes occur, while the ocean trenches are the convergent margins which record the deep focus earthquakes.

(iv) ***Anthropogenic Factors:*** Human overinteraction with nature is also one of the main causes of occurrence of many of earthquakes. The construction of reservoirs of multipurpose projects across the rivers; the extraction of minerals deep underground mining; blasting of rocks by dynamites, construction of roads, nuclear explosions, etc. lead to the occurrence of earthquakes. The Koyna earthquake of 1967, in the Satara District of Maharashtra and the Latur earthquake of 1993 (Osmanabad – Maharashtra) are some of the examples of earthquakes caused by the pressure of reservoir water.

Geographical Distribution of Earthquakes

The world distribution of earthquakes has been shown in **Fig. 8.5**. It may be observed from this figure that most of the earthquakes are recorded along *Pacific Ring of Fire* (convergent plate margins or oceanic trenches). About 68 per cent of all the earthquakes are recorded in the Pacific Ocean along the Ring of Fire. The mid-world mountain belt extends parallel to the equator from Mexico across the Atlantic Ocean, the Mediterranean Sea from Alpine-Caucasus, Elburz, Hindukush, Himalayan mountains and hills of North-east India. From North-east India along the border of Myanmar and the Islands of Andaman and Nicobar are also highly vulnerable to earthquakes. The mountains of Central Asia (Tien Shan, Altai, etc.) also have a high frequency of earthquakes. The Great Rift Valley of Eastern Africa, passing from south towards the Red Sea and Dead Sea is also known for more number of earthquakes (**Fig. 8.5**).

The Tohoku-Fukushima Earthquake

On March 11, 2011 an earthquake known as Tohoku earthquake with a magnitude of 9 was recorded along the north-eastern coast of Honshu Island of Japan (**Fig. 8.6**). The casualty was about 20,000 killed and over three thousand missing. More than 320,000 people still living in temporary homes. Fears of radiation leak led to a 20 km radius evacuation around the plant, while workers suffered

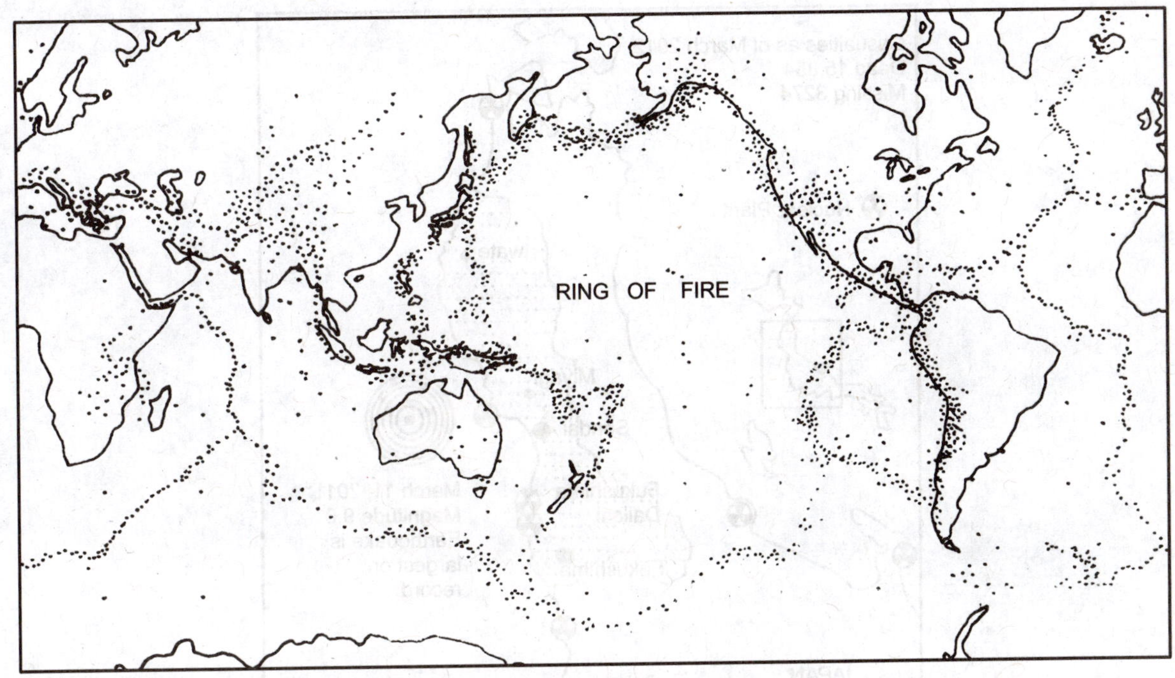

Fig. 8.5 World distribution of earthquakes

radiation exposure. About 320,000 people are still living in temporary homes. The Fukushima Nuclear Power Plant Disaster is considered to be the largest in Japan and the second largest in the world after the Chernobyl Disaster (April 26, 1986). It was Japans largest earthquake on record.

The resultant tsunami from the earthquake completely washed out the city of Sendai and seriously damaged the Fukushima and Daiichi nuclear power plants. Only two out of 54 reactors remained in operation. This earthquake resulted into huge tsunami. The six metre high tsunami wave entered the nuclear reactors which overheated the reactors. The flooding and earthquake damage hindered the rescue operation. Evidence soon arose of partial meltdown in the reactors, hydrogen explosion destroyed the upper cladding of the reactor building.

Table 8.7 The Most Disastrous Earthquakes (1901–2012)

Year	Location	Human Deaths
1908	Messina (Italy)	160,000
1920	Kansu (China)	180,000
1923	Sagami Bay (Japan)	250,000
1932	Tokyo (Japan)	163,000
1976	Tangshan (China)	750,000
2004	Sumatra (Indonesia)	250,000
2011	Tohoku (Japan)	>30,000

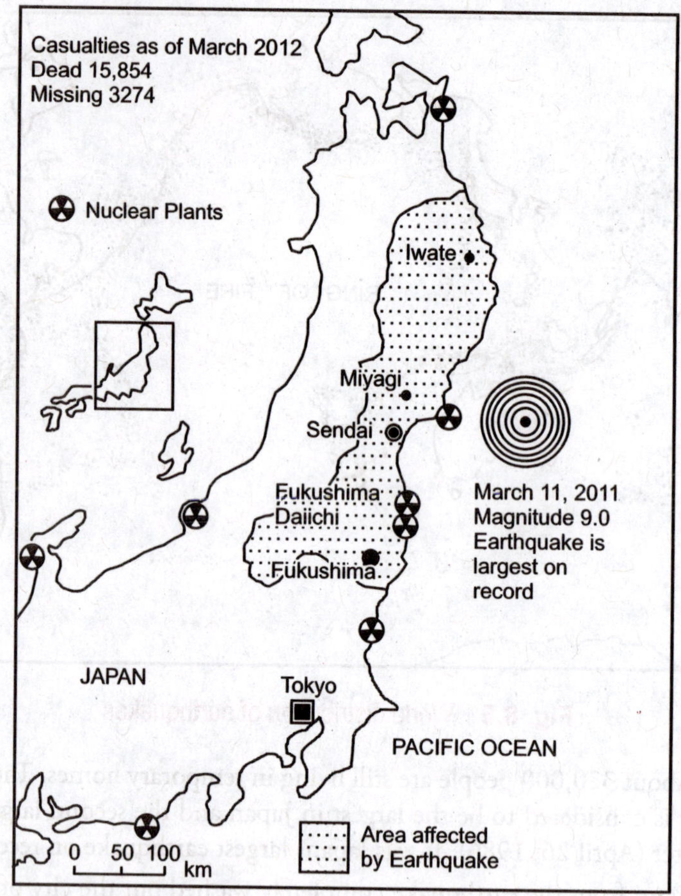

Fig. 8.6 Japan earthquake, March 11, 2011

Some of the most disastrous earthquakes recorded during the last century and the resultant human deaths have been given in Table 8.7.

Table 8.8 Major Earthquakes of the 20th and 21st centuries

Year	Place of Occurrence	Magnitude	Deaths
1905	Kangra Valley (India)	8.6	020,000
1908	Messina (Italy)	7.5	160,000
1915	Avezzano (Italy)	7.5	030,000
1920	Kansu (China)	8.5	180,000
1923	Kwanto-Tokyo (Japan)	8.2	163,000
1932	Kansu (China)	7.4	070,000
1932	Sagami Bay (Japan)	8.0	250,000

(*Contd.*)

Table 8.8 *(Contd.)*

Year	Place of Occurrence	Magnitude	Deaths
1934	Bihar (India)	8.4	010,700
1935	Quetta (Baluchistan)	7.6	060,000
1939	Chile	7.5	040,000
1939	Erzincan (Turkey)	8.0	040,000
1956	Kabul (Afghanistan)	7.6	025,000
1960	Agadir (Morocco)	5.9	014,000
1970	Chimbote (Peru)	7.8	067,000
1976	Italy	7.5	023,000
1976	Guatemala	7.5	023,000
1976	TangShan (China)	7.6	750,000
1978	Tabas (Iran)	7.7	025,000
1985	Mexico	8.1	010,000
1988	Armenia-Turkey border	6.9	026,000
1990	Iran	7.5	050,000
2001	India (Bhuj – Gujarat)	8.1	030,000
2004	Sumatra (Indonesia)	>9.0	250,000
2011	Tohoku (Japan)	>9.0	>30,000
2015	Gorkha Distt. (Nepal)	7.9	>15,000

The major earthquakes of the world during the last century, their magnitude and number of resultant deaths have been given in Table 8.8.

Earthquakes in India

As stated in the preceding paragraphs, most of the earthquakes in India occur in the Himalayan mountain belt and the Islands of Andaman and Nicobar. The Himalaya Mountain ranges are the region of great instability which is characterised by several faults and thrusts. The north-western and north-eastern corners of the Himalayas are particularly vulnerable as there are sharp changes in strikes, and the rocks are under great stress because of plates movements. The Indo-Gangetic alluvial plains are also greatly affected by earthquakes, originating in the Himalayan belt, but changes appear to be still taking place at the bottom of the Gangetic trough giving rise to the occasional earthquakes. The Sindh earthquake of 1819 and the Bihar earthquake of 1934 had their foci in this trough.

The Peninsular part of India was used to be considered as a stable block. The Koyana earthquake (1967), the Latur earthquake (1993) and the Jabalpur earthquake (1997) have, however, proved that the Peninsular India consist of several minor plates. The movements in these plates cause earthquakes of varying magnitudes.

The state of Gujarat, especially the Rann of Kachchh is another highly earthquake prone area of India. The Gujarat earthquake that occurred at 8.46 AM on 26th January, 2001 was one of the devastating earthquakes in India in recent years. It recorded 8.1 at the Richter Scale in which,

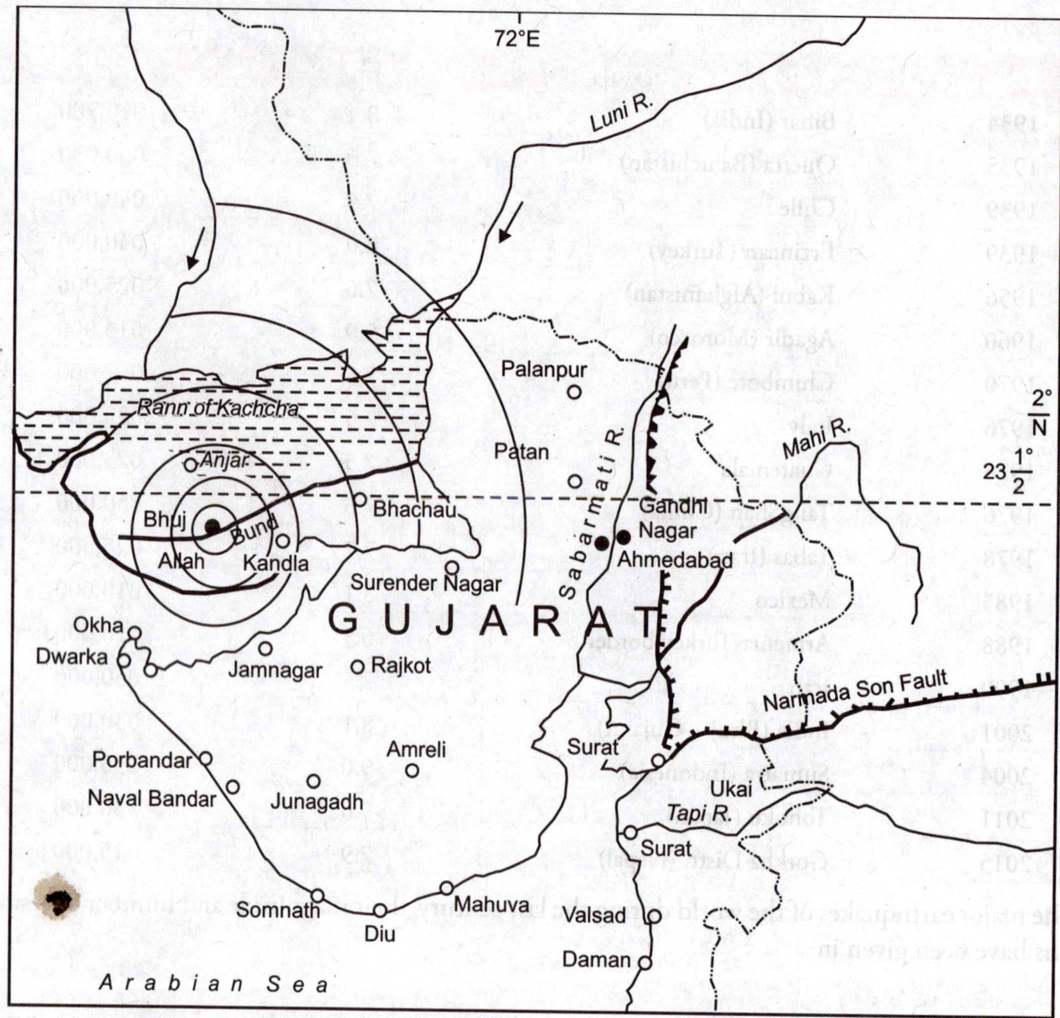

Fig. 8.7 Bhuj – Allah – Bund June 16, 1819 and Bhuj Earthquake – January 26, 2001

according to official records more than 30,000 people lost their lives and more than 1.67 lakh people were injured. Moreover, about 20 million population spread over 21 districts was adversely affected. The loss of property in this earthquake was enormous (**Fig. 8.7**).

In the opinion of seismologists, the Bhuj earthquake is a reawakening of the *Allah-Bund Fault* which came into existence as a result of 1819 earthquake. The main cause of this earthquake is attributed to the movement of the Indian Plate northward. The Indian Plate is moving in a north-east direction at the rate of about 5 cm per year against the Eurasian Plate along the Himalayas.

Seismic Zones of India

In general, the greater parts of India are highly vulnerable to seismic activity. On the basis of magnitude of damage risk, India has been divided into the following five damage risk zones. These earthquake zones have been shown in **Fig. 8.8**.

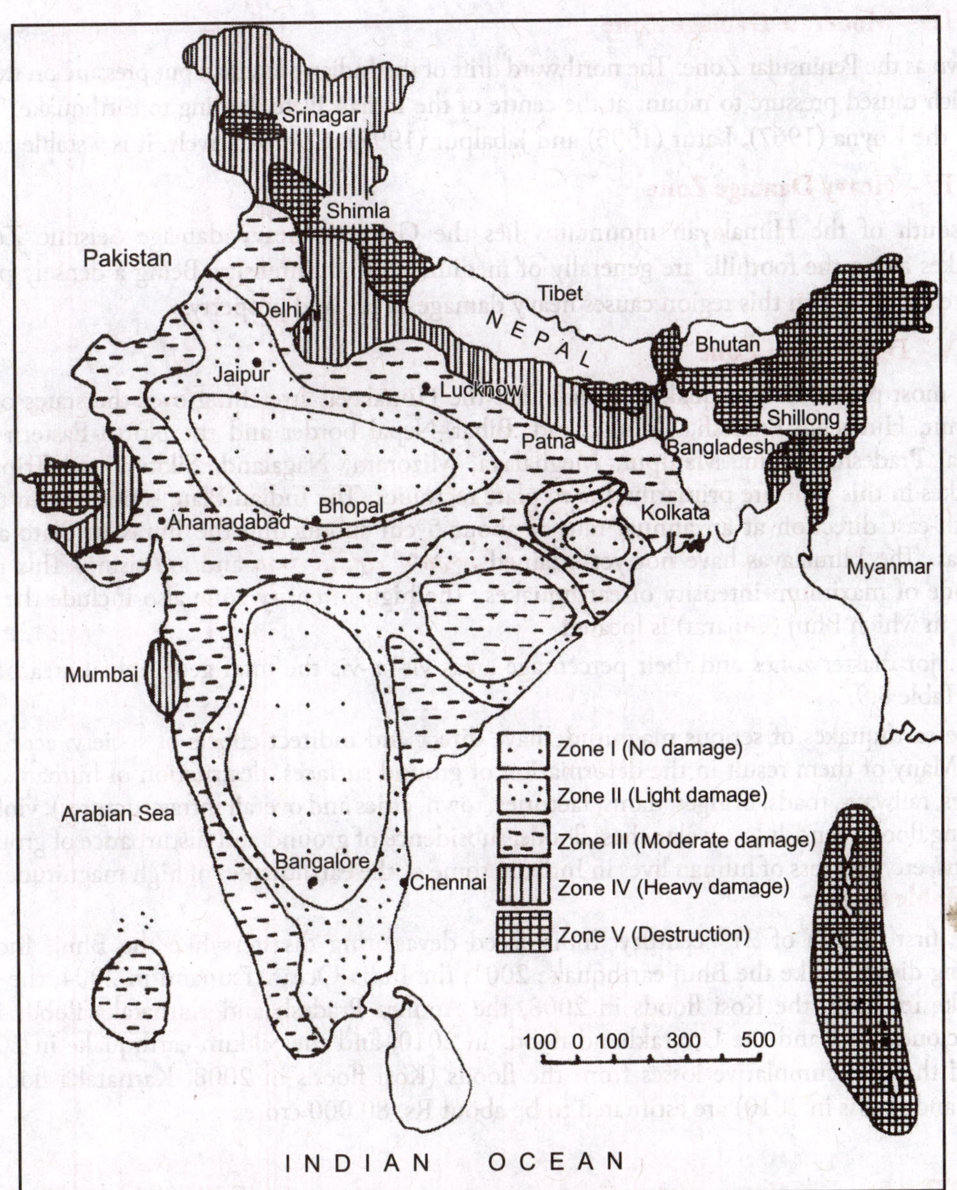

Fig. 8.8 Seismic Zones of India

1. Zone I–Least or No Damage Zone

The zone of least damage stretches over the Achaean formations of Tamil Nadu, Karnataka, Andhra Pradesh, western Madhya Pradesh and parts of Aravalli (Rajasthan). This region records earthquakes of less than three magnitude at the Richter Scale.

2. Zone II – Low or Light Damage Zone

The zone of light damage covers parts of the Chotanagpur Plateau, parts of Madhya Pradesh, Andhra Pradesh, and Tamil Nadu. It records, generally, earthquakes of low intensity.

3. Zone III – Moderate Damage Zone

It is known as the Peninsular Zone. The northward drift of the Indian Plate had put pressure on the Tibetan Plate which caused pressure to mount at the centre of the Indian Plate, leading to earthquake. This zone recorded the Koyna (1967), Latur (1993) and Jabalpur (1997). Comparatively, it is a stable zone.

4. Zone IV – Heavy Damage Zone

To the south of the Himalayan mountains lies the Gangetic heavy damage Seismic Zone. The earthquakes along the foothills are generally of medium to high intensity. Being a densely populated area, the earthquakes in this region causes heavy damage to life and property.

5. Zone V – Destruction Zone

The area most prone to earthquakes in India are the Himalayas stretching over the states of Jammu & Kashmir, Himachal Pradesh, Uttarakhand, Bihar–Nepal border and the North-Eastern states of Arunachal Pradesh, Assam, Manipur, Meghalaya, Mizoram, Nagaland, Sikkim and Tripura. The earthquakes in this zone are primarily due to plate tectonics. The Indian Plate is pushing in the north and north-east direction at an annual rate of about 5 cm subducting the Eurasian Plate along the Himalayas. The Himalayas have not yet attained *isostatic equilibrium* and are rising. This is known as the zone of maximum intensity of earthquakes. The high intensity zone also include the Rann of Kachchh in which Bhuj (Gujarat) is located.

The major diaster zones and their percentage areas vis–a–vis the total geographial area of India is given in Table 8.9.

All the earthquakes of serious magnitude have direct and indirect effects of society, economy and ecology. Many of them result in the deformation of ground surfaces, destruction of human structures (buildings, railways, roads, bridges, dams, factories, town, cities and overall infrastructures), violent fires, devastating floods, landslides, avalanches, floods, subsidence of ground and disturbance of groundwater conditions, etc. The loss of human lives in India in some of the earthquakes of high magnitude has been given in **Table 8.10**.

In the first decade of 21st century, India faced devastating disasters like the Bhuj, India faced devastating disasters like the Bhuj earthquake 2001, the India Ocean Tsunami in 2004, the Kashmir earthquake in 2005, the Kosi floods in 2008, the Andhra Pradesh and Karnataka floods in 2009, the Leh cloud burst and the Uttarakhand floods in 2010, and the Sikkim earthquake in 2011. It is estimated that the cumulative losses from the floods (Kosi floods in 2008, Karnataka floods 2009, Uttarakhand floods in 2010) are estimated to be about Rs. 80,000 crores.

Table 8.9 Disaster Zones and their percentage area vis–a–vis the Total Area of India

	Percentage of the Total Geographical Area of India
Seismic Zones – III, IV and V	59
Drought prone areas	68
Flood-prone areas, changing courses of rivers and river erosions	12
Cyclones	71% of the 7500 kms long coast of India are susceptible to cyclones.

Table 8.10 Major earthquakes and loss of human lives in India

Year	Place	Magnitude	Deaths
4th April, 1905	Kangra	8.6	20,000
5th January, 1934	Bihar–Nepal border	8.4	10,700
11th December, 1967	Koyna (Maharashtra)	6.5	01000
30th September, 1993	Latur (Maharashtra)	6.3	11,000
26th January, 2001	Bhuj (Gujarat)	8.1	>30,000
26th Dec. 2004	Sumatra (Indonesia)	9.3	>250,000
8th October, 2005	Muzaffarabad (POK)	6.5	>50,000
18th Sept. 2011	Mangan (Sikkim)	6.8	>100, one lakh houses collapsed
25th April, 2015	Nepal	7.9	>15,000

NEPAL EARTHQUAKE, 2015

Main Earthquake

Date: 25th April 2015 , **Time:** 11.41 am (IST)

Magnitude on Richter scale: 7.9

Epicenter : Barpak village near Lamjung (Gorkha District)

Casualty : Over 15,000

People injured : over 50,000

People affected : Over 8 million

Biggest Aftershock

May 12, 12.37 pm (IST)

Magnitude: 7.3 depth 15 km

Epicentre: Kodari Village in Dolakha District, 80 km east of Kathmandu and 50 km south-west of Mt.Everest.

Earthquakes are vibrations of earth, caused by the rupture and sudden movement if rocks that have been strained beyond their elastic limits. Most of the earthquakes as stated above occur along plate boundaries, i.e. oceanic ridges (divergent plate margins), oceanic trenches (convergent plate margins or subduction zones), and the transform faults on the oceanic ridges.

Convergent Plate Boundaries and the Nepal Quake

On the earth, the most widespread and intense earthquake activity occurs along the subduction zones of plate boundaries. Where the plates collide, are the areas of complicated geologic processes including igneous activity, crustal deformation and mountain building. The specific processes that are active along a convergent plate boundary depend up on the types of crust involved in the collission of the converging plates.

If both the converging plates contain continental crust (like the Indian and the Eurasian plates), neither can subside into the mantle, although one can override the other for short distance. The continental plates are made of Sial (Si + al). The Sial material is so buoyant that it cannot sink into the denser mantle (Sima) below. In such a case, both the continental masses are instead compressed, and the continents are ultimately fused with a single continental block, with a mountain range marking the line of suture. The Nepal earthquake is the result of the convergence of the Indian plate with Eurasian plate (**Fig.8.8-A**).

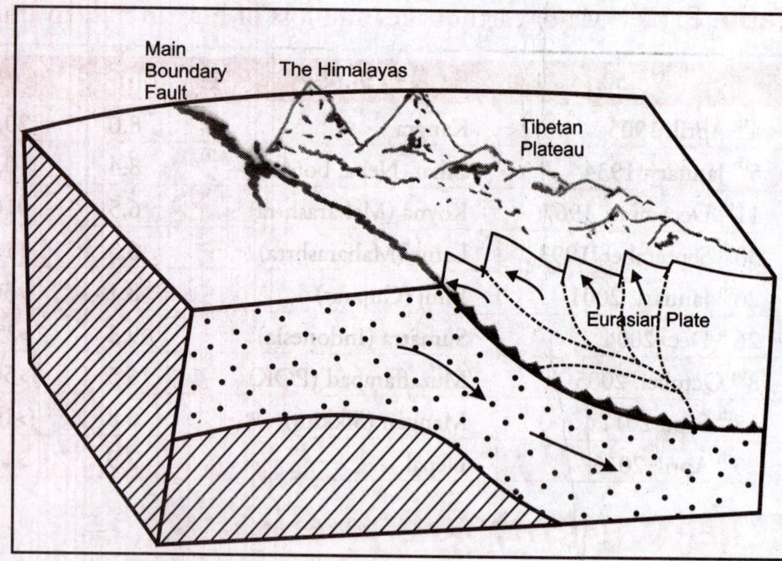

Fig. 8.8A Subduction of Indian Plate under Eurasian Plate

The 25th April, 2015, Nepal earthquake with a magnitude of 7.9 occurred as a result of the faulting on or near the Main Boundary Fault (between the lesser Himalayas and the Outer Himalayas or Siwaliks) where the Indian plate subducted the Eurasian plate. According to the seismologists, at this fault the Indian Plate is submerging the Eurasian Plate at the rate about 45 mm/year, towards the north-east, driving the uplift of the Himalayan Mountain ranges. Whenever, the subduction rate is high and sudden, an earthquake of serious magnitude occurs.

Consequences

According to initial estimate, based on the earthquake intensity mapping about 8 million people in 39 districts of Nepal have been affected, out of which over two million people live in the eleven severely affected districts.

Changes in Landforms

This earthquake has shifted the earth beneath the city of Kathmandu by about 3 meters (10 feet) south. The Mt. Everest is not directly above the Main Boundary Fault Line. Consequently its height is not much affected. There is, however, a big damage on top of the mountain, mainly because of avalanches, landslides and rapid slip of glaciers.

Damage to Life and Property

In this earthquake around 1.4 lakh buildings have been completely destroyed, and 1.2 lakh houses were partly damaged in Nepal. In total 10,395 government buildings were collapsed and over 13,000 partially damaged. Bhaktapur (south-east of Kathmandu) a 12th century heritage city was almost raised to the ground. This heritage city will have to be rebuilt almost entirely which may take years. **(Fig. 8.8-B)**.

Medical Complications

Delay in rescuing earthquake victims in far-flung interior and remote inaccessible areas have led to several medical complications. Many a times, it happens that some parts of body is under debris. This part does not get adequate blood supply than that part starts dying which results in the part turning gangrenous.

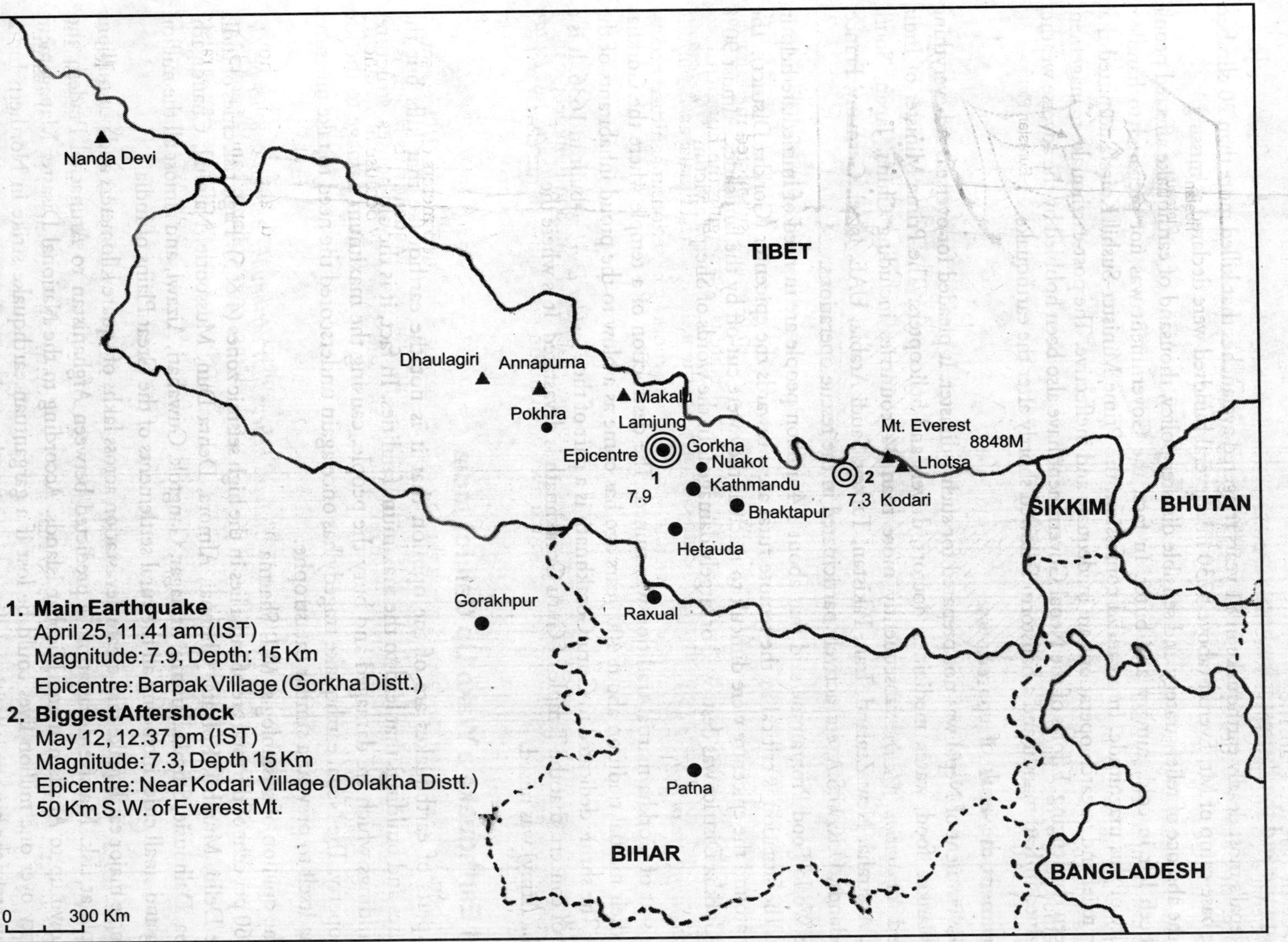

Fig. 8.8B Nepal Earthquake-25 April, 2015

Earthquake and the Everest Climbers

The Nepal's most deadly earthquake in 81 years triggered avalanches that killed more than 20 climbers on the base-camp of Mt. Everest (above 5230 m). Several hundred were declared as missing.

In the absence of relief strategy and sensible disaster policy, thousand of earthquake affected people were been left in cold, hungry and bitter. In fact, the Government was not prepared to handle a calamity of this magnitude. In a candid confession, the Prime Minister-Sushil Koirala admitted that rescue, relief and research operations are inadequate and ineffective. The post-earthquake management had been challenging. Efforts of the Nepal Government have also been hobbled by the adverse weather as it rained in Kathmandu and a hailstorm followed shortly after the earthquake.

Government of Nepal's Preparedness

The Government of Nepal was not prepared for such a disaster. It pleaded for overseas aid-everything from blanket, food, water, medicines, doctors, drivers and helicopters. The Prime Minister of India initiated *'Operation Maitri'* subsequently more than 34 countries including China, Japan, South Korea, Australia, New Zealand, Iran, Pakistan, Turkey, Saudi Arabia, UAE, Israel, Germany, France, Netherlands, U.K. U.S.A. etc. actively participated in the rescue operations.

The World Food Programme said that about 1.4 million people are in need of immediate help in Nepal. The situation is critical in the remote rural areas towards the epicenter (Gorkha District). The village around the epicentre were difficult to reach as they were cut-off by the landslides. Almost 90% of the Gorkha District was destroyed or largely damaged. In the words of Sherpa a victim *"The dead are gone, the living are in hell"*.

The seat of Gorkha martial tradition was ruined. The destruction of a temple where the Gorkhas began their martial tradition about 400 years ago has come as a blow to the proud inhabitants of the region. The shrine dedicated to Guru Gorakhnath is a part of the *Gorkha Durbar*-built in 1636. It is a matter of concern that the Temple of Guru Gorakhnath is devastated. It is where the *Guru Ji Ki Paltan* (Gorkha Army) was raised.

Nepal Earthquake a Wake Up Call for India

The experts of earthquakes are of the opinion that it is not the earthquake that kills but the structures and buildings that lead to the maximum fatalities. In fact, it is the old houses, structures and buildings which are damaged and bury the people, causing the maximum damage to the life and property. The Nepal earthquake tragedy has once again underscored the need to take measures in India itself to prevent a similar catastrophe.

In the opinion of seismologist M.L Sharma *'Indians believe that earthquake happen to other people'*. About 60 per cent of the total are of India lies in the high seismic zones (4 & 5). High risk cities of India include Delhi, Mumbai, Kolkata, Chennai, Almora, Dehra Dun, Mussoorie, Nainital, Chandigarh, Chamba, Dalhousie, Shimla, Jammu, Srinagar, Gangtok, Guwahati, Aizawl, and almost all the million and big and small cities including all the rural settlements of the Great Plains of India.

A single major earthquake may create devastation across lakhs of square kilometers and put millions of people at risk. Massive devastation is predicted between Afghanistan to Arunachal Pradesh and right down up to Anadaman and Nicobar Islands. According to the National Disaster Management Authority over one million lives could be lost if a gargantuan earthquake strike in Northern India. Unfortunately, the big one is waiting to happen; we just do not know where and when.

In India, one of the first areas that needs reform is the course structure of Civil Engineering education. Although about 85 per cent of houses in India have brick masonry walls made of fired/unfired bricks or stones, only 3 per cent of the undergraduate civil engineering and architecture curricula deals with these materials (Census of India, 2011). It is however, imperative to train the civil engineers in traditional material house designs of the people.

Another major concern is the multi-storey buildings that have mush-roomed in urban areas. These are built on a frame work of RCC beams and pillars with brick-walls added later. There should not be any compromise with the material in such multi-storeyed structures. Education and awareness about earthquakes and their consequences need to be given to masses in a big way on regular basis. Demonstrations in schools about how to protect ourselves in the eventuality of earthquake should be made a regular feature on the pattern of Japanese schools and colleges. Sooner our policy makers, planners, civil engineers, architects and authorities of disaster management address these issues the better for the people of India.

References:

Christopherson, R.W., 1995, **'Elemental Geosystems: A Foundation in Physical Geography'** Englewood Cliff, New Jersey, Prentice Hall.

Eiby, G.A. 1980, **Earthquakes,** New York, Van Nostrand Reinhold.

Hamblin, W.K. Et. al. **'Earth's Dynamic Systems'** 7th ed. Englewood Cliff, Prentice Hall.

Pakister, L.C., 1991, 'Washington, D.C., USA Government Printing Office.

Earthquake Prediction and Strategies to Combat

Prediction

Making a reliable forecast about the occurrence of an earthquake is still a difficult proposition. The seismologists are increasingly concentrating on the aspect of earthquake forecasting. One approach for making earthquake prediction is to examine the history of each plate boundary and determine the frequency of earthquakes in the past. On the basis of such data and information, seismologists construct maps that provide an estimate of expected earthquake activity. Areas that are quiet and overdue for an earthquake are termed as *seismic gaps*. The *seismic gaps* form a gap in the earthquake occurrence record and is, therefore, a place that possess accumulated strain.

The Chinese, on the basis seismographic studies on animal behaviour, made fairly reliable and accurate prediction about the Haicheng earthquake, 1975. The Chinese experts of earthquakes provided a list of indicative of animal behaviour for the prediction of earthquakes.. Before the earthquake of Haicheng, the cattle refusing to enter houses, corals and ducks refusing to enter water, snakes coming out of hibernation and fish jumping out of water. Chicken, mules, goldfish, mice all showed unusual behaviour just before the earthquake. The water of the wells rose by more than one metre, the dogs started barking and running for shelter inside the house, while, the livestock was restless. Just before the earthquake began to shudder, residents were awakened by brilliant red light that lit the early morning sky for hundreds of kilometres around. On the basis of these indicators, an accurate prediction was made and thus, lives of thousands of people were saved. Unfortunately, the very next year in 1976, the Tangshan earthquake could not be predicted in which more than 750,000 people lost their lives. Despite animal behaviour and other phenomena, effective earthquake prediction, which could save many lives and property damage is proving to be an elusive goal.

Strategy to Combat Earthquake Disasters

Earthquakes are the results of sudden forces about which a prediction cannot be made till date. Unlike other disasters, the damages caused by earthquakes are more devastating. Since it also destroys most of the transport and communication links, providing timely relief to the victims become difficult. It is not possible to prevent the occurrence of an earthquake; hence, the next best option is to emphasise on disaster preparedness and mitigation rather than curative measures as such. Some of the effective steps which can go a long way in reducing the damage from earthquakes are given below:

1. Establishing earthquake monitoring centres (seismological centres) for regular monitoring and fast dissemination of information among the people in the vulnerable areas.
2. Preparing a vulnerability map of the country and dissemination of vulnerability risk information among the people and educating them about the ways and means minimising the adverse impact of disasters.
3. Modifying the house types and building designs in the vulnerable areas and discouraging contribution of high rise buildings, large industrial establishments and big urban centres in such areas.
4. Making it mandatory to adopt earthquake-resistant designs and use light materials in major construction activities in the vulnerable areas.
5. An in-depth study of hotspots and tomography to make fairly reliable predictions about the occurrence earthquakes.
6. Earthquake disaster preparedness.
7. Rescue operations.
8. Relief operation after the earthquake. Effective rescue and relief camps establishment immediately after the earthquakes.
9. Recovery of disaster affected people from the mental, financial and social problems.
10. Rehabilitation of displaced people.
11. To restrict the lifting of underground water in the densely populated areas.
12. To restrict urban growth in the hilly areas of high seismic vulnerability.
13. To stop deforestation and overgrazing in the hilly areas.
14. To avoid the construction of large dams and reservoirs in the high seismic zones of hilly regions.
15. During the earthquake do not panic. Keep calm and behave intelligently. Try to reach the open space at the time of earthquake. Whenever, it is not possible, take cover under a desk, table or doorways. Stay away from glass windows and doors. Do not use candle, matches during or after the earthquake. If you are in moving car, stop as quickly as safety permits, but stay in the vehicle. Use a torch. Avoid places where there are loose electric wires and do not touch any metal object in contact with them.
16. During the earthquake, if there is fire, try to put it out. If you cannot, call the fire brigade.

Tsunami

Tsunami is a word of Japanese language which means *tsu* (harbour) with *nami* (wave). The word is both singular and plural. Tsunami caused by the sudden vertical movement of the Earth along faults (the same forces that cause earthquakes) are properly called seismic sea waves. Note that all seismic sea waves are tsunami, but not all tsunami are seismic sea waves.

The main causes of tsunami are:

(i) Under sea deep focus earthquakes of high magnitude.

(ii) Convergence of destructive plates in the ocean floor.

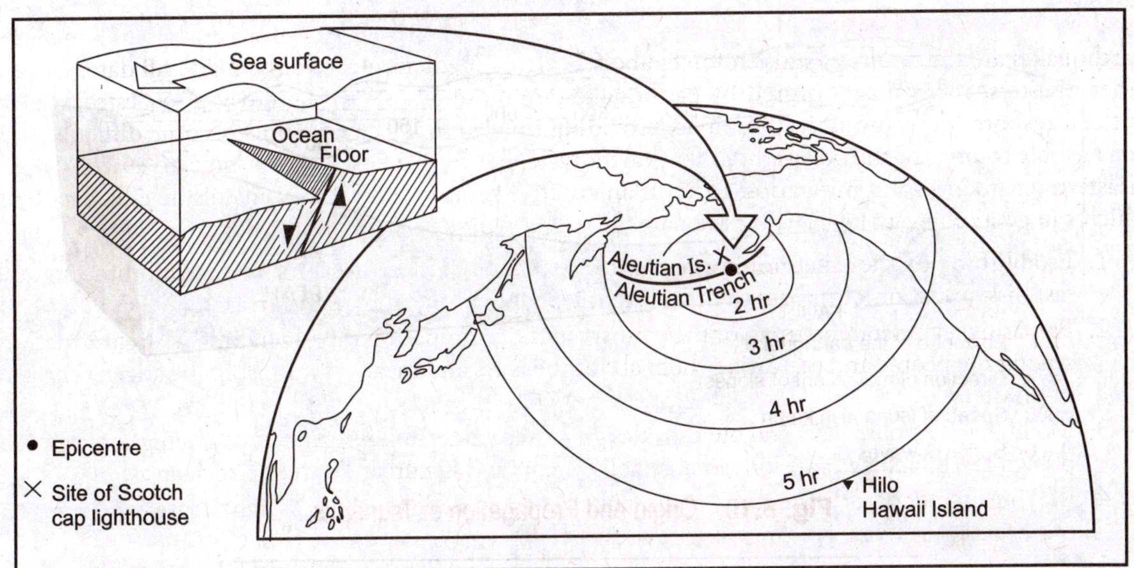

Fig. 8.9 Aleutian Island Tsunami, Ist April, 1946. The Aleutian Trench lifted the sea-surface above

(iii) Explosive volcanic eruptions in the seas/oceans.
(iv) Undersea massive landslides.

Origin of Tsunamis

Seismic sea waves originate on the ocean floor when Earth movement along faults displaces ocean water. Figure 8.9 shows the birth of a seismic sea wave in the Aleutian Islands, rupture along a submerged fault lifts the sea surface above. Gravity pulls the crest downward, but the momentum of the water causes the crest to overshoot and become a trough. The oscillating ocean surface generates progressive waves that radiate from the epicentre in all directions. Waves should also form if the fault movement were downward. In that case a depression in the water surface could propagate outward as a trough. The trough would be followed by smaller crests and troughs caused by surface oscillation.

Tsunamis have very long wavelength and very low amplitude, in deep ocean, they cannot be seen or detected from the air. Consequently, passengers on boats and ships cannot feel or see the tsunami as the killer waves pass by underneath at high speed. It may appear only as a gentle rise and fall of the sea in the open oceans. As the tsunami leaves the deep water of the open ocean and travel towards the shallow water, they are transformed in two ways, Firstly, their speed is reduced considerably and secondly they attain enormous height often exceeding 10 meters and occasionally may reach 30 metres. The origin propagation, speed and height of tsunamis in the open sea and shore of a sea have been depicted in Figs. 8.10 and 8.11. The wave energy spreads through an enlarging circumference as a tsunami expands from its point of origin (Figs. 8.10 and 8.11).

People on shore near the generating shock have reason to be concerned because the energy will not have dissipated very much. On April 1, 1946, a fracture along the Aleutian Trench generated a seismic sea wave that quickly engulfed the Scotch Cap lighthouse on *Unimark Island* in the Aleutians. The lighthouse (foundation 15 metres above sea level-height 36 metres) was completely destroyed, and the five coastguards operating the lighthouse died.

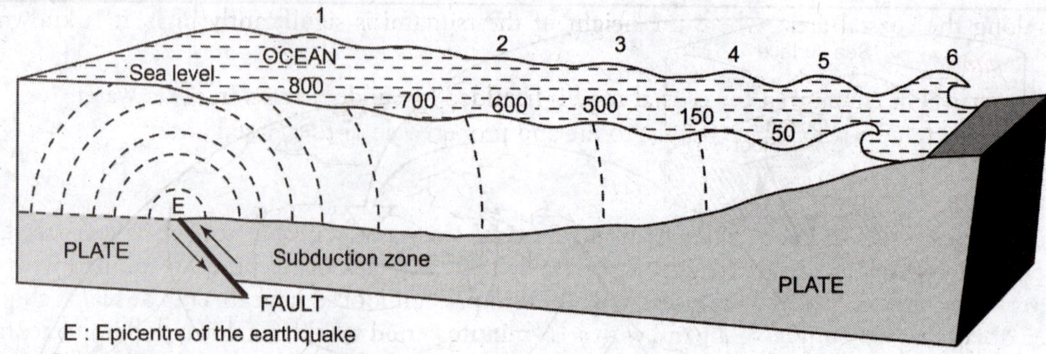

Fig. 8.10 Origin and Propagation of Tsunamis

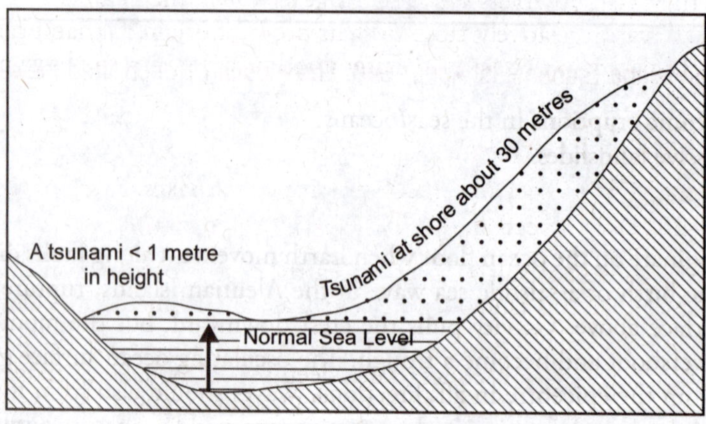

Fig. 8.11 Transformation of Tsunami-wave as it reaches a shore

The same seismic sea wave reached the Hawaiian Islands about five hours later. By this time the wave circumference was enormous and its energy more dispersed, but even so, successive waves surged onto Hawaiian beaches at 15 minute intervals for more than two hours. One 9-metre wave struck the town of Hilo. At least 150 people were killed in Hawaii Islands (USA) that morning.

Characteristics of Tsunami Waves

The salient characteristic features of tsunami waves are given below:

1. Tsunamis are high energy sea waves caused mainly by the deep focus earthquakes of high magnitude.
2. The wavelength of tsunami waves may be more than 100 km.
3. The wave height of a major tsunami in the deep oceans is very low, say about a metre or so.
4. The speed of tsunami increases with ocean depth and vice versa. Normally the speed of a tsunami varies between 500 to 1000 kms per hour.
5. The wavelength of the tsunami decreases as it approaches the shallow seas and coastal areas.

6. Along the coastal areas where the height of the tsunami is significantly high, it is known as '*tsunami run-up*'.
7. The arrival of tsunami in the coastal zone is heralded by sudden recession of sea water.
8. Tsunami waves create great damage to life and property along the coastal areas.

Encountering a Tsunami

The tsunami sea waves are very different from the tidal sea waves. Once a tsunami is generated, its steepness (ratio of height to wavelength) is extremely low. This lack of steepness, combined with the wave's very long period (5 to 20 minutes), enables it to pass unnoticed beneath ship at sea. A ship on the open ocean that encounters a tsunami with a 16-minute period would rise slowly and imperceptibly for about 8 minutes to a crest only 0.3 to 0.6 metre (1 or 2 feet) above average sea level and then ease into the following trough 8 minutes later. With all the wind waves around, such a movement would not be noticed.

As the seismic sea wave crest approaches shore, however, the situation changes rapidly and often dramatically. The period of the wave remains constant, velocity drops, and wave height greatly increases. As the crest arrives at the coast, observers see water surge ashore in the manner of a very high, very fast tide. In confined coastal waters relatively close to their point of origin, tsunami can reach a height of 30 metres (100 feet). The wave is a fast non-rushing flood of water, not the huge plunging breaker of popular folklore.

Major Tsunamis of the Last Few Decades

The greatest recent tsunami was associated with a massive earthquakes. Some of the major tsunami of the recent past (1990–2011) have been shown in **Fig. 8.12** (**Table 8.9**).

1. ***Nicaragua Tsunami:*** As a result of a serious earthquake it occurred on 2nd September, 1992. The maximum height of this tsunami sea waves was over 10 metres and the human casualty in Nicaragua was more than 170.
2. ***Flores Island (Indonesia):*** Consequent on a deep sea earthquake of more than 8 on Richter Scale, the Flores Island tsunami occurred on 12th December, 1992. The maximum height of the sea waves was more than 26 metres in which more than 1100 people died.
3. ***Papua New Guinea Tsunami:*** On July 12, 1993 a serious earthquake occurred in the south-West Pacific Ocean resulting into a tsunami. The height of the tsunami sea-waves was more than 15 metres. The number of deaths officially reported was 2500.
4. ***Okushiri (Japan):*** On July 12, 1993, an earthquake of high magnitude occurred in the Japan Sea near Okushiri. The height of the tsunami sea waves was more than 15 metres in which more than 2500 people lost their lives.
5. ***Peru Tsunami:*** ON 21st February, 1996, the north coast of Peru recorded an earthquake of high magnitude The tsunami wave height was more than five metres in which 15 people lost their lives.
6. ***Sumatra Tsunami (Simeulue – Indonesia):*** On December 26, 2004 an earthquake of 9.3 magnitude at the Richter Scale. This earthquake generated tsunami waves with a height of more than 15 metres. More than 250,000 people lost their lives and the damage was to property and ecology was enormous. This earthquake had its epicentre off the coast of Sumatra (Indonesia at 3.5° north and latitude and 95° east longitude. This place happens to be at the tri-junction of the Indian, Australian and Myanmarese (Burmese)

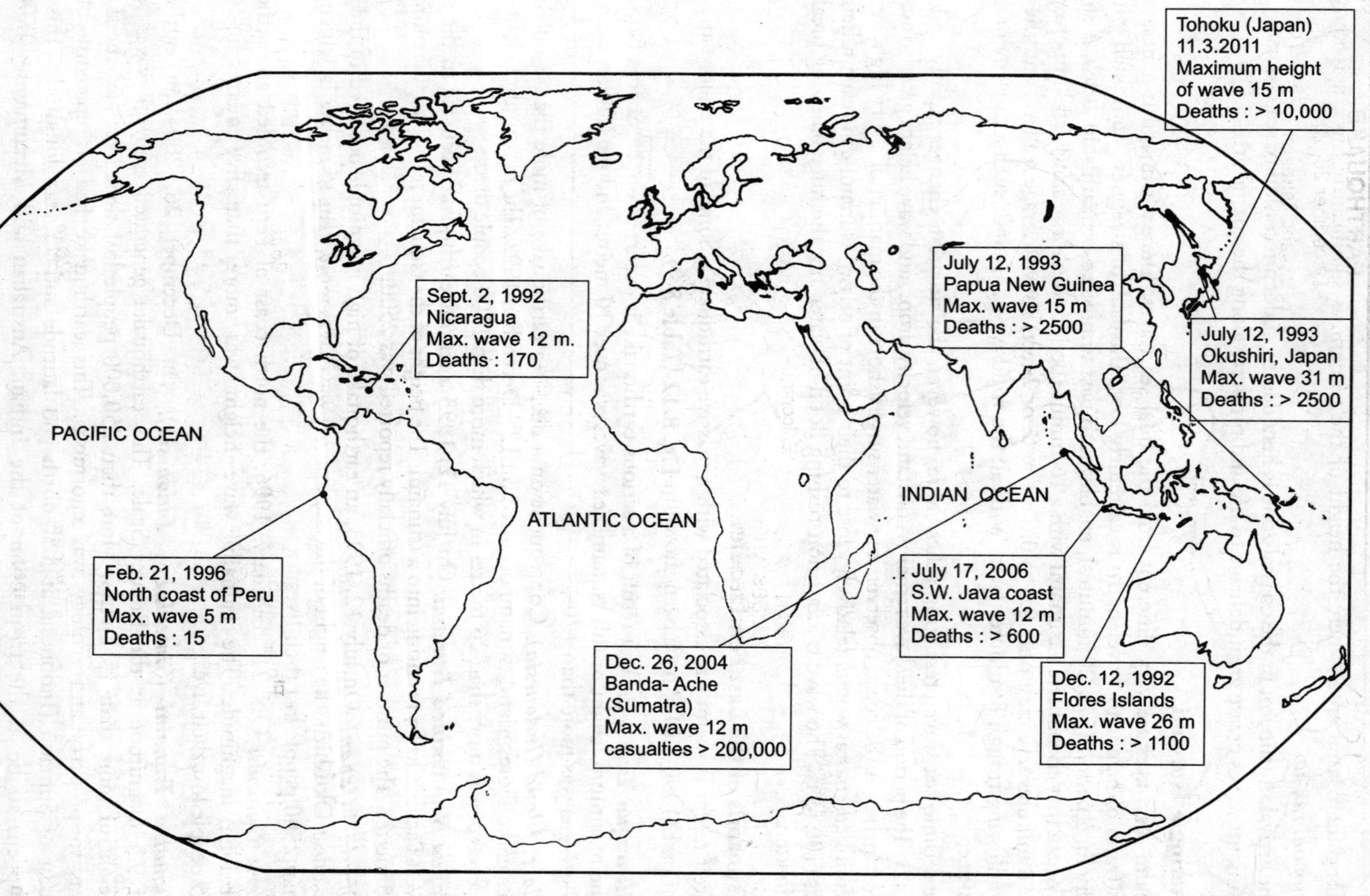

Fig. 8.12 Major Tsunamis – 1990–2012

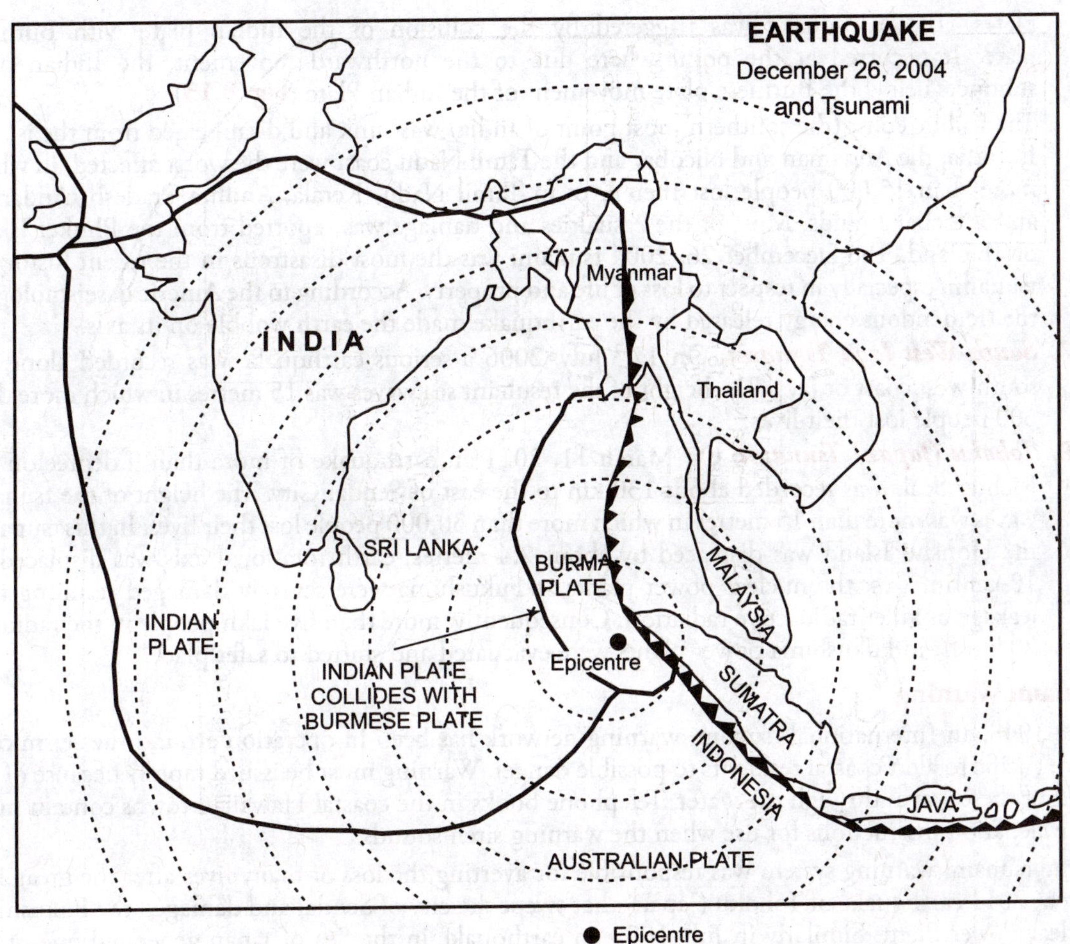

Fig. 8.13 Earthquake and Tsunami – 26th December, 2004

Table 8.11 Major Tsunamis of Recent Past (1990–2011)

Date of Tsunami	Place/Country	Maximum Height of Seismic Waves	Deaths
1. Sept. 2, 1992	Nicaragua	10 m	>170
2. December 12, 1992	Flores Island	26 m	>1100
3. July 12, 1993	Papua-New Guinea	15 m	>2500
4. July 12, 1993	Okushiri, Japan	15 m	>2500
5. Feb.21, 1996	North Coast of Peru	05 m	>15
6. Dec. 26, 2004	Simeulue – Banda Ache, Sumatra (Indonesia)	15 m	>200,000
7. July 17, 2006	S.W. Java (Indonesia)	>26 m	>600
8. March 11, 2011	Tohoku, Japan	>15	>10,000

plates. The earthquake was triggered by the collision of the Indian plate with Burmese plate. It occurred at the point where due to the northward movement, the Indian plate subducts below the Burmese plate movement of the Indian Plate (**Fig. 8.13**).

The Indira-Point (the southern most point of India) was sunk and disappeared from the island. In India, the Andaman and Nicobar and the Tamil Nadu coast were the worst affected, in which more than 15,000 people lost their lives in Tamil Nadu, Kerala, Andhra Pradesh, Andaman and Nicobar Islands. Most of the casualties and damage was reported from the Phuket Island of Thailand. The December 26, 2004 tsunami was the most disastrous in the recent history of tsunami, especially in respect to loss of life and property. According to the American seismologists the tremendous energy released by the earthquake made the earth wobble on its axis.

7. ***South-West Java Tsunami:*** On 17th July, 2006 a serious earthquake was recorded along the south-west coast of Java. The height of the resultant sea waves was 15 metres in which more than 600 people lost their lives.
8. ***Tohoku (Japan) Tsunami:*** On March 11, 2011 an earthquake of more than 9 degree on the Richter Scale was recorded about 130 km to the east of Sendai City. The height of the tsunami waves was more than 15 metres in which more than 30,000 people lost their lives. In this tsunami, the Honshu Island was displaced by about 2.4 metres, earth rotational axis was displaced by 10 centimetres, the nuclear power plants at Fukushima were severely damaged resulting into leakage of killer radioactive radiation. Consequently, more than five lakh people in the radius of 20 km from Fukushima power plants were evacuated and shifted to safer place.

Tsunami Warning

Since 1948, an International tsunami warning network has been in operation around the seismically active Pacific to alert coastal residents to possible danger. Warning must be issued rapidly because of the speed of these waves through the water. Telephone books in the coastal Hawaiian towns contain maps and evacuation instructions for use when the warning siren sounds.

The tsunami warning system was responsible for averting the loss of many lives after the great 11th March, 2011 earthquake of Tohoku (Japan) that swept the city of Sendai and damaged the Fukushima Nuclear Power Plant. Similarly in July 1993 an earthquake in the Sea of Japan generated one of the largest tsunami ever to strike Japan.

Management of Tsunami Disaster

The tsunami disaster management may be organised under two stages: (i) Pre-disaster stage, and (ii) post-disaster stage.

(i) ***Pre-tsunami Disaster Stage:*** In this stage, the following steps may be taken to avert and to minimise the danger to life and property.

1. Demarcation and mapping of areas vulnerable to tsunami.
2. Demarcation of the subduction zones where tsunami-generic earthquakes may occur.
3. People should not be allowed to construct houses and settlements in the tsunami vulnerable areas.
4. Development and protection of mangroves, corals, and coastal sand-dunes.
5. Installation of tsunami warning system along the coastal cities and towns, and islands of the Pacific Ocean, Atlantic and Indian Ocean.
6. Preparedness for timely evacuation of people living in the tsunami vulnerable areas.

(ii) ***Post-Tsunami Disaster Stage:*** In case the tsunami struck, the following steps should be taken to minimise the damage to life and property and to provide relief to the affected people.

1. Rescue and evacuation of the stranded alive people.
2. Immediate medical relief to the injured people.
3. Immediate relief and provisions of food and drinking water.
4. Rehabilitation of the displaced and affected people.
5. Avoid disaster area. Your presence may hamper rescue and other emergency operations.
6. Help people who require special assistance, e.g. infants, elderly people, those without transportation, people with disabilities.
7. Stay out of building if water remains around it. Tsunami water can weaken the foundation, causing building to sink, floors to crack, or walls to collapse.
8. When re-entering buildings or homes, be very careful. Carefully watch every step you take.
9. Use battery-powered lanterns or flashlights when examining buildings. Battery powered lighting is the safest and easiest to use and it does not present a fire hazard for the user. Do not use candle or lighter. Check for gas leak.
10. Watch out for wild animals, especially poisonous snakes that may have come into buildings with the water.

If the above steps are taken together, the adverse effect of tsunami may be reduced substantially.

Tsunami Warning System in India

An elaborate warning system in India has not been developed till date. It was after the earthquake of 2001 that the government allocated substantial amount to develop a network of tsunami warning system along the coast of Bay of Bengal, Arabian Sea and the Islands of Andaman and Nicobar. It is hoped the system will function effectively to give timely warning to the people living in the vulnerable coastal areas.

Landslides

Landslide has been defined as a sudden, rapid, down-slope movement of a cohesive mass of regolith and/or bedrock in a variety of mass movement under the influence of gravity. Landslides are fairly common phenomena and occur on small scale nearly everywhere. Large slides are less numerous, but commonly develop on steep slopes of weak shale rocks. They can move in a matter of seconds or slip gradually over a period of weeks and months.

Many landslides come to rest on a valley floor and in many instances dam the stream flowing through the valley, forming lake behind dam. Such lakes are temporary because the impounded water soon overflow the barrier and rapidly erode through the unconsolidated rock debris. This may result in catastrophic flooding down-stream as the lake is almost instantly drained.

Landslides are rarely on a scale comparable to seismic, volcanic or tsunami events. Many of the landslides are slow moving. They are destructive but they present little threat to life. The intensity and magnitude of landslide, however, depend on the geological structure and type and compactness of rocks. Earth flow, mass movement, mud-flow, rotational slip, rock-fall and debris avalanches are all examples of landslide.

Landslides generally happen where they have occurred in the past, and in identifiable hazard locations. Areas that are typically considered safe from landslides include areas that have not moved in the past; relatively flat areas away from sudden changes in slope; and areas at the top of a long ridge. Houses built at the toe of steep slopes are often vulnerable to slides and debris flow. The major causes of landslides are given below:

Causes of Landslides

As stated above, landslides are caused by the physical forces as well as my anthropogenic factors. In brief, the major causes of landslides are given below:

1. ***Earthquakes:*** Earthquakes are the most important cause of landslides, especially in the young folded mountains like the Himalayas, Rockies, Andes, Alps, etc. In India landslides are more frequent in the Greater Himalayas, Lesser Himalayas, Siwalik, Western Ghats, Eastern Ghats, Hills of North East India, Satpura and Vindhyan Mountain ranges (Fig. 8.14).
2. ***Rainfall, Snowfall and Sleet:*** Occurrence of heavy or/and continuous rainfall may lead to landslides in the areas of pervious and porous rocks. The Nashri area along the National Highway

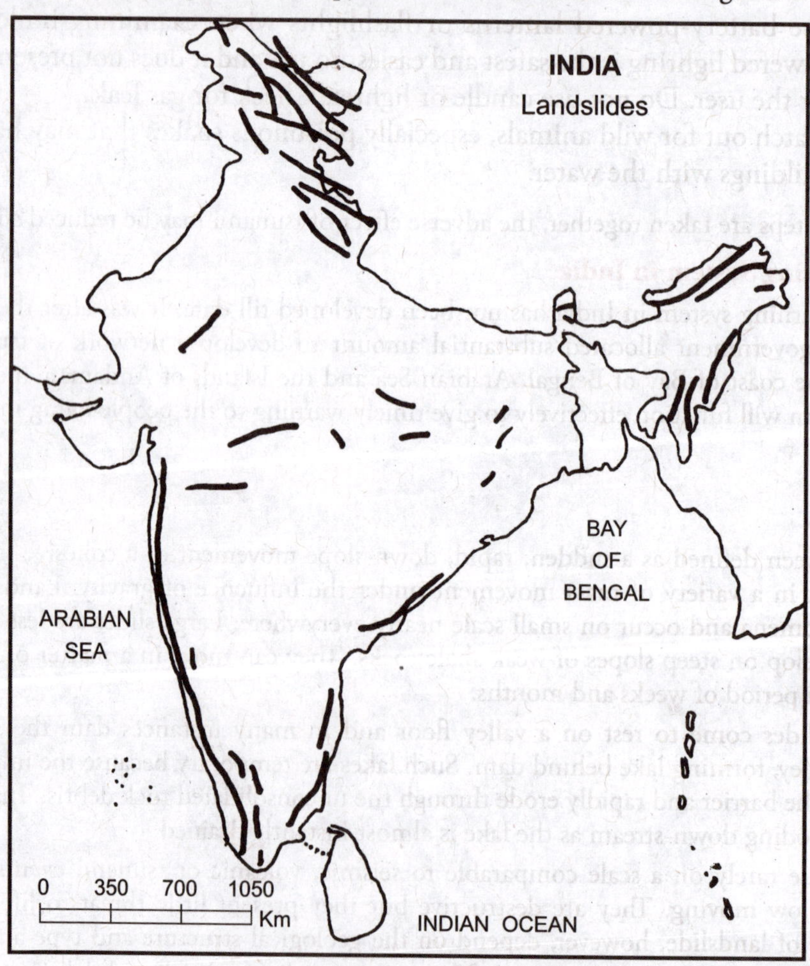

Fig. 8.14 Landslides Prone Areas

NO 1-A between Batote-Ramban and Banihal (Jammu & Kashmir State) is highly vulnerable to landslides, especially during the rainy and the winter seasons. The National Highways are disrupted and the vehicular traffic comes to a standstill causing great hardship to the civilian and military personnels (**Fig. 8.15**).

3. ***Mining, Quarrying and Road-cutting for Roads and Highways:*** The continuous extraction of coal, other minerals and building materials, and construction of roads along the steeper slopes in the mountainous areas create a condition favourable for the occurrence of landslides. Such landslides may be observed throughout the Himalayas, the Hill states of North East India, Nilgiri, and the Eastern and Western Ghats.
4. ***Construction of Houses on Vulnerable Slopes:*** Unplanned growth of towns and settlements in the hilly areas without testing of soils and rocks is also an important cause of landslide. The eastern slopes of Nainital (Uttarakhand) along the Mall Road is subsiding because of the

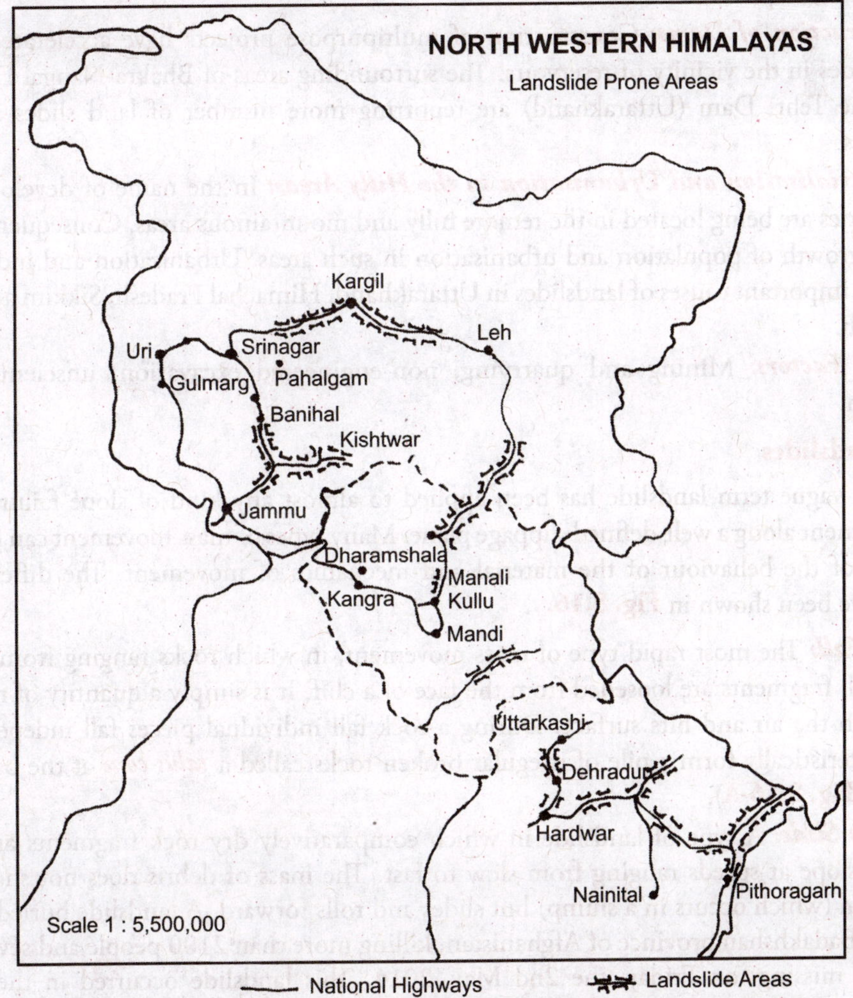

Fig. 8.15 Landslides in North-west Himalayas

heavy load of multi-storied buildings (hotels) and residential structures. The cities of Chamba (Himachal Pradesh), Shillong (Meghalaya), Aizawl (Mizoram), Gangtok (Sikkim), Pahalgam (J & K) are facing this type of adverse situation.

5. ***Deforestation:*** Deforestation, overgrazing, irrational land-use practices and other human activities are also largely responsible for landslides in hilly and mountainous areas. Deforestation has been quite significant in the Doda District of Jammu & Kashmir, Almora, Chamoli, Dehradun, Pithoragarh, Uttarkashi districts (Uttarakhand), Darjeeling (W. Bengal), Itanagar, Pasighat regions (Arunachal Pradesh), Khasi region of Meghalaya, and the greater parts of Eastern and Western Ghats. The reduction in forest cover has accelerated the rate of landslide in the hilly areas.
6. ***Shifting Cultivation:*** The slash and burn agriculture known as *Jhuming* in North East India is also significantly responsible for landslides in the states of Manipur, Mizoram, Meghalaya, Nagaland, Tripura, etc.
7. ***Construction of Dams:*** Construction of multipurpose projects have accelerated the rate of landslides in the vicinity of reservoirs. The surrounding areas of Bhakra-Nangal Dam (Punjab) and the Tehri Dam (Uttarakhand) are reporting more number of land slides in the recent decades.
8. ***Industrialisation and Urbanisation in the Hilly Areas:*** In the name of development, more industries are being located in the remote hilly and mountainous areas. Consequent upon is the rapid growth of population and urbanisation in such areas. Urbanisation and industrialisation are the important causes of landslides in Uttarakhand, Himachal Pradesh, Sikkim and Arunachal Pradesh.
9. ***Other Factors:*** Mining and quarrying, non-engineered excavation, unscientific land-use pattern.

Types of Landslides

Although the vague term landslide has been applied to almost any kind of slope failure. Landslides involve movement along a well-defined slippage plane. Many types of mass movement can be recognised on the basis of the behaviour of the material and mechanics of movement. The different types of landslides have been shown in **Fig. 8.16.**

(i) ***Rock Fall:*** The most rapid type of mass movement, in which rocks ranging from large masses to small fragments are loosened from the face of a cliff. It is simply a quantity of rock that falls through the air and hits surface. During a rock fall individual pieces fall independently, and characteristically form a pile of irregular broken rocks called a *talus cone* at the base of a steep slope (**Fig. 8.16-A**).

(ii) ***Debris Slide:*** A type of landslide in which comparatively dry rock fragments and soil move down-slope at speeds ranging from slow to fast. The mass of debris does not show backward rotation (which occurs in a slump) but slides and rolls forward. A landslide buried Argo village in the Badakhshan province of Afghanistan, killing more than 2100 people and several hundred people missing, on Friday, the 2nd May, 2014. This landslide occurred in the Hindukush mountain. The area between Batot and Banihall (Chenab gorge is also highly vulnerable to land Slides). (**Fig. 8.16-B**).

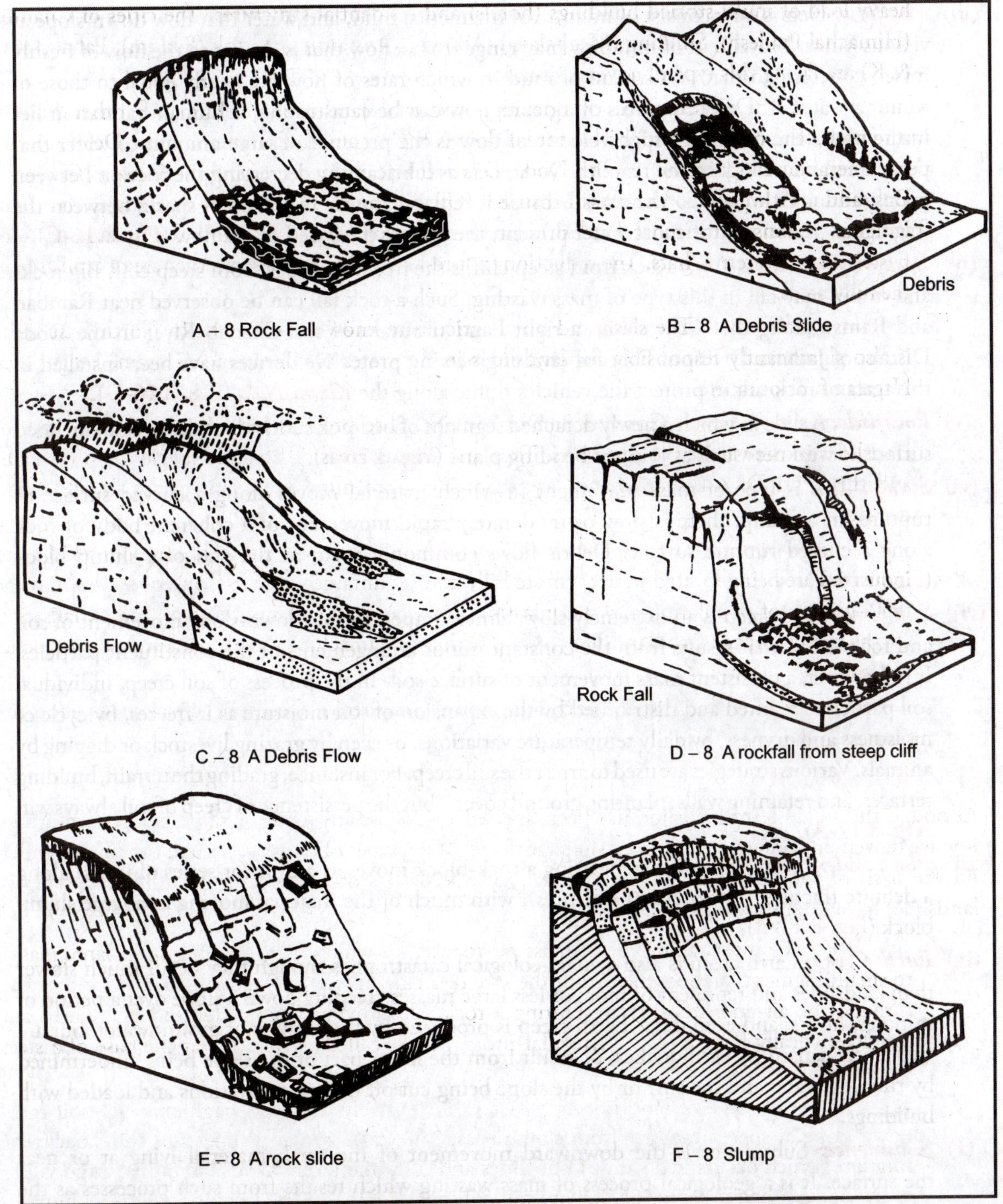

Fig. 8.16 Types of Landslides

(iii) ***Mudflow:*** Debris flow consist of mixture of fragments, mud, and water that flow down-slope as viscous fluids. Movement of mudflow may range from a flow that is similar to the flow of freshly mixed concrete, to that of a stream of mud in which rates of flow are nearly equal to those of running water. The consequences of a debris flow can be catastrophic if human habitation lies in the path. The reason for high velocity of flow is the presence of large amount of water that penetrates and soaks into the regolith. Water acts as lubricant by decreasing the friction between grains, and adds weight to the mass because it replaces the air in the open spaces between the fragments, Therefore, the more water present, the greater the speed of the flow **(Fig. 8.16-C).**

(iv) ***Rockfall from Steep Cliff:*** Rock from steep cliff is the free fall of rock from steep cliff. Big rocks and stones may fall in this type of mass wasting. Such a rock fall can be observed near Ramban and Ramsu along the *Khuni-Nala*, a right hand tributary of the Chenab River in the Doda District of Jammu Division. Especial civil engineering protective devices have been installed in this tract of rock-fall to protect the vehicles traffic along the *Khuni-Nala* **(Fig. 8.16-D).**

(v) ***Rockslide:*** A slide in which a newly detached segment of bedrock suddenly slides over an inclined surface of weakness such as joint or bedding plane (**Fig. 8.16-E**).

(vi) ***Slump:*** This is type of mass movement in which material moves along a curved surface of rupture. In a slump, there is slow or moderately rapid movement of a coherent body of rock along a curved rupture surface. Debris flows commonly occur at the end of a slump block **(Fig. 8.16-F).**

(vii) ***Soil Creep:*** Soil creep is an extremely slow, almost imperceptible down-slope movement of soil and rock debris that results from the constant minor arrangements of the constituent particles. It is, however, a persistent mass movement of surface soil. In the process of soil creep, individual soil particles are lifted and distributed by the expansion of soil moisture as it freezes, by cycle of moistness and dryness, by daily temperature variations, or even by grazing livestock or digging by animals. Various strategies are used to arrest the soil creep. For instance, grading the terrain, building terraces, and retaining walls, planting ground cover – but the persistence of creep of soil always win (**Fig. 8.17-A**).

(viii) ***Block slide:*** In this type of mass wasting a rock-block moves as a unit (or series of units) along a definite fracture, (or system of fractures), with much of the material moving as a large slump block (**Fig. 8.17-B**).

(ix) ***Earth Creep:*** Earth creep is also a vital geological catastrophes though they occur much slower than landslides and represent of more or less large masses creeping down a slope over a period of minutes, hours, and even days. Earth creep is produced by the activity of groundwater, but are frequently caused by earthquakes, or result from the lower part of the slope being undermined by running water and the surf or by the slope being cut off during excavations and loaded with buildings.

(x) ***Subsidence:*** Subsidence is the downward movement of the earth material lying at or near the surface. It is a geological process of mass wasting which results from such processes as the withdrawal of groundwater, geothermal fluids, oil and natural gas. The extraction of coal, salt, sulphur and other solids through mining also lead to subsidence. It is a frequent phenomenon in the *karst* (limestone) topography and the areas of underlain permafrost.

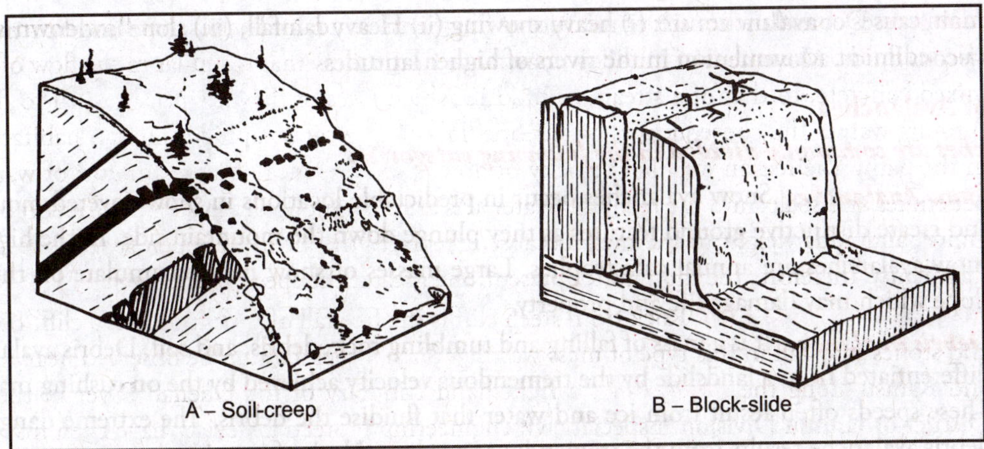

Fig. 8.17 Soil-creep and Block-slide

Steps to Reduce Risk from Landslides

Landslides are the results of endogenetic and exogenetic forces. They are generally sudden about which prediction cannot be made. Some of the important steps which can reduce the risk to life and property by landslides are given below:

1. ***Mapping of the Landslide Prone Areas:*** The delineation of landslide prone areas is imperative. Demarcation of such areas on the maps can help in the stabilisation of slope and reducing the frequency of landslide. Construction of houses, felling of trees and grazing in landslide prone areas should be prohibited or restricted.
2. ***Retaining Walls:*** Strong retaining walls along the road sides should be constructed to stop debris flow downward. In the construction of retaining wall should not obstruct the natural drainage.
3. ***Engineering Structures:*** Buildings and other engineering structures in the landslide prone areas should be constructed after soil testing with foundations.
4. ***Surface Drainage Control:*** Steps should be taken to control the natural drainage in the landslide prone areas so that the seepage of rainwater can be reduced.
5. ***Planting of Trees:*** Afforestation in the vulnerable areas is an effective way of durable landslides control. Planting of trees can help appreciably in binding the top layer of the soil, thereby reducing the frequency and intensity of landslides.
6. ***Scientific Management of Land and Forest Resources:*** Scientific management of land, forest and water resources in the upper reaches of rivers in the hilly areas, and public awareness about the landslide disasters can go a long way in the stabilisation and reduction of the number of landslide.

Avalanches

The sudden and rapid movement of ice, snow, earth or rock down a slope is known as avalanche. Avalanches are an obvious and important mechanism of mass wasting in mountainous parts of the earth. They are also highly significant on continental margins and deltas. Avalanches occur when the shear stresses on a potential surface of sliding exceeds the shear strength of the same plane. Avalanches damage the roads, traffic chaos, and destroy the houses and settlements which lie in path of avalanche.

The main causes of avalanches are: (i) heavy snowing (ii) Heavy rainfall, (iii) slope undercutting, and (iv) deltaic sediment accumulation in the rivers of higher latitudes.

Types of Avalanches

Avalanches are commonly divided in the following categories:

(i) ***Snow Avalanches:*** Snow avalanches occur in predictable locations in snow-covered mountains and create distinctive ground features as they plunge down the mountain side. In the highlands snow avalanches are annual catastrophes. Large masses of snow may accumulate on the steep slope which may damage life and property.

(ii) ***Debris Avalanche:*** It is a mass of falling and tumbling rock, debris, and soil. Debris avalanche is differentiated from a landslide by the tremendous velocity achieved by the on rushing materials. These speeds often result from ice and water that fluidise the debris. The extreme danger of a debris avalanche results from the tremendous speeds and lack of warning.

(iii) ***Dry Avalanche:*** This type of avalanches occur in winter when snow-drifts on the ridges and steep slopes grow so large after heavy snowfalls without thawing that any vibration of air, even the loud call cause them to break off. These avalanches come down, simultaneously filling the air with snow-dust which forms a veritable cloud.

(iv) ***Wet Avalanches:*** This type of avalanches occur generally during the winter season, after heavy snowfalls or during intensive thawing and also during spring thawing. Such avalanches consist of more or less sticky, waterlogged snow. These avalanches have a very uneven surface and produce snow cloud as they come down.

(v) ***Glacial Avalanches:*** These are the terminal parts of hanging glaciers sometimes breaking away from the main mass and rolling down to the foot of the slope as a chaos of fragments. As the name indicates these avalanches consist of ice.

Most of the avalanches in India occur in the Mountain range of Karakoram, Greater and Lesser Himalayas in the states of Jammu & Kashmir, Himachal Pradesh and Uttarakhand.

Strategy to Control Avalanches

The avalanches may be controlled by adopting the following steps:

(i) ***Hard Measures:*** Such measures are designed and adopted to prevent or to block or deflecting avalanches with protective structures. Such structures have been constructed near Ramsu and Ramban in the Doda District of Jammu and Kashmir State.

(ii) ***Soft Measures:*** Software measures provide safety by eliminating the probability of avalanches by removing snow deposits on slope with blasting and by predicting the occurrence of avalanches and recommending evacuation from hazardous areas.

(iii) ***Preventive Measures:*** Such measures include creating preventive structures. These structures are meant to prevent the occurrence of avalanches. These steps include: planting of trees, stepped terraces, avalanche control fences, suspended fences, retaining walls, deflecting structures, snow-sheds, etc.

In addition to the above measures, a timely prediction and forecasting can reduce the damage to life and property in the avalanche prone areas.

Climatic Disasters Cyclones

Cyclone is a dynamically or thermally caused low-pressure area of converging air flows. The cyclones may be divided into (i) the tropical cyclones, and (ii) temperate cyclones.

Tropical Cyclones

A cyclonic circulation originating in the tropics, with winds between 30 and 64 knots (39 to 73 mph); The tropical cyclones are known by different names in different parts of the country. They are called as *hurricanes* in the Gulf of Mexico, Gulf of California, USA – North America; *typhoons* in China; *Taifu (Tofu)* in Japan; *Baguio* in Philippines; *Willy-Willy* in north and east Australia and only *cyclones* in the Indian Ocean (Bay of Bengal, Arabian Sea and Madagascar).

Characteristics of Tropical Cyclones The main characteristics of a tropical cyclone are as under:

(i) The isobars in a tropical cyclone are circular in shape.
(ii) The diameter of a tropical cyclone varies from 150 to 500 kilometres and vertically from surface to about 12 km.
(iii) The central area of a tropical cyclone is known '*Eye*' of the cyclone.
(iv) They develop over the warm waters of lower latitudes.
(v) They derive their energy from the latent heat.
(vi) They occur in the Northern Hemisphere in the autumn season.
(vii) They give torrential rainfall.
(viii) They are most destructive and cause heavy damage to life and property in their path.

Origin of Tropical Cyclones The origin of tropical cyclones is not well understood. These cyclones are, however, quite different from that of the temperate cyclones. The air of the tropics is essentially homogeneous, with no fronts. In addition, the warm air and warm sea ensure an abundant supply of water vapour into the atmosphere, and thus the necessary latent heat to fuel these storms. The tropical cyclones originate within a warm, humid air mass between 8° and 25° N and South in both the hemispheres. A tropical cyclone usually develops from a small tropical depression. The cariolis effect also helps in the origin of tropical cyclones.

The trade wind belt is typically a relatively shallow layer of warm, moist air above which is a deep layer of warmer, dry subsiding air. This forms the trade wind inversion – characteristic that limits the vertical development of clouds. The inversion is sometimes interrupted by low-pressure trough, which allows thunderstorm development behind the wave. Increased convection and the normal pattern of high-altitude winds cause the trough to deepen on an isolated low pressure system is formed. If the pressure continues to fall, winds accelerate and a tropical storm is born. In this process, the role of cariolis effect is quite significant (**Fig. 8.18**).

The following conditions are required for the origin and development of a tropical cyclone:

1. Large and continuous supply of warm and moist air.
2. Significant cariolis force.
3. Existence of weak tropical trough.

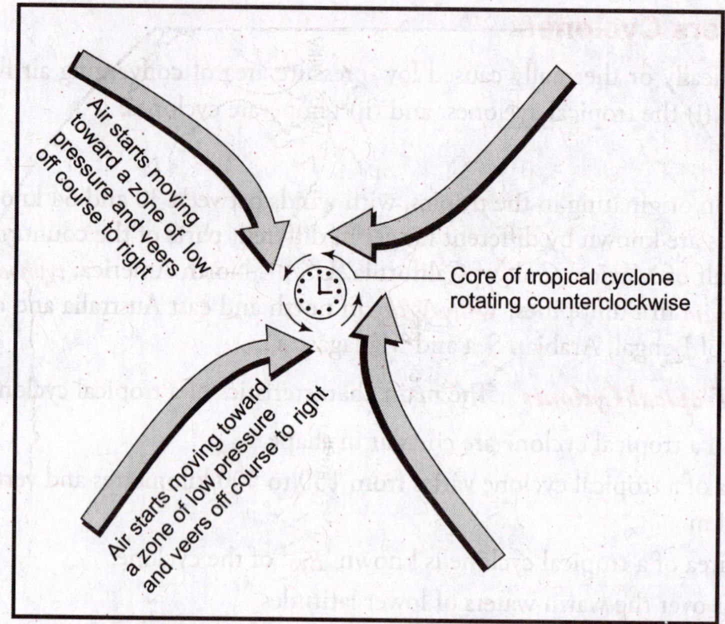

Fig. 8.18 The dynamics of a tropical cyclone, showing the influence of the cariolis force

4. Upper level outflow at a height of about 9000 to 15000 metres above the sea level, there must be an anticyclone circulation so that the ascending air currents within the cyclone may continue to be pumped on it in order to maintain the low pressure at the centre of the cyclone.
5. Weak vertical wind at the surface.
6. Small atmospheric vortices in Inter-tropical Convergence Zone: These atmospheric vortices initiate the forming process of a tropical cyclone.

After its origin, a tropical cyclone moves slowly at first, usually moving from east to west in low latitudes. As it gains strength, the speed increases and its path under the effect of coriolis force curves gradually toward the subtropical and temperate regions. As long as the storm remains over warm water (ocean water), it can grow in intensity. A storm can travel far north along the east coast of the United States and the east coast of China and Japan, because it follows the warm ocean currents of the *Gulf Stream* and the *Kuro Siwo* (Japan) respectively. When a storm moves over the cold *Labrador Current* of the North Atlantic Oceans, and the *Oya Siwo* Current of the Pacific Ocean, it dissipates rapidly. If it moves over land, increased friction with the land surface and loss of the energy supply causes the storm to dissolve quickly.

Tracks of Tropical Cyclones Tropical cyclones occur on the western margins of the oceans in the regions of warm tropical waters. They start over the tropical oceans between latitudes of 8° and 25° N and S on the eastern sides of continents. They are absent along the equator due to the weakness of the Cariolis effect. On an average 20 tropical cyclones occur each year. There are six general regions of the highest frequency of tropical cyclones **(Fig. 8.19)**:

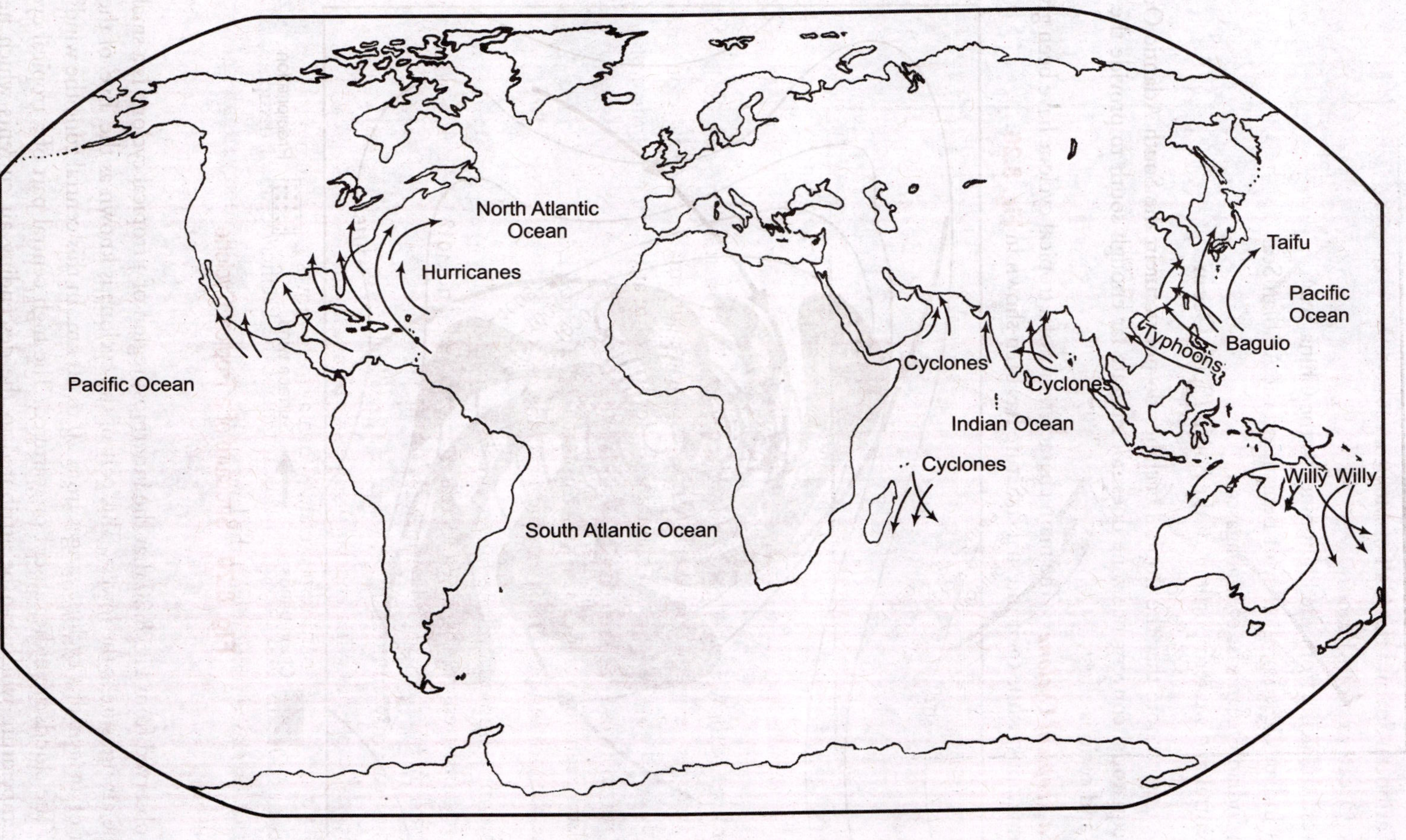

Fig. 8.19 Tracks of Tropical Cyclones

1. The Caribbean Sea and the Gulf of Mexico.
2. Pacific Ocean west of Mexico
3. The western Pacific from the Philippines to the China Sea.
4. North Indian Ocean in the Bay of Bengal and the Arabian Sea.
5. South Indian Ocean east of Madagascar.
6. The central and western portions of the South Pacific Ocean.

It is interesting to note that the tropical cyclones do not occur in the South Atlantic Ocean. It is because the equatorial convergence zone does not migrate far enough south to provide the necessary convergence and coriolis effect.

Structure of a Tropical Cyclone The main characteristics of a tropical cyclone have been given in the preceding paragraphs, while their internal structure has been shown in **Fig. 8.20**.

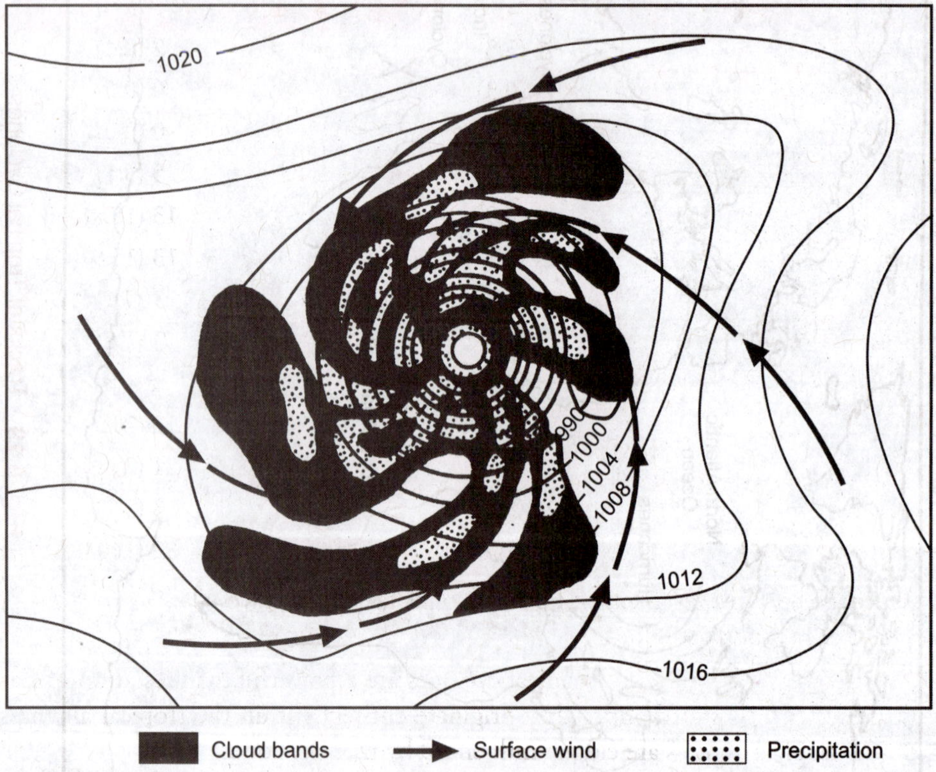

Fig. 8.20 Structure of a Tropical Cyclone

It may be observed from Fig. 8.20 that the innermost region of a tropical cyclone is a small circular area where the air pressure is the lowest. This part of the cyclone is known as the 'Eye' of the cyclone. The diameter of an 'eye' of a cyclone ranges from 20 to 40 km. In this central zone the winds are light and variable. The clouds are either absent or scattered. The high central part of a tropical cyclone has the highest temperature which can be attributed to the descending air currents which heat up by compression. In this central calm area, the sky is blue and there is intermittent sunlight against the background of spiralling clouds about 12 kilometres high. These clouds consist of bands which have been shown in Fig. 8.20 as dark-shaded elongated patches sprawling away from the central region of the cyclone. The central core of the tropical cyclone is surrounded by walls of cumulonimbus clouds. The highest velocities of winds are always recorded adjacent to the centre of a tropical cyclone. Moreover, the heaviest rainfall is also recorded in the vicinity of this region. The winds gradually slow down of uniform rate from the eye-wall in the centre where the rainfall practically ceases.

The frequency and tracks of cyclonic storms in India have been given in **Table 8.12**.

Table 8.12 Frequency of Cyclonic Storms in India

Months	Bay of Bengal	Arabian Sea
January	4 (1.3)	2 (2.4)
February	1 (0.3)	0 (0.0)
March	4 (1.30)	0 (0.0)
April	18 (5.7)	5 (6.1)
May	28 (8.9)	13 (15.9)
June	34 (10.8)	13 (15.9)
July	38 (12.1)	3 (3.7)
August	25 (8.0)	1 (1.2)
September	27 (8.6)	4 (4.8)
October	53 (16.9)	17 (20.7)
November	56 (17.8)	21 (25.6)
December	26 (8.3)	3 (3.7)
Total	314 (100.00)	82 (100.00)

Data in brackets are the percentages to total number of storms taking place in a year.

Social Relevance of Tropical Cyclones Tropical cyclones are a powerful manifestation of Earth's energy and moisture system. As stated above they originate entirely within the tropical air-masses. The people living in the tropical regions are closely influenced by these cyclones.

The tropical cyclones are violent and destructive types of storms. They commonly generate storm tides leading to coastal inundation. In general, tropical cyclones are the most destructive. The damage to life and property caused by them are enormous. According to the experts of weather and climate, by far the greatest damage to life and property is caused by the tropical cyclones. The destructive nature of tropical cyclones may be appreciated from the following destructive cyclones.

In Bangladesh, on 13th November, 1970 a tropical cyclone with a wind velocity of 200 km per hour roared up the mouth of Padma (Ganga) River, carrying with it masses of sea-water up to 12 metres in height. Another great storm (tropical cyclone), which struck in May 1991 killed more than 200,000 people and almost the same number in the cyclone of 1997. The Hudhud cyclone on 12th October 2014 caused severe damage to Vishakhapatnam, Srikakulam (Andhra Pradesh), Gopalpur, and Ganjam districts (Odisha). The Katrina Hurricane (August, 2005) was the costliest, and the third most deadliest in which about two thousand people lost their lives. It was followed by Rita Hurricane in September, 2005 in which the New Orleans city of Louisiana and Houston City of Texas State was submerged and almost the entire population was evacuated.

Recently, the *Sandy Hurricane* of North America created havoc condition in some of the states of USA. On Monday, the October 29, 2012, Sandy Hurricane (a gigantic tropical cyclone) took the shape of a disaster in the most powerful country of the world (USA). The diameter of this hurricane was supersize, over 1517 km. Moving northward, it met low pressure of the strong polar jet stream which increased its intensity. Moreover, higher tides were observed because of the Full Moon period which accelerated the flooding of the coastal areas. The adversely affected areas included the states of Washington D.C., Pennsylvania, New Jersey, New York, New England, Maine, Rhode (USA) and the north-eastern states of Canada. The consequent flood and freezing temperatures killed more than one hundred people. More than 40 lakh people had to stay without light for a few days. Life in New York, the commercial capital of the country was jeopardised as several parts of the city were submerged under water (**Fig. 8.21**).

The main advantage from the tropical cyclones are:

(i) They resultant rainfall from a tropical cyclone recharges ponds, lakes underground water table.
(ii) They add moisture to dry soil conditions.
(iii) The streams are flushed of pollution.
(iv) The local water-bodies are restored.
(v) They contribute to the precipitation regime and help in maintaining the water budget.

Thunderstorms

A tropical storm associated with thunder, lightning and very heavy rainfall or hail is known as thunderstorm. It represents an extreme condition of atmospheric instability, often associated with the passage of a cold front or due to intense heating of the ground surface and the resulting convectional uplift of air. In a thunderstorm, tremendous energy is liberated by the condensation of large quantities of water vapour. This process locally heats the air causing violent up-draughts and downdraughts as the rising parcel of air pulls the surrounding air into the column and as the frictional drag of raindrops pulls air towards the ground. As a result, giant cumulus-nimbus clouds can create dramatic weather moments-squall-line of heavy precipitation, lightning, thunder, hail-blustery winds and tornadoes (**Fig. 8.22**).

Thousands of thunderstorms occur on earth at any given moment. The equatorial regions experience many of them, as exemplified by the city of Kampala in Uganda. This city records on an average about 242 thunderstorms days a year – a record.

Thunderstorms and Hails in India

Thunderstorms Thunderstorms occur at variable frequency in different parts of India. Every location is vulnerable to thunder and lightning from time to time. Lightning occurs when the voltage gradient within a cloud or between clouds overcomes the electrical resistance of air. The result is large and powerful spark that partially equalizes the separation. Cloud to cloud lightning causes the sky to light up more or less uniformly. Cloud to surface lightning also occurs on rare occasions. This may result in blowing out electrical appliances in the buildings. It can start forest fires. The tremendous increase in temperature during a lightning stroke causes the air to expand explosively and produce the sound of thunder. Since the speed of sound is lower than that of light, thunder is heared with time lag after the flash of lightning.

Thunderstorms with associated showers of rain and hail are the predominant weather phenomena, generally, before and after the monsoon season. When sufficient moisture is not present in the air, as over north-west India, only dust storms may result. Thunderstorms, with associated squalls, are of short duration, but some are very violent and destructive like the *Kalbaishakis* of Bengal. Dust-storms or *Andhis* occur over north-west India. Some violent thunderstorms are accompanied with hail, especially in northern and central India and occasionally in the interior Peninsular India. The frequency of hailstorms is small in winter, but increases generally as the season advances to summer. During monsoon season (season of general rains), hailstorms are practically absent from the whole country.

Hail: Hail consists of ice pellets formed in concentric layers. It occurs only in Cumulo-nimbus clouds where updrafts can reach nearly 160 km/hr and where there is abundant supply of super cooled water. Initially an updraft carries water droplet above the freezing level to form the core of the hailstone. At some point the pellet falls from the updraft and collides with a film of liquid water. If the pellet is again lifted above the freezing level by an updraft, the same freezes to form a second layer of ice. This sequence can repeat a number of times resulting in the formation of several ice layers consisting of alternating zones of clear and milky ice. This process continues till it falls as hail either due to a downdraft or due to it growing too heavy to remain suspended by thunderstorm's updraft.

The number of days with hail is about 6-7 per year over Jammu and Kashmir, Himachal Pradesh and Uttrakhand,, but it decreases to 1 in 2 years over the adjoining plains. Over Bihar, Chhattisgarh, Jharkhand, Madhya Pradesh, Maharashtra, Uttar Pradesh and West Bengal, hailstorms occur 1 or 2 occasions in a year, and pose a potential hazard to Rabi crops. Protection against violent hailstorm is possible by adopting artificial hail suppression methods. It is difficult to forestall a hailstorm, since its occurrence is sporadic and confined to very limited areas in a thunderstorm. It is a highly localized phenomena.

Western Disturbances

The western disturbances are the low pressure depressions which originate from the Mediterranean Sea and enter India after crossing Turkey, Syria, Iraq, Iran, Afghanistan and Pakistan. The jet streams plays an important role in bringing the western disturbances to India. Their frequency is high between November and May. The average frequency of these western disturbances is 2 in November and May, and 4 or 5 from December to April. These disturbances result in light rains that are beneficial to Rabi crops. The human efficiency also increases at the arrival of western disturbances. In winter months, the disturbances are also followed by cold waves over northern and central India. These cold waves, and the resultant fog and frost are injurious to sugarcane, vegetables and orchards.

Cold Waves and Frost

A cold wave occurs when there is fall in temperature by 6° to 8°C from the normal temperature. When the temperature falls by more than 8oC that is termed as a severe cold wave condition.

In general, cold weather begins in India by early December. During the winter months, under the influence of western disturbances, night temperatures fall by 7°-8°C below normal in northern India, and about 5°C below normal over the Peninsular India. The ground temperatures are usually much lower than that of air temperatures. Under such cold wave conditions, the crops may be subject to sub-zero temperatures. Consequently, there is great damage to vegetable, orchards, sugarcane and standing Rabi crops due to cold waves and ground frost. The frost hazard is greatest in northern Punjab, being 10-20 days in December, January and February. Southward and eastward of this area, frost occurrence decreases rapidly.

The temperature to which air must be cooled to become saturated is known as dew point. Frost forms when the dew point of the air is below freezing. Thus frost forms when water vapour changes directly from gas to solid stage without entering the liquid state. Very small ice crystals are deposited over surfaces. A frost hazard is produced when a cold air mass moves into the region or when sufficient radiation cooling takes place on a clear night. The former may inflict widespread damage to the standing *Rabi* crops, vegetables and orchards.

The Indian Meteorological Department makes timely forecasting to enable the farmers to adopt protective measures. Irrigation or spraying with water helps to mitigate frost damage in the field. The use of heaters in orchards also help to raise the temperature by about 5°C. Valleys in which cold air stagnates are subject to frost to a greater extent, especially in the grape fields of Madhya Pradesh and Maharashtra. While laying out orchards and tea gardens, such valleys should be avoided. Trees planted as shelterbelts or shade trees protect the crops during the period of mild frost. Valuable crops can also be protected by covering the ground with suitable material, e.g. mulch, paper, and plastic, to reduce the cooling of the ground through radiation.

El Nino (Southern Oscillation) and Indian Monsoon

A southward flowing nutrient poor current of warm water off the coast of Chile and Peru (South America), caused by a break down of trade wind circulation. ENSO is an acronym for the coupled phenomena of El-Nino and the Southern Oscillation. The Southern Oscillation is a reversal of airflow between normally low atmospheric pressure over the western Pacific and normally high pressure over the eastern Pacific. This reversal airflow is caused by the occurrence of El Nino.

The world's most extensive region of warm ocean water with a sea surface temperature of over 27°C is located in the western equatorial Pacific Indonesian region. The heavy rainfall and associated heating of the atmosphere over this huge 'warm pool is the source of atmospheric heating. But the eastern equatorial Pacific is normally colder than the western part mainly due to the influence of Northeasterly Trade winds and the cold water current along the coast of Chile and the upwelling of the cold deep water off the coast of Peru. During the normal conditions, viz. in a Non El Nino year, the trade winds converge near the equator and the flow creates a warm surface current that moves from east to west along the equator. This results in the piling up of thick layer of warm surface water that produces higher sea levels (by about 40 cm) in the western Pacific (Indonesia, etc.). Sea surface temperatures of the western Pacific are about 8°C higher than that of eastern Pacific Ocean. But a strong cold Peruvian (Humboldt) Current, upwelling of cold water and lower sea levels characterize the eastern Pacific.

Periodically a phenomenon called as Southern Oscillation that is a global scale seesaw in surface pressure with centres of action near Indonesia-North Australia in one side and southeast Pacific region in the other side occurs, when it occurs, the above mentioned normal situation greatly changes. Pressure rises in the Indonesian region. This reversal creates a major change in the equatorial current system with warm water flowing eastward. This eastward shift of the warmest water marks the onset of El-Nino that sets up changes in atmospheric circulation. This represents the warm phase of Southern Oscillation. Thus, El Nino is a recurrent event of anomalous warming of the eastern equatorial Pacific in which temperatures are significantly above normal. El Nino is named after a Peruvian Christmas festival where the warming of the waters off Peru is said to occur near the birthday of 'The Boy' (El Nino) or the Christ child.

The meteorologists refer to the two phenomena of El Nino and Southern Oscillation that are atmospheric and oceanic parts of global system of climatic fluctuations as ENSO. The reverse phenomenon of the cooling of the eastern Pacific is called as La Nina (The Girl).

El Nino is a disruption of the ocean-atmospheric system in the tropical Pacific having important consequences for weather and the globe. Among these consequences are increased rainfalls across the southern tier of the U.S.A. and in Peru, which cause destructive flooding in South America, and drought in Indonesia and Australia, sometimes associated with devastating bush fires in Australia and the islands of South-east Asia.

At the occurrence of El Nino, maize production has been found to be much higher in Argentina as compared to other years. The close relationship of ENSO variability and occurrence of widespread droughts in the Sahel region of Africa have also been reported.

Lightning and Thunder

An estimated 8 million lightning strikes occur each day on earth. Lightning refers to flashes of light caused by enormous electrical discharges – tens to hundreds of million of volts – which briefly superheat the air to temperatures of 15,000°C – 30,000° C. The violent expansion of this abruptly heated air sends shock waves through the atmosphere – the sonic bang, known as thunder. The greater the distance a lightning stroke travels, the longer the thunder echoes. Lightning at great distance from the observer may not be accompanied by thunder and is called as ***heat-lightning***.

Lightning poses a hazard to aircraft and to the people, animals, plants and structures. Thousands of people are killed all over the world and several thousand receive injuries each year from thunder and lightning.

Tornadoes

Tornado is an intense vortex in the atmosphere with abnormally low pressure in the centre and a converging spiral of high velocity winds. In other words, it is an intense, destructive cyclonic rotation, developed in response to extremely low pressure, associated with ***mesocyclonic*** formation. A mesocyclone can range up to 10 km in diameter and rotate over thousands of metres vertically within the parent cloud. As a mesocyclone extends vertically and contracts horizontally, wind speeds accelerate in an

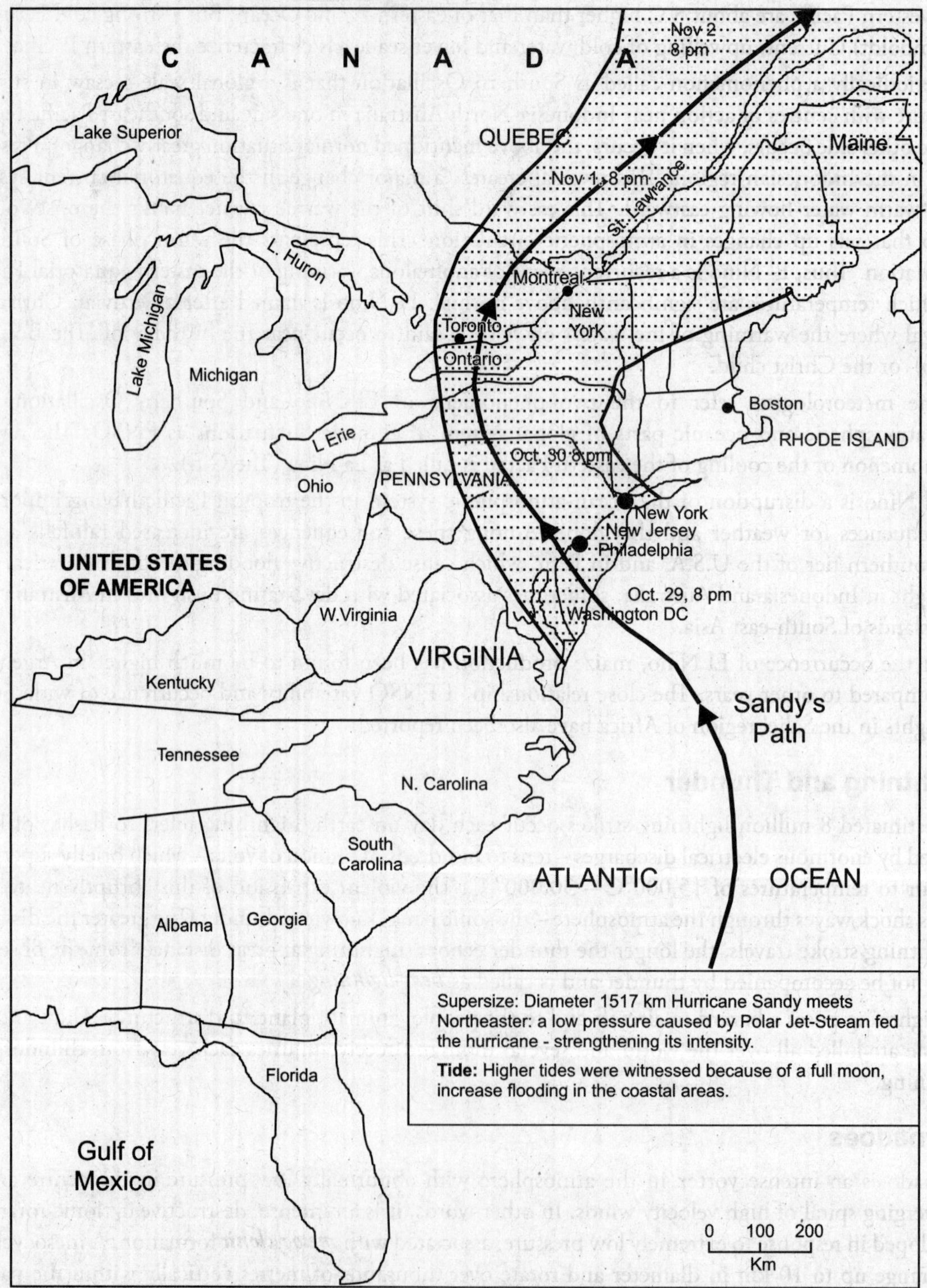

Fig. 8.21 Path of Sandy Hurricane, 29th October, 2012

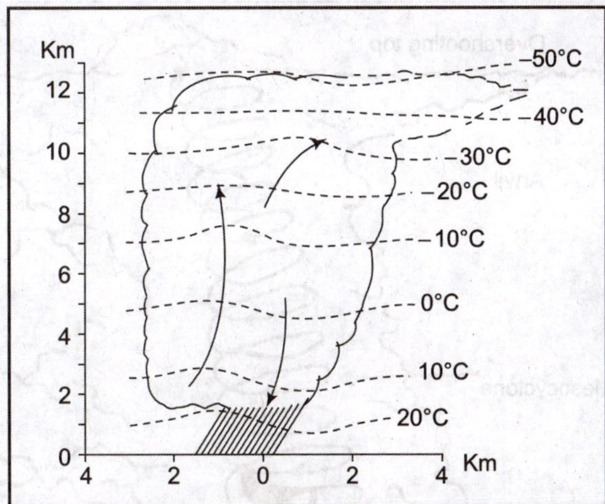

Fig. 8.22 Mature stage of thunderstorm (after Byers)

inward vortex (much as ice skates accelerate while spinning by pulling their arms in closer to their bodies). A well-developed mesocyclone most certainly will produce heavy rain, large hail, blustery winds and lightning; some mature meso-cyclones will generate tornado activity.

A more moisture-laden air is drawn up into the circulation of a mesocyclone, more energy is liberated, and the rotation of air becomes more rapid. The narrower the mesocyclone, the faster the spin of converging parcel of air being sucked into the rotation. The swirl of mesocyclone itself is visible, as are smaller, dark-grey funnel clouds that pulse from the bottom side of the parent cloud. The terror of this stage of development is the lowering of funnel cloud to Earth – a tornado (Fig. 8.23).

For the development of tornadoes, several prerequisites are essential.

1. There must be a mass of very warm, moist air present at the surface.
2. There must be an unstable vertical temperature structure.
3. There must be a mechanism present to start rotation.

In USA, the Great Plains is the foremost tornado region of the world. In fact, the Great Plains of USA is often called the Tornado Alley. Most of the tornadoes occur in the months of April (26) and May (18), and March (13). All the other months record two to six tornadoes except the month of July in which the average frequency is only one.

Tornadoes also occur in the Great Plains of India, generally in the months of April and May. They also occur in the Hwang Ho and Yangtse-Kiang basins of China.

Arctic Hurricanes

Arctic Hurricanes, also known as 'polar lows' are explosive storms that develop and die over a few days. They originate when cold air from the Arctic flows south over warmer water, the air takes up heat, expand and rise, generating convection currents that sometimes snowball into storms.

An Arctic Hurricane is a small-scale, short-lived atmospheric low pressure system (depression) that is found over the ocean areas pole-ward of the main polar front in both the Northern and Southern Hemispheres. The system usually have horizontal length scale of less than 1000 km and exist for no

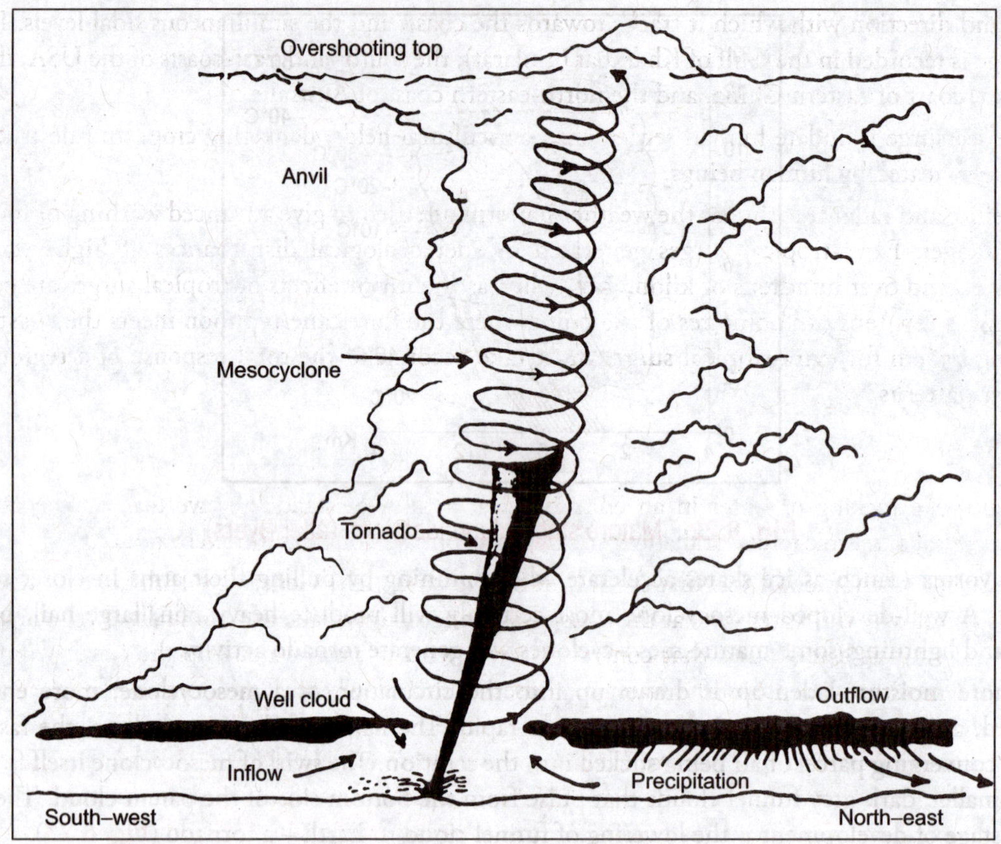

Fig. 8.23 Development of Mesocyclone and Tornado in a "Supercell" (after Donald Ahrens C., *Meteorology Today*, West Publishing Co., 1988)

more than a couple of days. They are part of larger class of meso-scale weather systems. They can be difficult to detect using conventional weather reports and are hazard to high-latitude operations, such as shipping and gas and oil platforms. Arctic hurricanes have been referred to by many other terms, such as polar meso-scale vortex, polar lows, Arctic lows, and cold air depression.

Surge, Sea-surge or Storm Surge

Changes in sea level generated by extreme weather events are known as sea surges. A sea surge is generated due to interaction of air, sea and land. The cyclone provides the driving force in the form of very high horizontal pressure-gradient and very strong surface winds. The sea water flows across the coast with strong winds and heavy downpour.

Sea surge appear on sea level records as distortions of the regular tidal patterns, and are most severe in regions of extensive shallow water. When maximum surge levels coincide with maximum high-water levels on spring tides, very high total sea level results. Low-lying coastal areas are then vulnerable to severe flooding. In tropical regions severe surges are occasionally generated by cyclones, hurricanes, and typhoon. The actual sea-surge levels depend on the intensity of the meteorological disturbances, the speed and direction with which it tracks towards the coast, and the simultaneous tidal levels. In India sea surge is recorded in the Gulf of Khambat (Gujarat); the south- and East-coasts of the USA, the coast of Japan, coast of eastern China, and the north-eastern coast of Australia.

The sea-surge inundate human settlements, agricultural fields, damaging crops and destruction of structures created by human beings.

Satellite and radar tracking of the weather patterns are used to give advanced warning of imminent flood danger. Extra-tropical surges generated by meteorological disturbances at higher latitudes, usually extend over hundreds of kilometres, whereas the major effects of tropical surges are confined to within a few tens of kilometres of the point where the hurricane/typhoon meets the coast. Flood warning system for extra-tropical surges must take account of the total response of a region to the weather patterns.

Seich

Pendulum-like rocking of water in an enclosed area; a form of standing wave that can be caused by meteorological or seismic forces, or that may result from normal resonances excited by tides.

The seiche phenomenon was first studied in Switzerland's lake Geneva by 18th century researchers curious about why the water level at the ends of the long, narrow lake rises and falls at regular intervals after wind-storms. They found that constant breezes tend to push water into the down wind end of the lake. When the wind stops, the water is released to rock slowly back and forth at the lake's resonant frequency, completing a crest-trough-crest cycle in a little more than one hour. At the ends of the lake, the water rises and falls a foot or two; at the centre it moves back and forth without changing height. This kind of wave is called a standing wave because it oscillates vertically with no forward movement. This kind of activity can occur in confined areas of ocean ranging in size from bays and harbour to entire ocean basins. Lake side property may occasionally be threatened, but damage from seiches along ocean coast is rare.

Floods

Flood has been defined as a high water level along a river channel or on a coast that leads to inundation of land which is not normally submerged. River floods which involves inundation of the floodplain may be caused by the following factors:

(i) **Precipitation:** Heavy rainfall in the upper catchment areas of the concerned river causes sudden increase in volume of water downstream. Consequently, the rivers inundate and cross their banks and spread the surrounding areas. A flood situation may also develop, when precipitation is very prolonged and follows a period of wetter than average conditions; when the snow-pack melts and snow-melt floods are an annual feature of many river regimes; when rain falls on snow and accelerates snowmelt; or when ice and snowmelt are combined. On 16th June, 2013 the cloud–burst in the catchment of Mandakni river resulted into heavy damage to life and property and even the holy shrine of Kedarnath was partly damaged.

(ii) **Drainage of Ice-dammed lakes:** When the stream of a river is dammed by ice, the snowmelts after a few days, which can lead to the release of great volumes of water. Such floods are frequent in Iceland, the Scandinavian countries and Siberian rivers.

(iii) **High Tides:** In addition to the above causes, floods in the coastal areas may be caused by high tides, especially in combination with river floods. The city of Mumbai was submerged under water in 2005 because of torrential rains and high tides at the time of New Moon.

(iv) **Storm surges:** large sea-waves produced by submarine earthquakes, volcanic eruptions, landslides, tornados and tropical cyclones are also the important causes of coastal floods.

(v) **Deforestation:** Large scale deforestation in the upper catchment is perhaps the most important anthropogenic factor of rivers floods and inundation. The frequent floods in the valley of Kashmir, Punjab, Haryana, Uttar Pradesh, Bihar, West Bengal, the Brahmaputra Valley (Assam) and the Manipur Valley are attributed to the felling of trees by man.

(vi) **Unplanned urbanisation:** Rapid urbanisation, especially in the flood prone areas is also responsible for heavy floods. The rainwater resulting from torrential rainfall is quickly disposed of through the city storm drains. Moreover, the percolation of water in the soil is very low in the urban areas. Thus, urbanisation is directly and indirectly responsible for floods.

(vii) **Agricultural encroachment in hilly areas:** Under the pressure of population in many parts, the slope have been brought under cultivation. The eroded soil goes to the river, making its channel shallow. The shallow channels have low water discharging capacity. At the time of heavy rainfall such channels are inundated which lead to frequent floods.

(viii) **Shifting cultivation:** Shifting cultivation is also an important cause of river floods. Shifting cultivation in India is largely confined to those hilly and mountainous regions where the average annual rainfall is generally high. After the harvest of the crops, the land is left fallow. At the occurrence of heavy rains the soil slumps downward into the river channels, making their bed shallow. The shallow river channels are not able to discharge the increased volume of rainwater. Consequently, there is inundation and increase in the frequency of floods.

(ix) **Landslides and Blocking of river channels:** Blocking of natural flow of the rivers by landslides and avalanches, caused by earthquakes or by anthropogenic factors is also an important cause of flash floods. The clearance of such landslide blockades causes sudden flash floods in the downstream section of the rivers. Similarly breaches in the dams constructed across the river also cause occasional floods of various magnitudes. The Kosi flood in Bihar in 2009 was mainly due to the breach in river embankment.

(x) **Mismanagement of land resources:** Monoculture (cultivation of only one crop in a field year after year) exhausts some of the nutrients of the soil. Under such a condition, the compactness of the soil diminishes. At the occurrence of rainfall the rate of erosion in such agricultural regions accelerates. The silt goes to the river channels, making their bed shallow, which are not able to discharge the enormous volumes of heavy and prolonged rain water.

Floods in India

Floods are frequent in India. Excepting the hilly and mountainous regions, floods occur in almost all the states and regions of the country. The frequency of floods is however, more devastating in the rivers of Assam, Bihar, West Bengal, Uttar Pradesh, Punjab, Haryana, Gujarat, Rajasthan, coastal Odisha, Andhra Pradesh and Tamil Nadu (**Fig. 8.24**).

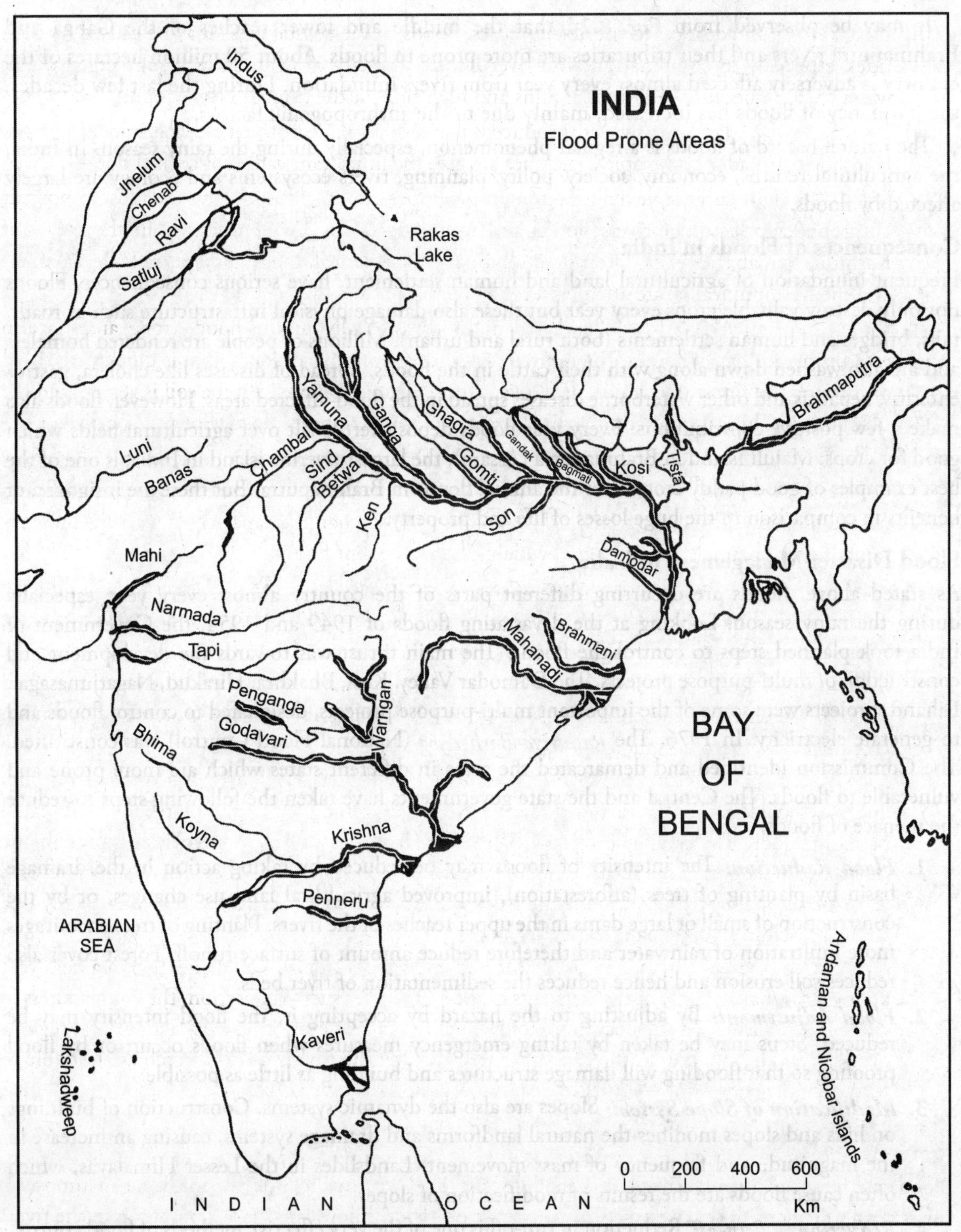

Fig. 8.24 Floods in India

It may be observed from Fig. 8.24 that the middle and lower reaches of the Ganga and Brahmaputra rivers and their tributaries are more prone to floods. About 50 million hectares of the country is adversely affected almost every year from rivers inundation. During the last few decades, the frequency of floods has increased, mainly due to the anthropogenic factors.

The natural hazard of floods is a regular phenomenon, especially during the rainy season. In India, the agricultural returns, economy, society, polity, planning, rivers ecosystems and ecology are largely affected by floods.

Consequences of Floods in India

Frequent inundation of agricultural land and human settlement, have serious consequences. Floods not only destroy valuable crops every year but these also damage physical infrastructure such as roads, rails, bridges and human settlements (both rural and urban). Millions of people are rendered homeless and are also washed down along with their cattle in the floods. Spread of diseases like cholera, gastro-enteritis, hepatitis and other waterborne diseases spread in the flood-affected areas. However, floods also make a few positive contributions. Every year floods deposit fertile silt over agricultural fields which good for crops. Majuli Island in Brahmaputra (Assam), the largest riverine island in India, is one of the best examples of good paddy crops after the annual floods in Brahmaputra. But these are insignificant benefits in comparison to the huge losses of life and property.

Flood Disaster Management in India

As stated above, floods are occurring different parts of the country almost every year, especially during the rainy season. Looking at the devastating floods of 1949 and 1954, the Government of India took planned steps to control the floods. The main thrust was towards the development and construction of multi-purpose projects. The Damodar Valley, Kosi, Bhakhra, Hirakud, Nagarjunasagar, Rihand, projects were some of the important multi-purpose projects, designated to control floods and to generate electricity. In 1976, The *Rashtriya Barh Ayog* (National Flood Control) was constituted. The Commission identified and demarcated the areas in different states which are more prone and vulnerable to floods. The Central and the state governments have taken the following steps to reduce the menace of floods:

1. ***Flood Reduction:*** The intensity of floods may be reduced by taking action in the drainage basin by planting of trees (afforestation), improved agricultural land use changes, or by the construction of small or large dams in the upper reaches of the rivers. Planting of trees encourages more infiltration of rainwater and therefore reduce amount of surface runoff. Forest cover also reduces soil erosion and hence reduces the sedimentation of river beds.
2. ***Flood Adjustment:*** By adjusting to the hazard by accepting it, the flood intensity may be reduced. Steps may be taken by taking emergency measures when floods occur; or by flood proofing so that flooding will damage structures and building as little as possible.
3. ***Modification of Slope System:*** Slopes are also the dynamic systems. Construction of buildings on hills and slopes modifies the natural landforms and drainage systems, causing an increase in the magnitude and frequency of mass movement. Landslides in the Lesser Himalayas, which often cause floods are the results of modification of slopes.
4. ***Reduction in Run-off***: Reduction in run-off is one of the very effective methods of flood control. Run-off can be reduced by inducing and increasing infiltration of the surface water into the soils

and underground water-table. This can be done by large scale afforestation, especially in the upper catchment of the rivers.

5. ***Costruction of Dams:*** Dams and multipurpose projects are being constructed across the river channels to store the surplus water in the reservoirs. A number of such reservoirs have been constructed in India, during the First Five Year Plan. For example, Bhakhra – Nangal Dam (Sutlej River). Hira-Kud Dam (Mahanadi), Nagarjunasagar (Krishna River), Rihand Dam, Damodar, Kosi projects, etc. A series of storage reservoirs are also effective control measures which are very popular in USA and Germany. In India, the Damodar Valley Corporation, designed on the pattern of Tennessee Valley Authority (TVA), is a multipurpose project in which a series of dams have been constructed to reduce the discharge of water at the time of floods.
6. ***Divert the Flood Water:*** Flood diversion system means the diversion of flood water in low lying areas, canals, and artificially constructed channels, lakes, etc. In India such efforts have been made to regulate the discharge of the Ghaggar River, Damodar River, Sutlej River etc. during the period of flood.
7. ***Channel Improvements:*** The carrying capacity of the channels of the rivers more prone to floods can be improved by drudging, deepening, and widening. The water of such rivers may also be diverted into flood-canals. In fact, diversion canals serve as a temporary storage and hold water as its flood waves move downstream. Thus, they help in reducing the severity of the floods.
8. ***Construction of Embankments:*** The central and state governments have constructed a number of embankments along the rivers to reduce the menace of floods. The length of the embankments constructed is more than 12 thousand kilometre long so far (1912). Such embankments have been constructed along the banks of the Bagmati, Beas, Brahmaputra, Chambal, Gandak, Ganga, Ghagra, Godavari, Kaveri, Kosi, Krishna, Mahananda, Mahanadi, Narmada, Penneru, Ravi, Sabarmati, Son, Sutlej, Tapi Tista, Yamuna, rivers, and their tributaries. The most important embankment is that of the Kosi River in India. These embankments have saved many of the important towns and cities of India, like, Allahabad, Kanpur, Dibrugarh, Jalpaiguri, Mlada, Mirzapur, Munghyr, Murshidabad, etc. (**Fig. 8.25**).
9. ***Flood Plain Zoning:*** Flood plain zoning is also an important step to control the floods. It is based on information regarding flood plains, particularly the identification of roadways in relation to land use. Detailed maps of flood prone areas need to be prepared, based on systematic study of terrain, topography, soil, drainage, and land use. In fact, some areas are more prone to floods than that of others. Different zones, on the basis of field studies and detailed maps are identified and delineated as shown in **Fig. 8.26**.

   It may be observed from **Fig. 8.26 'A'** is the main channel (water course) of the river. It is the flood way which is totally prohibited zone. No construction work should be allowed in this zone. Area '**BB**' is the regulatory flowing fringe and marks the extreme inundation design flood. This is called the restrictive zone. Beyond that is the secondary hazard zone marked by '**CC**'. This is the extent of the largest flood expected. The Central Flood Control Board of India, mooted the idea in 1957 to demarcate flood zones to prevent indiscriminate settlement in flood plains.

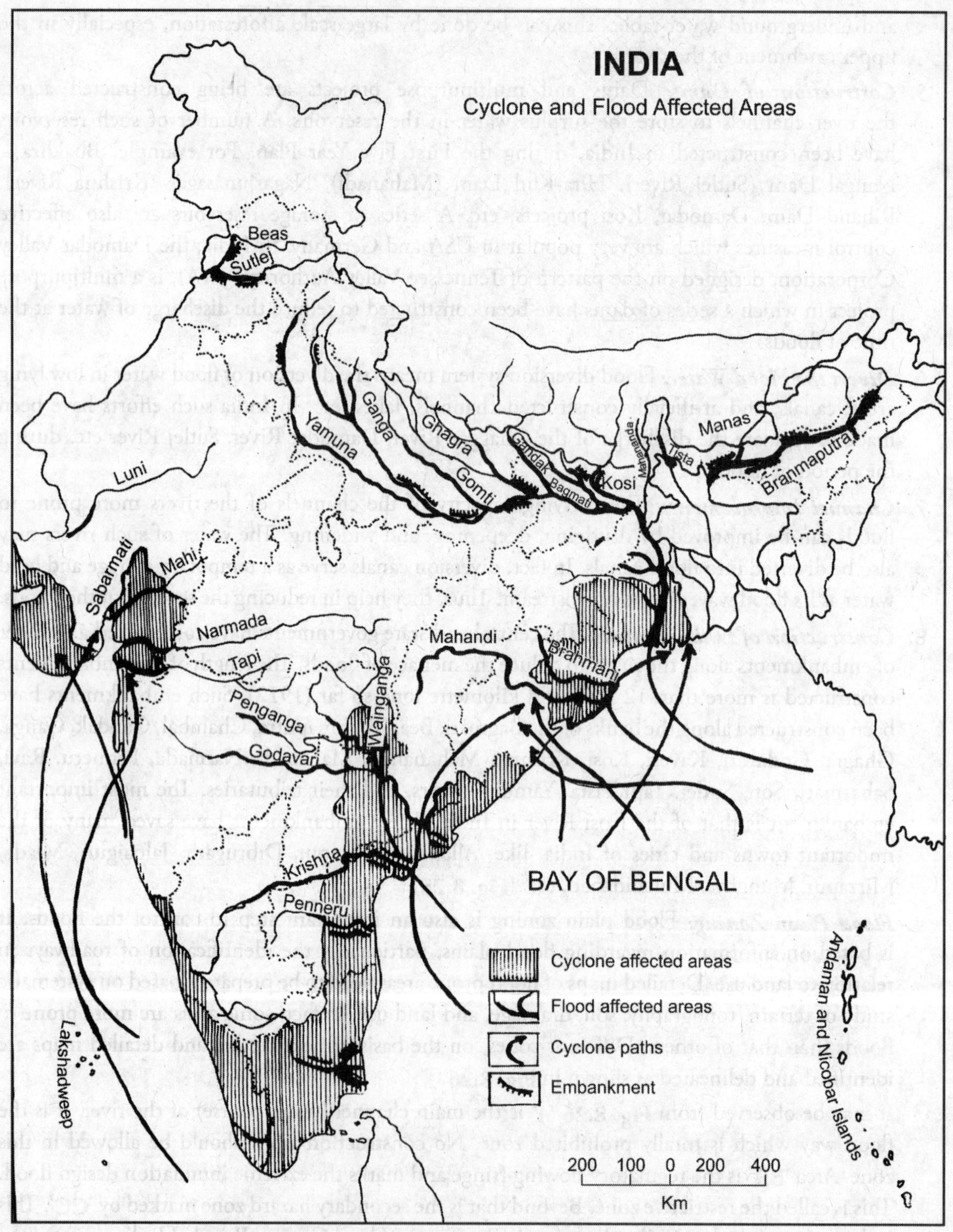

Fig. 8.25 Flood and cyclone affected areas and river embankments

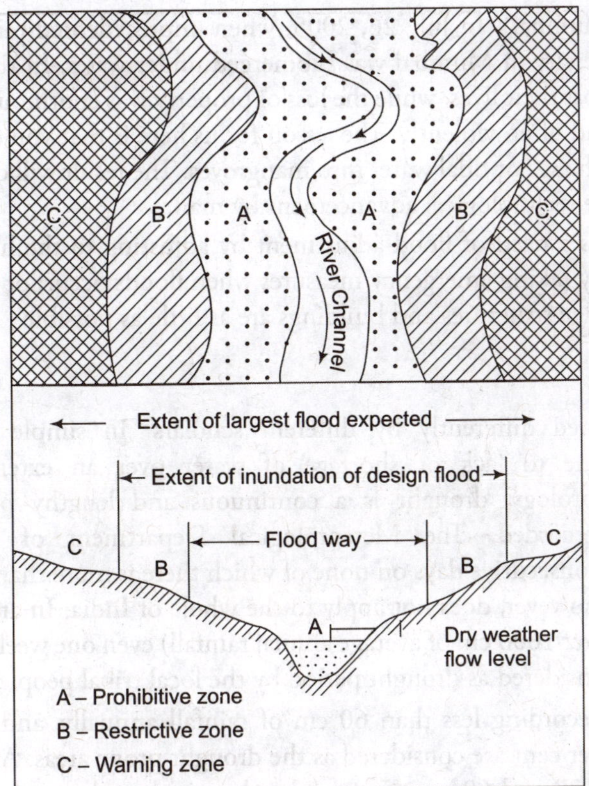

Fig. 8.26 Zoning of Flood Prone Areas

10. ***Modification of Groundwater Systems:*** The use of groundwater resources is constantly increasing. As we drill tube-wells and pump groundwater discharge, many of the buildings get subsided. The underground water-table has been lowered in the eastern district of Haryana. Contrary to this the water-table is rising in the western parts of Haryana because of the presence of gypsum layer underneath. The pumping out of water by tube-wells is disturbing the underground water table which is creating many problems in the states of Punjab and Haryana. The waterlogged conditions in the western parts of Haryana is attributed to the over-irrigation and high water-table.
11. ***Modification of Shorelines:*** The supply of sand and development of sea-beaches, etc. depend on modification of shorelines. Oil spills are also becoming a major problem in modifying shoreline ecology. The shorelines of Gulf of Khambat, Gulf of Mannar, Koromandal Coast, etc., have been significantly modified which is resulting into serious damage to mangrove, accelerating the menace of sea-surge floods at the time of cyclones. The sea-coasts and their marine ecosystems need to be conserved to reduce the damage from transgression of sea water.
12. ***Legal Measures:*** In addition to the steps given above, legislative measures are taken to restrict the construction of industrial and residential units in the flood prone areas. In India, large number of structure houses, slums, and industrial structures have been constructed in the bed

of Mithi River (Mumbai). In July 26, 2005, when unprecedented rainfall about 70 cm fell in only 12 hours, the city of Mumbai was submerged under water. In this deluge more than two thousand people lost their lives, while the loss of property was enormous. Nature has its own way of coming back and often violently. The lesson for us here is that you cannot interrupt the flow of rainwater into the sea or tidal water into mangroves. The result will only be disastrous. Nature is supreme, despite technological advancement by man.

In brief, there is a need of flood adjustment by adjusting to the hazard by accepting it; by land use zoning; by taking emergency measures when floods occur; or by flood proofing so that flooding will damage structures and buildings are as little as possible.

Drought Hazards

Drought has been defined differently by different scholars. In simple terms, a '*drought*' is a condition of dryness due to lack or shortage of water over an extended period. According to the experts of meteorology, drought is a continuous and lengthy period during which no significant rainfall is recorded. The Meteorological Department of India defined drought as a period of at least 22 consecutive days on none of which there is more than 0.25 mm (0.01 inch) of rainfall. This definition, however, does not apply to the whole of India. In areas like Mawsynram and Cherrapunji (recording over 1000 cm of average annual rainfall) even one week recording less than 0.25 mm of rainfall may be considered as drought period by the local tribal people.

In general, the areas recording less than 60 cm of rainfall annually, and where the variability of rainfall is more than 20 per cent are considered as the drought prone areas. Areas where the variability of rainfall varies between 20 and 60 per cent are the chronic drought prone areas of the country. In brief, in India droughts are more frequent in the areas where the average annual rainfall is less than 60 cm and the variability of rainfall is over 20 per cent, provided canal or tube-well irrigation is not available. The variability of rainfall over greater parts of the country is more than 20 per cent, and thus over 50 per cent of the country is vulnerable to droughts.

According to the Ministry of Agriculture and the Ministry of Environment, a drought prone area is defined as one in which the probability of drought year is greater than 20 per cent. A chronic drought prone area is one in which the probability of a drought year is greater than 40 per cent. A drought year occurs when less than 75 per cent of the average annual rainfall is recorded.

Types of Droughts

The meteorologists have classified the droughts in the following categories:

1. ***Meteorological Drought:*** It is a situation when there is a prolonged period of inadequate rainfall, marked with erratic distribution of the same over time and space.
2. ***Agricultural Drought:*** It is also known as soil moisture drought, characterised by low soil moisture that is necessary to support the crops, thereby resulting in crop failures. Moreover, if an area has more than 30 per cent of its gross cropped area under irrigation, the area is excluded from the drought-prone category.
3. ***Hydrological Drought:*** It results when the availability of water in different storages and reservoirs like aquifers, lakes, ponds, etc. falls below what the precipitation can replenish.

4. ***Ecological Drought:*** When the productivity of a natural ecosystem falls due to shortage of water and as a consequences of ecological distress, damages are induced in the ecosystem.

On an average, one in every five years is drought year in India, while in the Western Rajasthan every third year is a drought year. Although over 50 per cent of the area has high variability of rainfall, there are three main areas which are highly vulnerable to droughts in India. A brief description of the drought prone areas of India has been given in **Fig. 8.27**.

(i) **The arid and semi-arid areas of Rajasthan**: This is a contiguous region, covering the greater parts of northern Gujarat, Rajasthan, south-western Haryana, south-western Punjab and the Agra Division of Uttar Pradesh. The average annual rainfall in this region is less than 60 cm, while the variability of rainfall is 25 to 65 per cent. The excavation of the Indira Gandhi Canal and tubewell irrigation in some parts have modified the ecosystems in this region.

(ii) **The rain-shadow areas of the Western Ghats**: This drought-prone area lies to the east of the Western Ghats in the states of Maharashtra, Andhra Pradesh, Karnataka. The average annual rainfall in less than 60 cm, while the variability of rainfall varies from 30 to 40 per cent in this region.

(iii) **Other drought prone areas**: There are isolated tracts, covering an area of about one lakh sq km in different parts of the country which are drought prone. These areas include the Kalahandi region of Odisha, Bankura and Purulia districts of West Bengal, Palamu plateau of Jharkhand, the plateau of Mirzapur and Bundelkhand (U.P.), Baghelkhand of Madhya Pradesh, Coimbatore, Madurai and Tirunelveli districts of Tamil Nadu, parts of Ladakh, Himachal Pradesh and Uttarakhand.

Though droughts are recurring physical phenomena and their severity was more during the Medieval and British periods, droughts are quite frequent even in the 21st century. Some of the serious droughts of the last decade of the 20th and the 21st centuries have been described as follows.

The Maharashtra drought of 1965–66, and 2013, the Bihar drought of 1966–67, the Kalahandi drought of 1996–97 and the continuous deficient rainfall in Andhra Pradesh, Karnataka and Western Tamil Nadu during the last decade forced a number of farmers to commit suicide. The drought of 2009 over greater parts of the country resulted into serious drought disaster. The Maharashtra and Kathiawad (Gujarat) drought of 2013 is also quite serious under which the cropped area has decreased by about 50 per cent. Under the desperate condition of shortage of water, the farmers are committing suicide, looking towards the sky for the mercy of clouds. The masses are thirsty struggling to get drinking water, the situation seems quite alarming some districts of Maharashtra, Gujarat, Rajasthan and Madhya Pradesh.

Causes of Droughts

Deficient rainfall in some regions of the country is the main natural cause of drought. The more serious are the man-made factors – poor (or no) water management strategy, indiscriminate exploitation of surface and ground water by industries and the agricultural sector. Large scale deforestation and non-eco-friendly developmental projects. Some of the important causes of droughts have been given in the following:

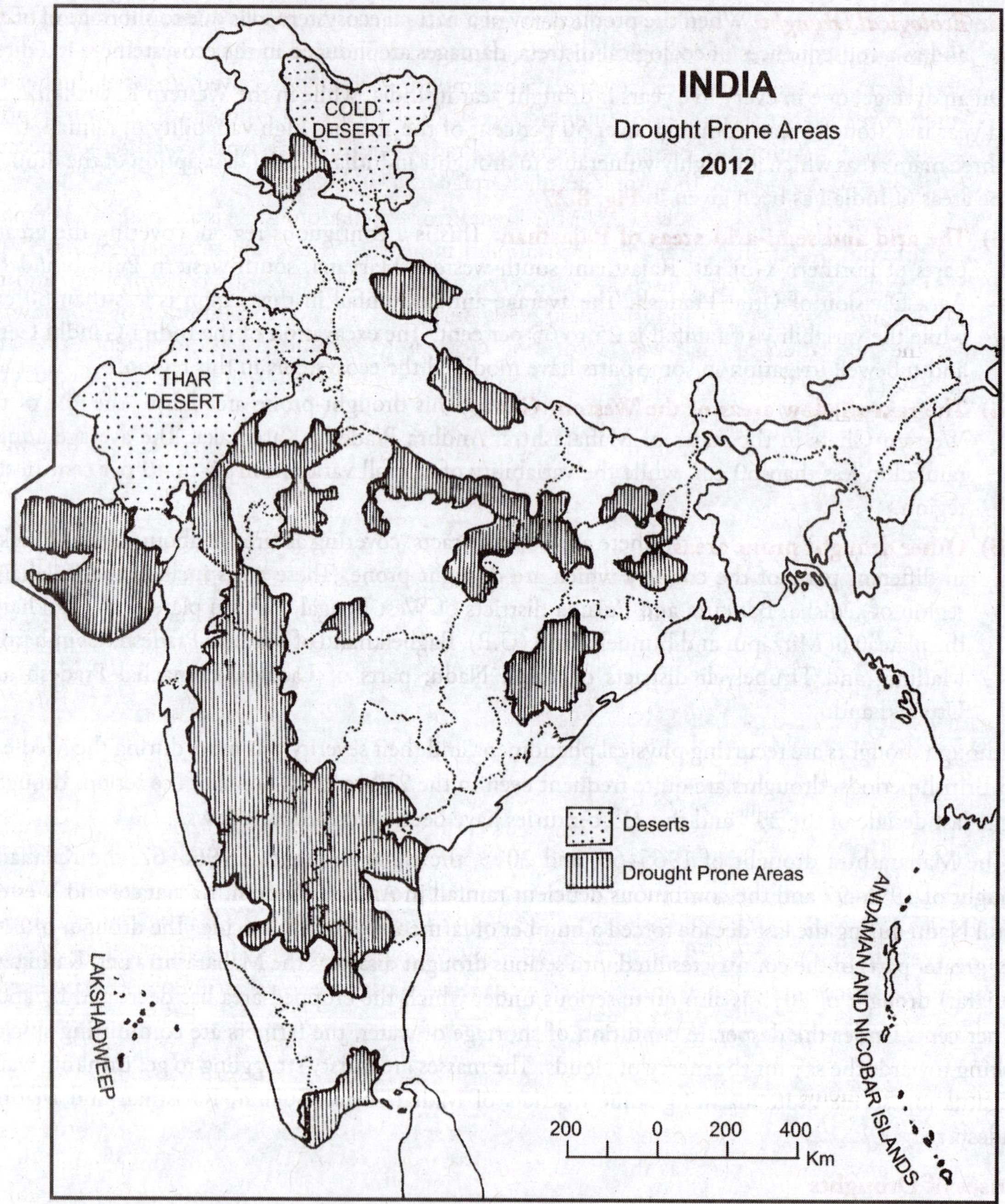

Fig. 8.27 Drought Prone Areas of India

1. ***Rainfall deficiency:*** In the meteorological sense rainfall below the average and its erratic distribution are largely responsible for droughts. As stated above, the regions with low rainfall and high variability are the most drought prone areas of the country.

2. ***Large scale deforestation:*** Large scale deforestation to meet the growing demand of food of the teeming millions and raw material for industries have depleted the forest cover. There is a direct correlation between the forest cover and the amount of rainfall received. In brief, higher the forest cover, higher the amount of rainfall received and vice-versa. Thousands of natural spring in the states of Jammu & Kashmir, Himachal Pradesh and Uttarakhand have dried up because of deforestation, creating the problems of shortage of drinking water.
3. ***Excessive use of groundwater:*** Under the pressure of population, there is an increasing demand for drinking water and water for irrigation and industries. According to experts about 85 per cent of the groundwater is used for irrigation, 5 per cent for domestic consumption, and the remaining 10 per cent for industrial and other purposes. This overconsumption of groundwater for the cultivation of high water requiring crops is responsible for the deficiency of water. Moreover, the industries are polluting the surface and underground water reducing the quantity of good quality water.
4. ***Lack of water-harvesting:*** In most of the states of the country excepting Tamil Nadu, water harvesting is not done seriously. Consequently, even a heavy rainfall recording states like Meghalaya, and Nagaland water scarcity is felt even during the rainy season.
5. ***Absence of long-term planning to combat deserts:*** There is no comprehensive policy about the water resource. In fact, water should be declared as a national resource and steps should be taken for its judicious and rational utilisation.
6. ***Rapid growth of population and consumerism:*** Rapid growth of population and unchecked consumption of resources to meet the greed of rich people and the ambition of middle class to raise their standard of living are also responsible for the depletion of water resources.

Consequences of Droughts

The organic life, and sustainability of the ecology and environment largely depend on the availability of water. A drought or deficiency of water adversely affects all forms of life. Thus, droughts have cascading effects on economy, society and ecology. Crop failure leading to scarcity of food-grains (*akal*), fodder (*trinkal*), inadequate rainfall, scarcity of water (*jalkal*), and often shortage of all three (*trikal*). Large-scale deaths of livestock and other animals, migration of humans and livestock are the most common phenomenon to be seen in the drought affected areas. Scarcity of water compels people to consume contaminated water resulting into spread of many waterborne diseases like gastro-enteritis, cholera and diarrhoea.

Droughts have both immediate as well as long term-disastrous consequences on the social and physical environments. *Some of the adverse consequences of drought have been given in the following:*

1. ***Ecological impact:*** Ecosystems and biodiversity are adversely affected. Some of the species of plants and animals perish as they cannot bear the extreme drought conditions. Some animals migrate to other places and hence there is a marked decrease in the population of certain animal species. In the ecosystem, there is stiff competition for food.
2. ***Economic impact:*** In a drought year there is a marked decrease in agricultural production. The fodder crops wither, and consequently, there is decrease in livestock production. The industrial production of agro-based and forest-based industries also goes down because of shortage of water and raw materials.

3. ***Demographic impact:*** Drought leads to depopulation of region and temporary or permanent out-migration of affected people and their livestock. There is frequent migration of the people from the Rajasthan and Gujarat towards the *Tarai* regions of Uttar Pradesh and Uttarakhand or to the urban places like Delhi, Ahmedabad and the cities of Punjab and Haryana.
4. ***Political consequences:*** A successful monsoon over the greater part of the country provides a good chance to the ruling party to win the next elections.
5. ***Desertification:*** Desertification refers to the persistent degradation of dry-land ecosystems by climatic variations and human activities. Desertification affects the livelihoods of millions of people, including the large proportion of poor people in arid and semi-arid regions. The United Nations Convention to Combat Desertification (UNCCD) defines desertification as:
   "*land degradation in arid, semi-arid and dry sub-humid areas resulting from various factors, including climatic variations and human activities.*"

   There are about two billion people living in the deserts and semi-desert areas of the world. Continuous drought conditions may change the nature of dry-land ecosystem. Prolonged droughts cause desertification and spread of deserts in the adjacent areas.
6. ***Soil erosion:*** In a drought year the extreme dry conditions may accelerate the rate of erosion in the affected arid and semi-arid regions.
7. ***Degradation of forests:*** The people dependent on forests, fell more trees for fuel-wood and charcoal to be sold in the market for their survival.
8. Fall in agricultural employment.
9. Scarcity of drinking water food grains and fodder.
10. Spread of water-borne disease due to the shortage of good quality drinking water.
11. Deaths due to starvation, undernourishment and malnutrition.
12. Degradation of moral values and increase in the rate of crimes.
13. Growth of fatalism, pessimism, and belief in supernatural powers and superstitions.
14. The worst affected people are those who are below the poverty line. They become desperate. The money-lenders advance loans at higher rates of interest.
15. Under distress, a lot of people, especially marginal and small farmers tend to commit suicide. Farmers in Maharashtra, Madhya Pradesh, Gujarat, Andhra Pradesh, Karnataka, Odisha and Chhattisgarh, and even in the agriculturally advanced states like Punjab and Haryana have committed suicide.

Strategy for Drought Management

The following steps can reduce the impact of drought conditions:

1. Afforestation is the most important and effective step to reduce the frequency of droughts. Israel has achieved a big success in combating deserts by planting drought-resistant plants and trees.
2. Rain-water harvesting
3. Watershed management
4. Introduction of scientific dry farming:
5. Development of drought resistant species of plants and trees.

6. Effective implementation of Drought-Prone Area Programmes (DPAP).
7. Construction of water-reservoirs and drilling of wells and tube-wells.
8. Diversification of agriculture.
9. Restructuring of cropping patterns and crop combinations.
10. Livestock and dairy development programmes.
11. Development of alternate sources of energy.
12. Interlinking of rivers: The distribution of rainfall is not uniform in India. During the rainy season, some of the rivers are in spate, while some regions may be in the grip of severe droughts. The problem of droughts and floods can be largely solved through an inter-basin linkage or through national water grid by connecting the different rivers of the country.

Cloudburst

A cloudburst is a sudden rainfall which can be quite unexpected, very abrupt, characterized with flash flood. In other words, cloudburst is an extreme amount of precipitation, sometimes with hail and thunder, which normally lasts no longer than a few minutes but is capable of creating havoc conditions of flood, landslides, avalanches, solifluction, mudflow, earthflow, debris- avalanche, rock fall, subsidence, slumps, soil creep, and mass wasting.

Generally, cumulus-nimbus clouds which can extend up to a height of 15 km above the sea level, are involved in a cloudburst. In some cloudbursts, up to 13 centimeters (5 inches) of rain can fall in one hour, often in the form of extremely large droplets. In brief, the term cloudburst is used to describe sudden heavy, brief and usually unpredictable rainfall.

The hard rain characteristic of a cloudburst is caused by a phenomenon known as ***Langmuir Precipitation***, in which drops of rain fuse together to create large drops as they fall, falling more quickly as they grow. The Langmuir Precipitation process is applicable only to those clouds which do not extend beyond the freezing point. The temperature in the uppermost part of the cloudburst seldom falls below 5°C. The occurrence of precipitation from such cumulus- nimbus clouds involves the coalescence of cloud droplets of different sizes. Since the rate of fall of these unequal rain-drops is different, they collide with each other within the cloud, and the larger drops grow at the expense of smaller ones. The size of the rain drops become sufficiently large which fall faster, and results into cloudburst. Sometimes, the rain in a cloudburst falls so fast and is so large that it is actually scary, frightening and painful.

According to the meteorologists the rainfall rate is equal to or greater than 10 cm (3.94 inches) per hour in a cloudburst. The associated convective (cumulus – nimbus) clouds, have great vertical extension. During a cloudburst, more than 20 mm (2 cm) of rainfall may fall in a few minutes. At the occurrence of a cloudburst loss of property and human life is frequent which may take the shape of disaster and catastrophe. The Uttarakahnad cloudburst on 16th June, 2013 is an example of large scale destruction of human life and economic structure.

Because of the amount of rainfall involved, a cloudburst can be quite dangerous, especially if it persists for several hours. Flashflood is common with cloudburst, and in areas with arroyos, washes, and other gullies, these geological features can quickly fill with water, sweeping away any people and animals which might be in the region. Flooding can also render streets unusable, and in extreme cases it can shut down entire city (like Kedarnath, Rambara, Gaurikund, Guptkashi, etc.) as people struggle to cope with the influx of water. The Uttarakhand cloudburst known as Himalayan Tsunami of 16th June, 2013 is an example of one of the worst cloudburst disasters in the recent history of India.

Often, these rainstorms appear in the summer season, and in the farming communities, they are sometimes welcomed, as a cloudburst can irrigate the withering crops very thoroughly. Most people try to avoid being caught out in the weather. Drowning have also been linked with cloudbursts, even without widespread flooding, because people can become disoriented when caught outside in severe weather. The extremes of rainfall in cloudbursts have been given in the Table 8.13.

Table 8.13 Extremes of Rainfall in cloudbursts

Duration	Rainfall	Location	Date
1 minute	38.10 mm (1.5 inches)	Basse-Terre, Guadeloupe (West Indies)	26 November, 1970
15 minutes	198.12 mm (7.9 inches)	Plumb Point, Jamaica	12th May, 1916
1 hour	250 mm (9.84 inches)	Leh, Ladakh, India	August 5, 2010
10 hours	940 mm (37 inches)	Mumbai, India	July 26, 2005
20 hours	2329 mm (91.69 inches)	Ganges Delta, India	January, 1966

In the Indian subcontinent, a cloudburst usually occurs when a moisture laden monsoon cloud drifts northward, from the Bay of Bengal or Arabian Sea across the plains, then on to the Himalaya and bursts, bringing rainfall as high as 75 millimeters per hour.

Table 8.14 Cloudburst Damage in India in recent past

Year	Place of cloudburst	Deaths
August, 1998	Gowalpara	400
July, 1970	Alaknanda Basin	500
15th August, 1997	Chirgaon-Shimla District	115
August, 17, 1998	Milpa Village, Kumaun Division	250
July 26, 2005	Mumbai cloudburst	>5000
August 6, 2010	Leh-Ladakh	>1000
June 16, 2013	Kedarnath cloudburst	Several thousands
July, 2015	Sonmarg (J & K), Badrinath (Uttarakand)	>100

Uttarakhand Cloudburst (Himalayan Tsunami)

Uttarakhand '*the abode of gods*' with its magnificent snow-covered peaks, pristine forests and awe-inspiring rivers, is a place of sacred in Indian culture. Millions of tourists and pilgrims pay homage to the state of Uttarakhand every year. Despite all these attractions, the state of Uttarakhand is highly vulnerable ecosphere. There are sudden cloudbursts, landslides, avalanches, and flash floods in the state. Nature demands both space and respect. This point is to be borne in mind while designing any developmental project and promotion of tourism.

Cloudbursts, landslides and flash floods are an almost annual feature in Uttarakhand. The cloudburst of 16th June 2013, however, was unparallel disaster in the modern history of the state of Uttarakhand, resulting into enormous loss of life, property, crops and infrastructure. With many highways damaged, bridges washed away, electricity and phones networks down, hotels and motels destroyed, rural settlements and towns buried and numerous ravaged places continued to be marooned. Looking at the colossal loss of life, property and infrastructure the cloudburst disaster has been given the name of '*Himalayan Tsunami*'. The Uttarakhand cloudburst affected about 48,000 sq km area of Bhagirathi, Alaknanda catchment, especially that of Mandakni River, the Kedarnath Shrine, Rambara, Gaurikund, and Guptkashi towns (**Fig.8.28**).

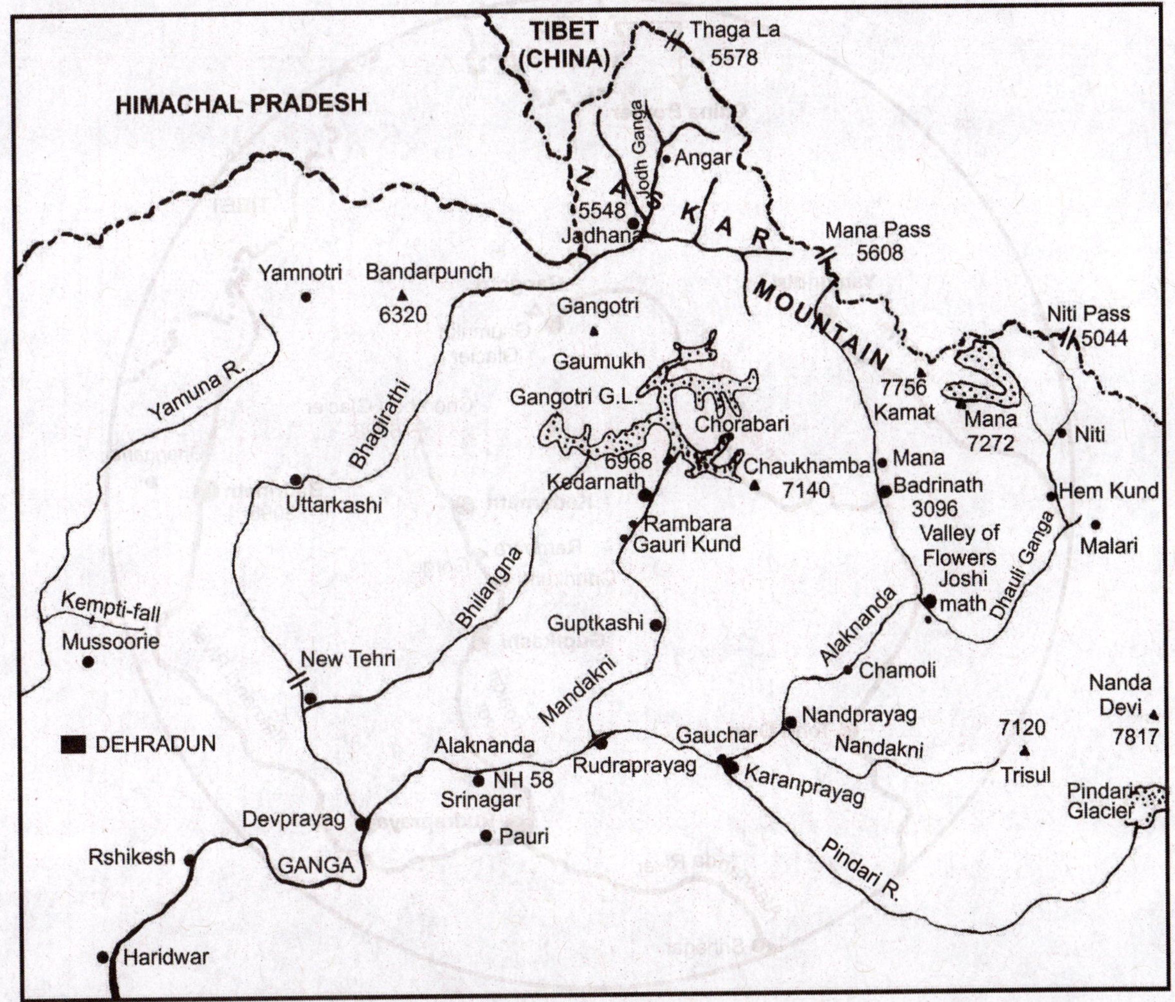

Fig. 8.28 Cloudburst Region of Uttarakhand (16th June, 2013)

As stated above, cloudburst is a natural phenomenon. It is a manifestation of excessive rainfall in a short duration of time (minutes or few hours). But excessive rainfall provides only a partial explanation for why the *Deo-Bhumi* (abode of the gods), Uttarakhand has been devastated in the cloudburst of 16th June 2013. According to experts of environment and ecology, the disaster might have been waiting to happen. The illegal constructions on the hills, the exponential growth of rickety structures that serve as hotels which are shoddidly maintained, the lackadaistical attitude towards warnings of natural catastrophes are largely responsible for this disaster of Mandakni, Bhilangna, Alaknanda and Bhagirathi rivers **(Fig.8.29)**. One can observe the extension and development of National Highways, construction of multistoried buildings, hotels, motels, *sarais, dharamshalas* (inns), rest-houses, factories, picnic spots, tourist camping grounds, over 150 dams across the rivers in the region of poor soil stability and fragile ecosystems which have compounded the vulnerability of the region to natural disasters. The ambitious

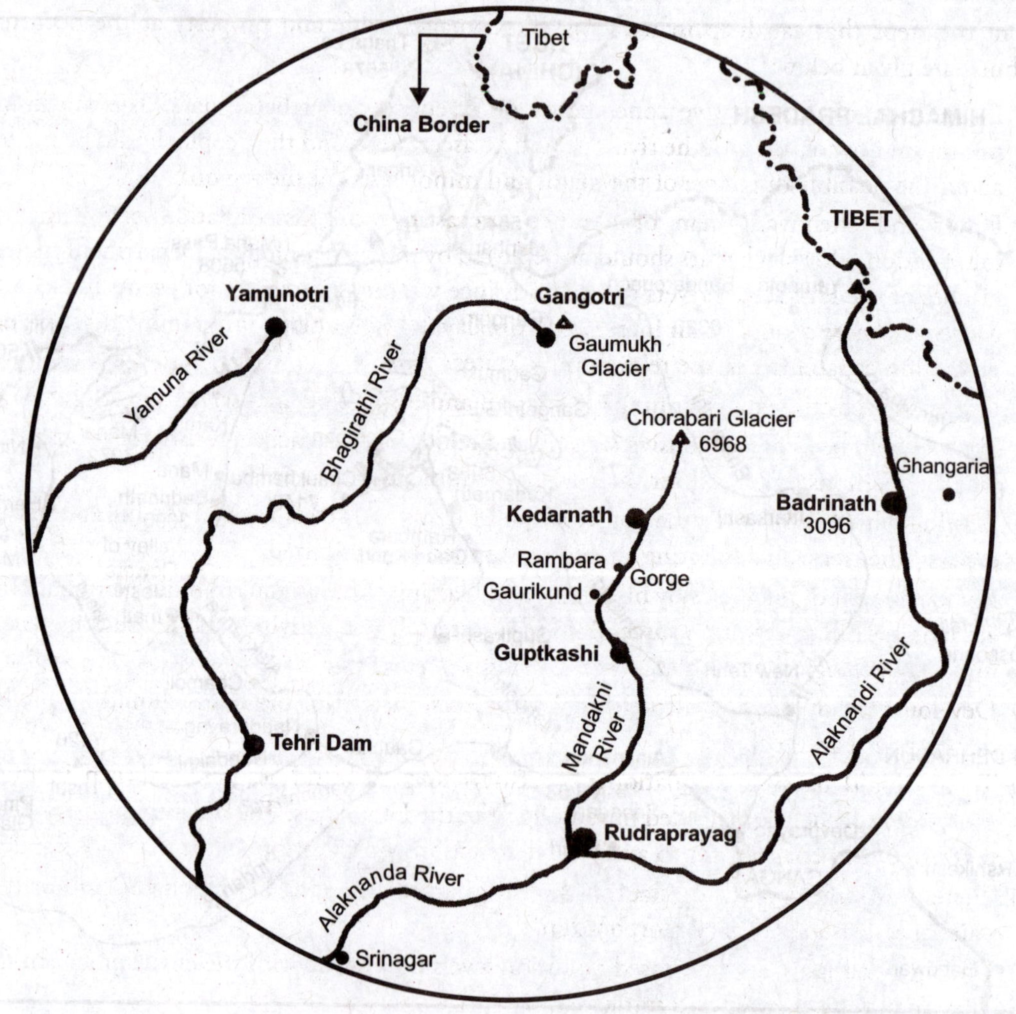

Fig. 8.29 Bhagirathi, Mandakni, Alaknanda Basins, the worst affected Region of 'Himalayan Tsunami' 16th June, 2013.

target of the decision makers and planners to convert the state of Uttarakhand into the '*Urjapradesh*' (Energy Province) and the 'Tourist Capital of India' is, however, against the principles of ecology, and environment.

Moreover, the indiscriminate deforestation, mindless construction of buildings, blasting of rocks for the construction of roads, lack of implementation of environmental laws and the indifferent implementation of Environmental Impact Assessment, have made the state of Uttarakhand highly vulnerable to disasters, natural calamities and catastrophe. In fact, the devastating floods in Uttarakhand have proved that taming natural forces through human interventions is all but a myth. There is an urgent need to adopt a long term planning, based on the principles of ecology for sustainable development not only in Uttarakhand but in all the hilly and mountainous states of the country.

Management of Cloud Burst Disasters

Some of the steps that can help in reducing the damage to life and property at the occurrence of cloudburst are given below:

(i) Delineation of eco-sensitive zones based on scientific and reliable data. The maximum and minimum flow of water in the rivers should be ascertained and the people should be made aware about the possible discharge of the major and minor rivers of the region.

(ii) Better and effective system of weather forecasting and dissemination of weather related information. Doppler-radars should be deployed by the Meteorological Department in the upper reaches of the Himalayan rivers to make advance weather forecasting for events like cloudburst. Moreover, there should be an integrated Himalayan Meteorology Programme that will enhance prediction capabilities in the relevant hilly states.

(iii) Proper site selection and planning of the rural and urban settlements.

(iv) There should be a comprehensive renewal and relook at construction techniques of roads, houses and the methods employed for the development of infrastructure.

(v) Blasting which is done for the construction of dams and roads weaken the hills and shakes the roots of the trees. Such blasting should be stopped or minimized.

(vi) Encroachment of river beds by buildings, and blasting of mountains to build National Highways are making hill states more susceptible to disasters. These activities should be done keeping in mind the ecological principles.

(vii) Development of minor hydro-electricity projects, instead of big dams should be preferred in development and planning.

(viii) There should be strict regulation of cultural (religious) and aesthetic tourism in the fragile ecosystems of the young folded mountains, like the Himalayas. The tourism industry need to be converted into eco-tourism to avert the destruction and catastrophe like that of Uttarakhand.

(ix) There is an urgent need to establish the Bhagirathi-Alaknanda Development Authority on the pattern of Damodar Valley Corporation.

(x) Uncontrolled jams, and increased pollution levels play havoc with the environment in the hills. They should be checked and mitigated.

(xi) There should be state-level and district level Disaster Management and Mitigation Centres to combat the humongous natural calamity, like that of the Himalayan Tsunami of 16th June -2013.

(xii) Mushrooming of resorts, motels, restaurant, etc. should be stopped in the ecologically sensitive areas as these activities involve huge deforestation and mining which are directly or indirectly responsible for soil erosion, landslides, loss of ground water, and change in the courses of rivers. Cloudburst have their worst effects on roads, buildings, rural and urban settlements located along the banks of rivers, especially along the steep banks.

(xiii) Human resource and physical infrastructure needed to tackle natural disaster, should be strengthened. Moreover, there should by credible mechanisms for ensuring compliance with environmental regulations.

(xiv) Relief operations too need to be ramped to a comparable level of the Himalayan Tsunami, of 16th June 2013.

(xv) There should be no discrimination while providing relief and rehabilitation measures. Calls from influential people and politicians should not be entertained by the persons engaged in rescue operation.

(xvi) The post cloudburst should include quick action of rescue of stranded alive people buried under thick cover of debris, regolith and boulders to evacuate them to safer places. Immediate medical help should be provided to survivors. Rescue and evacuation of stranded alive people, recovery and rehabilitation of the affected people also need to be done at war footing.

(xvii) Tourism to a great extent contributes to excessive and unchecked development around shrines. In fact, most religious places are littered with make-shift shops, hotels, and *dhabas* that come up as temporary shelters for quick commerce, but because of their endorsement by local religious authorities, become 'regularized'. The state government should take strict and effective action against such encroachment.

(xviii) In the post-cloudburst operation control of epidemics in the low lying areas is required. In the waterlogged areas diseases like malaria, chikungunya, and dengue may be prevented by anti-malaria sprays, fumigation against mosquitoes and provisions of chlorine bottled water to the flood affected people.

(xix) The Sant Samaj (religious community) should work as a pressure group to check the construction of multistory buildings, hotels, motels, *sarais*, and *dhramshalas* in the eco-sensitive areas.

(xx) In the cloudburst affected areas water supply, electric poles and telecommunication systems need to be restored at a priority basis.

(xxi) The sensitivity to environment and ecology at a time of global warming is both a necessity against disaster and a new way to forge a different, less destructive form of development. Unfortunately, the state of Uttarakhand has not even defined minimum environmental flows for rivers. Such laxity is bound to result into large scale destruction and disasters.

If these steps are taken together, the consequent damage to the life and property from natural calamities like cloudburst may be minimized appreciably.

Polar Vortex

Polar vortex is also known as 'polar cyclone', 'Arctic-hurricane', 'polar low' or 'polar tornado'. The polar vortex was first described as early as 1853 and was scientifically discovered in 1952 with radiosonde observations at an altitude higher than 20 km or beyond the tropopause. It is a large scale cyclone located either near the North Pole and the South Pole. On the Earth the polar vortices are located in the middle and upper troposphere and the stratosphere. They surround the polar high pressure and lie in the wake of polar front. The rotation speed of the atmosphere is much greater at the poles than that of the planet Earth. The vortex is most powerful in the Southern Hemisphere's winter, when the temperature gradient is steepest, and diminishes or can disappear in summer. The polar vortex is bounded by the jet stream which has, for some reason (blink blink wink wink) has wandered south. The polar jet-stream wandered south in the Northern Hemisphere. This fact was documented in the vortexes of 2006, 2009, 2010 and 2014 (**Fig. 8.30**). They generally occur in the winter season and get and weaken in the summer due to their reliance up on the temperature differential between the equator and the poles.

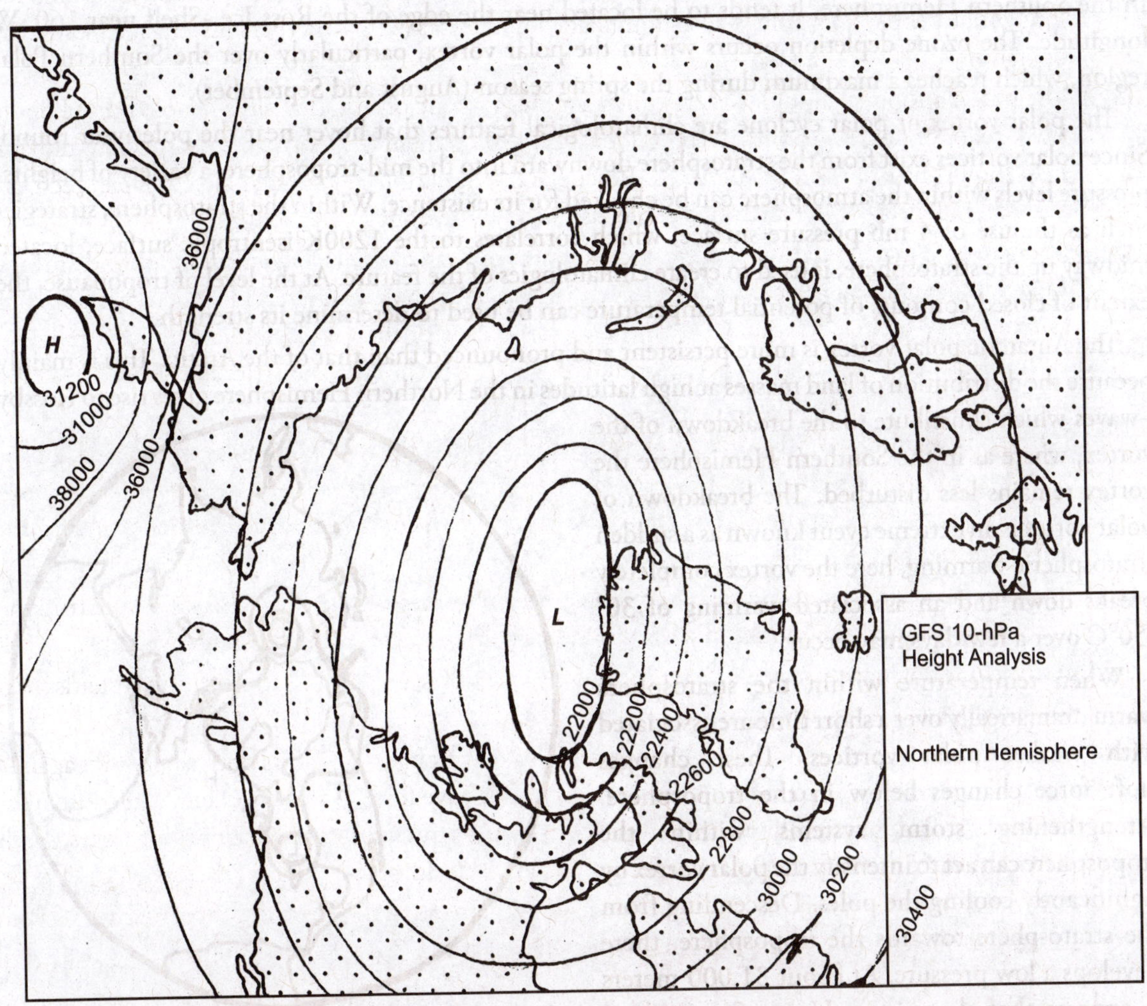

Fig. 8.30 Temperature Analysis showing the warm area (Low Pressure) and cold area (High Pressure)

Origin

The origin of polar vortex and its affects on the Earth's temperature are still not fully explained by the scientists. The scientists however, agree that the polar vortex is caused when an area of low pressure sits at the rotation pole of the planet. This causes air to spiral down from higher altitudes (Stratosphere and upper Troposphere) in the atmosphere, like water going down a drain'. A polar vortex is a persistent, large-scale cyclone located near one or both of a planet's geographical pole.' In size the polar vortex extend usually span up to 1000 km in which the air is circulating in a counter clockwise in the Northern Hemisphere and clockwise in the Southern Hemisphere. As in the case of other cyclones, the rotation of polar vortex is caused by the Coriolis effect.

The polar vortex in the Northern Hemisphere has two centres: (i) one near the Baffin Island (Canada), and (ii) the other over north-east Siberia to the north of Baikal Lake (**Fig. 8.30-31**). In the Southern Hemisphere, it tends to be located near the edge of the Ross Ice -Shelf near 160° W longitude. The ozone depletion occurs within the polar vortex, particularly over the Southern Polar region, which reaches a maximum during the spring season (August and September).

The polar vortex or polar cyclone are climatological features that hover near the poles year round. Since polar vortices exist from the stratosphere downward into the mid-troposphere, a variety of heights/ pressure levels within the atmosphere can be checked for its existence. Within the stratosphere, strategies such as the use of 4 mb pressure surface, which correlates to the 1200K isentropic surface, located midway up the stratosphere, is used to create climatologies of the feature. At the level of tropopause, the extent of closed contours of potential temperature can be used to determine its strength.

The Antarctic polar vortex is more persistent and pronounced than that of the Arctic. This is mainly because the distribution of land masses at high latitudes in the Northern Hemisphere gives rise to Rossby –waves which contribute to the breakdown of the vortex, where as in the Southern Hemisphere the vortex remains less disturbed. The breakdown of polar vortex is an extreme event known as a sudden stratospheric warming, here the vortex completely breaks down and an associated warming of 30° -50°C over a few days may occur.

When temperature within the stratosphere warm dramatically over a short time are associated with weaker polar vortices. These changes aloft force changes below in the troposphere. Strengthening storm systems within the troposphere can act to intensify the polar vortex by significantly cooling the poles. Descending from the stratosphere towards the troposphere, there develops a low pressure. At about 31,000 meters it appears that there is an Upper Stratosphere Lower Mesosphere Disturbance that could lead to a Sudden Stratospheric Warming.

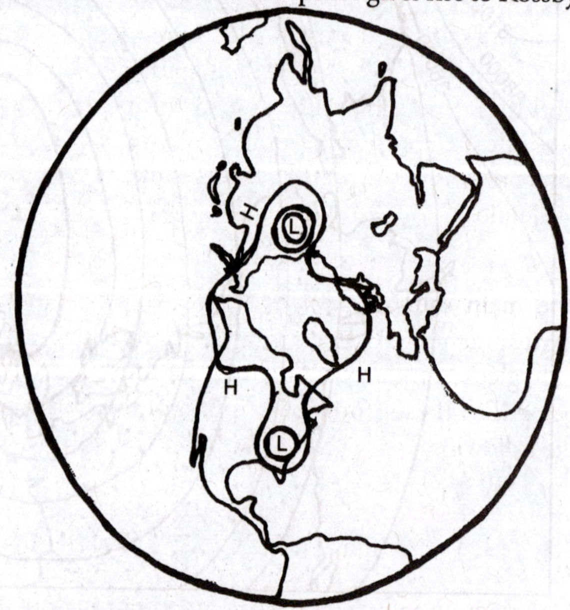

Fig. 8.31 Two centres of Polar Vortex in the Northern Hemisphere, and the Polar Jet-streams

Shape

The Arctic vortex is elongated in shape, with two centres, one roughly over the Baffin Island in Canada, and the other over north-east Siberia. In rare events, the vortex can push further south as a result of axis interruption. The January 1985 Arctic outbeak was a meteorological event, the result of the shifting of the polar vortex further south than is normally seen. In such a case, the cold the polar air from the north is pushed up to the Gulf of Mexico in North America. In such a situation a record low temperature is recorded. It happened in North America in the month of December-2013 and January 2014. The frequency of polar vortex is increasing significantly which is being attributed to the global warming, environmental pollution and greenhouse gases.

Climate change could be the cause of record cold weather. The polar vortex extends vertically for twenty to thirty kilometers. A well developed polar vortex produces extremely cold conditions leading to heavy snowfall. The temperature may fall to less than –60°C. In fact in January 2014, the occurrence of polar vortex the temperature went down to below –52°C at Chicago and –50° at New York and Baltimore (USA) and -60°C at Montreal and Toronto (Canada). The civic life was completely disarrayed, several dozens of people got buried under ice and many more died because of cold and exposure, thousands of flights were cancelled and the airports remained closed for several days. The frequency of polar vortex is increasing for the last few decades.

BIOLOGICAL HAZARDS AND DISASTERS

Epidemics

Epidemic is a widespread occurrence of an infectious disease in a community at a particular time. In other words it is sudden, widespread occurrence of a disease. It has been defined as an occurrence of disease that is temporarily of high prevalence. An epidemic occurring over a wide geographical area is called pandemic. Pandemic is an epidemic disease prevalent over a whole country or large part of the world. The rise and decline in epidemic prevalence of an infectious disease is a probability phenomenon dependent upon transfer of an effective dose of the infectious agent from an infected individual to a susceptible one. At present, diseases like HIV and cancer have also been included in the definition of epidemic.

Causes of Epidemics

The main causes of epidemics are (i) environmental pollution (water, air and soil pollution), (ii) environmental disasters like flood, drought, earthquake, tsunami, transgression of sea, and (iii) unhygienic conditions. Some of the important epidemic diseases are malaria, dengue, cholera, small-pox AID/HIVs. A brief description of the causes and consequences of the epidemics has been given in the following:

Major Diseases and Epidemics

Malaria

Malaria is an infectious disease, prevalent mainly in the regions of hot and humid climate. It is caused by protozoan parasites belonging to the genus plasmodium. These parasites are transmitted to humans by the bite of various species of mosquitoes.

In malaria, a serious, acute and chronic relapsing infection, characterised by periodic attacks of chills and fever, anaemia, and enlargement of spleen occurs.

Malaria occurs throughout the tropical and sub-tropical regions of the world, where climatic conditions are favourable for the vector (mosquito).

Malaria is a big health problem in India. It frequently occurs in the states of Assam, Bihar, Chhattisgarh, Madhya Pradesh, Uttar Pradesh, Uttarakhand, Punjab, Haryana, Rajasthan, Andhra Pradesh, Karnataka, Tamil Nadu, Malabar and Konkan coasts and the states of Kerala, Odisha, Tamil Nadu and West Bengal. Recently, the Indira Gandhi Canal Command area (Western Rajasthan) is reporting high number of malaria cases.

Natural calamities, especially floods, help in the growth of marshes, swamps, stagnant pools, and other large and small bodies of standing water. These are the ideal breeding places for Anopheles mosquito.

The epidemic of malaria may be controlled by removing the stagnant waters in the locality, and by following the principles of hygiene. Use of mosquito net, while sleeping is also a good preventive step of malaria.

Dengue and Chikungunya

Dengue is a type of fever which is also called as '*Break-bone Fever*' or '*Dandy Fever*'. Diseases like malaria, dengue and chikungunya are seasonal and show fluctuating trends in various seasons in different years. The dengue virus is carried by the yellow-fever mosquito, *Aedes aegypti*. The Asiatic tiger mosquito is another prominent carrier of the virus. There have been recent breakouts of dengue and chickengunya. In brief, dengue is characterised by fever and extreme pain in and stiffness of joints (hence the name '*break-bone fever*'. A mosquito becomes infected only if it bites an infected individual (humans and monkeys) during the first three days of the victims illness. Dengue viral infection may remain asymptomatic or manifest either as undifferentiated febrile illness (viral syndrome).

Signs and Symptoms The incubation period of dengue and chikungunya are two to five days. Symptoms of the disease include a fever up to 40°C, a petechial rash of the trunk and occasionally the limbs, and arthritis affecting multiple joints. Other nonspecific symptoms can include headache, conjunctival infection, and slight photophobia. Typically, the fever lasts for two days and then ends abruptly. However, other symptoms – namely joint pain, intense headache, insomnia, and an extreme degree of prostration – last for a variable period; usually for about 5 to 7 days. Patients have complained of joint pains for much longer time periods; some as long as two years, depending on their age.

Common laboratory tests for chikungunya virus isolation, and serological tests.

Virus isolation provides the most definitive diagnosis but takes 1–2 weeks for completion and must be carried out in Biosafety level 3 laboratories. The technique involves exposing specific cell-lines to samples from whole blood and identifying dengue/chikungunya virus-specific responses.

Dengue/Chikungunya virus is indigenous to tropical Africa and Asia, where it is transmitted to humans by the bite of infected mosquitoes, usually of the genus *Aedes*. Dengue is prevalent in parts of Asia (especially South and South-East Asia), countries of Equatorial Africa, South and Central America, Cuba and other island of West Indies. In India, the dengue virus was first isolated during the 1950s. Outbreaks have been reported from the various parts of the country, primarily from the urban areas. The main areas of concentration of dengue epidemic are Andhra Pradesh, Assam, Bihar, Delhi,

Haryana, Karnataka, Maharashtra, Punjab. Rajasthan, Tamil Nadu, Uttarakhand, Uttar Pradesh, and West Bengal. Every year, during the rainy season, a large number of dengue cases are reported even from the National Capital Region of the country.

Prevention The most effective means of prevention are protection against contact with the disease-carrying mosquitoes and mosquito control. Wearing bite-proof long sleeves and trousers (pants) also offer protection. In addition, garments can be treated with pyrethroids, a type of insecticides that often has repellent properties. Securing screens on windows and doors will help to keep mosquitoes out of the house.

There are no specific treatment of dengue/chikungunya. There is no vaccine currently available. Chloroquine is gaining ground as possible treatment for the symptoms associated with dengue/Chikungunya, and as an anti-inflammatory agent to combat the arthritis associated with Chikungunya virus.

For the prevention, and control of vector-borne diseases including malaria, dengue and chikungunya, the Government of India is implementing an integrated National Vectorborne Disease Control Programme under the over-arching umbrella of National Rural Health Mission. The main strategy for prevention and control of vectorborne diseases advocates for integral vector control, early ease detection and complete treatment.

Cholera

Cholera is an infectious and often fatal bacterial disease of the small intestine, typically contracted from infected water supplies and causing severe vomiting and diarrhoea. The victim suffers from massive diarrhoea with rapid depletion of body fluids and salts. The germ *vibro* enters the body via the mouth, usually in contaminated water or foods, and causes an infection in the small intestine.

Cholera often rises to epidemic proportions in South Asia particularly in India, Pakistan, and Bangladesh, and the countries of South-East Asia. It is more prevalent in the flood affected and flood prone areas.

Smallpox

Smallpox is an acute infectious disease caused by virus. It is characterised by fever and an eruption that, after passing through the stages of papule, vesicle, and pustule, dries up, leaving or less distinct scars. The characteristics eruptions may be so profuse as to be confluent, especially on the face, or so scanty that the lesions are missed altogether.

Smallpox arises from contact, direct or indirect, with another case of the disease. There are no natural animal carriers or natural propagation of the virus outside the human body. The virus is very stable and can survive for long periods outside the body. Most victims are infected by contact with an infected person by inhalation of the virus expelled in the breath or mouth- spray.

Smallpox was one of the world's most dreaded epidemic until 1977, when it was declared eradicated. No cases were reported from 1977 to 1980. Smallpox is estimated to have caused 20 lakh deaths in 1967 in the world. In India, the great smallpox epidemic in 1950 killed 25 lakh people.

AIDs/HIVs

AIDS (Acquired Immuno Deficiency Syndrome) is a disease of the immune system caused by the human immunodeficiency virus (HIV). HIV slowly attacks and destroys the immune system, the body defence against infection. It leads to affected person to a variety of other infectious diseases and certain malignancies that eventually cause death. AIDS is the final stage of HIV infection, during which time fatal infections and cancers arise. AIDS was first reported in 1981 by investigators in New York and California (USA).

HIV is transmitted by direct transfer of body fluids, such as blood and blood products, semen, and other genital secretions, or breast milk, from an infected person to an uninfected person. The main cellular target of HIV is a class of white blood cells critical to the immune system known as helper T cells.

HIV/AIDS spread to epidemic proportions in the 1980s, particularly in Africa, where the disease may have originated and where it has spread primarily through heterosexual contact. Spread was facilitated by several factors, including increasing urbanisation and long distance travel in Africa, international travel, changing sexual mores, and intravenous drug use.

According to UNO estimate over 40 million people throughout the world were infected with AIDS in 2012. People living in Sub-Saharan Africa accounted for more than 70 per cent of all infections. This epidemic is spreading in India, South East Asian countries Latin America and West Indies, USA and Canada. It is more prevalent among the blacks and the homosexuals. In India, the states of North East India, especially Manipur, Nagaland, Andhra Pradesh, Odisha are regularly reporting the cases of HIV.

Eutrophication

A natural processes in which lakes receive nutrients and sediment and become enriched; the gradual filling and natural aging of water-bodies. Pollution of water of rivers, lakes, ponds and reservoires due excess sediment load particularly suspended load in the direct result of accelerated rate of soil erosion. These chemicals and nutrients cause phenomenal growth of some aquatic plants. These dissolved substances adversely affect the physical and chemical properties of water. The water becomes unusable. Excess amount of chemicals and sediments also cause deaths of various aquatic organisms.

Famines

A relatively sudden event involving mass mortalities from starvation within a short period. Famine is typically distinguished from chronic hunger, understood as endemic nutritional deprivation on a persistent basis (as opposed to seasonal hunger, for example). The main characteristics of famine are:

(i) sharp price increase in staple foodstuffs, (ii) de-capitalisation of household assets, (iii) gathering of wild-foods, (iv) borrowing and begging, and (v) outmigration.

Causes of Famines

The main causes of famines have been described briefly in the following:

1. ***Natural calamities:*** Any aspect of physical environment's natural functions that may adversely affect human society to cause social disruption may be an important cause of famines. The earthquakes, snowstorms, floods, droughts, and epidemics are such natural hazards. The impact of these hazards is more serious in the developing and poor countries. India is not an exception to this.

2. ***Overpopulation:*** Apart from the natural calamities, droughts, floods, etc. overpopulation is one of the most important causes of famines. Overpopulation exists where there is an excess of population, overutilized or potential resources; that is to say, overpopulation occurs when resource development fails to keep pace with population growth. While there is no simple measure of overpopulation, it is usually distinguished by low per capita incomes, low and declining standard of living, high levels of unemployment, pronounced outward migration, and high density of population. In extreme cases, its symptoms may be hunger, malnutrition and famine. Inevitably, overpopulation strikes hardest at those occupying the lowest level in society – the landless, the marginal farmers, and unskilled workers.
3. ***Crop Failure:*** Crop failure may be due to failure or excessive rainfall or drought conditions. Failure of crops is an important cause of famines, especially in the developing countries.
4. ***Poverty and Unemployment:*** In any country or region if a certain proportion of the potentially active population is out of work at any given time, such a population is known as unemployed. Unemployment reduces the food purchasing power and the people may be in the grip of famine. In brief unemployment contributes to the spread of famine conditions.
5. ***Ineffective Public Distribution System:*** As stated above, it is the people who are generally below the poverty line who suffer most in a situation of famine. The administration can reduce the miseries of such people by an effective Public Distribution System (PDS) through which the edibles and essential commodities are provided at a cheaper rate.

Hunger and famine in particular, is intolerable in the modern world because it is unnecessary and unwarranted (Sen and Dreze, 1989). Famine causation has often been linked to natural disasters, population growth and war, producing a reduction in food supply. But some major famines (for example, Bengal in 1943) were not preceded by a significant decline in food production or absolute availability, and in some cases have been associated with food export. Thus famine is a social phenomenon rooted in the institutional and political economic arrangements which determine the access to food by different classes and strata.

Recent analyses have focused on access to and control over food resources. Sen (1981) argues that what we eat depends on what food we are able to acquire. Famine therefore is a function of the failure of socially specific entitlements through which individuals command bundles of commodities. Entitlements vary in relation to property rights, assets distribution, *class* and *gender*. Famine is therefore a social phenomena rooted in the institutional and political economic arrangements which determine the access to food by different classes and strata. Mass poverty and mass starvation are obviously linked via entitlement.

According to Karl Marx, the sole causes of famine are (i) the private property, and (ii) class ridden society. The means of production (private property) is owned by a few in the society. Those who own the means of production, they exploit the labourers/workers (those who do not own means of production). The owners of means of production '*hire and fire*' the workers. This process ultimately reduces the purchasing power of the poor people who finally become the victims of famines. Thus the capitalist mode of production is responsible for the exploitation, undernourishment, poverty and famines in the society.

In brief, mass poverty results from long-term changes in entitlements associated with social production and distribution mechanisms; famine arise from short-term changes in these same mechanisms. Famine and endemic deprivation correspond to two forms of public action to eradicate them:

(i) Famine policy requires entitlement protection ensuring that they do not impact up on vulnerable groups (i.e. landless labourers, women and marginal farmers).
(ii) Chronic hunger demands entitlement promotion to expend the command that people have over basic necessities (Sen and Dreze, 1989).

Since 1945 India has implemented a successful anti-famine policy, and yet has conspicuously failed to eradicate endemic deprivation; conversely, China has overcome hunger problem, but failed to prevent massive famine in the 1950s. Africa has witnessed a catastrophic growth in the incidence of both mass starvation and chronic hunger. The famine vulnerable countries of the world have been shown in **Fig. 8.32**.

It may be observed from **Fig. 8.32** that the worst affected areas of famine lie in the continent of Africa. The Sahel region, stretching over Somalia, Ethiopia, Sudan, Chad, Niger, Nigeria, Mali, Mauritania, Burkina Faso and Madagascar record one famine year after almost every two years. The deaths in the famines of the decade of 1990s were in millions. The other highly vulnerable areas to famines are Mongolia, western parts of China, parts of Afghanistan, Iran, Baluchistan, Sindh (Pakistan), Bangladesh, Myanmar, parts of India Central American countries and parts of Bolivia and Paraguay (**Fig. 8.32**).

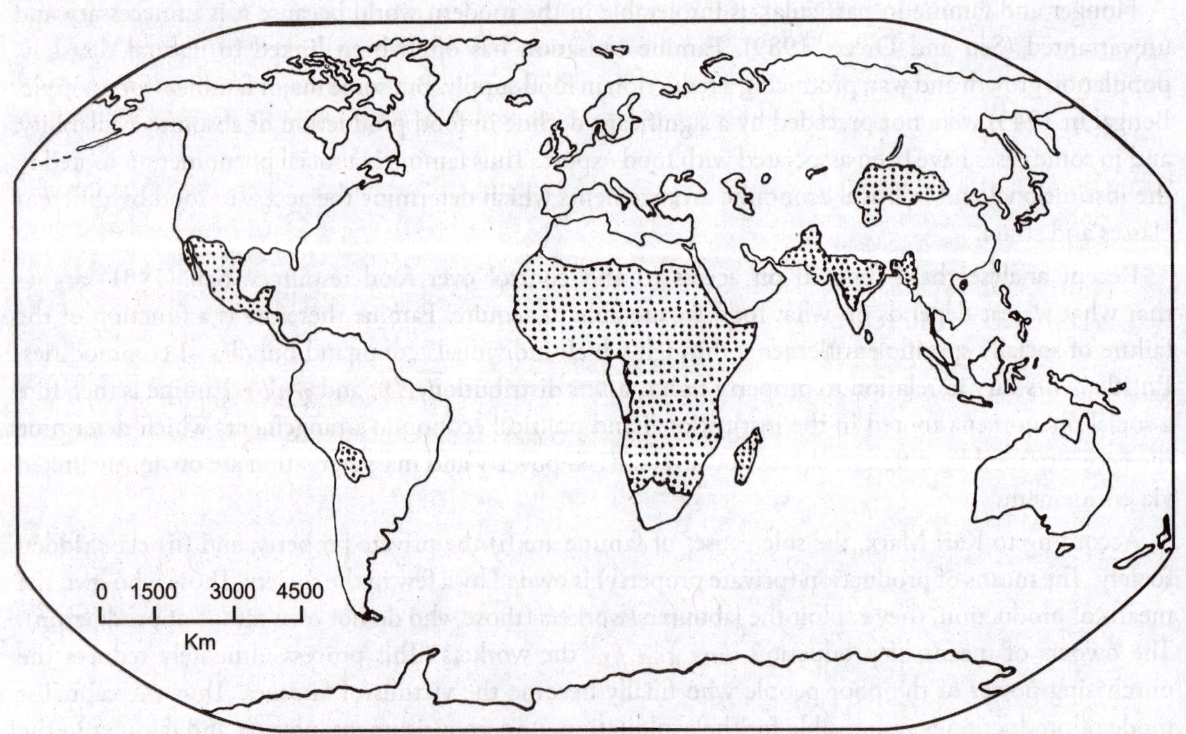

Fig. 8.32 Famine Prone Areas of the World

In India, the frequency of famines was very high during the Mediaeval and British period, but after Independence a number of projects were launched to reduce the famine conditions. A large number of dams, multi-purpose projects and irrigation projects, the fast means of transportation and communications have largely overcome the problems of famine. Still there are, however, some areas which are vulnerable to famine condition. The famine prone areas of India have been shown in **Fig. 8.33.**

It may be seen from **Fig. 8.33** that the greater parts of the states of Odisha, Jharkhand, Chhattisgarh, Madhya Pradesh, Rajasthan, Andhra Pradesh, and some parts of Gujarat, Maharashtra Bihar and Uttar Pradesh are vulnerable to famines. The famine prone areas: These areas are areas where the per capita income is low and the purchasing power of the people is very low. The unequal development and regional significant variations in per capita income that Naxalites are spreading their area of influence. In fact, these poverty ridden areas are infested with Naxalites creating many administrative problems by their violent attacks on the police and politicians. It was because of the Naxalites attack that some of the important leaders of Congress like Mahendra Karma, Nand Kumar Patel and his son including many important statelevel leaders were brutally killed on 25th May, 2013 in Jagdalpur region of Chhattisgarh. In fact, Bastar of Chhattisgarh has become one of the worst war zones in the world.

Wildfire (Forest Fire)

A wildfire is an uncontrolled fire in an area of combustible vegetation that occurs in the natural forests, countryside or a wilderness area. Wildfire is also known as forest fire, bush fire, grass-fire, hill fire, vegetation fire, peat-fire, and veld-fire.

A wild-fire differs from other fires by its extensive size, the speed at which it can spread out from its original source, its potential to change direction unexpectedly, and its ability to jump gaps such as roads, rivers and firebreaks. Wildfires are characterised in terms of the cause of ignition, their physical properties such as speed of propagation, the combustible material present, and the effect of weather on the fire.

Wildfires are a common occurrence in Australia, especially during the long summers usually experienced in the southern regions such as Victoria, and New South Wales. Due to Australia's hot and dry climate, wildfires (bushfire in Australia) pose a great risk to life infrastructure during all times of the year. In the United States, there are typically between 60,000 and 80,000 wildfires that occur each year, burning 3 million to 10 million acres of land depending on the year.

Wildfires can cause extensive damage, both to property and human life, but they also have various beneficial effects on wilderness areas. Some plant species depend on the effects of fire for growth and reproduction, although large wildfire may also have negative ecological effects.

Characteristics of Wildfire

The name wildfire was once a synonym for Greek fire but now refers to any large or destructive conflagration. The main characteristics of wildfire are:

1. They take place outdoors in areas of grassland, woodlands, bush-lands, scrubland, peat-land, and other wooded areas that act as a source of fuel.
2. All wildfires can be characterised in terms of their physical properties, their fuel type, and the effect that weather has on the fire.
3. The wildfires can be large or very small, i.e. 0.5 km to 400 square kilometres, they can also be as small as 0.25 acre or less.

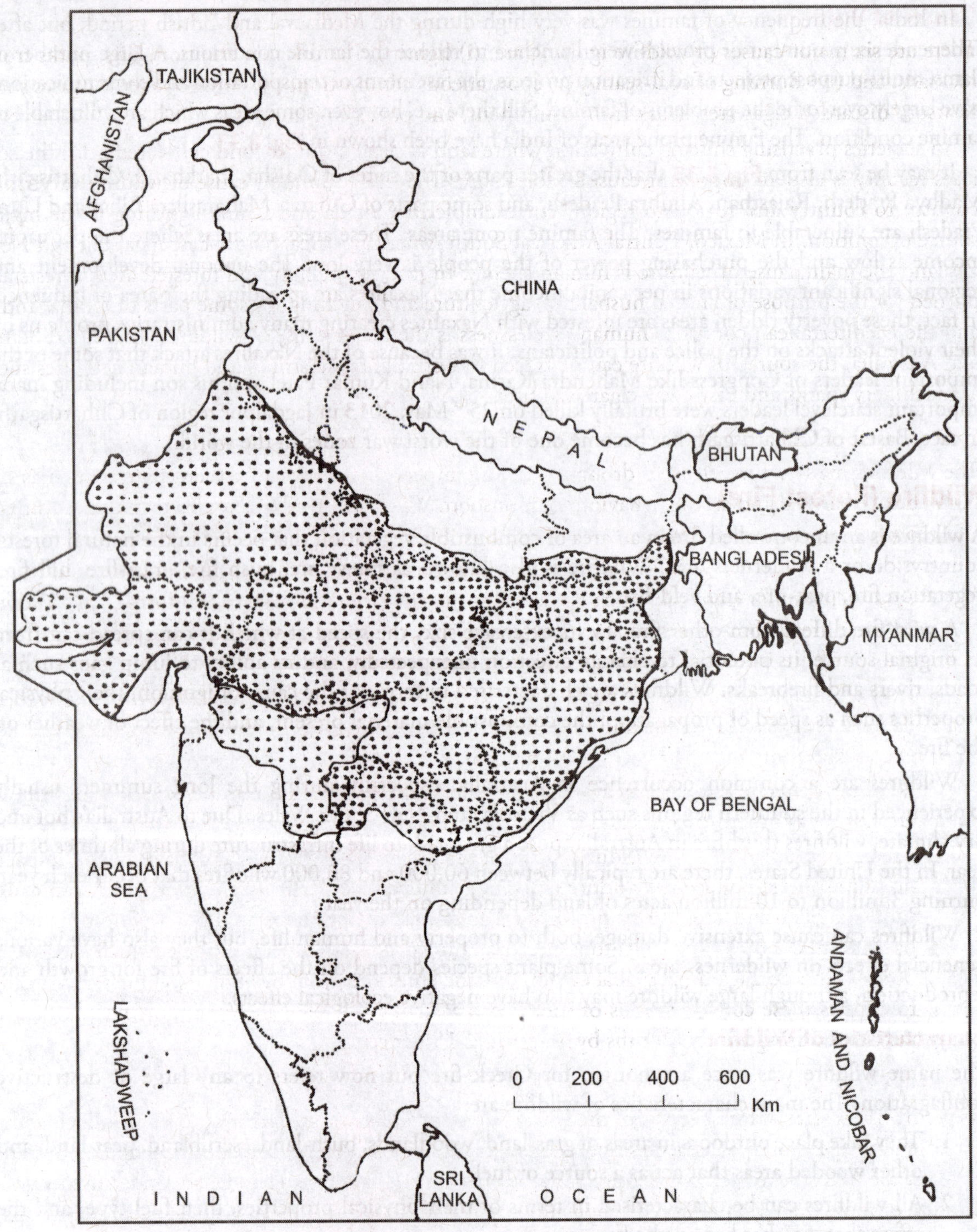

Fig. 8.33 Famine Prone Areas of India

Causes of Wildfire

There are six major causes of wildfire igniting are: (i) lighting, (ii) volcanic eruption, (iii) sparks from rockfalls, and (iv) Burning of coal-seams, (v) spontaneous combustion, (vi) Anthropogenic causes such as arson, discarded cigarettes, spark from equipment, and power line arcs.

In societies practising shifting cultivation where land is cleared quickly and cultivated until the soil loses fertility is also an important cause of forest-fire. The most common cause of wildfire vary from country to country and region to region. For example in Canada and China lightning is the major source of ignition. In Mexico, Central America, South America, Africa, South-East Asia, Fiji and New Zealand the main cause of wildfire is human agency. In fact, in the hilly and forested areas forests are burned for the purpose of animal husbandry, agriculture and ranching. In some parts of China, India and the Mediterranean countries human carelessness is the major cause of wildfires. In United States and Australia, the source of wildfire can be traced to both lightning strikes and human activities such as machinery sparks and cast-away cigarette butts.

Consequences of Wildfire

The wildfires many a times lead to drought, rise in temperature, snowmelt, cyclic changes such as El-Nino, delayed arrival and erratic behaviour of monsoon. Wildfire also adversely affects the environment and ecology.

(i) ***Effect on Ecology*** Wildfires are frequent in the forest areas of hot and humid climates. Many ecosystems suffer from too much fire, such as the chaparral in southern California. The wildfire in these areas upset the natural cycles, destroy native plant communities, and encouraged the growth of fire-intolerant vegetation and non-native weeds.

In the Amazon Rainforest, drought, logging, cattle ranching practices, and shifting cultivation damage fire-resistant forests and promote the growth of flammable brush, creating a cycle that encourages more burning.

Wildfires generate ash, destroy available organic nutrients and cause an increase in water runoff, eroding away other nutrients and creating flash flood conditions.

(ii) ***Atmospheric Pollution*** Wildfires can affect climate and weather and have major impacts on atmospheric pollution. Wildfire emissions contain fine particulate matter which can cause cardiovascular and respiratory problems. Forest fires in Indonesia in 1977 were estimated to have released 2.83 billion short tons of carbon dioxide (CO_2) into atmosphere, which is between 30% – 40% of the annual global carbon dioxide emissions from burning fossil fuels. According to experts these concentrations of sooty particles could increase absorption or incoming solar radiation during winter months by as much as 15 per cent.

Forest Fires in India

As per the latest state of forest report of the Forest Survey of India, the actual forest cover of India is about 19.27% of the geographical area, corresponding to about 63.3 million hectares. Only 38 million hectares of forest are well stocked (crown density above 40 per cent).The forests of India are under tremendous pressure of more than 1.24 billion of population. Forest fires are a major cause of degradation of India's forests. While statistical data on fire loss are weak, it is estimated that the proportion of forest areas prone to forest fires annually range from 33 per cent in some states to cover 90 per cent in other. About 90 per cent of the forest fires in India are caused by humans. The normal fire season in India is from the month of February to mid June. India witnessed the most severe forest fires in the recent time during the summer of 1955 in the hills of Uttar Pradesh and Himachal Pradesh. The fires were very severe and attracted the attention of whole nation. An area of 677,700 hectares was affected by forest fires **(Fig.8.34)**.

According to the Forest Survey of India, data on forest fire attribute around 50 per cent of the forest areas as fire prone. This however, does not mean that country's 50 per cent area is affected by fires annually. Very heavy, heavy and frequent forest fire damages are noticed only by 0.8 per cent, 0.14 per cent and 5.16 per cent of the forest areas respectively. Thus, only 6.17 per cent of the forests are prone to severe fire damage. In absolute term, out of 63 million hectares of forest area of around 3.73 million hectare can be presumed to be affected by fires annually.

Prevention of Wildfire (Forest Fire)

Wildfire prevention refers to the preemptive methods of reducing the risk of fires as well as lessening its severity and spread. Effective prevention techniques allow supervising agencies to manage air quality, maintain ecological balances, protect resources and limit the effects of future uncontrolled fires. North America firefighting policies permit naturally caused fires to burn to maintain their ecological role, so long as the risk of escape into high-value areas are mitigated. However, prevention policies must consider the role that humans play in wild fires, since, for example, 95 per cent of forest fires in Europe are related to human involvement. Sources of human-caused fire may include arson, accidental ignition, or the uncontrolled use of fire in land-clearing and agriculture such as slash-and-burn farming in Southeast Asia.

Strategies of wildfire prevention, detection, and suppression have varied over the years, and international wildfire management experts encourage further development of technology and research. One of the more controversial techniques is controlled burning: permitting or even igniting smaller fires to minimise the amount of flammable material available for a potential wildfire. While some wildfires-burn in remote forested regions, they can cause extensive destruction of homes and other property located in the wild-land–urban interface: a zone of transition between developed areas and underdeveloped wilderness.

Wildfire prevention programmes have been started in many of the developed and developing countries. The wildfires may be prevented by adopting the following steps.

(i) Burn the vegetation-fuel periodically.
(ii) To remove the cuts of trees by handcrews in order to clean and clear forest.
(iii) Prevent fuel-build-up.
(iv) Develop access in the forest area.
(v) Controlled burns.
(vi) In the forests buildings should be constructed of flame resistant materials.
(vii) Strict patrolling in the fire-prone forest areas. Skilled workforce to implement the rules and regulations of Forest Act.
(viii) The tourists and people should not throw the cigarette-buts in the forests which may ignite forest-fire.

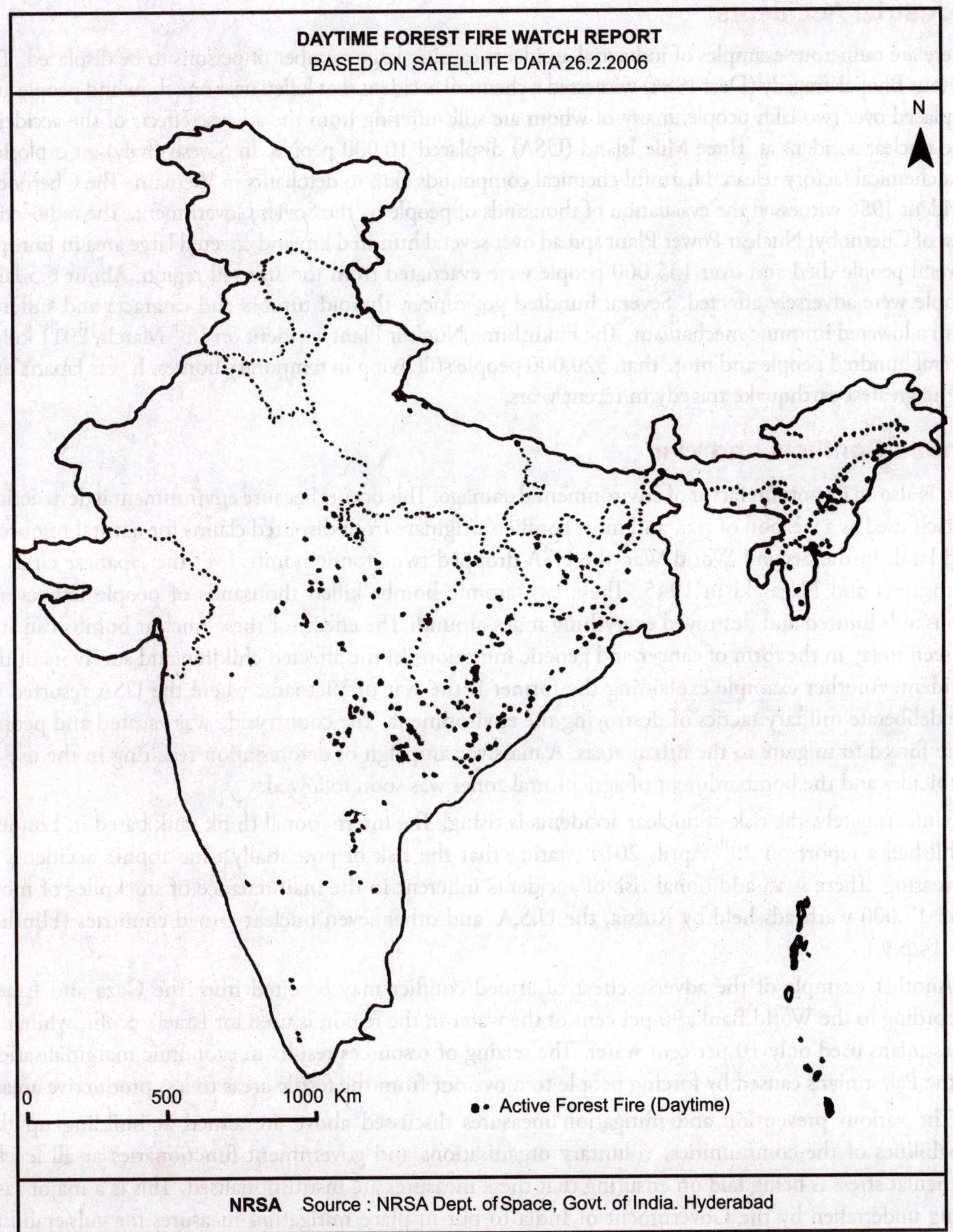

Fig. 8.34 Forest Fires in India

Industrial Accidents

There are numerous examples of industrial accidents causing large number of persons to be displaced, The famous Bhopal Tragedy (Dec. 1984) witnessed a chemical accident that killed over one thousand people and displaced over two lakh people, many of whom are still suffering from the adverse effects of the accident. The nuclear accident at Three Mile Island (USA) displaced 10,000 people. In Seveso (Italy) an explosion in a chemical factory released harmful chemical compounds akin to defoliants in Vietnam. The Chernobyl accident 1986 witnessed the evacuation of thousands of people by the Soviet Government. The radioactive dust of Chernobyl Nuclear Power Plant spread over several hundred km and covered large area in Europe. Several people died and over 135,000 people were evacuated from the affected region. About 6.5 lakh people were adversely affected. Several hundred got cancer, thyroid tumors and cataracts and suffered from a lowered immune mechanism. The Fukushima Nuclear Plant accident on 11th March, 2011 killed several hundred people and more than 320,000 people still living in temporary homes. It was Japan's one of the greatest earthquake tragedy in recent years.

Armed Conflicts and War

War is also an important factor of environmental damage. This occurs because environmental destruction is itself used as a weapon of war, and most conflicts originate from disputed claims for natural resources and land. In the Second World War, the USA dropped two atomic bombs over the Japanese cities of Hiroshima and Nagasaki in 1945. These two atomic bombs killed thousands of people left several thousands injured and destroyed everything miles around. The effects of these nuclear bombs can still be seen today in the form of cancer and genetic mutations in the affected children and survivors of the incident. Another example explaining the former is the war of Vietnam, where the USA resorted to the deliberate military tactics of destroying the environment. The countryside was vacated and people were forced to migrate to the urban areas. A massive campaign of deforestation resulting in the use of herbicides and the bombardment of agricultural zones was soon followed.

Unfortunately, the risk of nuclear accidents is rising. The international think tank based in London published a report on 29th April, 2014, stating that the risk of potentially catastrophic accidents is increasing. There is an additional risk of accidents inherent in the maintenance of stockpiles of more than 17,000 warheads held by Russia, the U.S.A. and other seven nuclear armed countries (Hindu–1.4.14,p.9.).

Another example of the adverse effect of armed conflict may be cited from the Gaza and Israel. According to the World Bank, 90 per cent of the water in the region is used for Israel's profit, while the Palestinians used only 10 per cent water. The seizing of resources results in economic marginalisation of the Palestinians caused by forcing people to move out from the fertile areas to less productive areas.

The various prevention and mitigation measures discussed above are aimed at building up the capabilities of the communities, voluntary organisations and government functionaries at all levels. Particular stress is being laid on ensuring that these measures are institutionalised. This is a major task being undertaken by the Government of India to put in place mitigation measures for vulnerability reduction.

Distribution of World Natural Resources

DEFINITION OF A RESOURCE

A thing that fulfills the needs of people is known as a resource. Resource may be natural, like mineral ores, water, soils, natural vegetation or man-made like labour, skills, finance, capital, technology, infrastructure and working environment. Resources may be classified into a number of ways, like renewable and non-renewable resources, exhaustible and non-exhaustible resources, biotic and abiotic resources, energy and mineral resources, potential and developed resources.

CLASSIFICATION

Non-Renewable Resource

Any resources that is present in the Earth's crust in fixed amount and cannot be replenished is known as non-renewable or exhaustible resource. Minerals like coal, crude-oil, natural gas, iron-ore, manganese, copper, bauxite, mica, uranium etc. are the examples of non-renewable resources.

Renewable Resource

Any resource that is naturally replaced on a seasonal basis by the growth of living organisms, or by other natural processes, is known as a renewable resource. In other words, a recurrent resource which is not diminished or marginally diminished, is known as a renewable resource. Such resources may be restored over a short period of time. Solar-energy, hydro-electricity, tidal, wind and geothermal energy are examples of renewable resources. Such resources may be used without endangering future consumption, as long as the use does not outstrip production of new resources as in the case of fishing. However at present, due to various factors, renewable energy alone cannot fulfil our energy needs. They cannot fulfill our energy needs. Nuclear energy, however, may become a major source of renewable energy in future to fulfill the shortage.

ENERGY RESOURCES

The technological progress and the standard of living of modern society is closely related to the consumption of energy. In the contemporary world, the standard of living of the people is judged by the level of energy consumption. In general, higher the level of energy consumption, higher is the standard of living of the people. However, a shortage of energy looms, as coal, petroleum and natural gas are increasingly getting exhausted, and they may become even more scarce in the near future. In such a scenario, hydro-power, solar energy and nuclear energy are the suitable alternate sources of energy.

Electricity is a clean source of energy. It is generated from water, coal, mineral oil, natural gas and atomic minerals. Electricity is relatively cheap, transportable, pollution free and renewable. Electric power is therefore increasingly becoming popular. In India, the per head/per annum consumption of electricity is about 350 kWh which is much below the per head consumption in the world at 1000 kWh and USA at 7000 kWh.

Water as a Resource

Hydro-electricity development in India commenced at the end of the 19th century with the commissioning of electricity supply in Darjeeling during 1897, followed by the commissioning of a hydropower station at Sivasamudram in Karnataka during 1902. In the pre-Independence era, the power supply was mainly in the private sector, that too restricted to the urban areas. With the formation of State Electricity Boards during the Five Year Plans, a significant step was taken in bringing about a systematic growth of power supply industry all over the country. A number of multi-purpose projects came into being, and with the setting up of thermal, hydro and nuclear power stations, power generation started increasing significantly.

The Ministry of Power in India, is primarily responsible for the development of electrical energy in the country. The construction, and operation of power projects and generation and transmission of power are entrusted to the National Thermal Power Corporation (NTPC), the National Hydro-electric Power Corporation (NHPC), the North-Easten Electric Power Corporation (NEEPCO), and the Power Grid Corporation of India Limited (PGCIL). The Power Grid is responsible for all the existing and future transmission projects in the Central Sector and also for the formation of the National Power Grid. The installed power generation capacity of India has increased from about 1400 MW in 1947 to 174, 361 MW (2011).

Coal as a Resource

Coal is an abundant, cheap but exhaustible source of energy. The consumption of coal in the world is more than 5 billion tons per year, accounting for about 35 per cent of worldwide carbon dioxide emissions. There are four types of coal, namely, (i) peat, (ii) lignite, (iii) bituminous, and (iv) anthracite.

Peat develops with the decay of plants in bogs. Compressed peat yields lignite—a low grade coal, often called brown coal. When coal is buried deeply, moisture expelled and the material subjected to increased temperatures, a firmer bituminous coal results. Bituminous coal is the most popular in metallurgy and is referred as soft coal. Further compression yields anthracite, the highest quality and hard coal. The high grade coal used in the steel industry is frequently called coking coal. It results from the heating of coal in the absence of oxygen which burns off volatile gases.

The distribution of coal in the world is highly unequal. China is the leading producer of coal, accounting for about 29 %, followed by U.S.A., India, Australia and Russia (**Fig. 9.1**). In India, Raniganj (West Bengal), Jharia, Daltenganj (Jharkhand), Sarguja, Korba (Chhattisgarh), Singrauli (M.P.), Talcher (Odisha), Wardha (Maharashtra), Singreni (Andhra Pradesh), Neyveli (Tamil Nadu), Marpalana, Barmer (Rajasthan), Kalakot and Nichahom (J & K), Lakhuni (Assam), Darrangiri (Meghalaya), and Vaekala (Kerala) are the major places of coal deposits (**Fig. 9.2**). The leading producers and consumers of coal have been given (**Table 9.1-9.3**).

Table 9.1 Leading Coal Producing Countries of the World

Country	Percentage of Total Production
1. China	29.0
2. U.S.A.	20.7
3. India	7.5
4. Australia	7.0
5. Russia	5.2

Table 9.2 Leading Consumers of Coal in the World

Country	Percentage of Total Consumption
1. China	27.1
2. U.S.A.	20.3
3. India	8.0
4. Germany	5.2
5. Russia	4.6

Table 9.3 Major Coal Fields of the World

Country	Coal Mines
1. China	Shanxi (Shansi), Shaanxi (Shensi), Sichuan, Fushun, Shenyang, Sinkiang
2. U.S.A.	Arkansas, Colorado, Illinois, Indiana, Iowa, Kentucky, Michigan, Montana, New Mexico, North Dakota, Ohio, Oklahoma, Pennsylvania, Pittsburg, West Virginia (Appalachian), Utah, Wyoming
3. India	Bokaro, Daltenganj, Deograh, Giridih, Jharia, Hutar, Kalakot, Karanpur, Korba, Neyvelli, Ramgarh, Raniganj, Singreni, Singrauli, Sohagpur, Talcher, Umaria, Wardha Valley.
4. Australia	Bowen Basin, Brisbane, Canberra, Sydney, New-Castle (New South Wales), Fingal (Tasmania), Ipswich (Queensland), Gippsland (Victoria), Pagingo
5. Russia	Moscow-Tula, Chokot Basin (Eastern Siberia), Irkutsk Basin, Lena-Basin, Kizel, Komi-Ukhta (Pechora Basin), Kuznetsk (Kuzbas), north-eastern Siberia, Irkutsk, Ob-Basin, Sakhalin Island, Tunguska-Basin, Tyumen (Ob- Basin). Upper Lena, Vladivostok, Yakut-Basin, Zyryanska Basin
6. Poland	Upper Silesian and Lower Silesian Fields
7. Germany	Ruhr, Saxony, Leipzig, Magdeburg, Dresden, Saar, Bavaria, Cologne
8. U.K.	Cumberland, Durham, Derbyshire, Lancashire, Leicestershire, Northumberland, Nottinghamshire, South Wales, Warwickshire
9. Canada	Alberta, Vancouver (British Columbia)

(Contd.)

Table 9.3 (*Contd.*)

Country	Coal Mines
10. France	Pas de Calais and Nord (North-eastern France), Franco-Belgian Coalfields, Alsace-Lorraine Fields, Central Massif
11. Belgium	Franco-Belgian --coalfields
12. Brazil	Southern Brazil
13. South Africa	Transvaal, Natal
14. Chile	Concepcion
15. Others	Argentina, Columbia, Mexico, Nigeria, Myanmar, Nigeria, Peru, Spain, Uruguay

Looking at the exhaustible nature of coal, it is imperative to make its use judiciously.

Japan is a leading importer of coal. The west European countries import about 34 per cent of the coal in the world. Over 50 per cent of the total coal import is by Japan.

Coal mining industry in India is facing several pressing problems. Some of the important problems of coal mining industry are given below:

1. Uneven distribution

The distribution of coal in India is highly uneven. Most of the good quality coal is confined to the states of Jharkhand, Chhattisgarh, Madhya Pradesh, Odisha and West Bengal. This involves high transportation coast to carry coal to the different parts of the country.

2. High ash content

Indian coal is relatively inferior as it contains 20 to 30 per cent ash content.

3. Deep coal seams

Being more deep, the mining cost of coal in India is relatively higher.

4. Obsolete technology

The latest mining technology for mines is available in a limited number of mines. In India, coal mining is more hazardous as compared to that of the developed countries.

5. Frequent fires in mines

There are heavy losses due to fires in the mines.

6. Environmental pollution

Mining and use of coal leads to serious problem of environmental pollution.

Oil (Petroleum) as a Resource

It was in 1857 that oil was first produced commercially. The first well of crude oil was dug in 1857 at Ploesti, 60 km to the west of Bucharest (Romania). In 1859, petroleum was produced at Titsuville-Pennsylvania, north of Pittsburgh (USA). Subsequently, it was produced at Baku (Azerbaijan) and the Caspian region of Russia in 1863.

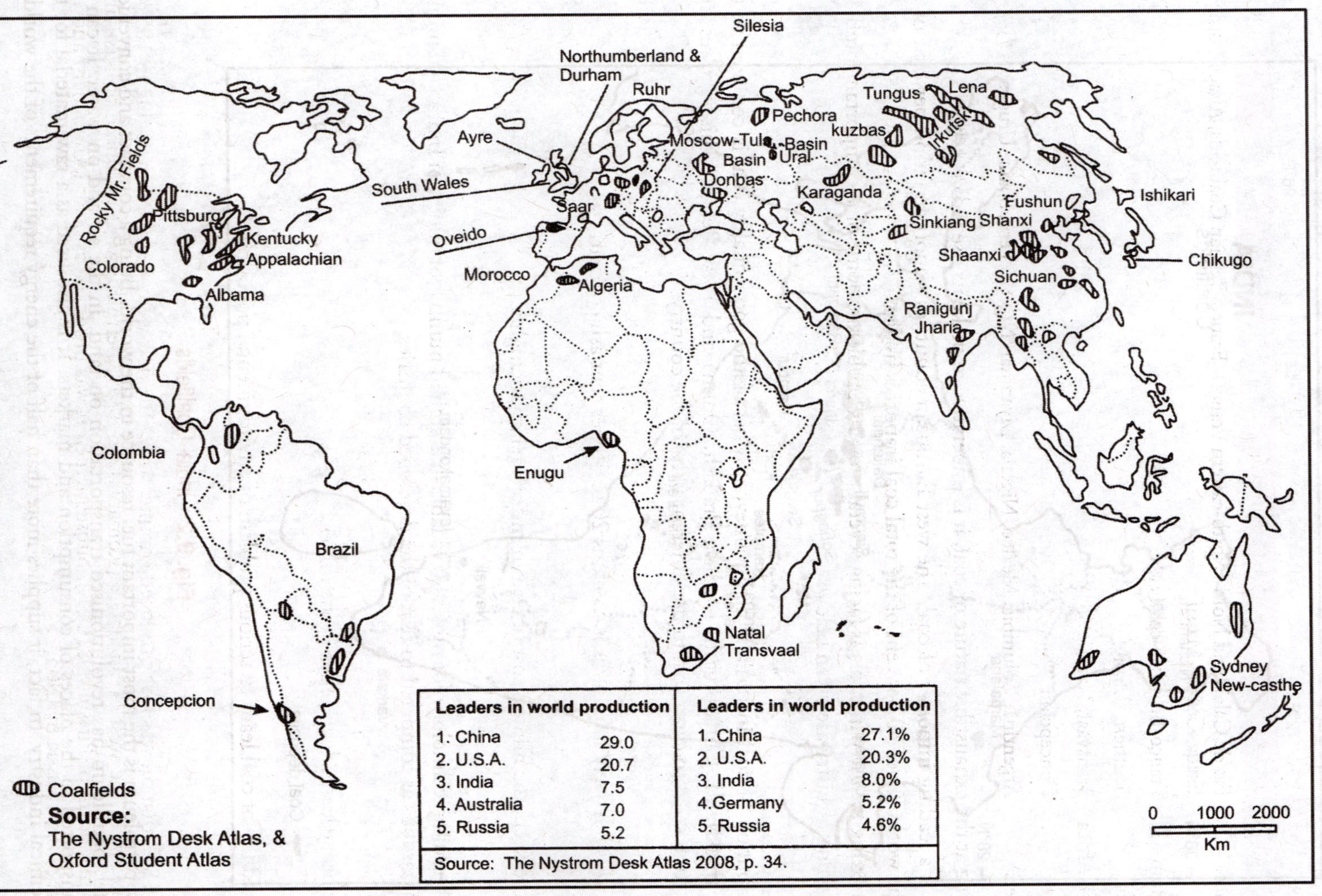

Fig. 9.1 World–Distribution of coal

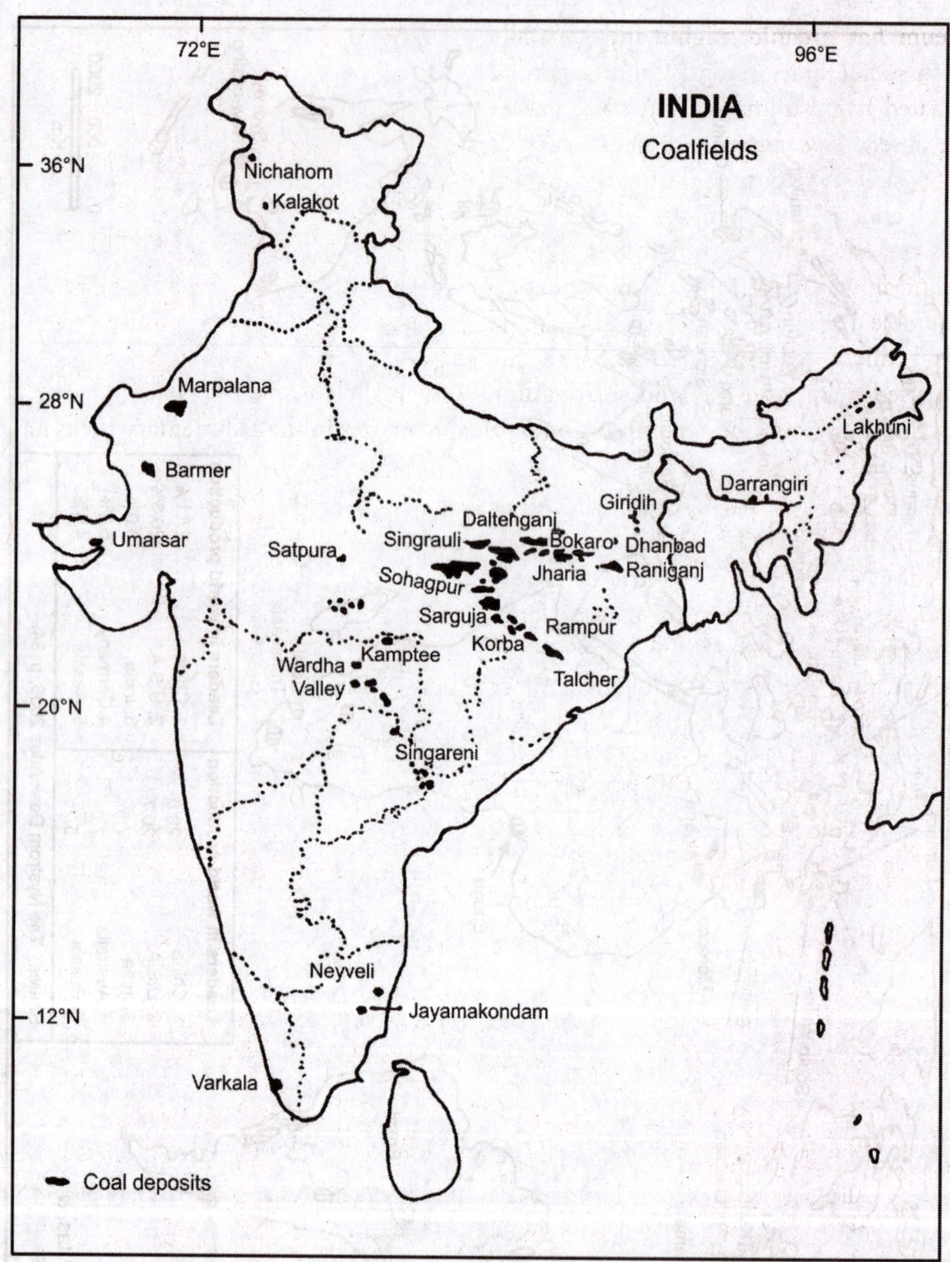

Fig. 9.2 India–Coalfields

Today, petroleum is the most important fuel resource in the world. Being a compact and convenient liquid fuel, petroleum has revolutionised transportation on land, in the air and on water. It can be easily transported to the places of consumption and markets. It is also used as a raw material for the petro-chemical industry. In fact, it supplies more than half of the energy requirements of the world at present.

Petroleum has organic origins and generally is found in sedimentary basins. Oil and natural gas originated from animal or vegetable matter contained in shallow marine sediments, such as sands, silts, and clay deposited during the periods when land and aquatic life was abundant in various forms, especially, the microscopic forms of fauna and flora. Conditions for oil formation were favourable during the Tertiary Period. Dense forests and microorganisms flourished in the gulfs, estuaries, deltas and the land surrounding them during this period. The decomposition of organic matter in the sedimentary rocks has led to the formation of oil.

Table 9.4 Crude Oil (Petroleum) – Leading Producers in the World

Country	Percentage of Total Production
1. Saudi Arabia	12.3
2. Russia	11.7
3. United States	8.1
4. Iran	5.4
5. China	4.9

At present, over 50 per cent of the oil is found in the Gulf countries of South-West Asia. Saudi Arabia alone contributes over 12 per cent of the oil-production of the world, followed by Russia (11.7%), U.S.A. (8.1%), Iran (5.4%) and China (4.9%). The United States of America is the leading consumer (25.2%), Japan (7.0%), China (6.6%), Germany (3.5%) and Russia (3.3%). The oil producing centres in different countries of the world and that of India have been shown in **Figs. 9.3 and 9.4,** while the leading producing and oil consuming countries have been given in **Tables 9.4 to 9.6.**

Table 9.5 Crude Oil (Petroleum) – Leading Consumers in the World

Country	Percentage of Total Consumption
1. United States	25.2
2. Japan	7.0
3. China	6.6
4. Germany	3.5
5. Russia	3.3

Table 9.6 Major Petroleum Producing Centres

Country	Oil Producing Centres
Algeria	Bougie, Edjele, Hassi Massould, Hassi R'Mel
Australia	Alice Spring (Northern Territory), Bass Strait, Moonie (Queensland), Daly Basin (Northern Territory), Port Hedland (Western Australia)
Brunei	Northern shore of Brunei
Brazil	Amazon Basin, coastal Brazil
Canada	Alberta, Athabasca, Saskatchewan
China	Daqing (Taching), Dakang (Takang), Sandung (Shantung), Panshan, Yumen, Karmi in Xinjiang (Sinkiang), Kashi (Kashgar)
Egypt	Sinai Peninsula

(Contd.)

Table 9.6 (*Contd.*)

Country	Oil Producing Centres
India	Bombay High, Digboi, Gulf of Khambat, K G Basin, Upper Assam
Indonesia	Jambi, Minas, Palembang, Kalimantan (Borneo Island), Balikpapan
Iran	Agha-Jari, Bahregan, Gach-Saran, Lali, Marun, Masjid-e-Sulaiman
Iraq	Alwand, Basra, Kirkuk, Mosul
Libya	Marsa Brega, Zelten, Ras Sidar, Sirte-Basin, Tobruk
Malaysia	Sarawak, East coast of Peninsula of Malaysia
Mexico	Cludad Madero, Poza Rica, Reynosa
Nigeria	Niger Delta
Russia	Bashkiria, Grozny, Kuybyshev, Maikop, Nizhnevartovsk, Perm, Sakhalin Island, Tataria, Tomsk
Saudi Arabia	Abqaiq, Ain Dar, Al-Hufuf, Burgan, Dahran, Dammam, Dharhan, Ghawar, Jubail, Mina-al-Ahmadi, Safania
U.K.	North Sea
U.S.A.	Alaska, Arkansas, California, Illinois, Kentucky, Louisiana, Michigan, New Mexico, Ohio, San Joaquin, Texas, Wayoming
Venezuela	Aruba, Lagunillas, Maracaibo Lake

The major exporters of oil and petroleum include: Angola, Algeria, Iran, Iraq, Kuwait, Indonesia, Libya, Nigeria, Qatar, Saudi Arabia, United Arab Emirates (UAE) and Venezuela.

In India, most of the crude oil is obtained from the Bombay High, Digboi, Naharkatiya, Moran-Hugrijan (Assam) Ankleshwar, Gulf of Khambat, Khambat, and Kalol, (Gujarat), and the Barmer district of Rajasthan. Crude oil is also obtained from the Godavari-Krishna Delta and the state of Tripura. India is however, not self reliant in crude oil and petroleum. India imports over 70 per cent of its demand mainly from the Gulf countries.

Natural Gas as a Resource

Natural gas is one of the important sources of energy. Natural gas burns clean and is easy to use. It is relatively cheap to buy and transport. Its storage and distribution is however, complicated. Natural gas may occur in association with crude-oil in the upper most part of an oil trap. The larger fields of natural gas often have no oil. The major constituents of natural gas are a mixture of gaseous hydrocarbons, of which methane alone may make up 80 to 90 per cent. The other gases include ethane, propane and butane.

The leading producers, consumers and mining centres of natural gas have been plotted in Fig. 9.5, while the leading producers and consumers have been given in Tables 9.7 – 9.9. It may be seen from Table 9.7 that Russia with a percentage share of 22.8 is the leading producer of natural gas, followed by U.S.A. (20.7%), Canada (7.1%), U.K. (3.9%) and Algeria (3.1%). Australia, China, India, Indonesia, Iran, Iraq, Saudi Arabia, Turkmenistan, Uzbekistan, and

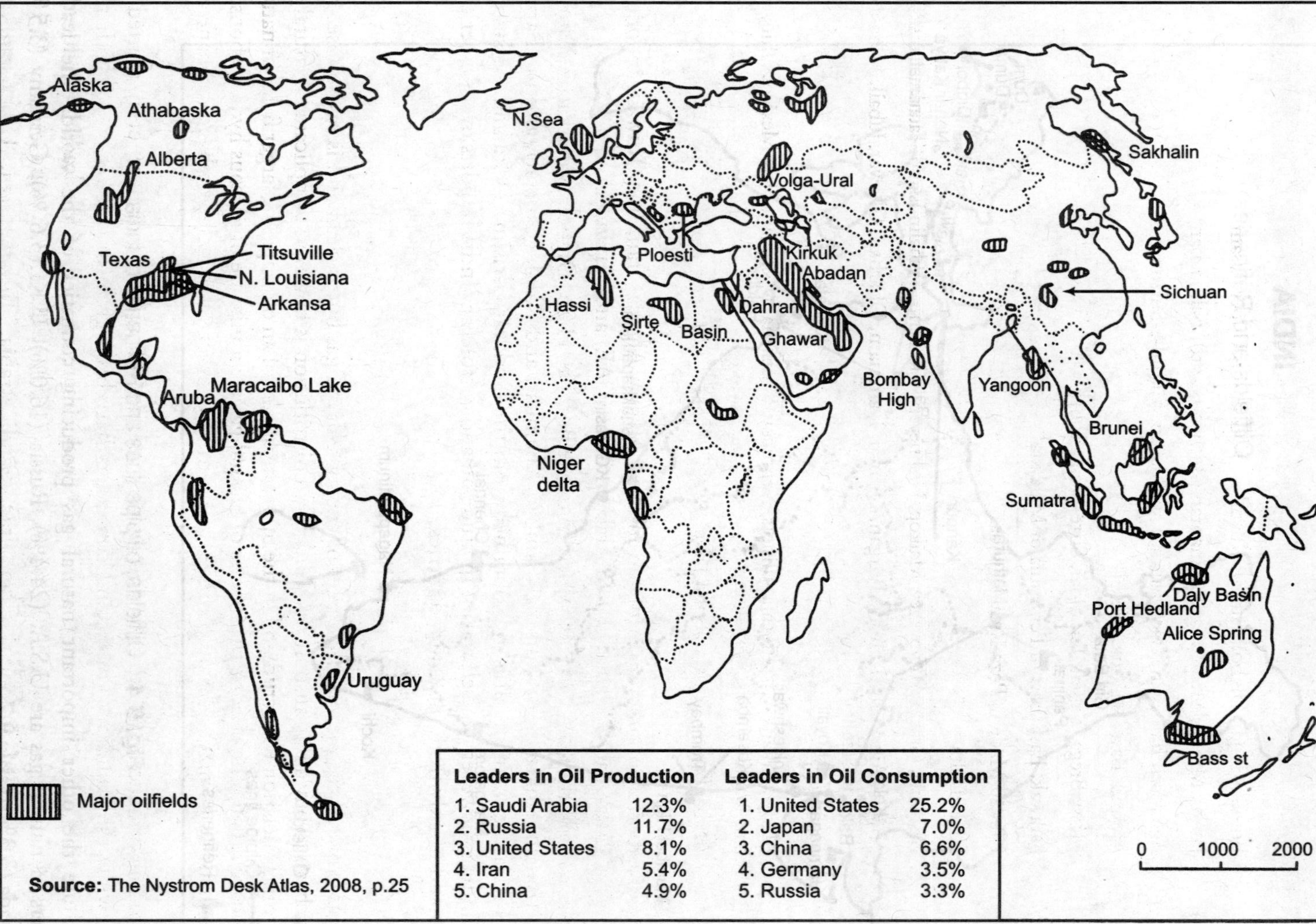

Fig. 9.3 World–Major oilfields

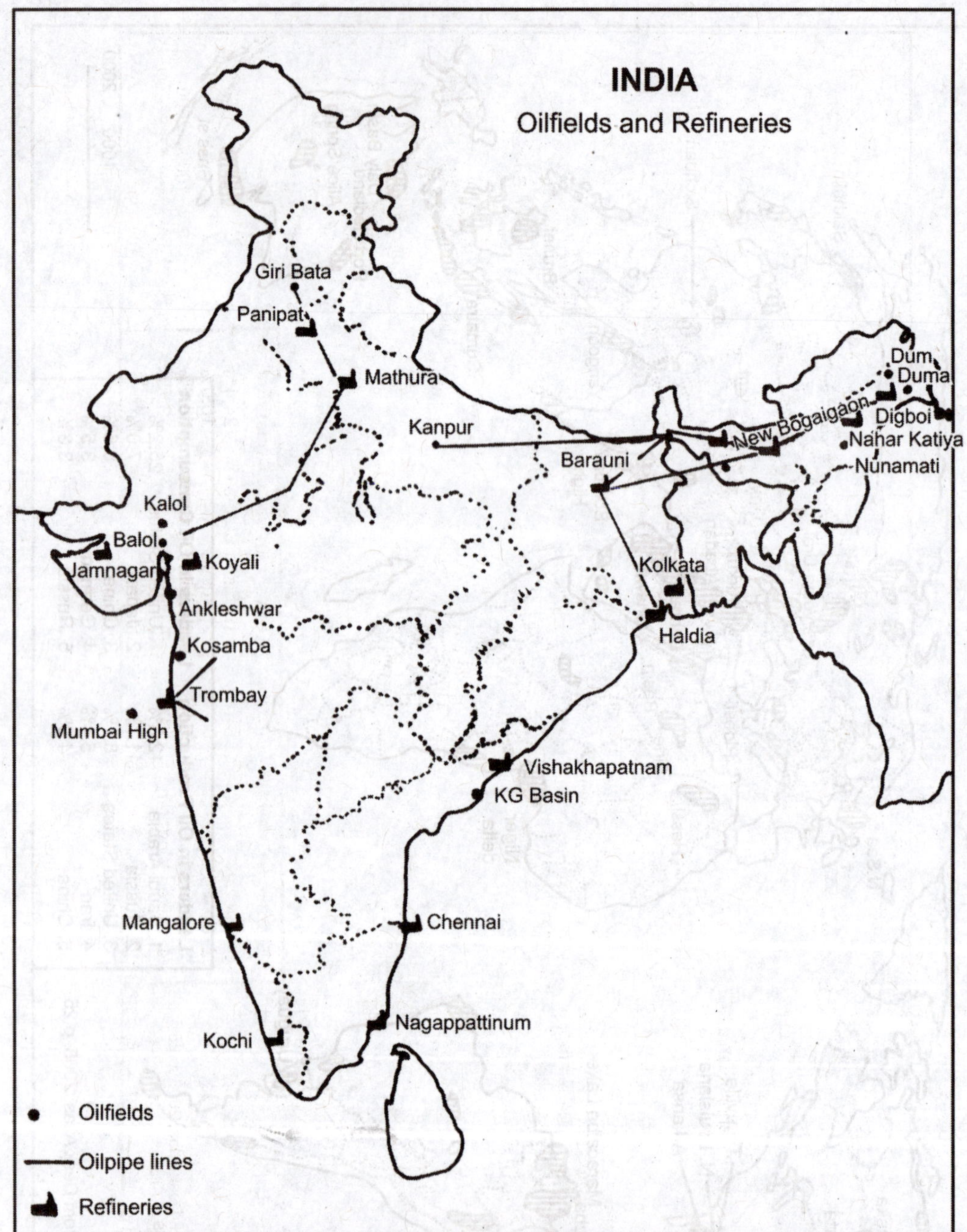

Fig. 9.4 Oilfields, oil pipe lines and Refineries of India

Vietnam are the other important natural gas producing countries of the world. The leading consumers of natural gas are U.S.A. (24.4%), Russia (16.0%), U.K. (3.6 %), Germany (3.5 %), and Canada (3.3%) **Table 9.7**.

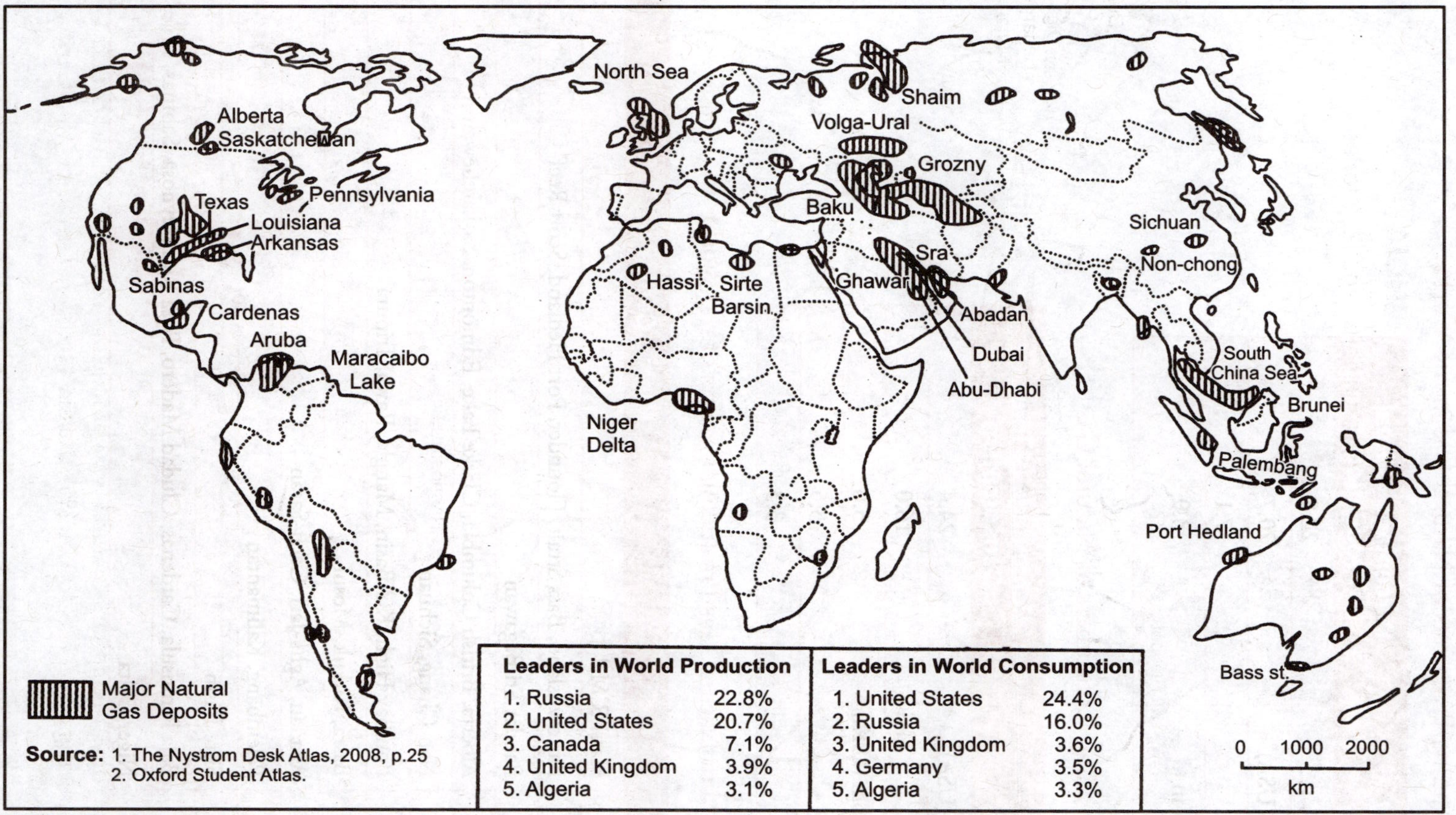

Fig. 9.5 World–Leading producers and consumers of natural gas

Table 9.7 Leading Producers of Natural Gas in the World

Country	Percentage of Total Production
1. Russia	22.8
2. United States (USA)	20.7
3. Canada	7.1
4. United Kingdom (U.K.)	3.9

Table 9.8 Leading Consumers of Natural Gas

Country	Percentage of Total Consumption
1. United States (USA)	24.4
2. Russia	16.0
3. United Kingdom (U.K.)	3.6
4. Germany	3.5
5. Canada	3.3

Table 9.9 Major Natural Gas Producing Centres of the World

Country	Mining Centre
1. Algeria	Hassi R'Mel
2. Australia	Barrow Island, Bass Strait, Flounder, Port Hedland, Scott Reef
3. Brunei	Bandar Sri Begawan
4. Canada	Alberta, British Columbia, Clarke Lake, Edmonton, Saskatchewan
5. China	Nan-Chang, Sichuan
6. India	Bombay High, KG Basin, Mangla, Rawa, Tripura
7. Iraq	Basra, Kirkuk, Mosul
8. Iran	Abadan, Agha-Jari, Gach-Saran
9. Indonesia	Palembang, Kalimantan
10. Libya	Sirte Basin
11. Mexico	Baja Peninsula, Cardenas, Cludad Madero, Poza Rica Reynosa, Sabinas
12. Nigeria	Niger Delta

(*Contd.*)

Table 9.9 *(Contd.)*

Country	Mining Centre
13. Netherlands	North Sea, Rhine Delta
14. Romania	Danube Delta
15. Russia	Grozny, Volga-Ural region, Shaim, Sakhalin
16. Saudi Arabia	Burgan, Dahran, Dammam, Ghawar, Jubail
17. U.K.	North Sea
18. U.S.A.	Albama, Arkansas, California, Colorado, Houston, Indiana, Kansas, Louisiana, Montana, Ohio, Prudhoe Bay (Alaska)
19. Venezuela	Aruba, Maracaibo Basin

HYDROPOWER

Running water from rivers has long been utilised by man as a source of power for the grinding of flour. The development of hydro-turbine, dynamo and cement helped in the tremendous development of hydroelectricity. Its generation requires (i) large volume of water, (ii)regular and reliable supply of water, (iii) presence of a gorge for the construction of dams, (iv) space for reservoir in the mountains, (v) large market, and (vi) adequate funds for the structure of dams. Looking at the given factors, it is clear that certain parts of the world are better suited by relief, and climate for the generation of hydroelectricity. The hydroelectric power generation is largely confined to the following regions:

1. Mountainous Regions

The glaciated mountainous regions which have waterfalls, steep-sided valleys and lakes are more suitable for the development of hydroelectricity.

2. Climate

Tropical and temperate regions with moderate to heavy rainfall favour the development of hydro-power.

3. Regions with Large Demand of Electricity

Regions with minerals and industrial development have more demand for electricity. Thus, large market is a factor which leads to the development of hydroelectricity.

The hydro-electricity potential is not uniformally distributed around the world. Some of the countries like Switzerland, USA, Sweden, Norway, Finland, Russia, U.K., China, India, Brazil, Congo Republic, Egypt, Indonesia, Malaysia, Japan. New Zealand, etc. have more potential for hydro-electricity development. In many of the countries like South America, hydroelectricity potential has not been adequately developed because there is less demand for electricity. In general, the development of hydroelectricity is more in the developed countries as compared to the developing countries.

India has developed hydroelectric power. The uneven distribution of rainfall in the Indian subcontinent, with long droughts and frequent floods make dam construction an essential feature of water management for flood control, water storage and irrigation. In India hydroelectricity accounts for about 23 per cent of total electricity.

In India, a number of multi-purpose projects aim at water storage, flood control, irrigation, hydro-electric generation, checking soil erosion, development of inland navigation of waterlogged areas, development of fisheries and tourism. Some of the important multi-purpose projects of India are given in **Table 9.11**.

Table 9.11 India-Major Hydroelectricity and Irrigation Projects

Project	Location	Beneficiary States
1. Banasagar Project	Son River	Madhya Pradesh, Uttar Pradesh, Bihar
2. Bhakra Nangal Dam	Satluj River	Punjab, Haryana, Himachal Pradesh, Rajasthan
3. Beas Project (Pong Dam)	Beas River	Punjab, Haryana and Rajasthan
4. Bhima Project	Bhima River	Maharashtra
5. Chambal Project	Chambal River	Madhya Pradesh and Rajasthan
6. Damodar Valley Project	Seven dams on Damodar and its tributaries	Jharkhand, and West Bengal
7. Dul-Hasti	Chenab River	Jammu & Kashmir
8. Gandak	Gandak River	Bihar and Uttar Pradesh
9. Ghataprabha Project	Ghataprabha	Karnataka
10. Hirakud	Mahanadi	Odisha
11. Jayakwadi	Godavari River	Maharashtra
12. Kakrapara Project	Tapi River	Gujarat
13. Kangasabati	Bankura District on Kangasabati and Kumari River	West Bengal
14. Kosi	Kosi River	Bihar
15. Mahi Project	Mahi River	Gujarat

(Contd.)

Table 9.11 *(Contd.)*

Project	Location	Beneficiary States
16. Malprabha	Malprabha	Karnataka
17. Nagarjunasagar	Krishna River	(Seemandhra and Telangana)
18. Narmada Project (Indira Sagar Dam)	Narmada River	Gujarat, Madhya Pradesh, Maharashtra and Rajasthan
19. Parmbikulam	Annamalai Hills	Tamil Nadu and Kerala
20. Pochampad	Godavari	Telangana
21. Rajghat Dam	Betwa	Madhya Pradesh and Uttar Pradesh
22. Ramganga Project	Chusit Stream	Uttar Pradesh
23. Salal Project	Chenab River	Jammu & Kashmir
24. Sardar Sarovar	Narmada in Gujarat	Gujarat, Madhya Pradesh, Maharashtra and Rajasthan
25. Tawa	Tawa River(a tributary of Narmada River)	Madhya Pradesh
26. Tehri Dam	Bhagirathi River	Uttarakhand
27. Thein Dam	Ravi River	Punjab
28. Tungbhadra Project	Tungbhadra River(a tributary of Krishna River)	Telangana and Karnataka
29. Ukai Project	Tapi River	Gujarat
30. Upper Krishna Project	Krishna	Karnataka

THERMAL ELECTRICITY

Thermal electricity is produced with the help of coal, petroleum and natural gas. About 65 per cent of the total electricity produced in India is thermal in character (Table 9.12).

Advantages of Thermal Power

The main advantages of thermal energy are as under:

1. Thermal energy can be generated in the areas not suitable for the generation of hydro-electricity.
2. Coal, diesel and natural gas can be transported to the areas of isolation and relative isolation.
3. It can be generated when weather conditions are adverse.
4. The gestation period of thermal power plant is short.

However, thermal energy is not eco-friendly, as it emits enormous quantity of carbon-dioxide. Moreover, it is based on valuable exhaustible resources.The major thermal power plants in India is given in Table 9.12.

Table 9.12 India–Major Thermal Power Plants

State	Thermal Power Plants
1. Andhra Pradesh	Bhadrachalam, Kothagudam, Manuguru, Nellore, Ramagundam, Vijayawada
2. Assam	Bongaigaon, Chandrapur, Namrup
3. Bihar	Barauni, Kahalgaon
4. Chhattisgarh	Korba
5. Delhi	Badarpur, Indraprastha, Rajghat,
6. Gujarat	Ahmadabad, Banas, Dhuvaram, Gandhinagar, Kachchh, Kandla, Mahuva, Porbandar, Sabarmati, Shahpur, Sikka, Ukai, Utaran, Wankbori
7. Haryana	Faridabad, Panipat, Yamuna-Nagar
8. Jammu & Kashmir	Kalakot
9. Jharkhand	Bokaro, Chandrapur, Subarnrekha
10. Maharashtra	Ballarshah, Bhusawal, Chandrapur, Chola, Dhabol, Khapar-Kheda, Koradi, Nasik, Paras, Parli, Trombay, Uran
11. Manipur	Loktak
12. Odisha	Balimela, Talcher
13. Punjab	Bhatinda, Rupnagar
14. Tamil Nadu	Ennore, Mettur, Neyveli, Tuticorin
15. Uttar Pradesh	Bahraich, Dorighat, Gorakhpur, Harduaganj, Jawaharpur, Kanpur, Mau, Moradabad, Obra, Panki, Parichha, Tundla
16. West Bengal	Birbhum, Bundel, Durgapur, Farakka, Gauripur, Kalaghat, Kolkata, Murshidabad, Titagarh, Santaldih

NUCLEAR ENERGY

Nuclear energy is a form of energy which uses nuclear reactions to produce steam to turn generators. Looking at the exhaustible nature of fossil fuels, nuclear energy development has become very vital for economic development. The first nuclear power station was built in Britain in 1956 at Calder Hall. At present, there are more than 400 nuclear power plants in the world. Most of them are in U.S.A., France, U.K. Germany, Russia, Japan, China, Sweden, Belgium, Switzerland, Italy, Australia and India.

Nuclear Power in India

Nuclear power is the fifth largest source of electricity in India after thermal, hydroelectric and renewable sources of electricity.

India has 22 nuclear reactors in operation at seven sites, having an installed capacity of 6780 MW and producing a total of 30,292.91 GWh of electricity. 11 more reactors are under construction to generate an additional 8,100 MW.

Nuclear Power Corporation of India Limited (NPCIL) is a government-owned corporation of India based in Mumbai which is responsible for the generation of nuclear power for electricity. NPCIL is administered by the Department of Atomic Energy, Govt. of India.

The Union Cabinet last year cleared the proposal of building of 10 new nuclear power plants to add 7000MW to India's nuclear power generation capacity. These will be the indigenous 700 MW

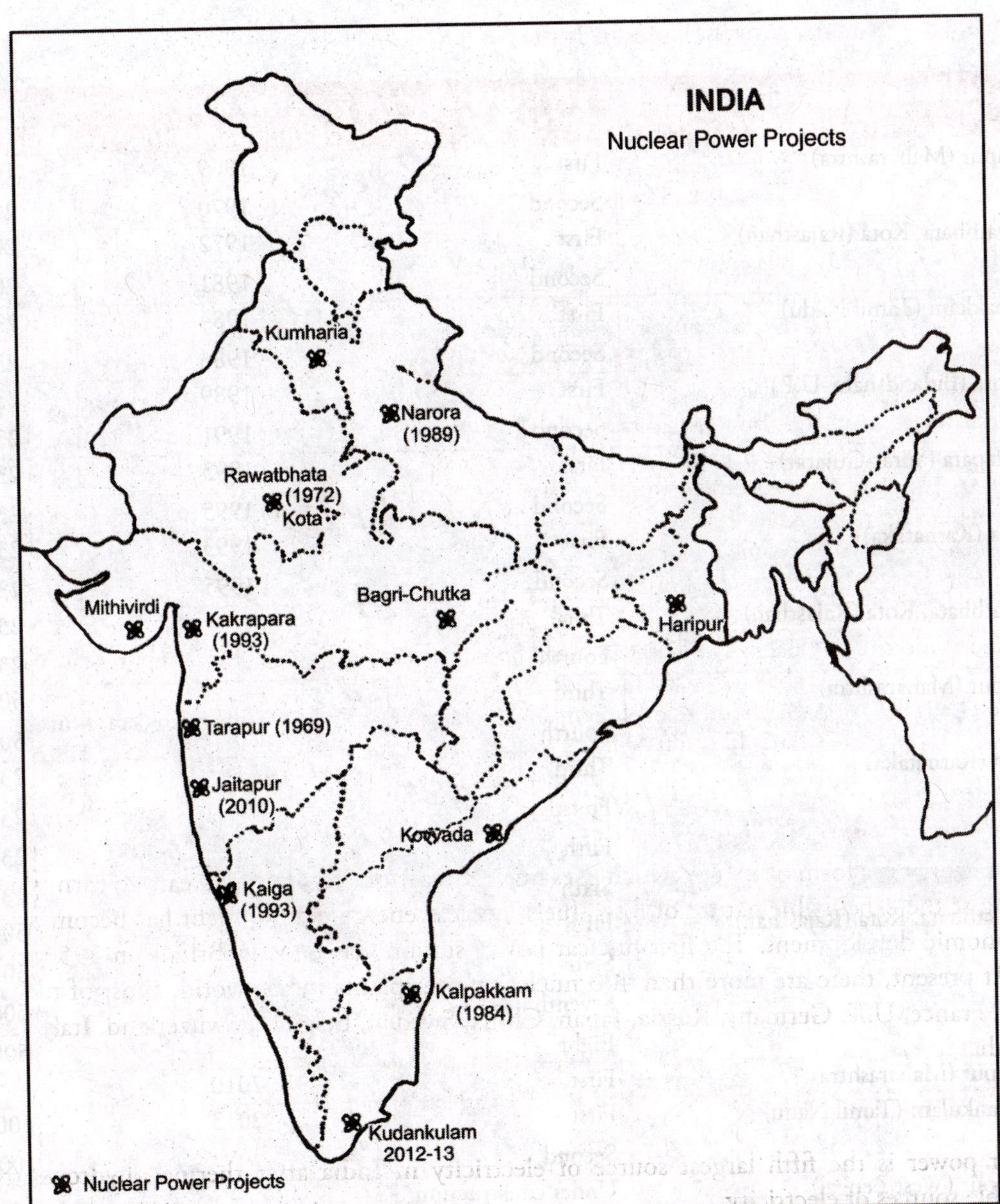

Fig. 9.6 India–Nuclear Power Projects

pressurised heavy water reactors. India and Russia signed a pact for setting up the last two units of the Kudankulam nuclear power plant with Moscow's help in Tamil Nadu.

Nuclear energy originates from the splitting of uranium atoms – a process called fission. This generates heat to produce steam, which is used by a turbine generator to generate electricity. Because nuclear power plants do not burn fuel, they do not produce greenhouse gas emissions. With no carbon emissions, it will remain an important clean energy resource for the future.

Table 9.13 Nuclear Power Plants in India

Nuclear Power Station	Unit	Year of Commissioning	Capacity
1.Tarapur (Maharashtra)	First Second	1969 1970	160 200
2.Rawatbhata, Kota (Rajasthan)	First Second	1972 1981	200 200
3.Kalpakkam (Tamil Nadu)	First Second	1984 1986	235 235
4.Narora (Bulandshahr-U.P.)	First Second	1989 1991	235 235
5.Kakrapara (Surat-Gujarat)	First Second	1993 1995	235 235
6.Kaiga (Karnataka)	First Second	1993 1995	235 235
7.Rawatbhata, Kota (Rajasthan)	Third Fourth	-	235 235
8.Tarapur (Maharashtra)	Third Fourth	-	500 500
9.Kaiga (Karnataka)	Third Fourth Fifth Sixth	-	235 235 235 235
10.Rawatbhata, Kota (Rajasthan)	Fifth Sixth Seventh Eight	-	500 500 500 500
11.Jaitapur (Maharashtra)	First	2010	-
12.Kudankulam (Tamil Nadu)	First Second	2013	1000 1000
13.Haripur (West Bengal)	Under construction	-	-
14.Bagri-Chutka (Madhya Pradesh)	‘	-	-
15.Kovvada (Andhra Pradesh)	“	-	-
16. Mithivirdi (Bhavnagar-Gujarat)	“	-	-
17. Kumharia (Haryana)	“	-	-

The Atomic Energy Institution at Trombay was established in 1954. This was renamed as the ‘Bhabha Atomic Research Centre (BARC)’ in 1967. The first nuclear power station with a capacity of 160 MW was set up at Tarapur near Mumbai in 1969. Subsequently, the Rawatbhata Atomic Plant (200 MW) near Kota was set up in 1972, which was followed by the establishment of Narora (1989), Kaiga (Karnataka), and Kakrapara in Gujarat in 1993, Jaitapur (Maharashtra) in 2010, Kudankulam

(Tamil Nadu) in 2013. The new sites of nuclear power plants include Bagri or Chutka (M.P.), Haripur (W. Bengal), Kawada (Seemandhra), Kumharia (Haryana) and Mithi Verdi near Bhavnagar Gujarat (**Fig.9.6**).

Nuclear energy, like other sources of energy, also cause environmental deterioration. The main disadvantage in this respect is that nuclear reactors produce radio-active wastes. According to environmentalists, the nuclear energy generation lead to more pollution. Nuclear plants are also opposed on moral grounds because of their close linkage with the development of nuclear weapons. In most of the developing and developed countries, the building of nuclear plants is opposed and obstructed by protest groups. About 25 per cent of the Europeans and 30 per cent of Japanese believe that nuclear plants are too dangerous to society and ecology.

Development of nuclear energy is imperative for the economic development of the country. But the disasters like Fukushima (Japan-2011) and Chernobyl (U.S.S.R.1986) have proved that it is full of risk. Thus it is a partial solution of the Indian energy crisis. Unfortunately, in India, in case of nuclear accident, the maximum fine that can be imposed by the regulator on an offending nuclear plant is Rs. 500/. This amount is too low to serve as a deterent against such infringements.

MINERAL RESOURCES

Minerals play a very vital role in the socio-economic development of a country. Iron-ore, manganese, copper, bauxite, gold, silver, lead, zinc, uranium and thorium are the mainstay of metal production and heavy industries in the world.

A brief description of some of the important minerals of the world has been given below:

Iron Ore

Iron ore is considered as the backbone of our present civilization. It is used all over the world. Iron ore is the foundation of our basic industries and the standard of living of the people of a country is often judged on the basis of consumption of iron ore.

There are several grades of iron ore based on purity and percentage of mineral content. Hematite, the highest grade ore is reddish in colour, containing up to 65 per cent of metal. The intermediate grade, magnetite is black in colour which has 50 to 60 per cent of metal content. The other categories of iron ore include, siderite, limonite and taconite. These categories have 20 to 40 per cent metallic content and therefore are not economically viable. The taconite, the lowest quality ore, requires crushing, magnetic separation, and heating to convert the ore into pellets that are marketable. The distribution and production of iron-ore are highly uneven. The leading producers and important mining centres of iron-ore have been shown in **Fig. 9.7, Table 9.14 & Table 9.15**.

Table 9.14 Iron Ore (Fe)—Leading Producers in the World

Country	Percentage of Total Production
1. China	32.5
2. Brazil	17.7
3. Australia	15.2
4. India	9.6
5. Russia	5.8
6. Ukraine	4.10
7. U.S.A.	2.9
8. South Africa	2.3
9. Canada	1.9
10. Others	8.0

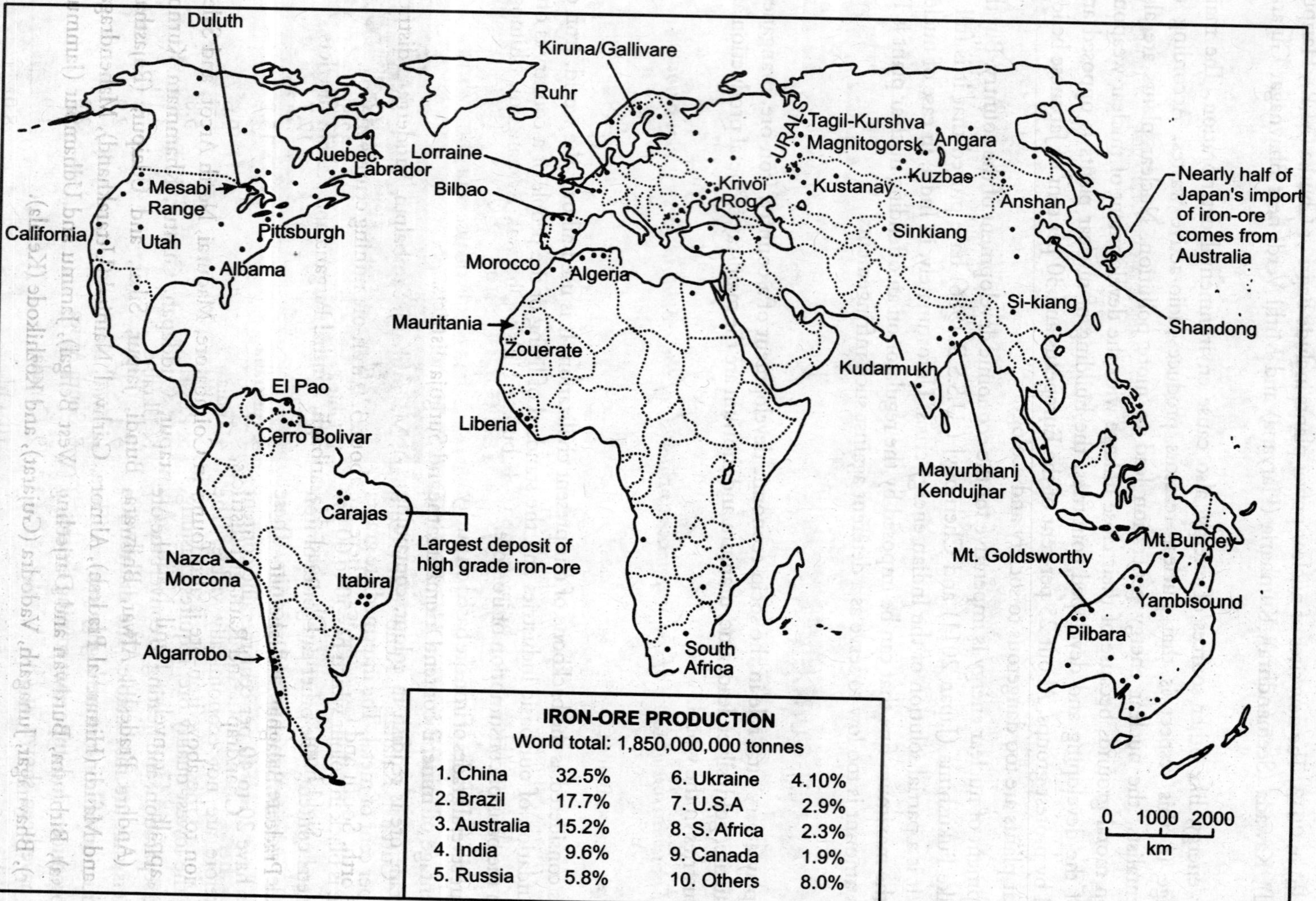

Fig. 9.7 World—major iron ore deposits

Table 9.15 Major Iron-Ore Mining Centres of the World

Country	Mining Centres
Brazil	Itabara
Australia	Mt. Bruce, Mt.Goldsworthy, Mt. Tom Price, Mt. Whaleback
China	Anshan (Manchuria), Chongquing (Chungking), Shandong (Shantung), Sinkiang, Xi-Jiang (Sinkiang), Guangzhou (Canton)
India	Badampahar, Bellary, Chikmagalur, Dalli-Rajhara, Durg, Goa, Kudermukh, Mayurbhanj
Russia	Magnitogorsk (Urals), Kuzbas, Angara (Siberia)
USA	Mesabi Range, Vermilion, Marquette Range (Lake Superior), Adirondacks (New York), Cornwall (Pennysalvania), Albama, Birmingham (Appalachian), California, Utah, Wyoming, Labrador, Eastern Quebec
Canada	
France	Lorraine, Normandy, Central Massif
Germany	Rhur Basin
Liberia	Bomi Hill, Mt. Nimba
Sweden	Kiruna, Callivare
Ukraine	Krivoi Rog
Mauritania	Zouerate
Chile	Algarrobo in Central Chile
Venezuela	Cerro Bolivar (Guiana Highlands)

In India, iron-ore is found in the following areas.

Karnataka: Bellary (Hospet), Chikmagalur (Bababudan Hills), Dharwar, Kamangudi, Shimoga, and Tumkur districts.

Chhattisgarh: Bastar, Bilaspur, Durg, Raigarh, and Surguja districts.

Odisha: Cuttack, Kalahandi, Kendujhar (Keonjhar), Mayurbhanj, Sambalpur, Sundergarh districts.

Goa: North, South and Central Goa. There are about 320 iron-ore mining centres in Goa.

Jharkhand: Sighbhum, Palamu, Dhanbad, Hazaribagh, Santhal Pargana and Ranchi districts.

Madhya Pradesh: Balaghat and Jabalpur.

Maharashtra: Chandrapur and Ratnagiri districts.

In addition to the above iron-ore is also found in Coimbatore, Madurai, North Arcot, and Salem, Tiruchirappalli, Tirunveli, (Tamil Nadu), Anantapur, Cuddapah, Guntur, Khammam Kurnool, Nellore, (Andhra Pradesh), Alwar, Bhilwara, Bundi, Jaipur, Sikar, and Udaipur, (Rajasthan), Kangra and Mandi (Himachal Pradesh), Almora, Garhwal, Nainital (Uttarakhand), Mahendragarh (Haryana), Birbhum, Burdwan and Darjeeling (West Bengal), Jammu and Udhampur (Jammu & Kashmir), Bhavnagar, Junagarh, Vadodra (Gujarat), and Kozhikode (Kerala).

Manganese

Manganese is found as a free element or in combination with iron-ore or mixed with some other minerals. Manganese constitute about 0.1 % of the Earth's crust. It is mainly used in the manufacturing of non-corrosive steel and ferro-manganese alloy. Nearly 10 kilograms of manganese is required for manufacturing one tone of steel. Thus, it is an important metal alloy, particularly in stainless steel. It is also used for the manufacturing of bleaching power, insecticides, paints, batteries and china-clay.

Table 9.16 Major Manganese Producing Countries

Country	Percentage of Total Production
1. South Africa	30
2. Australia	25
3. China	18
4. Brazil	10
5. Gabon	06
6. Ukraine	05
7. India	04
8. Others	02

Nearly 30% of the total manganese is produced in South Africa followed by Australia (25%), China (18%), Brazil (10%), Gabon (6%), Ukraine (5%) and India (4%) (Fig. 9.8).

The major manganese producing countries and manganese deposits in the world are given in Table 9.16 and Table 9.17

India is one of the leading producers of manganese in the world contributing about 4 per cent of the world production. The main reserves are found in Karnataka, followed by Odisha, Madhya Pradesh, Maharashtra and Goa. Minor manganese deposits are also found in Andhra Pradesh, Jharkhand, Gujarat, Rajasthan and West Bengal.

The main mining districts in Odisha are Sundergarh, Kendujhar, Kalahandi and Koraput.

Maharashtra : Nagpur and Bhandara districts,

Madhya Pradesh : Balaghat and Chindwara districts,

Karnataka : North Kanara, Shimoga, Bellary, Chitradurga, Dharwar, Chikmagalur and Bijapur districts,

Andhra Pradesh : Srikakulam, Visakhapatnam, Cuddapah and Guntur districts.

Table 9.17 World-Manganese Deposits

Country	Major Manganese Deposits Centres
Australia	Kimberley Plateau
Brazil	Amapa
Chile	Central Chile
China	Hunan, Guiz Hou
India	Balaghat, Sighbhum, Goa, Visakhapatnam
Japan	Honshu Island
Morocco	Bou-Azzer, Imini
Pakistan	Quetta
Philippines	Zambales
Russia	Outokumpu, Ural Mt.
South Africa	Postmasburg, Krugersdorp, Rustemburg
Spain	Betican Cordilleras
Turkey	Plateau of Anatolia
Ukraine	Chiatura, Nikopol
U.S.A.	Guyuna, Nye Butte, Kelloga Butte
Venezuela	Nadola
Zambia	Katanga, Nadola

Copper

The use of copper was started first by the Turks during the pre-historic period. Copper is a malleable and ductile metal. It is used for making electric wires, cooking utensils, coins and military products. The ratio of weight loss in copper refinery is extremely small, scarcely one per cent of the weight

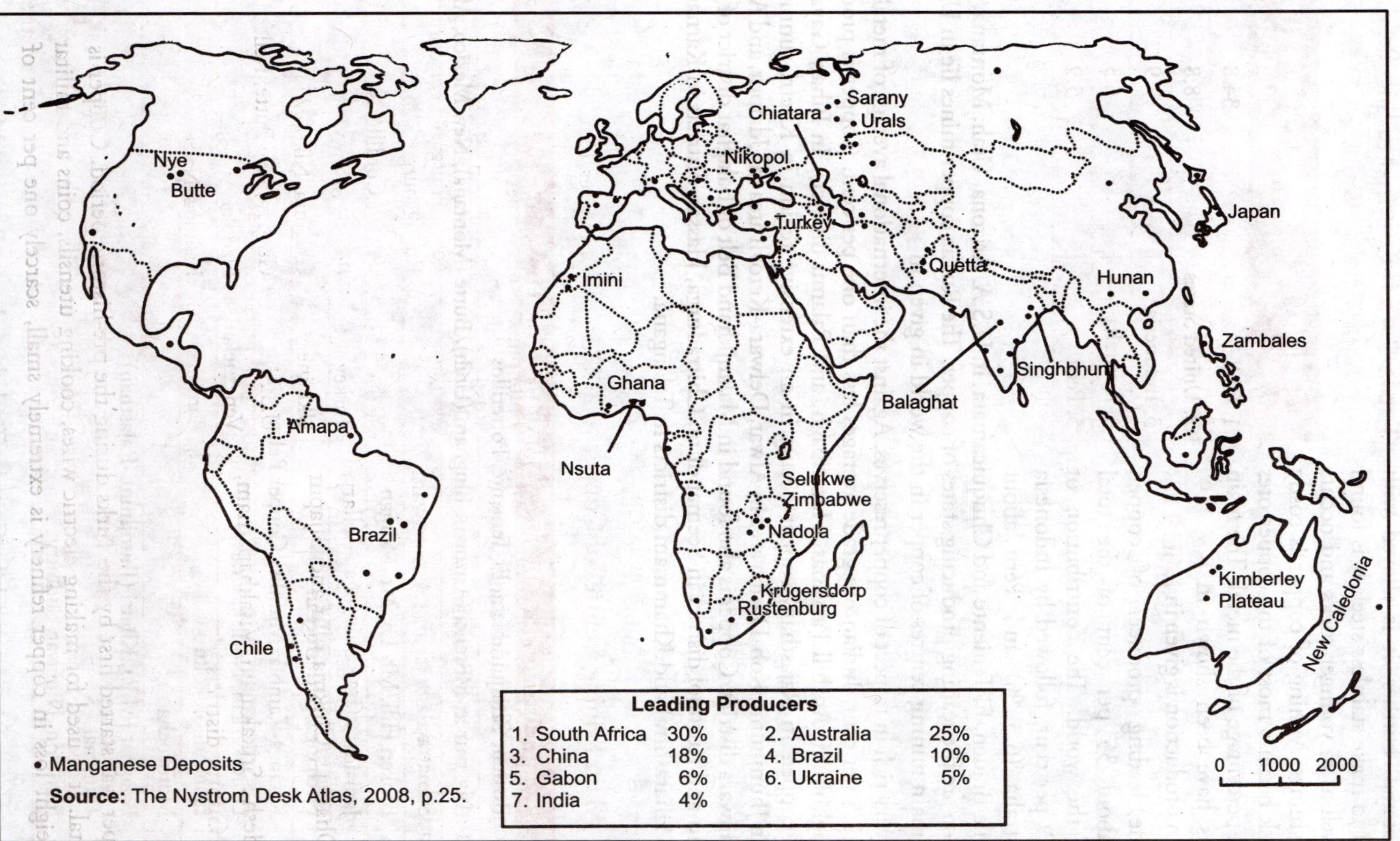

Source: The Nystrom Desk Atlas, 2008, p.25.

Fig. 9.8 World–Manganese deposits

of the raw material. Further, it is alloyed with iron and nickel to make stainless steel. It is found in ancient as well as in younger rocks and occurs in the form of mines. Mining of copper is costly and difficult task because most of the copper ores contain a small percentage of the metal. The main copper deposits have been shown in Fig. 9.9, while the rank in production is given in Table 9.18.

Chile is the leading producer of copper, contributing about 35 per cent of the total production of the world. The contribution of USA is about 9 per cent, followed by Indonesia (7.9 %), Australia (6.3 %) and Peru about (5.9 %). In Chile Braden, El Teniente and Chuquicamata, in U.S.A. Arizona, Utah, Montana, Nevada, and New Mexico are the leading producing states of copper. The Russia copper mines lie in Urals, and Balkhash. The main mining centres of copper in the world in given in Table 9.19.

Table 9.18 Copper-Leading Producers in the World

Country	Percentage of Total Production
1. Chile	34.8
2. United States	8.8
3. Indonesia	7.9
4. Australia	6.3
5. Peru	5.9

India is not very rich in respect of copper reserves. Against the international average of metal content (in the ore) of 2.5 per cent, Indian ore grade averages less than one per cent. Copper is produced in Jharkhand (Singhbhum, Anthill Parganas, Hazaribagh, and Palamu district). In Bihar, Gaya district is producer of copper. In Rajasthan, copper occurs in an extensive region in Khetri running from Singhana Belt in Jhunjhunu, Koh-Dariba area in Alwar, Delwara-Kerovli area in Udaipur, and Aguncha-Rampura in Bhilwara district. Copper is also found in Malanjkhand Belt of Balaghat district of Madhya Pradesh, Guntur and Kurnool district in Seemandhra, Chitradurga, Hassan districts in Karnataka and Chandrapur (Maharashtra) and Khammam districts in Telangana.

Table 9.19 Main Mining Centres of Copper

Country	Mining Centres
Chile	Braden, Chuquicamata, El-Teniente, Potrerillos
USA	Ajo, Bisbee, Morenci (Arizona), Bingham (Utah), Butte (Montana), New Mexico, Alaska
Indonesia	Sumatra
Australia	Broken Hill, Mt. Isa, Mt. Morgan
Jamaica	Jamaica
Zambia	Nechanga, Mt. Morgan
Zaire	Katanga-Zambia, Mufulira Copper Belt
Russia	Dzhezkazgan, Norilsk, Urals
Japan	Honshu, Shikoku
Peru	Morococha
India	Balaghat (M.P.), Khetri (Jhunjhunu-Rajasthan)
South Africa	Transvaal
Canada	Flin Flon, Nunavat, Sudbury

India imports copper from USA, Chile, Canada, Zimbabwe, Japan, Peru and Mexico.

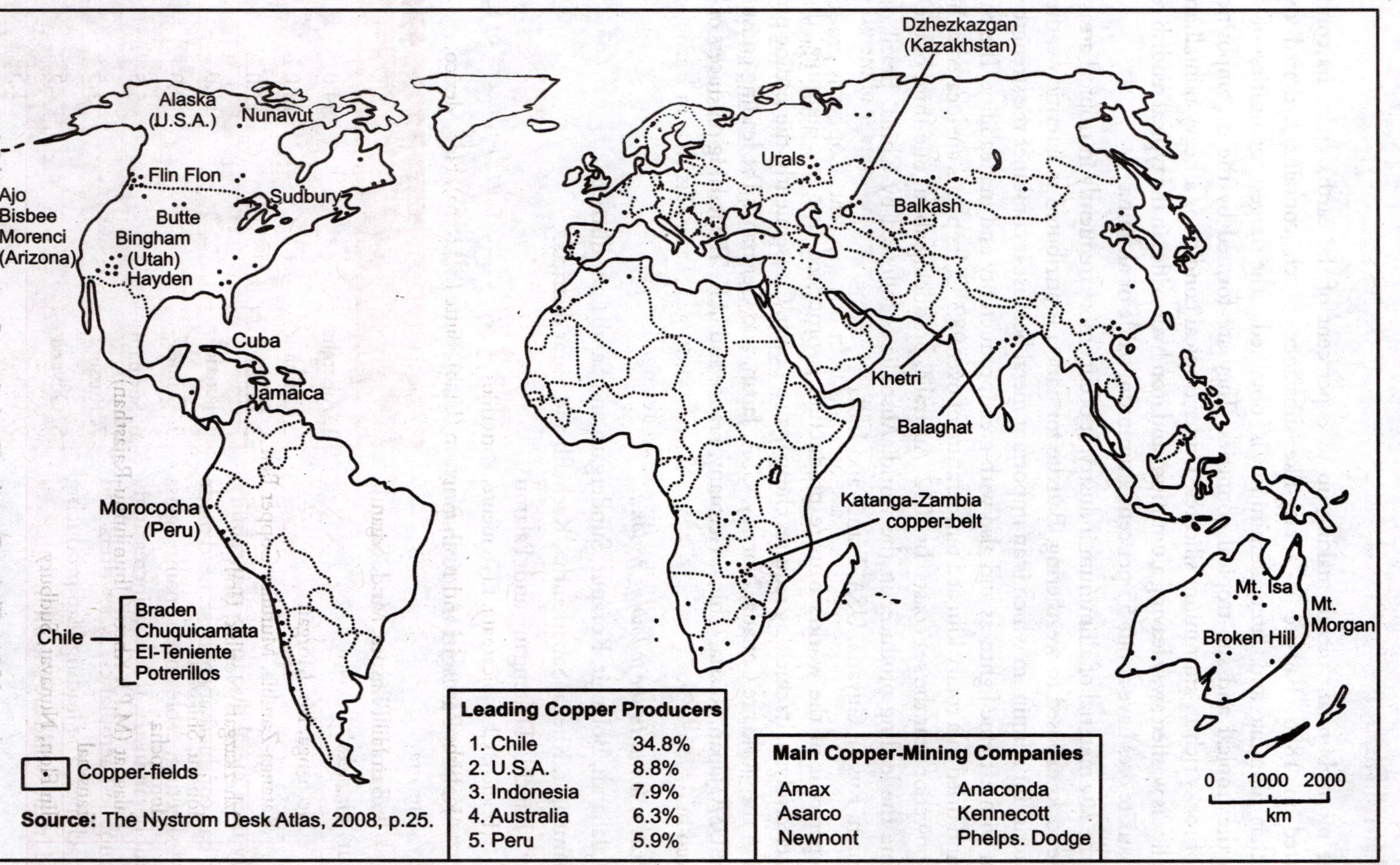

Fig. 9.9 World–Copper deposits

Bauxite (Aluminium)

Bauxite is the most abundant metal, making up to 8 per cent of the earth's crust. Its commercial use was started in 1886. Bauxite is a clay-like substance which contains hydrated oxide of aluminium, that alumina and later aluminium is obtained. The largest quantities of bauxite are found in the tropical and sub-tropical countries. They are formed by the decomposition of a wide variety of rocks rich in aluminium silicates. Under tropical conditions a heavy rainfall and deep weathering, silica is washed away leaving aluminium and iron hydroxides in the typical reddish regolith. The average bauxite ores have about 55 per cent aluminium oxide or alumina.

Bauxite is the raw material of aluminum industry. It occurs more frequently in tropical areas having clay-limestone rocks exposed to weathering. Bauxite formation is attributed to lateritic weathering. It is the raw material for aluminum which is an important metal because it combines the strength of such metals as iron with extreme lightness and also with great productivity and malleability. The bauxite is first crushed and dried in a rotary kiln at a temperature of over 982°C. Its plants are located either close of the hydro-power or near the sea coasts. In 2012, Australia, producing about one-third of the world's bauxite became the leading producer in the world. Australia is followed by China, Brazil, Jamaica, Guinea, Surinam, Russia, Guyana, USA, France and India.

About 95 per cent of the world's bauxite production is processed first into alumina, then into aluminum by electrolysis. Its smelting requires cheap hydro-power. Consequently, the leading producers of aluminum in the world are Canada, Norway, USA, Japan, and Germany. The leading consumers of aluminum are USA, Japan, Russia, China, Germany, France and U.K. The leading producers of bauxite have been given in Table 9.20.

In India, bauxite is found in the following regions:

Odisha: Kalahandi, Bolangir, Koraput, Sundergarh and Sambalpur districts.

Gujarat: Jamnagar, Kheda, Sabarkantha, Kachchh and Surat districts.

Jharkhand: Ranchi, Daltenganj and Palamu districts.

Maharashtra: Kolaba, Ratnagiri and Kolhapur districts.

Chhattisgarh: Bastar, Bilaspur, and Sarguja (Ambikapur) districts.

Table 9.20 Leading Producers of Bauxite in the World

Country	Percentage of Total Production
1. Australia	34.0
2. China	14.0
3. Brazil	12.0
4. Jamaica	11.0
5. Guinea	10.0
6. Surinam	5.5
7. Russia	3.5
8. Guyana	2.5
9. U.S.A.	1.5
10. France	0.5

Lead

Lead is widely used metal due to its malleability, heaviness and bad conductivity of heat. Lead oxide is used in lead sheeting, cable covers, paints, glass making and rubber industry. It is now increasingly used in automobiles, aeroplanes, typewriters and calculating machines. The leading lead producing centres of lead in the world are shown in Fig. 9.10 (Table 9.21).

In India, lead is found in the following areas: Andhra Pradesh: (Kurnool, Guntur districts), Telengana (Nalgonda and Khammam), Tamil Nadu (North Arcot Ambedkar, and South Arcot districts), Uttarakhand (Tehri, Garhwal and Pithoragarh districts), Jharkhand (Hazaribagh, Singhbhum, Ranchi and Palamu), Jammu and Kashmir (Baramulla and Udhampur), Madhya Pradesh (Hoshangabad, Shivpuri, and Gwalior), Chhattisgarh (Bilaspur, Ambikapur and Durg), West Bengal (Jalpaiguri and Darjeeling).

Table 9.21 Leading Lead Producing Countries of the world

Country	Percentage of Total Production
1. United States of America	18.0
2. Russia	17.0
3. Australia	12.0
4. Canada	10.0
5. Niger	5.0

Gold

Gold is a valuable metal which occurs in auriferous lodes and some of it is found in sands of several rivers. It is used for making ornaments and is known as international currency due to its universal use. The world distribution of gold has been shown in Fig. 9.11. India has limited deposits of gold. Gold in India occurs both in the native form as lodes and as alluvial gold in the sands of several rivers.

Karnataka is the leading producer of gold in India. There are three main gold fields in the country, namely, (i) Kolar Gold Field in Kolar District (Karnataka), (ii) Hutti Gold Field in Raichur District (Karnataka), and (iii) Ramgiri Gold Field in Anantapur District of Seemandhra. Small quantity of gold is also found from the sand of Subarnrekha River. Small quantities of gold are collected from rivers in Shimla and Bilaspur in Himachal Pradesh, Kargil area along the terraces of the Indus River and in alluvial and morainic deposits of Dras river in Jammu and Kashmir, Balaghat, and Seoni District of Madhya Pradesh, Bastar, Raipur and Raigarh in Chhattisgarh and parts of Purulia District of West Bengal.

Silver

Silver is a lustrous white metal, second only to gold as a precious metal through its value is very much less. Its beauty and resistance to corrosion make it desirable for fashioning into jewellery and other ornamental articles, but unlike gold, it tarnishes when it comes into contact with sulphur or sulphurous fumes, traces of which are always found in the air. It is however, very resistant to acetic acid attack and is widely used in making vats for vinegar, beer and industrial acids.

Only one-fifth of the world's silver is mined as argentite (silver ore) or as native silver. Silver was once widely used in making coins. The sterling silver, coins used in Britain before 1921, were made up of 50% silver with 40% copper for hardening purposes plus some nickel or zinc. Silver is ductile and malleable and, unlike gold, has fairly wide range of industrial applications. Silver is used in electro-plating, soldering and alloying, silver-ware silver-lined steel tanks and beer vats. Its thermal and electrical conductivity makes it a possible substitute for silver.

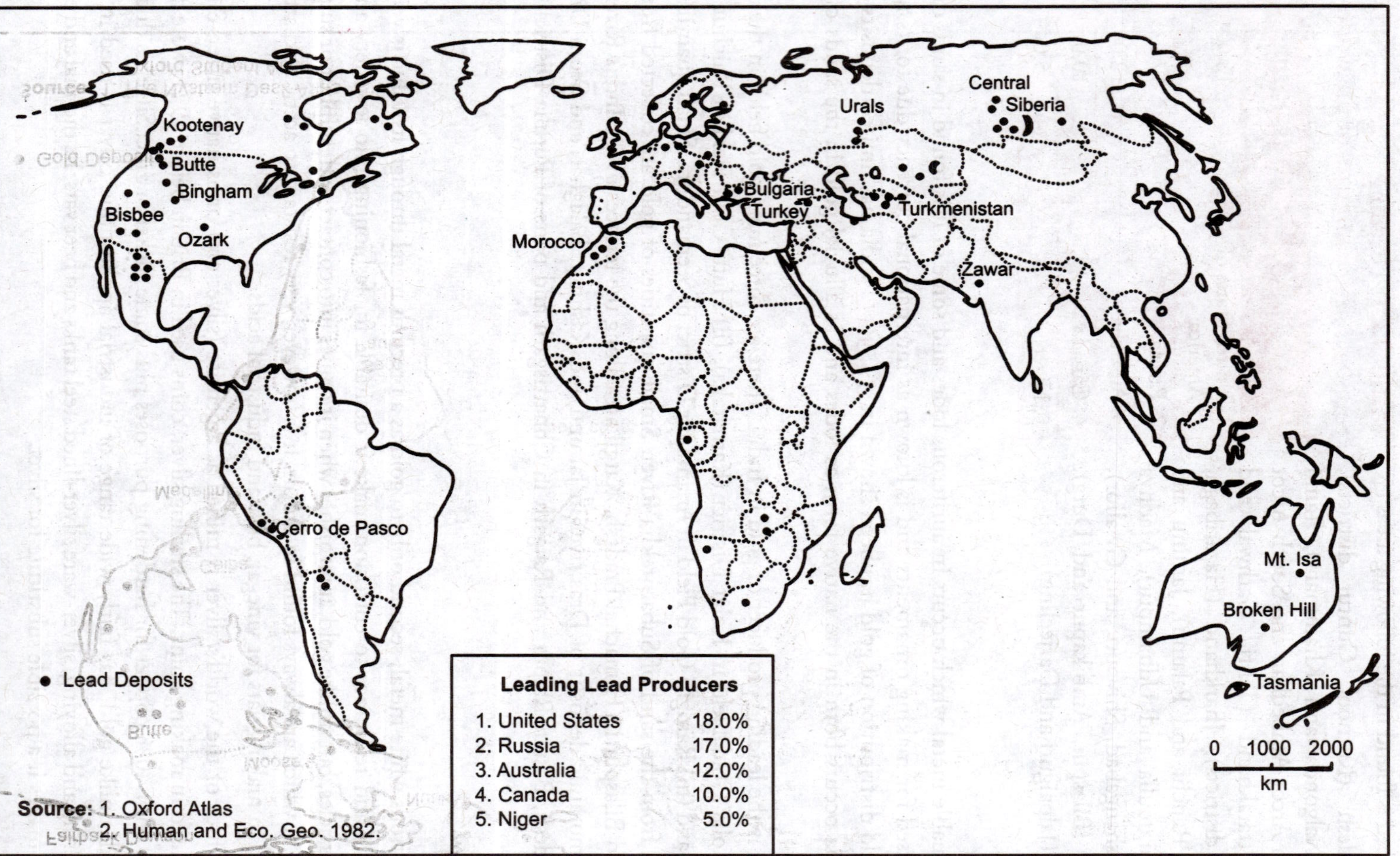

Fig. 9.10 World–Lead deposits

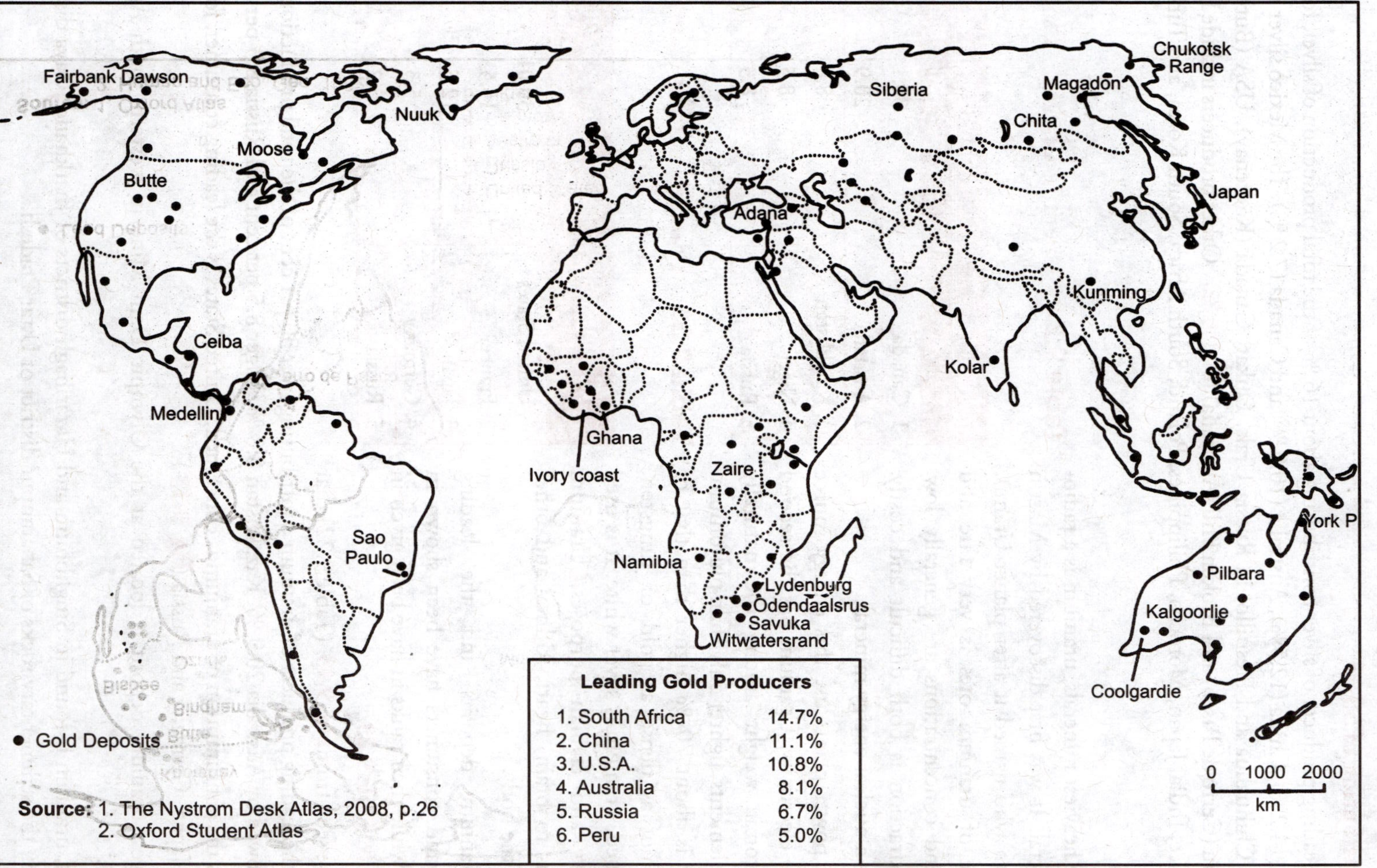

Fig. 9.11 World–Gold deposits

World Distribution of Silver

Peru is the leading producer of silver contributing about 16 % of the total production of silver, followed by Mexico (14.2%), China (12.5%), Australia (10.9 %) and Canada (7.2 %). The Mexico silver mining centres are Chihuahua and Fresnillo, in Russia Urals, Dukat, Canada (Kootenay), USA (Buttee and Tintic), Peru (Cerro de Pasco) and Broken Hill (Australia) (Fig. 9.12). Other producers include Bolivia, Chile, France, India, Japan, Morocco, Philippines, Poland, South Africa, South Korea, and Turkey.

Uranium

One of the heaviest minerals, uranium is a radio-active mineral. It was first discovered by Martin H. Klaproth who named it after planet Uranus. Occurrence of uranium ores is very rare and localized and concentrations are generally low, so their extraction is both difficult and costly. Uranium is a nuclear energy mineral.

Nuclear power plants use this energy source to generate electricity. Uranium has the second heaviest atomic weight among the naturally occurring elements, lighter only than plutonium. Its density is about 70 % higher than that of lead, but not as dense as gold or tungsten. When refined, uranium is silver white. It is used for military and civilian purposes. Uranium is injurious to brain, heart, kidney and other systems of the body.

The uranium deposits and the leading producers and consumers have been shown in Fig. 9.13 , while their ranks in have been given in Table 9.22 & Table 9.23 .

Table 9.22 Uranium-Leading Producers in the World

Country	Percentage of Total Production
1. Canada	30.1
2. Australia	20.9
3. Kazakhstan	8.8
4. Niger	8.5
5. Russia	8.3

Table 9.23 Uranium-Leading Consumers in the World

Country	Percentage of Total Consumption
1. United States	30.01
2. France	15.5
3. Japan	12.5
4. Germany	5.3
5. Russia	5.2

It may be seen from Fig. 9.13 (Table 9.22) that Canada is the leading producer of uranium contributing over 30 per cent of the total production of the world, followed by Australia 20.9 %, Kazakhstan 8.8 %, Niger 8.5 per cent and Russia 8.3 per cent.

So far as the consumption of uranium is concerned, United States is the leading consumer, followed by France, Japan, Germany and Russia (Fig. 9.13).

The largest uranium deposit is located at the Olympic Dam Mine in western South Australia (Fig. 9.13).

In India, uranium is found in Singhbhum and Hazaribagh districts of Jharkhand, Gaya district of Bihar and in the sedimentary rocks of Saharanpur district of Uttar Pradesh.

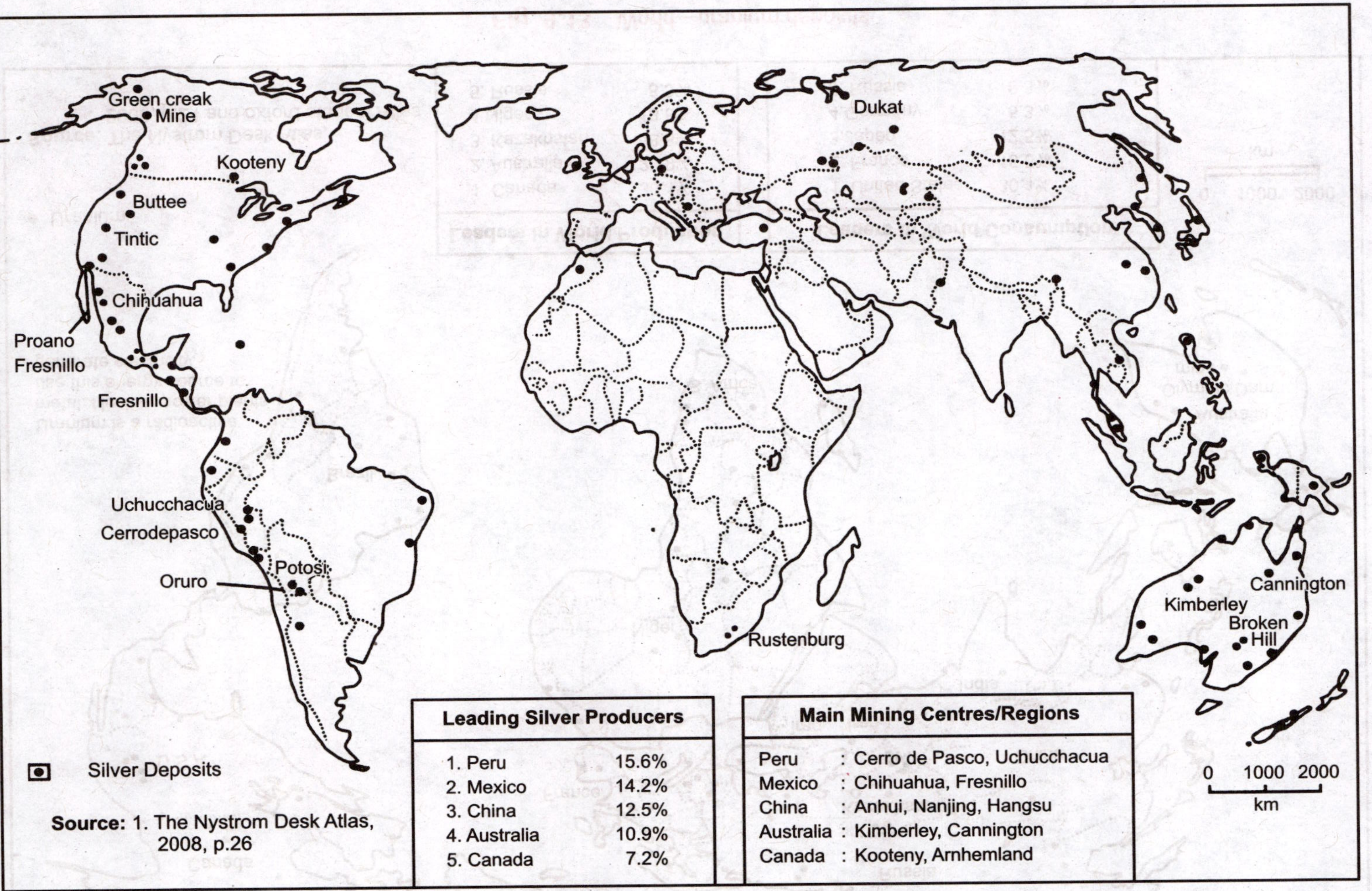

Leading Silver Producers	
1. Peru	15.6%
2. Mexico	14.2%
3. China	12.5%
4. Australia	10.9%
5. Canada	7.2%

Main Mining Centres/Regions	
Peru	: Cerro de Pasco, Uchucchacua
Mexico	: Chihuahua, Fresnillo
China	: Anhui, Nanjing, Hangsu
Australia	: Kimberley, Cannington
Canada	: Kooteny, Arnhemland

Fig. 9.12 World–Silver deposits

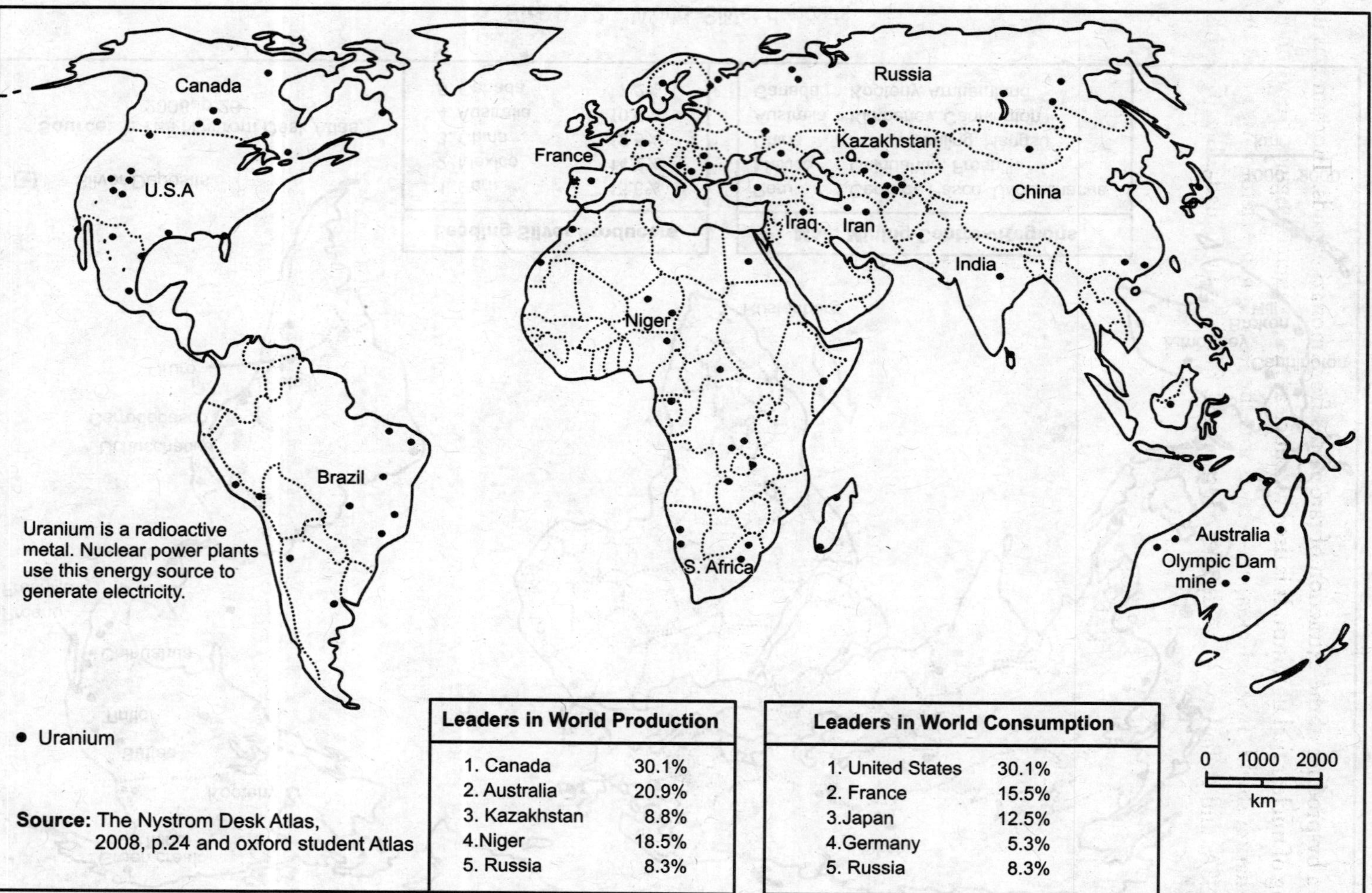

Fig. 9.13 World—uranium deposits

Thorium

Thorium is a by-product of the extraction of rare earths from monazite sands. Thorium was used for the breeding of nuclear fuel uranium. It is used as a nuclear fuel in aircraft engines. Thorium is a very effective radiation shield. India's Kakrapara-1 reactor is the world's first reactor which uses thorium. Australia, USA, and India have large deposits of thorium, followed by Canada, Brazil, South Africa and Turkey.

Locational Factors of Economic Activities

Economic activities are divided by economists and geographers into (i) Primary, (ii) Secondary, and (iii) Tertiary. An account of the features and locational factors of these activities are discussed in this chapter.

PRIMARY ACTIVITY

Primary activity means the extraction of product from the nature. About five hundred years ago, primitive economic activities were practiced virtually everywhere. Primary activity includes food-gathering, hunting, nomadic herding, sedentary agriculture, dairying, forestry, poultry, sericulture, apiculture, aquaculture, fishery and mining. The primary activities are closely influenced by the physical factors, terrain, topography, climate (temperature and precipitation), drainage, soils, natural vegetation, land use practices and soil management. The socio-economic and political institutions also influence the primary activities, agricultural practices and cropping patterns.

Food Gathering

Primitive gathering persists primarily in isolated pockets in the low latitudes, including the territories of some of the Red Indian tribes dispersed in the Amazon Basin (Brazil, Peru, Ecuador, and Venezuela). There are some isolated pockets in Congo Basin, and the interior parts of South-East Asia (Cambodia, China, Indonesia, Laos, Malaysia, Myanmar, New Guinea, Papua, Philippines, Thailand, Vietnam, etc.). Of all the primary activities, food - gathering requires the least amount of capital investment and effort, but considerable space is required. A very low man-land ratio occurs in such food gathering areas. Primitive gatherers still live in the Stone Age, such like their ancestors 100 centuries before. Their overall health is generally poor, life expectancy is short and standard of living is significantly low.

Hunting

Hunting is a primarily a communal activity, often requiring planned, large scale expeditions and a very well developed division of labour. Tracking down wild animals and protecting families against enemies can be conducted more effectively in groups. Hunters generally do not have domesticated food-plants and animals (except dog), permanent settlements or high population densities. The tools and implements utilized by hunters include a variety of traps, snares, and lethal weapons. Hunting is primarily a communal activity, often requiring planned large scale expeditions and a very well developed division of labour. At present hunting is practiced mainly in high latitudes, particularly in the Arctic region and the dense forests of the equatorial region, i.e. Amazon Basin, Congo Basin and countries of South East Asia **Fig. 10.1**.

Pastoral Nomadism

Pastoral nomads' or nomadic herding is a more advanced activity than either food -gathering or hunting. Nomadic herding activity encompasses the single largest territory on earth. There are about 15 million pastoralists, spread over about 26 million sq km twice the area of land devoted to cultivation. Nomadic herding is practiced mainly in the arid and semi-arid areas of Central Asia, South-West Asia, Sahara, Sahel -region of Africa, Sudan and Madagascar, Mongolia, Tibet, western China, Lower reaches of the Nile Valley. The nomadic areas of Old World (Africa, Asia and Europe) have been shown in **Fig. 10.2**. Subsistence herding is also practiced on the southern margins of Tundra (Eurasia) and Alaska (U.S.A.).

The animals kept by the nomadic herders are cattle, camels, goats, horses, reindeer, sheep, and yaks. Meat plays a small role in the diet of the nomadic herders, because animals are rarely killed except on special and ceremonial occasions.

The nomadic herders migrate regularly with their livestock and cattle in search of fodder and water. Their economy is livestock based. The status of a person is judged by the number of cattle he is keeping. In the mountainous areas like Alps, Caucasus, Tienshan, Altai, Himalayas and Rocky mountains seasonal migration or transhumance is practiced.

Livestock Ranching

Livestock ranching is carried on in the regions with relatively flat surface and plains where natural grasses grow luxuriously. It is practiced mostly in the temperate and tropical grasslands. The leading areas of temperate grazing are stretching in the Steppes in Eurasia, Prairies in North America, Pampas in Argentina and Uruguay (South America), Velds in South Africa and Downs in Australia (**Fig. 10.3**).

The movements of stock are normally confined to the ranch although there may be seasonal movement of transhumance to distant pastures. The ranch is a permanent base. Livestock ranching have all suffered from overgrazing. At times, most of these areas experience disastrous droughts. Improvements in breeds of stocks, prevention of over-grazing and conservation of water resources are, however, necessary if these regions of temperate grasslands continue to develop the trade in animal products.

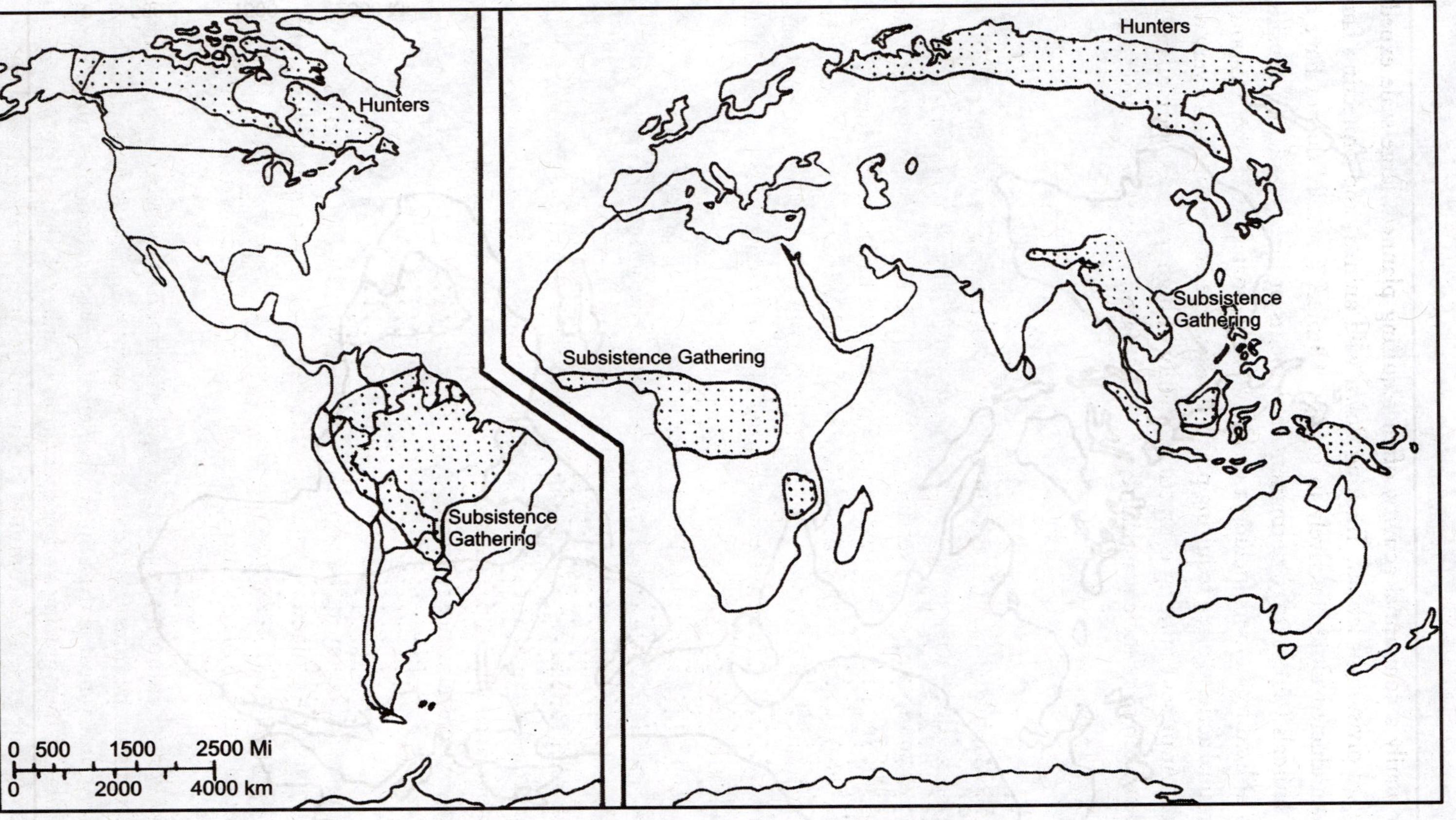

Fig. 10.1 Subsistence Gathering and Hunting

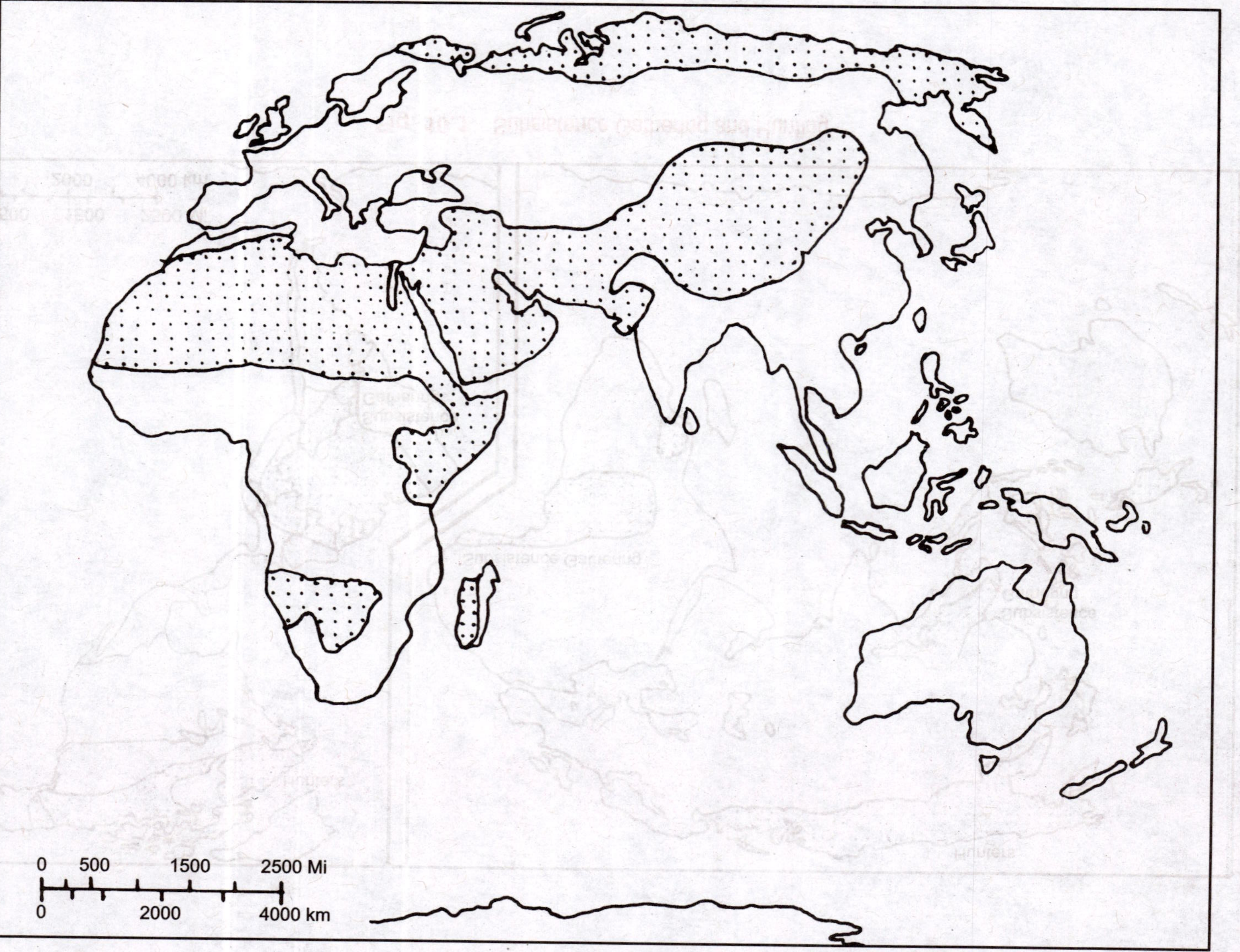

Fig. 10.2 Subsistence Herding–Pastoral Nomadism

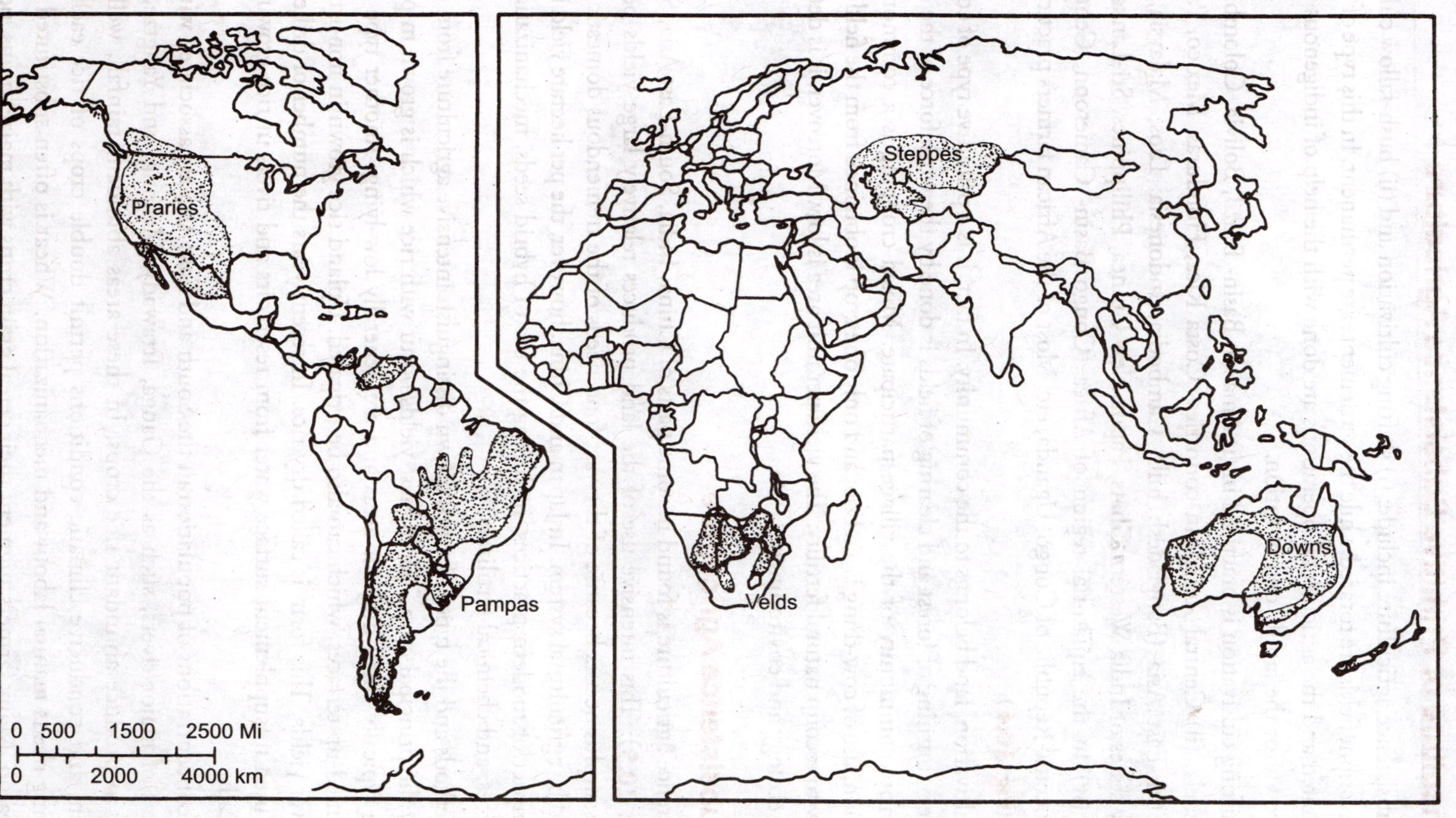

Fig. 10.3 World Distribution of Livestock Ranching

Shifting Agriculture or Primitive Subsistence Agriculture

The primitive subsistence agriculture include: (i) shifting cultivation and (ii) bush-fallow cultivation. In the shifting cultivation, fields are rotated while the settlements are permanent. In this type of agriculture, crops are not rotated and the agricultural operations are done with the help of indigenous technology. The crops are grown for the family consumption.

At present shifting cultivation is practiced in (i) Amazon Basin- Brazil, Bolivia, Colombia, Guyana, Surinam, Venezuela, (ii) Central American countries- Costa Rica, Honduras, Mexico, Panama, (iii) countries of South-East Asia (Bangladesh hills, Cambodia, Indonesia, Laos, Malaysia, Myanmar, North-East hilly states of India Western Ghats, Papua-New Guinea, Philippines, Sri-Lanka, Thailand, Vietnam), and (iv) In the equatorial region of Africa (Congo Basin- Cameroon, Central African Republic, Democratic Republic of Congo, Uganda, etc. Most of the African farmers practice rotational bush-fallowing (**Fig. 10.4**).

In shifting cultivation, land belongs to the community. In fact, it is a primitive type of communism. The felling of trees, burning of forest and clearing of fields is done by the work force of the community in which the entire community of the village participate. Mixed cropping is a common feature in shifting cultivation, use of cow-dung is a taboo, and only one crop is obtained from the field after which it is left as fallow to recoup natural fertility. The yield per unit area is low. Moreover, it is detrimental to the ecosystems, ecology and environment.

Intensive Subsistence Agriculture

Intensive subsistence agriculture is found in some parts of China, India, South-East Asia, South Korea and Japan (**Fig. 10.5**). This intensive use of the land produces relatively large yields per acre, but frequently little surplus occurs because of the vast food needs of the tremendous domestic population that is supported by agricultural system. In Japan and China, however, the per hectare yield is very high, owing to the impact of modern practices, including the use of hybrid seeds, mechanization, modern irrigation practices, and chemical fertilizers.

Cropping methods and the types of crops grown distinguish intensive agriculture from other types. Rice is typically the principal crop. The highest yields occur with rice which is grown in paddy fields. These fields are typically small dug-out areas and are generally low-lying. Another type of paddy is created by dammed-up terraces, which can also be irrigated. Upland rice grown in non-irrigated areas provides far lower yields. This form is called dry rice. In recent years the number of drilled wells and electric pumps used to supplement surface water from reservoirs and rivers in rice-growing areas has grown dramatically.

The highest concentrations of population in the South and East Asia are associated with the flood plains and deltas of major rivers, such as the Ganga, Irrawady, Mekong, and Yangtze, as a result of their ability to produce abundant rice crops. In these areas abundant rainfall, well developed irrigation system and conducive climatic conditions permit double crops of rice each year. This multiple cropping needs manual labour and mechanization. Wheat is often substituted with wheat in the winter season. Many farmers augment their cereal grain crops with maize, beans, peas, melons,

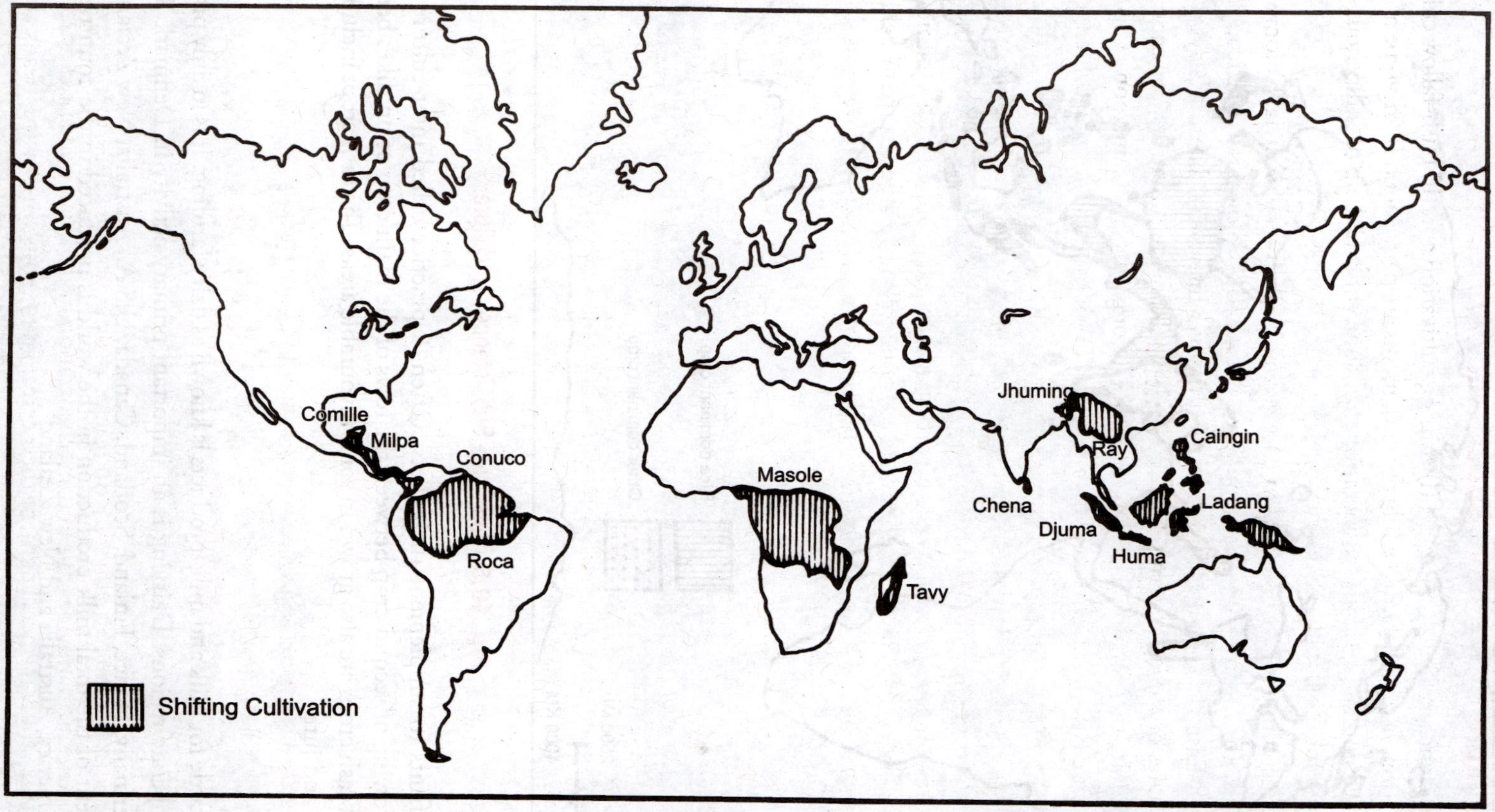

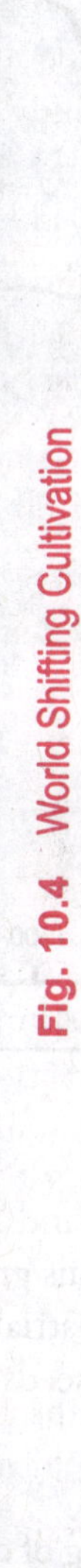

Fig. 10.4 World Shifting Cultivation

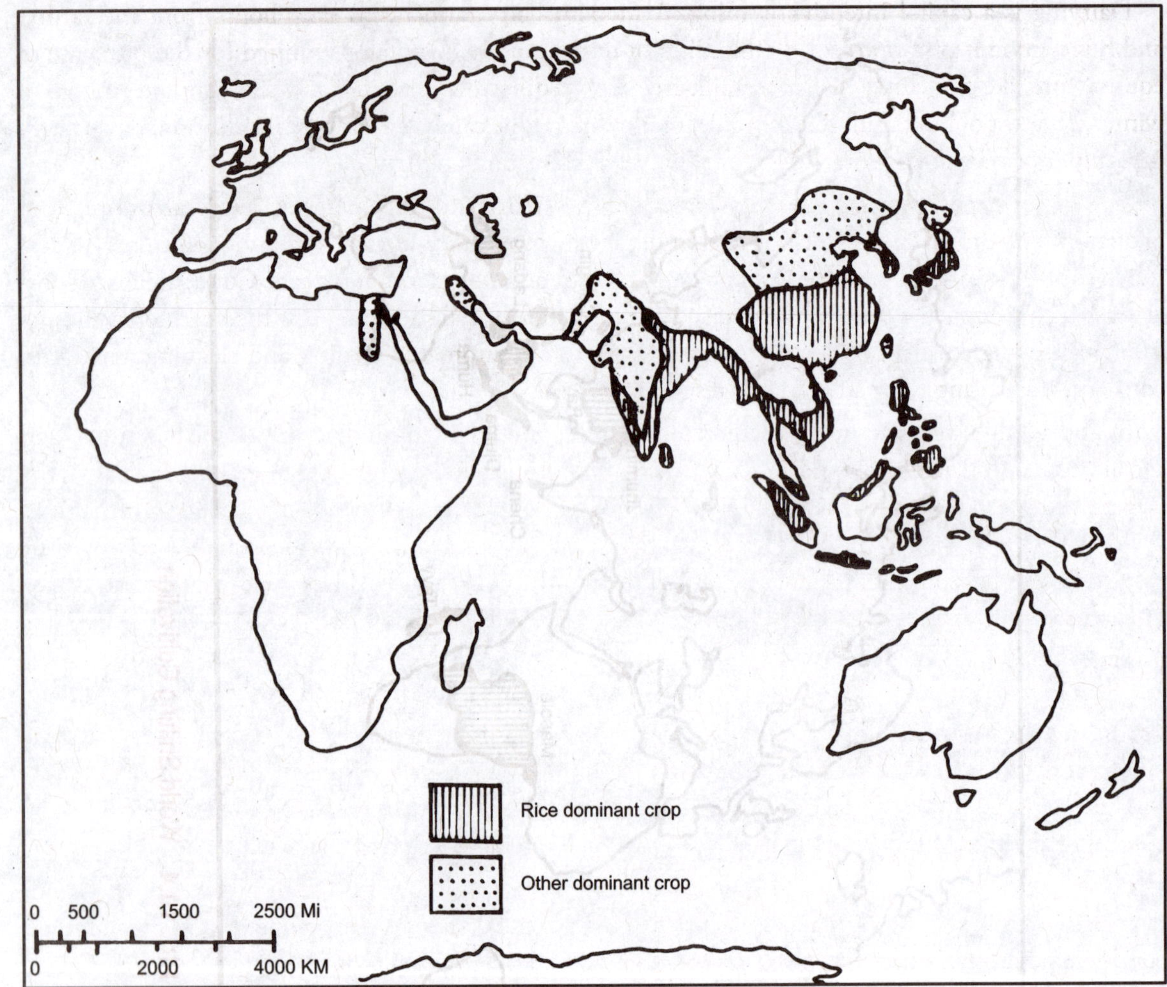

Fig. 10.5 Intensive Subsistence Agriculture

vegetables and fruits to supplement their diets. Often, a practice called inter-culture permits the simultaneous growing of second crop between the rows of the main crop or on dikes between paddy fields. Industrial cash crops are also grown in some favourable areas. The cash crops include sugarcane, cotton, oilseeds and jute.

Dairying

The keeping of cattle for milk and milk-products is known as dairy farming. It is mainly practised in the countries of temperate regions. Dairying is an important primary activity in Denmark, Belgium, the Netherlands, Germany, France, Finland, Scotland, Canada, U.S.A., Australia, New Zealand and Japan. Nearly 80 per cent of the total milk production in the world is produced in the countries of Europe, Russia, Anglo-America, Australia and New Zealand.

Dairying is a capital intensive farming. A modern dairy farm needs long hours from the farmer and huge amount of money for the building of infrastructure. Capital is required for the purchase of equipments like mulching machine, milk-freezers, feeding-towers, barns and silos for the storage of winter. The cost of bulk milk cooling and storage tanks alone can be enormous. In addition, dairy farms typically have several large tractors, plows, harvesters, wagons, and trucks.

The main breeds kept in the dairy farms are Holstein-Friesian, Guernsey, Jersey, Ayrshire from Scotland, and Brown Swiss from Switzerland. These cows under normal healthy conditions yield as much as 3000 kg of milk per year which fetches handsome amount to the farmers. Cows remain indoors at least 5 to 6 month a year, and the trend is for indoor housing throughout the year. Even though modern milking parlors and loafing barns typically have automated feeding and cleaning apparatus, constant monitoring is required by the respective farmers.

In India, the important milch breeds include Gir, Sindhi, Red-Sindhi, Sahiwal, Thaeparkar and Deoni. The Gir is native of Saurashtra. It is now found in several parts of Gujarat and Rajasthan. The Red Sindhi breed has a distinct red colour and hails from the Sindh Province of Pakistan. The Sahiwal breed has its origin in Montogomery (Faisalabad) Pakistan. India has imported exotic breeds. Some foreign breeds have been crossed with Indian breeds. The maximum yield of milk per lactation at the military farms in India is about 6000 kg while the average yield is 2600 kg.

Plantation Agriculture

The term plantation agriculture was originally applied specifically to the British settlements in America and then to any large estate in North America, West Indies and South -East Asia. In America and West Indies, the plantation agriculture was carried on by the Negro work-force, living on estates under the control of managers and proprietors.

Plantation is generally a large scale capital intensive enterprise in agriculture. It involves the existence of regular work-force under the control of a more or less elaborate management, and frequently a considerable capital outlay, although some of the plantation crops such as tea, coffee, cocoa arecanut, spices, rubber, qaat, banana, jute and sugarcane are also grown in small holdings also.

Plantation agriculture is practiced mainly in the tropical regions to grow cash crops. The crops planted include tea, coffee, cocoa, rubber, coconut, sugarcane, cotton, banana, oil-palm, Manila-hemp, vanilla, spices etc.

As stated above, plantation farms are generally large and are found mainly in the thinly populated areas. The size of farm of tea, coffee, cocoa and rubber varies from 10 hectares in Malaya to 60,000 hectares in Liberia. In these estates, a large disciplined but unskilled labour force is necessary. In the past slavery was the solution of the problem, and later indentured workers, particularly Indians were taken to sugarcane and rubber plantation estates of West Indies, Mauritius, Kenya, and Malaysia. The technical and managerial stag has invariably been European on the plantation estates.

The plantation crops have to be processed before leaving the estate. There are a number of reasons for this processing. First, the yield of many crops decline quickly after harvesting; secondly, the processing gives a product of higher value per unit weight that can be transported over long distances; and thirdly, many of the crops are perishable in their unprocessed forms. The need for processing plantation crops differ from crop to crop, but as a matter of fact, the more complex the process the more likely the crop is to be produced on plantation estate rather than on small holdings. The annual crops are more suited for plantation than perennial trees or bush crops. The plantation agriculture is however, based on exploitation of workers and labourers.

The leading producers of plantation crops have been shown in **Fig. 10.6**. The main producers of plantation crops are Brazil, Colombia, Costa Rica, Honduras, Mexico, Nicaragua, Panama, Peru, and Venezuela in North and South America; Cameroon, Ethiopia, Ghana, Ivoire Coast, Kenya, Liberia, Sierra-Leone, Madagascar, Nigeria, Rawanda, Tanzania, Togo, Uganda etc. (Africa); China, India, Indonesia, Malaysia, Myanmar, New Guinea- Papua, Philippines, Sri Lanka, Thailand, Vietnam (Asia). There is increasing international demand of all the plantation crops.

Mediterranean Type of Agriculture

The Mediterranean agricultural typology is confined to the coastal areas of the Mediterranean Sea in Europe, Asia Minor (coastal Turkey), Valley of California, Cape Province of South Africa, Central Chile, Tasmania and coastal Victoria (Australia) and southern New Zealand.

The Mediterranean region records hot summer and mild-rainy winters. This region is known for the cultivation of citrus fruits, fig, olive, vine, cork, cereals and fodder crops. Wheat is the important cereal crop, followed by barley, oats, oilseeds and fodder crops. The fragmentation and small size of holdings are the main problems of the Mediterranean agriculture.

Mixed Farming (Commercial Crops and Livestock)

In mixed farming, crops and animals occur in various combinations. It should not be confused with mixed cropping (sowing two or more than two crops in the same field in one season). The role of crops is particularly crucial in that they provide multiple roles as feed for animals, as a cash crop, and as a food supply for farm families. It is practiced mainly in U.S.A. Canada, Europe, Australia, New Zealand, Russia and South Africa.

Mixed farming is essentially associated with the densely populated, industrialized, and urbanized societies. Mixed farming yields fairly high agricultural returns because of efficient methods of farming, excellent infrastructure and reliability of precipitation.

The main characteristics of mixed farming are that farms produce both crops and livestock and the two enterprises are interwoven and integrated. The average size of holding in mixed farming is about 100 hectares in USA and about 15 hectares in England. These farms are mostly operated by family labour. Hired farm labour is, however, uncommon. Moreover, tenant farming is unusual. Mixed farms are characterized by high expenditure on machinery and farm buildings.

Mixed farming has a three-fold advantage. In the first place, it protects the farmers against the risk of poor prices and disease. In the second place, it spreads labour requirements more evenly throughout the year. Thirdly, it helps in the maintenance of soil fertility. The farmers keep livestock, beef-cattle, and hogs. The rising labour cost has however, made it increasingly difficult to keep a variety of livestock and grow a wide range of crops.

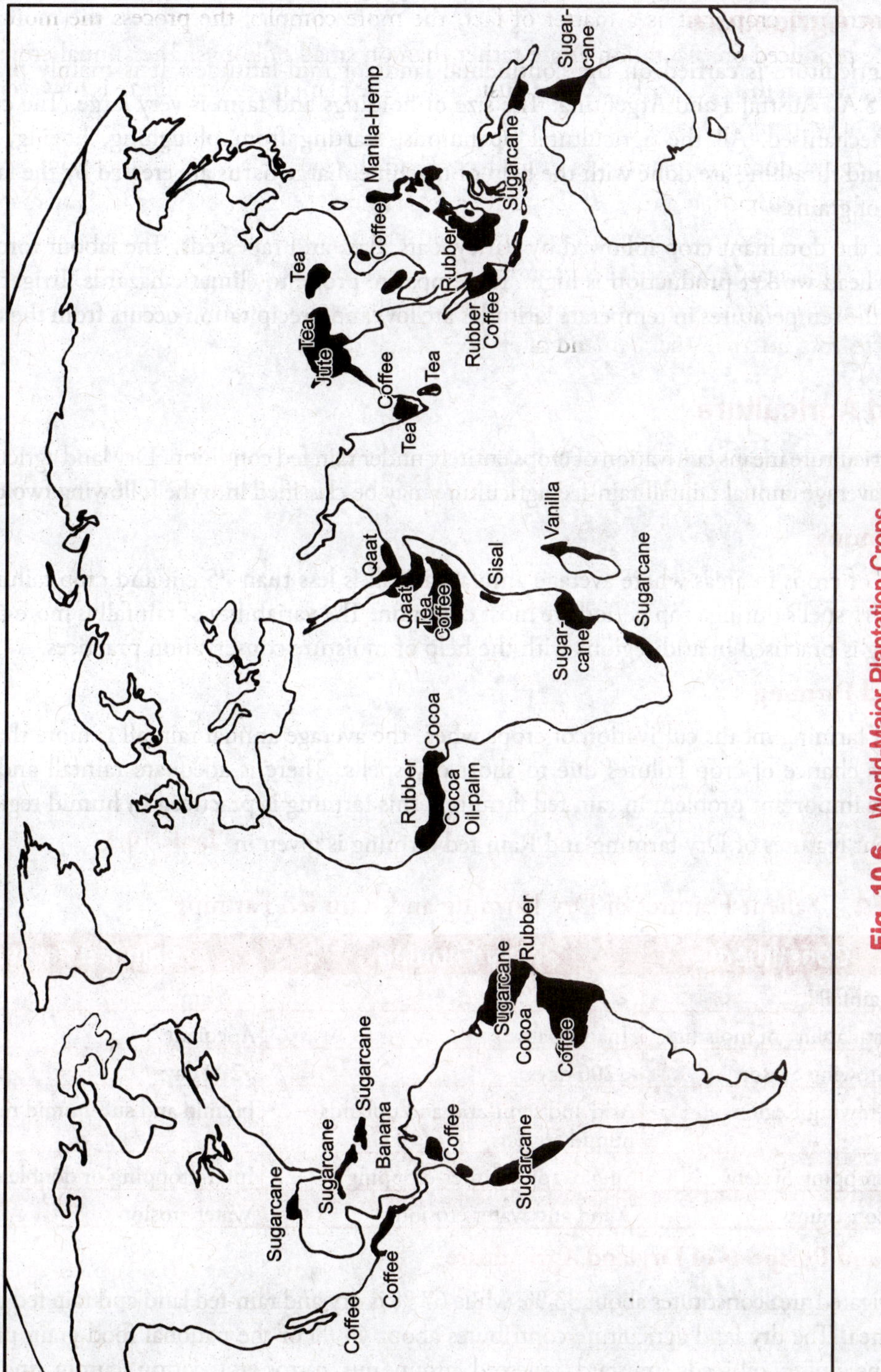

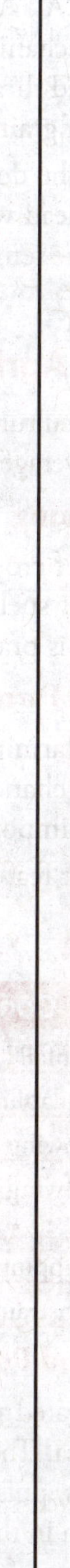

Fig. 10.6 World-Major Plantation Crops

Extensive Agriculture

Extensive agriculture is carried on the continental lands of mid-latitudes. It is mainly practised in Canada, U.S.A., Australia and Argentina. The size of holdings and farm is very large. The cultivation is highly mechanised. All the agricultural operations, starting from ploughing, hoeing, spraying, harvesting and thrashing are done with the help of machine. Large barns are erected by the farmers for the storage of grains.

Wheat is the dominant crop followed by barley, oats, flax, and rapeseeds. The labour force is small but the per head worker production is high. The crops are prone to climatic hazards. Irrigation is not required as the temperatures in temperate latitudes are low and precipitation occurs from the temperate cyclones.

Dry Land Agriculture

Dry land agriculture means cultivation of crops entirely under rain fed condition. Dry land agriculture. On the basis of average annual rainfall rain-fed agriculture may be classified into the following two categories:

1. Dry Farming

Cultivation of crops in areas where average annual rainfall is less than 75 cm and crop failures due to prolonged dry spells during crop period are most common. The variability of rainfall is more than 50%. Dry farming is practised in arid regions with the help of moisture conservation practices.

2. Rain Fed Farming

This type of farming means cultivation of crops where the average annual rainfall is more than 75 cm. There is less chance of crop failures due to short dry spells. There is adequate rainfall and drainage becomes the important problem in rain fed farming. This farming is practiced in humid regions.

The salient features of Dry farming and Rain fed farming is given in **Table 10.1**.

Table 10.1 Salient Features of Dry Farming and Rain fed Farming

S.No.	Constituents	Dry Farming	Rain fed Farming
1	Rainfall	< 75 cm	>75 cm
2	Availability of moisture	Inadequate	Adequate
3	Growing Season	< 200 days	>200 days
4	Growing Regions	Arid and semi-arid and uplands humid regions	Humid and sub-humid regions
5	Cropping System	Single crop or inter-cropping	Inter-cropping or double cropping
6	Constraints	Wind and water erosion	Water erosion

Problems and Prospects of Dryland Agriculture

In India, irrigated area constitutes about 33 %, while 67 % is dry and rain-fed land and rain fed of the total cultivated area. The dry land agriculture contributes about 44 % of the national food-grain production. Coarse grains, pulses, oil seeds (mustard, rapeseed, groundnut, castor etc), cotton, cumin, and spices are mainly grown in the dry land farming. The major part of milk, meat, mutton, wool, hides, bone-meal etc. are also obtained from dry-farm regions.

Dry farming areas are characterized by very low and highly variable and uncertain yields. The main problems of dry farming regions are given below:

(i) Uncertain and erratic rainfall.
(ii) Late onset and early withdrawal of monsoon.
(iii) Prolonged dry-spells during the crop period.
(iv) Low moisture retention capacity.
(v) Poor soil fertility condition.
(vi) Technological and developmental constraints.
(vii) Inadequate infrastructure and availability of credit and banking facilities.

Strategy for Dry Land Agriculture

The agriculture of the dry lands may be made more remunerative by adopting the following strategy:

1. Emphasis on short duration of leguminous and cover crops.
2. Animal husbandry, with pastures management.
3. Dairy farming.
4. Agro-forestry.
5. Apiculture.
6. Cottage industry.

Watershed Management

Watershed may be defined as a natural unit of land whose runoff collects and flows out of the area through a single outlet into a river or water-body. It is a drainage basin of the first or second order of tributaries of a river. The size of watershed may vary from a few hectares to several thousands of hectares. In fact, watershed is a physical, biological, economic and social system. A drainage basin is demarcated by the water-divides or ridges. Watershed or catchment basin area are generally synonyms. Watershed is comparatively smaller in area as compared to the catchment or basin.

The Government of India launched a Watershed Management Programme in the Seventh Five Year Plan to make a judicious use of available water and to develop dry land areas on the basis of watershed. For soil and water conservation measures, watershed is demarcated into sub-watersheds and micro-watersheds. Micro-watersheds are the basis for planning and execution. In the beginning, there was a plan to develop 4000 watersheds in different agro-climatic regions. *The watershed management programme has the following features:*

(i) Soil and Water Conservation Measures: Soil and water conservation measures on the watershed basis include all those measures which are effective in preventing or delaying the movement of soil and weathered material.

(ii) Scientific Dry Farming: The agricultural activities like contour ploughing, pre-monsoon ploughing, mulching, development of new varieties according to agro-climatic zones, weed control, integrated nutrient management and integrated pest management improve the production in dry land areas.

(iii) Animal Husbandry and Development of Dairying: Proper animal husbandry, artificial insemination, economic assistance to the milk producing cooperative societies are to be adopted.

(iv) Development of Social Forestry and Agro-forestry.

Objectives of Watershed Management

Following are the main objectives of watershed management programme:

1. To protect, conserve and improve the land resources.
2. To conserve the available water resources and to make a judicious use of the water resources.
3. To utilize the available natural resources for improving agriculture and allied activities including agro-based and cottage industries.

There is a need for multi-pronged approach to maximize crop production and also to make agriculture, ecosystems and ecology sustainable.

The following steps may go a long way in achieving the objectives of watershed management.

(a) Water harvesting, (b) location specific technology for crop production, (c) adoption of inter-cropping and mixed cropping, (d) afforestation on cultivable waste and marginal lands, (e) to develop dry land horticulture, (f) more efficient use of the surface and underground water, (g) development of dairying and pasture management, (h) development of goat and sheep farming, (i) popularization of sericulture and mulberry cultivation, (j) processing of farm and horticulture products, (k) training programmes for farmers.

Sustainable Agriculture

Definition

There are many definitions of sustainable agriculture. According to one definition sustainable agriculture is a form of agriculture aimed at meeting the needs of the present generation without endangering the resource base of the future generation. In order to feed the fast growing population more food has to be produced and this has to be done without degradation of the resource base. According to some experts, sustainable agriculture is minimal dependence on chemical fertilizers, pesticides and insecticides. It is also considered as a system of cultivation with the use of manures and rotation of crops.

Salient Features

Sustainable agriculture is a balanced management system of renewable resources including soil, wildlife, forests, crops, fish, livestock, plant genetic resources and ecosystems without degradation and to provide food, livelihood for current and future generations maintaining or improving productivity and ecosystem services of these resources. Sustainable agriculture system has to be economically viable both in the short and long term perspective. Sustainable agriculture has to be economically viable both in the short and long term perspectives. Natural resources not only provide food, fibre, fuel, fodder, and industrial raw material but also perform ecosystem services such as detoxification of noxious chemicals within soils, purification of waters, favourable weather and regulation of hydrological process within watersheds. Sustainable agriculture has to prevent land degradation and soil erosion. It has to be replenish nutrients and control weeds, pests and diseases through biological and cultural methods.

Sustainable agriculture is also known as enforcing organic farming or natural farming or permaculture. It is known as eco-farming as ecological balance is given importance. It is also called organic farming as organic matter is the main source of nutrient management. But some scientists consider that it is a misconception to think that sustainable agriculture is farming without chemical inputs. It is considered by some as integrated, low input and highly productive farming system.

Organic Farming

It is an agricultural system in which all types of agricultural products are produced organically, including grains, staple food, pulses, oilseeds, dairy, poultry, meat, fibers, cotton, jute, vegetables, horticulture, flowers and processed food products.

Organic farming avoids the use of chemical fertilizers, unsecticides, pesticides and weedicite.

Organic farming heavily relies on scientific rotation of crops, cow-dung, animal manure, green-manure, organic-waste, compost-manure, and biological control of pests and diseases, and repeated ploughing and pulverization of soil. Some of the farmers adopt mixed cropping of the soil exhaustive and soil enriching crops, like millets with pulses, wheat with gram, and cotton with legumes.

Advantages and Disadvantages of Sustainable Agriculture

The main advantage of sustainable agriculture are (i) ecological balance, (ii) low cost of cultivation, (iii) clean environment and (iv) nutritious food without pesticide residues. The conversion process from modern agriculture to sustainable agriculture usually takes three to six years. The sustainable agriculture movement was started in 1981. There is insufficient data to recommend sustainable agriculture. Much is now subjective and even hypothetical. There is no well founded body of knowledge. Doubts are expressed by some scientists whether it is possible to produce adequate food and other requirements for the teeming million of population without the use of chemical fertilizers and chemical pesticides. The use of limited quantities of fertilizers and discrete application of small quantities of target specific pesticides at critical stages of crop damage will be in agreement with the principle of sustainable agriculture.

Crop Rotation

The selection of optimal crop rotation is important for successful sustainable agriculture. Crop rotation is very important for soil fertility management, weed, insect and disease control. Legumes (pulses) are essential in any rotation and should comprise 30 to 50 per cent of the crop land. A mixed cropping, pasture and livestock system is desirable or even essential for the success of sustainable agriculture.

Table 10.2 Differences between Modern Agriculture and Sustainable Agriculture

Particulars	Sustainable Agriculture	Modern Agriculture
Plant nutrients	Farmyard manure, compost, green-manures, bio-fertilizers, and scientific rotation of crops	Chemical fertilizers are used
Pest control	Cultural methods, crop rotation and biological methods are used	Toxic chemicals, insecticides and pesticides are used
Inputs	High diversity, renewable and biodegradable inputs are used	High productivity and low diversity chemicals are used.
Ecology	Stable ecology, sustainability of land and other resources.	Fragile ecology, modern agriculture is highly exploitative. Water bodies are degraded.
Use of resources	The rate of extraction from forests, fisheries, underground water sources and other renewable resources do not exceed the rate of generation	The rate of extraction exceeds the rate of regeneration. Felling of trees, deforestation, overgrazing and pollution of water bodies takes place
Quality of food material	Food materials are safe	Food materials contain toxic residues.

Forestry

The management of woodland to provide, timber, fuel wood and forest products for sale is known as forestry. Forestry has traditionally been regarded as an extractive or robber industry. Forests which once covered about 60 per cent of the Earth's land surface, have been greatly reduced by clearance for agriculture, settlements, industries and infrastructure. At present about 25 per cent of the land surface is covered by forest.

Classification of Forest Areas

The forest areas of the world may be classified into: (i) Tropical Hardwood Forests, (ii) Coniferous Forests (Fig. 10.7).

Tropical Hardwood Forests The tropical hardwood forests include the evergreen rain forests of the equatorial region and the monsoon forests. In monsoon forests the trees are deciduous, shedding their leaves in the dry season. The majority of the trees are broad leaved and yield valuable hardwoods. Some tropical trees are noted for their extreme hardness, e.g. teak, sal, ironwood, and rosewood are so heavy and difficult to work that they have to be killed by ring-barking several years before they are felled. The wood of some of the trees are so heavy that they will not float in water and rivers. The main commercial species are teak, greenheart, logwood, ebony, mahogany, rosewood and iron-wood.

(i) The tropical hardwood forests are found in the Amazon Basin (Selvas'), Congo Basin, Guinea-coast (Ghana, Togo, Liberia), Madagascar, Indonesia, Malaysia, Papua New Guinea, Thailand, Vietnam and, Assam Andaman and Nicobar Islands, Nicobar, Western Ghats.

(ii) The coniferous forests are largely confined in the Northern Hemisphere. They cover a broad belt in both North and South America and Eurasia to the north of temperate hardwood belt. They also grow on upland and mountains or in areas of sandy or porous soil in the milder temperate areas because they are better adapted to withstand cold and drought than the broadleaved trees. The main areas of conifers are (i) Western North America, Central and Eastern North America, Northern Europe, Asiatic Russia and in Southern Continents in Chile, the western Brazilian Plateau, and the North Island of New Zealand (Fig. 10.7).

Coniferous forests Conifers are tall, straight, evergreen trees with narrow, needle-like leaves, and take their name from the cones in which they bear their seeds. Only a few conifers, such as the *larch*, are deciduous. Most coniferous trees are softwoods and are light in weight, which make them easier to cut and transport. Their height may be up to 30 metres or more. These forests are moderately dense. They however, do not have the wide buttress roots which make tropical trees so difficult to fell. The main varieties of conifers include spruce, pine, fir and larch families.

The forest cover is shrinking fast. There is an urgent need to conserve the forests. Some of the important steps which may go a long way in the conservation of forests are: (i) afforestation, (ii) improved cutting practices, (iii) forest protection (iv) reduction of wastage, (v) use of alternatives of wood, and (vi) recycling of the available resources.

Agroforestry

Agroforestry, the word coined in early seventies, has made its place in all the developed and developing countries of the world. A few definitions of agroforestry are as under:

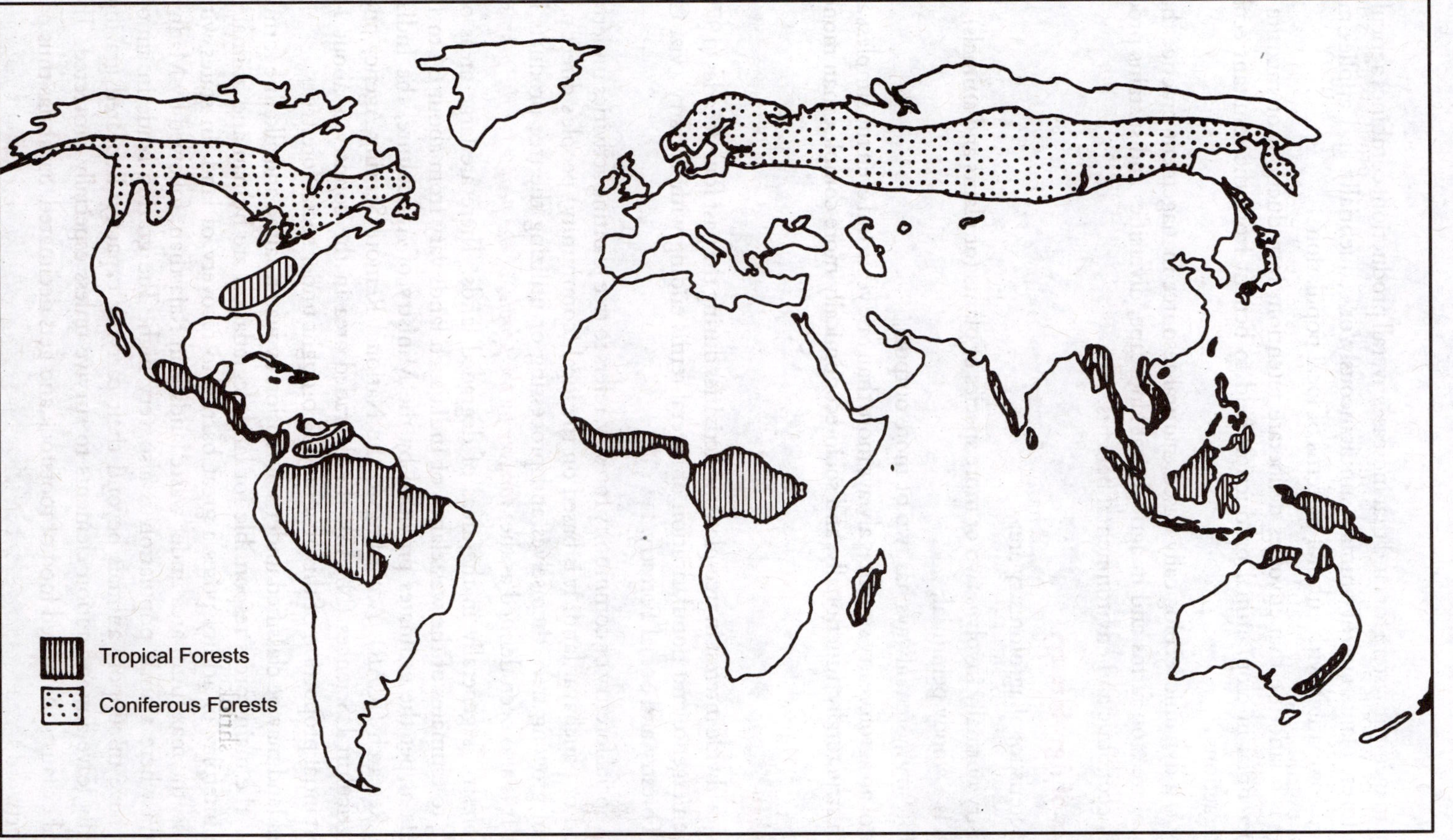

Fig. 10.7 Major Forest Areas of the World

Definitions

'A sustainable management system for land that increases overall production, combines agricultural crops, tree crops and forest plants and/or animals simultaneously/or sequentially and applies management practices that are compatible with cultural patterns of local population'.

'Agroforestry is a land-use that involves deliberate retention, introduction, or mixture of trees or other woody perennial in crop/animal production field to benefit from the resultant ecological and economical interactions'.

'Agroforestry is a dynamic, ecologically based, natural resource management practice that, through the integration of trees on farms and in agricultural landscape, diversifies and sustains production for increased social, economic and environmental benefits.'

Characteristics of Agroforestry

The main characteristics of agroforestry are:

1. agroforestry normally involves two or more species of plants (or plants and animals), at least one of which is a woody perennial;
2. an agroforestry system always has two or more outputs;
3. the cycle of an agroforestry system is always more than one year; and even the simplest agroforestry system in structurally, functionally, and socio-economically more complex than mono-cropping system.

Types of Forestry

The escalating worldwide interest in tree-planting activities during the past four decades (1970 onwards) resulted in the emergence and popularization of several terms ending with 'forestry', viz. Community Forestry, Farm Forestry and Social Forestry.

Social Forestry Social forestry or community forestry, refers to tree planting activities undertaken by the community land or panchayat land. It is based on the local (community) people's direct participation in the process of growing trees themselves and processing or utilizing the tree products locally in a systematic way. It is also been defined as the '*forestry by the people, of the people for the people*'.

The social forestry is generally in the areas of degraded lands. There are large areas of degraded land. According to estimates of the wastelands of India such lands vary from about 64 to 188 million hectares in India as per the estimates provided by the Ministry of Agriculture, the Indian Council of Agricultural Research (ICAR). According to the National Remote Sensing Agency and National Academy of Agricultural Sciences (NAAS), the degraded area in the country is about 120 million hectares. A substantial proportion of this area may be brought under social forestry.

The degraded land may be classified under soil erosion by water, saline and alkaline formations, and mining activity. The main forces responsible for land degradation are human and animal population pressure where interplay of aridity poses a great barrier to recovery of land. In states with arid and semi-arid regions, the maximum area under waste lands is in Rajasthan, followed by Madhya Pradesh, and Maharashtra where animal population is also very high. The grazing lands in almost all parts of the country have to support animals beyond their carrying capacity. Repeated grazing/browsing by animals hardly leave any vegetation elements to survive unless especially protected. The repeated biomass removal exhausts the stored food of rootstock and gets decimated. Savannas thus pass through steppe into deserts.

The demographic pressure in India shows that the human population has crossed 1.21 billion mark in 2011 with a population density 382 per sq km with a maximum in Bihar (1102) followed by West Bengal (1029) and Kerala 859 per sq km. The only weapon that can be used in the war against hunger, inadequate shelter, and environmental degradation is the adoption of agro-forestry practices.

Agroforestry, in true sense, has been realized as the need of the hour. It does not confine to regional, geographical or agro-climatic boundary.

Agroforestry for Food, Fuel and Fodder

Owing to increase in population of human and cattle, there is increasing demand of food as well as fodder, particularly in developing countries like India. Each year farmers of the world must now attempt to feed 81 million more irrespective of weather. It is important to note that there will be 19% decline in cropland per head by the end of this century due to population explosion. Therefore, there is slight scope to increase food production by increasing the area under cultivation. A management system, therefore, needs to be devised that is capable of producing food from marginal agricultural land and is also capable of maintaining and improving quality of producing environment.

The different aspects in which agroforestry can help in enhancing the productivity of our lands to meet the demand of ever-growing human and livestock population are discussed here.

A. Food

1. Food for man from trees and fruits, nuts, and cereal substitutes.
2. Enhanced food and feed production from crops associated with trees through nitrogen fixation, better access to soil nutrients brought to surface from deep tree roots, improved availability of nutrients due to high cation-exchange capacity of soil and its organic matter.
3. Enhanced sustainability of cropping systems through soil and water conservation by arrangements of trees to control run-off and erosion.
4. Feed for livestock from trees.
5. Micro-climate improvement due to trees, particularly shelter-belts and wind-breaks.

B. Water

1. Improvement of soil-moisture retention in rain-fed croplands and pastures through improved soil structure and micro-climate effect of trees.
2. Regulation of stream flow, reducing food hazards and a more even supply of water through reduction of run-off and improvement of interception and storage in infiltration galleries.
3. Improvement in drainage from the waterlogged or saline soils by trees with high water requirements.

C. Energy

1. Fuel-wood for direct combustion.
2. Production of charcoal, oil and gas.
3. Ethnol produced from fermentation of high–carbohydrate fruits.
4. Oils, latex and other combustible saps and resins.

D. Shelter

1. Building materials for shelter construction
2. Shade trees for people, livestock and shade-loving crops.
3. Wind-breaks and shelter-belts for protection of settlements, crop lands, pastures and road-ways.
4. Fencing: Live fences and fence posts.

E. Cash

1. Direct cash benefits from sale of tree products.
2. Indirect cash benefits from increased productivity.

Demerits of Social and Agroforestry

The negative effects of social forestry and agro-forestry are given below:

1. ***Competition:*** The major yield-decreasing effects at the tree-crop interface arise from competition for light, water and nutrients. While availability of light may be the most limiting factor in many situations, particularly those with relatively fertile soils and adequate water availability, the relative importance of light will decrease in semi-arid conditions as well as on sites with low fertility soils. The trees exhaust the soil nutrients reducing the yield per unit area of the main crops.
2. ***Pests and Diseases:*** The effect of tree—crop interactions on pests and disease incidence is a potentially important one, but is rather unexplored. Bacterial and fungal diseases may increase in shaded, more humid environments. For example, the incidence of diseases increases greatly under conditions of heavy shading. The main reasons for this are probably greater relative humidity and decreased wind both of which tend to favour fungal growth.

Table 10.3 A Comparison of Agroforestry and Social Forestry Systems

Points of difference	Agroforestry	Social-forestry
1. Components	It combines with the production of agricultural crops, forest plants and animals fodder species simultaneously or sequentially on the same unit of land.	It includes forest crops including fruit, fodder, fuel-wood, small timber to meet the multifarious demands of the society.
2. Need for intensive research before implementation	A definite package of technology has to be developed before implementation. Research efforts have been lacking.	Not required as compared to agroforestry. Cultivable waste and fallow lands are utilized for raising forest crops.
3. Consideration before raising	Crop inter-relationship to provide photothermic quantum needed by the farmer. Crop, rooting behavior and intensive study on the mutual effects is necessary before implementation.	Forest crops are raised either independently or in combination with other forest crops including legumes and grasses. This does not require deep research on the interrelationship.
4. Economic considerations	Combined yield of trees and agricultural crops should be better than individual and combination should be supplementary.	Social demands and requirements are more important than any economic consideration.
5. Plantation site	Dryland, waterlogged, alkaline, saline and nearly all cultivable areas and forest blocks.	Around field-bunds, farm-pond, habitation, unproductive land, village community land (Gram-Samaj-Bhumi).
6. Co-operation and management	Willing cooperation in different management is complicated, unless well tried before implementation.	Willing co-operation is natural to cover unproductive barren areas.

Source: Vyas, A.K., 2011, ***Introduction to Agriculture***, 5th ed. New Delhi, Jain Brothers, p.202.

3. ***Expansion of Root-network:*** The roots of the agroforestry trees make the agricultural land significantly unproductive from the agricultural point of view.

In order to overcome the above shortcomings, an integrated approach is necessary for research and development of agroforestry that is acceptable to farmers'/society and is able to improve their livelihood besides having potential of more biomass production and micro-climate improvement. This approach should be region specific as the socio-economic conditions of farmers/people and climatic conditions are area specific. There is also need to give importance to specific zones like coastal areas, where coastal zones agriculture is practised. In such areas, agroforestry which can impart sustainability to the productivity and can protect the fragile coastal ecosystems from degradation. A comparison of agroforestry and social forestry systems is given in Table 10.3.

Agroforestry is thus not only the option, but an imperative, in view of the global problem of natural resource degradation and expected climatic change. Its role in carbon sequestration, bioremediation, production system diversification is expected to ensure sustainable production and a healthy environment.

Fishing

Fish are a vital source of food. Fisheries include fish, whales, seals, pearls, crustaceans (i.e. lobsters, crabs, prawns, shrimps), mollusks (i.e. oysters, mussels, cockles, clams), sponges and seaweeds. The marine resources are however, an inexhaustible resource. In fact, fishing like mining is a 'robber industry'. If a man catch fish at a rate faster than nature can replace them, there will eventually be very few left. Overfishing and especially the wasteful killing of immature fish must be checked, not just by individual countries, but, as fish know no national boundaries, on an international basis.

The productivity of fish varies from latitude to latitude from ocean to ocean. The major determinants of fish products are as under: (i) the depth of water, (ii) the ocean currents, (iii) the temperature and salinity of the oceans, and (iv) the amount of plankton or fish food present.

Conditions Favourable for Fishing Grounds

Fishing is done in all the seas and oceans of the world. But most of the commercial grounds are located in the temperate latitudes. Commercial fishing is little developed in the tropical waters (**Fig. 10.8**). The major determinants of fishing grounds are as under.

1. ***Temperate Latitudes:*** In the high latitudes, there is abundant supply of phytoplankton. The phytoplankton are tiny plant organism which form the food of zooplankton (microscopic animals), which in turn become the food of fish. The fish in turn eaten by larger fish and sea mammals, i.e. seals and whales (**Fig. 10.9**).
2. ***Cool Climate:*** The sea water temperature less than 20°C is more conducive for the fast multiplication of fish. In fact, the largest fishing grounds of the world are found in the regions where the oceanic surface temperature is between 10°C to 15°C.
3. ***Availability of Cheap Labour:*** For the catching, cleaning, cutting, salting, smoking, pickling, drying or canning and marketing of fish cheap labour is imperative.
4. ***Availability of Market:*** Big market is also required for the development of fish industry.

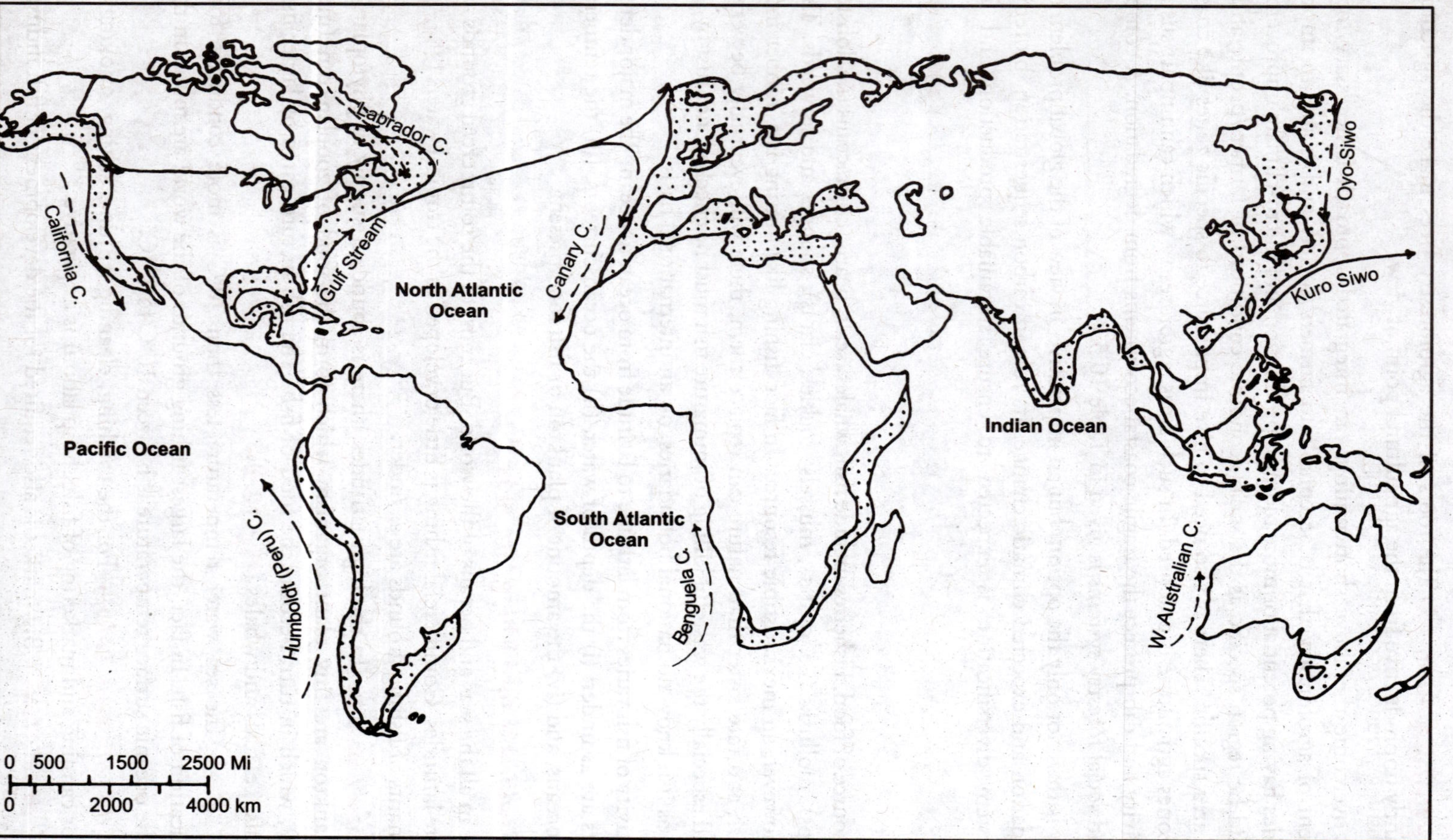

Fig. 10.8 Major Fishing Grounds of the World

Major Fishing Grounds

The significant fishing grounds of commercial fishing of the world are:

1. ***North East Atlantic Ocean:*** This fishing region extends from Iceland to the Mediterranean shores. In this region fisheries is a highly organized basis by the European countries (**Fig. 10.8**).
2. ***North Sea:*** Herring is the dominant species in the North Sea. More than million tonne of fish is caught from this region annually.
3. ***North West Atlantic:*** This region stretches from New Foundland to New England (USA) coastal seas of the North West Atlantic. The Grand Bank, George's Bank, Sable Bank, are the main fishing areas of this region. The merger of Gulf Stream and the Labrador Currents create ideal conditions for the fast multiplication of fish in this region.
4. ***The North East Pacific:*** It covers the continental shelf from Alaska to California. The main fish in this region are salmon.
5. ***The North West Pacific:*** This fishing ground covers from Bering Strait to the East China Sea. Salmon is the main fish of this region.
6. ***Other Fishing Grounds:*** Fishing is also done in the India Ocean, coasts of Chile and Peru and the countries of South East Asia.

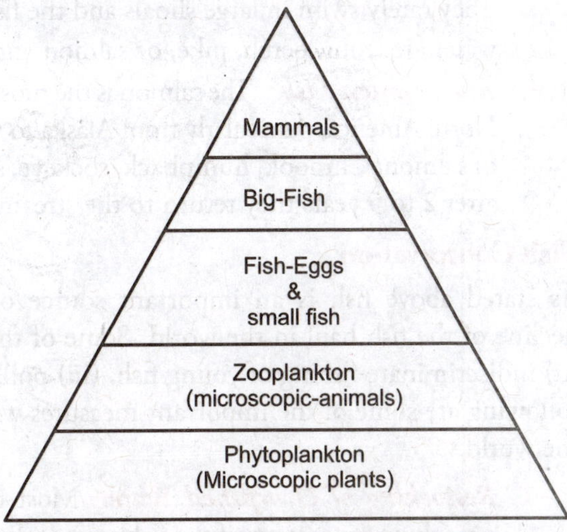

Fig. 10.9 The Food-pyramid of marine life

Fish Species

There are two main types of fish, namely (i) salt-water fish which spent their entire lives in the oceans and seas, and (ii) the fresh water fish which are found in inland streams, rivers and lakes. (iii) There are some anadromous fish, chiefly the salmon, which are spawned in the inland rivers, but spend most of their lives in the seas and only return to rivers to spawn and die.

(i) ***Salt Water Fish*** There are thousand of species of salt water fish in the seas and oceans, but the most numerous is the herring. The herring is found in large shoals which may be 15 km in length and 6 km in width and comprises as many as about 700,000 herrings. They swim between 15 and 30 meters below the surface and are caught by drift, usually at night, because they swim deeper during the day.

The mackerel is another important pelagic fish about 60 cm in length. It is tasty but perishable and is best consumed fresh. It is mainly found in the Mediterranean Sea, North Sea, Baltic Sea, and the Yellow Sea. They are caught by seine nets or purse seine.

Other pelagic fish caught in temperate waters are sardine, pilchards, brisling, anchovies, cod and menhaden. These species are usually smaller in size. These fish are caught in by trawl nets.

Other white fish include the flatfish, brill, catfish, dogfish, dab, hake, haddock, halibut, sole, and tuna or tunny.

(ii) ***Fresh Water Fish*** The fresh water fish are less important from the commercial point of view. They rarely swim in large shoals and the fishing areas are rather restricted. The main fish of fresh water are trout, perch, pike, or salmon and carp in rivers and lakes.

(iii) ***Anadromous Fish*** The salmon is the most important fish in this category. It is extensively fished in North America, particularly from Alaska to Oregon on the Pacific coast. There are five major species of salmon: Chinook, humpback, sockeye, silver and chum. The young salmon lives in the sea but after 2 to 5 years they return to the stream where they were born to lay their own eggs or die.

Fish Conservation

As stated above fish is an important source of nutritious food. There are many reasons for the decline of the fish haul in the world. Some of the important causes of fish decline are (i) overfishing, (ii) indiscriminate fishing of young fish, (iii) pollution of water, and (iv) ignorance of fish culture. The following are some of the important measures which can go a long way in the conservation of fish in the world.

1. ***Restocking of Overfished Water:*** Most coastal areas and inland waters have overfished and restocking is necessary if the fish are not disappear entirely. This can be done by transferring small fish from areas well-populated with fish or by introducing new species. Such young fish should be shielded from predators and allowed to get well-established before fishing recommences.
2. ***Forbid Indiscriminate Fishing:*** The killing of immature fish should be forbidden. In some countries, the size of all fish brought into a port has to be checked and offenders can be officially cautioned and fined.
3. ***Artificial Fertilization of Eggs:*** Scientists have successfully experimented with the artificial fertilization of eggs in special hatcheries and then transferred them from the breeding ground.
4. ***Protection from Pollution:*** Fish can not survive in polluted water. There should be legislation against those industries responsible for pollution. This step will help tremendously in preserving the fish pollution both in rivers and coastal waters.
5. ***International Agreement on Fisheries:*** As fish know no boundaries, it is essential to devise some form of international control over fishing and to minimize the coastal pollution.
6. ***Researches in World Fisheries:*** A systematic research about fisheries is imperative for the sustainability of this resource. In this direction research need to be done about the salinity of oceans, temperature of water, fertility of the micro-organisms or plankton, data on number and type fish caught, fishing method, greater use of fish, sea mammals and other marine products. If all the above steps are taken together, the fish resource may be made more viable and sustainable.

SECONDARY ACTIVITIES (MANUFACTURING)

The primary products obtained from the nature are processed through industries to make them usable. The secondary activities are known as manufacturing. In fact, the agricultural, mineral and energy resources are processed in factories and industries. Manufactured goods often take very different forms which are more useful and valuable than the original raw materials from which they are made. For example, sugarcane is processed into sugar in sugar factories, cotton is converted into cloths in textile mills, and iron-ore is smelted into iron and steel. All these processing and manufacturing are the secondary activities.

Classification of Industries

Numerous types of goods are manufacture by man with the help of technology. The manufacturing industries, however, may be classified into three categories, known as: (i) primary, (ii) secondary, and (iii) tertiary industries.

1. Primary Industries

In this category are included the production of power from coal and oil or the production of agricultural commodities to form food-stuffs or industrial raw materials like the smelting of bauxite to make aluminum.

2. Secondary Industries

The secondary industries include, heavy industries, e.g. (i) engineering, metal goods, heavy chemicals, ship-building, locomotives, and (ii) light industries, e.g. electrical equipments, plastics, textiles/garments, cosmetics and toilet articles. Basically they include all re-processing of partially manufactured goods to make more complex products, e.g. the use of cloth in clothing, the use of iron parts in manufacture of machinery, and the use of paper to make books.

3. Tertiary Industry

It includes trade, commerce, transportation, entertainment, personal service, tourism, administration etc.

Locational Factors of Industries

Different industries are located at different places. The location of an industry is influenced by several physical and socio-economic factors. These determinants are known as the locational factors of industries. The major determinants of location of industries are: (i) availability of raw material, (ii) availability of sources of energy, and power (coal, electricity, petroleum, natural gas, hydro, nuclear power etc), (iii) availability of labour (skilled and unskilled), (iv) capital, (v) entrepreneurship, (vi) market (domestic and international), (vii) managerial skill, (viii)political stability, (ix) climate, and (x) national policy and preferential treatment, (xi) Industrial inertia or the failure of industry to move machinery from one area to another when locational advantages and disadvantages change is called industrial inertia. (xii) good transportation network, and (xiii) cost of building and infrastructural network.

Textile Industries

Textile is one of the oldest industries of the world. It is based on pure raw material and therefore may be located in the region of raw material or market. Location of textile industry is also affected by the transportation cost. The lightness and ease to transport of fibres means that raw materials location is of negligible advantage.

Modern, mechanized textile manufacturing was first developed in Britain, as a result of invention of spinning and weaving machines. From Britain the techniques of modern textile spinning, weaving, dyeing, printing and finishing spread to other parts of Europe, USA, China, India, Japan and the rest of the world. Textile manufacture is now one of the most widely distributed industries of the world for the following reasons.

(i) Clothing is one of the basic needs of the world population. Everyone needs clothing and therefore there is a constant demand for textiles all over the world. These can be most cheaply and economically supplied by local manufacture.

(ii) Mechanization has meant that textile manufacture can be done using unskilled labour. It is therefore an ideal industry for countries where there is no background of industrial skills. Textile industries are always among the first to be developed by underdeveloped countries.
(iii) Cotton is grown in a very large number of tropical and subtropical countries.
(iv) Fibers are relatively light, non-perishable and easily transportable.
(v) Textile industries are located mainly in relation to power and labour supplies. Thus the raw material location is of negligible advantage.

Cotton Textile Industry in the World

Cotton textile industries are largely confined to USA, Britain, China, India, Central Asian Republics, Egypt, France, Germany, Japan, Netherlands, Russia, Ukraine, Thailand, South Korea, Indonesia, Malaysia, Sri Lanka, Pakistan, Brazil, Argentina, South Africa, Nigeria. The important cotton textile industrial centres of the world have been shown in **Fig. 10.10**.

Cotton Textile Industry in India

The first modern cotton textile mill was started in 1818 at Fort Gloster near Kolkata. The attempt however, failed and a new textile mill was started by the Bomaby Spinning and Weaving Company Ltd. In 1851. After 1858 mills began to be set up in Ahmadabad, Mumbai, Pune, Sholapur, Kanpur, Nagpur, Chennai and Coimbatore. At present, having more than 425 textile mills, cotton textile is the first ranking industry of India.

In India,the location of cotton textile industry is mainly influenced by the availability of raw material, proximity to the market, availability of capital, nearness of seaport, moist climate and cheap and skilled labour. The concentration of cotton mills is in Mumbai, Ahmadabad, Vadodra, Surat, Bhavnagar, Rajkot, Sholapur, Nagpur, Pune, Bhopal, Indore, Ujjain, Gwalior, Jabalpur, Agra, Bareilly, Kanpur, Meerut, Modinagar, Moradabad, Hathras, Varanasi, Haora, Kolkata, Murshidabad, Patna, Amritsar, Ludhiana, Phagwara, Hissar, Bhiwani, Beawar, Bhilwara, Bangaluru, Mysore, Pondicherry, Chennai, Coimbatore, Erode, Madurai, Tuticorin, Alwaye, Alleppey, Kochi, Trichure, etc. **(Fig. 10.11)**.

Export

India is the second largest exporter of cotton textiles in the world. India exports cotton goods to Russia, France, Germany, United Kingdom, United States, Norway, Sweden, Australia, Nepal, Ethiopia, Sudan, Tanzania, and Sri Lanka. The Cotton Textile Promotion Council helps in the exports of textile goods.

Problems

Cotton textile industry is confronted with numerous problems at present. Some of the important problems of textile industry have been given in the following:

1. ***Shortage of Raw Material:*** Raw Material determines about 35 per cent of the total production cost of textile goods. The country is deficient in good quality cotton. The long staple cotton is imported from Egypt, Sudan, Pakistan, Turkmenistan, Uzbekistani and United States of America. Fluctuation in prices and uncertainties in the availability of raw material causes low production and sickness to the cotton factories.
2. ***Obsolete Machinery:*** Most of the textile mills in India are working with the outdated machinery. Obsolete machinery leads to low output and poor quality of goods. It is one of the main reasons why Indian textiles are not able to face competition in the international market.

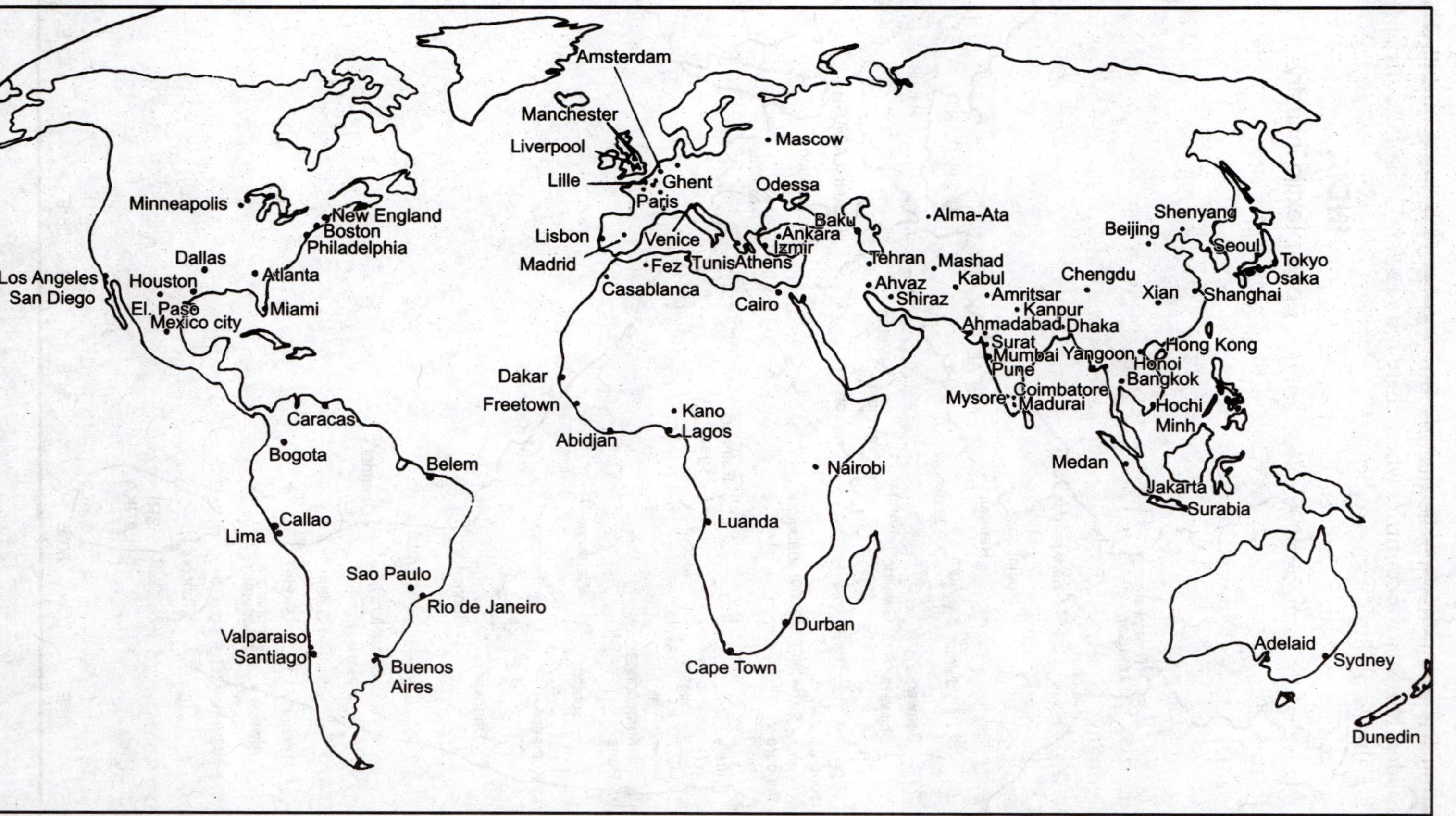

Fig. 10.10 World–Cotton Textile Industry

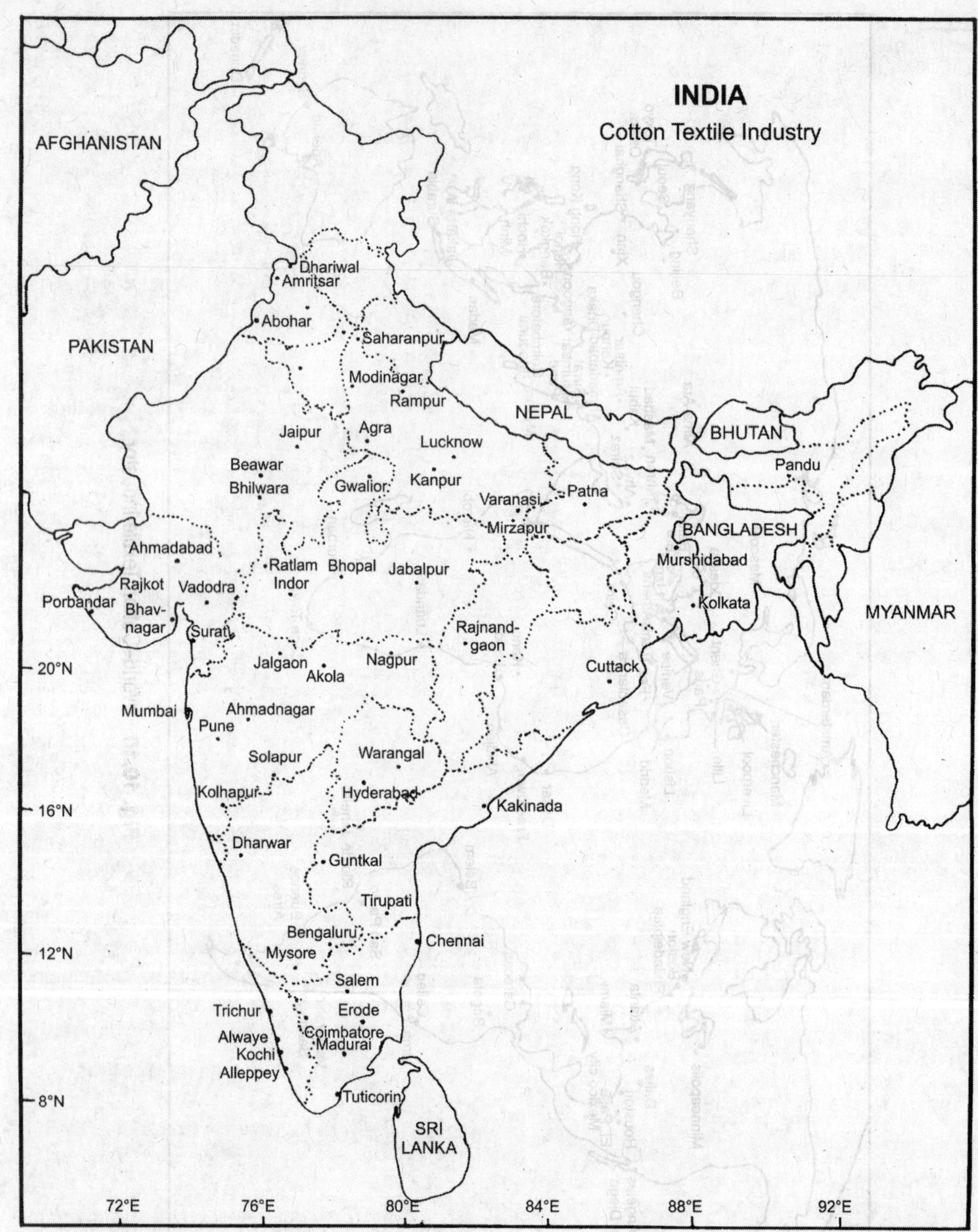

Fig. 10.11 India: Main Centres of Textile Industry

3. ***Shortage of Power:*** The textile mills are facing acute shortage of power. This leads to loss of man hours, low production and loss in the mills.
4. ***Competition in the International Market:*** The Indian cotton textile goods are facing stiff competition in foreign markets from China, South Korea, Japan, Malaysia, Indonesia, Taiwan, and Thailand.
5. ***Sick Mills:*** In India more than one hundred cotton mills are sick and incurring great losses.
6. ***Strikes and Lockouts:*** Frequent strike and lockouts also affect the production and efficiency of cotton mills adversely.
7. ***Slow Pace of Modernization:*** Most of the cotton textile mills of India are not able to modernize their machinery and management. Consequently, the efficiency is low and the cost of production of cotton goods is relatively high. All these problems need to be addressed on a priority basis to make the textile industry more profitable and sustainable.

Iron and Steel Industry

Out of all the metallurgical industries, iron and steel industry is the most important. Iron and steel are capable of more extensive application than any other metal. Iron has great strength and toughness, great elasticity, relatively high ductility, low cost and alloy-ability. The following factors are the main determinants in the location of iron and steel industry.

(i) Availability of Iron Ore

The availability of high grade iron-ore like hematite and magnetite are of vital significance for the location of iron and steel industry. Most of the iron and steel industries of U.S.A. are located near the Mesabi Range (near Superior Lake) and the Appalachian Mountain, and in the Ural Mts. of Russia.

Although iron-ore-fields exercise considerable attraction on the industry, there are many important iron-fields which have no local smelting industry. For example, in the remote and sparsely populated region of Schefferville (Canada); while in the Mauritania desert there is insufficient market potential to set up iron and steel industry.

(ii) Availability of Coal

In the establishment of iron and steel industry, the availability of coal is also very important. Many of the steel plants have been located in the Appalachian, Saar Basin, Silesia Basin, Wales, Donets Basin, Karaganda, Kuzbas, Raniganj and Jharia coal deposits region.

(iii) Coastal Locations

At present, many large scale iron and steel plants have been located along the coastal locations. The steel plants of north-east Australia, England, Germany, Japan, USA, South Africa, South Wales, Spain, Glasgow (Scotland), New Manglore (Karnataka) and Vishakhapatnam (Andhra Pradesh), are the examples of coastal locations of iron and steel industry. Thus coastal sites have become more important as iron ore, coal and alloy metals are all easily assembled.

Major Steel Plants of the World

Iron and steel industry is well distributed in the developed and the developing countries of the world. Some of the important iron and steel industrial centres of the world are:

Pittsburgh, Buffalo, Cleveland, Detroit, Duluth, Gary, Chicago, Atlanta, Seattle and Birmingham (USA) near the iron ore deposits. Similarly, iron and steel industries have been located near Ruhr Basin (Germany), Lorraine (France), Chelyabinsk, Magnitogorsk in Ural Mountains (Russia), Donbas

(Ukraine), Karaganda (Kazakhstan), Kuzbas (Russia), Anshan, Shenyang, (Manchuria), Shanghai -China, Kimberley Plateau and Pilbara, Whyalla, Port Kembla (Australia), Rasht (Iran), Salvador, Curitiba, Rio de Janeiro, Minas Gerais in Brazil (**Fig. 10.12**). In India most of the iron and steel plants are located near the iron –ore and coal deposits. The main steel plants of India and the Chotanagpur region are Bhilai, Bhadravati, Bokaro, Burnpur, Dhanbad, Daitari, Dolvi (Maharashtra), Durgapur, Gopalpur, Jamshedpur, Kalinganagar, Paradip, Rourkela, Salem, Vijaynagaram, and Vishakhapatnam (**Figs. 10.13 & 10.14**).

Table 10.4 World-Major Industrial Regions

Industrial Region	Main Industries
Europe Bohemia (Germany)	Iron and steel, heavy machinery, mining equipments, electric goods, light machinery, consumer goods, agricultural machinery (Fig. 10.12)
Lorraine (N. East France)	Iron and steel, textile, heavy and light machinery, consumer goods, brewery, and food processing.
Moscow (Russia)	Iron and steel, cotton and woollen textiles, engineering goods, assorted machinery, automobiles, electric goods, pharmaceutical and food processing.
Po-Basin (Italy)	Automobiles electric goods, consumer goods, porcelain, precision instruments, agricultural machinery, financial services.
Ruhr Basin (Germany)	Iron and steel, heavy machinery, petrochemicals, mining equipments, consumer items.
Saar Basin (France)	Iron and steel, automobiles, electric goods, electronics, chemicals, agricultural machinery, textiles and food processing.
Cardiff-Swansea (Wales-U.K.)	Ship building, iron and steel, heavy machinery, mining equipments, automobiles, petrochemicals, light machinery, consumer goods, food processing
Glasgow (Scotland)	Ship building, Iron and steel, automobiles, electronic goods, agricultural machinery, chemicals, textiles, and food processing.
Manchester, Liverpool, New Castle (England)	Ship-building, woollen and cotton textile, light machinery, utensils, electronic goods, textiles.
Volga Region (Russia)	Petrochemical, textiles, agricultural machinery, mining equipments.
Industrial Regions of North America	Iron and steel, electric appliances, grains milling, automobiles, petrochemicals, engineering goods, consumer goods, fir-trade, heavy machinery, precision instruments, brewing, ceramics, fruits-packing, dairy products, and food processing.
Buffalo, Cleveland, Detroit, Duluth, Gary, Milwaukee, Toledo (Great Lakes Region)	Iron and steel, electric appliances, grains milling, automobiles, petrochemicals, engineering goods, consumer goods, fir-trade, heavy machinery, precision instruments, brewing, ceramics, fruits-packing, dairy products, and food processing.
Brazil	Industrial centres, Curitiba, Rio de Janeiro, Sao-Paulo, Salvador, Santos.
Colombia	Medelin, Bagota, Kali
Peru	Callao, Lima, Chimbote, Tacha
Argentina	La Plata, Buenos Aires, Parana
South Africa	Johannesburg, Durban, Cape Town
India	Bhilai, Bhadrawati, Bokaro, Burnpur, Daitari, Dhanbad, Dolvi, Gopalpur, Jamshedpur, Kalinganagar, Paradip, Rourkela, Salem, Vijaynagar, Vishakhapatnam, Mumbai, Ahmadabad, Chennai, Kolkata, Delhi,etc.

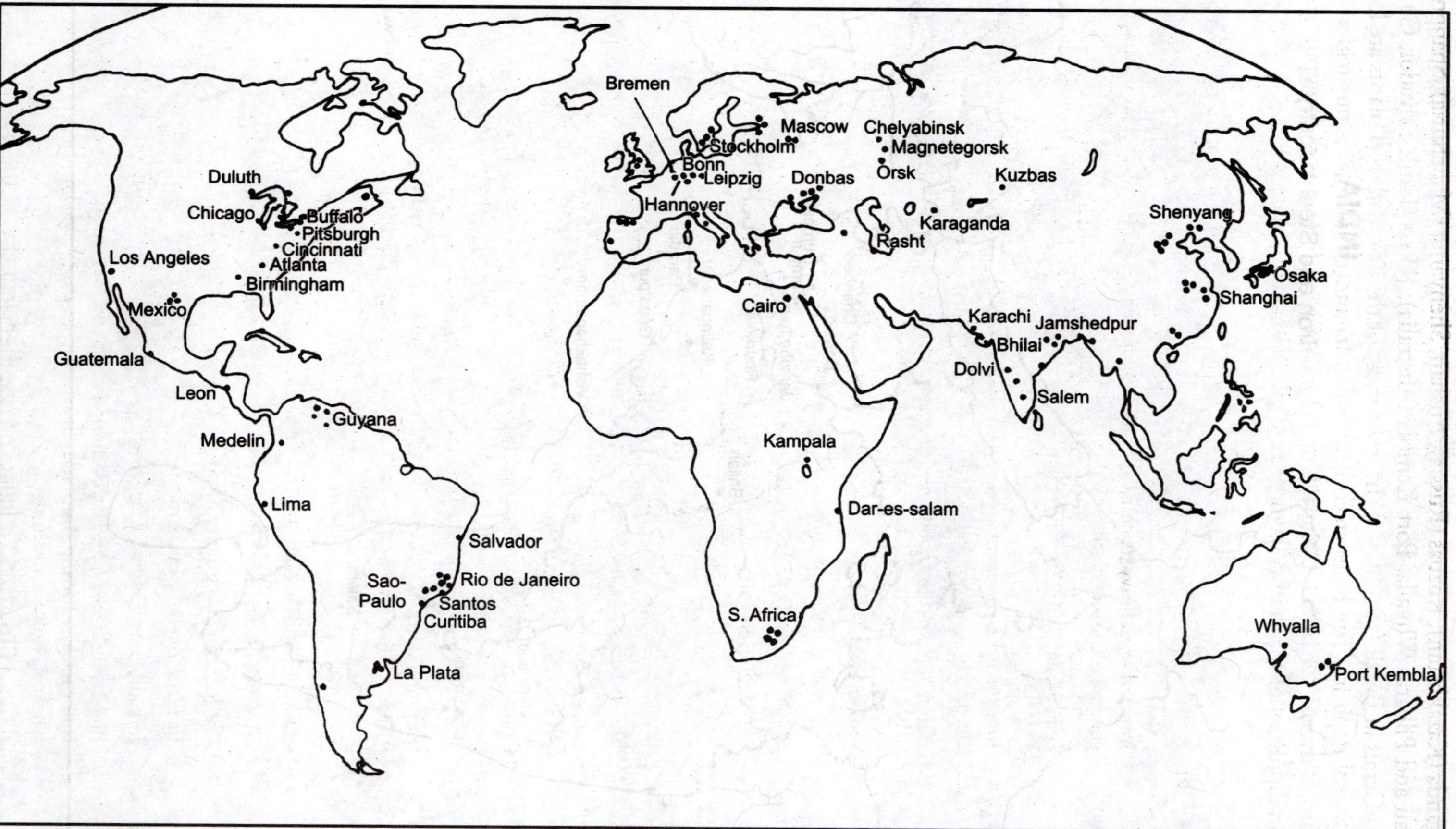

Fig. 10.12 World Iron and Steel Industry

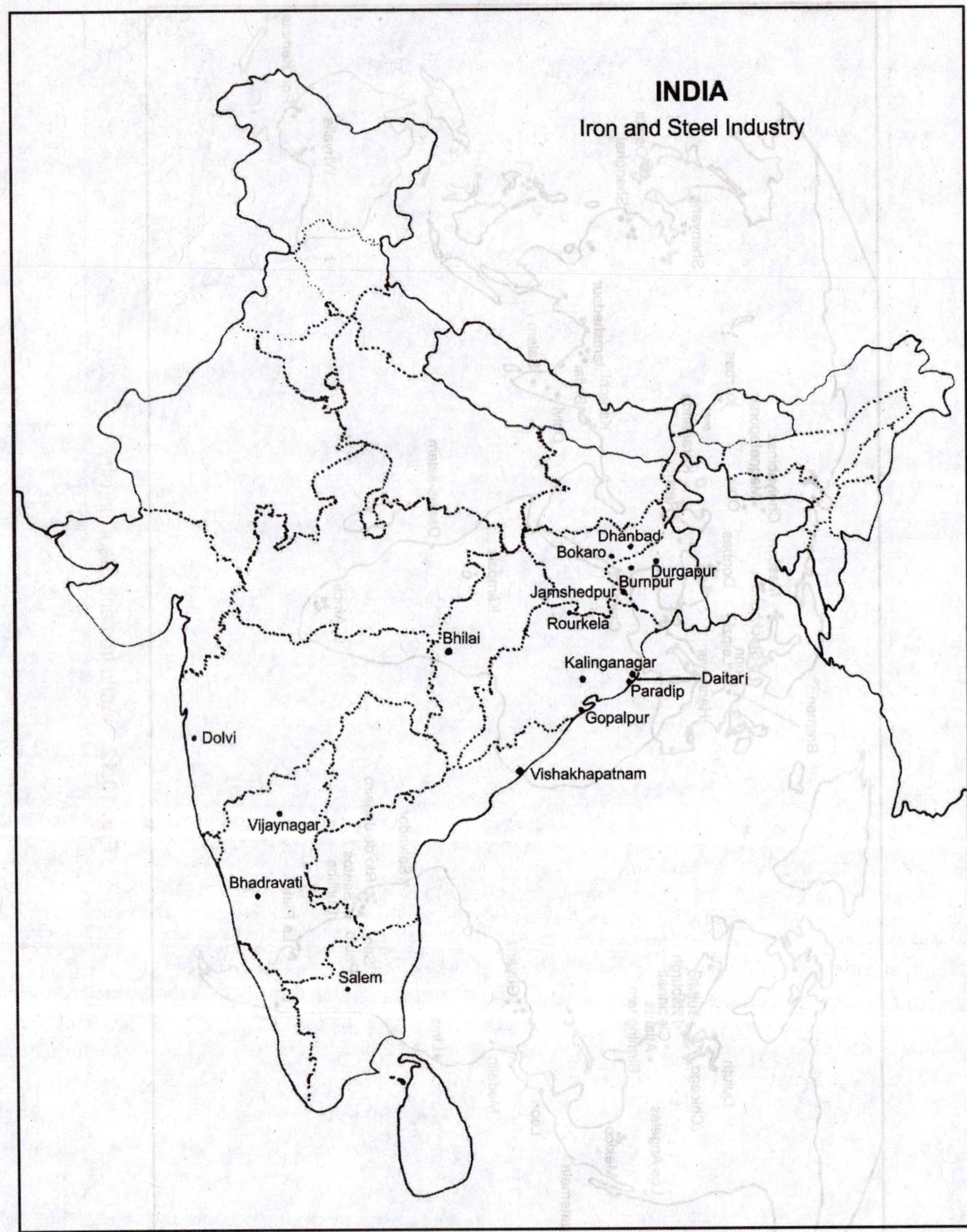

Fig. 10.13 India Iron and Steel Industry

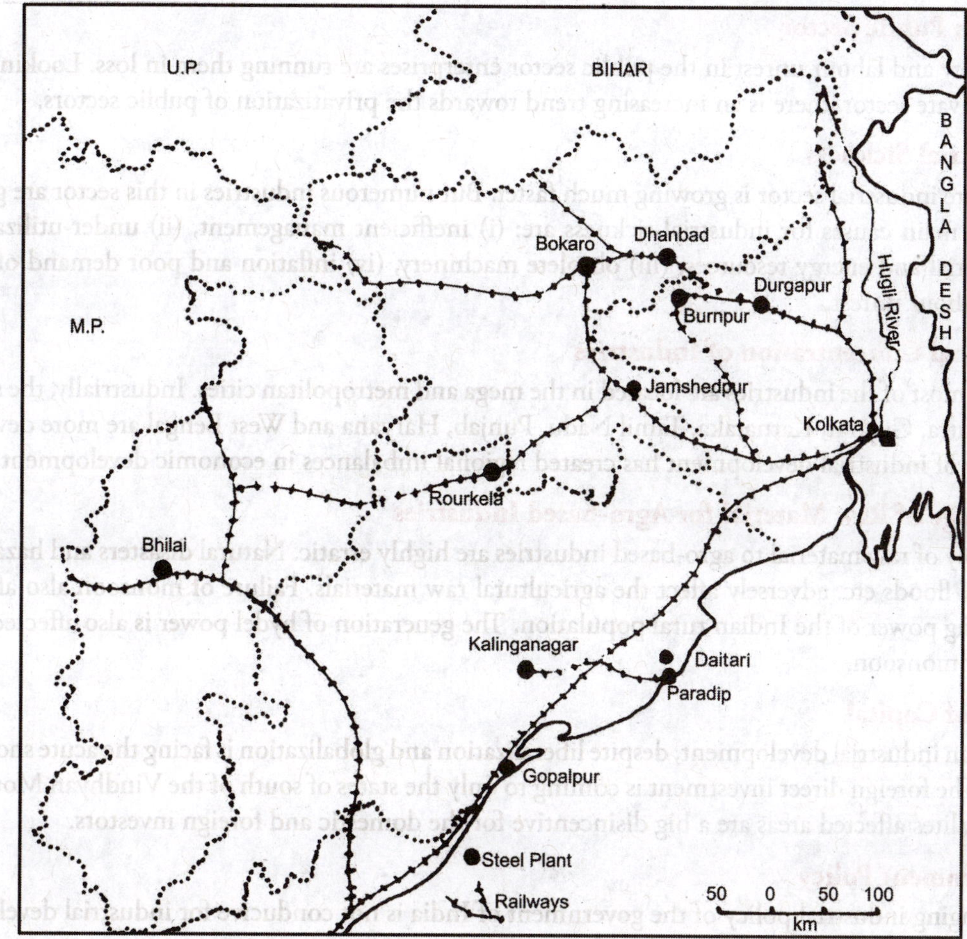

Fig. 10.14 Iron and Steel Plants of Chhotanagpur Region

Industrial Problems of India

India is one of the emerging industrial forces in the world. Being in the transitional phase, India is facing a number of problems. The main industrial problems of India has been given in the following:

1. Inadequate Industrial Infrastructure

The basic structure, roads, electricity, transport equipments are not adequate to accelerate the industrial growth of India. The energy crisis is affecting the production efficiency of the industries adversely. The road and rail transport are over-burdened and there are many bottlenecks in transport of raw material and finished goods.

2. Inadequacy of Raw Material

Some of the raw material used in copper, aluminum and iron and steel industries are not adequately available. India is importing heavy quantities of crude oil, natural gas, phosphate to sustain its petrochemical industries. There is shortage of good quality of cotton, jute, wool and silk for the textile industries.

3. Loss in Public Sector

Inefficiency and labour unrest in the public sector enterprises are running them in loss. Looking at the loss in private sector, there is an increasing trend towards the privatization of public sectors.

4. Industrial Sickness

The private industrial sector is growing much faster. But numerous industries in this sector are growing sick. The main causes for industrial sickness are: (i) inefficient management, (ii) under-utilization of raw material and energy resources, (iii) obsolete machinery, (iv) inflation and poor demand of goods, and (v) labour unrest.

5. Regional Concentration of Industries

In India, most of the industries are located in the mega and metropolitan cities. Industrially, the states of Maharashtra, Gujarat, Karnataka, Tamil Nadu, Punjab, Haryana and West Bengal are more developed. This type of industrial development has created regional imbalances in economic development.

6. Shortage of Raw Material for Agro-based Industries

The supply of raw material to agro-based industries are highly erratic. Natural disasters and hazards like droughts, floods etc. adversely affect the agricultural raw materials. Failure of monsoon also affect the purchasing power of the Indian rural population. The generation of hydel power is also affected by the failure of monsoon.

7. Lack of Capital

The Indian industrial development, despite liberalization and globalization is facing the acute shortage of capital. The foreign direct investment is coming to only the states of south of the Vindhyan Mountains. The Naxalites affected areas are a big disincentive for the domestic and foreign investors.

8. Government Policy

The changing industrial policy of the government of India is not conducive for industrial development in the country.

All the above problems need to be addressed at the priority basis to have a balanced industrial development in the country.

TERTIARY ACTIVITY

The tertiary sector of Indian economy is weak as compared to Japan, Germany, U.S.A., China etc. Activities associated with tertiary sector, i.e. retail and wholesales, transportation and distribution, entertainment (movies, T.V. radio, music, theatre, etc.), media, insurance, banking, healthcare and law need much improvement to overcome the industrial problems of India.

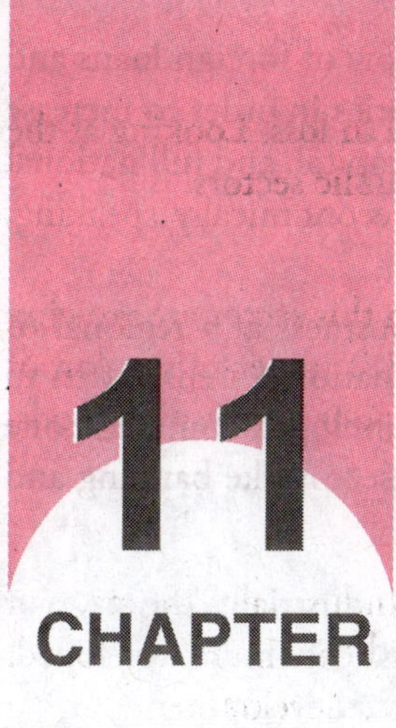

Chapter 11 Contemporary Socio-Economic Issues

GLOBALISATION AND LIBERALISATION

Effects on Indian Society

Globalisation

The concept of interactions of natural and human phenomena at a global scale is known as globalisation. It refers to the trend toward the growing interconnectedness of different countries of the world. It is primarily an interchange of economic, social, cultural, political, technological attributes that take place between societies, communities, nations and countries. In other words, it is a process by which a society opens up to outside influences in the fields of economy, production, distribution, trade, culture, art, music, fashion, traditions and the way of life.

Though the interconnectedness of countries is going on from times immemorial, this process was termed as 'Globalisation' for the first time around the second half of the 20th century. Much of the literature on Globalisation has appeared since the late 1970s and 1980s. The contemporary Globalisation differs from the process that could be observed in the past, primarily in terms of quantum of interchange and interconnectedness. Everything happens much faster today than it did in the past. The current process of Globalisation, which is popularly described as gradual removal of barriers to trade and investment between nations, is said to aim to achieve economic efficiency through competition, while seeking broader objectives of economic and social development.

The most important form of globalisation is economic globalisation. It results mostly from a free movement of capital, labour, technology, information and products which effect economy, culture, social and political environment. In the context of Indian economy, it implies several features like removal of protective methods to enable foreign players to freely compete in the Indian market. Further, it means allowing foreign investment without much restriction along with inflow of foreign loans and Non-Resident Indians (NRI) payments. It also means reduction in customs duties in order to increase both export and import. There is free movement of goods, services, labour and capital, and full national treatment for foreign investors as well as nationals working overseas so that economically speaking, there are no foreigners. In brief, it is the borderless world.

From the point of view of business firm, it means that instead of doing business at a regional or national level, it can now get raw material, labour and markets from the international arena, often to its advantage. If labour and raw material are expensive in more affluent and developed countries, one could shift to places where these factors of production are cheaper. In service sector like banking and insurance, it could just mean transferring relevant data to another computer.

The salient features of present day globalisation are:

1. National economies have become more open and more closely integrated.
2. World trade has grown significantly.
3. International capital flows have grown even faster.
4. Ideas, technologies and cultural attributes are exchanged at a higher acceleration.
5. There is greater volume of exchanges of goods and services.
6. There is greater variety of things being exchanged.
7. New services have entered in the international market. For example, an Indian architect may design a building in African countries or a Japanese architect may design a building in France or in the Gulf Countries.
8. Use of internet and mobile phones have made it possible to communicate anywhere around the globe instantly. This accelerated the growth and development of knowledge of societies.
9. While globalisation is seen as a factor of economic growth, it is also known to increase the income gap between and within the countries, increase poverty, and aggravate environmental degradation.

Liberalisation

Liberalisation has been defined as the general reduction in the role of the state in economic governance. It is the withdrawal by the state from some economic sectors and its replacement by the private sector.

The salient features of liberalisation are:

1. Decline in the public sectors in basic and key industries, banking, insurance, etc.
2. Decline in the role of state in provision of public social services like education, housing and health care.
3. Future development through wider participation of the private sector.

Privatisation

Privatisation largely means selling of public owned assets to private ownership by stages. Privatisation can be done using any or all of the following techniques:

1. Public offering of shares—All or part of the shares of public limited company are offered for sale to public.
2. Private sale of shares—All or part of a state-owned enterprise is sold to private individuals or group of purchasers.

3. New private investment in a state-owned enterprise—private share issues are subsidised by the private sector or public.
4. Entry of the private sector into public sector—private groups allowed to get into areas reserved for the public sector such as the power and telecommunications sectors in India.
5. Contracting out the services of utilities to private operators or contractors for operation and maintenance, while retaining ownership with the government in the case of water, sewage treatment, etc.
6. Sale of government or state enterprise assets as private sale instead of shares.
7. Reorganisation or fragmentation of subsidiary units of a company.

Arguments in favour of Liberalisation, Privatisation and Globalisation in India

Following arguments are in favour of liberalisation, privatisation and globalisation:

1. Raising the rate of economic growth of India to about 8 per cent or more.
2. Growing competitiveness in industrial sector to face global challenge.
3. Reduction in poverty and inequality in the distribution of income and wealth.
4. It enhances the efficiency, productivity and profitability of public sector.
5. It is promoting private sector investment in important areas.
6. It promotes the flow of foreign direct investment.
7. It generates more rural and urban employment.

Arguments against Liberalisation, Privatisation and Globalisation

Following are the arguments against globalisation, liberalisation and privatisation in India:

1. The agricultural sector is ignored as compared to industries and tertiary sectors.
2. The policy has been adopted under the pressure of World Bank and International Monetary Funds which is considered as a surrender of the Indian economy to these international financial bodies.
3. Globalisation has increased the dependence of the economy on foreign technology and has failed to improve indigenous technology.
4. Globalisation has increased indebtedness of the country on foreign assistance.
5. Globalisation has led to the loss of economic sovereignty of the country.
6. Globalisation has aggravated the problem of unemployment by introducing large scale retrenchment of workers without making any adequate provision for alternative scope of employment.
7. There is much stress on privatisation.
8. Globalisation has been encouraging a dangerous trend of consumerism by the production of luxury goods.
9. Globalisation failed to arrest the rising trend of prices (inflation), check fiscal deficit, control subsidies and the controlling of non-plan expenditure of the government.

Social Relevance of Liberalisation and Globalisation

The socio-economic implications of liberalisation and globalisation are multidimensional. The economic dimensions of globalisation are, however, more prominent and far-reaching. The impact of globalisation on the work of people, employment, working conditions, income, social status of families, society, liberty and social security, female empowerment, identity, and culture are numerous. *Some of the important consequences of liberalisation and globalisation on economy, employment and culture have been described briefly in the following:*

1. **Reduction in Public Spending**: The government expenditure in India has declined in public spending from 11% in 1960s to about 4.5% in 2012. The consequences of reduction in public spending has adversely affected employment and development of social services like education, health-care and housing.
2. **Decrease in Social Security System**: The moving of public sector into private sector means the state is moving away from economic planning and leaving the economic decisions to the market-forces. Liberalisation and globalisation thus resulted in casualization or informalization of the work force, causing low wages for workers and exploitation of workers.
3. **Job Insecurity**: The Transnational and Multinational Corporations have evolved a vendor system for their productions. The companies give out their work to labourers through contractors, who in turn deliver the output to the company. This results in job insecurity of the labourers and worsening of labour welfare since there is no monitoring for their welfare.
4. **Displacement of Unskilled and Semi-skilled Workers**: Increased mechanization and use of new technology demand more skilled labour and thus displace unskilled workers.
5. **Feminisation of Labour**: Women have entered the labour force in large number in countries that have embraced liberal economic policies. The overall economic activity rate of women for the age group 24–54 approached over 72% in 2012. The highest absorption of women has been witnessed in the export oriented industrial sector. Investors have demonstrated a preference for women in the soft industries such as apparel, shoe, ornaments-selling, toy-making, data-processing and semi-conductors assembling.
6. **Poverty**: Liberalisation and globalisation have resulted in the widening of inequalities in the income of the rich and the poor. The main cause of this widening disparity is contractualization of works and skill-based segregation of work. Liberalisation, privatisation and globalisation are very uneven process, with unequal distribution of profits.
7. **Effect on Agriculture**: Globalisation has adversely affected the income of farmers of the developing countries mainly because the increase of costs of production.
8. **Lowering of Underground Water-table**: The underground water table is being increasingly lowered because of too much pumping out of water by millions of tube wells as the new seeds of rice and wheat demand more irrigation. The High Yielding Varieties are vulnerable to pest attacks resulting in more use of pesticides. The indiscriminate use of chemical fertilizers has changed the soil chemistry resulting into degradation of agricultural land, water resource, ecosystems, ecology, sustainability of resources and environment.
9. **Change in Land Use of Million and Mega Cities:** Globalisation and liberalisation have adversely affected the over all infrastructure of the mega and million cities. The clearance of slums and

changes in the urban land use created more problems for the urban poor. The slum dwellers like hawkers, street-dwellers, destitute have been pushed out of the city to the peripheries. The income of these people declined and their poor standard of living has further deteriorated.

10. **Migration of Workers**: There is unprecedented scale of human displacement. About 16 per cent of the workers of the world are crossing international borders in search of jobs and employment. Indian labour is not an exception to this.
11. **Commercialization of Indigenous Knowledge**: Liberalisation and Globalisation invade the territories and resources of indigenous people which may lead to destruction of their way of life. The big corporates get access to indigenous knowledge and patent it for their gain and profit.
12. **Effect on Cultures and Traditions**. Liberalisation and Globalisation have not only affected our lifestyles, it has also affected the fine arts, literature, music, dance, movies, news, media, TV programmes, entertainment and life style. Satellite cables, phones, walkman, VCDs, DVDs and other entertainment technology has made the life in urban and rural areas more fast, enjoyable but full of tension.
13. **Easy Communication**: The information technology made the communication easier, faster and cheaper.
14. **Development of Hybrid Culture**: The globalisation may lead to single world culture or homogenized culture. The global interactions may produce inventive new cultural forms or hybrid culture.
15. **Resurgence of Cultural Nationalism**: Liberalisation and Globalisation also give rise to active cultural campaigning to defend local identities. Nations reject global cultural integration and people remain loyal to local histories, identities, customs and traditions. It is leading to cultural clash. Thus the overall impact of globalisation, liberalisation and privatisation are numerous. Change is the law of nature, but the change should not be at the cost socio-cultural values of the country.

POVERTY AND HUNGER

Definition of Proverty

There is no unanimity about the definition of poverty. Poverty is a peculiar problem which varies in space and time, from country to country and from region to region. In fact, there cannot be a common definition of poverty which can be accepted everywhere in the world. In the opinion of leading social scientists, poverty is a situation where a section of the society, having no fault of their own, is denied of even basic necessities (food, clothing and shelter) of life. In other words, poverty is the perceived deprivation with respect to basic human needs. 'These basic human needs can be adequately nourished, the need to be decently clothed, the need to be reasonably sheltered, the need to be minimally educated, and the need to be mobile for purposes of social interaction and participation in economic activity.'

Poverty Line

Normally poverty is defined with poverty line. The poverty line divides the population of the country as poor and non-poor. In India, the poverty line is defined on the basis of private consumption expenditure for buying both food and non-food items. Thus, the poverty line defines a threshold income. Households earning below this threshold are considered poor. Different countries have different methods of defining the threshold income depending on local socio-economic needs. In India, the Planning Commission releases the poverty estimates in India.

The Indian Poverty Line

In 2011, the Suresh Tendulkar Committee defined the poverty line on the basis of monthly spending on food, clothing, housing, education, health, electricity and transport. According to one estimate in 2014, a person who spends ₹ 30.50p in rural areas and ₹ 46.25p in urban areas a day is defined as living below the poverty line.

The Planning Commission of India made an estimate of poverty line in July 2014. As per the latest available information, the poverty line at all India level for 2013-2014 is estimated at a monthly per capita consumption expenditure (MPCE) of ₹ 1927 per month for rural areas and ₹ 1407 for urban areas. The issue of poverty can be analyzed from a number of perspectives. One of them is the perspective of (i) absolute poverty and (ii) relative poverty.

Absolute and Relative Poverty

Absolute Poverty

The concept is not related to the income and the distribution of consumption expenditure, which is usually done in the measure of relative poverty. Absolute poverty refers to being unable to meet minimum human needs, such as adequate food, clothing, health-care, education and shelter, even by developing world standards. It also includes social deprivation, such as denial of employment, participation in social institutions, and education. In the measure of absolute poverty, the absolute minimum consumption basket includes consumption of food grains, vegetables, milk products and other important items which are necessary for attaining healthy living with access to other important non-food items. People whose consumption expenditures are found below this threshold limit are usually considered as poor. For example, the one-dollar consumption expenditure per capita purchasing power parity (PPP) dollars is the absolute poverty line accepted internationally. The concept of absolute poverty is very much relevant to poor and less developed countries of the world where large scale poverty prevails.

Thus poverty is a denial of choices and opportunities, a violation of human dignity. It means lack of basic capacity to participate effectively in society. It means not having enough to feed and clothe a family, not having a school or clinic to go to, not having the land on which to grow one's food or job to earn one's living, and having access to credit. It mean insecurity, powerlessness and exclusion of individuals, households and communities. It means susceptibility to violence, and it often implies living on marginal or fragile environments, without access to clean water.

Relative Poverty

The concept of relative poverty is associated with the issues of inequality. Not every country (or population) has the same standard of living and per capita income. In comparison to other countries, a country is generally poorer or richer. Most underdeveloped countries are considered poor because their per capita GNP is much lower than that of most developed countries. For example, the per capita income of USA in 2011 was over $45,000 and that of U.K. was $28,000 and thus U.K. can be considered as poor as compared to USA.

The problem of international disparity in poverty is further aggravated by the presence of large internal disparities in poverty levels within the country, regardless of weather it is poor or rich in the aggregate. The internal disparity in underdeveloped countries appears greater than that in the developed countries.

In relative poverty, the extent of income or consumption of the last quintile population (the poorest) could be compared with the richest quaintile showing a wide gap between the two.

Causes of Poverty

There are many causes of poverty. These causes are invariably interrelated and complicated. Some of the important causes of poverty are given below:

(i) Overpopulation

Overpopulation is one of the important causes of poverty. Malthus (1798) was the first economist who emphasized overpopulation as the main cause of poverty, undernourishment and starvation. Although the Malthusian position has certain validity, it lacks a sound logical basis. It cannot explain why so much affluence exists in the midst of abject poverty in the developing countries. It also does not explain why so much poverty exists in countries with tremendous amount of resources but with a relatively small population.

(ii) Unequal Distribution of Means of Production

In the opinion of Karl Marx and Frederick Engels, poverty exists not because of overpopulation but because of unequal distribution of productive resources such as land and capital available in the society. The unequal distribution of resources excludes certain population groups from having secure access to productive resources. As a result they cannot be productive and are forced into poverty. The situation gets worse in socio-economic environment in which employment opportunities are extremely limited, which is the case in most underdeveloped countries. Marxists do not deny the excess population growth adds to the problem of poverty, affecting those who are deprived and owning the resources.

(iii) Rapid Growth of Population

Excessive population growth aggravate the problem of poverty in societies where resources are limited, land property is stagnating, technological development is at a rudimentary stage, and resource distribution is quite uneven. High population growth often deplete available resources before they are fully developed and made more productive than what exists at the present state of technological development. Population growth also tends to aggravate the situation of unequal resource distribution because it leads to a greater degree of competition for limited resources among the population. But in this competition, not everybody has the same chance (probability) of winning. It is almost certain that the well-to-do class will win the competition because they can outbid the poor and deprived.

(iv)Agricultural Development and Food Production

Another significant cause of persistent poverty in most of the underdeveloped and developing countries is low level of agricultural land productivity (crop yield per unit area). Land productivity in developing countries remained stagnant. Land productivity in developing countries is several times lower than that in developed countries such as Denmark, Japan and the Netherlands.

(v) Resource Distribution

The unequal distribution of means of production (land, forests, minerals, and capital) are also largely responsible for the poverty in developing countries. In most of the developing countries, land is the basic source of livelihood, income, and social status. In spite of the fact that industrial and service activity has expanded in these countries, the agricultural sector (land) remains the most important source of employment and livelihood. It has been reported that inequality in resource distribution leads to : (i) the exclusion of a large number of people from useful activities thus making them much less productive than they could be with secure access to resources; (ii) the underutilization and low productivity of resources available in a given society; and (iii) the lack of incentives among those who possess minimal or resources of their own and depend on others for their subsistence. None of these situations helps in enhancement of productivity and thus reduce poverty.

Regional Patterns of Poverty in the World

According to the U.N. and World Bank, the people earning less than one American Dollar a day are in the group of extreme poverty, while the people who earn less than two American Dollars a day are also poor. On the basis of these criteria, about one billion people live in less than one dollar a day, and about 2.6 billion people live in less than two dollars a day. Thus about 37.1 per cent of the world population is either below the extreme poverty or below the poverty line. U.S.A. is a well developed country in which any person earning less than $28 a day is considered to be below the poverty line.

The regional distribution of poverty in the world has been shown in **Fig.11.1.** It may be observed from **Fig.11.1** that the continent of Africa is worst affected in the world in respect of poverty, hunger and malnutrition. Excluding the countries of Algeria, Egypt, Libya, Morocco, Tunisia and South Africa, the greater parts of Africa are in the grip of poverty and hunger. Poverty is also significant in Afghanistan, Bangladesh, India, Myanmar, Laos, Cambodia, Mongolia, Pakistan and in the countries of Central America.

Incidence of Poverty in India

On the basis of NSS data, various estimates of the extent of poverty have been made by different scholars. Among those who estimated the level of poverty in India, the names of B.S. Minhas, V.N. Dandakar and N.Rath, P.K. Bardhan, M.S. Ahulwalia and the Planning Commission of India are noteworthy. About 26 per cent of the total population of India is below the poverty line. The state-wise variations in the levels of poverty have been plotted in **Fig.11.2. (Table 11.1)**.

Table 11.1 India-Poverty Ratio at State Level

State	Rural	Urban	Rural-Urban Combined
1. Andhra Pradesh	32.3	23.4	25.8
2. Arunachal Pradesh	36.4	21.8	34.4
3. Assam	36.4	21.8	34.8
4. Bihar	55.7	43.7	54.4
5. Chhattisgarh	53.6	35.1	48.6
6. Goa	47.9	25.6	38.1
7. Gujarat	39.1	20.1	31.8
8. Haryana	24.8	22.4	24.1
9. Himachal Pradesh	25.0	4.6	22.9

Contd.

Table 11.1 *(Contd.)*

10. Jammu & Kashmir	25.0	4.6	22.9
11. Jharkhand	55.7	43.7	54.5
12. Karnataka	37.5	25.9	33.4
13. Kerala	20.2	18.4	19.7
14. Madhya Pradesh	53.6	35.1	48.6
15. Maharashtra	47.9	25.6	38.1
16. Manipur	36.4	21.8	34.4
17. Meghalaya	36.4	21.8	34.4
18. Mizoram	36.4	21.8	34.4
19. Nagaland	36.4	21.8	34.5
20. Odisha	60.8	37.6	57.2
21. Punjab	22.1	18.7	20.9
22. Rajasthan	35.8	29.7	34.4
23. Sikkim	36.4	21.8	34.4
24. Tamil Nadu	37.5	19.7	28.9
25. Tripura	36.4	21.8	34.5
26. Uttar Pradesh	42.7	26.2	41.5
27. West Bengal	38.2	24.4	34.4
28. Andaman & Nicobar	37.5	19.5	28.9
29. Chandigarh	22.1	18.7	20.9
30. Dadar Nagar & Haveli	47.9	25.6	38.1
31. Daman & Diu	47.9	25.6	38.1
32. Delhi	14.69	14.69	14.69
33. Lakshadweep	20.2	18.4	25.4
34. Pondicherry	37.5	19.7	28.9
All India	41.8	25.7	37.1

Note: 1. Poverty Ratio of Assam is used for Arunachal Pradesh, Manipur, Meghalaya, Mizoram, Nagaland, Sikkim and Tripura.

2. Poverty Line of Maharashtra and expenditure distribution of Goa are used to estimate poverty ratio of Goa.

3. Poverty Line of Himachal Pradesh and Expenditure distribution of Jammu & Kashmir are used to estimate Poverty Ratio of Jammu & Kashmir.

4. Poverty Ratio of Tamil Nadu is used for Pondicherry and Andaman and Nicobar Islands.

5. Urban Poverty Ratio of Punjab is used for both rural and urban poverty of Chandigarh.

It may be seen from Table 11.1 that over 57 per cent of the total population of Odisha is below the poverty line followed by Bihar and Jharkhand (54.4%), Chhattisgarh (48.6%) Madhya Pradesh (48.6%), and Uttar Pradesh over (41%). The lowest percentage of poverty in is the state of Kerala (19.7%) followed by Punjab (20.9%), Himachal Pradesh (22.9%), Jammu & Kashmir (22.9%), and Haryana (24.1%).

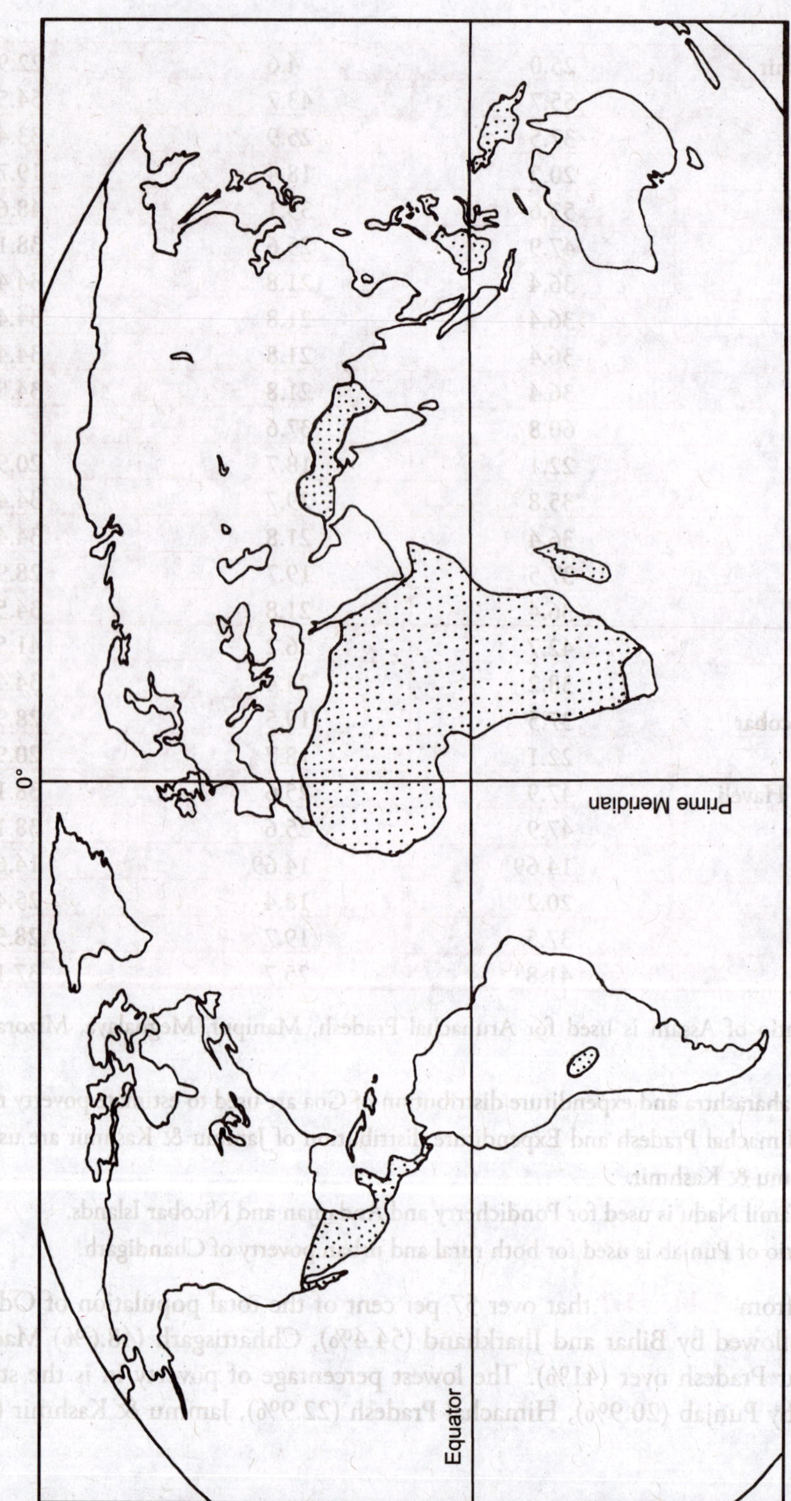

Fig. 11.1 Regions of Poverty and Hunger in the World

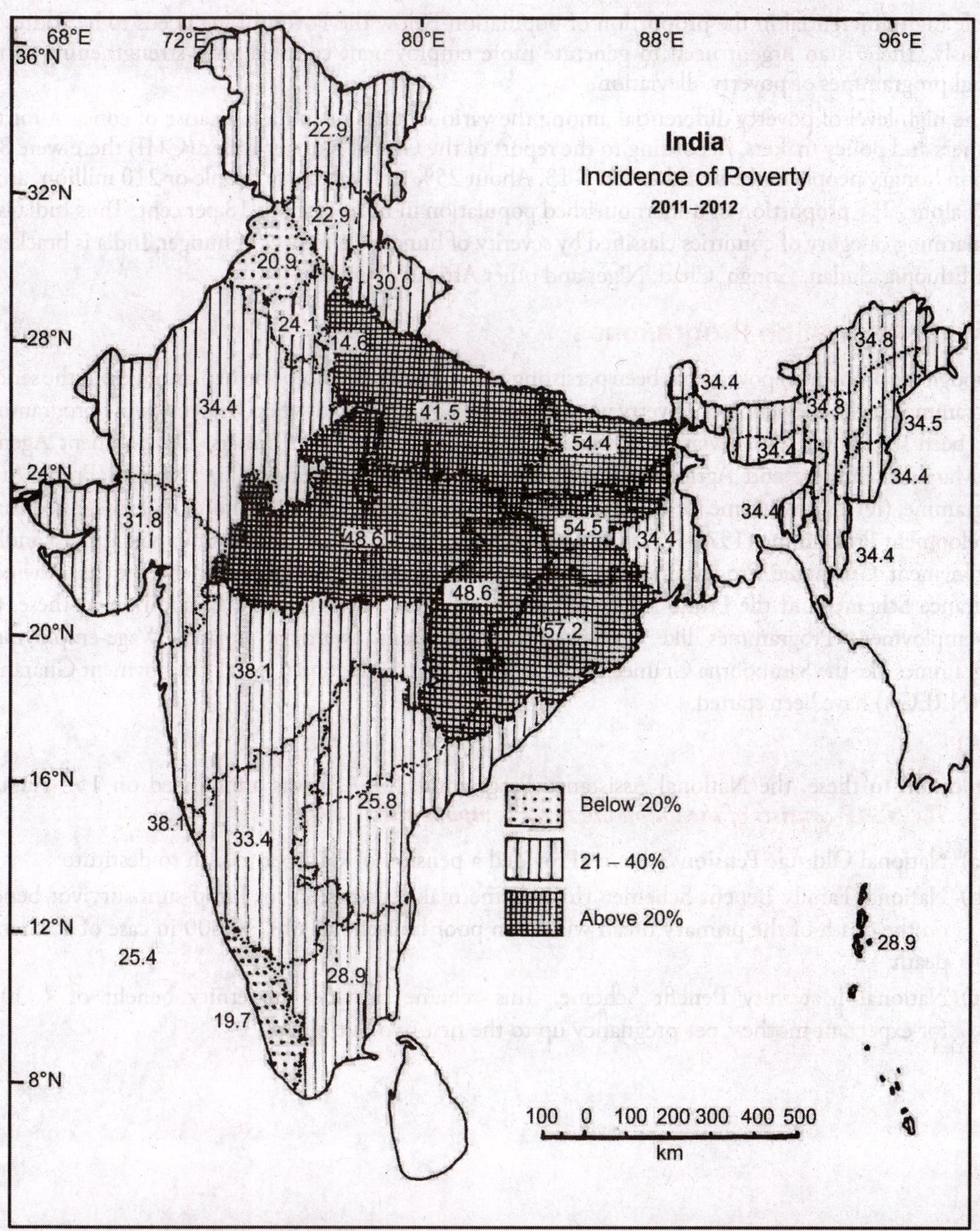

Fig. 11.2 India–Level of Poverty at the State Level

The states with more than 30% Below the Poverty Line (BPL) population are Madhya Pradesh, (48.6%), Uttar Pradesh (41.5%), Maharashtra (38.1%), Assam and Rajasthan (34.4%), West Bengal (34.4%), Karnataka (33.4%) and Gujarat (31.8%).

The high differential in the proportion of population Below the Poverty Line needs to be addressed seriously. There is an urgent need to generate more employment coupled with strengthening of the special programmes of poverty alleviation.

The high level of poverty differential among the various states of India is a cause of concern for the planners and policy makers. According to the report of the Global Hunger Index (GHI) there were 842 million hungry people in the world in 2011-13. About 25% of the hungry people or 210 million, are in India alone. The proportion of undernourished population in India is about 18 per cent. Thus India is in the alarming category of countries classified by severity of hunger. In respect of hunger, India is bracketed with Ethiopia, Sudan, Congo, Chad, Niger and other African countries.

Poverty Alleviation Programmes

Although the problem of poverty has been persisting in India since the inception of planning, but the serious programme for the alleviation of poverty were introduced only in recent years. The following programmes have been started for the alleviation of poverty in India: (i) Marginal Farmers' Development Agency, (ii) Marginal Farmers and Agricultural Labourers Development Agency, (iii) Drought Prone Areas Programme, (iv) Crash Scheme for Rural Employment, and Food Work Programme, (v) Integrated Rural Development Programme (1978-79), (vi) National Rural Employment Programme, (vii) Rural Landless Employment Guarantee Programme. In 1993-94, two new programmes, namely, the Employment Assurance Scheme, and the Prime Minister Rozgar Yojana were introduced. In addition to these, the Self-employment Programmes like the Swarnajayanti Gram Swarojgar Yojana, Wage-employment Programmes like the Sampoorna Grameen Rojgar Yojana and the National Rural Employment Guarantee Act (NREGA) have been started.

NSAP

In addition to these, the National Assistance Programme (NSAP) was announced on 15th August, 1995. ***The NSAP consists of the following three components:***

(a) National Old Age Pension Scheme: Provided a pension of ₹ 75 per month to destitute.

(b) National Family Benefit Scheme: This scheme makes provision for lump-sum survivor benefit on the death of the primary bread winner in poor households of ₹ 10,000 in case of accidental death.

(c) National Maternity Benefit Scheme. This scheme provides maternity benefit of ₹ 300/- for expectant mothers per pregnancy up to the first two live births.

Major Crops and Cropping Patterns in India

INTRODUCTION

Agriculture is the largest private enterprise in India. There are more than 10 crore farm holdings in the country which has been and will continue to be the lifeline of the Indian economy at least in the foreseeable future. It contributes nearly 17 per cent to the national GDP, sustains livelihood of about two-thirds of the population, accounts for 52 per cent of the national workforce and forms the backbone of the agro-based industry. Moreover, agriculture is a social sector where non-trading concerns like food and nutritional security, employment and income generation, poverty alleviation, gender equity, ecology and environment play a significant role. Contribution of agriculture to our nation's security at the time of economic sanction and in strengthening the national sovereignty is well recognized. Yet, it has remained, so far, an unorganized sector.

India through modern agricultural technologies, has moved from an era of chronic food shortage and 'begging bowl' status during 1960s, when our annual food imports were around 8 -10 million tones, to a level of food self-sufficiency, buffer stocks and even food exports from 1990s. With reference to 1950, the productivity gains are nearly 3.5 times in food-grains, 1.6 times in fruits, 2.1 times in vegetables, 5 times in fish, 1.8 times in milk, and 4.8 times in egg production at present.

CLASSIFICATION OF CROPS

Classification of Indian Crops

1. Arable Crops

Crops which require preparatory tillage e.g. rice, wheat, barley, sugarcane, sugarbeet, cotton, potato, etc.

2. Alley Crops

Crops which are grown in alleys/passages formed by trees or shrubs, established mainly to hasten soil fertility restoration, increase soil fertility and reduce soil erosion. Arable crops like sweet-potato, *urad*, turmeric and ginger are grown in the passages formed by the rows of eucalyptus, poplar and cassia.

3. Augmenting Crops

Crops which are grown to supplement the yield of the main crops e.g. Japanese mustard with barseem, Chinese cabbage with mustard. Here Japanese mustard and Chinese cabbage help in getting higher yield in the first cutting.

4. Avenue Crops

Crops which are grown along farm road and fences e.g. *Arhar*, *Dhaicha*, and *Sisal*.

5. Border Crops/Barrier/Guard Crops

Crops which help to protect another crop/crops from trespassing of animals or restrict the speed of wind and are mainly grown as border e.g. safflower (thorny oilseed crop) is planted around the field of chickpea.

6. Break Crops

Crops which are grown to break the continuity of agro-ecological situation of the field under multiple cropping systems. For example, legumes and pulses in rice-wheat crop combination.

7. Cash Crops

Crops which are grown to sale to earn hard cash e.g. Jute, Cotton, Sugarcane and Tobacco.

8. Catch/Contingent/Emergency Crops

Such crops are cultivated to catch the forthcoming season when main crops is failed. They mature in short duration e.g. green-gram, cowpea, onion and radish.

9. Cleaning Crops

Maize, potato and vegetables.

10. Cole Crops

Crops which are grown to make the field clean e.g. maize, cabbage, potato and sugar beet.

11. Commercial Crops

Crops grown for commerce, e.g. rubber, tea, coffee, cocoa, coconut etc.

12. Contour Crops

Crops which are grown on or along the contour lines to protect the land from erosion e.g. marvel grass.

13. Complementrary Crops

Crops which are grown to benefit each other in inter-cropping e.g. *Jowar* (millets) with *Lobiya*. *Jowar* (millets) receives nitrogen from *Lobiya* and *Lobiya* requires support from *Jowar (millets)*.

14. Competitive Crops

Such crops compete to each other and are not suitable for inter-cropping e.g. maize with cucurbit (*Tori*).

15. Cover Crops

The crops which are grown to protect the soil surface from erosion through their ground covering foliage and/or root-mats e.g. *Lobiya*, ground-nut, *Urad*, sweet potato.

16. Energy Crops

Crops which are grown to obtain liquid energy such as ethanol and alcohol e.g. sugarcane, potato, maize, tapioca.

17. Exhaustive Crops

Crops which leave the soil of the field exhausted after growing, e.g. rice, wheat, maize, millets etc.

18. Fouling Crops

Crops whose cultural practices allow the infestation of weeds intensively e.g. direct rice sown by broadcast method.

19. Ley Crops

Any crop or combination of crops grown for grazing or harvesting for immediate or future feeding to livestock e.g. *Barseem* with mustard.

20. Mulch Crops

Mulch crops are grown to conserve soil moisture. For example, cow pea and groundnut.

21. Nurse Crops

Crops which help in the nourishment of other crops by providing shade and acting as climbing sticks e.g. *Rai* in peas, *Jowar* (millets) in cow pea.

22. Paired Row Crops

Each third row is called paired row cropping. It is suitable for dryland and objective is to conserve soil moisture.

23. Restorative Crops

Such crops provide a good harvest along with enrichment or restoration of soil fertility e.g. legumes, pulses, *Barseem* etc.

24. Riparian Crops

Grown along irrigation and drainage channels or waterbodies e.g. waterbind-weed, para-grass. They protect the soil from erosion.

25. Skip Crops

In skip cropping, a line is left unsown in the regular row series of sowing. Such cropping is known as skip cropping.

26. Smother Crop

Crops which are able to smother (suppress) the population and growth of weeds by providing dense foliage and quick growing ability e.g. cow pea, mustard.

27. Soiling Crops

Crops grown to harvest while they are still green and fed fresh to livestock in stalls e.g. *Barseem, Rizka* etc.

28. Trap/Decoy Crops

Crops grown to trap insect-pests and soil-borne harmful biotic agents such as parasitic weeds e.g. cotton red-bug is trapped by growing Bhindi around the cotton and weed.

29. Truck Crop

Grown to market fresh e.g. *Bhindi* (ladies finger), spinach.

30. Ware Crops

Crops which are grown for temporary storing as intact in warehouse for future use or sale, e.g. potato.

MAJOR CROPS OF INDIA

India has great diversity in geo-climatic conditions. Consequently, there is great variation in the cropping patterns and their combinations in the country. Each crop has its minimum, maximum and optimum temperatures for growth and performance. The geographical conditions required for the cultivation of major staple and cash crops in India have been concisely presented in the following:

Rice (*Oryza sativa*)

One of the three most important crops in the world, forms the staple diet of 2.7 billion people. It is grown in all the continents except Antarctica, occupying about 150 million hectares, producing 573 million tones paddy with an average productivity of 3.83 tonnes per hectare. India has the largest area under rice cultivation, while China is the largest producer of rice. In India, it accounts for more than 40 per cent of food-grain production, providing direct employment to 70 per cent people in rural areas. Being the staple food for more than 65 per cent of the people, our national food security hinges on the growth and stability of rice production. Annual rice is grown in 44.6 million hectares. Its production was 20.6 million tones in 1950-51 to 97.2 million tones milled rice in 2007-08. The impressive growth is mainly owing to wide adoption of high yielding, semi-dwarf varieties, increased use of irrigation, chemical fertilizers, insecticides and pesticides and improved package of cultural practices.

Environmental Requirements

Rice is grown in different parts of the world from 39° S (Australia) to 50° N latitude in China and Japan (**Figs. 12.1 & 12.2**). In India, it is grown from 8° N to 34° N latitude under varying climatic conditions. It is grown in areas ranging from below the sea-level as in Kuttanad Valley of Kerala to altitude above 2000 m in Kashmir Valley. Depending on the pattern of rainfall distribution, it is cultivated as a rain-fed upland crop in Jharkhand and Odisha and parts of West Bengal (Purulia and Bankura districts).

The optimum climatic requirements for its normal growth include 20°-35°C temperature throughout the crop duration. Rice grows in all type of soils, however, soils capable of holding water for a longer period such as heavy soil (clay, clay-loam and loamy) are most suited for its cultivation. The most important group of soils for successful cultivation includes alluvial soils, red soils, laterite or lateritic soils and black soils. It is grown normally in soils with soil reaction ranging from 5 to 8 pH.

Systems of Rice Cultivation

The traditional rice farming systems in India broadly include wetland (lowland) and dry land (upland) systems. Cultural practices developed for varied forms of these systems depending on soil type, season, rainfall pattern, irrigation and other growing conditions have been in practice for centuries. However, the diffusion of High Yielding Varieties of rice since the mid-sixties have changed the crop management practices. There are in all three major systems of rice cultivation in India, given below:

Dry Cultivation This system is confined mainly to rain- fed ecosystem with no supplementary irrigation facilities. The land is usually prepared with the help of draught animals after receiving the first rain of the season. Land is ploughed using disc- harrow twice to obtain a fine tilth and uproot the weeds. Seeds are sown either by broadcast or drilling in time. In general, traditional tall varieties combining early maturity and drought tolerance are preferred and hardly any chemical fertilizers are used. All cultural practices right from land preparation, seeding to harvesting and threshing are carried out manually.

Wet Cultivation This system is prevalent in areas, where adequate water supply is assured either through rainfall or irrigation or both. The land is ploughed thoroughly and puddle in 3-5 cm standing water. Puddling besides making field soft for transplanting helps in reducing percolation losses of water and controlling weeds. Puddling is done largely by bullock-drawn country-made plough and wooden plank. It can also be done, as is the practice in large farms, with power tiller or tractor-mounted cage wheels depending on soil condition.

Around 45% of rice is grown under irrigated condition, predominantly as transplant crop. Direct seeding of germinated seeds in wet soil (puddled field) is also practiced in areas with abundant irrigation water and problems of labour availability. About 25-day-old seedling (4-5 leaf stage) uprooted from the nursery-beds are transplanted about 3-4 cm deep.

Rice is essentially a summer (*kharif*) crop which is sown in June to August and harvested from November to December. This crop is locally known as *aman*, *sali* and *agahani*. But in Assam, West Bengal, Odisha, Bihar and Tamil Nadu it is also grown as autumn and summer crop.

Varieties

India has over 3000 varieties of rice out of which some are short duration varieties. The short duration varieties need only 60 to 75 days to yield harvest. Due to increasing use of High Yielding Varieties, many of the indigenous varieties have almost disappeared. Among the HYVs mention may be made of IR-5, IR-8, IR-20, IR-22, Taichung native, etc.

Area

About 43 per cent of the total area under cereals is devoted to rice crop. This area has increased from about 300 lakh hectares in 1950-51 to 450 lakh hectares in 2010-11. Although each state of the country has some area under rice cultivation, West Bengal, Uttar Pradesh, Madhya Pradesh, Chhattisgarh, Odisha and Bihar account for over 60 per cent of rice area in India **(Fig.12.3)**. West Bengal has the

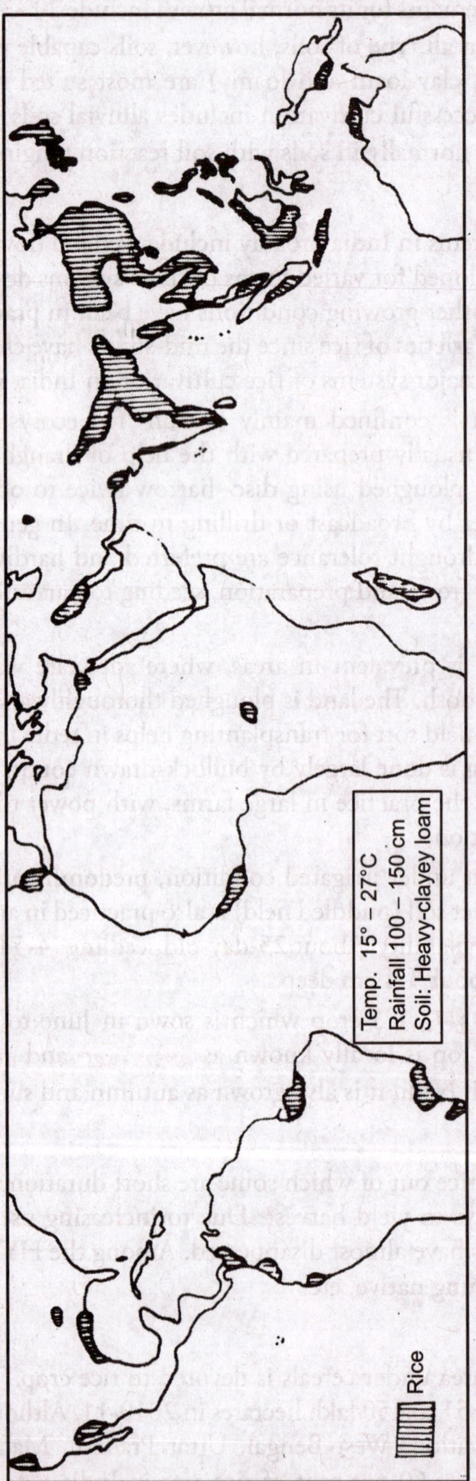

Fig. 12.1 World Rice Producing Regions

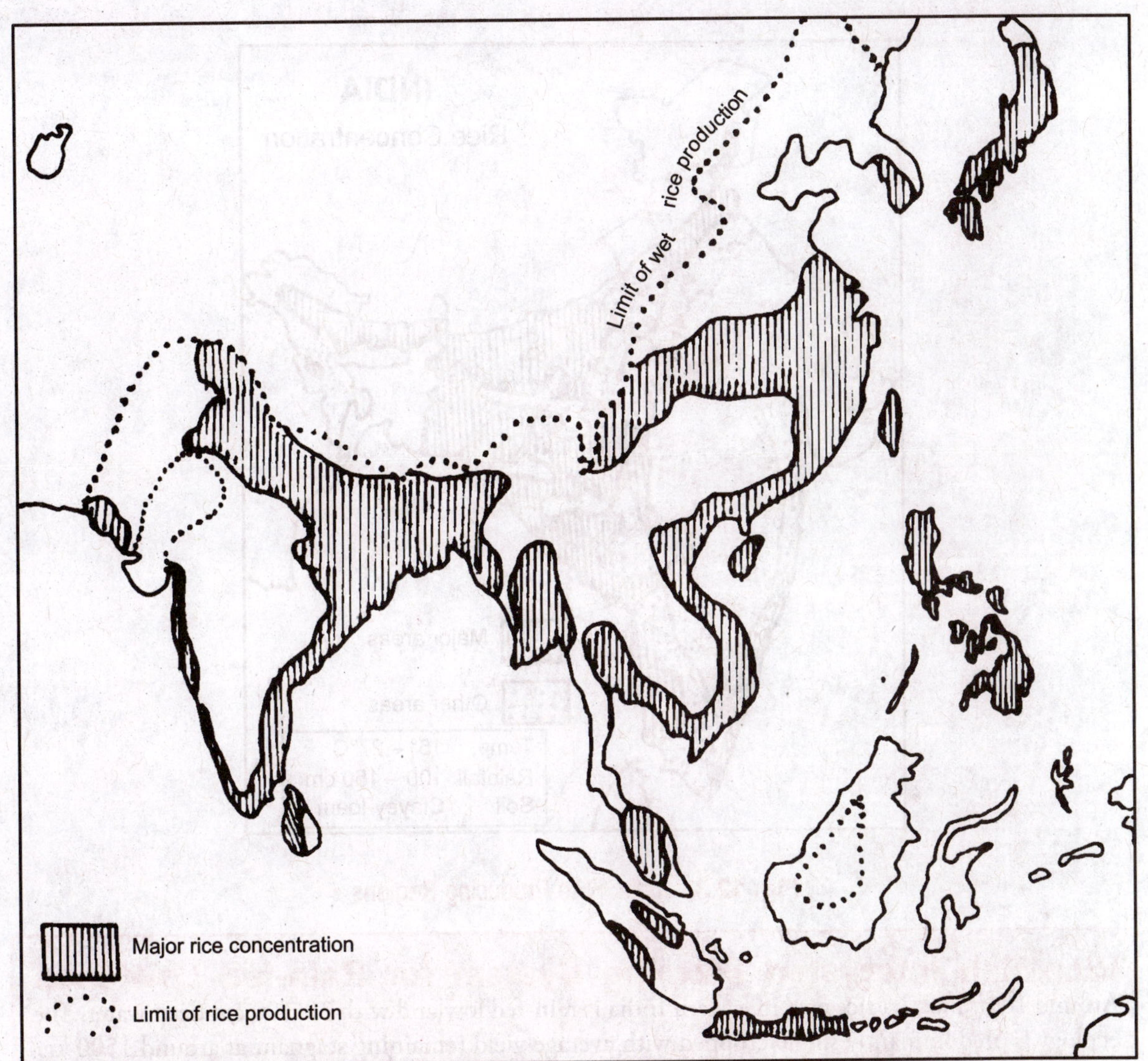

Fig. 12.2 Rice Producing Regions of South East Asia

largest area under rice cultivation followed by Uttar Pradesh, Andhra Pradesh, Punjab, Tamil Nadu, Bihar, Odisha and Madhya Pradesh. The other important rice growing states include Assam, Haryana, Jammu & Kashmir, Karnataka, and Maharashtra.

Yield

The average yield of rice in the country is about 2000 kg per hectare which is more than 3 times than that of 1950-51. This yield is however, much lower as compared to Egypt (6500 kg/ha), USA (6500 kg/ha), and Japan (6400 kg/ha). The low yield of rice in India may be attributed to mismanagement of water supply, primitive methods of cultivation and less application of modern agricultural inputs.

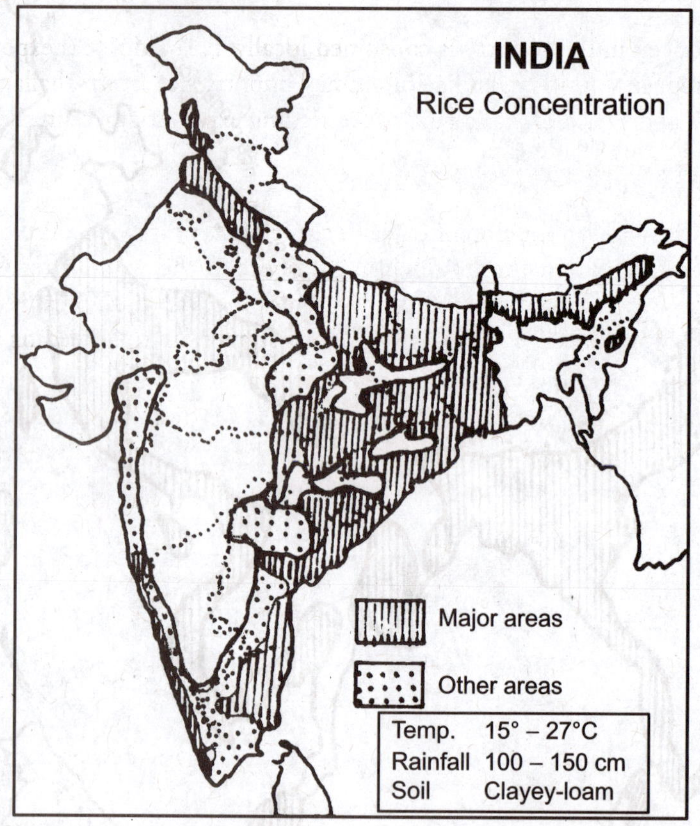

Fig. 12.3 India: Rice Producing Regions

Rice-Fish Integrated Farming System for Rain-fed Lowlands

Around 10 million ha rice area in eastern India is rain-fed lowland with 30-100 cm deep water. The ecology is predominantly single cropped with average yield remaining stagnant at around 1500 kg/ha for a long time. Considering the scope of converting the constraint into opportunity, the Central Rice Research Institute, Cuttack, has developed rice-based integrated farming systems involving various mutually beneficial components like fish or prawn, vegetable and fruit crops. The rice–fish farming comprises 2.5 m wide bunds raised to 1 m in all around the main field and a water storage system in the form of 2 length-wise side trenches with gentle slope (0.5%) connecting a wide pond refuge at water end. The fish-stock should regularly be fed with oilcake and rice polish mixture, besides regular manuring and liming of water body. Winter crops like watermelon, vegetables, green-gram, cowpea, sesame etc. can be raised successfully after rice preferably on opposite side of the pond refuge. Besides, papaya, banana, okra, ridge-gourd etc. in rainy season; and radish, tomato, carrot, pumpkin, bean, cauliflower and cabbage in winter season can be raised on bunds successfully to maximize productivity. This system of rice farming is found to be 3 times more productive and 4 times more economical than only rice-fish culture.

Trade

Most of the rice produced in the country is consumed locally. Basmati rice is exported Gulf countries, Russia, and east European countries. India sometimes imports rice from Thailand, Myanmar, USA, Bangladesh, Malaysia and Sri Lanka. Thailand is the leading exporter of rice in the world.

Wheat (*Triticum aestivum*)

Wheat is the second most important crop of India. It contributes nearly one-third of the total foodgrain production. India stands third in the production of wheat in the world after China, and USA. It contributes nearly one-third of the total food production of the country. Wheat is consumed mostly in the form of pan-backed bread, called *chapati/roti*. Wheat straw is used for feeding the cattle.

The area under wheat has steadily gone up since the start of Green Revolution in 1964-65 and its production and productivity have increased tremendously. The wheat area has risen from 12.5 million ha in 1965-66 to over 28 million ha in 2010-11. Another major change that has occurred in wheat cultivation since Independence is that the proportion of area under irrigated wheat has increased greatly. It has gone up from 34% in 1965 to 51% in 1970 and almost 90% in 2010-11. Thus, the crop has now become largely irrigated as compared to being primarily rain-fed earlier.The total world wheat production is estimated at 606 million tones from 217 million ha during 2010-11 to which India contributed about 12 per cent.

Environmental Requirements

In India wheat is a winter (*Rabi*) crop. Wheat may be grown between 12°C-25°C. The sowing is done between October to December and harvesting in the beginning of summer. The reasonably high temperatures (about 25°C) at both ends of the crop season determine the duration available for wheat cultivation, which ranges from 100 days in down south to more than 145 days in north-western plains and 180 days in the hills (Himachal Pradesh, Uttarakhand and Jammu & Kashmir). Normally wheat is sown when the average daily temperature falls to around 22°-23°C which happens only in November in most wheat growing areas. Sowing wheat while the temperatures are high (around 25°C) results in poor germination, reduced tillering and early onset of flowering, thereby exposing the floral parts to cold damage. High temperatures in October do not permit early seeding of the main crop. Early seeding increases the incidence of root rot and seeding-blight fungi and severely restricts tillering capability crop duration and yield potential of most varieties. Very high temperature during the grain-ripening period can result in grain shriveling.

Wheat needs 50-75 cm of rainfall. In case of less rainfall, controlled irrigation facilities should be available. The annual rainfall in the wheat growing regions of India ranges from 12.5 cm to 100 cm but most of it is received in summer during the monsoon. In winter, when wheat is in the field, the rainfall ranges between 3 and 7 cm only. As such to achieve high yield, irrigation is essential, which enables the application and utilization of required inputs. However, availability of irrigation facilities varies widely in different parts of the country. The proportion of irrigated wheat in Punjab Haryana and Rajasthan is more than 97%, where as in Himachal Pradesh and Karnataka it is only 20% and 52% respectively. In Uttar Pradesh 97.5%, Bihar it is 90.7%, while in Madhya Pradesh it is 78% of wheat area is irrigated. Prevalence of several wheat diseases, viz. rusts, loose smut, karnal-bunt etc. are also the other important constraint of wheat cultivation in India.

Light loam, sandy loam, and clayey loam are well suited for wheat cultivation. In India, most of the wheat is grown in the alluvial soils of the Great Plains. Wheat field requires good preparation through multiple ploughing before the seeds are sown.

Irrigation

Wheat sown under irrigated conditions requires 4 to 6 irrigations, depending on the soil and weather conditions. Heavy deep soils with good water-holding capacity may require only 4 heavy (7 to 9 cm) irrigations whereas 6 to 8 irrigation may be required in sandy soils. Higher temperatures during any of the crop growth period may necessitate additional irrigation. Adjustment need to be made for rainfall during crop season.

Fertilization

To achieve high productivity levels use of synthetic fertilizers is essential. It should be remembered that large quantities of plant nutrients are removed from the soil along with the harvest of grain and straw. The nutrients removed from the soil include large quantities of N. P. K. along with small amounts of several other elements. The fertilizer dose recommended for the timely sown irrigated wheat is 80-150 kg/ha nitrogen (N), 40-60 kg/ha phosphorous and 40kg/ha potassium (K).

The wheat distribution regions of the world have been shown in **Fig. 12.4**. There are more than 250 million hectares of land under wheat cultivation and the annual production is about 400 million tones. The major wheat growing countries of the world are China, U.S.A., India, Canada, Australia, Argentina, Russia, Ukraine, France and Turkey. About 20 per cent of the annual wheat output finds its way into the international market. In Asia, China, India, Pakistan,Turkey and Japan are the major producers of wheat.

The geographical distribution of wheat in India has been shown in **Fig. 12.5**. About 90 per cent of wheat production in India comes from five states, namely, Uttar Pradesh, Punjab, Haryana, Madhya Pradesh and Rajasthan.

With the increased emphasis on intensive cropping and high yields, the rotation of patterns have undergone drastic changes all across the country, particularly in Punjab, Haryana and western Uttar Pradesh where rice is now extensively grown in *Kharif* and is followed by wheat in the *Rabi* season. Similarly, wheat is now extensively cultivated after rice in eastern Uttar Pradesh and Bihar. Hence the rice-wheat rotation has become extremely important.

The sugarcane-wheat and cotton–wheat rotations are also common in several parts in northern India under irrigated conditions. Soybean-wheat has become important in Madhya Pradesh and Maharashtra. Wherever more irrigation water is available, a legume crop is grown between two cereal crops to enrich the soil as well as to get the needed pulses.

Varieties

The main varieties of wheat grown in India are DBW 17, PBW 550, PDW 291, TL 2908, etc.

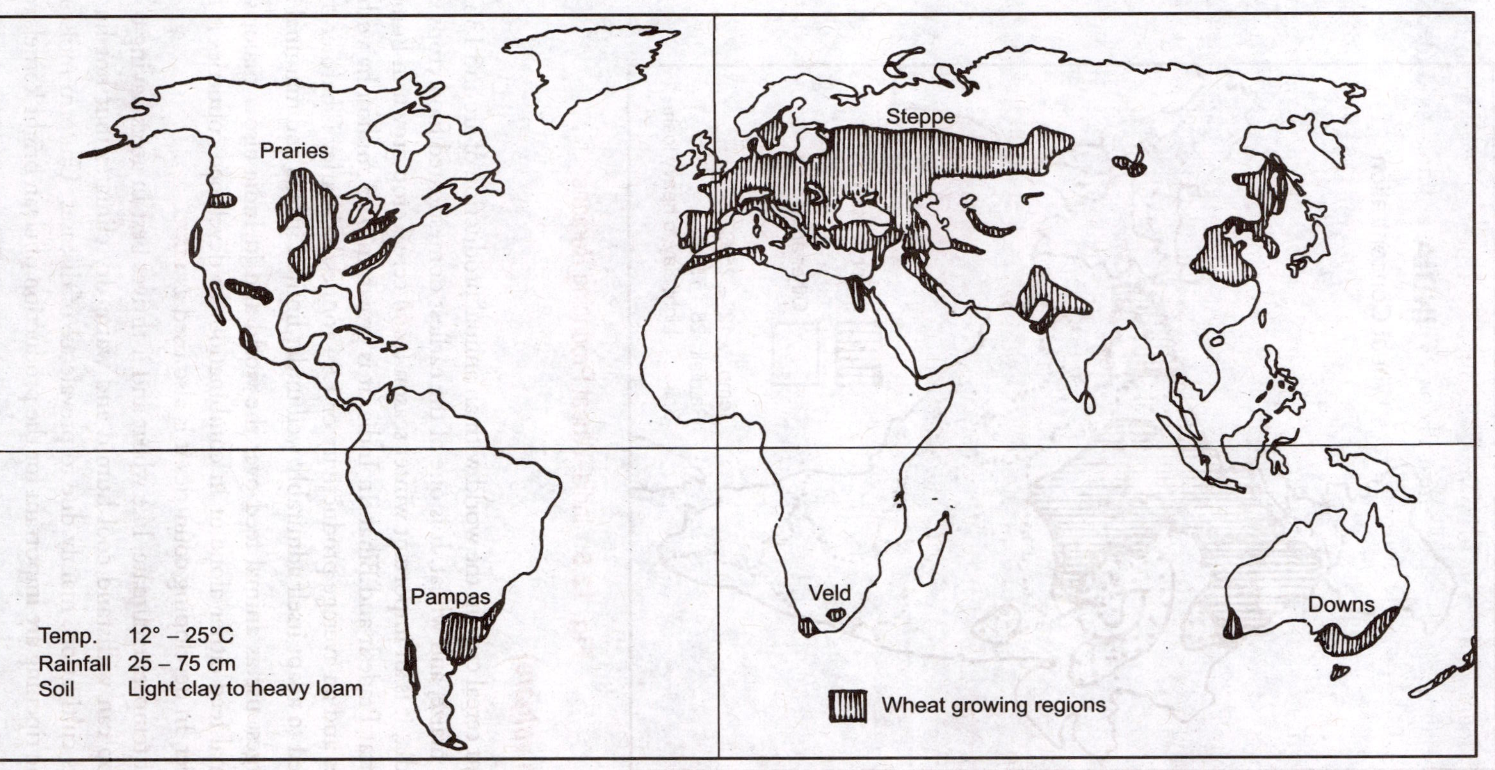

Fig. 12.4 World–Wheat–Producing Regions

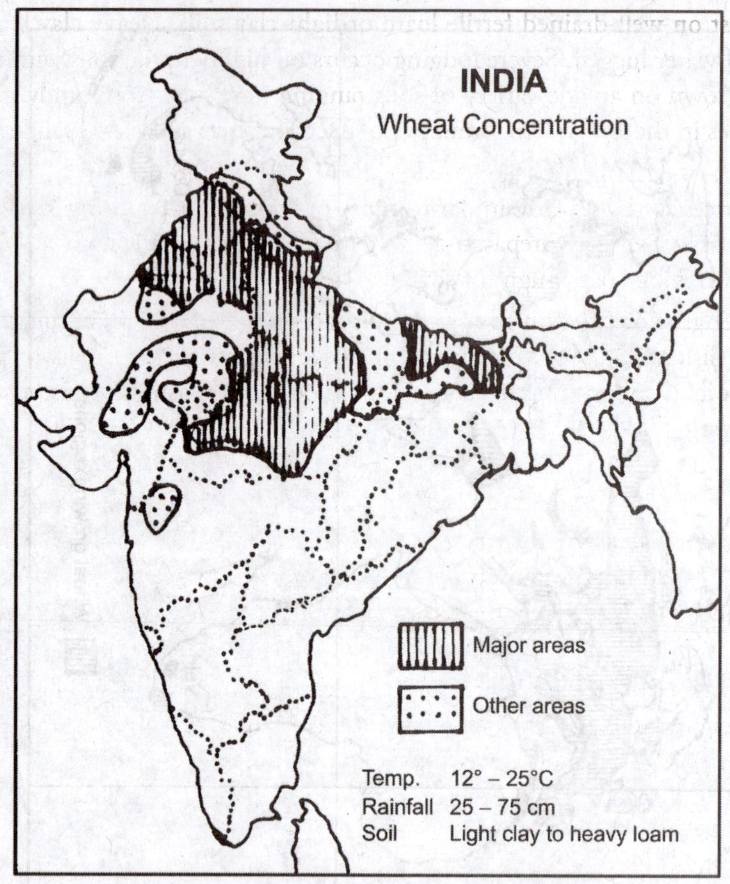

Fig. 12.5 India–Wheat Producing Regions

Barley (*Hordeum vulgare*)

Barley is an important cereal crop in the world with an annual production of around 136 million tones, ranking next to rice, maize, and wheat. It is one of the earliest domesticated food crops since the dawn of civilization. In India, it is an important winter season (*rabi*) cereal crop grown in Punjab, Rajasthan, Madhya Pradesh, Uttar Pradesh and Bihar. In India, it is grown in 0.63 million ha with a production of 1.20 million tones and an average productivity of 1.94 tonnes/ha. Barley is hardier than wheat and is inherently equipped to adapt itself admirably well under limited inputs and marginal lands.

Barley has the largest use as animal feed over the world and in India also a major share of barley grain is used as animal feed either alone or in combination. In developed countries it is used for the manufacturing of beer. In developing countries it is also used as *sattu*.

Barley is a crop of temperate climate, like wheat and it thrives best in areas having cool dry winters low rainfall. The crop can withstand cool humid and warm dry climates, but hot humid climate is not favourable for its cultivation, mainly due to prevalence of diseases. Uniform moisture supply and bright sunshine at the ripening are important for the production of clean bright kernels required by the malting industry.

Barley thrives best on well-drained fertile loam or light clay soils. Heavy clay loams are unsuitable for its cultivation, if water logged. Severe lodging occurs on highly fertile soils with excess of nitrogen. In India, barley is grown on a wide variety of soils ranging in texture from sandy to heavy loams and on the terraced slopes in the hill. It was found to be successful crop on coastal saline soils of Sundarban in the West Bengal.

Cultivation practices for barley are similar to those of wheat, but requiring less inputs. Barley does not require a very fine seed-bed preparation and therefore ploughing with a soil-turning plough, levelling and one harrowing are enough for sowing.

Barley is generally grown either on conserved soil moisture from the preceding monsoon season or under restricted irrigation. Usually, it needs two or three irrigations. One or two extra irrigations are required on sandy soils. Waterlogging in the field must be avoided as it causes severe yellowing as well as reduction in tillering.

Maize or Corn (*Zea Mays*)

Maize is the most versatile crop with wider adaptability in varied agro-ecologies. Globally, it is cultivated on nearly 150 million hectares in about 160 countries, having wider diversity of soil, climate, biodiversity and management practices that contributes nearly 37% (9782 million tones) in the global grain production.

Maize crop is grown both in the tropical and temperate countries and its field may be found from low altitude to a height of about 2000 meters in the tropical and subtropical countries. Globally it is cultivated on nearly 150 million hectares in about 160 countries having wider diversity of soil, climate, biodiversity and management practices that contribute nearly 37 per cent in the global grain production. The United States of America (USA) has the highest harvest of maize in the world that contributes nearly 20 per cent of the total production in the world. The other major countries that contribute significantly to the global maize production are China, Brazil, Mexico, India, Indonesia and Argentina (Fig. 12.6). The USA has the highest average yield about 9.6 tonnes per hectare which is double than the global average productivity of 4.92 tonnes per hectare. The average yield in Argentina, China, Brazil, Mexico and India are 6.47' 4.85,3.7, 2.53, and 2.43 tonnes per hectare respectively.

In India, maize is the fourth most important food crop after rice, wheat and millets. It is cultivated in about 8 million hectares under a wide range of agro-ecological situations. It contributes nearly 8% in the national food basket. In addition to staple food for human being and quality feed for animals, maize serves as a basic raw material as an ingredient to thousands of industrial products that include starch, oil, protein, alcoholic beverages, food sweeteners, pharmaceutical, cosmetic, film, textile, gum, package and paper industries etc.

Maize is cultivated throughout the year in different parts of the country for various purposes including grain, fodder, green cobs, sweet corn, baby corn, pop corn etc.

Geo-climatic Conditions Required

Maize requires average temperature between 21°C and 27°C. Temperature below 10°C or above 35°C is harmful for the crop. It performs well in the region where the rainfall is between 50–75 cm. Bright sunshine after rainfall is useful for healthy growth of the crop.

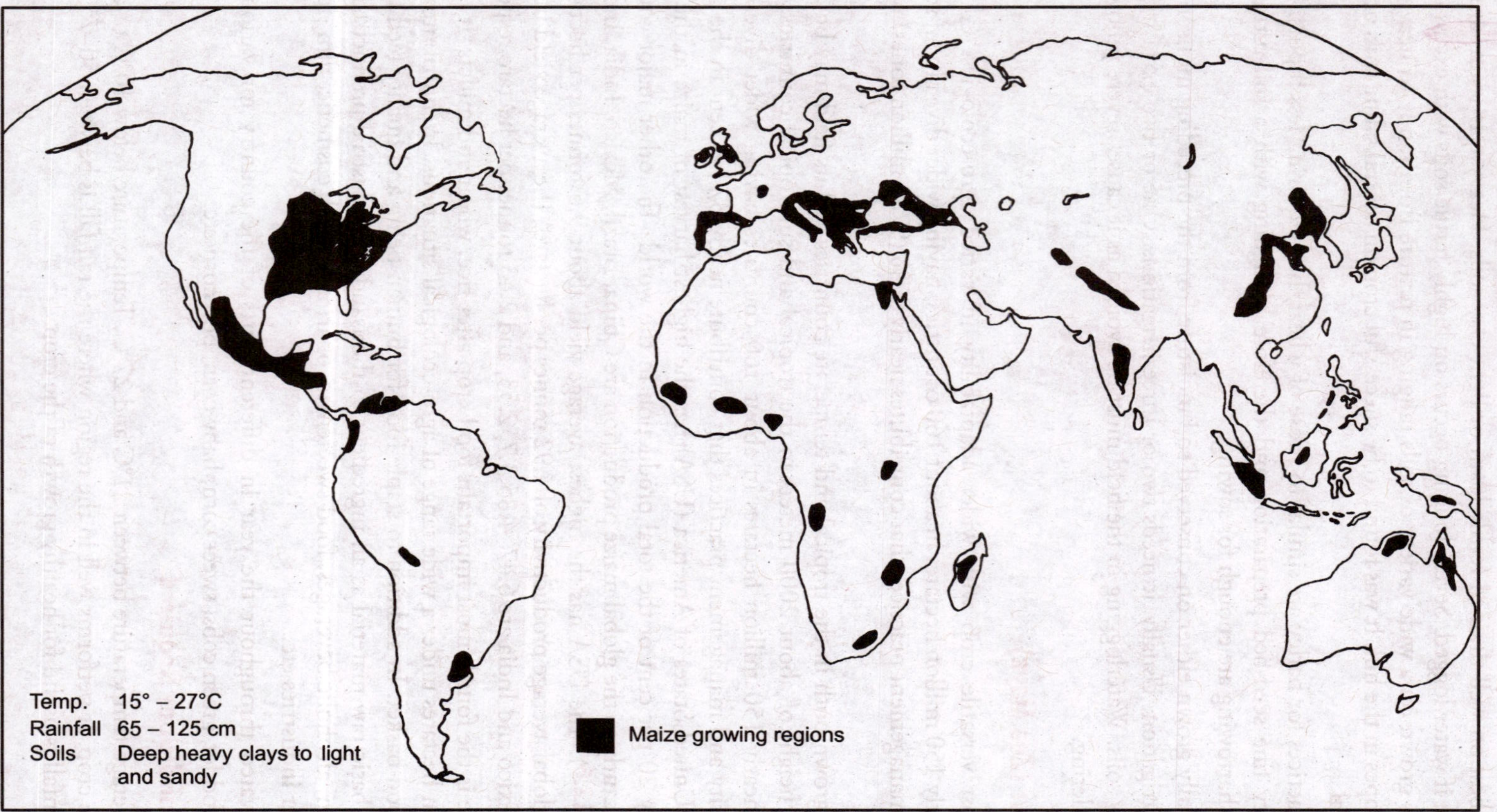

Fig. 12.6 Maize Growing Regions of the World

Time of Sowing

Maize can be grown round the year in all seasons, viz. *kharif* (monsoon), post monsoon, *rabi* (winter) and spring. For higher productivity in *kharif* season, the farmers having sufficient irrigation facilities, it is desirable to complete the sowing 12-15 days to onset of monsoon. However, in rain-fed areas, the sowing time should be coincided with the onset of monsoon.

Maize is cultivated mainly as a *kharif* crop, while in some parts of the country it is grown as a *rabi* crop.

Maize can be grown successfully in wide range of soils, ranging from loamy sand to clay loam. However, soils with good organic matter content having high water holding capacity with neutral pH are considered good for higher productivity. The soil should be well-drained.

The per hectare yield of maize is less than that of wheat and rice but higher than *jowar* (millet) and *bajra* (bulrush millet). The United States of America is the leading producer of maize (corn) followed by China, Brazil, Mexico, Russia, Romania India and South Africa. The United States of America is the leading exporter of maize.

Maize is largely grown in north India. The highest concentration of the crop is found in Uttar Pradesh, Rajasthan, Madhya Pradesh, Bihar, Himachal Pradesh, Jammu and Kashmir, and Punjab which together account for about 70 per cent of the total area. The major maize-growing states that

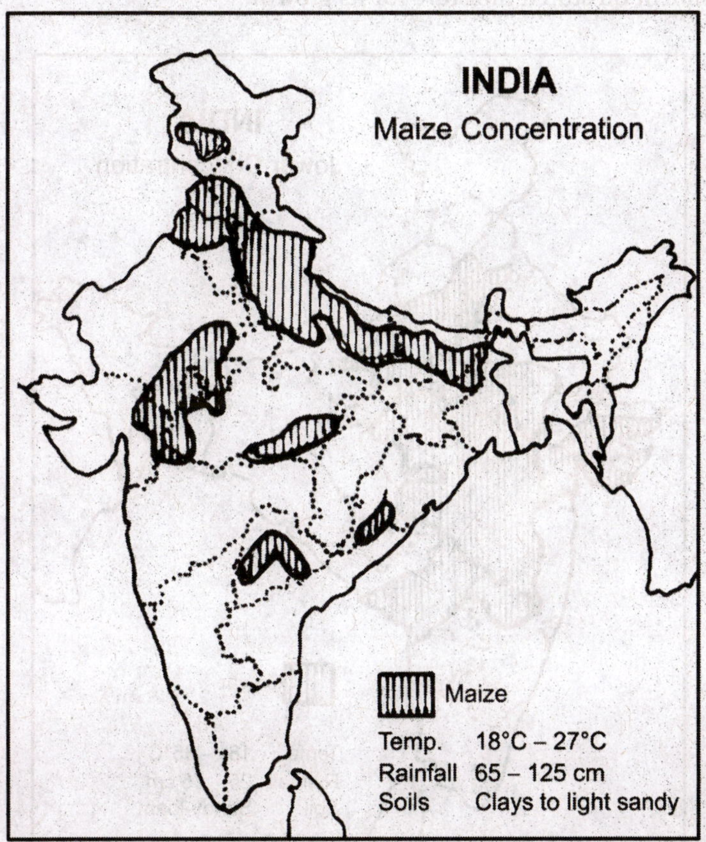

Fig. 12.7 India–Maize Producing Regions

contribute more than 80% of the total maize production are Andhra Pradesh (21%), Karnataka (17%), Rajasthan (10%), Maharashtra (9%), Bihar (8.5%), Uttar Pradesh (6%), Madhya Pradesh (5.5%), and Himachal Pradesh (4.4%) (**Fig. 12.7**).

Millets /Jowar (*Sorghum bicolor*)

Millets were the first crops to be cultivated prior to the plough age. Millets are an important staple food crops in some of the developing countries of the world. The millets are categorized as major and minor millets, based on size of seeds and the extent of cultivation. Sorghum (*Jowar*) and pearl millet are considered as the major millets. Other millets include finger millet, foxtail millet, proso millet, kodo-millet, little millet, etc. However, realizing the excellent nutritional composition of these grains, they are now called as nutritious grains or nutria cereals.

Sorgham (*Sorgham bicolor*), popularly known as *jowar*, is one of the most important food and fodder crops in India and occupies third place in area and production. In general, the area under millets is decreasing. The area under sorghum has gradually declined from 18 million ha in 1960 to 8.5 million ha in 2010.

Grain sorghum (millet) is grown over a variety of soils from light to medium deep black soils. However, the cultivation of *Rabi* (winter) sorghum in India is more or less confined to black soils (*Regur-soil*) and dependent on stored moisture for its growth.

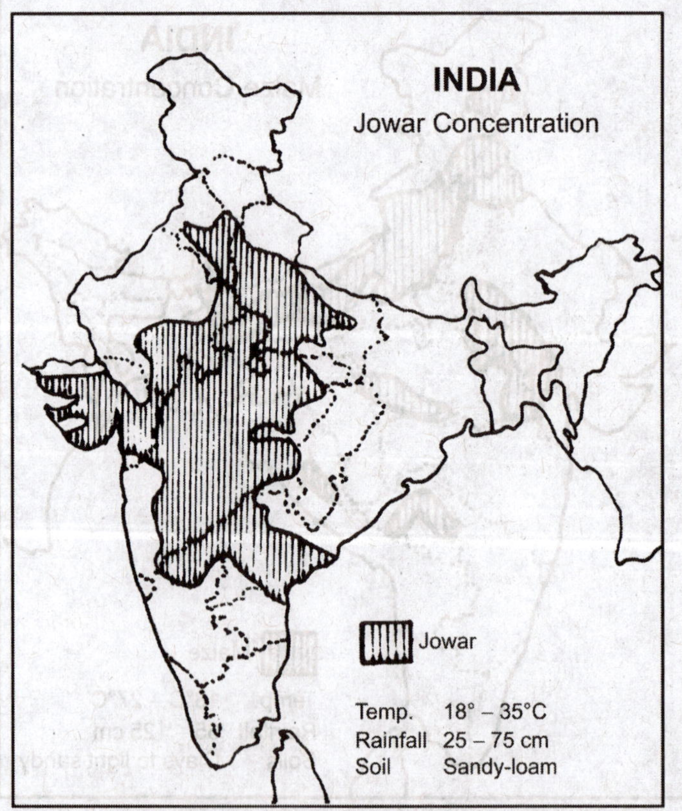

Fig. 12.8 India–Millets Producing Regions

Sorghum is considered as drought hardy crop and hence rated as an important component of dry land agriculture. The cultivation of sorghum is confined to areas where annual rainfall is ranging from 40 to 100 cm per annum.

The main areas of millets concentration are Rajasthan, Uttar Pradesh, Madhya Pradesh, and Gujarat (**Fig. 12.8**). It is an important *Rabi* (winter) crop in Andhra Pradesh, Maharashtra and Karnataka. In Tamil Nadu sorghum is grown through out the year, i.e. in *kharif* (summer season), *rabi* (winter season) and *Zaid* (spring season).

Bajra/Pearl-Millet (*Pennisetum Typhoideum*)

Known as bulrush millet, *Bajra* is one of the important staple food crop of India. In India, it is grown in about 10 million hectares, producing about 7.5 million tones of grains. Bajra grows well in the region where the temperature varies between 25° to 30°C. The crop requires about 30 to 50 cm of annual rainfall. Heavy rainfall exceeding 75 cm is however, unsuitable for the *Bajra* crop. It is the most drought-and heat tolerant crop with highest water-use efficiency. The crop is grown mostly during *Kharif* season from June to October.

Improved varieties/hybrids are quite diverse especially for maturity duration and as a result, it is possible to choose appropriate variety depending on the geographical conditions. Since 1985, as many as 38 new hybrids of *Bajra* were developed and released by public and private sectors. Among the varieties, Raj 171, ICMV 221, Pusa Composite 334, Pusa 383 and Samrudhi are popular.

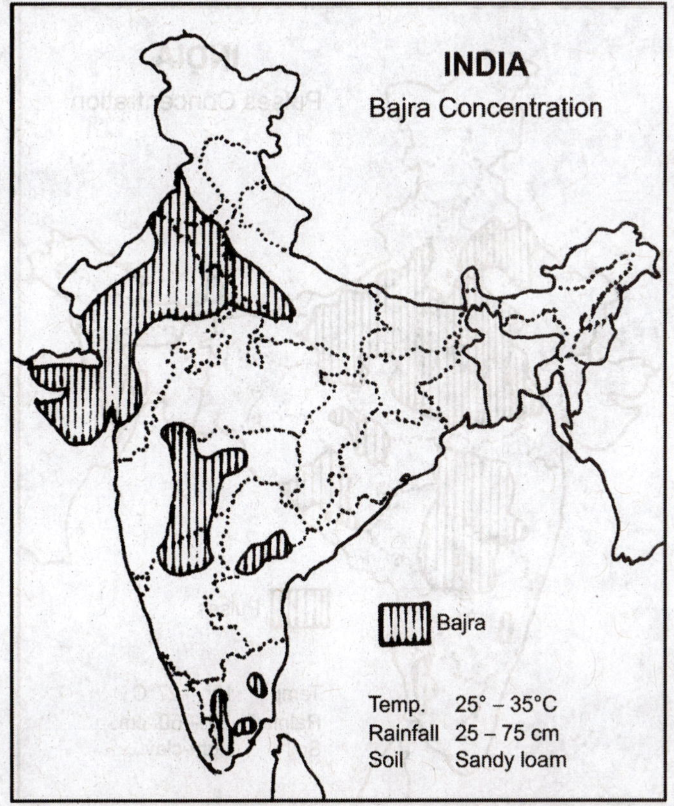

Fig. 12.9 India–Bajra Producing Regions

The average yield of *Bajra* is about 650 kg per hectare. It is grown mainly in Rajasthan, Maharashtra, Gujarat, Uttar Pradesh, Haryana, Karnataka, Tamil Nadu and Andhra Pradesh (Fig. 12.9).

It is grown in a wide range of soils ranging from light soils on sand dunes in Rajasthan to red loams in Karnataka, Tamil Nadu and parts of Maharashtra and on black soil in Andhra Pradesh.

Major *Bajra* produce is consumed locally and only a small quantity enters in the inter-state market. A small quantity of produce is exported to the countries of East Africa, South-West Asia and European countries.

There has been gradual decline in the area of *Bajra*. Due to its low yield per hectare and less remunerative value, it is finding less popularity amongst the farmers.

Pulses (Legumes)

Pulses are important source of dietary protein, and have unique property of maintaining and restoring soil fertility through biological fixation of nitrogen. Pulses help in making soils fertile and sustainable by improving their physical properties. Pulse crops add up to 40 kg nitrogen per hectare.

India grows pulses on about 23 million ha area and produces nearly 14-15 million tonnes of pulse grains. The commonly grown pulse crops are Bengal-gram or chick-pea or gram, *arhar* or pigeonpea or *tur*, green-gram or *mung*, bean, black-gram or *urad*-bean, *masoor* or lentil, *matar* or pea, *khesari*, cowpea, *moth*-bean, French-bean or *rajmah*.

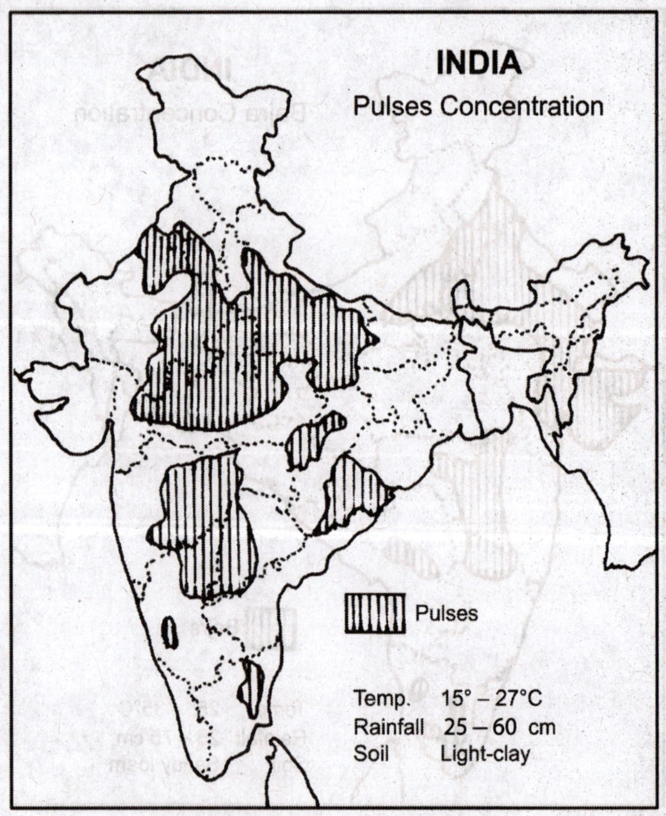

Fig. 12.10 India–Pulses Producing Regions

Bengal Gram/ or Chickpea or Gram (*Cicer arietinum*)

Bengal gram is grown in all types of soils, ranging from heavy clay to light loam. The optimum temperature for its growth ranges from 15° to 25°C. The soil should be well-drained sandy loam to deep heavy loams. This crop does not need a fine seed-bed. The land should be ploughed by soil turning plough soon after harvest of rainy season (*kharif*) crops.

Bengal gram is commonly rotated with maize, pearl-millet, rice, cotton, soybean, sorghum, sunflower. In intercropping it is grown with linseed, wheat, barley, mustard, safflower etc. Recently, a few varieties have been developed that can be sown up to the second week of December **(Fig. 12.10).**

Pigeon-pea or *Arhar*/ *Tur* (*Cajanus cajan*)

Pigeon pea is a native crop of India. It is cultivated throughout in tropical and subtropical regions and warmer temperate regions from 30° N to 30° S. Plant is woody perennial, but often grown as an annual crop.

Pegion-pea (*Arhar*) is consumed extensively as *dal*. In some parts of India green-pods are used as vegetables. The pod husk and seed husk are used as feed for cattle. The dry sticks are used as fuelwood or for thatching purposes. The deep root open the soil to improve physical properties of the soil. The plans shed large amount of leaves which add organic matter to soil.

Pigeon-pea is cultivated in wide range of climatic conditions in tropical areas with a temperature range of 20°-35°C. The plant is sensitive to frost during stages of growth. In frost prone areas like Punjab, Haryana and west Uttar Pradesh short duration varieties are grown, as they escape frost. It is grown on a wide variety of soils from sandy to heavy clay loams that are well-drained. The plant also thrives in regions of heavy rainfall and under irrigation, provided there is no standing water on the ground even for a few days.

In India, pigeon-pea occupies 3.75 million ha area with production of 3.1 million tones. It is mainly grown in Maharashtra, Karnataka, Andhra Pradesh, Uttar Pradesh, Madhya Pradesh, Gujarat, Odisha, Tamil Nadu, Chhattisgarh, and Bihar. In Punjab, Haryana, Gujarat, and western Uttar Pradesh, early maturing varieties are grown. The average yield of pigeon-pea is 1200-1500 kg/ha and that of long duration pigeon-pea is 1800 to 2500 kg/ha.

Green Gram (*Vigna radiate*)

Green-gram or *moong* is of ancient cultivation in India. The grains are generally used as *dal* or to make flour. The straw and husk as fodder for cattle. The germinated grains are used as sprouts. Unlike other pulses, it does not produce flatulence.

Being a tropical crop it cannot tolerate low temperature. It thrives well at 25°-35°C. In the northern plain it can be grown in spring, summer and *kharif* whereas in southern parts it can be grown throughout the year as the variation in temperature is not much. Green-gram is cultivated on a wide variety of soils, ranging from sandy to heavy loam. Deep, well-drained loam soils of the alluvial tracts are, however, ideal. The crop also performs well on shallow and eroded soils and is considered as a good cover crop. It is very sensitive to water-logging. There is generally no need of a fine bed for sowing this crop. When the crop is grown as an intercrop, the tillage requirement of the main crop decides the field operations. It is desirable to have a weed-free seed-bed with adequate drainage facilities during *kharif*. For spring or summer cultivation, irrigation should be given soon after harvesting the *rabi* crop.

Black-gram or *Urad*-bean (*Vigna mungo*)

Black-gram or *urad*-bean is of ancient cultivation in India. The crop is extensive cultivated in the country. Black-gram, occupies 3.2 million ha area and contributes about 1.33 million tones to pulse production. It is cultivated mainly as a *kharif* crop almost in all states and has a premier place in hill agriculture. In the northern plains, it is also cultivated during spring as a catch crop. In southern and south-eastern regions, it is cultivated in rice fallow during *rabi*. The grains are used as *dal* or made into flour. Various preparations are made from its flour, e.g. *papad, dosa, vada* etc.

Black-gram is grown in a wide variety of soils. In fact, it has a wide range of adaptability. During *kharif*, it is cultivated throughout the country. Black-gram needs relatively heavier soils than green-gram. Well drained, moisture retentive, deep loam soils free from excessive soluble salts are ideal. The crop, however, thrives well on marginal lands and protects eroded soils. It is grown as a rain-fed crop in the warm plains as well as in the foot-hills and up to an altitude of 2000 m.

Lentil or *Masur* (*Lens culinaris*)

Lentil or *masur* is one of the oldest crops that originated in the Near East and the Mediterranean region. It had spread to Europe, India and China.

Lentil is grown on a wide range of soils ranging from light loamy, sandy to heavy clay soil in northern parts, and moderately deep, light black soils in Madhya Pradesh and Maharashtra. Its range of cultivation extends to an altitude of 3500 m in north-west hills. The optimum temperature for its growth and development ranges from 15° to 25°C.

Lentil is generally grown as rain fed crop during *rabi* after rice, maize and pearl millet. In intercropping it is grown with barley, linseed and mustard. It is also grown as an intercrop in autumn-planted sugarcane.

French Bean or *Rajmah* (*Phaseolus vulgaris*)

French bean or *rajmah* is widely cultivated in the tropics, sub-tropics and temperate regions. It is a native of Mexico and Guatemala. It has spread to Europe, Africa and other parts of the world.

The crop can be grown in light loamy sand to clay soil under adequate moisture. It is highly sensitive to frost and water logging. The ideal temperature range for proper growth of this crop is 15°-27°C. If the temperature crosses above 30°C, the flower drop is a serious problem. Similarly, below 5°C the flowers and developing pods are damaged. Field should be well prepared for sowing. The crop is sown in the first week of July in the hills, in the second fortnight of March in lower hills and in the second fortnight of October in plains. The main areas of its cultivation are Madhya Pradesh, Maharashtra, Gujarat, and Andhra Pradesh.

Oilseed

India is among the fifth largest vegetable oil economies in the world after USA, China, Brazil, and Argentina. In the agricultural economy of India, oilseeds are important next only to food grains in terms of area, production and value. At present, India accounts for about 12-15% of world's oilseeds area, 7-8% of world's oilseeds output and 9-10% of world's edible oils consumption. The diverse agro-ecological conditions in the country are favourable for growing all the nine annual oilseeds which include seven edible oilseeds, viz. groundnut, rapeseed-mustard, soybean, sunflower, sesame, and safflower, and two non-edible sources, viz. castor and linseed (**Fig. 12.11**).

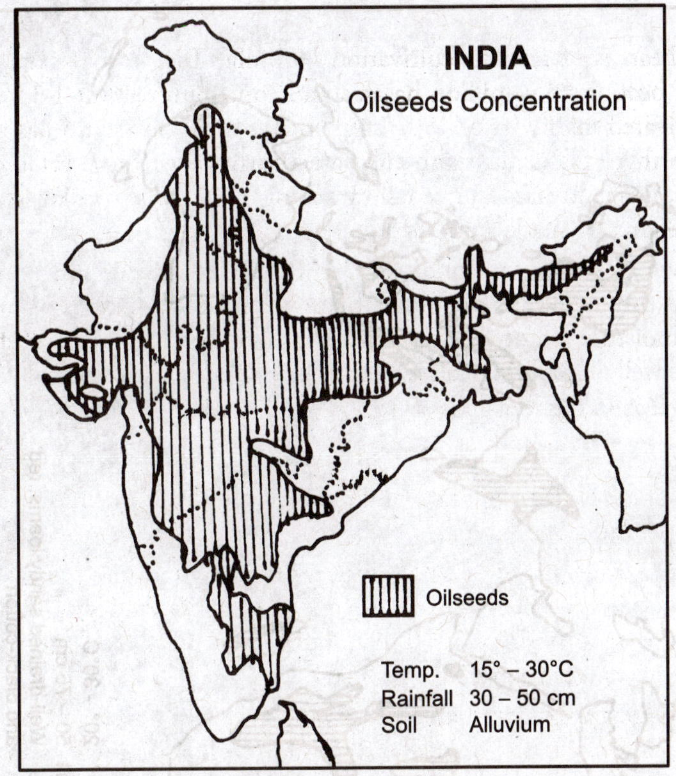

Fig. 12.11 India–Oil Seeds Producing Regions

Madhya Pradesh, Gujarat, Rajasthan, Andhra Pradesh, Maharashtra, Karnataka, Tamil Nadu and Uttar Pradesh account 90% of oilseeds area and production in the country. Among different oilseeds, groundnut, rapeseed-mustard, and soybean account for nearly 80% of oilseeds area and 88% of oilseeds production of the country.

Groundnuts or Peanut (*Arachis hypogoea*) *and* Groundnut (*Arachis hypogaea*)

Groundnut is believed to be a native of Brazil. The oil content varies from 44% to 50% depending upon the varieties and geo-economic conditions. Its oil finds extensive use as a cooking medium, both as refined oil and *vanaspati ghee*. It is also used in soap making, and in manufacture of cosmetics, lubricants, stearin and their salts.

Climate and Soil Groundnut is grown throughout the tropics. Its cultivation is also extended to the subtropical countries, lying between 45°N and 35°S, and up to an altitude of 1000 meters. The crop can be grown successfully in places receiving a minimum rainfall of 50 cm and a maximum of 125 cm. The rainfall should be well-distributed during the flowering and pegging stages of crop. The groundnut crop, however, cannot stand frost, long and severe drought of water stagnation.

Although groundnut is grown on a wide variety of soil types, the crop does best on sandy-loam, loamy soils. It also performs well in well-drained black soils. Heavy and stiff clays are unsuitable for groundnut cultivation as the pod development is hampered in these soils.

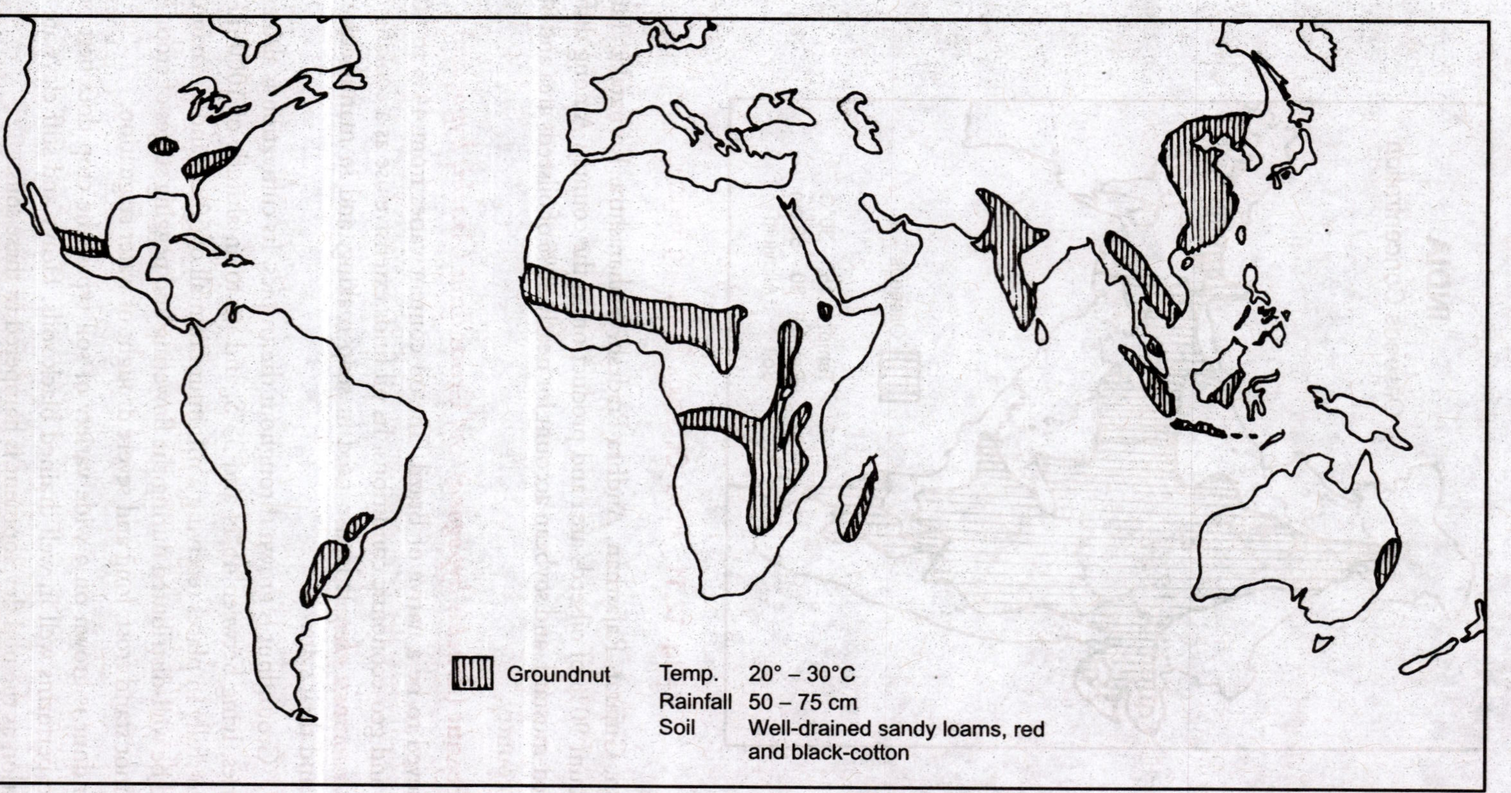

Fig. 12.12 World Distribution of Groundnuts

Groundnut is raised mostly as a rained *kharif* crop, being sown from May to July, depending upon the monsoon rains. In winter *(rabi)*, groundnut is sown in the southern states during November-December, mostly in the rice fallow. Summer groundnut is raised in the states of Gujarat, Maharashtra, and Madhya Pradesh. In these states, it is sown during the second fortnight of January up to the first fortnight of February.

The total world groundnut production is about 48 million tones from 22 million hectares. The major groundnut producing countries of the world are China, India, Nigeria, USA, Indonesia, Argentina, Sudan, Senegal, and Myanmar. With 6.3 million hectares and 9.20 million tones of nuts in shell, India shares 28% area and 19% production of groundnut of the world.

Nearly 81% of the area and 84% of the production are concentrated in the four states, viz. Gujarat, Andhra Pradesh, Tamil Nadu and Karnataka. The other producing states are Rajasthan, Maharashtra, Madhya Pradesh, Odisha, and Uttar Pradesh.

Groundnut or peanut is a leguminous plant. Groundnut, in fact, is not a nuts but a type of bean. Groundnut originated in Brazil, but are now grown very widely in the tropical and sub-tropical areas. They require warm temperature around 25°C and light to moderate rainfall of about 40 cm in the coastal areas of high humidity and about 70 cm in the drier interior regions. Groundnuts give good returns in sandy soil.

Groundnut is grown mainly in the dry tropical and sub-tropical climates, in the savanna regions of West Africa, in the monsoonal climates of China and India where sandy soils are the most important determinant.

The groundnut is an annual crop, and because it is a leguminous crop which adds valuable nitrogen to the soil, it is often grown in rotation with other crops like millets, maize or cotton crop.

Groundnut is a labour intensive crop. Fertilizer is applied with the seeds when they are planted and the nuts are picked by hand. The outer shells are usually removed in the producing regions to minimize transport cost and the nuts are sacked for export. The exported nuts are crushed to obtain the oil in the importing countries.

China, India, U.S.A. Argentina, Brazil, Benin, Gambia, Ivory-Coast, Ghana, Guinea, Guinea-Bissau, Ethiopia, Liberia, Mali, Niger, Nigeria, Sierra Leone, Sudan, Togo, Indonesia, Malaysia, and Thailand are the important producers of groundnuts (**Fig. 12.12**).

India is the largest producer of groundnuts in the world. It is grown in the drier parts of the Peninsular India, i.e., Andhra Pradesh, Karnataka, Maharashtra, Gujarat, Rajasthan, Haryana and Punjab.

Rapeseed (*Brassica rapa*) and Mustard (*Brassica juncea*)

Rapeseed–mustard is the third most important oilseed crop after soybean and groundnut, contributing nearly 20-25% of the total oilseed production in the country. Rapeseed-mustard group of crops are being cultivated in almost all the states of the country.

The rapeseed and mustard crops are tropical as well as of temperate zones and require relatively cool temperatures for satisfactory growth. In India, they are grown in the *rabi* season from September-October to February-March. The rapeseed and mustard grow well in the areas having 25 to 40 cm of rainfall. *Sarson* and *taramira* are preferred in low rainfall areas, whereas *raya* and *toria* are grown in medium and high-rainfall areas respectively.

Mustard is usually cultivated as a sole crop in rain fed areas of *kharif* fallows. However, it is intercropped with wheat. It is also an important crop in different crop sequences in rain fed and irrigated areas.

Usually rapeseed-mustard crops are harvested as soon as 75% of pods turn yellow. *Toria*, which takes 75 to 90 days to mature, is the earliest crop to be harvested. The moisture in the seed should be around 30%. Harvesting can be done with the help of serrated sickle leaving about 15 cm high stubble in the field. The mechanical reaper or harvester can also be used in large fields.

Under good management, seed yields of 800-1500 kg/ha under rain fed conditions and 2000 kg/ha under irrigated conditions can be expected.

It is predominantly cultivated in Rajasthan, Uttar Pradesh, Haryana, Madhya Pradesh, and Gujarat. Its cultivation is also done in Karnataka, Tamil Nadu and Andhra Pradesh.

Sugarcane (*Saccharum spp*)

Sugarcane belongs to bamboo family of plants. It is the main source of sugar, *gur* and *khandsari*. It also provides raw material for manufacturing alcohol. Bagasse (the crushed cane residue), is used for the manufacturing of paper. It is also an efficient substitute for petroleum products and a host of other chemical products. The upper green part of sugarcane is used as a nutritious fodder for cattle.

Sugarcane contributes nearly 78 % to the total sugar pool at the global level. It is the prime source of sugar in India; also holding the prominent position as the commercial cash crop of India. It occupies about 3.5% (95 million hectares) of the total cropped area in the country. Uttar Pradesh has the largest area (45.3 million hectares) under sugarcane, which is 43% of the total sugarcane area of the country.

Sugarcane is a continual *Kharif* crop which remains in the field from 10 to 12 months depending on the geographical and socio-economic conditions. It requires hot and humid climate with an average temperature ranging between 20° to 35° C. and a rainfall of about 100 cm. In areas of scanty rainfall it needs six to 10 irrigations almost after every fortnight during the summer season. Short cool dry winter season during harvesting is ideal. Frost and fog are detrimental to sugarcane. In northern India where the winters are severe and fog is frequent in winters, the per unit yield of sugar is low. In fact, fog and frost lead to red-rot disease and reduce the sugar content in the crop. The hot and dry winds like *loo* are also injurious to the crop.

Heavy soils with good drainage are preferred for sugarcane cultivation though it grows well in medium—and light textured soils also with assured irrigation. In Peninsular India, it is grown on brown or reddish loams, laterite and black cotton soils.

Sugarcane can be grown in a wide range of climates from warm tropical south to foothills of Himalayas. However, its height is strongly influenced by the age of the crop and the season. For good bud-sprouting, moist soil and temperature range of 21°-25°C are necessary, whereas emergence and tillring occur best at 30°-35°C with relative humidity of about 50% and bright sunshine. Temperature above 50°C arrests its growth, and that below 20°C slows it markedly, and less than 10°C with severe frost proves fatal during its germination and establishment. The crop does its best in tropical region, receiving a rainfall of 75 to 120 cm. In the absence of adequate rainfall, controlled irrigation should be available.

Brazil is the leading producer of sugarcane, followed by India, China, and Cuba. The other producers of sugarcane are Mexico, Pakistan, Tanzania, Mozambique, Myanmar, Thailand, Guatemala, Honduras, Nicaragua, Costa Rica, Panama (**Fig. 12.13**).

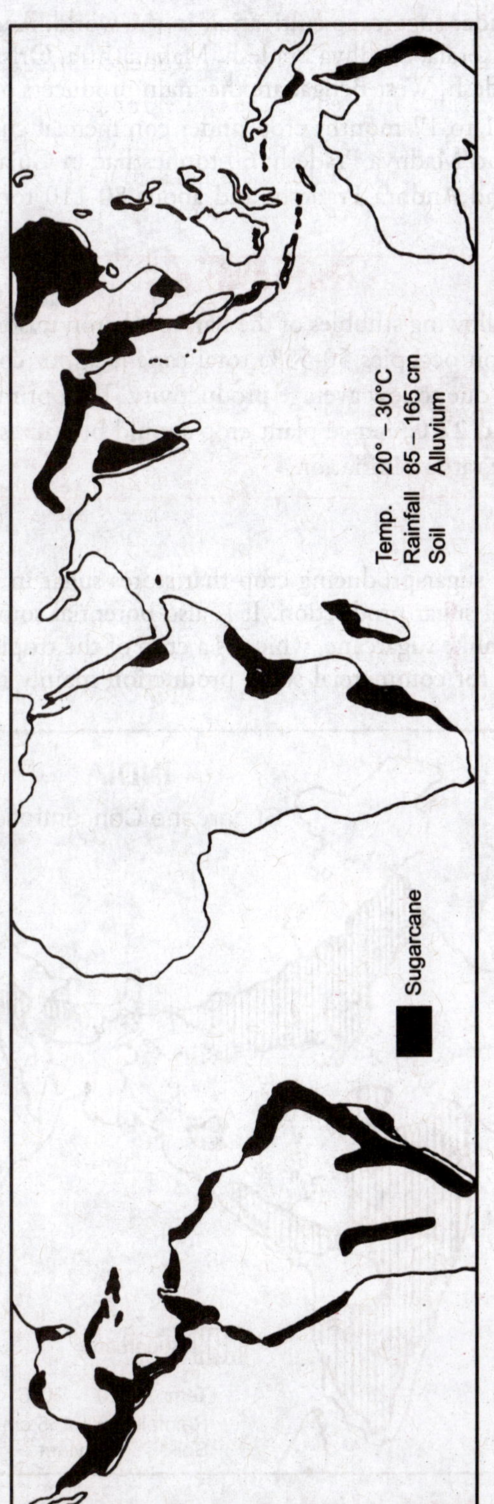

Fig. 12.13 World Distribution of Sugarcane Production

India has the largest area under sugarcane cultivation in the world. Andhra Pradesh, Assam, Bihar, Gujarat, Haryana, Karnataka, Kerala, Madhya Pradesh, Maharashtra, Orissa, Punjab, Rajasthan, Tamil Nadu, Uttarakhand, Uttar Pradesh, West Bengal are the main producers of sugarcane (Fig.12.14).

The average cane yield of 1·1 to 12 months crop under commercial cultivation is about 42 tonnes per hectare in Assam, Bihar, and Madhya Pradesh; 60 tonnes/hac in Gujarat and West Bengal, 80-90 tonnes /hac in Maharashtra and Andhra Pradesh, and about 80-110 tonnes/ha in Maharashtra and Andhra Pradesh.

Ratooning

Ratooning is the method of allowing stubbles of the harvested crop to sprout and form the basis for the next crop. In India, ratoon occupies 50-55% total cane area but contributes to only 30-35% of the total cane production, due to low average productivity. The optimum temperature for quick sprouting of stubble is around 27°C, hence plant crop should be harvested from mid-February to mid-March to obtain profuse ratoon initiation.

Sugarbeet (*Beta vulgaris*)

Sugarbeet is also an important sugar-producing crop that stores sugar in roots. It accounts for nearly 22 per cent of the world's total sugar production. It is also potential source of ethanol which is now blended in automobile fuel. Unlike sugarcane, which is a crop of the tropics is essentially a crop of the temperate regions. It is grown for commercial sugar production mainly in European countries; USA

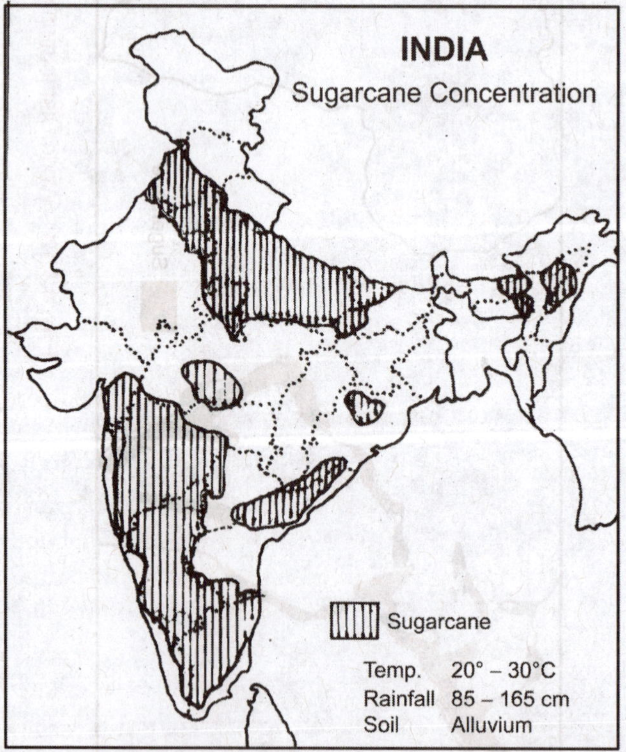

Fig. 12.14 India–Sugarcane Producing Regions

and Canada in North America; Chile in South America; Egypt and Morocco in Africa; and China, Iran, Japan, Syria and Pakistan in Asia. In India, Maharashtra, Karnataka, Andhra Pradesh, Tamil Nadu and Gujarat are the potential areas for winter sugarbeet in the country. The Kashmir Valley has a good scope for the generation of a beet-based sugar-industry.

Geo-climatic Requirements

Sugarbeet requires cool climate, good rainfall or irrigation and bright sunshine during its growth period. The optimum temperature for seed germination is 15°C and for growth and sugar accumulation, it is 21°C. Higher temperatures i.e. above 30°C retard accumulation of sugar but favour rapid growth. Winter sugarbeet is a 6-7 month crop. In India it is sown in October and harvested in April-May.

Sugarbeet grows best in loams and clayey loams with a nearly-neutral pH reaction. It has high tolerance to soil salinity and alkalinity but does poorly in acid soils. Clayey and waterlogged soils are unsuitable for sugarbeet cultivation.

Sugarbeet is susceptible to a number of soil-borne diseases. Their control through chemicals is difficult and costly, and therefore, a long rotation period to prevent built up of diseases is of considerable importance as a prophylactic measure. A rotation of 3-5 years would be minimum need for this crop. Some possible rotations are cowpea (fodder)- sugarbeet-cotton-sugarcane (plant)- sugarcane (ratoon), early maize or rice-sugarbeet- *sani-dhaincha* (green manure) etc.

Sugarbeet is sown in lines, 50 cm apart, on flat beds or on ridges which are kept 10-12 cm high and 20 cm wide. The seed bed is prepared like that of wheat crop. Thus, the land is prepared to a good tilth by repeated ploughing and planking. In India, it is sown in during the first fortnight of October. It does not tolerate delay in sowing as the crop sown after October gives lower root yield and sugar content.

The crop requires 7-10 irrigations in subtropics and 10-12 irrigations in tropics depending upon the weather. Sugarbeet is sensitive to inadequacy of water and therefore timely irrigation is essential to ensure a good yield of roots.

Beet-pulp, a residue obtained after extraction of sugar, is a highly valuable cattle feed that can largely replace barely-grains in feed concentrates. Beet-pulp can be fed to cattle as fresh or in dried form. The mixing of molasses with pulp improves its palatability.

Beet-tops are highly nutritious cattle-feed and are known to improve milk-yield of cows.

Cotton (*Gossypium spp.*)

Usually referred as 'white gold' and one of the important commercial crops, cotton plays a pivotal role in economic, political and social affairs of the world. It is cultivated in 60 countries. The leading producers of cotton are China, USA, India, Brazil, Pakistan, Azerbaijan, Turkmenistan, Uzbekistan, Turkey, Mexico, Colombia, Peru, Egypt, Sudan, Kenya, Ethiopia, Nigeria, and Mozambique (Fig. 12.15). These countries contribute about 90% of the total world production. Asian countries, China (30%), India (19%), and Pakistan (8%) account for 57% of the world cotton production. India ranks first in the world in area with 9.56 million ha under cotton crop and second in total production after China which reached the level of about 320 lakh bales in 2010-11.

Cotton is the major cash crop of India which accounts for 65% of the fibre used in the textile industry. The organized sector of the Indian textile industry constitutes the largest single industrial segment in the country in terms of annual value of output and labour employed.

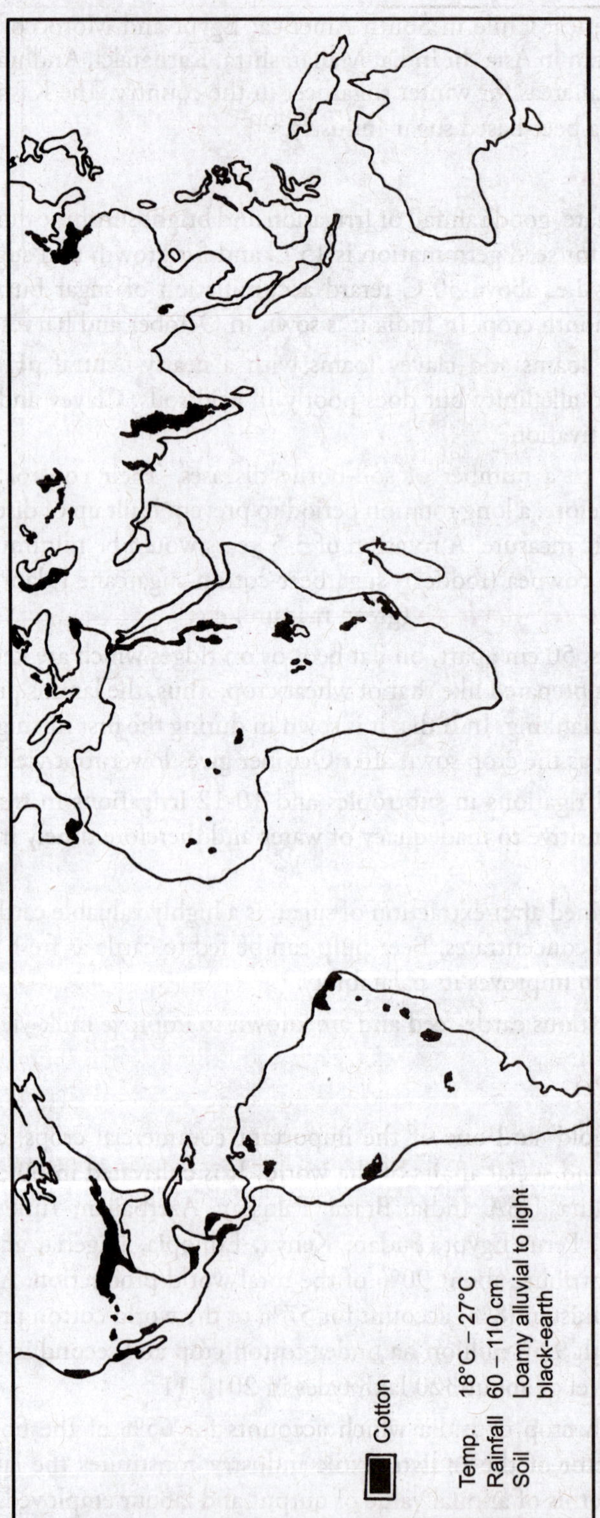

Fig. 12.15 World–Cotton Producing Regions

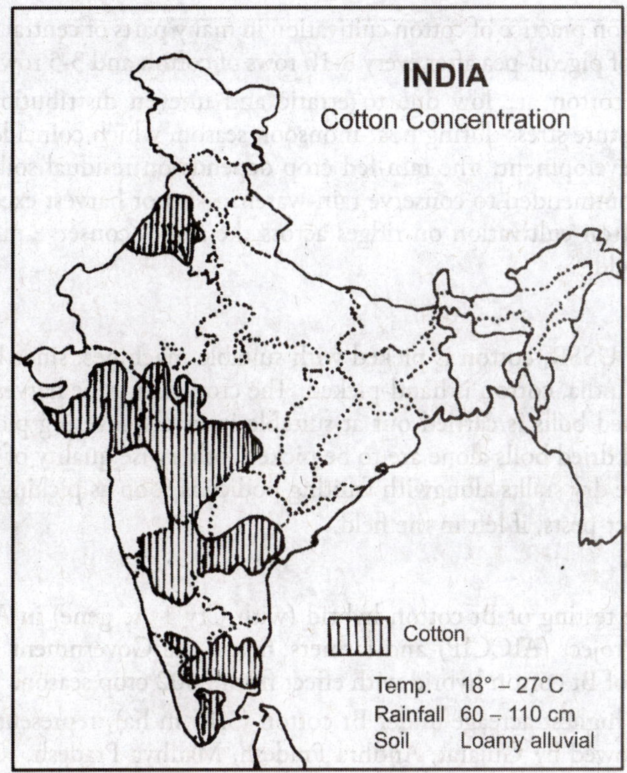

Fig. 12.16 India–Cotton Producing Regions

Cotton, a semi-xerophyte, is grown in tropical and subtropical conditions. A minimum temperature of 15°C is required for better germination at field conditions. The optimum temperature for vegetative growth is 21°-27°C and it can tolerate temperature to the extent of 43°C, but temperature below 21°C is detrimental to the crop. Warm days and cool nights with large diurnal variations during the period of fruiting are conducive to good boll and fiber development. It requires about 50 cm of rainfall. In case of scanty rainfall, irrigation is required. Cotton is grown on a variety of soils, ranging from well-drained deep alluvial soils in the Northern Plains to black clayey soils in the Peninsular India (**Fig. 12.16**).

Cotton is grown as mono-cropping, mixed cropping, inter-cropping and rotation or sequence cropping which depends on the amount and distribution of rainfall. Depending upon the climate and crop-growing period, cotton needs 70-120 cm water. The water requirement is low during first 60-70 days after sowing and highest during flowering and boll development.

Crop Season

Cotton sowing season varies considerably from zone to zone and is generally early (April-May) in the northern plains, and is monsoon based in the peninsular India. The pre-monsoon dry sowing, practiced in parts of Maharashtra, Gujarat, Madhya Pradesh during the last week of May or in early June, have been found to give higher *kapas* (unginned-cotton) yield.

The type of cropping system adopted, i.e. mono-cropping, mixed cropping, relay cropping, inter-cropping and rotation of sequence cropping, depends upon the amount and distribution of rainfall, length of growing season and the type of soil.

The common cultivation practice of cotton cultivation in many parts of central and south India is strip cropping of 1 or 2 rows of pigeon-pea after every 8-10 rows of cotton and 3-5 rows of finger millet (*ragi*).

Yield from rain-fed cotton are low due to erratic and uneven distribution of rainfall. Rainfed cotton suffers from moisture stress during post-monsoon season, which coincides with critical periods of flowering and boll development. The rain-fed crop depends on residual soil moisture, and several measures have been recommended to conserve rain-water in-situ or harvest excess run-off and recycle it at critical phases. Cotton cultivation on ridges across the slopes conserve more water, reduces soil erosion and improves yield.

Harvesting

In the USA and former USSR, cotton is picked with suitable machines, since holdings are very large and labour is scarce. In India, cotton is hand-picked. The crop cannot be harvested at one stretch and the picking of the opened bolls is carried out at suitable intervals covering picking season of several weeks. Well-opened and dried bolls alone are to be picked, otherwise quality of fibre will not be good. It is better to remove the dry stalks alongwith fruiting bodies as soon as picking is completed, because they usually harbor insect-pests, if left in the field.

Bt. Cotton in India

In India, after extensive testing of Bt cotton hybrid (with Cry 1 Ac gene) in All-India Co-ordinated Cotton Improvement Project (AICCIP) and farmers' fields, the Government of India has approved commercial cultivation of Bt cotton hybrid with effect from 2002 crop season.

Maharashtra has the highest acreage under Bt cotton (3.15 m ha), representing 42% of Bt cotton area of the country followed by Gujarat, Andhra Pradesh, Madhya Pradesh, Karnataka, Tamil Nadu and other states.

Due to large scale cultivation of Bt cotton and less usages of pesticides since 2002, in India changes in insect pest complex are evident. Mealy-bugs and Mired-bugs are emerging as potential threat. During the last few years, the pest caused serious damage in the state of Punjab and Haryana. Other affected states with this pest are Rajasthan, Gujarat, Maharashtra, Andhra Pradesh and Madhya Pradesh.

An emerging Player in Cotton Trade

After partition (1947), Indian Union was left with only 60% of the crop production but it had over 95% of the cotton-based industry. This has led to a serious situation related to raw material availability (that undivided India enjoyed). However, India continued to export some quantity of coarse, short staple *desi*-cotton. The country made remarkable advances in cotton production, especially after the advent of hybrid cotton from the mid-seventies. Consequently, India could not only meet the domestic demand in full form its own production but could also generate surplus for export in years of bumper crops. India is gradually emerging as a major player in the world cotton trade.

Plantation Crops

The term 'Plantation agriculture' was originally applied specifically to the British settlements in America and then to any large estate in North America. West Indies and the South East Asian countries which was cultivated by Negro or other coloured labour, living on the estate under the control of proprietor or managers. It represents the development of agricultural resources of the tropical countries in accordance with the methods of secondary occupation or western industrialism. It is a large scale enterprise in agriculture. Plantation involves the existence of a regular force under the control of a more or less elaborate management and frequently a considerable capital outlay, although some of the plantation crops, except tea and rubber are also grown in small holdings by small farmers.

The plantation agriculture is practised mainly in the tropical countries to grow cash crops. Because plantations have usually established in the sparsely populated areas, labour has to be imported and provided with housing, food, education, postal and medical facilities. In the past slavery was the solution, and later indentured labourers, particularly Indians, went to sugarcane plantaion in various parts of the British Empire. Indians also provided much labour to the rubber estates of Malaysia, tea gardens of Sri Lanka and the sugarcane of the West Indies. Some of the important plantation crops are rubber, tea, coffee, cocoa, oil-palm, areca-nut, coconut, cotton, sugarcane, jute, Manila-hemp and vanila.

Socio-Economic Implications of Plantation Agriculture

Plantation has certain common characteristics that qualify it as both an economic and social institution of continued relevance in the modern world. It is an important continuous economic and social factors.

1. Plantation agriculture is an export based agricultural system to carry on production at a high profit level.
2. The high profit comes at the cost of those workers and laboures who are under paid by the employers.
3. Plantation system ignores the social aspirations, family relationships, and even the religious beliefs of plantation workers.
4. The labour has to stay at the plantation estates away from the community and family and thus it is against family integration and creates a situation of dependence on management by labourers.
5. Plantation agriculture is based on large, disciplined, and unskilled imported labour force which some times causes special and psychological problems.
6. The imported labour suffers many psychological problems.
7. The surplus and excess supply of labour creates unemployment and under-employment.
8. The plantation, whether it is owned by a foreign corporation or by a local government, must ensure a steady supply of workers. Because a shortage of labour at a critical moment at the harvesting or processing of a crop can be economically disastrous.
9. In many areas the selection of plantation crops are not conducive environmentally.
10. Looking at the problems faced by the big estates of plantation system, the small farmers are shifting to annual crops instead of perennial crops.

Tea (*Camellia sinensis*)

Tea is the world's most popular beverage, being favoured by at least 50 per cent of the world population. It is the national drink of China, Japan, India, Sri Lanka, Great Britain and Russia.

India has about 45 lakh hectares of land under its cultivation. The major tea growing states in India include Assam (53%), West Bengal (24%), Tamil Nadu (11.0%), and Kerala about 8%). Tea is also grown on a small scale in Tripura, Karnataka, Himachal Pradesh, Uttarakhand, Sikkim, Bihar, Manipur, Odisha, Nagaland and Arunachal Pradesh.

The tea industry in India is more than 160 years old, generating a revenue of over ₹ 6000 *crore*. It employs more than one million workers directly and looks after 4 million dependents of these employees. Of the working population directly employed by the tea gardens, nearly 50% are women. The production of tea in India has increased from 250 million kg in 1947 to 755 million kg in 2011, recording a substantial increase.

Factors of tea cultivation Tea is a native to the subtropics of Asia. It is grown widely in both the subtropics and the high elevations within the tropics. Tea is an evergreen plant (actually, a tree crop pruned to form bushes and tender-new- leaves) that grows best where temperatures range between 20° to 27°C. Few plants require as much moisture as tea. Over 200 cm of rainfall, well distributed throughout the year is desirable. Humidity must also be high to assure abundant leaf formation. Tea cultivation is extremely sensitive to soil quality. It grows well on the undulating—well-drained fertile soils. Tea plantation requires deep, fertile alluvial soil with a good water holding capacity. There are however, a number of small pockets of old red soil which are mostly rich loam.

Tea growing areas in India In Darjeeling, tea is grown on sedimentary soils in the hill slopes at an elevation of 600-2000 m. The temperature in these hills usually does not exceed 25°C. During winter, the temperature dips to about 5°-6°C. Unlike in the other regions, winter is very cold and dry, and at higher elevations, snowfall and frost may occur. In South India, tea areas are located on the hilly terrains. About 32% of the tea areas in the south India are at an elevation on the hilly terrain. The cultivated tea near to equator produces almost the same yield throughout the year, but farther from the equator, harvest in winter gradually declines and at latitudes beyond about 16°C temperature, there is complete winter dormancy, the length of dormant period increases progressively with increasing distance from the equator.

Process of tea cultivation Young tea plants are grown in nurseries under protective conditions. The saplings are transplanted in the fields when they are about one year old. Plucking leaves begins usually when plants are three year old. The highest yields are achieved at six years. Tea bushes are constantly pruned to generate tender new leaf growth, which is the only part of the plant that is harvested. Once tea leaves are plucked, they must be processed quickly at a nearby factory. The leaves that are completely processed (i.e. withered, fermented, and fired) make black tea, the major product in the world trade. Green-tea is produced when withered leaves undergo a steaming to stop fermentation from occurring. Green-tea is extremely popular in Japan and China, where it is almost completely produced by small scale farmers.

Conventionally, tea is grown under shade trees in India. The beneficial effects of shade trees in tea fields have been well realized. These trees help to regulate temperature and humidity at bush level. They minimize the loss of water through evaporation and transpiration. They help to reduce the injury caused to tea leaves by UV radiation. They also help in minimizing soil erosion and increase the fertility of soil by adding 8-10 tonnes of organic matter/ha/year.

Harvesting is most important cultural operation which influences yield, productivity of labour and quality of tea. More han 70% of the labour force in any tea-garden is deployed for this work. Harvesting in tea involves the regular removal of young shoots comparising an apical bud and 2 or 3 leaves, immediately below it. Harvesting should be carried out when shoots attain maximum weight, without compromising on quality.

Leading tea producess India, China, Sri Lanka and Kenya are the leading tea producing countries, while India is the largest exporter of tea in the world **(Figs. 12.17-18).**

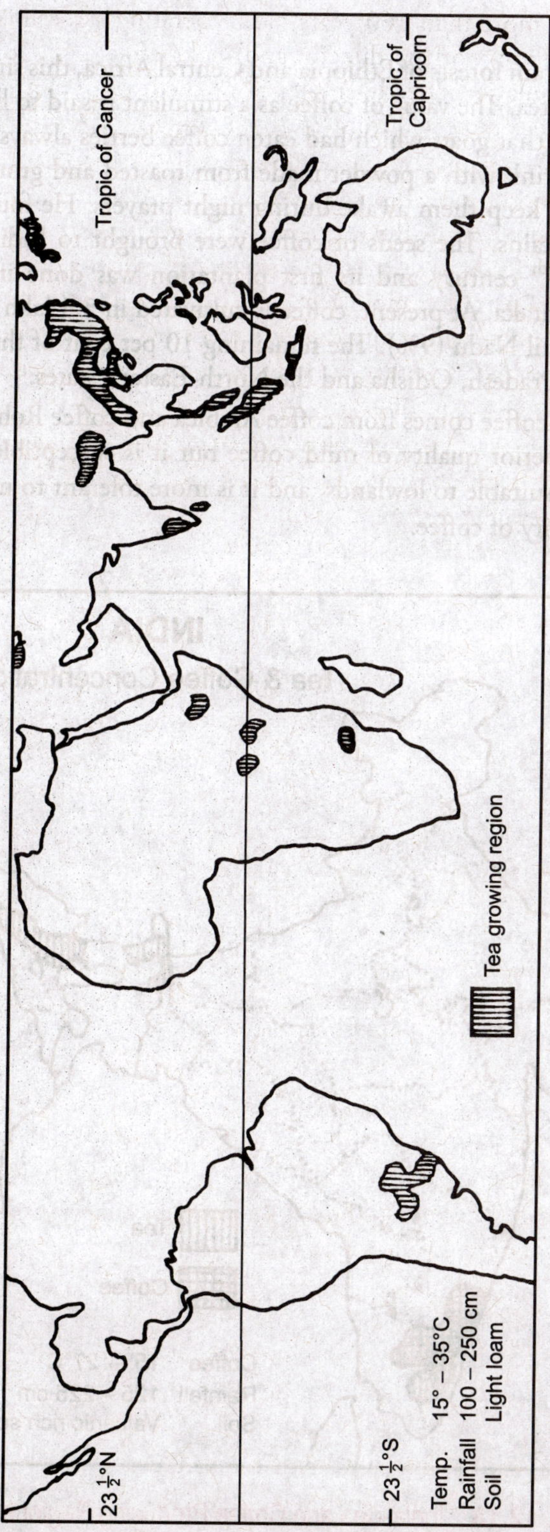

Fig. 12.17 World–Distribution of Tea Production

Coffee (*Coffea*)

Coffee, a native to the tropical rain forests of Ethiopia and Central Africa, this simulating beverage crop. Coffee is more expensive than tea. The value of coffee as a stimulant is said to have been discovered by an Arabian priest who noticed that goats which had eaten coffee berries always had restless nights. He tested his ideas by mixing a drink with a powder made from roasted and ground coffee beans which he gave to his subordinates to keep them awake during night prayers. He found this was because of the caffeine which coffee contains. The seeds of coffee were brought to India by the Muslim Fakir –Bababudan Sahib in the 17th century and its first plantation was done in the Bababudan Hills Chikamaglur District of Karnataka. At present, coffee is cultivated in 3.4 lakh ha, covering Karnataka (56%), Kerala (25%) and Tamil Nadu (9%). The remaining 10 per cent of the accounts for the non-traditional states like Andhra Pradesh, Odisha and the North-Eastern states.

Commercial production of coffee comes from coffee Arabica and coffee Robusta. Arabica is suitable for high lands, producing superior quality of mild coffee but it is susceptible to major diseases and pests. Robusta coffee is more suitable to lowlands, and it is more tolerant to major diseases and pests, producing rather inferior quality of coffee.

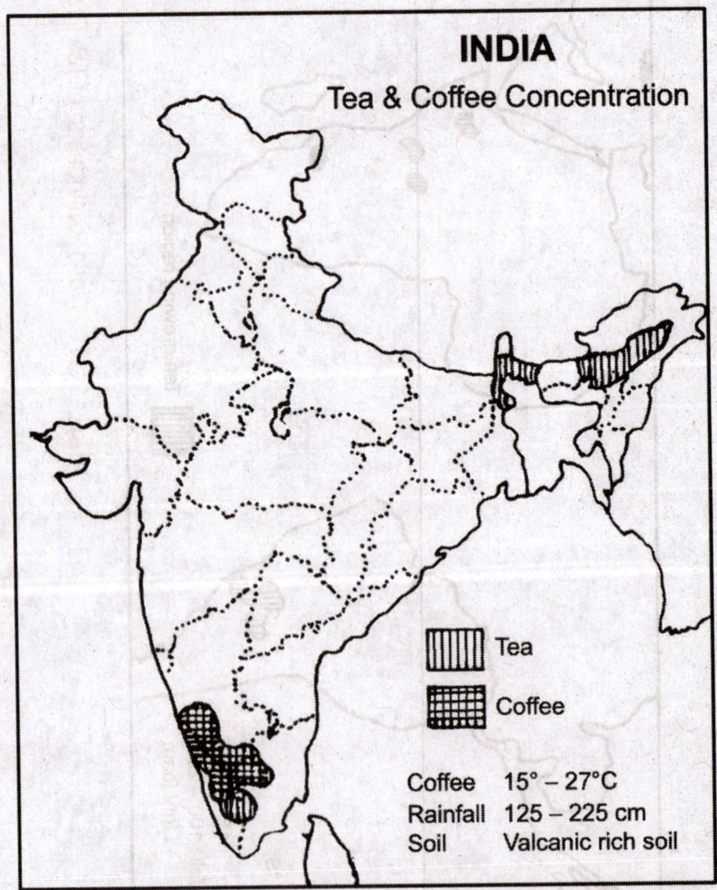

Fig. 12.18 India–Tea and Coffee Producing Regions

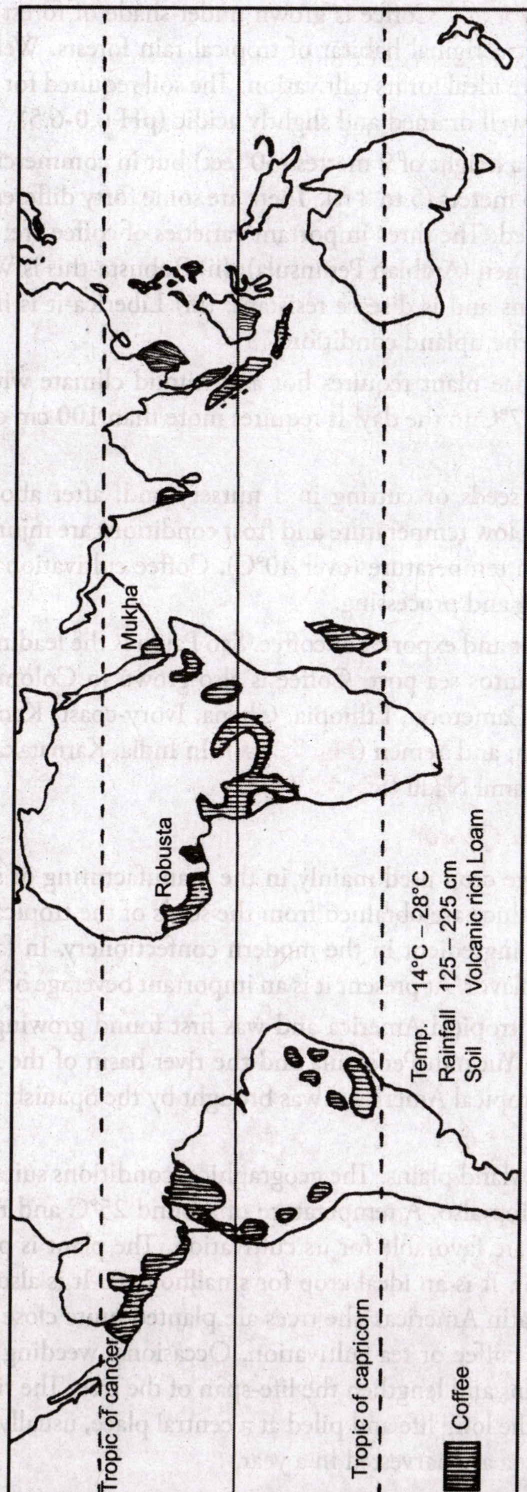

Fig. 12.19 World–Distribution of Coffee Production

Geo-climatic Conditions Required Coffee is grown under shade of forest to create suitable micro-climate, simulative to that of its original habitat of tropical rain forests. Well distributed rainfall and good shade of evergreen trees are ideal for its cultivation. The soil required for coffee plantation is deep-friable, rich in organic matter, well drained and slightly acidic (pH 6.0-6.5).

The coffee tree may grow to a height of 9 metres (30 feet) but in commercial cultivation it is usually pruned to a height of 1.5 to 2.5 meters (5 to 8 ft). There are some forty different species but three major types are commercially cultivated. The three important varieties of coffee are: (i) Arabica also known as Mocha coffee –native to the Yemen (Arabian Peninsula); (ii) Robusta-this is West African variety which can survive even arid conditions and is disease resistant; (iii) Liberica-it is indigenous to Liberia and suited to low land rather than the upland conditions.

Conditions for Growth Coffee plant requires hot and humid climate with a temperature ranging between 15°C in the night to 27°C in the day. It requires more than 100 cm of rainfall distributed over the greater part the year.

Coffee is propagated from seeds or cutting in a nursery and, after about six months plants are positioned 3 meters apart. Very low temperature and frost conditions are injurious to the crop and same is the condition with very high temperature (over 40°C). Coffee cultivation requires cheap labour for transplanting, plucking, drying and processing.

Brazil is the leading producer and exporter of coffee. Sao Paulo is the leading centre of coffee exports. The export is done through Santos sea-port. Coffee is also grown in Colombia, Mexico, El-Salvador, Guatemala, Jamaica, Angola, Cameroon, Ethiopia, Ghana, Ivory-coast, Kenya, Uganda, Zaire, India, Malaysia, Philippines, Vietnam, and Yemen (**Fig. 12.19**). In India, Karnataka is the leading producer of coffee followed by Kerala and Tamil Nadu (**Fig. 12.18**).

Cocoa or Cacao (*Theobroma Cacao*)

Cocoa is an important beverage crop used mainly in the manufacturing of soft drinks and chocolate. The raw material for these produce are obtained from the seeds of the tropical tree known as cocoa. Its main importance is as a basic ingredient in the modern confectionery. In fact it has great nutritional value and known for excellent flavor. At present it is an important beverage of the elites and intellectuals.

The cacao is indigenous to tropical America and was first found growing wild in lowland Central America, from Panama to the Yucatan Peninsula and the river basin of the Amazon and the Orinoco rivers (Venezuela). From the tropical America it was brought by the Spanish. The Spanish diffused it in the tropical African countries.

Cocoa thrives in tropical lowland plains. The geographical conditions suitable for banana cultivation are conducive for the cocoa crop also. A temperature of around 25°C and rainfall about 100 cm well distributed in all the months are favorable for its cultivation. The plant is propagated from seeds and grows best in forest conditions. It is an ideal crop for smallholders. It is also grown on large estates in some parts of Africa and in Latin America. The trees are planted quite close together (about 3 meters) and there is no pruning as in coffee or tea cultivation. Occasional weeding and manuring do help to improve the quality of the beans and lengthen the life-span of the tree. The ripe pods are removed from the trunk and branches with the long life and piled at a central place, usually near the main road or the railway line. Two crops of cocoa are harvested in a year.

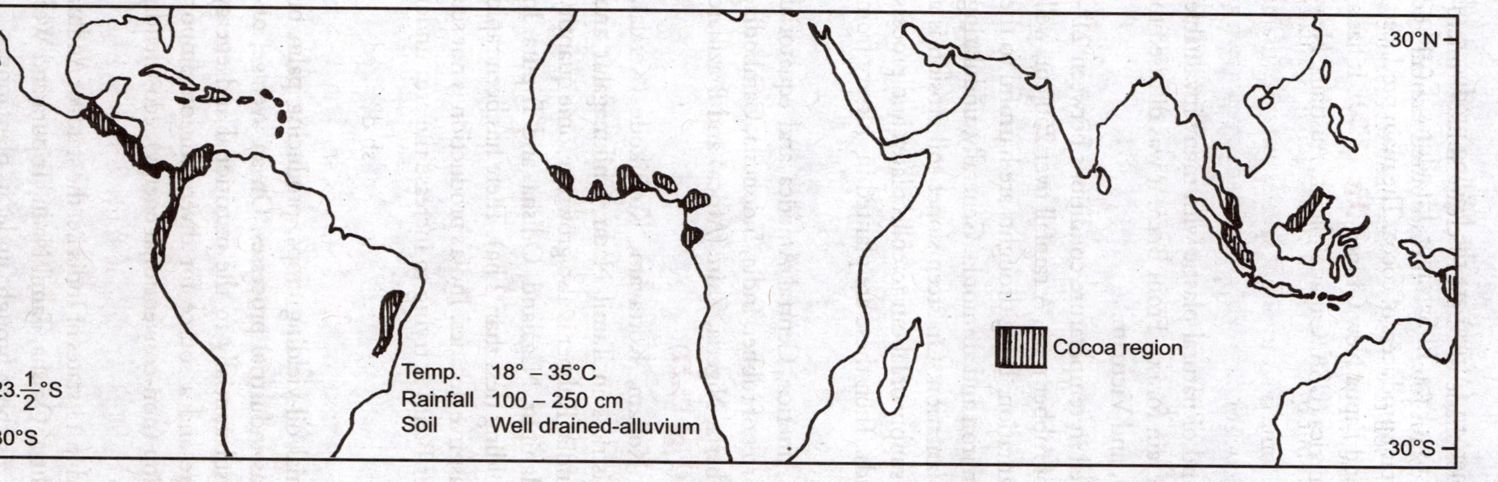

Fig. 12.20 World–Distribution of Cocoa Production

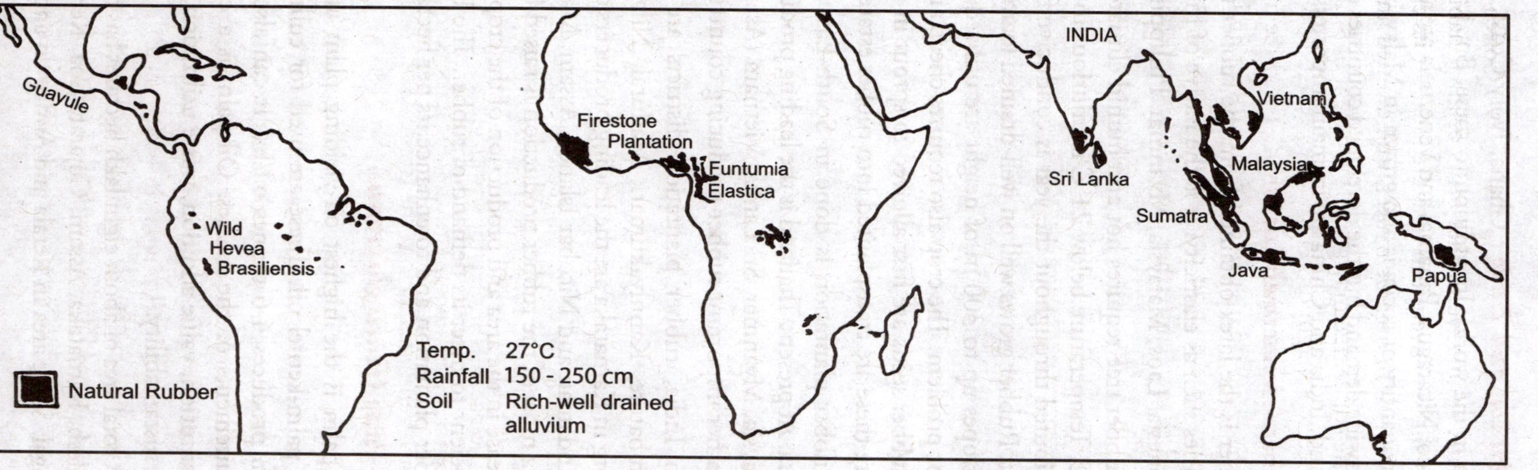

Fig. 12.21 World–Distribution of Natural Rubber Production

Production and Trade Ghana, Ivory Coast, Nigeria, Cameroon (Africa) are the leading producers of cocoa in the world. In addition to these, Brazil, Colombia, Costa Rica, El-Salvador, Honduras, Ecuador, Mexico, Nicaragua, Panama, and Venezuela are also the important producers of cocoa. The main producers some quantity of cocoa is also grown in Malaysia, Indonesia and Papua New Guinea **(Fig.12.20)**. It has a worldwide demand but the developed countries of Europe, America (USA, Canada), Japan, Australia, New Zealand, India and China are its main importers.

Rubber (*Hevea brasiliensis*)

Rubber is the latex obtained from the rubber tree. It is a kind of natural plastic with many invaluable qualities such as elasticity. It is the native of the Amazonian rain forests. From Brazil it was diffused to Indonesia, Laos, Malaysia, Myanmar, Philippines, Thailand, and Vietnam.

Rubber tree requires hot and humid climate. It grows well in temperature conditions between 21°-27°C. Temperature below 21°C is injurious to the growth of rubber trees. A rainfall over 250 cm, well distributed throughout the year is conducive for rubber plantation. Long droughts are harmful to the plant. Rubber grows well on well-drained loamy soils, rich in iron and ammonia. Generally, undulating hill slopes up to 300 m of height are utilized for rubber plantation. On steep slopes soil erosion is a major problem. The crop also requires cheap and abundant supply of labour to collect latex and process it. Rubber seeds are first allowed to sprout in river-bed sands. Then these are planted in nursery from where these are transplanted into rubber estates.

Rubber plantation is done in South-East Asia, South America, Central America and equatorial Africa. At present Thailand is the leading producer and exporter of rubber. India, Indonesia, Cambodia, Malaysia, Myanmar, Sri Lanka, Vietnam (Asia), Ghana, Liberia, Nigeria, Zaire (Africa) and Brazil are the other important rubber producing countries of rubber (**Fig. 12.21**).

In India, rubber plantation districts are Ernakulam, Kollam, Kottayam, Kozhikode (Kerala), Coimbatore, Kanniyakumari, Madurai, Nilgiri, Salem districts in Tamil Nadu, Chikmagalur and Coorg in Karnataka are the leading producers of rubber in India. Rubber is also grown in some quantity in Andaman and Nicobar Islands, Assam, Maharashtra, Manipur, Nagaland, Odisha, and Tripura. In India most of the rubber production is raised from small holding (less than 2 ha). There has been rapid increase in the area and production of the crop during the last five decades. India's production is not self sufficient to meet its demand of rubber. The Indian Rubber Board is trying to increase the area under rubber plantation and to enhance its per hectare yield.

Oil-Palm (*Elaeis guineensis*)

Oil-palm is the highest oil-yielding plant among perennial oil-yielding crops, producing palm oil and palm-kernel oil. These are used for culinary as well as industrial processes. On an average, oil-palm produces 4-6 tonnes oil/ha. It can also contribute substantially to the nutritional and energy requirements of the masses. Oil-palm is a crop for future and a source for diversification, import substitution, value addition, waste utilization, eco-generation (non-conventional energy), eco-friendly and sustainability.

A total area of about eight lakh hectares has been identified in 11 states of India i.e. the states of Andhra Pradesh, Karnataka, Assam, Gujarat, Goa, Kerala, Maharashtra, Odisha, Tamil Nadu, Tripura and West Bengal. Some area in Kerala and Andaman and Nicobar has also been brought under its plantation.

Oil-palm is a humid tropical palm which thrives well where annual temperature ranges 29°-33°C (maximum) and 24°-25° (minimum) an evenly distributed rainfall of 250-400 cm, and relative humidity more than 80%. It can be grown up to 900 m above the mean sea level.

Oil-palm is propagated mainly through seeds. Seeds are extracted from fruits. Since seeds have dormancy, pre-heating of seeds is done in a heating room for 80 days at 40°C. Then the seeds are soaked for 5 days in running water and kept in cool places. The germination commences in 10-12 days. These sprouts are put in polybags.

Oil-palm requires sufficient irrigation, as it is fast growing crop with high productivity and biomass production. Oil-palm starts bearing bunches two and half to 3 years after planting. Wherein the bunch is mature and ready for harvesting, fruits in bunch turn yellowish-orange, and 5-10 fruits from each bunch drop on their own. Harvesting should be done at 10-12 days interval during rainy season. It should be done at closer intervals of 6-7 days as ripening is hastened after rains.

The yield of palm-oil depends on variety, age and management practices. From the fifth year onwards, the average yield may be 20-25 tonnes per hectare per year. To obtain good quality raw palm oil, the fruits are processed within 24 hours after harvesting.

Cashew-nut (*Anacardium occidentale*)

Cashew is cultivated widely throughout the tropics for its kernels. In India, it is grown in the west coast, east coast and a few plain areas of Karnataka, Tamil Nadu, Kerala, Andhra Pradesh, Maharashtra and Madhya Pradesh. The highest productivity is recorded in Maharashtra with 1.5 tonnes per hectare.

Cashew tolerates wide range of geo-climatic conditions. The plantation of cashew is restricted to altitude below 700 m where the temperature does not fall below 20°C for prolonged periods. However, the best production is recorded upto the altitude of 400 m with at least 9 hour sunlight/day from December to May. Cashew grow well at reasonably high temperatures and does not tolerate prolonged periods of cold and frost, especially during the juvenile period. Temperature above 35°C is however, between the flowering and fruiting period could adversely affect fruits setting and retention.

Cashew can adapt very well to dry conditions as it is hardy and drought resistant. However, its varieties perform very well where atleast a minimum of 60 cm of rain is recorded in a year. Cashew is very sensitive to water- logging and hence heavy clay soils with poor drainage conditions are unsuitable for its cultivation. Cashew grows in almost all the soils (sandy loams, laterite soils and coastal sands) except the excessive alkaline and saline soils. Cashew responds well to supplementary irrigation during the summer months (April to June).

Planting of soft wood grafts is usually done during monsoon season (July-August) both in the west coast and the east coast. Therefore land preparation such as clearing of bushes and other wild growth, digging of pits for planting should be done during the pre-monsoon season (May-June).

Cashew is commonly grown in sloppy lands both in the west and east coasts. Soil erosion and leaching of plant nutrients are generally expected under such topographical conditions. To overcome this problem, preparing terraces around the plant/tree trunk and opening of catch-pits are highly essential. Therefore, cultural operations should be restricted to one meter depth and 2 meter radius around the trunk of the tree so that the applied nutrients are in the root zone.

Manures and fertilizers promote the growth of plant and advance the onset of flowering in young trees. The ideal period for fertilizer application is immediately after cessation of heavy rains. It is grown under rainfed conditions. However, in homestead gardens, supplementary irrigation during summers at fortnight interval increases the yield.

Cashew plants start bearing fruits three years after planting. They provide full yield by tenth year and continue giving remunerative yields for a further period of 20 years. Cashew nuts are harvested during February-May. Only fully mature nuts should be harvested. Usually, the nuts are picked after they fall off from the trees. The best quality of nuts are obtained where freshly fallen fruits are collected. On an average a tree provides 2 kg nuts at the age of 3-5 years, 4 kg (6-10 years), 5-10 kg at 11-15 years, and more than 10 kg at 15-20 years.

Arecanut (*Areca catechu*)

Arecanut or betel nut or *supari* (Areca catechu) is chewed both as new nut and after processing. While ripe arecanut is favoured in Assam, Kerala, and Northern parts of West Bengal, *Chali* is more popular in western and northern parts of India. Processed green nut *kalipak* is the choice of Karnataka and Tamil Nadu. Owing to the medicinal properties, it is used in treating leucoderma, cough, fits, worms, anaemia and obesity. Arecanut is of utmost importance in many religious ceremonies. Tannins in arecanut are being used for dyeing clothes, ropes and for tanning leather. Plastic, hard boards and craft paper of satisfactory strength can be made from its husk. The leaf sheath is a good material for making throw-away cups and plates, playboards, decorative veneer panels and picture mounds. Its stem forms a useful building material in the village. Arecanut is mostly grown in Kerala, Karnataka, Assam, West Bengal and Tamil Nadu.

Jute (*Corchorus capsularis*)

Jute is one of the important cash crops of India. It is grown in the north-eastern states, viz. West Bengal, Assam, northern Bihar, south-east Odisha, Tripura, Meghalaya and eastern Uttar Pradesh (Fig. 12.22).

The main concentration of jute cultivation is in Bangladesh and India. The other major jute growing areas are China, Thailand, Myanmar, Indonesia, Brazil and Nepal. Africa and Indo-Myanmar region has been identified as the primary and secondary centres.

Jute is an industrially oriented crop. About 95% of fibres being utilized in industry and the remaining 5% are retained by farmers for domestic use. About 72% of the jute goods are consumed domestically and the remaining 18% are exported to countries like United Kingdom, Japan, South-West Asia, China, South, Korea, Africa, USA, Canada, Argentina, CIS, Australia and New Zealand.

Geo-Climatic Conditions Required: Jute requires a warm and humid climate, with temperature fluctuating 25°C and 35°C, the optimum being 34°C. Incessant rains or waterlogged conditions are definitely harmful. Though the white jute varieties can stand water-logging to some extent during the later stage of growth, *tossa* jute varieties cannot. In the seedling stage waterlogging is not tolerated by both the species. Areas receiving early showers in late February or early March, followed by relatively short dry spell are suitable for sowing of white jute varieties. Rain below 100 cm is not harmful. Alternative sunshine and rainy days are most conducive to growth. The dry spell proceeding the onset of the monsoon enables the essential weedings and thinning operations to be carried out.

The newer grey alluvial soils of good depth, receiving silt from the annual flood, is ideal for the cultivation of jute. Jute is however, widely grown in sandy loam and loam soils and heavy clays are unsuitable. Soils with a low pH give a poor crop, the optimum pH being around 6.4.

Jute requires a clean clod free field with fine tilth. The land is therefore ploughed, cross-ploughed and planked several times. All weeds thoroughly removed. Rough cropping is advantageous as it facilitates the intercultural operations.

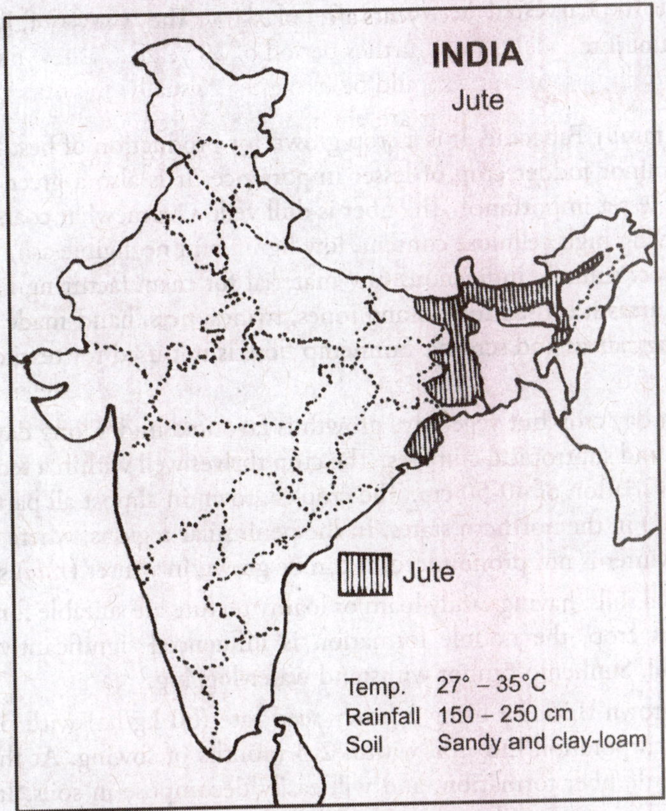

Fig. 12.22 India–Jute Producing Areas

Mesta (*Hibicus sabdariffa*)

The fiber of mesta is obtained from stems of *kenaf* and *roselle*. There are about 400 species under the Hibiscus distributed in the tropical and subtropical regions of the world, of which 36 species had been observed in India, Pakistan, Bangladesh Sri Lanka and Myanmar. Tropical Africa appears to be a major centre of diversity for mesta crop. The major mesta-growing countries are India, China, Thailand, Malaysia, Indonesia, Philippines, Egypt, Sudan, Brazil and Australia. In India, the area under mesta at present, is around 0.15 million ha. Of which more than 90-95% is under roselle. The average annual production is around 0.84 million bales. The leading producers of mesta are Andhra Pradesh (36%), followed by Maharashtra, Odisha, Bihar and West Bengal.

It requires warm and humid climate with a temperature of 20°C-30°C and its rainfall requirement is between 50 and 75 cm. Mesta however, does not withstand prolonged water stagnation. Mesta can be grown on a variety of soils including new and old alluvium. Light textured, well-drained soil having adequate organic matter produces higher fiber yield. Acid soils need to be amended for better growth of the plants.

Mesta when broadcast, requires 10-12 kg of seeds/ha. The seedlings are to be annually thinned twice to a spacing of 15-18 cm between plants when plants are 10-12 cm tall. Though the farmers practice broadcasting for maximum utilization of soil moisture, it is not advocated as the intercultural operations become difficult, time consuming, labour intensive and costly.

Mesta plants are to be harvested between 140-145 days. The harvesting and retting of mesta is almost similar to that of jute.

Sunhemp (*Crotalaria juncea*)

Sunhemp belongs to family Fabaceae. It is a crop grown for production of best fibers. It is also a green manuring crop and minor fodder crop of lesser importance. It is also a green manuring crop and a minor fodder crop of lesser importance. The fiber is dull yellow, somewhat coarse, strong and durable. Owing to be fibre having high cellulose content, low lignin and negligible ash, the paper industry has identified it as the most suitable indigenous raw material for manufacturing tissues paper and paper for currency. In rural areas it is used for making ropes, twines, nets, hand-made paper and *tat pattis*. It is also used for making canvas and screens. Sunhemp fibre is not used for textile purposes, unlike jute and mesta.

Sunhemp is a short day crop but vegetative growth is favoured under long day conditions. The crop grows best in tropical and subtropical climates. The crop thrives well within a temperature range of 20° to 30°C. and rainfall variation of 40-50 cm. The crop is grown in almost all parts of India. It is grown in rainy season (*kharif*) in the northern states. In the peninsular regions, where the climate is more or less equable and the winter is not pronounced, it can be grown in winter (*rabi*) season also.

Well-drained alluvial soils, having sandy loam or loamy texture are suitable for sunhemp cultivation. Being the leguminous crop, the nodule formation is influenced significantly by the calcium and phosphate status of soil. Sunhemp cannot withstand water-logging.

A sunhemp crop grown thick by using a heavy seed rate (60 kg/ha) with profuse branching and foliage is ready for incorporation into soil within 2-3 months of sowing. At this time, the stalk will be tender with very little fiber formation, and will easily decompose in soils. It fixes 50-60 kg N/ha through root nodules. The crop is either ploughed in as it stands or is cut close to ground and ploughed in as it stands and levelled with a wooden plank (*suhaga*). In double cropped rice, the green-manuring crop is cut and is incorporated into the soil. Green-manuring with sunhemp is practiced invariably in every type of soil. It is particularly found suitable in reclaiming saline-alkaline soils.

Sunhemp fibre, because of its chemical constituents, can be an excellent raw material for good quality paper making. It produces good quality bleachable pulps, the strength of which equals to that of hardwood pulp also. The fibres are utilized for the manufacturing of cordage (ropes, cords, especially in a ships rigging).

Ramie (*Boehmeria genus*)

Remie is a semi-perennial type best fibre crop which produces longest (12 cm and the strongest textile fibre of plant origin. According to Vavilov (1951) is indigenous to central and western China. The crop is grown in parts of Assam, Arunachal Pradesh, Himachal Pradesh (Kangra Valley) and Nilgiri Hills area of Tamil Nadu. Rime is a cellulosic fibre containing 86-87% cellulose.

Deep, fertile loamy or sandy loam soils are suitable for the successful cultivation of the crop. Land is to be ploughed 2-3 times and levelled to facilitate drainage. The plot shoud be free from clods and weeds. In flat planting, generally small furrows of 5-7 cm depth are opened with wheel hoe and rhizomes are placed horizontally and covered with soil. Ridges protect the rhizomes from water stagnation and the furrows act as micro-drainage channels during peak rainfall and also conserves moisture during dry period. The period between May to September is the best for its cultivation.

The growth of ramie crop during winter is retarded and uniform and the canes are not suitable for fibre extraction. Thus in a rain-fed plantation, the winter crop is cut close to ground during March/April with the onset of pre-monsoon showers, for uniform growth of subsequent crop. This operation is called stage back and extremely important for getting good fibre yield in subsequent cuts.

The use of fibre depends primarily on its gum content. If the gum content is less than 4 %, it can be used for manufacturing of fibric. The fibre can be blended with natural fibre like cotton, silk, wool and also with synthetic fibres to produce yarns. It can also be used for the manufacturing of apparel and cordage. It has great pharmaceutical and chemical industries.

Sisal (*Agave sisalana*)

Sisal introduced from Mexico, is a semi-perennial succulent plant which yields a creamy-white fibre from its leaves. Sisal plants consists of a rosette of swords-shaped leaves with a terminal spine. The short stem (bole) during the early stage of growth is almost concealed by the surrounding sessile, thick, broad and very long leaves. The fibre is often referred to as hard fibre.

The major sisal producing countries in the world are Brazil, Kenya, Tanzania, Madagascar, Angola, Haiti, and China. In India it is grown in Odisha, Madhya Pradesh, Andhra Pradesh, Maharashtra, Jharkhand Bihar, and the western parts of West Bengal.

Sisal is a native to tropical and sub-tropical America and Caribbean Islands with the maximum concentration in Mexico.

Sisal is usually grown in hot and humid regions. It can withstand dry period of some duration and also high atmospheric temperature. Sisal prefers a rainfall of not less than 100 cm per annum and the rainfall should be evenly distributed. Sisal needs plenty of light and sunshine for good growth.

Sisal can grow in a wide range of soils. The soil should be friable, well-drained, dry, permeable and sandy-loam. The soil should not be too acidic and low in nutrient.

For the cultivation of Sisal, land should be prepared by uprooting trees and bush growth. Top soil should be disturbed as little as possible and infertile sub-soil should not be exposed. Ploughing to a depth of 15-20 cm is adequate.

Sisal plants rarely set seeds. Propagation of sisal is done by bulbils and suckers which are asexual source of propagation. The sisal plant produces nearly 500-2000 bulbils. Bulbils are collected from mid-February to mid-April.

The process of extracting the fibre from leaf tissues of sisal is called decortications. Extracting of fibre is preferably done on the same day or within 48 hours from the time of harvesting. Decorticated fibre is washed in clean water and dried in the sun for removing moisture. It is also used for reinforcement in composite materials for manufacturing of low cost composite building materials. Composite panels and corrugated sheets made of sisal fibre composites have been developed by the Central Building Research Institute, Roorkee. The high strength and durability has opened the scope of sisal for manufacturing of geotextiles.

Sisal fibre is used for manufacturing cordage—rope, twine, floor covering, steel rope, carpets, etc. because of its strength. Due to its durability, ability to stretch, and its affinity for dyes, it can be used for industrial fabric. It is also used for low cost and speciality paper. Geotextiles, mattresses, carpets and wall coverings and other handicrafts.

Flax (*Linum Usitatissimum*)

Linseed is a dual purpose crop. The fibre comes from stems of flax types and the oil from the seeds of linseed types. The flax fibres are valued for its strength and durability which are superior to those of cotton. They are soft, showy and posses light water absorbency. It has low elasticity and is stronger when wet than when dry. It is resistant to high temperature, moisture and mildew. Flax made of flax launder well. It is grown in the temperate and subtropical regions of the world.

Flax is woven into fine fabrics such as lawns, cambric and drills, canvass, and buckrams. It is used in stitching, making twines and nets for fishing ropes, carpet backing, sails, wrapping cloth and house furnishings. It is good raw material for tissue-paper, fire-fighting hosepipes, knapsacks and water-bags.

Flax is a crop of temperate zone. A cool, humid climate with temperature ranging from 10° to 20° C with a relative humidity 65% during growing period is preferred as it promotes the stem height which is the most desirable character in flax. In hot and dry climate, flax types tend to branch and grow as linseed types. Flax requires 15-20 cm rainfall during its growth period. Drought and higher temperature affect vegetative growth. The ideal geographical regions envisaged for successful flax production in India are the valleys of Himalayan range whose winter simulates a European summer. The agro-climatic conditions of Kangra Valley of Himachal Pradesh during *rabi* had been found to be very congenial for flax cultivation. The high humidity and occasional cloudy conditions favours the vegetative growth whereas the warm and dry season during April after harvesting of the crop facilities retting and drying.

Rich loams or clay loams are considered best. Heavy clay or light soils are unsuitable. Fertile, well drained soils with neutral to slightly acidic soils reaction are suitable for flax cultivation.

Tobacco

Tobacco is an important cash crop of India. This was brought to India by the Portuguese in 1508. Since then its cultivation spread to different parts of the country and at present India is one of the leading producers of tobacco in the world. Tobacco is mainly used for smoking-bin the form of cigarette, bidi, cigar, cheroot, hookah, *kheni*, *pan-parag, etc.* It is also used for manufacturing insecticides. The main areas of its cultivation in India are Andhra Pradesh, Maharashtra, Gujarat, Uttar Pradesh, Bihar, Tamil Nadu, Karnataka, Kerala, Odisha, Madhya Pradesh, Rajasthan and West Bengal **(Fig. 12.23)**.

Tobacco is grown in the varied geo-ecological conditions of the tropical and sub-tropical regions. Tobacco can withstand a temperature varying from 16° to 35°C, but the ideal temperature is between 18°–25°C. It normally requires rainfall between 100-250 cm. The soils should be well-drained.

In India, the two main varieties of tobacco grown are:

(i) *Nicotiana tobacum* – a better quality tobacco which mainly used in cigarettes and cigar. The plant is tall and has long broad, leaves with pink flowers. About 90 per cent of total tobacco production in India is of this type.

(ii) *Nicotiana rustica*: It needs cool climate and is mainly grown in northern and north-eastern India. It is grown mainly for *hookah*, chewing and snuff. It accounts for about 10 per cent of the total tobacco production of the country.

About 80% of the total production of tobacco is used within the country and the remaining 20 per cent is exported. India is the fourth largest exporter of tobacco in the world. It is exported to Russia, U.K., Japan, Germany, Egypt, Sri-Lanka, Nepal, Bhutan, South-West Asian countries, Indonesia, Malaysia and Philippines.

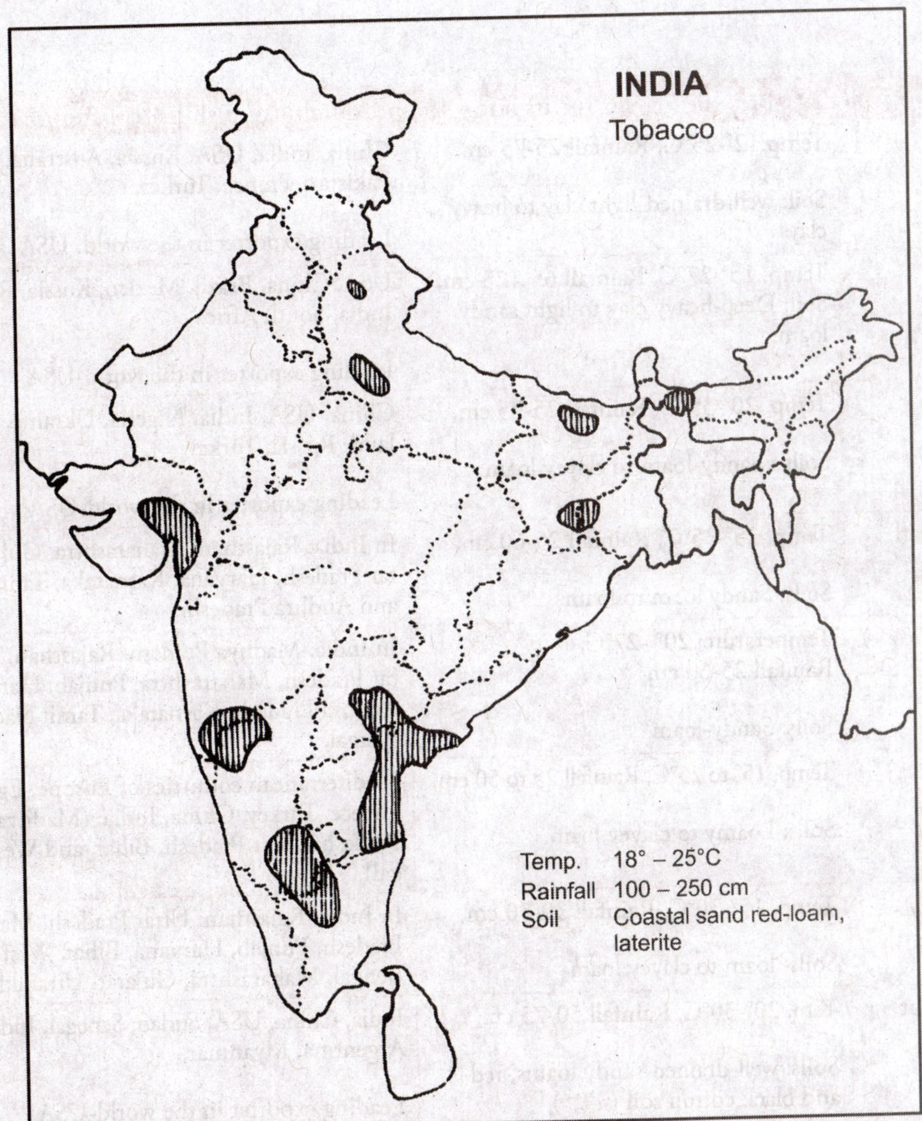

Fig. 12.23 India: Tobacco Producing Regions

Table 12.1 Geo-climatic Conditions Required for the Major Crops.

Crop	Geo-climatic requirements	Leading Producers
1. Rice	Temperature: 15°-27°C Rainfall : 100-150 cm Soil :Heavy-clayey to –clayey-loam	China, India, Indonesia, Bangladesh, Thailand, Japan, Myanmar, Vietnam, Malaysia, Pakistan, Sri-Lanka. Leading exporter in the world: Thailand

(*Contd.*)

Table 12.1 (*Contd.*)

Crop	Geo-climatic requirements	Leading Producers
2. Wheat	Temp.12°-25°C, Rainfall:25-75 cm, Soil: well-drained-light clay to heavy clay.	China, India, USA, Russia, Australia, Canada, Pakistan, France, Turkey. Leading exporter in the world: USA
3. Maize	Temp. 15°-27°C, Rainfall 65-125 cm, Soil: Deep-heavy clay to light sandy loam.	USA, China, Brazil, Mexico, Russia, Romania, India, South Africa. Leading exporter in the world-USA
4. Millets	Temp. 20°-35°C, Rainfall 25-75 cm, Soils : Sandy-loam to clayey loam.	China, USA, India, Nigeria, Ukraine, Thailand, Russia, Turkey. Leading exporter in the world-USA
5. Bajra (pearl millet)	Temp. 25°-35°C, Rainfall 25-60 cm, Soils: Sandy loam to loam	In India: Rajasthan, Maharashtra, Gujarat, Uttar Pradesh, Haryana, Karnataka, Tamil Nadu, and Andhra Pradesh.
6. Pulses (*Kharif*)	Temperature; 20° -27°C, Rainfall 25-60 cm Soils: Sandy-loam	In India: Madhya Pradesh, Rajasthan, Uttar Pradesh, Maharashtra, Punjab, Haryana, Andhra Pradesh, Karnataka, Tamil Nadu, West Bengal,
7. Lentil (*Rabi*)	Temp. 15° to 25°C, Rainfall 25 to 50 cm, Soils: Loamy to clayey loam.	Mediterranean countries of Europe, Egypt, Greece, Turkey, China, India: (Madhya Pradesh, Uttar Pradesh, Bihar, and West Bengal),
8. Oilseeds	Temp. 15°-30°C, Rainfall 30-50 cm, Soils- loam to clayey loam	In India: Rajasthan, Uttar Pradesh, Madhya Pradesh, Punjab, Haryana, Bihar, West Bengal, Maharashtra, Gujarat. Uttarakhand.
9. Groundnut	Tem. 20°-30°C, Rainfall 50-75 cm, Soils: well-drained-sandy loams, red and black cotton soil (*regur*)	India, China, USA, Sudan, Senegal, Indonesia, Argentina, Myanmar. Leading exporter in the world-USA
10. Sugarcane	Temp. 20°-35°C, Rainfall 85-165 cm, Soils: Well-drained alluvium, black, red and brown *regur* soils.	Brazil, India, China, Pakistan, Thailand, Mexico, Cuba, Colombia. Leading exporter-Brazil.
11. Sugarbeet	Temp. 10°-25°C, Rainfall 25-50 cm. Soil: well-drained-loamy soil.	France, USA, Germany, Russia, China, Ukraine, Poland, Turkey, Leading exporter in the world; France
12. Cotton	Temp. 18°-27°C, Rainfall 60-110 cm. Soils: well-drained loam, and *regur* (black-earth)	China, USA, India, Brazil, Pakistan, Uzbekistan, Egypt, Turkey. Leading exporter in the world-USA

(*Contd.*)

Table 12.1 (*Contd.*)

Crop	Geo-climatic requirements	Leading Producers
13. Tea	Temp. 15° -35°C, Rainfall 100-250 cm Soils:well-drained, light loamy soil.	India, China, Sri-Lanka, Kenya, Indonesia, Bangladesh, Turkey. Leading exporter in the world: India.
14. Coffee	Temp. 15°-28°C, Rainfall 125-225 cm, Soil-well-drained alluvial soil.	Brazil, Colombia, Indonesia, Vietnam, Ivory-Coast, Mexico, Ghana, Cameroon, India. Leading exporter in the world-Brazil
15. Cocoa	Temp. 18°-35°C, Rainfall 100-250 cm, Soils: well-drained alluvium.	Ivory-Coast, Ghana, Indonesia, Brazil, Cameroon, Nigeria, Ecuador, Costa-Rica. Leading exporter in the world: Ivory-Coast
16. Rubber	Temperature-27°C, Rainfall 150-250 cm Soils: rich-well-drained alluvial soil.	Thailand, Indonesia, Malaysia, India, China, Sri-Lanka, Liberia, Brazil. Leading exporter in the world: Thailand.
17. Jute	Temp. 25°-35°C Rainfall about 150-250 cm Soil: Well drained alluvial soil.	Bangladesh, India, China, Thailand, Myanmar, Brazil and Nepal. Leading exporter-Bangladesh
18. Flax	Temp. 10°-20°C, Rainfall 15-20 cm, Soil: Rich loam or clayey loam.	In India: Himachal Pradesh, Uttarakhand and the Jammu Division of J & K.
19. Coconut	Temp. 27°C, Rainfall 100-250 cm, up-to 600 m above the sea level, soil lateritic red, sandy alluvial sandy.	In India: Kerala (55%), Tamil Nadu, Andhra Pradesh, Karnataka, Goa, Gujarat and Maharashtra.
20. Oil-palm	Temp. 27°-33°C (maximum), 22°-24°C (minimum), Rainfall 250-400 cm well distributed in the year. Soil: Deep-loamy and alluvial soil.	India: Andhra Pradesh, Karnataka, Assam, Gujarat, Goa, Kerala, Maharashtra, Odisha, Tamil Nadu, Tripura and West Bengal.
21. Clove	Temperature 25°35°C, Rainfall 200-250 cm, Soil: red alluvial soil.	In India: Kerala, Tamil Nadu, Karnataka, Andaman and Nicobar
22. Black Pepper	Temp. 15°C to 40°C, Rainfall 200-300 cm. Height up-to 1500 m above sea level. Soil: rich in hums, red-loam to sandy loam, and red lateritic sandy loam.	In India: Kerala, Karnataka, Tamil Nadu, Andaman and Nicobar Islands and Pondicherry
23. Cardamom	Temp. 10°-35°C, Rainfall 150-400 cm, height 600-1500 m, soil: well-drained lateritic.	In India: Kerala (60%), Karnataka (30%), Tamil Nadu (10 %).
24. Turmeric	Temp. 20°-30°C, Rainfall 150-250 cm, Soil: well-drained clayey loam or red loamy soil.	In India: Andhra Pradesh, Karnataka, Kerala, Odisha, Tamil Nadu, and West Bengal.

Horticulture

Horticulture is a branch of agriculture relating to the cultivation of fruits, vegetables, ornamental plants, flowers and garden crops. Horticulture crops like field crops are at present grown on an extensive scale.

Horticulture crops generally receive intensive culture. The present day horticulture may be classified into a number of general divisions given below:

Classification

1. ***Olireculture:*** It deals with the cultivation of vegetables.
2. ***Pomology:*** The term pomology is often applied to fruit growing. In a strict sense, this term refers to the fruits, e.g. apple and pear but in a broad viewpoint, it includes all sorts of fruits.
3. ***Floriculture:*** This deals with the cultivation of ornamental plants. The range of flowers grown both outdoors and under glass is very extensive.
4. ***Aboriculture:*** Aboriculture is the growing of and caring for trees for aesthetic purposes, e.g. specimen trees, street and avenue trees and shade trees.
5. ***Landscape gardening and design:*** The landscape and designing branches of horticulture embrace ornamental plants, trees and shrubs in relation to the adornment of many different kinds of places, e.g. private homes, public grounds, golf course and cemeteries.
6. ***Processing and manufacturing:*** A good proportion of horticultural crops are prepared as products e.g. canned goods, frozen-pack fruits and vegetables, jams, jellies, dehydrated foods, wines, unfermented juices, vinegars and perfumes.
7. ***Nursery business:*** The nursery business is concerned with the propagating and growing of young trees, shrubs and plants for sale.
8. ***Seed trade:*** Good seed is basic to successful horticulture. Seeds of many types of vegetables and flowers are produced commercially.
9. ***Storage and marketing:*** There are two main types of storages viz. common storage and cold storage. Many horticultural crops need storage for off-season supply. The marketing of crops and products is significant phase of commercial horticulture.

India has favourable climates and soils for growing a large number of horticulture crops such as fruits, vegetables, potato, tropical tuber crops, mushrooms, ornamental plants, medicinal and aromatic crops, and plantation crops, covering coconut, arecanut, cashew nut, etc.

There is a growing awareness about the advantages of the horticulturcal crop production, and this bound to go up with the increase in socio-economic status of the people. Its role in the country's nutritional security, poverty alleviation and employment generation is becoming increasingly important.

India, today, is the second largest producer of fruits and vegetables in the world, contributing 10 and 14% of the total world production of fruits and vegetables respectively. The availability of flowers has increased significantly in all the cities, as indicated by the growing number of florists and sizable export of cut-and dried flowers. India is a treasure house of medicinal and aromatic plants. It is the largest producer, consumer and exporter of spices and spice products in the world. In fact India is at the brink of a *Golden Revolution*. Diversification in horticulture is one of the best options as there are numerous advantages of growing horticulture crops. The main advantages of horticulture are given in the following:

1. produce higher biomass than field crops per unit area,
2. are highly remunerative for replacing subsistence farming and thus alleviate poverty level in rain-fed, dry land, arid and coastal agro-ecosystems,
3. have potential for development of wastelands through planned strategies,
4. need comparatively less water than food crops,
5. provides higher employment opportunity,
6. are important for nutritional security,
7. are environmental friendly,
8. are high value crops with high potential of value addition,
9. have high potential for foreign exchange earnings, and
10. make higher contribution to GDP.

Fruit Crops

India has great diversity in geo-climatic and socio-economic conditions. Consequently a large variety of fruits are grown in India. Of these, mango, banana, citrus, pineapple, papaya, guava, *sapota*, jackfruit, litchi and grapes (tropical and sub-tropical fruits), apple, pear, peach, plum, apricot, almond, and walnut (temperate fruits) and aonla, ber, pomgranet, fig, phalsa (arid zone fruits) are important.

India accounts for 10 per cent of total production of fruits. It leads the world in the production of mango, banana, *sapota*, and acid lime.

Mango

Mango is a tropical as well as semi-tropical plant which grows almost all over India excluding the high mountainous areas above 600 m, and desert areas. Mango performs well in the frost free dry period at the time of flowering and sufficient heat during the ripening of fruits. The bearing is not good if the humidity is high throughout the year. Frost at the time of flowering is very injurious. Rainfall and cloudy weather at the time flowering are also injurious to mango crop. Mango grows well in areas with an annual rainfall of 75 to 150 cm. with little or no irrigation. With adequate irrigation it grows even in drier areas. Wind storms at the time of fruit maturity are injurious since they cause heavy fruit drop.

Mango is the most important fruit accounting for about 38% of area and 22% of the total fruit production. India's share in the world production is about 55 per cent. The major mango grower states of India are Uttar Pradesh, Andhra Pradesh, Odisha, West Bengal, Maharashtra, Gujarat, and Karnataka.

Citrus

Citrus fruits rank second in the total area with about 5 lakh ha accounting for about 13% of the fruit area. Limes, lemons, sweet orange are the main citrus fruits grown in India. Citrus fruits are grown mainly Maharashtra, Andhra Pradesh, Punjab, Haryana, Karnataka, and the states of North-East India. During the last three decades there had been a substantial increase in the area under citrus fruits. One of the major introduction in citrus has been *kinnow* which has established very well in Punjab, Haryana, Rajasthan and Himachal Pradesh.

Banana

Banana is essentially a tropical plant, requiring a warm humid climate. It grows successfully at elevations up to 800 m in Assam and up to 1500 m in South Indian. In warm dry weather, the plant stops growth and in the cold weather it is damaged by frost. In fact, a great deal of banana cultivation in India is located close to the coastal areas. About 150 to 250 cm of rain, well distributed through out the year is desirable for banana. It however, can stand rain up to 400 cm. Stagnation of water is injurious and may cause diseases like Panama-wilt.

In India, banana ranks third in area with about 5 lakh hectare, covering about 12.5% of the total area under fruits. Most of the banana is produced on small scale basis. A unique feature of banana cultivation in the country is that *Dwarf Cavendish* banana is grown in dry climate where leaf-spot is not a serious problem, unlike in other banana growing countries. The phenomenal increase in production has been due to use of density planting, use of tissue-cultured seedlings and drip irrigation. The major producing states of banana are: Tamil Nadu, Maharashtra, Karnataka, Gujarat, Andhra Pradesh, Assam, Bihar and Madhya Pradesh.

Guava

It is a subtropical and tropical fruit. It requires a distinct winter for developing good fruit quality which is influenced greatly by the climate. It can withstand drought but only a mild frost. It does not thrive if the annual rainfall is more than 250 cm. It does not do well where the winter is warm. It can grow well up to an elevation of 500 m. It requires dry atmosphere at flowering and fruiting but high temperature at fruit development causes fruit drop.

In India, guava is the fifth important fruit covering an area of 1.5 lakh ha with a total production of 18 lakh tones. It is grown in almost all the states and the Union Territories of India.

Apple

It is essentially a temperate fruit. It requires chilling below 5°C for a period of 2-3 months and therefore, it is generally grown at an elevation from 500-2000 m in India. The most optimum temperature range for growth of apple is 15°-20°C.

Apple is the fourth major fruit crop of the country, occupying a total area of 2.30 lakh ha with a total production of 13.8 lakh tones. It is grown mainly in Jammu & Kashmir, Himachal Pradesh, Uttarakhand, and Arunachal Pradesh.

Papaya

Papaya is a tropical plant but it also does very well in a mild tropical climate. It is very sensitive to frost. Papaya does not like strong hot and dry winds. Dry climate at the time of ripening is preferable. Under high humidity the fruit quality is said to be inferior. In high rainfall areas with poor drainage of soil the cultivation of papaya is impossible due to death of the plant caused by collar disease. It can grow well up to an elevation of 300 m and a temperature range between 15°-40°C.

It requires warm and dry summer and cool winters. Bright sunshine helps in the development of papaya. Papaya ranks sixth in area and production. It is mainly grown in Andhra Pradesh, Karnataka, Maharashtra, Gujarat, Tamil Nadu, Madhya Pradesh, Punjab, Haryana, Uttar Pradesh.

Grape

Grape occupies about 1.15% of the total area and 2.6% of the total production. It is grown in Maharashtra, Andhra Pradesh, Karnataka and Tamil Nadu. It is also grown in limited area in the northern states.

Litchi

Litchi has great economic significance because of its high returns and export potential. The area under litchi has increased significantly after 1990. The states of Uttarakhand, Bihar, West Bengal, Assam, Punjab, and Haryana are the important producers of litchi.

Arid Fruits

The arid zone of the country are becoming potential areas of *aonl*a, *ber*, pomgranet, date palm, and fig.

In addition to these, there are a large number of indigenous fruits such as jackfruit, jamun (Syzygium cumini), bel (*Aegle marmelos*), kamrakh (*Averrhoa carambola*), phalas, wood-apple (*Limonia acidissria*), mulberry (*Morus alba*), and lasoda (*Cordia mixa*). These fruits have diverse uses, besides being hardy and well-adapted to different agro-climatic conditions and stress situations.

In recent years, olive and kiwi fruits have been successfully introduced in the temperate areas of Jammu and Kashmir, Himachal Pradesh and Uttarakhand.

Pineapple

About 0.50 lakh hectare of area is under pineapple in India. Pineapple needs a temperature between 20° to 30°C, and an average rainfall of about 150 cm. The main growers of pine apple are the states of Meghalaya, Tripura, Kerala, West-Bengal, Bihar, Tamil Nadu, Karnataka, and Andaman and Nicobar.

Vegetable Crops

India is the second largest producer of vegetable after China. Vegetables contribute about 13.5% to the total world production. India occupies first position in cauliflower, second in onion and third in cabbage.

At present about 60 lakh hectares area is under vegetable cultivation. The main vegetable producing states are West Bengal, Odisha, Uttar Pradesh, Bihar, Maharashtra, Gujarat, Punjab, Haryana, Uttarakhand, and Himachal Pradesh.

Tomato

Tomato is a warm season crop. The plants cannot stand severe frost. The crop does well under average monthly temperature of 21° to 23°C but commercially it may be grown at temperatures ranging from 18° to 27°C. Temperature and light intensity affect the fruit set, pigmentation and nutritive value of the fruit.

Tomato as the most important crop is grown across the length and breadth of the country. The area under its cultivation is about 4.7 lakh hectare with a production of 85 lakh tones. Bihar, Karnataka, Odisha, Maharashtra, Madhya Pradesh, Andhra Pradesh, Punjab, Haryana, Uttar Pradesh, and Karnataka are the main tomato producing states of India.

Brinjal

Brinjal is the second most important vegetable crop in India. It is grown almost throughout the country, covering an area of about 5 lakh ha with a total production of 80 lakh tones. The major brinjal growing states are West Bengal, Odisha and Bihar.

Cabbage

The cabbage thrive in a relatively moist climate. It is grown mainly as a winter crop in the plains in India. It is grown mainly in northern India where the winter temperature is relatively low. In the hills it is taken as a spring and early summer crop. In some parts even two crops of cabbage are taken.

Cabbage is the third major vegetable crop primarily grown in the winter season. The total area under cabbage cultivation in India is 2.5 lakh ha with a production of 56 lakh tones. The major cabbage growing states are West Bengal, Odisha, Bihar, Assam, Karnataka, Uttar Pradesh, Punjab and Haryana.

Onion

Onion is the forth most important commercial crop of the country. It occupies about 4.8 lakh ha with a production of about 55 lakh tones. The major onion producing states include Gujarat, Maharashtra, Karnataka and Uttar Pradesh. Onion is grown in *kharif*, late *kharif*, and *rabi* seasons. More than 50 per cent production comes from the *rabi* crop.

Cauliflower

Cauliflower produces best curds in a cool and moist climate. There are, however, varieties which withstand a sufficiently high temperature. The foliage of cauliflower can withstand a sufficiently high temperature. The foliage of cauliflower can withstand snow but the curd is damaged. The optimum monthly temperature is 15°-20°C.

Cauliflower is the fifth most important vegetable of the country primarily grown in the winter season. It is grown over an area of 2.6 lakh hectare with a production of 47 lakh tones. With a wide range of heat tolerant varieties, cauliflower can now be grown virtually all over the country.

Potato

The potato has a wide range of seasonal adaptability. It is a cool season crop and is moderately tolerant to frost. The young plants grow best at a temperature of 24°C. Later growth is favoured at a temperature of 18°C. Tuber production is maximum at 20°C and decreases with the rise in temperature. At about 30°C the tuber production stops totally. Short days are beneficial for tuber production. It can be cultivated up to an elevation of 2300 m. It can be grown as a summer crop in the hills and as winter crop in plains.

In the world, India ranks fifth in area and production of potatoes with 225 lakh tones from 13 lakh hectares. Potato is grown in India in almost all the states and under diverse geo-climatic conditions. Nearly 90% of potatoes are grown in the vast Northern Plains of India during winter season between October to March. About 6% area under potato cultivation is in the hills, where it is grown during long summer days of April to October. Uttar Pradesh, West Bengal, Himachal Pradesh, Uttrakhand, and Bihar are main producers of potatoes contributing about 75% of the total production of the country. The major producing states of potato are Uttar Pradesh, Bihar, West Bengal, Punjab, Haryana, Karnataka, Assam and Madhya Pradesh.

Carrot

The carrot is a cool season crop though some of the tropical types tolerate quite high temperature. The colour development and growth of root are affected by temperature. Carrots grown at 10° to 15°C develop poor colour. Those grown at 15°-20° will develop a good colour. The highest temperature however, produces shortest roots and the longest roots are produced at the lowest temperature of 10°to 15°C. Carrots are mainly grown in the Northern Plains of India.

Peas

Peas thrive best in a relatively cool weather. In contrast to beans, peas are able to withstand relatively low temperature especially during the seedling stage. The plants may not stand a severe continued frost. The flowers and young pods are badly affected by frost. Hot dry weather interferes with the setting of seed and lowers the quality of pods produced. Peas grow best in those regions where there is a low transition from cool to warm weather in the spring. The seeds can germinate at a minimum temperature of 5°C and the optimum temperature for germination is about 22°C. At higher temperature the germination is rapid but loss of stand may result from various decaying organisms.

Dry-Fruits

Almond (Amygdalus communis)

Almond, an important temperate nut fruit of the country, is mostly grown in Jammu and Kashmir, and Kinnaur (Himachal Pradesh). Most of the existing orchards in Jammu and Kashmir are seedling origin and attain giant size which makes orchard management difficult. The vegetatively propagated plants start bearing only after 3-4 years. Damage to blossom due to early spring frosts is a major constraint. With identification of mid and late blooming types and introduction of late blooming varieties, this problem is likely to be overcome. However, the productivity and quality can be improved by proper irrigation, pruning and cultural practices.

The site for almond cultivation should have proper soil and air drainage. It must be free from hailstorm and frost in spring. Almond grows 750-3000 m above mean sea level. It has very exacting climatic requirement compared to any other fruit. At the blossoming stage the blossoms can withstand up to -2.2° to -3°C for a short time only, but if low temperature continues for many hours, they are damaged.

The main varieties of almond are Makhdoom, Parbat, Waris, Shalimar, Afghanistan are recommended for Jammu and Kashmir, where as Neplus-Ultra and Texas (Mission) for dry temperate zone. The Katha, Drake, and Peerless are suitable for the Himachal Pradesh.

Almonds are ready for harvesting when they change from green to yellowish with cracks or when splitting at suture starts from pedicel end.

Walnut (*Juglan sp.*)

Walnut is the most important temperate nut fruit of the country. It is grown in Jammu & Kashmir, Himachal Pradesh and Uttarakhand. There are no regular orchards of walnuts in the country because the existing plantations are generally of seedling origin. The seedling trees attain giant size and start bearing nuts of variable size and shapes after 10-15 years, whereas vegetatively propagated plants are true to type and produce almost uniform-sized nuts after 4-5 years. They remain within manageable size. But the major constraint is low success in vegetative propagation. Walnuts earn valuable foreign exchange.

Walnut is sensitive to low temperature during spring and high temperature during summer. Walnut is performs better in the areas where springs are free from frost and there is not extreme heat in the summer season. At bloom, temperature of even 2°-3°C below freezing results in killing of a large number of young flowers. Hot summers with low humidity result in blank nuts. Walnut grows well in areas with well-spread rain of about 75 cm or more. Temperature 25°-30° near harvesting results in well filled kernels.

A well-drained silt loam soil having abundant organic matter is ideal. The soil should be free from rock, impervious clay, coarse sandy soil with hard pan, layers of gravel and fluctuating watertable. Alkaline soils should also be avoided.

The suitable varieties of walnut region-wise are: (i) Jammu & Kashmir-Lake English, Drainovsky, *Opex Caulchry*, (ii) Himachal Pradesh-Gobind, Eureka, Placentia, Wilson, and (iii) Uttarakhand-Chakrata Selections.

Generally walnuts are grown under rain fed conditions, but they need adequate water during 5-6 weeks after bloom. Inadequate moisture results in poor quality.

Walnuts are usually harvested when hull colour changes from green to yellowish with cracks or when splitting starts at suture from pedicel end. In Himachal Pradesh harvesting commences from August and extends up to the last week of September, whereas in Kashmir walnuts are harvested in September.

Table 12.2 Package of Practices for Cultivation of Fruit Crops

Crop	Time of Planting	Spacing (m)	Propagation Method	Varieties	Yield(q/ha)
1. Apple	Dec-Jan	5x5	By grafting and budding	Red delicious, Golden delicious, Royal delicious, Yellow-newton, Irish-peach	150-400
2. Mango	Rainy season	10-12	Seed, Inarching, Vineer grafting	Dashehari, Langra, Chausa, Bombay-green, Amarpali, Fazli, Alfanso, Pusa-Surya, Konkan-Ruchi	100 (10 years age), 500 (20 year age)
3. Guava	Onset of monsoon	4-5	Seeds, air-layering, inarching	L-49, Chittidar Allahabad, Safeda, Red-flesh, Lalit	70-100
4. Grape	January	3x3	Cutting/Layering/Budding	Anab-e-Shahi, Banglore blue, Banglore purple, Thompson seedless, Pusa Seedless,	300-400
5. Papaya	Onset of monsoon	2x2	Seeds, tissue culture	Honeydew, Pusa-delicious, Pusa-dwarf, Solo, Arka-Surya	30-70
6. Banana	Throughout the year except severe winter	2-2.5	Sword suckers	Poovan, Basrai, Rasthali, Robusta, Harichal	300-400

Spices

Among spices, black pepper, large and small cardamom, ginger, turmeric, and *chilli* are important. Of which, pepper and cardamom are confined to Kerala and Karnataka, while ginger, turmeric and *chilli* are widely cultivated across the country. There is a scope for extending area under black pepper in Tamil Nadu, Andhra Pradesh Karnataka and north-eastern states.

Black-Pepper (*Piper nigrum*)

Known as the king of spices, black-pepper is being cultivated on a large scale in India. India exports black-pepper to 75 countries. The North American region is the leading importer of Indian black-pepper. In India it is grown in Kerala, Karnataka, Tamil Nadu, Andaman and Nicobar Islands, and Pondicherry. India is also a major consumer of black-pepper.

Black-pepper is a crop warm and humid climate. It requires 200-250 cm of rainfall and a dry spell of about 50 days before flowering with the onset of rains and high humidity (75-95%). The hot and humid climate of the sub-mountainous tracts of the Western Ghats are ideal for its cultivation. It grows successfully up to 1500 m above the mean sea level.

Black-pepper is a climber. It needs standards for support. Pepper is also trained on coconut, areca-nut, jackfruit tree etc. in a mixed homestead farming. The crop is irrigated from November to December till the end of March to get better returns. It matures in about 180-200 days. The major products are white pepper, green-pepper, and bottled-green pepper.

Cardamom –small (*Elettaria cardamomum*)

Popularly, it is known as the queen of spices. It is dried fruit of a tall perennial herbaceous plant. In India, cardamom is cultivated in Kerala (60%), Karnataka (31%) and Tamil Nadu (9%). India is the leading producer and exporter of cardamom.

The natural habitat of cardamom is the evergreen forests of the Western Ghats. It is grown in areas receiving 150-400 cm of rainfall, and temperature 10°-35°C. It is successfully cultivated between 600-1500 m above the mean sea level. It is grown in the soils which are rich in humus content.The cardamom plantation need irrigation from the last week of January to mid-May.

Cinnamon (*Cinnamomum verum*)

Cinnamon is an evergreen tree reaching a height of 6-15 m. The dried inner barks of cinnamon are the products for commerce. The district of Cannanore of Kerala is the famous for cinnamon. It is cultivated in Kerala, Karnataka, and Tamil Nadu. Its cultivation is more prevalent in the hilly regions of the Western Ghats.

Cinnamon is a hardy plant. It tolerates a range of soil and climatic conditions. It is generally grown in the lateritic soils and sandy patches with poor nutrient status. It is cultivated up to a height of 1000 m above the mean sea level. It needs rainfall of 200-300 cm. It is mostly grown as an unirrigated crop.

Clove (*Syzygium aromaticum*)

Clove are the dried aromatic, fully grown unopened flower buds. Cloves have been used in India since the ancient times. It is an evergreen tree.

Clove grows well in rich, loamy soil of humid tropics. It can be grown successfully in all the areas except in coastal sandy belt. It performs well in the red soil of the midland of Kerala as well as in the hilly terrain of the Western Ghats.

Coriander (*Coriandrum sativum*)

It is used a common flavouring substance. The stems, leaves and fruits have a pleasant aroma. In medicines, its seeds are used as a carminative refrigerant and diuretic. In India, coriander is cultivated in Andhra Pradesh, Rajasthan, Gujarat, Madhya Pradesh, Karnataka, Tamil Nadu and Uttar Pradesh.

Coriander is a tropical crop. It requires frost-free climate particularly at the time of flowering and seed formation. Dry and moderately cool weather during seed formation increase yield as well as the quality of the produce.

In irrigated conditions, loamy soil is best suited for its cultivation, whereas in unirrigated areas black or heavy soil is better than loamy.

Last week of October is optimum sowing time for coriander. Delayed sowing reduces the plant growth and increases the incidence of diseases and pests. Depending upon the climatic conditions, moisture retaining capacity of soil and variety used, 4-5 irrigations. The crop should be harvested when about 50% seeds turn yellow. An yield of 12-25 q/ha under irrigated conditions and 7-8 q/ha under unirrigated conditions can be easily obtained. Clean and dried seeds filled in large bags are stored in damp-free aerated stores.

Cumin (*Cuminum cyminum*)

Cumin is an important spice mainly cultivated for flavouring vegetables, pickles, soups etc. The seeds are extensively used in Ayurvedic medicines prescribed for stomach pain and dyspepsia. In India, it is mainly grown in Gujarat and Rajasthan.

It grows well in moderately cool dry climate. Cumin crop is not suitable in the areas with high humidity and frequent rains, particularly after flowering period, as it increases the incidence of disease like blight and powdery mildew. The best soil for cumin crop is well-drained, loamy. It can also be cultivated on medium heavy as well as moderately saline soils with good-drainage. The field in which cumin crop has not been taken up at least during last three years should be selected.

Cumin requires less irrigations compared to other spices. First light irrigation is given immediately after sowing to wet the surface soil. The second irrigation should be applied at the time of germination. Depending up on the soil type and climatic conditions, the subsequent irrigations may be given at 15 -25 days interval. Avoid irrigation at the time of active seed filling because it increases the incidence of powdery mildew, blight and aphid infestation.

Harvesting is done by cutting the plants with sickle. The plants are stacked on clean threshing floor or tarpolin for drying in sun. After drying, seeds are separated by light heating with sticks or rubbing the plants between the places of lint free gunny bags or tarpolin pieces followed by winnowing. Dried and clean seeds are filled in bags and stored in damp-free aerated stores.

Ginger (*Zingiber officinale*)

It is one of the oldest spices with a distinct flavor and pungency. It has a wide range of uses that include culinary, flavourant in soft drinks, alcoholic, and non-alcoholic beverages, confectionery, pickles, pharmaceutical preparations. India is the largest grower of ginger in the world. Other countries cultivating ginger extensively are West Indies, Brazil, China, Japan, Indonesia, Malaysia, Pakistan, Myanmar, Thailand and Vietnam. In India, Kerala, Odisha, Andhra Pradesh, Himachal Pradesh, Meghalaya, Uttar Pradesh, Uttarakhand and West Bengal are the leading producers in India. About

60 per cent of the total area is confined to Kerala, accounting for 25 per cent of the country's total production.

Ginger grows well in warm and humid climate. It is cultivated up to 1500 m above the mean sea level. However, an optimum elevation for its successful cultivation is 300-900 m. Moderate rainfall at sowing till the rhizomes sprout, fairly heavy and well distributed showers during the growing period and dry weather about one month before harvesting are optimum requirements for its successful cultivation. Early planting helps in better growth and development of rhizomes and higher yields.

A rich soil with good drainage and aeration is ideal for its cultivation. It grows well in sandy and clayey loam, red loam and lateritic loam soils. Ginger should not be grown in the same site year after year.

Tamarind (*Tamarindus indica*)

Tamarind is an important tree of semi-arid tropical conditions. Every part of the plant is used for different purposes. The fruit pulp, sweetish/acidic in taste, is used for serving curries, *chutneys*, sauces and soups. Pulp is a carminative and laxative given as infusion in biliousness and febrile conditions. Because of its anti-scorbatic properties, pulp is used by sailors in place of lime or lemon juice. Tamarind Kernel Powder (TKP) is used as sizing material in textile and leather industry. Seeds are used as a source of carbohydrates for paper and jute products. Seeds yield a fatty oil which is used in paints and varnishes. Wood is used for making agricultural implements, tool handles, wheels, mallets and rice pounders. Tender leaves, flowers and young seedlings are eaten as a vegetable. In India, it is grown in Bihar, Jharkhand, Chhattisgarh, Odisha, Maharashtra, Katnataka, Andhra Pradesh, M.P., U.P. and Tamil Nadu. It is also grown in the sub-Himalayan tract.

Tamarind tree is well-adapted to semi-arid tropical regions, but it can be grown in heavy rainfall areas too, if drainage is provided. It is grown in areas where the temperature reaches 46°C (maximum) and 0°C (minimum). It needs rainfall between 75-150 cm. It is grown on gravelly to deep alluvial soils. It thrives best on deep loamy or alluvial soils. It can tolerate slightly saline and alkaline soils. This tree is also adaptable to poor soils.

Seedling plants start yielding in 8-10 years, whereas grafts and buddling in 4-5 years after planting. Harvesting is done during January-April, average yield being 25 tonnes of pods/ha.

Turmeric (*Curcuma longa*)

Turmeric is used as spice, dye, and in cosmetic industry and religious ceremonies. It is cultivated in Andhra Pradesh, Odisha, West Bengal, Tamil Nadu, Karnataka and Kerala. It is an erect, perennial herb grown as an annual crop.

Turmeric prefers a warm, humid, climate with a rainfall of 150 cm and temperature 20°-30°C. It thrives well up to 1200 m above the mean sea level. Well-drained sandy or clayey loam or red loamy soils having acidic to slightly alkaline pH are ideal for its cultivation.

Turmeric comes up well under sparse shade also. It can be grown as an intercrop in coconut gardens like ginger or as mixed crop with red gram, chilli, vegetables, maize and ragi.

Turmeric can be grown either as rain-fed crop (Kerala, Odisha, and north-eastern states) or an irrigated crop (Andhra Pradesh and Tamil Nadu) depending on location. In case of irrigated crop, depending on weather and soil conditions, 15-20 irrigations may be necessary at 7-10 days intervals.

Turmeric takes 7-9 months for harvesting. Drying up of the aerial portion indicates maturity. On an average, a yield of 25-30 tonnes/ha of fresh rhizomes may be obtained. The harvested rhizomes are washed well to remove adhering soil. The fingers are separated and cooked in boiling water for one hour under slight alkaline condition and sun-dried on bamboo mat or drying floor for 10-15 days. For boiling turmeric, usually copper galvanized/iron or earthern vessels are used. It takes 40-60 minutes of boiling to reach the correct stage (soft). Its important storage centres are at Alleppey, Durggirala, Nizamabad, Rajapuri, and Cuddapah. Value-aided products of turmeric are also made.

Table 12.3 Package of Practices for Cultivation of Vegetable Crops

Crop	Sowing	Spacing(cm)	Seed rate (kg/ha)	Varieties	Yield (q/ha)
1. Potato	Mid-October	50x20	20-25 (q/ha)	Kufri Kisan, Kufri-alandar,Kufri Sheetman, Kufri-Sinduri, Kufri-Jee-van, Kufri Janhara, Kufri-Ashoka	25-30q/ha
2. Tomato	June-July for winter crop and November for Spring Summer crop	75x60 for winter crop and 75x45 for spring summer crop	0.5	Pusa ruby, Pusa early dwarf, Red-cherry, Sunray, Marglobe, Pusa-Hybrid-4, Pusa Divya Nandi, Sankranthi	250q/ha to 400q/ha
3. Cauliflower	Early sowing June, mid-season-Sept. late season November	45x45	0.6	Early Pusa Katki, Pusa Kunwari, Patna Main, Late-Danis, Sutton's snowball	200-300
4. Cabbage	Early season Aug. Sept. Late season Sept.Oct.	45x45	0.5	Pride of India, Golden acre, Pusa -deepali	300-450
5. Onion	Oct.Nov.	15-20	25 kg for direct sowing and 8 kg for nursery	Pusa red, Pusa-ratnar, Nasik-red, Nasik-white, Patna-red, Poona-red	250-300
6. Radish	Sept.Oct.	15-20	10	Pusa-himani, Scarlet globe, Pusa chetki, Japanese white, Pusa-reshmi	150-250
7. Carrot	Aug.Nov.	15-20	6	Pusa-kesar, Pusa-meghali, Nantes	200-300

(*Contd.*)

Table 12.3 *(Contd.)*

Crop	Sowing	Spacing(cm)	Seed rate (kg/ha)	Varieties	Yield (q/ha)
8. Turnip	Aug.Sept.	10-15	4	Pusa-swati,Pusa-kanchan, Golden-ball,	200-250
9. Spinach	Oct.	25-30		Pusa-jyoti, Virginia savoy	70-100
10. Cucumber	June-July rainy season crop and Feb. for summer	150x75	2.5	Balam-khira, Khira-Poona, Straight-eight	80-100
11. Peas	Oct.Nov.	50 cm	80	Arkel, Bonneville, Vivek-matar	-
12. Bhindi (okra)	June-July for rainy season crop and Feb.March for summer crop	45-60	15-20	Pusa sawani, Pusa-makhmali, long-green, Hissar-unnat, Varsha, Uphar, Shital-Joyti	50-100

IRRIGATION SYSTEMS IN INDIA

The process of supply of moisture to crops and plants is known as irrigation. In greater, parts of India, agriculture is rain-fed, largely dependent on monsoon. The behaviour of monsoon is erratic and unpredictable, resulting into droughts. About two third of the total cultivated area in India needs irrigation facilities. In the incident of failure of monsoon, the crop fails or the production declines significantly. Irrigation makes the agricultural returns more reliable and at the same time helps in bringing new area under cultivation. Moreover, with the help of irrigation a farmer may get two or three crops in a year, thereby increasing the agricultural intensity. Moreover, the per hectare yield of irrigated area is higher as compared to the dry-farming areas. The irrigation potential of India is about 102 million hectares. About 84 per cent of the water resources of India are used for irrigation.

Irrigation Systems

Depending on the availability of surface and underground water, slope of land, nature of soil and types of crops grown in a region, a number of methods of irrigation are applied in India. The main sources of irrigation applied in different parts of India are: (i) canals, (ii) wells and tube-wells, (iii) tanks, and (iv) other sources (springs, drip, sprinkler, *kuhls, dhenkli, dongs*, *bokka,* etc.). The area irrigated by different sources of irrigation has been plotted in Fig. 12.24, while Table 12.4 gives the temporal changes in the percentage area under different sources of irrigation.

Table 12.4 Area and Sources of Irrigation (Area in Thousand Hectares)

Year	Canals	Wells & Tube-wells	Tanks	Other sources	Total
1950-51	8295 (44.0%)	5980 (31.7%)	3610 (19.1%)	970 (5.2%)	18,855 (100.0%)
2010-2011	15316 (28.88%)	33914 (62.0%)	2516.2 (4.16%)	2954 (4.96%)	54700 (100.0)

Source: Statistical Abstracts of India-2011-2012.

Canal Irrigation

Merits The distribution of rainfall in India is highly uneven. Over the greater part of the country, over 80 per cent of rainfall occurs during the season of South-West Monsoon (*Barsat*-season of general rains). Water is indispensible for human, animal and plant life. Water is essential for protoplasm. It is an important ingredient in photosynthesis. About 400 to 500 litres of water is necessary for the production of one kilo of plant dry matter. Water is also required for translocation of nutrients and dissipation of heat.

Canals used to be the most important source of irrigation before the Green Revolution in 1960s. In fact, in 1950-51 about 44 per cent of the total irrigated area was under canal irrigation. In 2010-2011, however, only about 28 per cent of the irrigated area is under canal irrigation. Canals are an effective source of irrigation in the plain areas. The main intensity of canal irrigation in the Northern Plain of India, especially in the states of Punjab, Haryana, and Uttar Pradesh. Canal irrigation is also done in the coastal and delta regions of the peninsular India and in the command areas of the multi-purpose projects.

The main canals of India are Upper Ganga Canal, Lower Ganga Canal, Sharda Canal, Easter Yamuna Canal, Agra Canal, Betwa Canal, Upper Bari Doab Canal, Sirhind Canal, Bhakra Canal, Bist-Doab Canal, Western Yamuna Canal, Krishna Delta Canal, Son Canal (Bihar), Kosi Canal, Gandak Canal, Mayurakshi Canal, Midnapur Canal, Chambal Canal, Mettur Canals and Indira Gandhi Canal (**Fig. 12.22**).

The merits of canal irrigation are given below:

1. Canals are a perennial source of irrigation as their source lies in the perennial rivers or reservoirs of dams.
2. Canals carry out a lot of sediments brought down by the rivers. This sediment deposited in the fields, enhances the fertility of agricultural land.
3. It is a cheap source of irrigation as the farmer has to pay the irrigation charges per annum.

In the long run, canal irrigation is quite cheap.

Demerits

1. The initial cost of construction of canal is very high.
2. The seepage of water and excessive irrigation of crops by farmers lead to waterlogged conditions.
3. The waterlogged areas work as the breeding grounds for mosquitoes.
4. There is pilferage and wastage of water.
5. Canal irrigation is suitable in the plain areas.

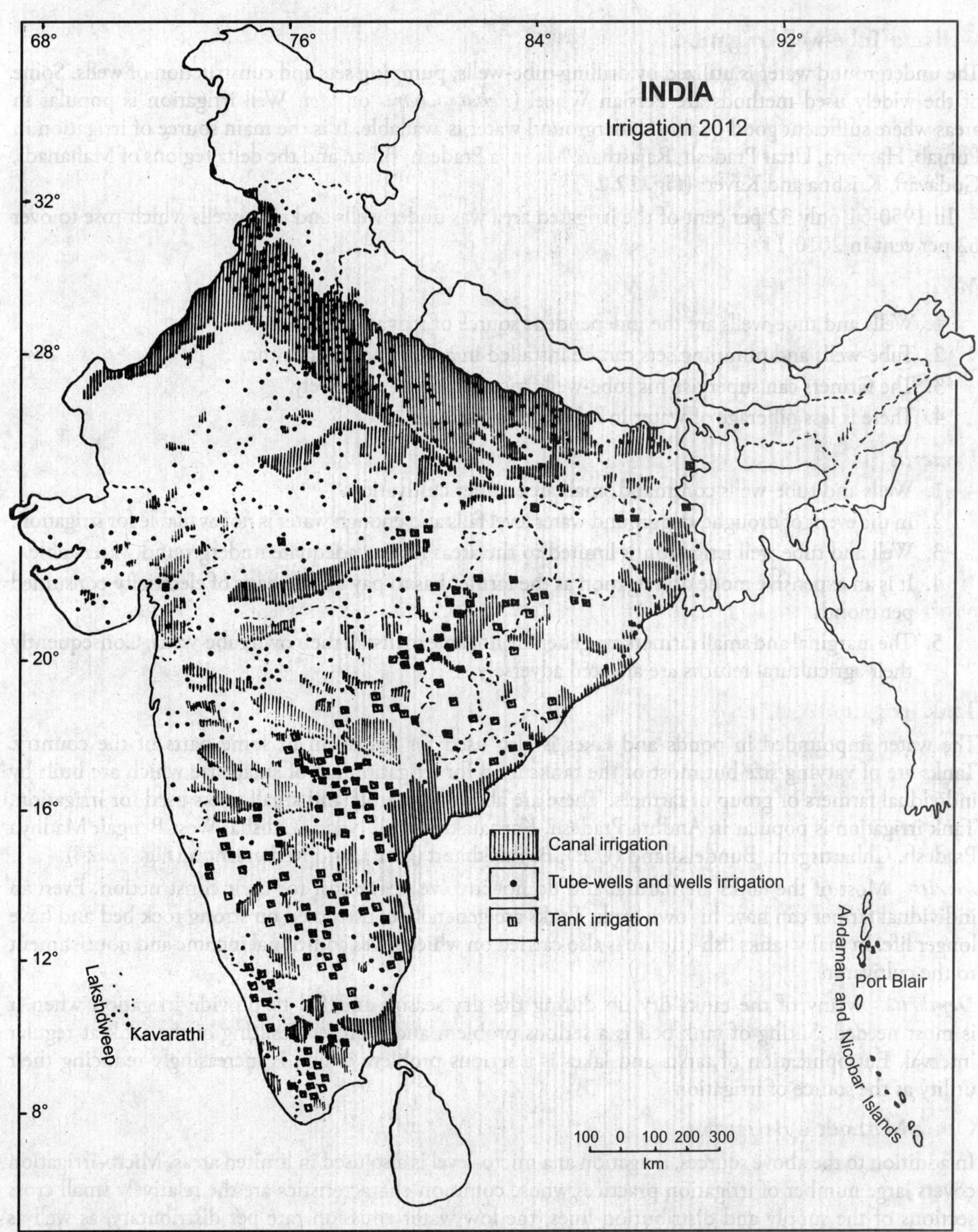

Fig. 12.24 Irrigated Area of India

Well and Tube-well Irrigation

The underground water is utilized by drilling tube-wells, pumping sets and construction of wells. Some of the widely used methods are Persian Wheel (*Rehat) Charas* or *Mot.* Well irrigation is popular in areas where sufficient good quality underground water is available. It is the main source of irrigation in Punjab, Haryana, Uttar Pradesh, Rajasthan, Madhya Pradesh, Bihar, and the delta regions of Mahanadi, Godavari, Krishna and Kaveri (**Fig. 12.24**).

In 1950-51 only 32 per cent of the irrigated area was under wells and tube-wells which rose to over 62 per cent in 2010-11.

Merits

1. Wells and tube-wells are the independent source of irrigation.
2. Tube-wells and pumping sets can be installed in a short period of time.
3. The farmers can supervise his tube-well irrigation more effectively.
4. There is less pilferage of water in tube-well irrigation.

Demerits

1. Wells and tube-wells command small area under cultivation.
2. In the event of drought, the ground water level falls and enough water is not available for irrigation.
3. Well and tube well irrigation is limited to the areas having adequate underground water-table.
4. It is an expensive mode of irrigation as the farmer has to pay on the basis of electricity consumed per month.
5. The marginal and small farmers are generally not able to install their own tube-wells. Consequently their agricultural returns are affected adversely.

Tank Irrigation

The water impounded in ponds and lakes is also used for irrigation in some parts of the country. Tanks are of varying size but most of the tanks used for irrigation are of small size which are built by individual farmers or group of farmers. There are about 5 lakh big and small tanks used for irrigation. Tank irrigation is popular in Andhra Pradesh, Karnataka, Tamil Nadu, Odisha, West Bengal, Madhya Pradesh, Chhattisgarh, Bundelkhand (U.P.), Baghelkhand (M.P.), and Maharashtra (**Fig. 12.24**).

Merits Most of the tanks are natural and do not involve heavy cost for their construction. Even an individual farmer can have his own tank. Tanks are generally constructed on strong rock bed and have longer life. In many tanks fish-culture is also carried on which gives additional income and nourishment to the cultivators.

Demerits Many of the tanks dry up during the dry season and fail to provide irrigation when it is most needed. Silting of tank bed is a serious problem and requires desilting of the tank at regular interval. Eutrophication of tanks and lakes is a serious problem which is increasingly reducing their utility as the source of irrigation.

Other Methods of Irrigation

In addition to the above sources, irrigation at a micro-level is also used in limited areas. Micro-irrigation covers large number of irrigation practices whose common characteristics are the relatively small cross sections of the supply and distribution lines, the low water emission rate per distributary, as well as localized delivery of water to limited area. As a rule, the micro-irrigation systems are stationary, solid set installations which are capable of supplying optimum amount of water to the crop. The important micro-irrigation systems use drip, micro-jet, and micro-sprinkler systems. Micro-irrigation is enjoying increasing popularity for the irrigation of the tree crops.

Drip Irrigation Drip irrigation is defined as the precise, slow application of water in the form of discrete or continuous or tiny streams or miniature sprays through mechanical devices called emitters or applicators located at selected points along water delivery lines. The drip irrigation was started first in Israel in 1940, especially for the irrigation of trees and orchards.

Drip irrigation has proved to be success in terms of economy of water and increased yield in a wide range of crops. The increase in the yield varies from 20% to 100%. The highest increase in yield of 100% has been banana, 50% in sugarcane, pomegranate and around 25% in grapes and cotton. This method saves 40-70 per cent water. Moreover, drip irrigation has given higher profitability as compared to conventional surface irrigation.

The experts agree on the point that drip irrigation system is quite economical and the investment is worth paying. The emphasis on drip irrigation should be in drought prone areas where irrigation is mostly through wells and horticulture crops.

Some of the disadvantages of drip-irrigation are: (i) high initial cost, (ii) restricted area of root growth, (iii) requirement of higher level of design, management and maintenance, and (iv) clogging of emitter. However, the limitations are not unsurmountable.

MISCELLANEOUS

Changes in Ice Caps and Water-bodies

Ice Cap

A dome shaped glacier with a generally outward and radial flow of ice is known as ice cap. The difference between ice cap and ice sheet is normally taken to be one of scale with the former being less than 50,000 sq. km. in area, while the ice-sheet is more than 50,000 sq km. The marginal regions of the ice cap may be drained by outlet glaciers which flow beyond the ice cap in U-shaped shallow valleys.

Ice sheet

It is a large dome-shaped glacier (over 50,000 sq km in area) with a generally outward and radial flow of ice. Ice sheets and ice caps are formed layer by layer from the snowfall of each year. With time the snow is compressed into ice. On a continental scale such ice sheets can exceed a thickness of 4 km. as they do in Antarctica. Antarctica alone has 91% of all the glacial ice on the Earth.

Antarctic Ice Sheet

Antarctica is a continent covered by a single enormous ice sheet. The edges of the ice sheet that enter bays along the coast form excessive *ice shelves*, with sharp ice cliffs rising up to 30 m above the sea. Large tabular islands of ice are formed when sections of the shelves break off and move out to sea.

The ice caps and ice sheets are melting and Antarctica's ice sheets are breaking up. The icebergs and ice-shelves move seaward. In March 2000, the second largest iceberg ever recorded broke free from the Ross Ice Shelf (Antarctica around 150°W) and floated into the Ross Sea. The huge ice-berg was 11,000 square kilometers in size, being about 300 kilometers in length and 37 kilometers in width.

If the ice sheet of Antarctica melts the sea level will rise by about 70 meters. The socio-economic consequences of ice-sheet melting may be catastrophic. What this will do to the global socio-economic system one can only guess. Some of the important consequences of ice cap, ice sheet and permafrost melting have been briefly described in the following:

1. The Changes in Plant and Animal Life

The melting of ice caps and permafrost are affecting the biosphere and bringing changes in plants and animals. For example, the population of penguins on Antarctica is decreasing which has dropped by about 40 per cent in the last quarter of the 20th century. The hypothesis is that the warmer temperatures make it harder for the penguins to find food and breed. Moreover, phytoplankton and zooplanktons which are the basic component of food chain are decreasing. Coral reefs are dying at an unprecedented rate. Vegetation, like lichen and mosses has started appearing on the steep slopes of mountains of Antarctica.

It has been observed that in Alaska, the melting of permanently frozen ground is changing the migratory patterns of the caribou (reindeer). In the National Park (USA), there is an unusual growth of spruce trees. Moreover, millions of birds have migrated towards north from the western coast of USA because of warmer water. Rates of natural migration and adaptation of species and plant communities, however, appear to be much slower than the rate at which climate is changing.

2. Spread of Tropical Diseases

Melting of cryosphere is the result of global warming. Extremes of heat and cold, and wet and dry conditions have been frequent in recent years. Down through the history such extreme events have often been followed by outbreaks of diseases. There is a possibility of increase in the cases of malaria by about 15 per cent. Other diseases, such as dengue fever, yellow-fever, Ebola fever, and viral-encephalitis would also increase. In fact, malaria is spreading even in the temperate countries of Europe.

3. Reduction in Biodiversity

According to some of the ecologists and environmentalists about one third of all ecosystems would shift to another type. The rapid change in ecosystems would greatly reduce biodiversity in many climatic regions and biomes.

4. Shift in Climatic Zones

Mid-latitude climate zones could shift pole-ward by as much as 550 km causing conversion of forest to grassland and scrubland. Some species of forest trees would not be able to migrate quickly enough and would die out.

5. Desertification

Desertification means the spread of desert like conditions which may be caused by climatic change or by human activities or both. As a result of climatic change and change in the precipitation patterns deserts would expand and the continental interiors in general, would become drier.

6. Effect on Agriculture

The beneficial agricultural effects include milder winters in northern regions as well as increased precipitation and faster crop growth in some areas. The grain belts of North America and Russia would expand northward. It may affect the international trade of grains also.

7. Effect on Coastal Population

About 50 per cent of the total urban population of the world is living along the coastal areas. In case of sea level rise, the low-lying coastal urban centres will be adversely affected. Cities like Aden, Amsterdam, Athens, Baltimore, Bangkok, Boston, Buenos Aires, Belfast, Chennai, Colombo, Copenhagen, Dhaka, Dubai, Dublin, Galveston, Halifax, Ho Chi Minh City, Hong Kong, Houston, Jakarta, Kandla, Kochi, Kolkata, Lagos, Lisbon, London, Los Angeles, Male (Maldives), Manila, Mumbai, Muscat, Nagasaki, New Orleans, New York, Okha, Philadelphia, Rio de Janeiro, Rome, Rotterdam, San Francisco, Seoul, Shanghai, Singapore, Surabaya, Sydney, Tianjin, Tokyo, Vancouver, Washington D.C., Yangon etc. will submerge under water.

8. Change in Lakes Ecosystems

Changing temperatures will have a detrimental effect on living organisms in the lakes, especially those which are in the higher latitudes. The warmer water kills the planktons on which higher life forms are dependent. In fact, less plankton mean less fish.

9. Submergence of Sea Beaches

The submergence of sea beaches and sea-resorts will adversely affect the domestic and international tourism.

10. Increase in the frequency of Tropical Cyclones

Because of sea level rise there will be more evaporation which shall induce more latent heat and water vapour in the troposphere (atmosphere). This process may lead to more stormy weather in the tropical latitudes.

11. Shift in Natural Vegetation Belts

Under the changed climatic conditions because of melting of ice caps, the rainfall pattern will change. A change in precipitation patterns will transform the belts of natural vegetation which shall ultimately affect the soil-belts and the agricultural practices.

Smart City (Intelligent City or Digital City)

The term 'smart city' is still a vague term as it has been defined differently by different urban geographers and planners. According to the British urban planners, 'smart city' is a dynamic concept, but a process by which cities become more 'liveable' 'resilient' and 'enjoyable' and which respond quicker to new challenges. In the opinion of Smart City Council 'A smart city is one that has digital technology embedded across all city functions'.

Objectives of Developing Smart Cities

(i) to overcome the problem urban growth,
(ii) to address the issues of climatic change,
(iii) to provide better facilities for economic and social life,
(iv) to reduce the problems of waste disposal and environmental degradation in urban cities towns and places.

Main Characteristics of a Smart City

1. A smart city uses physical infrastructure (roads, buildings, energy, health care, water, waste disposal, and other physical assets) more efficiently, supporting strong, healthy economic, social and cultural life.
2. A smart city creates an innovative environmental.
3. In a smart city, the people adapt effectively and promptly to changing circumstances.
4. There is emphasis on citizen's participation.
5. The building and infrastructure are designed and developed to reduce damage to ecology and environment.
6. In smart city internet shopping facility is available.
7. There is strong social networking.
8. There are provisions of entertainment even for 'geriatrics' or aging population (senior citizens).
9. The rate of crime is low.
10. Low rate of pollution, and
11. Life is more enjoyable.

At present, some of the smart cities include Barcelona (Spain), Boston and Chicago (U.S.A.), de Hague (the Netherlands), and Stockholm (Sweden).

On 25th January, India and U.S.A. had signed three memoranda of understanding for developing Ajmer, Allahabad and Vishakhapatnam. These cities are to be developed as smart cities as joined venture by the United States Trade and Development Agency (USTDA) and the Indian Urban Development Ministry.

The cities of Ajmer and Allahabad have the potential to develop into major hubs for cultural and religious tourism. They need development on various fronts and can be the models for the development of other cities. Vishakhapatnam was selected because being a coastal city, it has the potential to develop into a trading and tourist destination.

Criticism

The main arguments against the use of this concept are:

(i) The emphasis on the development of smart cities will lead to lope sided urban development in India.

(ii) The focus on smart cities may lead to new problems to human health and environmental degradation as man may be away from nature.

(iii) The smart cities concept is to promote globalized business. Such a business oriented model may result into cultural pollution.

Sustainable City

A sustainable city is a city designed and developed after environmental impact assessment. The inhabitants of a sustainable city require minimum input of energy, water and food. There is less emission of CO_2 and less water, air, soil and noise pollution. The waste disposal is also efficient, almost free from environmental degradation.

An eco-city is a city built off the principles of living means of the environment. The ultimate goa of eco-cities is to eliminate all carbon waste to produce energy through renewable resources, and tc incorporate the environment into the city. The objective of eco-city is also to stimulate economic growth, to eradicate poverty, hunger, malnutrition and to provide a conducive environment for good health, education and higher efficiency of the work force.

The concept of eco-city was developed by a group of urban ecologists' of Berkeley, under the guidance of Richard Register in 1975. In 1987, they started the journal of 'Urban Ecologist' in 1987. The urban ecology further advanced after the first International Eco-City Conference held at Berkeley (California) in 1990. Since then, the annual conferences of the Eco-City have been organized at Adelaide, Senegal, Brazil, China, Bangalore, San Francisco, Istanbul, Montreal, France and Abu Dhabi.

Salient Characteristics of Sustainable City

An eco-city has the following characteristics:

(i) Self-oriented economy: The resources needed are available locally.

(ii) Has completely carbon –neutral and renewable energy production.

(iii) Has planned and well developed transport system.

(iv) Resource conservation: Water and energy resources are utilized judiciously.

(v) Ensures decent and affordable housing.

(vi) Supports local agriculture especially horticulture and dairying.

(vii) Different agricultural systems such as agricultural plots within the city. This reduces the distance food has to travel from feed to fork.

(viii) Renewable energy resources, such as solar panels, wind energy and bio-gas created from sewage

(ix) Big parks, gardens, planting of trees, green lawns, spaces, green roofs, zero-energy buildings, natural ventilation system and eco-industrial parks to reduce the use of air conditioning.

(x) Optimum building density to make public transport viable but avoid the creation of urban heat islands.

(xi) Sustainable transport system to reduce greenhouse gases.

(xii) Promotes voluntary simplicity in life style, decreasing material consumption and increasing environmental awareness.

(xiii) The city design must be able to grow and evolve as the population grows.

(xiv) The rate of crime should be significantly low, and

(xv) Life even for the senior citizens should be enjoyable.

Adelaide and Melbourne (Australia), Belo Horizonre (Brazil), Alberta, and Calgary (Canada), Tianjin (China), Aalborg, Ballerup and Frederikshavn (Denmark), Freiburg (Germany), Clonburris (Ireland), Hacienda-Mombasa (Kenya), Songdo (Korea), Masdar City (Abu Dhabi), Bilbao (Spain), and Arcosanti, Douglas Ranch (Arizona), Treasure Island (San Francisco), Coyote Springs (Nevada), and Sonoma Mountain of California are some of the examples of sustainable cities.

Eco-City

An eco-city is a city built off the principles of living within the means of environment. The ultimate goal of many eco-cities is to eliminate all carbon waste to produce energy entirely through renewable resources and to incorporate the environment into the city. One of the objectives of eco-cities is also to stimulate economic growth, reducing poverty, organizing cities to have higher population densities, open spaces, higher efficiency and healthy environment.

The concept of eco-city was developed by Richard Register in Berkeley, California in 1975. The first conference of Eco-City was held in Berkeley (California) in 1990. Subsequently Eco-city conferences were held in Adelaide (Australia), Yoff (Senegal), Curitiba (Brazil), Shenzhen (China), Bangalore (India), San Francisco (U.S.A.), Istanbul (Turkey), Montreal (Canada), Nantes (France) and Abu-Dhabi (UAE).

Characteristics of Eco-City

The ideal eco-city fulfills the following requirements:

(i) Operates on a self-contained economy. Resources needed are found locally.
(ii) Has completely carbon –neutral and renewable energy production.
(iii) Has a well planned city layout and public transport system with segregated lanes for vehicles.
(iv) Resource Conservation: Maximum efficiency of water and energy resources.
(v) Provisions for the restoration of environmentally damaged urban areas.
(vi) Decent and affordable housing for all socio-economic, ethnic, minorities and religious groups.
(vii) Low rate of environmental and water pollution.
(viii) Supports local agriculture and produce.
(ix) Eco-cities have green roofs, and vertical landscaping.
(x) Promotes simplicity in lifestyle.
(xi) Environmental education and increasing awareness of environment.

Bills, Treaties, Plans, Agreements

This chapter is a compilation of important Bills, Treates and Agreements in the field of ecology and environment.

COMPENSATORY AFFORESTATION FUND BILL

The Parliament has passed the Compensatory Afforestation Fund Bill, 2016 after it was approved by the Rajya Sabha. The bill provides for establishment of funds under the public accounts of the Centre and State levels for compensatory afforestation.

Salient features

The bill establishes the National Compensatory Afforestation Fund (NCAF) under the Public Account of India, and a State Compensatory Afforestation Fund under the Public Account of each state. The NCAF will get 10% of funds collected and the remaining 90% will go to respective State Fund. The collected funds will be utilised for afforestation, regeneration of forest ecosystem, wildlife protection and forest related infrastructure development. The legislation will allow states to access nearly 42000 crore rupees that is lying idle and channel it into afforestation projects. It has provisions for administration of funds and utilization of funds by the user agencies to undertake plantations, protection of forests and forest-related infrastructure development.

NATIONAL DISASTER MANAGEMENT PLAN RELEASED

Prime Minister Narendra Modi released the National Disaster Management Plan (NDMP) in June 2016 to make India disaster resilient and reduce loss of lives. The first of its kind of national plan is based on the **four priority themes** of the "Sendai Framework for Disaster Risk Reduction 2015-30". They are:

(i) Understanding disaster risk (ii) Improving disaster risk governance (iii) Investing in disaster risk reduction and (iv) Disaster preparedness, early warning and building back better in the aftermath of a disaster.

Salient Features of the Plan

- The plan covers all phases of disaster management: prevention, response, mitigation and recovery.
- It provides for vertical and horizontal integration among all the Government agencies and departments.
- It also spells out the roles and responsibilities of all levels of Government right up to Urban Local Body (ULB) and Panchayat level.
- The plan also identifies major activities such as early warning, medical care, information dissemination, fuel, search and rescue, transportation, evacuation, etc. to serve as a checklist for agencies responding to a disaster.
- The plan incorporates provisions for strengthening disaster risk governance and lays down six thematic areas. They are integrated and mainstream disaster risk reduction, promoting participatory approach, capacity development, working with elected representatives, grievance redress mechanism and promoting quality standards, certification and awards for disaster risk management.

The National Disaster Management Plan has been mandated under Section 11 of the Disaster Management Act, 2005. As per the Act, the national plan must lay down the guidelines for preparation of state-level disaster management plans as well as plans by each Central ministry and department.

INDIA SIGNS PARIS AGREEMENT

The Union Cabinet gave its approval for signing the Paris Agreement adopted at the 21st Conference of Parties of UNFCCC held in Paris in December 2015. The Paris Agreement on climate change is considered as a milestone in global climate cooperation. It is meant to enhance the implementation of the Convention and recognizes the principles of common but differentiated responsibilities, equity and respective capabilities in the light of different national circumstances.

Key features of the Paris Agreement

Rights of Developing Countries: Acknowledges the development imperatives of developing countries and their rights to development. It also supports their efforts to harmonize development with environment and protecting the interests of the most vulnerable.

Sustainable Development: It recognizes the importance of sustainable lifestyles and sustainable patterns of consumption. In this regard developed countries take the lead and also highlight the importance of 'climate justice' in its preamble.

Implementation of the Convention: It reflects the principles of equity and common but differentiated responsibilities and respective capabilities especially in the light of different national circumstances.

Other Objectives: It further ensures that it is not mitigation-centric and includes other important elements such as adaptation, finance, loss and damage, technology, capacity building and transparency of action and support. Pre-2020 actions are also part of the decisions.

Financial support from Developed countries: They have been urged to scale up their level of financial support with a complete road map. The sole purpose of the financial support from developed countries is to achieve the goal of mitigating climate change jointly providing US 100 billion dollars by 2020. The financial support will be used for mitigation and adaptation by significantly increasing adaptation finance from current levels. It will further provide appropriate technology and capacity building support.

DRAFT NATIONAL WILDLIFE ACTION PLAN (NWAP-3) (2017-2031)

The first National Wildlife Action Plan (NWAP-1) was drafted and adopted in 1983. It was implemented from 1983 through 2001. On its completion and based on the new concerns and challenges viz. increased commercial use of natural resources, growth in human and livestock population, changes in the consumption patterns, rising interest in biodiversity conservation etc., the Plan was revised and a new Action Plan (NWAP-2) was put in place for the period 2002-2016. A review of NWAP-2 was undertaken and based on its evaluations and lessons learnt, a Plan for the period 2017-2031 is developed called National Wildlife Action Plan (NWAP-3)

Features of NWAP-3

The Plan is based on the premise that essential ecological processes that are governed, supported or strongly moderated by ecosystems, are essential for food production, health and other aspects of human survival and sustainable development.

Maintenance of these ecosystems which can be termed as 'Life Support Systems' is vital for all societies regardless of their stage of development. It also emphasizes on other two aspects of living resource conservation viz. preservation of genetic diversity and sustainable utilization of species and ecosystems which has direct bearing on our scientific advancements and support to millions of rural communities.

The Plan adopts landscape approach in conservation of all uncultivated flora and undomesticated fauna that has ecological value to mankind irrespective of where they occur. It accords special emphasis to rehabilitation of threatened species of wildlife while conserving their habitats which include inland aquatic, coastal and marine eco-systems. It also takes note of concerns relating to climate change on wildlife by integrating it in to wildlife management Planning

It underlines the fact that despite being one of 12 mega biodiversity countries of the world, national planning has not taken serious note of adverse ecological consequences of reduction and degradation of wilderness areas from the pressures of population, commercialisation and development projects. The plan has brought to focus the alarming erosion of our natural heritage comprising of rivers, forests, grasslands, mountains, wetlands, coastal and marine habitats arid lands and deserts.

INDIA BECOMES MEMBER OF SAWEN

The Union cabinet has given its formal approval for adopting the Statute of the South Asia Wildlife

Enforcement Network (SAWEN). With this, India will become member of SAWEN, a regional inter-governmental body in combating wildlife crime in the region and beyond. By becoming member of SAWEN, India will strengthen its ties with the member countries for controlling the trans-boundary wildlife crimes through coordination, communication, collaboration, cooperation and capacity building in the region.

What is SAWEN? SAWEN is a regional inter-governmental wildlife law enforcement support body launched in January, 2011 in Paro, Bhutan. It aims at working collectively as a strong regional inter-governmental body to combat wildlife crime by attainting common mutual goals and approaches for combating illegal trade in the region. SAWEN's regional network comprises of eight South Asia countries: Afghanistan, India, Pakistan, Nepal, Bhutan, Bangladesh, Sri Lanka and Maldives.

INTERNATIONAL SOLAR ALLIANCE (ISA)

ISA is India's first international and inter-governmental organization comprising of 121 Countries. The United Nations is its Strategic Partner. It was jointly launched by India and France in November 2015 during the United Nations climate change conference (COP21) in Paris. It has its headquarters in Gurgaon, India.

It seeks to empower solar-rich countries located between the tropic of Cancer and tropic of Capricorn to collaborate to harness solar energy and generate electricity.

It also aims to bring standardization in solar technologies and encourage research and development and also to improve access to energy and opportunities for better livelihoods in remote and rural areas.

20 NEW SITES ADDED TO THE WORLD NETWORK OF BIOSPHERE RESERVES IN 2016

The International Co-ordinating Council of the Man and the Biosphere (MAB) Programme of UNESCO added 20 sites to the World Network of Biosphere Reserves during its meeting in the capital of Peru on 18th and 19th March 2016. The newly adopted sites include 18 national sites and one transboundary site shared between Spain and Portugal. The Council also approved 9 extensions to existing Biosphere Reserves. Following the withdrawal of two sites at the request of Austria, this brings the total number of biosphere reserves to 669 sites in 120 countries, including 16 transboundary sites.

The Man and the Biosphere Programme was created by UNESCO in the early 1970s as an intergovernmental scientific endeavour to improve relations between people around the world and their natural environment.. New reserves are designated each year by the International Co-ordinating Council of the Programme, which brings together elected representatives of 34 UNESCO Member States.

The following sites joined the network in 2016

Monts de Tlemcen (Algeria)—The 8,225 ha reserve is situated in the Province of Tlemcen, an area of great biodiversity, which also has major archaeological sites, cultural landscapes and caves and covers the same area as the Tlemcen National Park.

Beaver Hills (Canada)—Located in the province of Alberta in western Canada, this morainic landscape developed its characteristic Boreal-zone features of abundant wetlands, shallow lakes and rock formations during the progressive retreat of glaciers some 12,000 years ago. Today, the reserve comprises a mixture of lands modified by agricultural activity, mixed wood forests, grasslands and wetlands.

Tsá Tué (Canada)—Located in Canada's Northwest Territories, the area is the homeland of the Sahtúto'ine (The Bear Lake People). It includes Great Bear Lake, the last pristine arctic lake, and part of its watershed. The Taiga that covers much of the site is important to wildlife species including the muskox, general moose and caribou.

Lake Bosomtwe (Ghana)—Situated in the Ashanti region of Ghana, Bosomtwe comprises one of six meteoritic lakes in the world. The southernmost section of the site overlaps with the northern section of the Bosomtwe Range Forest Reserve creating a combination of forest, wetland and mountain ecosystems. The biosphere reserve sustains 35 tree species, including some used for timber. The site is also home to a great diversity of wildlife and to a human population of over 50,000 inhabitants.

La Hotte (Haiti)—Located in the south-east of the country the biosphere reserve encompasses both terrestrial and marine areas. The region is considered a biodiversity hotspot due to its wide climate range: from humid to subtropical dry. The reserve covers six mountain peaks culminating at 2,347m, as well as a coastal and marine ecosystem in the north (Iles Cayemites) and south (Ile-à-Vache). It is home to more than 850,000 inhabitants, whose main economic activities are farming, agroforestry, fishing, commerce, and handcrafts.

Agasthyamala (India)—Located in the Western Ghats, in the south of the country, the biosphere reserve includes peaks reaching 1,868m above sea level. Consisting mostly of tropical forests, the site is home to 2,254 species of higher plants including about 400 that are endemic. It is also a unique genetic reservoir of cultivated plants especially cardamom, jamune, nutmeg, pepper and plantain. Three wildlife sanctuaries, Shendurney, Peppara, Neyyar and Kalakad Mundanthurai Tiger reserve are included in the site.

Balambangan (Indonesia)—The biosphere reserve in the province of East Java encompasses three national parks (Alas Purwo, Baluran and Meru) and one nature reserve (Kawah Ijen) with terrestrial and marine ecosystems featuring karst landscapes, savannah, and forests that are alpine/subalpine, upper, dry and lower montane (mountain), lowland, coastal and mangrove. The site also features seagrass beds, and coral reefs.

Hamoun (Iran)—Located in the southeast of the country, the biosphere reserve includes terrestrial and wetland ecosystems with a total of seven habitat types, including desert and semi-desert areas, as well as Hamoun Lake, with its marshlands and watersheds. The three wetlands of the biosphere reserve are the most important in the region. The area is a hot spot for migratory birds (183 species) and home to 30 mammal species, and 55 plant species.

Collina Po (Italy)—The biosphere reserve is located in the north Italian Piedmont Region and covers the whole Turin stretch of the River Po with its main tributaries and the Collina Torinese hillside. The river Po is the main reservoir of biodiversity in the Turin plain, partly due to the numerous wetlands along its course.

Barsakelmes (Kazakhstan)—The biosphere reserve is situated in the Sahara-Gobi Desert zone of the Aral Sea basin. The Aral Sea region is a priority area for wetland conservation and several bird migration routes converge over the region.

Belo-sur-Mer—Kirindy-Mitea (Madagascar)—Situated on the western coast of the island, the site includes watershed upstream and marine and coastal ecosystems downstream. It presents a mosaic of rich but fragile ecosystems such as dry forests, thickets, thorn forests, savannahs, salty swampy depressions known as "tannes", mangroves and coral reefs.

Isla Cozumel (Mexico)—Situated off the south-eastern coast of the country, Cozumel Island encompasses diverse marine and terrestrial ecosystems rich in amphibian and reptile species. The main terrestrial ecosystems are medium semi-deciduous forests and mangroves. The biosphere reserve forms part of the second largest reef system in the world, the Mesoamerican Reef, which is home to 1,192 marine species.

Atlas Cedar (Morocco)—Situated in the central Atlas Mountains, the biosphere reserve is home to 75% of the world's majestic Atlas cedar tree population. This part of the Atlas Mountains is rich in ecosystems and its peaks, reaching up to 3,700 metres, provide the region with critically important water resources.

Gran Pajatén (Peru)—Located in the Central Cordillera, the biosphere reserve is characterized by high altitudes and a pristine ecosystem. It encompasses the National Park del Río Abiseo, a UNESCO World Heritage site. The reserve is home to fauna and flora of rainforests characteristic of this part of the Andes and has a high level of endemism. It is the only place on earth where the yellow-tailed woolly monkey, previously thought extinct, is to be found.

Albay (Philippines)—Located at the southern end of the Luzon Island, the biosphere covers some 250,000 hectares. The terrestrial elevation of the site culminates at 2,462 metres and its marine part reaches a depth of 223 metres below sea level. The site's high conservation value is constituted notably by its 182 terrestrial plant species, 46 of which are endemic

Fajás de São Jorge (Portugal)—The biosphere reserve covers the entire Island of São Jorge, the fourth largest in the Azores Archipelago. At 1,053m, the Pico da Esperança is the island's highest elevation. The site's rugged coastal cliffs form a unique landscape of highland meadows, peat bogs and scrubs. The combination of high altitude and coastal ecosystems has resulted in a wealth of endemic terrestrial flora.

Tejo/Tajo (Portugal and Spain)—The biosphere reserve is located in the western part of the Iberian Peninsula shared between Spain and Portugal with the Tajo River as its main axis. It is characterized by low altitude and sharp relief. Vegetation in the site consists largely of cork oak formations and patches of scrub, as well as cultivated areas and pastures. The fauna is typically Mediterranean and includes many rare species.

Jozani-Chwaka Bay (Tanzania)—The biosphere reserve encompasses the only national park on the island of Zanzibar. The site is a biodiversity hotspot area including inter alia reef fish species, dolphins, the Zanzibar leopard (Panther pardus adersi), 168 species of birds including 30 of global and regional relevance.

Isle of Man (United Kingdom)—Located in the Irish Sea, the Island is home to more than 80,000 people. The hills hold important peat reserves and are deeply cut by wooded glens in the east. The site's marine environment is rich in biodiversity and harbours important populations of European eel, Atlantic cod and basking sharks, among others.

Extensions to Existing Biosphere Reserves

Trifinio Fraternidad (Honduras)—The extension concerns the Honduran part of the Tri-national Trifinio Fraternidad Biosphere Reserve between El Salvador, Guatemala and Honduras. It covers a surface area of 278,762ha including six national protected areas.

Toscana (Italy)—Designated in 2004 as the Selve Pisana Biosphere Reserve, the site is situated along the Mediterranean coast of Italy, west of Pisa. The extension should pave the way for the implementation of sustainable activities in agriculture, sylviculture and tourism.

Mount Hakusan (Japan)—The extension represents a four-fold increase of the site, which was designated as a biosphere reserve in 1980 and comprises alpine, subalpine, and montane zones around the 2,700 metre-high Mount Hakusan.

Yakushima and Kuchinoerabu Jima (Japan)—Designated in 1980 under the name of Yakushima, the biosphere reserve, 60km south of the Island of Kyushu, is known for its Yaku cedar primeval forest. It encompasses the area inscribed on the World Heritage List, also under the name of Yakushima, and now covers the entire island, as well as the island of Kuchinoerabu and the marine area surrounding both.

Mount Odaigahara, Mount Omine and Osugidani Biosphere Reserve (Japan)—Designated as Mount Odaigahara and Mount Omine Biosphere Reserve in 1980, the site in the Kii Peninsula of Honshu Island is a mountainous area in which forestry is more developed than agriculture. The extension increases the surface area of the site to 120,000 ha, compared to its initial 36,000ha.

Noroeste Amotapes – Manglares (Peru)—The biosphere reserve, off the northern coast of Peru was designated in 1977 under the name of Noroeste Bisophere Reserve. It now includes the Cerros de Amotape National Park, Coto El Angolo and Tumbes Mangroves Protected Area. The extension covers a surface area of 1,115,947ha.

Mont Sorak (Republic of Korea)—Designated in 1982, the reserve is located in the centre of the Baekdudaegan Mountain Range, which includes the highest peak in the country. With its extension, the biosphere reserve covers an area of 76,000ha and now encompasses inhabited areas, forests, and agricultural lands around Mount Sorak National Park.

Shinan Dadohae (Republic of Korea)—One thousand islands have been added to the archipelago biosphere reserve, situated in the south west of the country, which was designated in 2009.

Wester Ross (United Kingdom)—Formerly known as Beinn Eighe, the site, situated in the northwest of Scotland, was designated in 1976. With the addition of 530,000ha, the site now includes Loch Maree, which is of international importance due to its black-throated diver population.

THE GALAPAGOS ISLAND

The Galapagos Islands is a group of 19 volcanic islands on the Pacific Ocean that is home to a diverse population of animals.

Although Galapagos is a part of Ecuador, it is located in a remote place, at a distance of around 1,000 km from the South American continent. The wildlife on these islands includes a pretty unique variety of endemic species that include land iguana, the giant tortoise and the many types of finch, among others. Biologists believe that the reason behind this unusual wildlife is a combination of seismic and volcanic activities that formed the islands and the isolated location of the same.

Some of the most commonly seen animals in these islands include the giant tortoise, sea lions, lava lizard, green sea turtle, and red rock crabs among many others. The presence of avifaunal species is no less. The most commonly seen birds in the Galapagos Islands include greylag goose, black-bellied whistling duck, cinnamon teal, and white-cheeked pintail, among others.

The Galapagos Islands are a melting pot of marine species. Located at a place that is essentially a confluence of three ocean currents, the marine life of this place is unimaginably vast. Most commonly found species include whale, Galapagos damsel, Scalloped hammerhead shark, red-lipped or Galapagos batfish, spotted eagle ray, golden cownose ray, razor surgeonfish, king angelfish and more.

Being a part of the prestigious UNESCO World Heritage Sites list, the Galapagos Islands has now become a wildlife travellers' favourite and attracts scores of tourists from different parts of the world.

CORAL REEFS AFFECTED EN MASSE DUE TO EL NINO

El Nino is causing unprecedented and irreversible damage to coral reefs which protect more than 4000 species of fishes in the world and act as a natural barrier protecting islands from rough ocean waves. Corals are some of the most diverse ecosystems in the world housing tens of thousands of marine species. In India, nearly 208 species of corals are recorded. Corals are neither a plant nor a rock but is made up of thousands of tiny animals called polyps. In India, the Andaman and Nicobar Islands, Gulf of Mannar and Palk Bay, Lakshwadweep and Gulf of Kutch are coral reef hotspots.

Benefits of corals: Coral reefs provide shelter to nearly one quarter of all known marine species. They act as natural barriers protecting coastal cities, beaches and communities from the wrath of the ocean waves.

Red coral: It is highly valued as jewellery and grows only 2-3 cm in 20 years and is listed as a protected species by the Convention on International Trade in Endangered Species (CITES). Corals are also mined in large quantities to produce lime and construction material.

Coral bleaching underway: Corals get their colour and food from tiny photosynthetic algae called zooxanthelae. These algae live in the tissues of corals and when temperature rises, the algae is expelled. Without algae the corals gets bleached. Mass bleaching can affect thousands of species and also lead to deaths of corals causing land erosion and a major ecological balance.

FIVE YEAR NATIONAL BIOTECH STRATEGY

A five year strategy on biotechnology has been unveiled by the government. The National Biotechnology Development Strategy 2015-2020 focuses on areas of healthcare, food and nutrition, clean energy and education.

Key points of the strategy:

- Establish India as a world class bio-manufacturing hub
- Make this sector a $100 billion industry by 2025
- Launch of four major missions in healthcare, food and nutrition, clean energy and education
- Setting up five new biotech clusters, 40 biotech incubators and 20 bio-connect centres
- Create a strong infrastructure for R&D
- Build skilled workforce and leadership

INTERNATIONAL BIODIVERSITY DAY

Every year May 22 is being observed as International Biodiversity Day (IDB) across the world to promote conservation and sustainable use of biodiversity.

Objectives: (i) To step-up understanding and awareness about biodiversity issues. (ii) To make people aware about the importance of biodiversity on the one hand and its unprecedented loss on the other.

2016 Theme: "Mainstreaming Biodiversity; Sustaining People and their Livelihoods

The United Nations General Assembly (UNGA) had proclaimed 22 May as the International Biodiversity Day on 20 December 2000.

Pakke Tiger Reserve: The Pakke Tiger Reserve in East Kameng district of Arunachal Pradesh has won the 'India Biodiversity Award 2016'. The tiger reserve was selected in the conservation of threatened species category for its Hornbill Nest Adoption Programme. The Programme is a joint collaboration of Ghora-Aabhe Society, Nature Conservation Foundation and the State Forest Department. Under it, urban citizens contribute money to protect hornbill nests around Pakke Tiger Reserve.

WORLD BANK LAUNCHED AMBITIOUS CLIMATE CHANGE ACTION PLAN

The World Bank has unveiled an ambitious Climate Change Action Plan (CCP) to accelerate efforts to tackle climate change effectively by 2020. The Action Plan mainly seeks to help developing countries focus on increasing sources of renewable energy, develop green transport systems, decrease high-carbon energy sources and build sustainable, livable cities for growing urban populations.

Key Highlights

- Helps developing countries add 30 GWs of renewable energy.
- Expand universal access to early-warning systems in the case of disasters to 100 million people by the year 2020.
- World Bank to help in developing climate-smart agriculture investment plans for at least 40 nations.
- To design sustainable forest strategies for 50 countries
- Bring adaptive social protection social safety nets that can quickly support people affected by a disaster or an economic shock.
- Pilot a new approach in 15 cities that aims to integrating infrastructure, land use planning and disaster risk management.
- To quadruple funding over next 5 years starting 2016, to make transport systems more resilient to climate change
- To invest at least US $1 billion to promote energy efficiency and resilient buildings by 2020.
- To support financial sector like banking, capital and pensions market in the overall objective of sustainable development.

NORWAY BECOMES FIRST COUNTRY IN THE WORLD TO PROHIBIT DEFORESTATION

Norway has become the first country in the world to prohibit deforestation. In this regard, Norwegian Parliament had pledged to make government's public procurement policy deforestation-free. The step was taken by Norwegian Government based on official recommendations of Norwegian Parliament's Standing Committee on Energy and Environment as part of the Action Plan on Nature Diversity. Norway will no longer procure use or procure products that encourage deforestation. Under the pledge, Norwegian Government will also not award contracts to any company that cuts down and destroys forests. In addition, Norwegian lawmakers also committed to find a way to source essential products such as soy, palm oil, beef and timber that have little or no impact on ecosystems. The standing committee also has asked Government to frame separate biodiversity policy and use funds provided by Government Pension Fund Global to increase biodiversity protection.

BORNEAN ORANGUTAN DECLARED CRITICALLY ENDANGERED

Bomean orangutan, a primate species has been declared critically endangered by the International Union for Conservation of Nature and Natural Resources (IUCN). The declaration was based on the assessment for the IUCN Red List of Threatened Species. IUCN assessment has found that population of Bornean orangutans has dropped by nearly two-third since the early 1970s. It has projected that their population will further decline to 47,000 animals by 2025 representing population loss of 86%.

GENETIC RECOGNITION TAG TO KENDRAPARA SHEEP

The National Bureau of Animal Genetic Resources (NBAGR) has conferred rare and singular species genetic recognition tag to the threatened breed of Kendrapara sheep found in Odisha. The genetically rare status will help to boost conservation effort to protect these domesticated threatened sheep. Kendrapara sheep is found only in coastal Jagatsinghpur and Kendrapara districts of Odisha. Kendrapara sheep carries FecB mutation gene, which is responsible for prolificacy (multiple babies in same delivery) or multiple birth syndrome. This characteristic makes them distinctive from other species sheep species as they are not known for giving multiple births. They are primarily used for mutton production. Besides, their skin also has economic importance.

STEPS TAKEN BY UNION MINISTRY TO PROTECT WILDLIFE SPECIES IN INDIA

According to the Union Government, there are 909 entries of taxa (including species, families, genus, orders and classes) of animals, birds and plants in the various Schedules of the Wild Life (Protection) Act, 1972.

The steps taken by the Union Ministry of Environment, Forest and Climate Change (MoEFCC) to protect these species are as follows:

- The names of protected species of animals, birds and plants have been mentioned at Schedule I of Wildlife (Protection) Act, 1972.
- The Union Government has established a country-wide protected area network for protection of these species and their habitats of threatened flora and fauna under Wildlife (Protection) Act, 1972.
- The network includes 730 Protected Areas including 103 National Parks, 535 Wildlife Sanctuaries, 26 Community Reserves and 66 Conservation Reserves in different bio-geographic regions.
- Legal protection has been provided to wild animals under the provisions of the Wild Life (Protection) Act, 1972 against hunting and commercial exploitation.
- Special programmes like Project Elephant' and 'Project Tiger' have been launched for conservation of these endangered species and their habitats.
- Under the Wildlife (Protection) Act, 1972, the Central Bureau of Investigation (CBI) has been empowered to apprehend and prosecute wildlife offenders.

The Wildlife Crime Control Bureau (WCCB) has been set up to ensure co-ordination among various officers and State Governments for the enforcement of law for control of poaching and illegal trade in wildlife and its products. National Biological Diversity Act (NBA), 2002 has been enacted to ensure protection of threatened species and their habitats.

Under the Section 38 of the NBA, 2002 the species which are on the verge of extinction or likely to become extinct in near future as threatened species, are notified. Botanical Survey of India (BSI) has brought a number of endemic/threatened plants under cultivation (ex-situ conservation) in its and associated botanic gardens.

- India is a signatory to several major international conventions relating to conservation and management of wildlife.
- Some of these are Convention on Biological Diversity, Convention on International Trade in Endangered Species of Wild Fauna and Flora (CITES), Convention on the Conservation of Migratory Species of Wild Animals etc.
- India has a strong legal and policy framework to regulate and restrict wildlife trade. Trade in over 1800 species of wild animals, plants and their derivative is prohibited under the Wildlife (Protection) Act, 1972. India is also a member of the CITES (Convention on International Trade in Endangered Species of Fauna and Flora) since 1976. CITES is an international agreement between governments that aims to ensure that international trade in specimens of wild animals and plants does not threaten their survival. CITES works by subjecting international trade in specimens of selected species listed on Appendices to certain controls.
- Financial and Technical assistance is provided to State/Union Territory Governments for protection and Management of Protected Areas as well as other forests under various Centrally Sponsored Schemes.
- This financial and technical assistance is extended to the State Governments under various Centrally Sponsored Schemes, viz, 'Integrated Development of Wildlife Habitats', 'Project Tiger' and 'Project Elephant' for providing better protection and conservation to wildlife.
- The Wildlife (Protection) Act, 1972 provides for the creation of Protected Areas for the protection of wildlife and also provides for punishment for hunting of specified fauna specified in the schedules I to IV.
- In order to protect the migratory species throughout the range countries, a Convention on Conservation of Migratory Species (CMS) has been in force, under UNEP and also known as Bonn Convention.
- Bonn convention is a global platform for the conservation and sustainable use of migratory animals and their habitats. It brings together the States through which migratory animals pass, the Range States and lays the legal foundation for internationally coordinated conservation measures.
- India also signed non legally binding MoU with CMS on the conservation and management of Siberian Cranes, Marine Turtles, Dugongs and Raptors. India is temporary home to several migratory animals and birds. They include Amur Falcons, Bar headed Geese, Black necked cranes, Marine turtles, Dugongs, Humpbacked Whales, etc.
- The Ministry of Environment, Forest and Climate Change, launched the 'Asiatic Lion Conservation Project with an aim to protect and conserve the world's last ranging free population of Asiatic Lion and its associated ecosystem.
- India has submitted proposals regarding changes to the listing of various wildlife species in the CITES secretariat meeting, scheduled later this month in Geneva, Switzerland.The proposals

submitted are regarding changes in the listing of the smooth-coated otter, small-clawed otter, Indian star tortoise, Tokay gecko, wedge fish and Indian rosewood.

- Wetland (Conservation and Management) Rules 2010 have been framed for the protection of wetlands, in the States.
- The Centrally Sponsored Scheme of National Plan for Conservation of Aquatic Eco-System also provides assistance to the States for the management of wetlands including Ramsar sites in the country.
- The Wildlife Protection Society of India (WPSI) has launched Operation Kachhapa in September 1998 to try to stem the slaughter. The objective is to reduce turtle mortality and try to safeguard the future of the species by concentrating on three main activities
- Wildlife Institute of India, Bombay Natural History society and Salim Ali Centre for Ornithology and Natural History are some of the research organisations undertaking research on conservation of wildlife.
- A habitat conservation project has been taken up for the golden langurs - an endangered species - adjacent to Manas National Park in Assam It was undertaken at the Assam State zoo in Guwahati during 2011-12, funded by Central Zoo Authority
- The Indian Government has banned the veterinary use of diclofenac drug that has caused the rapid population decline of Gyps vulture across the Indian Subcontinent.Conservation Breeding Programmes to conserve these vulture species have been initiated at Pinjore (Haryana), Buxa (West Bengal) and Rani, Guwahati (Assam) by the Bombay Natural History Society.
- The National Board for Wildlife (NBWL) recently added four species- the Northern River Terrapin, Clouded Leopard, Arabian Sea Humpback Whale, Red Panda- to a Recovery Programme for Critically Endangered Species on the recommendation of a Standing Committee.
- The progamme is one of the three components of the centrally funded scheme, Integrated Development of Wildlife Habitats (IDWH). Started in 2008-09, IDWH is meant for providing support to protected areas (national parks, wildlife sanctuaries, conservation reserves and community reserves except tiger reserves), protection of wildlife outside
- The Centrally Sponsored Scheme 'Integrated Development of Wildlife Habitats' has been modified by including a new component namely 'Recovery of Endangered Species' and 16 species have been identified for recovery viz. Snow Leopard, Bustard (including Floricans), Dolphin, Hangul, Nilgiri Tahr, Marine Turtles, Dugong, Edible Nest Swiftlet, Asian Wild Buffalo, Nicobar Megapode, Manipur Brow-antlered Deer, Vultures, Malabar Civet, Indian Rhinoceros, Asiatic Lion, Swamp Deer and Jerdon's Courser.
- Taking serious note of alarming extinction of two Indian birds -- Great Indian Bustard and the Lesser Florican -- the Supreme Court constituted a high powered committee to urgently frame and implement an emergency response plan for the protection of these species.

MARRAKECH PROCLAMATION ADOPTED

The COP22 to the UNFCC, 12th session of COP of Parties to Kyoto Protocol (CMP 12), and first session of COP of Parties to the Paris Agreement (CMA 1) were held in Marrakech, Morocco in November 2016. Nearly 200 nations attending the COP22 to the UNFCC have adopted the Marrakech Action Proclamation for Climate and Sustainable Development.

Key Features of the Proclamation

- It is the urgent duty of countries to respond global warming which is warming the climate at an alarming and unprecedented rate.
- Countries affirmed their commitment to full implementation of the Paris Agreement
- It highlighted the need to support efforts aimed to reduce vulnerability of most vulnerable countries.
- The countries called for an increase in the volume, flow and access to finance for climate projects, alongside improved capacity and technology.
- It also called for strengthening cooperation among the countries to close the gap between current emissions trajectories.

The adaptation of Marrakech Action Proclamation sends out a strong signal to the world on climate action and shift towards a new era of action on climate and sustainable development.

WORLD'S FIRST SALT TOLERANT PLANT GARDEN

The world's first Genetic Garden of Halophytes (naturally occurring salt-tolerant plants) has been inaugurated at the coastal town of Vedaranyam in Tamil Nadu. The garden has been set up by M S Swaminathan Research Foundation. It will have over 1,500 species belonging to 550 genera and 117 families of Halophytes plants. Halophytes are salt-tolerant or salt-resistant plants and can thrive in soils or waters containing high salt concentrations. They constitute two per cent of terrestrial plant species. The alarming rise in the sea level has prompted agriculture scientists to call for the cultivation of saline-tolerant crops in the light of danger of sea intrusion. In future, these plants could mitigate impact of climate change as they by providing food for people, fodder for livestock and bio fuel.

COUNTRIES REACH HISTORIC AGREEMENT ON FATE OF ANTARCTICA

The countries that decide the fate of Antarctica reached an historic agreement on October 28, 2016, to create the world's largest marine protected area in the ocean next to the frozen continent.

The agreement comes after years of diplomatic wrangling and high-level talks between the U.S. and Russia, which had rejected the idea in the past.

The agreement covers an area about twice the size of Texas in the Ross Sea.

The deal was clinched after 24 countries and the European Union met in Hobart, Australia in the last week of October 2016. Decisions on Antarctica require a consensus among the 25 members, a hurdle which has confounded past efforts.

The marine protected area covers 1.6 million square kilometers (617,000 square miles). There will be a blanket ban on commercial fishing across about three-quarters of that area. In the remaining ocean zones, some commercial fishing will be allowed.

A small amount of fishing for research purposes will be allowed throughout the protected area.

The agreement represents the first step in what would become a worldwide network of marine reserves that would help protect the Earth's oceans.

The agreement will take effect from December 2017 and, for most of the reserve, will last an initial 35 years.

LIVING PLANET REPORT AND LIVING PLANET INDEX (LPI)

Living Planet Report

Every two years, Global Footprint Network, WWF and the Zoological Society of London publish the Living Planet Report, the world's leading, science-based analysis on the health of our planet and the impact of human activity. The Living Planet Report uses the Ecological Footprint and additional complementary measures to explore the changing state of global biodiversity and human consumption. The report documents the extent of human pressure on the planet, how that compares across nations, and how it is impacting the natural world.

Living Planet Index

The Living Planet Index (LPI) is an indicator of the state of global biological diversity, based on trends in vertebrate populations of species from around the world.

The LPI provides the general public, scientists and policy-makers with information on trends in the abundance of the world's vertebrates and offers insights into which habitats or ecosystems are declining most rapidly. This information can be used to define the impact humans are having on the planet and for guiding actions to address biodiversity loss.

The Living Planet Index was originally developed by WWF in collaboration with UNEP-WCMC, the biodiversity assessment and policy implementation arm of the United Nations Environment Programme.

The LPI measures biodiversity by gathering population data of various vertebrate species and calculating an average change in abundance over time. The LPI can be compared to the stock market index, except that, instead of monitoring the global economy, the LPI is an important indicator of the planet's ecological condition. The global LPI is based on scientific data from 14,152 monitored populations of 3,706 vertebrate species (mammals, birds, fishes, amphibians, reptiles) from around the world. From 1970 to 2012 the LPI shows a 58 per cent overall decline in vertebrate population abundance Population sizes of vertebrate species have, on average, dropped by more than half in little more than 40 years. However, it is the stronger decline in freshwater species that has had more influence on the global decline in this report.

Grim Outlook for India

The biennial report that tracks over 14,000 vertebrate populations of over 3,700 species from across the world highlights the pressure on water and land India faces because of unsustainable human activities.

Around 70% of surface water is polluted and 60% of ground water will reach critical stage -- where it cannot be replenished -- in the next one decade, the report prepared by World Wide Fund for nature (WWF) with other research institutions said.

The biggest reason for contamination is industrial and municipal waste.

It also pointed out that one-fourth of India's total land is facing desertification and about a third of land is getting degraded primarily because of depleting forest cover.

Key Highlights of the 2016 Living Planet Report

For decades scientists have been warning that human actions are pushing life on our shared planet toward a sixth mass extinction. Evidence in the *Living Planet Report* supports this.

The Concerns

- Wildlife populations have already shown a concerning decline, on average by 58 per cent since 1970 and are likely to reach 67 per cent by the end of the decade.
- Humanity has started feeling the impact of a sick planet—from social, economic and climate stability to energy, food and water security—all increasingly suffering from environmental degradation.
- The world is beginning to increasingly understand that a diverse, healthy, resilient and productive natural environment is the foundation for a prosperous, just and safe future for humanity.

The Positives

- Despite the alarming statistics, there is also evidence that things are beginning to change. While environmental degradation continues, there are also unprecedented signs that we are beginning to embrace a "Great Transition" toward an ecologically sustainable future.
- Despite 2016 set to be another hottest year on record, global CO_2 emissions have stabilised over the last two years, with some arguing they may even have peaked, and it looks like China's huge coal burning may have finally peaked too. Economists say this is likely a permanent trend.
- Rampant poaching and wildlife trafficking is devastating ecosystems, but the U.S. and more notably China have recently committed to a historic ban of domestic ivory trade

Meanwhile, according to the Living Planet report, we are entering a new era in Earth's history: the Anthropocene, an era, in which humans, rather than natural forces, are the primary drivers of planetary change. But we can also redefine our relationship with our planet, from a wasteful, unsustainable and predatory one, to one where people and nature can coexist in harmony.

What is the Anthropocene era?

The Earth's ecosystems have evolved over millions of years. This process has resulted in diverse and complex biological communities, living in balance with their environment. These diverse ecosystems also provide people with food, fresh water, clean air, energy, medicine and recreation. Over the past 100 years, however, nature and the services it provides to humanity have come under increasing risk. The size and scale of the human enterprise have grown exponentially since the mid-20th century. As a result, the environmental conditions that fostered this extraordinary growth are beginning to shift. To symbolize this emerging environmental condition, Nobel Prize winner Paul Crutzen (2002) and others have proposed that we have transitioned from the Holocene into a new geological epoch, calling it the "Anthropocene". During the Anthropocene, our climate has changed more rapidly, oceans are acidifying and entire biomes are disappearing – all at a rate measurable during a single human lifetime. This trajectory constitutes a risk that the Earth will become much less hospitable to our modern globalized society. Such is the magnitude of our impact on the planet that the Anthropocene might be characterized by the world's sixth mass extinction event. In the past such extinction events took place over hundreds of thousands to millions of years. What makes the Anthropocene so remarkable is that these changes are occurring within an extremely condensed period of time. Furthermore, the driving force behind the transition is exceptional. This is the first time a new geological epoch may be marked by what a single species (homo sapiens) has consciously done to the planet – as opposed to what the planet has imposed on resident species.

change. But we can also redesign our relationship with our planet, from a [illegible], unsustainable and predatory one, to one where people and nature can coexist in harmony.

What is the Anthropocene era?

The Earth's ecosystems have evolved over millions of years. This process has resulted in diverse and complex biological communities, living in balance with their environment. These diverse ecosystems also provide people with food, fresh water, clean air, energy, medicine and recreation. Over the past 100 years, however, nature and the services it provides to humanity have come under increasing risk. The size and scale of the human enterprise have grown exponentially since the mid-20th century. As a result, the environmental conditions that fostered this extraordinary growth are beginning to shift. To symbolize this emerging environmental condition, Nobel Prize winner Paul Crutzen [illegible] and others have proposed that we have transitioned from the Holocene into a new geological epoch, calling it the 'Anthropocene'. During the Anthropocene, our climate has changed rapidly, oceans are acidifying and entire biomes are disappearing, all at a rate measurable during a single human lifetime. This trajectory constitutes a risk that the Earth will become much less hospitable to our modern globalized society. Such is the magnitude of our impact on the planet that the Anthropocene might be characterized by the world's sixth mass extinction event. In the past, such extinction events took place over hundreds of thousands to millions of years. What makes the Anthropocene so remarkable is that these changes are occurring within an extremely condensed period of time. Furthermore, the driving force behind the transition is [illegible]. This is the first time a new geological epoch may be marked by what a single species (Homo sapiens) has consciously done to the planet — as opposed to what the planet has imposed on resident species.

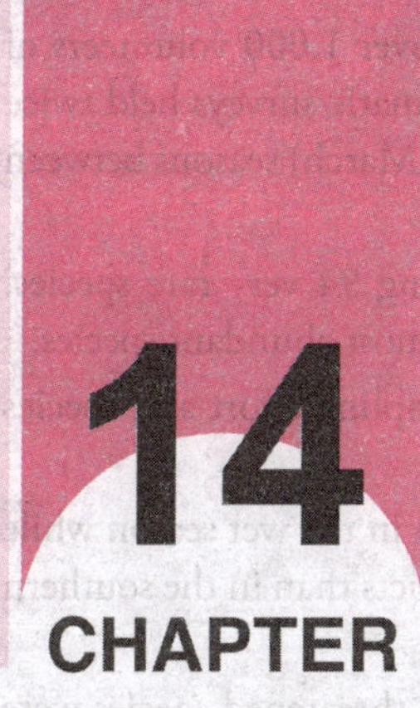

Latest Updates on Environment & Ecology

ANAMALAI TIGER RESERVE

- ICAR – Sugarçane Breeding Institute (ICAR-SBI), Coimbatore in collaboration with Anamalai Tiger Reserve, conducted a campaign on "Knowledge empowerment of tribals' and launched its STC (Scheduled Tribe Component) project at Attagatti in Anamalai Tiger Reserve (ATR),
- Unlike other tiger reserves, the Anamalai Tiger Reserve has diverse groups of indigenous people
- Referring to the 'Malasar' tribes who are of great help to the Forest Department in training the elephants with their profound knowledge and skill on handling Asian elephants
- The interventions by the Institute for implementing STC, was finalized based on a systematic need assessment by conduct of Focus groups among two tribes viz., 'Malasar' and 'Malai malasar' tribes

LIVING ROOT BRIDGES

- Meghalaya CM pitched for UNESCO recognition as the hill State marked its 50th year of creation.
- The Zoological Survey of India has underlined some green rules for the living root bridges of Meghalaya to get the UNESCO World Heritage Site tag.
- A living root bridge is like a suspension bridge formed by guiding the pliable roots of the rubber fig tree (Ficus elastica) across a stream or river and allowing the roots to grow and strengthen over time.
- They are common in the southern part of the northeast Indian state of Meghalaya.

KERALA BIRD ATLAS (KBA)

- The Kerala Bird Atlas (KBA), the first-of-its-kind State-level bird atlas in India, has created solid baseline data about the distribution and abundance of bird species across all major habitats, giving an impetus to futuristic studies.

- Conducted as a citizen science-driven exercise with the participation of over 1,000 volunteers of the birdwatching community, the KBA has been prepared based on systematic surveys held twice over 60 days a year during the wet (July to September) and dry (January to March) seasons between 2015 and 2020.
- The KBA accounts for nearly three lakh records of 361 species, including 94 very rare species, 103 rare species, 110 common species, 44 very common species, and 10 most abundant species.
- It is arguably Asia's largest bird atlas in terms of geographical extent, sampling effort and species coverage derived from the aggregation of 25,000 checklists.
- It was found that the species count was higher during the dry season than in the wet season while species richness and evenness were higher in the northern and central districts than in the southern districts.
- Most of the endemics were concentrated in the Western Ghats while the threatened species were mostly along the coast. The survey ignored the short duration passage of migrant species.

TWO SPECIES OF FUNGI ASSOCIATED WITH BASAL STEM ROT FOUND

- Researchers from Kerala have identified two new species of fungi from the genus Ganoderma that are associated with coconut stem rot.
- They have also genotyped the two fungi species, named *Ganoderma keralense* and *G. pseudoapplanatum* and identified genetic biomarkers.
- The DNA barcodes have been made publicly available in DNA sequence repositories so that future studies can use it for early detection of the pathogen. The research was published in the journal *Mycologia*.
- The butt rot or basal stem rot of coconut is known by several names in different parts of India: Ganoderma wilt (Andhra Pradesh), Anaberoga (Karnataka) and Thanjavur wilt (Tamil Nadu), to mention a few.
- The infection begins at the roots, but symptoms include discolouration and rotting of stem and leaves. In the later stages, flowering and nut set decreases and finally the coconut palm (Cocos nucifera) dies.

SPOT-BILLED PELICANS

- A nematode infestation has resulted in the mortality of over 150 spot-billed pelicans at Telineelapuram Important Bird Area (IBA) in Naupada swamp of Srikakulam district in Andhra Pradesh.
- The deaths of spot-billed pelicans started in December and at least 21 birds succumbed to the infestation in the past 72 hours alone.
- Over 150 spot-billed pelicans have succumbed to the infestation since December. Only adult birds have succumbed to the infestation till date.
- Until now, in South India, the Telineelapuram IBA is the prime winter sojourn for the spot-billed pelican for breeding. The same IBA is also a breeding habitat for the painted stork (Mycteria leucocephala).

- The nematode infestation would not spread from one species to another species as per the studies carried out by the experts in Karnataka State.
- The spot-billed pelican is capable of hunting huge fish from the water bodies and swamps and thus, it is vulnerable to infestation.
- Thousands of spot-billed pelicans and a few hundred painted storks migrate from the Siberian region to breed in the Telineelapuram IBA and a majority of them prefer to stay here instead of going back home.

LADAKH ADOPTED TWO ENDANGERED SPECIES

Ladakh adopted these species two years after it was separate Union created as a separate Union Territory (UT) from the erstwhile State of Jammu & Kashmir (J&K).

Black-Necked Crane

Black-necked Crane are scientifically known as Grus nigricollis. It is a medium-sized crane found in Asia. It breeds on the Tibetan Plateau and remote parts of India & Bhutan. In India, Black-necked crane are only found in Ladakh region. It was the State bird of J&K before it was made a UT in 2019. It is an endangered species.

Snow Leopard

Snow leopard is scientifically called as Panthera uncia. It is a felid of genus Panthera and is native to the mountain ranges in Central and South Asia. It has been listed as Vulnerable on the IUCN Red List as its global population is lesser than 10,000 mature individuals.

GENUS SEPTEMERANTHUS

- A new genus of a parasitic flowering plant has recently been discovered from the Nicobar group of islands.
- The genus Septemeranthus grows on the plant species Horsfieldia glabra (Blume) Warb.
- The parasitic flowering plants have a modified root structure spread on the stem of the tree and are anchored inside the bark of the host tree.
- The plant was found on the periphery of the tropical forest in one of the biodiversity hotspots referred to as the Nicobar group of islands separated from the Andaman group of Islands by a wide gap of 160 km with heavy tidal flows.
- The genus Septemeranthus has a distinct vegetative morphology, inflorescence, architecture and floral characters.
- The leaves of the plant are heart-shaped with a very long tip and the ovary, fruit and seeds are 'urceolate' (earthen pot-shaped). The flowers have five persistent bracts having conspicuous margins.
- The name Septemeranthus is derived from the Latin word 'septem' meaning 'seven', referring to the arrangement of flowers. The genus belongs to the family Loranthaceae, a hemi-parasite under the sandalwood order Santalales and is of widespread importance.

- Plants which are hemi-parasites are partially dependent on their host plants for nutrition. For instance, the newly discovered plant that derives nutrients from its hosts has green leaves capable of photosynthesis.

NATIONAL TIGER CONSERVATION AUTHORITY (NTCA)

The 19th Meeting of National Tiger Conservation Authority (NTCA) was held under the chairmanship of Union Minister for Environment, Forest & Climate Change

NTCA Meeting Highlights

- The 5th cycle of All India Tiger Estimation which is currently underway will help in taking correct policy decision.
- We have 51 tiger reserves in the country and efforts are being made to bring more areas under Tiger Reserve network.
- The tiger reserves are not just for tigers because more then 35 rivers originates from these areas which are crucial for water security.
- Today, 14 Tiger Reserves have been accredited under CA|TS and NTCA is working on getting other Tiger Reserves evaluated for CA|TS accreditation
- The environment minister unveiled the Action Plan for introduction of Cheetah in India, that has become extinct in independent India.
- The union minister also released a Water Atlas, mapping all the water bodies in the tiger bearing areas of India.
- Landscape wise information have been outlined in this water atlas which include, the Shivalik Hills and Gangetic plain landscape, Central Indian Landscape and Eastern Ghats, Western Ghats landscape, North Eastern Hills and Brahmaputra flood plains and Sundarbans.

National Tiger Conservation Authority (NTCA)

- NTCA has been constituted under section 38 L (1) of Wildlife (Protection) Act, 1972.
- Further, as per the section 38 L, sub section 2 of the said Act, the authority consists of the Minister in charge of the Ministry of Environment and Forests (as Chairperson), the Minister of State in the Ministry of Environment and Forests (as Vice-Chairperson), three members of Parliament, Secretary, Ministry of Environment and Forests and other members.
- The authority derives its power from section 38 O (1) of WLPA, 1972 and functions under the guidance of Chairperson, Vice-Chairperson and members.
- It was established in December 2005, following a recommendation of the Tiger Task Force, constituted by the Prime Minister of India for reorganised management of Project Tiger and the many Tiger Reserves in India.
- A programme for protection called, 'Tiger Protection Program' (popularly known as Project Tiger) was started in 1973, by the Government of India in co-operation with WWF.

CA/TS

- CA|TS is a set of criteria which allows tiger sites to check if their management will lead to successful tiger conservation.
- CA|TS is organised under seven pillars and 17 elements of critical management activity.
- CA|TS was developed by tiger and protected area experts.
- Officially launched in 2013, CA|TS is an important part of Tx2, the global goal to double wild tiger numbers by the year 2022.
- The long-term goal of CA|TS is to ensure safe havens for tigers.

How Does CA|TS Work and Who Is Using It?

- Sites taking part will initially be 'registered' (standards not yet attained) then, when all required standards are met, 'approved' (standards achieved).
- An approved site has achieved excellence in tiger site management.
- Sites are evaluated through an assessment and independent review process.
- Of the 13 tiger range countries Nepal, India, Bangladesh and Russia have registered and rolled out CA|TS, whilst discussion is ongoing with Bhutan, Indonesia, Thailand, Malaysia and China.

BHITARKANIKA NATIONAL PARK

- This larger national park is located in the northeast Kendrapara district of Odisha. It obtained the status of a Ramsar site in 2002. The area the second Ramsar site of Odisha after the Chilika Lake.
- The Park is surrounded by Bhitarkanika Wildlife Sanctuary, Gahirmatha Beach, Marine Sanctuary, separating swamp region as well as mangroves from the Bay of Bengal.

SOUTH ASIAN CONSULTATION ON POST-2020 GLOBAL BIODIVERSITY FRAMEWORK

- A two-day meeting of the South Asian Consultation Meeting on the Post-2020 Global Biodiversity Framework was held in New Delhi
- The meeting was attended by the representatives from Bangladesh, Bhutan, Maldives, Nepal, Sri Lanka and Pakistan in addition to representatives from the Secretariat of the Convention on Biological Diversity, Montreal; the Global Environmental Facility, Washington; French Embassy in New Delhi; UNDP-India; IUCN Offices in Canada and Singapore; National Geographic, USA and Campaign for Nature; Montreal in this virtual cum real meeting.
- The two-day regional consultation will help in developing strategies that would feed into the global meetings of CBD planned in March, 2022 in Geneva and for the 15th Conference of Parties of the CBD in China in April-May, 2022.

Meeting Highlights

- This Convention is a milestone towards developing South Asia perspective and calls for innovative financing methods from GEF.
- India has joined over 75 countries that are part of the 30 by 30 High Ambition Coalition (HAC) for Nature and People. In South Asia, already Pakistan and Maldives have joined.
- India urged other countries to join HAC and also requested GEF, Convention of Biological Diversity (CBD) and Campaign for Nature and others to ensure that timely and adequate resources for developing countries.

Global Biodiversity Framework

- The framework must aim to halt biodiversity loss by 2030 and achieve recovery by 2050, which requires additional investment in nature equivalent to between 0.7 and 1% of annual global GDP.
- Targets in the framework should be measurable, underpinned by science, and have explicit outcomes.
- The Post-2020 Global Biodiversity Framework (GBF) is a United Nations-led initiative to tackle its root causes and could have a similar impact as the Paris Agreement.
- Set to be finalized in early 2022, the GBF's draft sets out targets for protecting marine and land habitats, reducing pesticides and plastic waste, and increasing investments.
- The Post-2020 Global Biodiversity Framework (GBF) will set 21 targets and 10 milestones for governments to meet by the end of the decade.
- These include protecting a minimum of 30% of the world's oceans and land, reducing pesticide use by at least two-thirds, eliminating plastic waste, and increasing financial resources dedicated to biodiversity to at least US$ 200 billion annually.

CHILIKA LAKE

Chilika Lake, Asia's largest brackish water lagoon, witnessed over 10.74 lakh birds, including uncommon Mongolian gull, visiting the waterbody in Odisha this winter, according to a census report released

Water Bird Status Survey-2022 Highlights

- Spread over Puri, Ganjam and Khorda districts, Chilika Lake covers an area of around 1,100 sq km. However, compared to around 11.40 lakh birds of 190 species last year, 10,74,173 winged guests of 183 species to the lake were counted during the exercise
- As per the Water Bird Status Survey-2022 conducted in the Chilika, 10,74,173 water birds (107 species) and 37,953 individuals (76 wetland dependent species) were counted in the entire lagoon.
- Last year, the count in the Chilika was over 12 lakh. Members who were part of the census also reported sighting the Mongolian gull.
- The census was undertaken jointly by the Odisha State Wildlife Organisation, the Chilika Development Authority (CDA) and the Bombay Natural History Society.

- The increase in numbers for the greater flamingo at Nalabana mudflat indicates that the restoration at Nalabana is effective.
- This year's greater flamingo count was the highest in the last decade. It is largely due to appropriate management of mudflats.

WORLD WETLANDS DAY 2022

- The Prime Minister has expressed happiness over inclusion of two more wetlands, Khijadiya Wildlife Sanctuary in Gujarat and Bakhira Wildlife Sanctuary in UP in the Ramsar site list.
- The Union Environment Minister participated in the national level celebration of World Wetlands day 2022 held at Sultanpur National Park, a Ramsar site of Haryana.
- Two new Ramsar sites (Wetlands of International Importance), Khijadia Wildlife Sanctuary in Gujarat and Bakhira Wildlife Sanctuary in U.P were also announced
- Bakhira Wildlife Sanctuary in UP provides a safe wintering and staging ground for a large number of species of the Central Asian Flyway while Khijadia Wildlife Sanctuary is a coastal wetland with rich avifaunal diversity providing a safe habitat to endangered and vulnerable species.
- On the occasion, "National Wetland Decadal Change Atlas" prepared by the Space Applications Centre (SAC), Ahmedabad was also released highlighting the changes which have happened in Wetlands across the country in the past decade.
- The original Atlas was released by SAC in 2011 and has over the years been used extensively by all the State Governments also in their planning processes.
- World Wetlands Day is observed every year globally on 2nd February aiming to raise awareness about the vital role the wetlands play for people and the planet.
- February 2nd also marks the date of the adoption of the Convention on Wetlands in 1971 in the Iranian city of Ramsar.
- The theme of 'World Wetlands Day' this year is 'Wetlands Action for People and Nature', which is a call to take action for preservation of wetlands.
- Ramsar sites are wetlands of international importance as per UNESCO's 1971 Convention on Wetlands held in Ramsar, Iran. It came into force in 1975.
- The certification brings visibility to ecologically sensitive wetlands and helps in conservation.
- Any wetland site which has been listed under the Ramsar Convention that aims to conserve it and promote sustainable use of its natural resources is called a Ramsar Site.
- Last year (2nd February 2021) marked the 50th anniversary of the Ramsar Convention, the day which is also celebrated as World Wetlands Day.
- India on this occasion established the Centre for Wetland Conservation & Management which is the first in the country.
- It is set up under the Ministry of Environment, Forest and Climate Change (MoEF&CC), at the National Centre for Sustainable Coastal Management (NCSCM) in Chennai.

NATIONAL ADAPTATION FUND FOR CLIMATE CHANGE (NAFCC)

- The National Adaptation Fund for Climate Change (NAFCC) was established to support adaptation activities in the States and Union Territories (UTs) of India that are vulnerable to the adverse effects of climate change.
- NAFCC is implemented in project mode and till date, 30 projects are sanctioned in 27 States and UTs.
- The Ministry of Environment, Forest and Climate Change has demarcated the Hazard Line for the entire mainland coast of India under its Integrated Coastal Zone Management (ICZM) project.
- Further, Coastal Regulation Zone Notification 2019 has been notified to conserve and protect the unique environment of coastal stretches and marine areas to promote sustainable development.
- The NAFCC projects implemented in the states of Kerala, Tamil Nadu and Andhra Pradesh include activities relating to coastal areas and these projects are-
    1. Promotion of integrated farming system of Kaipad in coastal wetlands of North Kerala
    2. Management and rehabilitation of coastal habitats and biodiversity for climate Change Adaptation and Sustainable Livelihood in Gulf of Mannar, Tamil Nadu and
    3. Climate Resilient interventions in Dairy Sector in coastal and Arid areas in Andhra Pradesh.

CONSERVING MARINE RESOURCES

Government of India has already undertaken several initiatives focusing on the conservation of coastal and marine resources especially, wetlands, mangroves and coral reefs and their management through implementation of law and continuous monitoring.

A Few Examples Are :

i. The WildLife Protection Act of India (1972) provides legal protection to many marine animals. There are total of 31 major Marine Protected Areas in India covering coastal areas that have been notified under Wildlife Protection Act, 1972.

ii. The National Committee on mangroves, wetlands and coral reefs constituted in 1993 advise the Government on relevant policies and programmes regarding marine species.

iii. The Coastal Regulation Zone (CRZ) notification (1991 and later versions) prohibit developmental activities and disposal of wastes in the fragile coastal ecosystems.

iv. The Biological Diversity Act of India,2002 and the Biological Diversity Rules 2004, and the guidelines thereof advise the Government on matters related to the protection and conservation of biodiversity, sustainable use and equitable sharing of its components, Intellectual Property Rights, etc.

v. The Department of Fisheries, Govt. of India is implementing a flagship scheme namely the PradhanMantriMatsyaSampadaYojana (PMMSY) for sustainable and responsible development of fisheries sector in India. Two of the key objectives of the scheme are (a) harnessing of fisheries potential in a sustainable, responsible, inclusive and equitable manner and (b) Robust fisheries management and regulatory framework.

vi. The Centre for Marine Living Resources and Ecology (CMLRE), an attached office of Ministry of Earth Sciences (MoES) is mandated with the management strategies development for marine living resources through ecosystem monitoring and modelling activities.

INCOIS PREPARES COASTAL VULNERABILITY INDEX

Indian National Centre for Ocean Information Services (INCOIS) has carried out coastal vulnerability assessment for entire Indian coast at States level to bring out an Atlas comprising 156 maps on 1:1,00,000 scales to prepare a Coastal Vulnerability Index (CVI).

Know About CVI Index

- From this CVI, it can be delineated that Gujarat's 124 coastal km is going to get affected or 5.36%, Maharashtra 11 km or 1.22% and then Karnataka & Goa 48 km or 9.54%, Kerala 15 km or 2.39%, Tamil Nadu 65 km or 6.38%, Andhra Pradesh 6 km or 0.55 %, Odisha 37 km or 7.51% West Bengal 49 km or 2.56%, Lakshadweep Islands 1 km or 0.81%, Andaman Islands 24 km or 0.96 km and Nicobar Islands 8 km or 0.97%.
- While the maps determine the coastal risks due to future sea-level rise based on the physical and geological parameters for the Indian coast, the CVI uses the relative risk that physical changes will occur as sea-level rises are quantified based on parameters like: tidal range; wave height; coastal slope; coastal elevation; shoreline change rate; geomorphology; and historical rate of relative sea-level change.
- Coastal vulnerability assessments can be useful information for coastal disaster management and building resilient coastal communities.

Multi-Hazard Vulnerability Mapping (MHVM)

- A coastal Multi-Hazard Vulnerability Mapping (MHVM) was also carried out using parameters like sea level change rate, shoreline change rate, high-resolution coastal elevation, extreme water level from tide gauges and their return periods.
- This MHVM mapping was carried for the entire mainland of India on a 1:25000 scale.
- These maps depict the coastal low-lying areas exposed to the coastal inundation.

Indian National Centre for Ocean Information Services (INCOIS)

- INCOIS, which is an autonomous body under Ministry of Earth Sciences (MoES), has been issuing alerts on Potential Fishing Zone, Ocean State Forecast, Tsunami Early Warning, Storm Surge Early Warning, High Wave Alerts, etc., through dedicated ocean modeling, observations, computation facilities and the marine data center.

TAMIL NADU TO SET UP INDIA'S FIRST DUGONG CONSERVATION RESERVE

- Government of Tamil Nadu recently announced its plan to set up India's first Dugong Conservation Reserve in the Palk Bay on the southeast coast.
- Dugong or sea cow is an endangered marine mammal. It is facing extinction because of habitat loss, sea pollution, and loss of seagrass.
- Dugong is found in Gulf of Mannar and at Palk Bay in Tamil Nadu.
- Gulf of Mannar is a shallow bay area between south eastern end of Tamil Nadu and western Sri Lanka.

About Dugong

Dugong is a sea mammal and is the only living species of the order Sirenia. The mammal is restricted to coastal habitat because of seagrass, which is a major part of its diet. The IUCN has listed dugong as a "vulnerable to extinction species".

DEVIKA PROJECT

- Launched by the Prime Minister during his visit to Jammu in early 2019 under the National River Conservation Plan (NRCP).
- Under the project, bathing "ghats" (places) on the banks of the Devika River will be developed, encroachments will be removed, natural water bodies will be restored and catchment areas will be developed along with cremation ground.
- The project includes the construction of three sewage treatment plants, sewerage network of 129.27 km, development of two cremation ghats, protection fencing and landscaping, small hydropower plants and three solar power plants.

Devika River

- Devika river originates from the hilly Suddha Mahadev temple in Udhampur district of Jammu and Kashmir and flows down towards western Punjab (Pakistan) where it merges with the Ravi river.
- The river holds religious significance as it is revered by Hindus as the sister of river Ganga.

SEA BUCKTHORN BERRY ALSO KNOWN AS" LEH BERRY"

- The Ladakh Administration taking a decision to start the commercial plantation of "Leh Berry".
- The Council of Scientific and Industrial Research (CSIR) under the aegis of Union Ministry of Science & Technology is promoting "Leh Berry" which is an exclusive food product of the cold desert and also a means of wide-ranging entrepreneurship as well as self-livelihood.
- CSIR will also develop harvesting machinery to be used by local farmers and self-help groups, as currently only 10% of berry is being extracted from the wild sea buckthorn plant.

- Commercial cultivation of three medicinal plants will begin this spring season at the height of above 15,000 feet.
- This also includes "Sanjeevni Booty", locally known as "Sola" which has a very high life saving and therapeutic properties.

Seabuckthorn (Hippophae Rhamnoides)

- Popularly known as Leh berry or Chhermang or Cherma in Ladakh and Lauhul Spiti is a miracle 2-4 meter bush growing wild in high altitude areas of Ladakh region of Jammu and Kashmir
- Sea buckthorn has a rich history of use in treating numerous medical conditions.
- It has been called a "Wonder plant" in many Asian countries, including China, India, and Pakistan.
- The berries have been used for more than 2,000 years as a medicine and food additive in Europe, Russia, and Asia.
- Mythically believed to be the "Sanjivani Booti" from the Ramayana, Seabuckthorn berry found only in the snow-capped mystical hills of Leh - Ladakh where human feet rarely dare to step.
- The berry is a thorny shrub that contains a high amount of vitamin-C, Calcium along with Vitamin A, B1, B2, E and K.
- It also contains over 100 essential nutrients good for human growth process.
- Sea buckthorn (Himalayan Berry) is the only fruit in the world which contains Omega 3, 6, 9 and rarest omega 7.
- The Defense Research and Development Organisation (DRDO) has endorsed and recognizes the immense benefits of Sea Buckthorn.

MINISTRY OF POWER NOTIFIES GREEN HYDROGEN/ GREEN AMMONIA POLICY

- Prime Minister launched the National Hydrogen Mission on India's 75th Independence Day (i.e. 15th August, 2021).
- The Mission aims to aid the government in meeting its climate targets and making India a green hydrogen hub.
- This will help in meeting the target of production of 5 million tonnes of Green hydrogen by 2030 and the related development of renewable energy capacity.
- Hydrogen and Ammonia are envisaged to be the future fuels to replace fossil fuels.
- Government of India is taking various measures to facilitate the transition from fossil fuel / fossil fuel based feed stocks to green hydrogen / green ammonia.

The Policy Provides as Follows :

- Green Hydrogen / Ammonia manufacturers may purchase renewable power from the power exchange or set up renewable energy capacity themselves or through any other, developer, anywhere.
- Open access will be granted within 15 days of receipt of application.

- The Green Hydrogen / Ammonia manufacturer can bank his unconsumed renewable power, up to 30 days, with distribution company and take it back when required.
- Distribution licensees can also procure and supply Renewable Energy to the manufacturers of Green Hydrogen / Green Ammonia in their States at concessional prices which will only include the cost of procurement, wheeling charges and a small margin as determined by the State Commission.
- Waiver of inter-state transmission charges for a period of 25 years will be allowed to the manufacturers of Green Hydrogen and Green Ammonia for the projects commissioned before 30th June 2025.
- The manufacturers of Green Hydrogen / Ammonia and the renewable energy plant shall be given connectivity to the grid on priority basis to avoid any procedural delays.
- The benefit of Renewable Purchase Obligation (RPO) will be granted incentive to the hydrogen/ Ammonia manufacturer and the Distribution licensee for consumption of renewable power.
- To ensure ease of doing business, a single portal for carrying out all the activities including statutory clearances in a time bound manner will be set up by MNRE.
- Connectivity at the generation end and the Green Hydrogen / Green Ammonia manufacturing end, to the ISTS for Renewable Energy capacity set up for the purpose of manufacturing Green Hydrogen / Green Ammonia shall be granted on priority.
- Manufacturers of Green Hydrogen / Green Ammonia shall be allowed to set up bunkers near ports for storage of Green Ammonia for export / use by shipping. The implementation of this Policy will provide clean fuel to the common people

GOVERNMENT NOTIFIES GUIDELINES ON EXTENDED PRODUCERS RESPONSIBILITY (EPR) ON PLASTIC PACKAGING

- Ministry of Environment, Forest and Climate Change has notified the Guidelines on Extended Producers Responsibility on plastic packaging under Plastic Waste Management Rules, 2016.
- The guidelines on extended producer responsibility coupled with prohibition of identified single use plastic items, which have low utility and high littering potential, with effect from 1st July 2022, are important steps for reducing pollution caused due to littered plastic waste in the country.

EPR Guidelines and Benefits

- The Guidelines provide framework to strengthen circular economy of plastic packaging waste, promote development of new alternatives to plastics and provide further next steps for moving towards sustainable plastic packaging by businesses.
- Reuse of rigid plastic packaging material has been mandated in the guidelines to reduce the use of fresh plastic material for packaging.
- The enforceable prescription of minimum level of recycling of plastic packaging waste collected under EPR along with use of recycled plastic content will further reduce plastic consumption and support recycling of plastic packaging waste.

- The EPR guidelines will give a boost for formalization and further development of plastic waste management sector.
- In a significant first, the guidelines allow for sale and purchase of surplus extended producer responsibility certificates, thus setting up a market mechanism for plastic waste management.
- The implementation of EPR will be done through a customized online platform which will act as digital backbone of the system.
- The online platform will allow tracking and monitoring of EPR obligation and will reduce the compliance burden for companies through online registration and filing of annual returns.
- In order to ensure monitoring on fulfilment of EPR obligations, the guidelines have prescribed a system of verification and audit of enterprises.
- The Guidelines prescribe a framework for levy of environmental compensation based upon polluter pays principle, with respect to non-fulfilment of extended producer responsibility targets by producers, importers & brand owners, for the purpose of protecting and improving the quality of the environment and preventing, controlling and abating environment pollution.
- The funds collected shall be utilized for collection, recycling and end of life disposal of uncollected plastic waste in an environmentally sound manner.
- Under these producers, importers & brand owners, may operate schemes such as deposit refund system or buy back or any other model, in order to prevent mixing of plastic packaging waste with solid waste.

NDC-TIA INITIATIVE

- The NDC-TIA is a joint programme of seven organizations that engages India, China and Vietnam in promoting a comprehensive approach to decarbonizing transport in their respective countries.
- The project is part of the International Climate Initiative (IKI).
- The Federal Ministry for the Environment, Nature Conservation and Nuclear Safety (BMU) supports the initiative on the basis of a decision adopted by the German Bundestag.
- NITI Aayog is the implementing partner for the India component of the project.

NDC Transport Initiative for Asia (NDC-TIA)

- The NDC Transport Initiative for Asia (NDC-TIA) aims to promote a coherent strategy of effective policies for decarbonising transport co-ordinated among various sector ministries, civil society, and the private sector.
- The project engages in China, India and Vietnam over the period 2020-24.
- The goal is to enable the countries' transport sectors to contribute to achieving their Nationally Determined Contributions (NDCs) and increase ambition in transport sections of long-term strategies and 2025 NDCs.
- As a regional initiative, the project will disseminate knowledge in Asia and at the global level.

- It will disseminate and share experiences at international dialogue platforms such as the United Nations Framework Convention on Climate Change (UNFCCC) process.
- The NDC-TIA is a joint project of seven organisations, co-ordinated by Deutsche Gesellschaft für Internationale Zusammenarbeit (GIZ) GmbH and funded by the German Federal Ministry for the Environment, Nature Conservation and Nuclear Safety (BMU) under the International Climate Initiative (IKI).
- The implementing partner in India for the project is NITI Aayog.
- Project partners also include the World Resources Institute (WRI), Agora Verkehrswende (AGORA), the Partnership on Sustainable, Low Carbon Transport (SLoCaT), the International Council on Clean Transportation (ICCT) and the Renewable Energy Policy Network for the 21st Century (REN21).
- NDC-TIA is a part of ITF's work on Decarbonising Transport in India, which includes Decarbonising Transport in Emerging Economies – India component.

DISASTER MANAGEMENT PLAN OF MINISTRY OF PANCHAYATI RAJ RELEASED

- Union Minister of Rural Development & Panchayati Raj released the Disaster Management Plan of Ministry of Panchayati Raj
- The Ministry of Panchayati Raj has developed the Disaster Management Plan with an aim to develop disaster resilience at the grassroots level among the Panchayats and establish a framework to align the disaster management measures in rural areas to that of the National Disaster Management Authority'.
- Objective : To formulate Panchayat-level and village-level Disaster Management Plans to mitigate the challenges in the event of disaster.

Managing Disasters Comprehensively - Preparedness Strategy

- People's participation in preparedness for disaster management
- Mitigation activities at grassroots level.
- Active participation of the community is vital to carry out the activities relating to disaster management in rural areas.
- Community-based disaster management
- Convergence and collective action with programs and schemes of different Ministries / Departments.

Disaster Management Plan of Ministry of Panchayati Raj (DMP-MoPR) – Highlights

- The Ministry of Panchayati Raj (MoPR) has prepared this Disaster Management Plan (DMP) so that all Panchayati Raj Institutions along with communities can be prepared for any disaster.

- DMP–MoPR incorporates many innovations in addition to being in compliance with Disaster Management Act 2005, National Disaster Management Policy 2009, and guidelines issued by National Disaster Management Authority.
- DMP-MoPR would contribute to the efforts of the Government in bringing convergence in disaster management and planning in rural areas.
- DMP-MoPR has been prepared with larger perspective of community-based planning starting from Village to District Panchayat level.
- Under the Plan, every Indian village would have "Village Disaster Management Plan" and every Panchayat would have their Disaster Management Plan.
- All stakeholders including PRIs, elected representatives and functionaries of Panchayats etc. would participate in planning, implementation, monitoring and evaluation of the plan.
- This plan would be extremely useful for ensuring a participatory planning process for DMPs which is integrated with GPDP for addressing disasters across the country

PROTECTION OF GREAT INDIAN BUSTARDS

Important steps taken by the Government for protection of Great Indian Bustards in the country including details of captive breeding facilities are as given below:

- A site for establishment of a Conservation Breeding Centre for the Great Indian Bustard has been identified at Kota District, Rajasthan in consultations with State Forest Departments of Rajasthan and Gujarat, Wildlife Institute of India and international experts, under the project titled 'Habitat Improvement and Conservation Breeding of Great Indian Bustard-an integrated approach'.
- A satellite conservation breeding facility with incubator, hatcher, chick rearing and housing for captive birds has been set up at Sam, Jaisalmer, Rajasthan and is managed by WII Scientists, Rajasthan Forest Department with the technical assistance of the International Fund for Houbara Conservation and Reneco, Abu Dhabi.
- The Great Indian Bustard is listed in Schedule-I of the Wild Life (Protection) Act, 1972, thereby, according it highest degree of legal protection from hunting.
- The species has been identified for conservation efforts under the component 'Species Recovery Programme' of the Centrally Sponsored Scheme (CSS)-Development of Wildlife Habitat.
- Financial and technical assistance is provided to the State/Union Territory Governments under the Centrally Sponsored Scheme of Development of Wildlife Habitat for providing better protection to Great Indian Bustard and its habitat.
- Ministry has taken up an initiative on conservation breeding of the Great Indian Bustard in collaboration with Rajasthan, Gujarat and Maharashtra Forest Departments and technical support from Wildlife Institute of India, Dehradun.
- The Ministry with financial support from National Authority for Compensatory Afforestation Funds has sanctioned an outlay of Rs. 33.85 crores for the duration of five years for the programme titled 'Habitat Improvement and Conservation Breeding of Great Indian Bustard-an integrated approach'.

- The objective of this programme is to build up captive population of Great Indian Bustard and to release the chicks in the wild for increasing the population and also to promote in-situ conservation of the species.
- The Great Indian Bustard has been included in the Appendix I of Convention on Migratory Species (CMS) of the basis of proposal submitted by India.
- As per the studies conducted by Wildlife Institute of India, there are around 150 Great Indian Bustards left across the country which includes about 128 birds in Rajasthan and less than 10 birds each in the States of Gujarat, Maharashtra, Andhra Pradesh and Karnataka.

REJUVENATION OF 13 MAJOR RIVERS THROUGH FORESTRY

- The Centre envisages a Rs. 19,000–crore project to rejuvenate 13 major rivers by planting trees.
- These 'forestry' interventions are expected to increase the cumulative forest cover by 7,417.36 sq. km. in the vicinity of these 13 rivers and would prevent 50.21 million tonnes of CO_2–equivalent in 10–year–old plantations and 74.76 million tonnes CO_2–equivalent in 20–year–old plantations.
- They would help recharge groundwater, reduce sedimentation, generate Rs. 449.01 crore from non-timber and other forest produce as well as provide employment of 344 million man–days.
- The rivers are the Jhelum, Chenab, Ravi, Beas, Sutlej, Yamuna, Brahmaputra, Luni, Narmada, Godavari, Mahanadi, Krishna and Cauvery funded by the National Afforestation & Eco-development Board, (MoEF&CC)
- The two Ministries made public multiple voluminous Detailed Project Reports, for each of these rivers, prepared by the Indian Council of Forestry Research & Education, Dehradun, (ICFRE).

PROGRAMME ON SEAGRASSES

Seagrasses and its Benefits

- Seagrasses are flowering plants which are found in our sea beds and ocean floors.
- The major seagrass beds exist along our coastline of Gulf of Mannar and Palk Bay regions on the east coast, Gulf of Kachchh region on the west coast, the lagoons of islands in Lakshadweep in the Arabian Sea and Andaman and Nicobar Islands in the Bay of Bengal.
- Seagrass ecosystems are recognized globally for their ability to sequester carbon, nurture fish communities and support marine mammals such as sea cows or dugongs.
- Seagrasses have been studied for over two decades with the financial support of the Ministry of Environment, Forest and Climate Change and the State/UT Governments.
- Based on field surveys and satellite data, the National Centre for Sustainable Coastal Management has estimated the total extent of seagrass ecosystem in India to be 516.59 km^2.
- The CO_2 sequestration rate of seagrass ecosystem is estimated to be up to 434.9 tonnes/km^2/year with an annual net CO_2 sink of 0.75 million tonnes for an area of 517 km^2.

Projects Initiated

The Government initiated a project across the States of Andhra Pradesh, Maharashtra, and Odisha on enhancing climate resilience of India's coastal communities at a total cost of US $130.269 million which includes a grant of US$ 43.419 million by Global Climate Fund (GCF) covering 24 ecosystems in these selected States which aims to strengthen the climate resilience of coastal communities by protecting and restoring India's natural ecosystems such as mangroves and seagrasses.

IPCC SIXTH ASSESSMENT REPORT (AR6) ON CLIMATE CHANGE

- India welcomes the release of the Working Group II (WG2) contribution to the Sixth Assessment Report (AR6) of the Intergovernmental Panel on Climate Change (IPCC).
- The report reaffirms India's call for equity and climate justice and stated that the Developed countries must take the lead in urgent mitigation and providing finance for adaptation, loss and damage.

Key Findings of the Report and its Summary for Policymakers

- The Report affirms that climate change due to historical emissions is leading to serious impacts which are already being felt globally including in developing countries with low contribution to cumulative emissions.
- The Summary for Policymakers (SPM) underlines the need for climate action on the basis of equity and climate justice to ensure the well-being of humanity and the planet.
- The Report is a clarion call for the world to abandon their unsustainable production and consumption and move urgently to climate resilient development.
- The Report fully acknowledges the importance of losses and damages arising from climate change.
- The Report notes that future climate-resilient development pathways depend on climate risks, adaptation measures and the remaining carbon budget.
- The Report recognizes the key role of agriculture and the great importance of food security in adaptation.
- India faces multiple climate hazards and has high vulnerability to climate change.
- Lucknow and Patna, according to one of several studies cited in the IPCC report, are among the cities predicted to reach wet-bulb temperature (a metric of humidity) of 35°C if emissions continued to rise.
- Bhubaneswar, Chennai, Mumbai, Indore, and Ahmedabad are identified as at risk of reaching wet-bulb temperatures of 32-34°C with continued emissions.
- Overall, Assam, Meghalaya, Tripura, West Bengal, Bihar, Jharkhand, Odisha, Chhattisgarh, Uttar Pradesh, Haryana and Punjab will be the most severely affected, but if emissions keep rising, all States will have regions that experience wet-bulb temperature of 30°C or more by the end of the century.
- According to the IPCC report, global sea levels will likely rise 44-76 cm this century if governments meet their current emission-cutting pledges. With faster emission cuts, the increase could be limited to 28-55 cm.

- But with higher emissions, and if ice sheets collapse more quickly than expected, sea levels could rise as much as 2 m this century and 5 m by 2150.
- The impacts and the consequent limitations to adaptation would rise beyond 1.5 degree warming above pre-industrial levels.
- The Working Group I contribution to AR6 released in August, 2021 had made clear that developed countries need to rapidly decrease their emissions and reach net zero by 2050

Steps Taken by India

- India is already walking the path of climate resilient development with its combination of several adaptation-oriented development actions and its contribution to mitigation.
- At COP26, as the implementation of the Paris Agreement began, India reaffirmed its commitment to climate actions, including the goal of net zero by 2070, and the one-word mantra of L.I.F.E. = lifestyles for environment.
- India notes that future reports should strengthen the "solution space" and more comprehensively assess knowledge regarding effectiveness, costs and benefits.
- India firmly believes that climate change is a global collective action problem that can be solved only through international cooperation and multilateralism.
- India has taken tremendous actions to combat climate change by taking several initiatives including, inter-alia, setting up of International Solar Alliance, Coalition for Disaster Resilient Infrastructure, 'One Sun, One World, One Grid' and Infrastructure for Resilient Island States, raising the domestic renewable energy target to 500 GW by 2030, putting in place an ambitious National Hydrogen Mission and continuing efforts to decouple its emissions from economic growth.

Intergovernmental Panel on Climate Change (IPCC)

- It is an intergovernmental body of the United Nations responsible for advancing knowledge on human-induced climate change.
- It was established in 1988 by the World Meteorological Organization (WMO) and the United Nations Environment Programme (UNEP), and later endorsed by United Nations General Assembly.
- Headquartered in Geneva, Switzerland, it is composed of 195 member states.
- The IPCC provides objective and comprehensive scientific information on anthropogenic climate change, including the natural, political, and economic impacts and risks, and possible response options.
- It does not conduct original research nor monitor climate change, but rather undertakes a periodic, systematic review of all relevant published literature.
- Thousands of scientists and other experts volunteer to review the data and compile key findings into "Assessment Reports" for policymakers and the general public
- This has been described as the biggest peer review process in the scientific community.

- The IPCC is an internationally accepted authority on climate change, and its work is widely agreed upon by leading climate scientists as well as governments.
- Its reports play a key role in the United Nations Framework Convention on Climate Change (UNFCCC), with the Fifth Assessment Report heavily informing the landmark Paris Agreement in 2015.
- The IPCC shared the 2007 Nobel Peace Prize with Al Gore for contributions to the human understanding of climate change.

HISTORIC RESOLUTION ON PLASTIC POLLUTION ADOPTED BY 175 COUNTRIES

- The resumed session of fifth United Nations Environment Assembly (UNEA 5.2) held from 28th February 2022 to 2nd March 2022 in Nairobi, considered three draft resolutions to address plastic pollution.
- One of the draft resolutions under consideration was that of India.
- The draft resolution submitted by India called for immediate collective voluntary action by countries.
- About 175 countries have adopted a resolution at the fifth United Nations Environment Assembly (UNEA) to end plastic pollution.

Session Highlights

- India engaged constructively with all member states in UNEA 5.2 to develop consensus on the resolution for driving global action on plastic pollution by setting up of an intergovernmental negotiating committee for a new international legally binding treaty.
- On the insistence of India, the principle of national circumstances and capability while taking actions to address plastic pollution was included in the text of the resolution to allow developing countries follow their development trajectories.
- India also stood for not mandating the inter-governmental negotiating committee with development of targets, definitions, formats and methodologies, at this stage, pre-judging the outcome of deliberations of the Committee.
- The provision for immediate collective voluntary actions by the countries was also included to address plastic pollution on urgent and continual basis.
- The principal objectives of India's draft resolution were sufficiently addressed in the resolution on "End plastic pollution: Towards an international legally binding instrument" adopted in the resumed fifth session of UNEA, which concluded on 2nd March 2022.
- The resolution called for the member states to continue and step up activities and adopt voluntary measures to combat plastic pollution, including measures related to sustainable consumption and production.

- The measures might also include a circular economy approach, developing and implementing national action plans, while fostering international action and initiatives under respective national regulatory frameworks.
- Earlier, India had piloted a resolution on addressing single use plastic product pollution in the fourth United Nations Environment Assembly (UNEA) held in 2019, bringing global focus on the issue.

Steps Taken by India

- The Ministry of Environment Forest and Climate Change has put in place a ban on identified single use plastic items, which have low utility and high littering potential.
- The Guidelines on Extended Producers Responsibility on plastic packaging have also been notified.
- The single use plastic ban coupled with extended producer responsibility guidelines provide legal framework for addressing plastic pollution.

OLIVE RIDLEY TURTLES

- A record number of around 2,45,188 Olive Ridley sea turtles came ashore for mass nesting at the Nasi-1 and Nasi-2 islands of Gahirmatha marine sanctuary within Bhitarkanika National Park
- After two days of mass nesting at Gahirmatha, Olive Ridley turtles started arriving at the island from Gokharkuda to Podampeta in Rushikulya.
- Odisha witnessed a rare phenomenon of mass nesting, simultaneously in two places - Gahiramatha & Rushikulya.
- Gahirmatha beach is considered the world's largest nesting ground for endangered species.

Mass Nesting of Olive Ridley Turtles

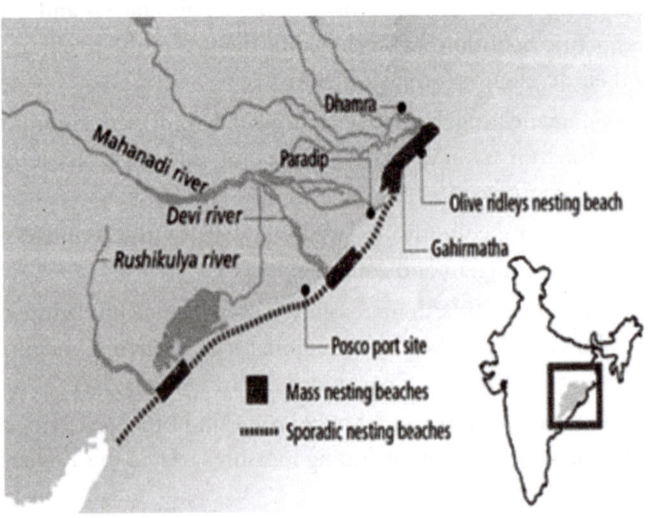

- Gahirmatha is the world's largest rookery for the endangered Olive Ridley sea turtles.
- Both Nasi-I and Nasi-II beaches are under the jurisdiction of the Defence Research and Development Organisation, which conducts missile tests from the nearby Wheeler Island.
- The turtles settled in the Gahrimatha and Rushikulya rookeries in Odisha to lay their eggs in the sand.
- Every year, they travel from the Indian Ocean only after the temperature starts to get warmer.
- Gahirmatha was declared a marine sanctuary covering 1435 square kilometers from Dhamra mouth to Hukitola island in 1997 by the government.

Know about Olive Ridley Sea Turtle

- It is also known commonly as the Pacific ridley sea turtle
- It is a species of turtle in the family Cheloniidae.
- The species is the second-smallest and most abundant of all sea turtles found in the world.
- It is found in warm and tropical waters, primarily in the Pacific and Indian Oceans, but also in the warm waters of the Atlantic Ocean.
- This turtle and the related Kemp's ridley turtle are best known for their unique synchronised mass nestings called arribadas, where thousands of females come together on the same beach to lay eggs.

SEAWEED PARK

- The Centre would establish a seaweed park with special economic zone status in Tamil Nadu.
- The project will be the first of its kind in India and will come up under the PM Kisan Sampada Yojana.
- The Centre has plans to implement projects worth 20-thousand crore rupees, under the PM Kisan Sampada Yojana.
- Seaweed, or macroalgae, refers to thousands of species of macroscopic, multicellular, marine algae.

Seaweeds

- Seaweeds are primitive marine, non-flowering algae without roots, stems and leaves.
- Seaweeds are generally anchored to the sea bottom or other solid structures by rootlike "holdfasts," which perform the sole function of attachment and do not extract nutrients as do the roots of higher plants.
- Large seaweeds form dense underwater forests known as kelp forests, which act as underwater nurseries for fish, snails and sea urchins.
- Seaweeds are abundant along the Tamil Nadu and Gujarat coasts and around Lakshadweep and Andaman & Nicobar Islands.
- As part of the Budget 2021 speech, Nirmala said that a multipurpose seaweed park will be established in Tamil Nadu soon to promote seaweed farming and cultivation.

FIRST EVER NTCA MEETING OUTSIDE NATIONAL CAPITAL HELD AT ARUNACHAL PRADESH

- The 20th Meeting of National Tiger Conservation Authority (NTCA) was held in Pakke tiger reserve in Arunachal Pradesh under the chairmanship of Union Minister for Environment, Forest & Climate Change
- For the first time in history the NTCA meeting happened outside the national capital.

National Tiger Conservation Authority (NTCA) Meeting Highlights

The Minister released

1. Standard operating procedure(SOP) for tiger reintroduction and supplementation in wild
2. Forest fire audit protocol for tiger reserves
3. Technical manual on MEE of Tiger reserves in India prepared by NTCA.

SOP for tiger reintroduction and supplementation in wild

- The NTCA has prepared a Standard Operating Protocol (SOP) to deal with the reintroduction and supplementation.
- The SOP takes into account, the scientific knowledge available on the subject as well as conditions that may be typical to India.

Forest Fire Audit Protocol for Tiger Reserves

- Forest Fires play a crucial role in maintaining the dynamics of forest.
- Fire can play a vital role in healthy forests, recycling nutrients, helping tree species regenerate, removing invasive weeds and pathogens and maintaining habitat for some wildlife.
- However, as populations and demands on forest resources have grown, cycle of fire has spun out of the balance and these uncontrolled and repeated fires at short succession are one of the major causes behind forest degradation and biodiversity loss.
- In order to help the tiger reserve managers assess their fire preparedness and manage complete life cycle of forest fires, the NTCA has prepared a Forest Fire Audit Protocol for Tiger Reserves and is now being released.

Management Effectiveness Evaluation (MEE) of Tiger Reserves in India

- India is amongst the selected countries in the world that have institutionalized the MEE Process.
- The globally accepted framework of Management Effectiveness Evaluation (MEE) of tiger reserves has paved way for successfully assessing the tiger conservation efforts in the country.
- The MEE exercise in tiger reserves was initiated in 2006 and four cycle has been completed.
- Since then a lot of experience has been gained and need was felt revisit and review the whole process.

- Accordingly, a committee was constituted by the National Tiger Conservation Authority to revisit and review the MEE criteria for the 5th cycle of MEE exercise starting 2022.
- Based on the suggestions made by the committee, the technical manual on Management Effectiveness Evaluation (MEE) of Tiger Reserves in India is being released by NTCA.

The National Tiger Conservation Authority (NTCA)

- NTCA was established in December 2005, following a recommendation of the Tiger Task Force, constituted by the Prime Minister of India for reorganised management of Project Tiger and the many Tiger Reserves in India.
- The Wildlife Protection Act of 1972 was amended in 2006 to provide for constituting the National Tiger Conservation Authority responsible for implementation of the Project Tiger plan to protect endangered tigers.
- The National Tiger Conservation Authority is set up under the Chairmanship of the Minister for Environment and Forests.
- NTCA has been constituted under section 38 L (1) of Wildlife (Protection) Act, 1972.
- The authority consists of the Minister in charge of the Ministry of Environment and Forests (as Chairperson), the Minister of State in the Ministry of Environment and Forests (as Vice-Chairperson), three members of Parliament, Secretary, Ministry of Environment and Forests and other members.
- The authority derives its power from section 38 O (1) of WLPA, 1972 and functions under the guidance of Chairperson, Vice-Chairperson and members.
- A programme for protection called, 'Tiger Protection Program' (popularly known as Project Tiger) was started in 1973, by the Government of India in co-operation with WWF.

UNITED NATIONS CONVENTION TO COMBAT DESERTIFICATION (UNCCD)

Union Minister for Environment, delivered National Statement at the 15th Session of the Conference of Parties (COP) of United Nations Convention to Combat Desertification (UNCCD) in Cote d'Ivoire.

UNCCD Highlights

- The fifteenth session of the Conference of the Parties (COP15) of the United Nations Convention to Combat Desertification (UNCCD) is being held in Abidjan, Côte d'Ivoire, from 9 to 20 May 2022.
- The COP15 theme, 'Land. Life. Legacy: From scarcity to prosperity', is a call to action to ensure land, the lifeline on this planet, continues to benefit present and future generations.
- Several global developments indicate support to the objectives of UNCCD, such as the launch of the UN Decade on Ecosystem Restoration (2021-2030) that aims at halting and reversing ecosystem degradation and loss.

- The importance placed on increasing area, connectivity and integrity of natural ecosystems is visible in the post-2020 Global Biodiversity Framework.
- For the first time, an Intergovernmental Working Group (IWG) on effective policy and implementation measures for addressing drought under the United Nations Convention for Combating Desertification (UNCCD) was established by decision 23/COP.14. India held the 14th COP in Delhi in 2019.

20TH LIVESTOCK CENSUS

- Union Minister of Fisheries, Animal Husbandry and Dairying Shri Parshottam Rupala released the Breed-Wise Report Of Livestock And Poultry based on 20th Livestock Census
- The breed-wise data collection was done along with 20th Livestock Census during the year 2019.
- It was for the first time in the country that breed wise data was collected by using tablet computers instead of paper mode which is indeed a unique attempt.
- The livestock as well as poultry birds were counted according to their breeds as recognized by National Bureau of Animal Genetic Resources (NBAGR).

Highlights of Breed-wise Report of Livestock and Poultry

- The report has covered 184 recognized indigenous/exotic & crossbred breeds of 19 selected species that are registered by the NBAGR (National Bureau of Animal Genetic Resources).
- There are 41 recognized indigenous whereas 4 exotic/crossbred breeds of cattle covered in this report.
- As per the report, the Exotic and Crossbred animal contribute nearly 26.5% of the total cattle population whereas 73.5% are Indigenous and Non-descript cattle.
- Crossbred Jersey has the highest share with 49.3% as compared to 39.3% of Crossbred Holstein Friesian (HF) in total Exotic/Crossbred cattle.
- Gir, Lakhimi and Sahiwal breeds have major contribution in total Indigenous Cattle.
- In Buffalo, the Murrah breed majorly contributes with 42.8% which is commonly found in UP and Rajasthan.
- In Sheep, there are 3 exotics and 26 indigenous breeds were found in the country. Among the pure exotic breeds, Corriedale breed majorly contributes with 17.3% and in the indigenous breeds the Nellore breed contribute the highest in the category with 20.0% share.
- In Goats, there are 28 indigenous breeds found in the country. The Black Bengal breed contributes the highest with 18.6%.
- In exotic/crossbred pigs, crossbred pig contributes 86.6% whereas Yorkshire contributes majorly with 8.4%. In indigenous pigs, Doom breed major contributes with 3.9%.
- In Horse & Ponies, the share of Marwari breed majorly contributes with 9.8%.
- In Donkeys, the share of Spiti breed contributes with 8.3%.

- In Camel, Bikaneri breed majorly contributes with 29.6%.
- In Poultry, desi fowl, Aseel breed majorly contribute in both backyard poultry and commercial poultry farm.

HIMALAYAN BIRD COUNT (HBC)

- As part of a global effort, scientists and birdwatchers in the Himalayan regions of India, Nepal and Bhutan came together and documented as many birds of the mountain range as possible.
- Uttarakhand reported the highest number of bird species, at 293, while the highest number of checklists (lists of birds seen and heard by birdwatchers), at 192, was uploaded from Jammu & Kashmir, according to the primary report from birdwatchers in the Himalayan regions of India, Nepal and Bhutan.
- Birdwatchers from Ladakh, Jammu and Kashmir, Himachal Pradesh, Uttarakhand, North Bengal, Sikkim, Arunachal Pradesh, as well as Nepal and Bhutan, took part in the initiative
- From the westernmost Ladakh to the easternmost Arunachal Pradesh, this is the first edition of the Himalayan Bird Count (HBC) which aims to celebrate the incredible bird diversity and bring attention to the threatened habitats of the region.
- The event is organised by Bird Count India, Bird Conservation Nepal and Bhutan's Royal Society for Protection of Nature working together to bring the Himalayan birding fraternity together for a common good.
- The organisations have collectively decided to do this event on "Endemic Bird Day" to spread awareness about Himalaya's bird biodiversity.
- The exercise was undertaken on May 14 and a total of 607 species were documented in just one day.
- A checklist includes birds seen and heard.
- Bird Count India is an informal partnership of organisations and groups interested in documenting and monitoring India's birds.
- The initiative encourages birdwatchers to upload their bird lists to eBird a global platform for bird observations.

RAMGARH VISHDHARI WILDLIFE SANCTUARY

- Ramgarh Vishdhari Wildlife Sanctuary was notified as a tiger reserve May 16, 2022, after a nod by the Union Ministry of Environment, Forest and Climate Change (MoEF&CC) in July 2021.
- It is now India's 52nd tiger reserve and Rajasthan's fourth, after Ranthambore, Sariska and Mukundra.
- There were an estimated 2,967 tigers in India in 2019, according to the National Tiger Conservation Authority.
- The newly notified tiger reserve includes the tiger habitat between Ranthambore Tiger Reserve in the northeast and Mukundra Hills Tiger Reserve on the southern side and facilitates dispersal of tigers from Ranthambore Tiger Reserve.

PURPLE REVOLUTION

- Centre's Aroma Mission, ably supported by CSIR, is changing the mind-set of farmers and more and more of them are taking up the cultivation of aroma crops like lavender, lemon grass, rose and marigold for extracting costly oils to be used in many industries.
- Purple Revolution has shifted focus to Agri-tech StartUps.
- Due to high monetary returns, farmers in hilly areas of Jammu and Kashmir are switching from traditional farming to aroma crops like lavender

Know about the Aroma Mission

- Aroma crops are both drought and pest resistant, and CSIR is providing all kind of technical support for promoting this Agri Start-up boon in the UT.
- CSIR is also planning to introduce the aroma crops in other hilly States with similar climatic conditions like Uttarakhand, Himachal Pradesh and in North-Eastern States.
- IIIM Jammu was helping the Start-ups in aroma and lavender farming to sell their produce.
- Last month the Ministry of Science and Technology inaugurated the country's first 'Lavender Festival' at Bhaderwah, the birthplace of India's Purple Revolution
- Aroma Mission is attracting Start-ups and agriculturists from across the country, and during Phase-I, CSIR helped cultivation on 6,000 hectares of land and covered 46 Aspirational districts across the country.
- In the second Phase of Aroma Mission, it is proposed to engage over 45,000 skilled human resources with the aim of benefitting more than 75,000 farming families across the country.
- CSIR-IIIM introduced lavender to farmers in Doda, Ramban, Kishtwar, Kathua, Udhampur, Rajouri, Pulwama, Anantnag, Kupwara and Bandipora districts of J&K.
- Lavender cultivation has employed about 5,000 farmers and young entrepreneurs in geographically remote areas of J&K.

STEPS TO PROMOTE RENEWABLE ENERGY IN THE COUNTRY

Steps to Promote Renewable Energy, Including Wind Energy, in the Country

- Permitting Foreign Direct Investment (FDI) up to 100 percent under the automatic route,
- Waiver of Inter State Transmission System (ISTS) charges for inter-state sale of solar and wind power for projects to be commissioned by 30th June 2025,
- Declaration of trajectory for Renewable Purchase Obligation (RPO) up to the year 2022
- Setting up of Ultra Mega Renewable Energy Parks to provide land and transmission to RE developers on a plug and play basis,
- Laying of new transmission lines and creating new sub-station capacity for evacuation of renewable power,

- Setting up of Project Development Cell for attracting and facilitating investments,
- Standard Bidding Guidelines for tariff based competitive bidding process for procurement of Power from Grid Connected Solar PV and Wind Projects.
- Government has issued orders that power shall be dispatched against Letter of Credit (LC) or advance payment to ensure timely payment by distribution licensees to RE generators.
- Conducting skill development programmes to create a pool of skilled manpower for implementation, operation and maintenance of RE projects.

INDIAN VIRTUAL HERBARIUM (IVH)

- With details of about one lakh plant specimens, IVH is the biggest virtual database of flora in the country
- Herbarium specimens are considered important tools for plant taxonomy, conservation, habitat loss and even climate change
- Prime Minister has recently described Indian Virtual Herbarium as an example of how digital tools can help us connect to our roots.
- Herbarium was an interesting collection of plants and preserved parts of plants.
- Developed by scientists of the Botanical Survey of India (BSI), the herbarium was inaugurated by Union Minister of Environment Forest and Climate in Kolkata on July 1. Since then, the portal ivh.bsi.gov.in has had nearly two lakh hits from 55 countries.
- Each record in the digital herbarium includes an image of the preserved plant specimen, scientific name, collection locality, and collection date, collector name, and barcode number.
- The digital herbarium includes features to extract the data State-wise, and users can search plants of their own States, which will help them identify regional plants and in building regional checklists.

PROJECT CHEETAH TO RE-ESTABLISH THE SPECIES IN ITS HISTORICAL RANGE IN INDIA

- The eight African Cheetahs set to travel from Namibia to Madhya Pradesh's Kuno Palpur sanctuary over the next few days have undergone preliminary health examinations .
- Cheetahs will be brought either to Jaipur or Gwalior airport by a chartered flight from Namibia around August 25. They will then be transported to Kuno by helicopter,
- Ministry involved - Ministry of Environment, Forest and Climate Change (MoEFCC)
- Aim - to introduce cheetahs in India.
- Why - India lost the species – Achinonyx jubatus – more than half a century ago.
- Reason - Hunters shot down the last of the big cats in India in 1952.
- Present status - cheetahs roam wild only in some parts of Africa and Iran.

African Cheetah Introduction Project in India

- Jan 2022 - The government released the 'Action Plan for Introduction of Cheetah in India'.
- As India will import 12-14 wild cheetahs from Africa (Namibia or South Africa)
- Introduce them in the Kuno-Palpur National Park in Madhya Pradesh.
- July 2022 - India and Namibia signed MoU, for establishing the cheetah into the historical range in India".
- August 2022 - IOC signed an MoU with the National Tiger Conservation Authority (NTCA)
- Indian Oil will be contributing Rs.50.22 crore in 4 years for the project components viz. Cheetah Introduction, its Habitat Management & Protection, Eco Development, Staff Training and Veterinary Healthcare
- The IOC will contribute the funds to the NTCA, which is the nodal agency authorised by the MoEFCC for funding, supervision and hand holding of Project Cheetah.
- Indian Oil to support "Project Cheetah" under CSR
- The cheetahs that are arriving are not Asiatic cheetahs but African cheetahs
- Asiatic cheetahs that went extinct in India

75 RAMSAR SITES IN 75TH YEAR OF INDEPENDENCE

- India adds 11 more wetlands to the list of Ramsar sites to make total 75 Ramsar sites covering an area of 13,26,677 ha in the country in the 75th year of Independence.
- The 11 new sites include: Four (4) sites in Tamil Nadu, Three (3) in Odisha, Two (2) in Jammu & Kashmir and One (1) each in Madhya Pradesh and Maharashtra. Designation of these sites would help in conservation and management of wetlands and wise use of their resources.
- India is one of the Contracting Parties to Ramsar Convention, signed in Ramsar, Iran, in 1971. India signed it on 1st Feb 1982.
- During 1982 to 2013, a total of 26 sites were added to the list of Ramsar sites, however, during 2014 to 2022, the country has added 49 new wetlands to the list of Ramsar sites.
- During this year itself (2022) a total of 28 sites have been declared as Ramsar sites.
- Based on the date of designation mentioned on Ramsar Certificate, the number is 19 for this year (2022) and 14 for previous year (2021).
- Tamil Nadu has maximum no. of Ramsar sites (14 nos), followed by UP which has 10 nos. of Ramsar sites.

Know about the New Ramsar Sites (added in 2022)

1. Tampara Lake - Odisha (Ganjam district)
2. Hirakud Reservoir -Odisha
3. Ansupa Lake - Odisha (Cuttack district)
4. Yashwant Sagar - Madhya Pradesh.

5. Chitrangudi Bird Sanctuary - Tamil Nadu.
6. Suchindram Theroor Wetland Complex- Tamil Nadu
7. Vaduvur Bird Sanctuary - Tamil Nadu
8. Kanjirankulam Bird Sanctuary - Tamil Nadu
9. Thane Creek - Maharashtra
10. Hygam Wetland Conservation Reserve - River Jhelum basin
11. Shallbugh Wetland Conservation Reserve - District Srinagar, UT of J&K.
12. Koonthankulam Bird Sanctuary - Tamil Nadu
13. Satkosia - Odisha.
14. Nanda Lake
15. Gulf of Mannar Biosphere Reserve -southeastern coastline
16. Ranganthittu bird sanctuary – Karnataka
17. Vembannur wetland - Tamil Nadu
18. Vellode Bird Sanctuary - Tamil Nadu
19. Sirpur wetland - Indore
20. Vedanthangal wetland - Tamil Nadu.
21. Udhayamarthandapuram Bird Sanctuary - Tamil Nadu

INDIA'S NEW CLIMATE ACTION GOALS

- India will achieve net-zero emissions latest by 2070.
- By 2030, India will ensure 50% of its energy will be sourced from renewable sources.
- India plans to generate 500 GW of renewable energy by 2030. This marks a 50 GW increase from its current target of 450 GW.
- India also committed to reducing its carbon emissions until 2030 by a billion tonnes.
- By 2030, India will reduce the carbon intensity of its economy to less than 45 per cent.
- India is largely on track to meet, and even exceed, its Paris Agreement targets: reduce emissions' intensity of its gross domestic product (GDP) by 33 to 35 percent from 2005 levels by 2030.

India's GHG Emission

- India is the third-largest emitter of GHGs in the world. India accounts for about 7% of today's global emissions.
- However, India has extremely low per-capita emissions that are far below the global average.

Sixth Assessment Report (AR6)

- The Sixth Assessment Report (AR6) had emphasised that to keep the temperature rising within 1.5°C, global emissions should be reduced by 45% from 2010 levels by 2030, on the way to net-zero 2050.

- However many high-emitter countries are short of the emissions reductions required by 2030 to restrict global temperature rise to well below 2°C or even the goal of 1.5°C above pre-industrial levels.

INTERNATIONAL SOLAR ALLIANCE (ISA)

- It is an action-oriented, member-driven, collaborative platform for increased deployment of solar energy technologies.
- Its basic motive is to facilitate energy access, ensure energy security, and drive energy transition in its member countries.
- The ISA was conceived as a joint effort by India and France to mobilize efforts against climate change through deployment of solar energy solutions.
- The Headquarters is in India with its Interim Secretariat being set up in Gurugram.
- A total of 106 countries have signed the ISA Framework Agreement.
- Out of 106 nations, 86 have signed and ratified the ISA Framework Agreement.
- All member states of the United Nations are eligible to join the ISA.
- The United Nations General Assembly (UNGA) has granted Observer Status to the International Solar Alliance (ISA).
- The ISA seeks to develop and deploy cost-effective and transformational solar energy solutions.
- To help member countries develop low-carbon growth trajectories, with particular focus on delivering impact in countries categorized as Least Developed Countries (LDCs) and the Small Island Developing States (SIDS).
- India and France launched the International Solar Alliance (ISA) to boost solar energy in developing countries.
- It was launched at the United Nations Climate Change Conference in Paris in November 2015 by the Indian Prime Minister and French President. Its secretariat is located in Gurugram, India. Hence, statement 1 is correct.
- At initial stage ISA was opened to membership of countries lying fully or partly between the Tropics of Cancer and Capricorn (torrid zone).
- In 2018, the membership of ISA was opened for all the UN members. However, all the member countries of the UN are not its members. Hence, statement 2 is not correct.
- Currently, 80 countries have signed and ratified the ISA Framework Agreement while 98 countries have signed the ISA Framework Agreement.

One Sun One World One Grid (OSOWOG)

- The new Global Green Grids Initiative One Sun One World One Grid (GGI-OSOWOG) has been announced at COP26.
- The new GGI-OSOWOG is an evolution of the International Solar Alliance's OSOWOG multilateral drive to foster interconnected solar energy infrastructure at a global scale.

- This initiative aims to tap solar energy and have it travel seamlessly across borders.
- The initiative will work towards accelerating the making of large solar power stations and wind farms in the best locations, linked together by continental-scale grids crossing national borders.
- Over 80 countries have endorsed the One Sun Declaration.
- This initiative will bring together an international coalition of national governments, financial organizations, and power system operators.
- It has been taken up under the technical assistance program of the World Bank.

CHANGTHANG WILDLIFE SANCTUARY

- In a unique and first-of-its-kind initiative, the Department of Science and Technology (DST) has undertaken to set up India's first-ever Night Sky Sanctuary in Ladakh.
- The proposed Dark Sky Reserve will be located at Hanle in Ladakh as a part of Changthang Wildlife Sanctuary.
- It will boost Astro tourism in India and will be one of the world's highest-located sites for optical, infrared, and gamma-ray telescopes.

LIST OF WORLD HERITAGE SITES IN INDIA IDENTIFIED BY UNESCO

A UNESCO World Heritage Site can be any place such as a forest, lake, building, island, mountain, monument, desert, complex or a city; which has a special physical or cultural significance.

Currently, there are 1092 World Heritage sites in the world. However 38 World Heritage Properties are in India out of which 30 are Cultural Properties and 7 are Natural Properties and one is named as mixed

Year wise Nomination of World Heritage Sites in India

1983

1. Agra fort (Uttar Pradesh)
2. Ajanta caves (Maharashtra)
3. Ellora caves (Maharashtra)
4. The Taj Mahal (Uttar Pradesh)

1984

5. Group of Monuments at Mahabalipuram
6. Sun Temple Konark (Odisha)

1985

7. Kaziranga National Park (Assam)
8. Keoladeo National Park (Rajasthan)
9. Manas Wildlife Sanctuary (Assam)

1986

10. Churches and Convents of Goa
11. Fatehpur Sikhri (Uttar Pradesh)
12. Group of Monuments at Hampi (Karnataka)
13. Khajuraho Group of Monuments (Madhya Pradesh)

1987

14. Elephanta Caves (Mumbai)
15. Great Living Chola Temples
16. Group of Monuments at Pattadakal (Karnataka)
17. Sundarban National Park (West Bengal)

1988

18. Nanda Devi National Park (Uttarakhand)

1989

19. Buddhist monuments at Sanchi (Madhya Pradesh)

1993

20. Humayun's Tomb, Delhi
21. Qutb Minar and its monuments, Delhi

1999

22. Mountain Railways of India

    The Mountain Railway of India consists of three railways: the Darjeeling Himalayan Railway located in the foothills of the Himalayas in West Bengal (Northeast India)the Nilgiri Mountain Railways located in the Nilgiri Hills of Tamil Nadu (South India) and the Kalka Shimla Railway located in the Himalayan foothills of Himachal Pradesh (Northwest India)

2001

23. Mahabodhi Temple Complex at Bodh Gaya (Bihar)

2003

24. Rock Shelters of Bhimbetka (Madhya Pradesh)

2004

25. Champaner-Pavagadh Archaeological Park (Gujarat)
26. Chhatrapati Shivaji Terminus (formerly Victoria Terminus) (Mumbai Maharashtra)

2007

27. The Red Fort Complex (Delhi)

2010

28. The Jantar Mantar, Jaipur (Rajasthan)
29. Western Ghats

2013

30. Hill forts of Rajasthan

    This includes six majestic forts in Chittorgarh; Kumbhalgarh; Sawai Madhopur; Jhalawar; Jaipur, and Jaisalmer.

2014

31. Rani-ki-Van (the Queen's Stepwell) at Patan, Gujarat
32. The Great Himalayan National Park (GHNP) (Himachal Pradesh)

2016

33. The architectural work of Le Corbusier, an outstanding contribution to the Modern Movement
34. Khangchendzonga National Park (Sikkim)
35. Archaeological site of Nalanda Mahavihara at Nalanda, Bihar

2017

36. Historic city of Ahmadabad (Gujarat)

2018

37. Victorian Gothic and art deco ensembles of Mumbai

2019

38. Jaipur (Rajasthan)

2021

39. Dholavira (Gujarat)

2022

40. Kakatiya Rudreshwar/Ramappa temple (Telangana)

INDIA'S DEEP OCEAN MISSION

India's ambitious 'Deep Ocean Mission' is all set to be launched this year under the Ministry of Earth Sciences. The Ministry has announced on July 27 that the Rs. 8,000-crore plan to explore deep ocean minerals will start from October. One of the main aims of the mission is to explore and extract polymetallic nodules. These are small potato-like rounded accretions composed of minerals such as manganese, nickel, cobalt, copper and iron hydroxide. They lie scattered on the Indian Ocean floor at depths of about 6,000 m and the size can vary from a few millimetres to centimetres. These metals can be extracted and used in electronic devices, smartphones, batteries and even for solar panels. The International Seabed Authority (ISA), an autonomous international organisation established under the 1982 United Nations Convention on the Law of the Sea, allots the 'area' for deep-sea mining. India was the first country to receive the status of a 'Pioneer Investor ' in 1987 and was given an area of about 1.5 lakh sq km in the Central Indian Ocean Basin (CIOB) for nodule exploration.

India has entered into 15-year contracts for exploration for polymetallic nodules, polymetallic sulphides and cobalt-rich ferromanganese crusts in the deep seabed with 29 contractors. Later it was extended for five more years till 2022. China, France, Germany, Japan, South Korea, Russia and also some small islands such as the Cook Islands, Kiribati have joined the race for deep sea mining. Most of the countries have tested their technologies in shallow waters and are yet to start deep-sea extraction.

ENVIRONMENT MINISTRY NOTIFIES NEW WETLAND RULES

The Union Environment Ministry notified the new Wetland (Conservation and Management) Rules 2017 which prohibit a range of activities in wetlands like setting up and expansion of industries, waste dumping and discharge of effluents.The new rules will replace the 2010 version of the rules. Wetlands can be defined as lands transitional between terrestrial and aquatic eco-systems where the water table is usually at or near the surface or the land is covered by shallow water.

They support rich biodiversity and provide wide range of ecosystem services such as water storage, water purification, flood mitigation, erosion control, aquifer recharge and others. There are at least 115 wetlands that are officially identified by the central government and of those 27 are identified as wetlands of international importance under Ramsar Convention which is an international intergovernmental treaty for conservation of wetlands. India is a party to the treaty.

The new rules stipulate setting up of a State Wetlands Authority in each State and union territories that will be headed by the State's environment minister and include a range of government officials.

These authorities will need to develop a comprehensive list of activities to be regulated and permitted within the notified wetlands and their zone of influence.

The State authorities will also need to prepare a list of all wetlands of the State or union territory within three months, a list of wetlands to be notified within six months, a comprehensive digital inventory of all wetlands within one year which will be updated every ten years.

To oversee the work carried out by States, the rules stipulates for setting up of **National Wetlands Committee,** which will be headed by the MoEFCC Secretary, to monitor implementation of these rules.

The Committee will also advise the Central Government on appropriate policies and action programmes for conservation and wise use of wetlands, recommend designation of wetlands of international importance under Ramsar Convention, advise on collaboration with international agencies on issues related to wetlands etc.

BONN CONVENTION

Migratory species are those animals that move from one habitat to another during different times of the year, due to various factors such as food, sunlight, temperature, climate etc. In order to protect the migratory species throughout the range countries, a Convention on Conservation of Migratory Species (CMS) has been in force, under UNEP and also known as Bonn Convention. Bonn convention is a global platform for the conservation and sustainable use of migratory animals and their habitats. It brings together the States through which migratory animals pass, the Range States and lays the legal foundation for internationally coordinated conservation measures.

India also signed non legally binding MoU with CMS on the conservation and management of Siberian cranes, marine turtles, dugongs and raptors. India is temporary home to several migratory animals and birds. They include amur falcons, bar headed geese, Black necked cranes, Marine turtles, Dugongs, Humpbacked Whales, etc.

INDIA IS HOME TO 1,256 SPECIES OF ORCHID, SAYS FIRST COMPREHENSIVE SURVEY

The Botanical Survey of India has come up with the first comprehensive census of orchids of India putting the total number of orchid species or taxa to 1,256.

The 1,256 species or taxa of orchids belong to 155 genera and 388 species are endemic to India.

Orchids can be broadly categorised into three life forms: epiphytic (plants growing on another plants including those growing on rock boulders and often termed lithophyte), terrestrial (plants growing on land and climbers) and mycoheterotrophic (plants which derive nutrients from mycorrhizal fungi that are attached to the roots of a vascular plant). About 60% of all orchids found in the country, which is 757 species, are epiphytic, 447 are terrestrial and 43 are mycoheterotrophic.

A State-wise distribution of orchid species point out that the Himalayas, North-East parts of the country and Western Ghats are the hot-spots of the beautiful plant species.

The highest number of orchid species is recorded from Arunachal Pradesh with 612 species, followed by Sikkim 560 species and West Bengal; Darjeeling Himalayas have also high species concentration, with 479 species.

While north-east India rank at the top in species concentration, the Western Ghats have high endemism of orchids.

The entire orchid family is listed under appendix II of CITES (Convention on International Trade in Endangered Species of Wild Fauna and Flora) and hence any trade of wild orchid is banned globally.

SPECIAL RHINO PROTECTION FORCE (SRPF)

The SRPF is basically a tiger protection force named after the rhino since the threat of poaching is more for the one-horned herbivore. Their job profile includes protecting the striped cat since Kaziranga is also a tiger reserve.

The Assam government would be paying the salaries of the SRPF members and the amount would be reimbursed by the National Tiger Conservation Authority, which recommended setting up of the special force.

The 430 sq.km. KNP (Kaziranga National Park) encompasses eight ranges under two wildlife divisions — Eastern Assam and Biswanath — straddling the river Brahmaputra.

Kaziranga National Park is located in Golaghat and Nagaon districts of Assam. In 1968 it was given National Park status and in 1985 it was declared UNESCO World Heritage Site (WHS) for its unique natural environment.

It is home to world's largest population of One Horned Rhinoceros i.e. about 68%.

The one horned rhinoceroses are listed as vulnerable on IUCN Red list of Threatened Species.

It is also recognized as an Important Bird Area (IBA) by Birdlife International for conservation of avifaunal species.

FOREST SURVEY REPORT (FSR) 2021

- Minister for Environment, Forest and Climate Change released the 'India State of Forest Report 2021' prepared by the Forest Survey of India (FSI) which has been mandated to assess the forest and tree resources of the country.
- The ISFR-2021 provides information on forest cover, tree cover, mangrove cover, growing stock, carbon stock in India's forests, forest fire monitoring, forest cover in tiger reserve areas, above ground estimates of biomass using SAR data & climate change hotspots in Indian forests.

ISFR-2021 – Major Findings

- The total forest and tree cover of the country is 80.9 million hectare which is 24.62 percent of the geographical area of the country. As compared to the assessment of 2019, there is an increase of 2,261 sq km in the total forest and tree cover of the country.
- Out of this, the increase in the forest cover has been observed as 1,540 sq km and that in tree cover is 721 sq km.
- Increase in forest cover has been observed in open forest followed by very dense forest. Top three states showing increase in forest cover are Andhra Pradesh (647 sq km) followed by Telangana (632 sq km) and Odisha (537 sq km).
- Area-wise Madhya Pradesh has the largest forest cover in the country followed by Arunachal Pradesh, Chhattisgarh, Odisha and Maharashtra. In terms of forest cover as percentage of total geographical area, the top five States are Mizoram (84.53%), Arunachal Pradesh (79.33%), Meghalaya (76.00%), Manipur (74.34%) and Nagaland (73.90%).
- 17 states/UT's have above 33 percent of the geographical area under forest cover.
- Out of these states and UT's, five states/UTs namely Lakshadweep, Mizoram, Andaman & Nicobar Islands, Arunachal Pradesh and Meghalaya have more than 75 percent forest cover while 12 states/ UTs namely Manipur, Nagaland, Tripura, Goa, Kerala, Sikkim, Uttarakhand, Chhattisgarh, Dadra & Nagar Haveli and Daman & Diu, Assam, Odisha, have forest cover between 33 percent to 75 percent.
- Total mangrove cover in the country is 4,992 sq km. An increase of 17 sq Km in mangrove cover has been observed as compared to the previous assessment of 2019.
- Top three states showing mangrove cover increase are Odisha (8 sq km) followed by Maharashtra (4 sq km) and Karnataka (3 sq km).
- Total carbon stock in country's forest is estimated to be 7,204 million tonnes and there an increase of 79.4 million tonnes in the carbon stock of country as compared to the last assessment of 2019.

Know the Methodology

- FSI has adopted using the vector boundary layers of various administrative units upto districts level as provided by Survey of India along in order to ensure comprehensive compatibility with the geographical areas as reported in Census, 2011.
- The biennial assessment of forest cover of the country using mid-resolution satellite data is based on interpretation of LISS-III data from Indian Remote Sensing satellite data (Resourcesat-II) to monitor forest cover and forest cover changes at District, State and National level.
- This information provides inputs for various global level inventories, reports such as GHG Inventory, Growing Stock, Carbon Stock, Forest Reference Level (FRL) and international reporting to UNFCCC targets under CBD Global Forest Resource Assessment (GFRA) for planning and scientific management of forests.
- The accuracy level achieved in the current assessment is the significantly high. The accuracy of forest cover classification has been assessed 92.99%. The accuracy of classification between forest and non-forest classes has been assessed 95.79% against internationally accepted accuracy of classification of more than 85%.

Other Significant Features of ISFC 2021

- In the present ISFR 2021, FSI has included a new chapter related to the assessment of forest cover in the Tiger Reserves, Corridors and Lion conservation area of India.
- In this context, the decadal assessment of change in forest cover within Tiger Reserves, Corridors and Lion conservation area helps in assessing the impact of conservation measures and management interventions that have been implemented over the years.
- For decadal assessment, change in forest cover, during the period between ISFR 2011 (data period 2008 to 2009) and the current cycle (ISFR 2021, data period 2019-2020) within each Tiger Reserves has been analysed.
- A new initiative of FSI has also been documented in the form of a chapter, where the 'Above Ground Biomass' has been estimated.
- FSI, in collaboration with Space Application Centre (SAC), ISRO, Ahmedabad, initiated a special study for estimation of Above Ground Biomass (AGB) at pan-India level, using L- band of Synthetic Aperture Radar (SAR) data.
- The results for the States of Assam and Odisha (as well as AGB maps), were presented earlier in ISFR 2019.
- The interim results for AGB estimates (and AGB maps) for the entire country are being presented as a new chapter in ISFR 2021. The detailed report will be published after completion of the study.
- FSI in collaboration of with Birla Institute of Technology & Science (BITS) Pilani, Goa Campus has performed a study based on 'Mapping of Climate Change Hotspots in Indian Forests'.
- The collaborative study was carried out with the objective to map the climatic hotspots over the forest cover in India, using computer model-based projection of temperature and rainfall data, for the three future time periods i.e. year 2030, 2050 and 2085.

ALL INDIA TIGER ESTIMATION 2018

The report, *Status of Tigers Co-predators & Prey in India, 2018*, released by Prime Minister Narendra Modi, shows that the number of tigers in the country have increased to 2,967 (range: 2,603-3,346) in 2018 from 2,226 (range: 1,945-2,491) in 2014.

As per the latest census the population of the tiger has increased to 2,967. "In five years, the number of protected areas increased from 692 to over 860, community reserves from 43 to over 100

This is a 33 per cent increase over the 2014 census. With this, India has achieved the target set in 2010 St Petersburg Declaration of doubling tiger population by 2022.

St. Petersburg Declaration

29 July is celebrated across the world as Global Tiger Day to create awareness about tiger conservation and protection of natural habitat of tigers.

This day act as a reminder of agreement signed by countries at Saint Petersburg Tiger Summit in Russia in 2010, to raise awareness about decline of global tiger population.

Signatories declared an agreement that governments of tiger-populated countries would double animal's population by 2022.

14TH RHINO CENSUS 2022

In Kaziranga National Park Assam

- The population of the Greater One-horned or Indian Rhinoceros in the Kaziranga National Park and Tiger Reserve has been estimated at 2,613 which is 200 more than the number recorded in 2018.
- Of the rhinos estimated, 1,823 were adults, 365 were subadults, 279 juveniles and 146 calves. The females outnumbered the males by 183.
- This was the first time drones were used to survey the animals in three compartments of the park.

In Orang National Park Assam

- It recorded an increase of 24 rhinos over the figure of 101 in 2018.

In Pobitora Wildlife Sanctuary Assam

- It recorded five more rhinos than in 2018. Of the 107 rhinos counted, 50 were females, 30 males and 27 calves.

The census at Manas National Park and Orang National Park also completed . Assam has an estimated 2,645 rhinos in all. Manas National Park and Kaziranga National Park are two World Heritage Sites in Assam. Manas is also a tiger reserve.

The IUCN Status of

Greater One-Horned Rhinoceros — Vulnerable

Javan Rhinoceros — Critically Endangered

Sumatran Rhinoceros — Critically Endangered

GOVERNMENT LAUNCHES ASIATIC LION CONSERVATION PROJECT

The Ministry of Environment, Forest and Climate Change, launched the 'Asiatic Lion Conservation Project with an aim to protect and conserve the world's last ranging free population of Asiatic Lion and its associated ecosystem. The budget of the project for the next three years will be funded through a centrally sponsored scheme, the Development of Wildlife Habitat, with the contributing ratio of 60:40 for central and state share.

The Asiatic Lion Conservation Project will strengthen the ongoing measures for conservation and recovery of Asiatic Lion with the help of state-of-the-art techniques, regular scientific research studies, disease management, modern surveillance techniques. It will be supplemented with sufficient eco-development works ensuring a stable and viable lion population in India.

ASIAN WATER BIRD CENSUS

The Asian Waterbird Census (AWC) is an integral part of the global water bird monitoring programme, the International Waterbird Census (IWC), coordinated by Wetlands International.

Waterbirds are one of the key indicators of wetlands health. Wetlands provide feeding, resting, roosting and foraging habitats for these charismatic species. India coordinates bird-watching at Sultanpur Bird Sanctuary, Haryana, India. This year three new species- Greater flamingo, Grey-headed lapwing, and Blue-cheeked bee-eater were spotted.

Every January, thousands of volunteers across Asia and Australasia visit wetlands in their country and count waterbirds. In India, the AWC is annually coordinated by the Bombay Natural history Society (BNHS) and Wetlands International.

The AWC was initiated in 1987 in the Indian subcontinent and since has grown rapidly to cover major regions of Asia, from Afghanistan eastwards to Japan, Southeast Asia and Australasia. The census, thus covers the entire East Asian – Australasian Flyway and a large part of the Central Asian Flyway.

The Census has the Following Objectives:

- To obtain information on an annual basis of waterbird populations at wetlands in the region during the non-breeding period of most species (January), as a basis for evaluation of sites and monitoring of populations
- To monitor on an annual basis the status and condition of wetlands
- To encourage greater interest in waterbirds and wetlands amongst citizens
- Till date, more than 6,100 sites of 27 countries have been covered with active participation of thousands of volunteers.

DOLPHIN CENSUS 2022

WWF-India, in partnership with the Department of Forests and Wildlife Preservation, Punjab conducted the first ever organised Indus River Dolphin Survey across Beas river (Beas Conservation Reserve).

Gangetic dolphin census was conducted in Ganga, Gandhak and Ghagra rivers. The majority of population lives in the state of Bihar. Vikramshila Gangetic Dolphin sanctuary is its only sanctuary in Bihar.

- The population of dolphins in Odisha has increased from 544 in 2021 to 726 in 2022 revealed the annual dolphin census
- Gahirmatha is home to the State's largest population of dolphins, even more than Chilika.
- As per the 2022 dolphin census, Gahirmatha Marine Sanctuary and nearby areas in Bhitarkanika saw dolphin count skyrocket to 540 from 342 last year.
- These included 45 Irrawaddy, 135 bottlenose, 332 humpback, 13 striped and 15 spinner dolphins.
- However, the count of dolphins in Chilika Wildlife Division saw a dip from 188 in 2021 to 167 in 2022.

Indus Dolphin – Endangered

Irrawaddy Dolphin – Endangered

Gangetic Dolphin – Endangered

CROCODILE CENSUS 2022

The population of the saltwater or estuarine crocodile (*Crocodylus porosus*) has increased in the water bodies of Odisha's Bhitarkanika National Park and its nearby areas in Kendrapara district, with forest officials counting 1,784 crocodiles in this year's annual reptile census.Last year, they had sighted 1,742 crocodiles.

In 1975, the Union Ministry of Forest and Environment, in collaboration with the United Nations Development Programme, had started a crocodile breeding and rearing project in Dangamala within the Bhitarkanika Park.

The three species of crocodilians—saltwater, Mugger and Gharial— breeding programmes had been started in 1975 in 34 places in West Bengal, Madhya Pradesh, Uttar Pradesh, Bihar and other states in India and Nepal.

But the saltwater crocodile conservation programme in Bhitarkanika is the most successful one, as in 1975, Bhitarkanika was the home of only 96 crocodiles.

Breeds of Crocodiles

Mugger Crocodile(Vulnerable) – found in marshes

Gharial(Critically endangered) – freshwater

Saltwater crocodile(Least concern)

GOVERNMENT DECLARES 56,825 SQ KM AREA IN WESTERN GHATS AS ECO-SENSITIVE

The Environment Ministry has identified over 50,000 square kilometres, spread across six states in Western Ghats, as Ecologically Sensitive Area (ESA).

In exercise of the powers conferred by section 3 of the Environment (Protection) Act, 1986 (29 of 1986)...the Central Government hereby notifies the identified area of 56,825 square kilometres, spread across six states, namely, Gujarat, Maharashtra, Goa, Karnataka, Kerala and Tamil Nadu, as the Western Ghats Ecologically Sensitive Area," the draft notification said.

Earlier, following the recent Kerala floods, the National Green Tribunal (NGT) had restricted six states from giving environmental clearance for activities that could harm eco-sensitive areas.

In 2011, a committee headed by ecologist Madhav Gadgil, had recommended 64% of the area come under ESA, but it was dropped after protests from various states.

Another expert committee, in 2013 headed by former ISRO chairman K Kasturirangan had suggested that 37 per cent (60,000 hectares) of the Western Ghats should be declared as ESA. This too was not implemented.

The calls to declare the Western Ghats as ESA got louder after the Kerala floods. Many environmental experts including Gadgil had blamed it on the rampant destruction of the Western Ghats and the mindless construction and mining activities in ecological fragile areas in the state.

Western Ghats

Western Ghats, also known as Sahayadri which sprawls across six states over a distance of approximately 1,500 kilometres from Tapti river in the north to Kanyakumari in the south is considered a treasure trove of rare flora and fauna including 7,402 species of flowering plants, 1,814 species of non-flowering plants, 139 mammal species, 508 bird species, 179 amphibian species, 6,000 insects species and 290 freshwater fish species.

In 2012 it was listed as a UNESCO World Heritage Site and is one of the eight "hottest hot-spots" of biological diversity in the world.

COMPOSITE WATER MANAGEMENT INDEX (CWMI) – BY NITI AAYOG

India is suffering from the worst water crisis in its history, with about 60 crore people facing high to extreme water stress and about 2 lakh people dying every year due to inadequate access to safe water.

The report, titled 'Composite Water Management Index (CWMI)released by Minister for Water Resources, further said the crisis is only going to get worse. By 2030, the country's water demand to be twice the available supply, implying severe water scarcity for hundreds of millions of people and an eventual 6 per cent lose in country's GDP.

CWMI is an important tool to assess and improve the performance of states Union territories in efficient management of water resources.

CWMI has been developed by NITI Aayog comprising nine broad sectors with 28 indicators covering various aspects of ground water restoration of water bodies, irrigation, farm practices, drinking water policy and governance. For the purposes of analysis, the reporting states were divided into two groups.

(i) 'North Eastern and Himalayan states' and

(ii) 'Other States' - to account for the different hydrological conditions.

According to the report, Jharkhand, Haryana, Uttar Pradesh and Bihar are the worst performing states in water management.

DAM SAFETY ACT 2021

India has 5,264 large dams in the country while 437 dams are under construction. In addition to these dams, there are thousands of other small and medium dams in the country. Of the total large dams, 293 dams are more than 100 years old and 1,041 dams are more than 50 years old. In the absence of a proper legal framework, safety and maintenance of these large number of dams are a cause of concern. The dam Safety Act, 2021 provides for proper monitoring inspection, operation and maintenance of all specified dams in the country. Dam Safety Act 2021 provides for a national committee on dam safety and national dam safety authority. At present, both these authorities exist under the central water commission (CWC), however, they lack a legal mechanism to enforce their orders.

It will also create a national dam safety authority as a regulator to implement policy, guidelines, and standards for dam safety. It will maintain and publish data of all dams and resolve inter-state disputes. It will also fix the accountability of dam maintenance with penal provisions.

The Act will also create dam safety committees and dam safety organisations at state level with specialist officers.

The institutional framework for dam safety as provided under the dam safety act 2021 includes the following:

National Committee on Dam Safety (NCDS)

The Act provides for constitution of a National Committee on Dam Safety which shall evolve dam safety policies and recommend necessary regulations as may be required for the purpose.

National Dam Safety Authority (NDSA)

The Act provides for establishment of National Dam Safety Authority as a regulatory body which shall discharge functions to implement the policy, guidelines and standards for dam safety in the country.

State Committee on Dam Safety (SCDS)

The Act provides for constitution of a State Committee on Dam Safety by State Government.

It will ensure proper surveillance, inspection, operation and maintenance of all specified dams in that State and ensure their safe functioning.

It further provides that every State shall establish a "State Dam Safety Organisation", which will be manned by officers from the field dam safety preferably from the areas of dam-designs, hydro-mechanical engineering, hydrology, geo-technical investigation, instrumentation and dam-rehabilitation.

State Dam Safety Organization (SDSO)

The Bill provides that every state having specified number of dams will establish a State Dam Safety Organization which will be manned by officials with sufficient experience in the field of dam safety.

Other Duties and Functions

The Bill lays down that all specified dams will fall under jurisdiction of the SDSO of the State in which the dam is situated.

For specified dams owned by CPSUs or where a dam is extended in two or more states or where a dam owned by one state is situated in other state, NDSA shall be construed as SDSO.

BLUE FLAG BEACHES IN INDIA

1. Kovalam Beach, Tamil Nadu
2. Eden Beach, Puducherry
3. Golden Beach – Odisha
4. Shivrajpur Beach – Gujarat
5. Kappad Beach – Kerala
6. Ghoghla Beach – Diu
7. Radhanagar Beach – Andaman and Nicobar
8. Kasarkod Beach – Karnataka
9. Padubidri Beach – Karnataka
10. Rushikonda Beach – Andhra Pradesh
11. Kovalam Beach – Tamil Nadu
12. Eden Beach – Puducherry

About Blue Flag Certification

- The Blue Flag Certification is awarded by a non-profit organization called the Foundation for Environmental Education (FEE).
- The Blue Flag is an eco-label and blue flag beaches should provide clean and hygienic bathing water, along with basic infrastructure for tourists.

- Operators of beaches or boating tourism that have been awarded the 'blue flag' are allowed to display the blue flag logo.

About the Foundation for Environmental Education (FEE)

- The FEE is headquartered in Copenhagen, Denmark.
- It was founded in 1981 as the Foundation for Environmental Education in Europe (FEEE).
- Currently, it has 77 member countries.

Blue Flag Certification in India

- In June 2018 it was reported that Chandrabhaga beach on the Konark coast of Odisha is not only India's but also Asia's first beach to get the Blue Flag certification.
- This project was initiated in 2017-2018 as a part of developing model beaches in each coastal UT or state in India.
- In 2019, the Ministry of Environment, Forest and Climate Change (MoEFCC) had identified 13 beaches in the country for blue flag certification, from which 8 were showcased.
- This required relaxing certain rules of the Coastal Regulation Zone notification, to enable certain construction activities on the beaches.

CITES (CONVENTION ON INTERNATIONAL TRADE IN ENDANGERED SPECIES ON WILD FAUNA AND FLORA)

CITES (Convention on International Trade in Endangered Species on Wild Fauna and Flora) is an international agreement between governments. Its aim is to ensure that international trade in specimens of wild animals and plants does not threaten their survival.

The trade is diverse, ranging from live animals and plants to a vast array of wildlife products derived from them, including food products, exotic leather goods, wooden musical instruments, timber, tourist curios and medicines.

CITES is an international agreement to which States and regional economic integration organizations adhere voluntarily. States that have agreed to be bound by the Convention ('joined' CITES) are known as Parties. Although CITES is legally binding on the Parties – in other words they have to implement the Convention – it does not take the place of national laws. Rather it provides a framework to be respected by each Party, which has to adopt its own domestic legislation to ensure that CITES is implemented at the national level.

OPERATION KACHAPA TO STEM LOSS OF TURTLES

Wildlife Protection Society of India launched Operation Kachhapa in September 1998 to try to stem the slaughter. The objective is to reduce turtle mortality and try to safeguard the future of the species by concentrating on three main activities

- To improve patrolling of non-fishing zones and the protection of nesting sites.
- To support legal action on turtle conservation and fishing law violations.
- To build public support and awareness of sea turtle conservation issues.

Operation Kachhapa has had a significant impact on the number of sea turtle deaths and public awareness of the problem. But construction activity along the coast is relentless and sadly thousands of turtles still die every year from the illegal fishing boats that ply off the coast of Orissa.

Conservation of the Olive Ridley Sea Turtle was launched by the Wildlife Protection Society of India in collaboration with the Odisha State Forest Department

International trade in these turtles and their products is banned under CITES Appendix-I. To reduce accidental killing in India, the Odisha government has made it mandatory for trawls to use Turtle Excluder Devices (TEDs), a net specially designed with an exit cover WCCB was awarded by CITES for its Operation Save Kurma to combat the proliferating illegal trade of live turtles . The Olive ridley is well known for its 'arribadas', or annual mass nestings.

Other Turtle species:

- Leatherback (Vulnerable),
- Loggerhead (Endangered),
- Hawksbill (Critically Endangered),
- Green Turtle(Endangered)
- Olive Ridley(Vulnerable)

PARIVESH LAUNCHED

Prime Minister, Narendra Modi, launched PARIVESH (Pro-Active and Responsive facilitation by Interactive, Virtuous and Environmental Single-window Hub)

PARIVESH is a Single-Window Integrated Environmental Management System, developed in pursuance of the spirit of 'Digital India' initiated by the Prime Minister and capturing the essence of Minimum Government and Maximum Governance.

PARIVESH automates the entire process of submitting the application and tracking the status of such proposals at each stage of processing.

"PARIVESH" is a workflow based application, based on the concept of web architecture and it has been rolled out for online submission, monitoring and management of proposals submitted by Project Proponents to the Ministry of Environment, Forest and Climate Change (MOEFCC), as well as to the State Level Environmental Impact Assessment Authorities (SEIAA), to seek various types of clearances (e.g. Environment, Forest, Wildlife and Coastal Regulation Zone Clearances) from Central, State and district-level authorities. The system has been designed, developed and hosted by the Ministry of Environment, Forest and Climate Change, with technical support from National Informatics Centre, (NIC), New Delhi. The main highlights of PARIVESH include - single registration and single sign-in for all types of clearances (i.e. Environment, Forest, Wildlife and CRZ), unique-ID for all types of clearances required for a particular project and a single Window interface for the proponent to submit applications for getting all types of clearances (i.e. Environment, Forests, Wildlife and CRZ clearances).

GLOBAL ENVIRONMENT OUTLOOK 2019 (6TH EDITION)

Global Environment Outlook (GEO) is a series of reports on the environment, issued periodically by the United Nations Environment Programme (UNEP). The United Nations Environment Program (UNEP) has released the sixth edition of the Global Environment Outlook (2019) titled 'Healthy Planet, Healthy People'.

The report calls on the decision makers to take immediate action to address pressing environmental issues to achieve the Sustainable Development Goals as well as other internationally agreed environment goals, such as the Paris Agreement. UN Environment launched the first Global Environment Outlook (GEO) in 1997. By bringing together a community of hundreds of scientists, peer reviewers and collaborating institutions and partners, the GEO reports build on sound scientific knowledge to provide governments, local authorities, businesses and individual citizens with the information needed to guide societies to a truly sustainable world by 2050. This flagship report shows how governments can put the world on the path to a truly sustainable future. It emphasizes that urgent and inclusive action is needed by decision makers at all levels to achieve a healthy planet with healthy people.

KHANGCHENDZONGA BIOSPHERE RESERVE

The Khangchendzonga Biosphere Reserve has become the 11th Biosphere Reserve from India that has been included in the UNESCO designated World Network of Biosphere Reserves (WNBR).

The decision to include Khangchendzonga Biosphere Reserve in WNBR was taken at the 30th Session of International Coordinating Council (ICC) of Man and Biosphere (MAB) Programme of UNESCO held at Palembang, Indonesia, from July 23-27, 2018. India has 18 Biosphere Reserves and with the inclusion of Khangchendzonga, the number of internationally designated WNBR has become 11, with 7 Biosphere Reserves being domestic Biosphere Reserves.

Khangchendzonga Biosphere Reserve in Sikkim is one of the highest ecosystems in the world, reaching elevations of 1, 220 metres above sea-level. It includes a range of ecolines , varying from sub-tropic to Arctic, as well as natural forests in different biomes, that support an immensely rich diversity of forest types and habitats. The core zone – Khangchendzonga National Park was designated a World Heritage Site in 2016 under the 'mixed' category. Over 118 species of the large number of medicinal plants found in Dzongu Valley in north Sikkim are of ethno-medical utility.

India has 18 Biosphere Reserves and with the inclusion of Khangchendzonga, the number of internationally designated WNBRs has become 11, with 7 Biosphere Reserves being domestic Biosphere Reserves.

There are total 11 biosphere reserves of India which have been recognized internationally under Man and Biosphere Reserve program:

1. Nilgiri
2. Gulf of Mannar
3. Sundarban
4. Nanda Devi
5. Nokrek
6. Pachmarhi

7. Similipal
8. Achanakmar - Amarkantak
9. Great Nicobar
10. Agasthyamala
11. Khangchendzonga

MAB PROGRAMME & INDIA'S BIOSPHERE RESERVE PROGRAMME

Launched in 1971, UNESCO's Man and the Biosphere Programme (MAB) is an Intergovernmental scientific programme that aims to establish a scientific basis for the improvement of relationships between people and their environments. The Biosphere Reserve Programme in India is guided by MAB programme as India is a signatory to the landscape approach supported by MAB programme.

The financial assistance is in the ratio of 60:40, but for the North Eastern and Himalayan states it is 90:10. The State Government prepares the Management Action Plan, which is approved and monitored by the Central MAB Committee.

COP 25 SUMMIT, MADRID (SPAIN) 2019

- COP25 is the 25th meeting of the conference of parties (COP) to the United Nations Framework Convention on Climate Change (UNFCCC).
- It took place in Madrid (Spain) in December 2019.
- The prime aim of the COP 2019 was to finalize the rulebook for the Paris Agreement.
- The Katowice rulebook that was the outcome of the COP24 could not bring resolution to all the issues related to global climate change action.
- Hence, a conference of parties met at the 25th meeting of UNFCCC to bring a finalized copy of the rulebook of the Paris Agreement.

Paris Agreement

The Paris Agreement was signed in the COP21 of the UN Climate Change Conference of UNFCCC aiming to reduce and mitigate greenhouse gas emissions (GHGs.)

Conference of the Parties (COP26) 2021

- The 26th UN Climate Change Conference of the Parties (COP26) was held in Glasgow.
- The Sixth Assessment Report (AR6) of the Intergovernmental Panel on Climate Change released in August 2021 had sounded an alert for the nations of the world over global temperature rise and associated risks.
- The report notes how human influence has warmed the atmosphere, ocean and land which is in turn leading to widespread and rapid changes in the atmosphere, ocean, cryosphere and biosphere.
- This is contributing to the increasing intensity and frequency of extreme climate events like droughts, extreme rainfall, rising sea levels and heatwaves.

- The 12th Emissions Gap Report released by the UN Environment Programme notes huge gap between the updated emissions reduction pledges made by countries for 2030 and what is needed to keep the rise in global temperature to 1.5 degrees C or even 2 degrees C.

COP26 Goals

- To achieve global net-zero by the middle of the century and keep 1.5 degrees within reach.
- To adapt to protect communities as well as natural habitats from the impact of climate change.
- Mobilisation of finances for the stated goals.
- To work together so that the rules could be listed out in detail and help in the fulfilment of the Paris Agreement.

Initiatives Announced at the Glasgow Summit

- Ending deforestation by 2030 under New York Declaration of Forests.
- The New York Declaration on Forests is a voluntary and non-legally binding political declaration adopted in 2014.
- The Declaration pledges to halve the rate of deforestation by 2020, end it by 2030, and restore hundreds of millions of acres of degraded land.

GANGETIC DOLPHIN

Dolphins are one of the oldest creatures in the world along with some species of turtles, crocodiles and sharks. The Ganges river dolphin was officially discovered in 1801.

Ganges river dolphins once lived in the Ganges-Brahmaputra-Meghna and Karnaphuli-Sangu river systems of Nepal, India, and Bangladesh. But the species is extinct from most of its early distribution ranges.

The Ganges river dolphin can only live in freshwater and is essentially blind. They hunt by emitting ultrasonic sounds, which bounces off of fish and other prey, enabling them to "see" an image in their mind. They are frequently found alone or in small groups, and generally a mother and calf travel together. Calves are chocolate brown at birth and then have grey-brown smooth, hairless skin as adults. Females are larger than males and give birth once every two to three years to only one calf.

It is the apex of the aquatic food chain in the river eco-system, it is essentially blind and uses echolocation. It can never live in the sea, thus recent rising salinity in Sunderbans region of India is causing a decrease in population. Vikramshila Gangetic Dolphin Sanctuary (VGDS) in Bihar is India's only sanctuary for the Gangetic dolphin and the National Dolphin Research Centre (NDRC), Patna is India's and Asia's first Centre for Dolphin conservation.

Status

- National Aquatic animal
- Schedule I of WPA, CITES Appendix I
- IUCN – Endangered
- Irrawaddy Dolphin - endangered

LIVING PLANET REPORT 2020

- It is a collaboration between WWF International and the Zoological Society of London
- This is the 13th edition of the biennial publication tracking wildlife populations around the world.

Findings

- The population of vertebrate species declined by around 68 per cent between 1970 and 2016.
- Living Planet Index was used by the report to calculate this decline.
- Wildlife populations in freshwater habitats suffered a decline of 84 per cent, equivalent to four per cent per year, particularly in Latin America and the Caribbean.
- The average two-thirds decline in global populations of mammals, birds, amphibians, reptiles and fish in less than 50 years in large parts is due to the same environmental destruction, which is contributing to emergence of zoonotic diseases such as Covid-19.
- 75 per cent of earth's ice-free land has been significantly altered, most of the oceans polluted and over 85 per cent area of wetlands lost all due to human activity.
- One in five plants is threatened with extinction.
- India has 2.4 per cent global land share, about eight per cent global biodiversity and around 16 per cent global population
- However, it has lost 12 per cent of its wild mammals, 19 per cent amphibians and 3 per cent birds over last five decades.
- India's ecological footprint per person is less than 1.6 global hectares (gha) / person (smaller than that of many large countries). But, its high population size have made the gross footprint significantly high.

Living Planet Report

It is a comprehensive study of trends in global biodiversity and the health of the planet. The report presents a comprehensive overview of the state of the natural world through the Living Planet Index (LPI).

Living Planet Index

It is a measure of the state of the world's biological diversity based on population trends of vertebrate species in terrestrial, freshwater and marine habitats.

ENVIRONMENT MINISTRY NOTIFIES CRZ REGULATIONS 2019; REPLACES CRZ NORMS OF 2011

The Union Ministry of Environment, Forest and Climate Change(MoEFCC) notified the 2019 Coastal Regulation Zone (CRZ) norms, replacing the existing CRZ norms of 2011 as per the recommendation suggested by the Shailesh Nayak committee which was constituted in 2015 by MoEFCC. The new CRZ norms, issued under Section 3 of the Environment Protection Act, 1986, aim to promote sustainable development based on scientific principles taking into account the natural hazards such as increasing sea levels due to global warming.

The norms also seek to conserve and protect the environment of coastal stretches and marine areas, besides livelihood security to the fisher communities and other local communities in the coastal area.

The 2019 norms replace the existing CRZ norms of 2011.

Salient Features of CRZ Regulations 2019

Allowing FSI as per current norms in CRZ areas: As per CRZ, 2011 Notification, for CRZ-II (Urban) areas, Floor Space Index (FSI) or the Floor Area Ratio (FAR) had been frozen as per 1991 Development Control Regulation (DCR) levels.

Densely populated rural areas to be afforded greater opportunity for development: For CRZ-III (Rural) areas, two separate categories have now been stipulated as below:

CRZ-III A - These are densely populated rural areas with a population density of 2161 per square kilometre as per 2011 Census. Such areas shall have a No Development Zone (NDZ) of 50 meters from the HTL as against 200 meters from the High Tide Line stipulated in the CRZ Notification, 2011 since such areas have similar characteristics as urban areas.

CRZ-III B - Rural areas with population density of below 2161 per square kilometre as per 2011 Census. Such areas shall continue to have an NDZ of 200 meters from the HTL.

Tourism infrastructure for basic amenities to be promoted: Temporary tourism facilities such as shacks, toilet blocks, change rooms, drinking water facilities etc. have now been permitted in Beaches. Such temporary tourism facilities are also now permissible in the "No Development Zone" (NDZ) of the CRZ-III areas as per the Notification. However, a minimum distance of 10 m from HTL should be maintained for setting up of such facilities.

(CRZ Clearances streamlined: The procedure for CRZ clearances has been streamlined. Only such projects/activities, which are located in the CRZ-I (Ecologically Sensitive Areas) and CRZ IV (area covered between Low Tide Line and 12 Nautical Miles seaward) shall be dealt with for CRZ clearance by the Ministry of Environment, Forest and Climate Change. The powers for clearances with respect to CRZ-II and III have been delegated at the State level with necessary guidance.

A No Development Zone (NDZ) of 20 meters has been stipulated for all Islands: For islands close to the main land coast and for all Backwater Islands in the main land, in wake of space limitations and unique geography of such regions, bringing uniformity in treatment of such regions, NDZ of 20 m has been stipulated.

All Ecologically Sensitive Areas have been accorded special importance: Specific guidelines related to their conservation and management plans have been drawn up as a part of the CRZ Notification.

Pollution abatement has been accorded special focus: In order to address pollution in Coastal areas treatment facilities have been made permissible activities in CRZ-I B area subject to necessary safeguards.

INTERGOVERNMENTAL PANEL ON CLIMATE CHANGE (IPCC)

The Intergovernmental Panel on Climate Change (IPCC) is an intergovernmental body of the United Nations, dedicated to providing the world with an objective, scientific view of climate change, its natural, political and economic impacts and risks, and possible response options.

The IPCC was established in 1988 by the World Meteorological Organization (WMO) and the United Nations Environment Programme (UNEP), and later endorsed by the United Nations General Assembly.

Membership is open to all members of the WMO and UN. The IPCC produces reports that contribute to the work of the United Nations Framework Convention on Climate Change (UNFCCC), the main international treaty on climate change.

The objective of the UNFCCC is to "stabilize greenhouse gas concentrations in the atmosphere at a level that would prevent dangerous anthropogenic (human-induced) interference with the climate system

UNFCCC COP 27

- 27th session of the Conference of Parties (COP27) of the United Nations Framework Convention on Climate Change (UNFCCC)
- Location - Sharm el-Sheikh (Egypt's coastal city)
- Date - 6 to 18 November 2022.
- Participants - 45,000 registered participants from 195 member countries.
- The Sharm-El-Sheikh Adaptation Agenda outlines 30 Adaptation Outcomes to build resilience for four billion people that are most vulnerable to climate, by 2030.
- Last year, PM Modi, at the 26th edition of the COP in Glasgow, Scotland, committed to India becoming net-zero, or in effect carbon neutral, by 2070 along with Panchamrita

Five Commitments made by the Prime Minister of India at the Global Conference (Panchamrit)

1. To raise the non-fossil fuel based energy capacity of the country to 500 GW by 2030.
2. By 2030, 50% of the country's energy requirements would be met using renewable energy sources.
3. The country will reduce the total projected carbon emission by one billion tonnes between now and the year 2030.

4. The carbon intensity of the economy would be reduced to less than 45% by 2030, Modi said as the fourth point.
5. The country would become carbon neutral and achieve net zero emissions by the year 2070.

India's Participation in COP27

- India is determined to press developed countries into making good their unfulfilled commitment to deliver $100 billion a year of climate finance by 2020 and every year thereafter till 2025.
- The Environment Minister of India Shri Bhupender Yadav is leading the Indian delegation to COP-27.
- India is hosting a pavilion with the theme of LiFE- Lifestyle for Environment at COP 27.
- LiFE aims to have a substantial impact on the health and wellbeing of the planet.
- LiFE movement is India's contribution to handling global climate crisis.
- The LiFE movement seeks to transform persons into 'pro-planet people', who would adopt sustainable lifestyles in the modern world.

About Mission LiFE

- The Prime Minister of India gave the mantra of LiFE to the world in 2021 at COP 26 in Glasgow and this movement has since been widely supported by world leaders.
- India has spearheaded Mission LiFE as a global mass movement that harnesses the power of individual and collective action across the world to address the climate crisis.
- It aims to resurrect the delicate balance between man and nature by encouraging a shift from mindless and wasteful consumption to mindful and deliberate utilisation to protect and preserve the environment.
- Mission LiFE is designed with the objective to mobilise at least one billion Indians and other global citizens to take individual and collective action for protecting and preserving the environment in the period 2022 to 2027.
- Within India, at least 80% of all villages and urban local bodies are aimed to become environment-friendly by 2028.

MANGROVE ALLIANCE FOR CLIMATE (MAC)

- India joined the Mangrove Alliance for Climate (MAC) at the 27th Summit of the Conference of Parties (COP27) at Sharm el-Sheikh in Egypt.
- UAE, Indonesia, Australia, Japan, Spain and Sri Lanka are the other MAC supporters.

About Mangrove Alliance for Climate (MAC)

- Spearheaded by the United Arab Emirates (UAE) in partnership with Indonesia, MAC was launched at the COP27 Summit in Egypt to scale up and accelerate the conservation and restoration of the mangrove forests.

- The alliance will raise awareness about the role of mangroves as a "nature-based solution to climate change".
- The alliance will be amplified at the G20 Summit that will be held between November 15 and 16 in Bali under the presidency of Indonesia.
- The MAC seeks to scale up, accelerate conservation, restoration and growing plantation efforts of mangrove ecosystems for the benefit of communities globally, and recognize the importance of these ecosystems for climate change mitigation and adaptation,

About Mangrove Forests

- A mangrove is a shrub or a small tree that grows along the coastlines and has roots in salty sediments, often underwater.
- They also grow in swamps. Mangrove forests can survive extreme weather conditions and require low oxygen levels to survive.
- The mangroves cannot survive freezing temperatures and thus are found mainly in tropical and subtropical latitudes.
- Sundarbans in West Bengal in India is the largest mangrove forest in the world.
- UNESCO celebrates July 26 as the International Day for the Conservation of the Mangrove Ecosystem to raise awareness about mangrove ecosystems and to promote their conservation.

Benefits of Mangroves

- Mangrove forests can store ten times more carbon per hectare than terrestrial forests. Also, they can store carbon up to 400 per cent faster than land-based tropical rainforests.
- When the mangroves are cut, the carbon stored in these plants gets released into the air. So, preserving them to keep the carbon emissions levels low is necessary.
- Once the plants die, they take the stored carbon into the soil. This is called "Blue Carbon".
- Mangrove forests act as natural barriers against rising tides and storms.
- They also provide breeding grounds for marine biodiversity and 80% of global fish populations depend on healthy mangrove ecosystems.

Presence of Mangroves in India

- India contributes to nearly half of the total mangrove cover in South Asia.
- Mangroves cover in the country is 4,992 square km, which is 0.15 per cent of the country's total geographical area. Since 2019, the cover has risen by only 17 sq km.
- West Bengal has the highest percentage of mangrove cover in India, mainly because it has Sundarbans, the largest mangrove forest in the world. It is followed by Gujarat and Andaman, and Nicobar islands.
- Other states that have mangrove cover are Maharashtra, Odisha, Andhra Pradesh, Tamil Nadu, Goa and Kerala.

MIDDLE EAST GREEN INITIATIVE SUMMIT 2022

- Kingdom of Saudi Arabia and Arab Republic of Egypt hosted the Middle East Green Initiative Summit 2022 on the sidelines of COP 27
- Objective - to create infrastructure needed to reduce emissions and protect the environment.

About Middle East Green Initiative

- The first Middle East Green Initiative (MGI) Summit was hosted by HRH Mohammed bin Salman, Crown Prince and Prime Minister in Riyadh on 25 October 2021.
- It facilitated a first-of-its-kind regional dialogue on climate, with leaders in attendance from 28 countries agreeing to work together to tackle climate change.
- This year global leaders will assemble again to discuss and build on the region's first climate alliance.
- Various initiatives undertaken by the Middle East Green Initiative, relate directly to encouraging sustainable consumption practices like planting of 50 billion trees across the Middle East that lead to employment opportunities and strengthening the resilience of countries.
- The Arab Republic of Egypt is developing a Green Ammonia facility to be used as bunker fuel to serve the Suez Canal Maritime traffic.
- The efforts of Egyptian Governments in establishing green fuel production in the country in the pursuit of net-zero shipping is worth appreciating.

Steps Taken by India

- India has also initiated a number of coalitions such as International Solar Alliance
- India has also initiated Leadership group in Industry transition (Lead IT) track along with Sweden with focus on hard to abate industrial sectors
- Coalition for Disaster Resilient Infrastructure for easy and faster mobilization of technology, finance and necessary information for Small Island Developing States.

THE INTERNATIONAL DAY FOR BIOSPHERE RESERVES – 3RD NOVEMBER

- November 3 will be the first 'The International Day for Biosphere Reserves', to be celebrated beginning 2022.
- An event showcasing the contribution of the biosphere reserves to sustainable development will be organised at UNESCO Headquarters in collaboration with all the regions of the World Network of Biosphere Reserves.

Biosphere Reserve (BR)

- Is an international designation by UNESCO for representative parts of natural and cultural landscapes extending over large area of terrestrial or coastal/marine ecosystems or a combination thereof.
- They are sites for testing interdisciplinary approaches to understanding and managing changes and interactions between social and ecological systems, including conflict prevention and management of biodiversity.
- Biosphere reserves are nominated by national governments and remain under the sovereign jurisdiction of the states where they are located.

World Network of Biosphere Reserves

- The World Network of Biosphere Reserves (WNBR) was formed in 1971, as a backbone for biodiversity conservation, ecosystem restoration, and living in harmony with nature.
- The World Network of Biosphere Reserves of the MAB Programme consists of a dynamic and interactive network of sites of excellence.
- There are now 738 properties in 134 countries, including 12 in India, four in Sri Lanka, and three in the Maldives.

Biosphere Reserves in India

- There are 18 Biosphere reserves in India as of 2022, of which 12 are also part of the UNESCO MAB Programme.
- In India, the first biosphere reserve was designated by UNESCO in 2000, namely, the blue mountains of the Nilgiris stretching over Tamil Nadu, Karnataka and Kerala.

List Of Biosphere Reserves (BR) In India

S. No.	Name of the BR & total geographical area (Km^2)	Date of Designation	Location in the State (s)/Union Territory
1.	Nilgiri (5520)	1-8-1986	Part of Wyanad, Nagarhole, Bandipur and Mudumalai, Nilambur, Silent Valley and Siruvani hills in Tamil Nadu, Kerala and Karnataka.
2.	Nanda Devi (5860.69)	18-1-1988	Part of Chamoli, Pithoragarh and Almora districts in Uttarakhand.
3.	Nokrek (820)	1-9-1988	Part of East, West and South Garo Hill districts in Meghalaya.

4.	Manas (2837)	14-3-1989	Part of Kokrajhar, Bongaigaon, Barpeta, Nalbari, Kamprup and Darang districts in Assam.
5.	Sunderban (9630)	29-3-1989	Part of delta of Ganges & Brahamaputra river system in West Bengal.
6.	Gulf of Mannar (10500)	18-2-1989	India; part of Gulf of Mannar extending from Rameswaram island in the North of Kanyakumari in Tamil Nadu.
7.	Great Nicobar (885)	6-1-1989	Southern most island of Andaman and Nicobar Islands.
8.	Similipal (4374)	21-6-1994	Part of Mayurbhanj district in Orissa.
9.	Dibru-Saikhova (765)	28-7-1997	Part of Dibrugarh and Tinsukia districts in Assam.
10.	Dehang-Dibang (5111.5)	2-9-1998	Part of Upper Siang, West Siang and Dibang Valley districts in Arunachal Pradesh.
11.	Pachmarihi (4981.72)	3-3-1999	Part of Betul, Hoshangabad and Chhindwara districts in Madhya Pradesh.
12.	Khangchendzonga (2619.92)	7-2-2000	Part of North and West districts in Sikkim.
13.	Agasthyamalai (3500.36)	12-11-2001	Part of Tirunelveli and Kanyakumari districts in Tamil Nadu and Thiruvanthapuram, Kollam and Pathanamthitta districts in Kerala.
14.	Achanakmar-Amarkantak (3835.51)	30-3-2005	Part of Anuppur and Dindori districts of Madhya Pradesh and Bilaspur district of Chattisgarh.
15.	Kachchh (12,454)	29-1-2008	Part of Kachchh, Rajkot, Surendranagar and Patan districts in Gujarat.
16.	Cold Desert (7,770)	28-8-2009	Pin Valley National Park and surroundings; Chandratal & Sarchu; and Kibber Wildlife Sanctuary in Himachal Pradesh.
17.	Seshachalam (4755.997)	20-9-2010	Seshachalam hill ranges in Eastern Ghats encompassing part of Chittoor and Kadapa districts in Andhra pradesh.
18.	Panna (2998.98)	25-8-2011	Part of Panna and Chhattarpur districts in Madhya Pradesh.

Biosphere Reserves that are part of Man and the Biosphere (MAB)

1. Nilgiri, Tamil Nadu-Kerala
2. Gulf of Mannar, Tamil Nadu
3. Sundarban, West Bengal
4. Nanda Devi, Uttarakhand
5. Nokrek, Meghalaya
6. Pachmarhi, Madhya Pradesh
7. Similipal, Odisha
8. Achanakmar-Amarkantak, Madhya Pradesh-Chhattisgarh
9. Great Nicobar, Andaman & Nicobar Island
10. Agasthyamala, Karnataka-Tamil Nadu-Kerala
11. Khangchendzonga, Sikkim
12. Panna, Madhya Pradesh

GANGETIC DOLPHIN

According to Uttar Pradesh Government, dolphins have started coming back to the Ganga river with improvement in the quality of its water through the Namami Gange programme

About the Gangetic Dolphin

- The Gangetic dolphin is a fresh-water species, and one of the few river dolphins found in the world.
- It inhabits the Ganges-Brahmaputra-Meghna and Karnaphuli-Sangu river systems of Nepal, India, and Bangladesh.
- Common Names: Blind dolphin, Ganges dolphin, Ganges susu, hihu, side-swimming dolphin, South Asian River Dolphin
- Scientific name: Platanista gangetica
- The Gangetic dolphin has been recognized as India's National Aquatic Animal and is the official animal of the Indian city of Guwahati.
- It feeds majorly on fishes and is are usually found in counter current systems of the main river channel.
- Its eyes lack lens, and as a result, this species is also referred to as the "blind dolphin".
- They have a highly developed bio sonar system that facilitates them to hunt for fish even in murky waters.
- Being a mammal, the Ganges River dolphin cannot breathe in the water and must surface every 30-120 seconds.
- Because of the sound it produces when breathing, the animal is popularly referred to as the 'Susu'.

- The population of the Ganges dolphin is estimated to be a few hundred.
- IUCN Status: Endangered.
- It is placed in Schedule-I of the Wildlife (Protection) Act.
- It is listed on CITES Appendix I, which lists species that are the most endangered among CITES-listed animals and plants.

Vikramshila Gangetic Dolphin Sanctuary

- It is located in Bhagalpur district of Bihar, India.
- The sanctuary is a 60 kilometers stretch of the Ganges River from Sultanganj to Kahalgaon in Bhagalpur district. Notified as Vikramshila Gangetic Dolphin Sanctuary in 1991, it is the protected area for the endangered Gangetic dolphins in Asia.
- Once found in abundance, only a few hundred remain, of which half are found here.

Appendix

Countries on Equator

Ecuador, Colombia, Brazil, Gabon, Congo, Democratic Republic of Congo, Uganda, Kenya, Somalia, Maldives, Indonesia, Kiribati.

Countries on Prime Meridian

United Kingdom, France, Spain, Algeria, Mali, Burkina Faso, Ghana and Togo.

Earth's Extremes (Hottest, Coldest, Deepest etc.)

Wettest spot	Mawsynram (Meghalaya) and Mount Waialeale, Hawaii (annual rainfall 1168 cm)
Driest spot	Atacama Desert, Chile (South America), rainfall barely measurable
Coldest spot	Vostok, Antarctica, –88°C, recorded in 1960, –92°C recorded in 2014
Hottest spot	Azizia, Libya, 58°C, recorded in 1922
Northernmost town	Ny-Alesund, Spitsbergen, Norway
Southernmost town	Ushuaia, Argentina
Largest gorge	Grand Canyon, Colorado River, Arizona-349 km long, 6–28 km wide and 1.6 km deep
Deepest gorge	Hell's Canyon, Snake River, Idaho, 2408 m deep
Strongest surface wind	Mount Washington, New Hampshire, 231 mph recorded in 1934
Deepest Point	Mariana Trench, North Pacific Ocean, 11,033 metres
Highest point	Mount Everest, Himalayas (China-Nepal border-8848 metres
Lowest point	Dead Sea (Israel-Jordan border) about 400 metres below the sea level

Extremes of Sea-Level Pressure Readings

Pressure mb	Event
1083.8	Highest recorded. *Agata*, Siberia, Russia (Former Soviet Union), December 31, 1968
1078.2	Highest recorded in North America, Northway, Alaska, January 31, 1989

1063.9	Highest in the lower 48 states, Miles City, Montana, December 24, 1983
870	Lowest recorded. Typhoon Tip, Pacific Ocean near Guam, October 12, 1979

Geographical Distribution of Forests in India

Geographical Region	Percentage of Total Forest Area
1. Peninsular Plateau and Hills	57.00
2. Himalayan Region	18.00
3. Western Ghats and Western Coastal Plains	10.00
4. Eastern Ghats and Eastern Coastal Plains	10.00
5. The Great Plains of India	5.00
Total	100.00

India: Area under Forests

Forest Group	Area in Million Hectares	Percentage of Total Area
1. Tropical Moist Deciduous	23.680	37.00
2. Tropical Dry Deciduous	18.304	28.60
3. Tropical Wet Evergreen	5.120	8.00
4. Subtropical: Moist Hill (pines)	4.224	6.60
5. Tropical Semi-evergreen	2.624	4.1
6. Himalayan Moist Temperate	2.176	3.4
7. Others	7.872	12.30
Total	64.00	100.00

India: Area under National Parks and Wildlife Sanctuaries

Protected area	Percentage of geographical area
National parks	1.19
Wildlife sanctuaries	3.60
Conservation and country reserves	0.04
Total protected area	4.83

Age of Maturity of Selected Trees

Tree	Age of Maturity
1. Pine	20 years
2. Beech	30 years
3. Teak	60 years
4. Sal	65 years
5. Sheesham	70 years
6. Spruce	>100 years
7. Birch	>100 years
8. Larch	>100 years
10. Duglas Fir	200 years

Recent Revolutions in India

1. Black Revolution	Petroleum Production
2. Blue Revolution	Fisheries
3. Brown Revolution	Honey-bee (Apiculture)
4. Evergreen Revolution	Over-all Development of Agriculture
5. Grey Revolution	Housing Development/Fertilizers
6. Golden Revolution	Horticulture
7. Golden Fibre Revolution	Jute
8. Green Revolution	Agriculture
9. Pink Revolution	Prawn, Onions, Pharmaceutical
10. Red Revolution	Meat and Tomato
11. Round Revolution	Potato
12. Silver Fibre Revolution	Cotton
13. Silver Revolution	Poultry and Eggs
14. White Revolution	Dairy Development
15. Yellow Revolution	Oil-seeds

List Of Spices

Common name	Botanical name	Part used	Medicinal properties
Chillies	Capsicum annuum	Fruits	As a flavourant, rich in Vitamin C and good appetizer, used in the preparation of neuralgia and rheumatic disorder
Cinnamon	Cinnamon zeylanicum	Bark	As a flavourant, dye, leaves are used in pharmaceutical products, soap and dental preparations and perfumes.
Clove	Eugenia caryophyllus	Flower buds	Used as a culinary spice, in cigarettes, toothpaste and mouth wash and perfume industry.
Coriander	Coriandrum sativum	Seed and leaves	Used for garnishing currie, sausages; seeds are carminative and diuretics, oil is used in perfumes.
Ginger	Zingiber officinale	Rhizome	Used in food preparation, alcoholic beverages, stimulant and carminative.
Fennel	Foeniculum vulgare	Seeds and leaf	Dried seeds are used in curry powder, pickles, confectionary, oil is used as stimulant and carminative.
Pepper	Pipper nigrum (king of spices)	Seeds	As a representative, flavourant, used in medicines and insecticides, oil of pepper is used in perfumes.
Saffron	Crocus sativus	Flowers	As a flavouring and dyeing agent in Indian dishes, in Ayurvedic and Unani system of medicine.
Small cardamom	Elettaria cardamom (Queen of spices)	Fruits	As a flavourant and masticatory; a powerful stimulant, strengthens nervous system, and reduces depression.
Turmeric	Curcuma longa	Rhizome	As a flavourant, dye, medicines.

Unique Animals of India

Pigmy-hog, black-buck, lion-tailed macaque, Nilgiri-tahr, golden-langurs etc.

Typical Animals of India

Herbivorous

Elephants, rhinocerous, deers-musk-deer, bara-singha, dancing-deer (sambhar), thamin and Kashmiri-stag, antelopes (black-buck, four-horned antelope or chausingha, Indian-gazelle, chinkara, blue-cow-nilgai, bison, wild-buffalo, Himalayan-ibex or wild-goat, wild-boar, wild-ass, Nilgiri-tahr.

Carnivorous Animals

Lion, tiger, leopard, stripped hyaena, wolf, black bear (Himalayan), sloth-bear, monkeys, apes, Nilgiri-langur, lion-tailed monkeys, Hanuman-monkey, Indian giant squirrels.

Birds

Pea-fowl, jungle fowl, patridge, quail, great Indian-bustard, duck, pigeon, sandgrouse, storks, pelican, eagle, crane, owl, hornbill, etc.

Reptiles

Crocodiles, alligators, lizards, and several species of snakes, etc.

Important Institutes & their location

INSTITUTE	LOCATION
Birbal Sahni Institute of Paleontology (BSIP)	Lucknow
Botanical Institute of India (BSI)	Kolkata
Central Arid Zone Research Institute (CAZRI)	Jodhpur
Central Coconut Research Station (CCRS)	Kasaragod (Kerala)
Central Coffee Research Institute (CCRI)	Chikmagalur (Karnataka)
Centre for Finger Printing and Diagnostic (CDFD)	Hyderabad
Central Drug Institute (CDRI)	Lucknow
Central Food Technology Research Institute (CFTRI)	Mysore
Central Institute for Medicinal and Aromatic Plants (CIMAP)	Lucknow
Central Jute Technology Research Institute (CJTRI)	Kolkata
Central Potato Research Institute (CPRI)	Shimla
Central Rice Research Institute (CRRI)	Cuttack
Forest Research Institute of India (FRII)	Dehra Dun
Food Research Institute of India (FRII)	Dehra Dun
Institute of Bio-resources and Sustainable Development (IBSD)	Imphal (Manipur)
Indian Council of Agricultural Research (ICAR)	New Delhi
International Crops Research Institute For Semi-arid Tropics (ICRISAT)	Hyderabad
Indian Institute of Science and Technology (IIST)	Bangalore
Institute of Rain and Moist Deciduous Forests (IRMDF)	Jorhat (Assam)
Institute of Wood Science and Technology (IWST)	Bangalore
National Bureau of Plant Genetic Resources (NBPGR)	New Delhi
National Brain Research Centre (NBRC)	Gurgaon (Haryana)
National Botanical Research Institute (NBRI)	Lucknow
National Environmental Engineering Research Inst. (NEERI)	Nagpur
National Institute of Immunology (NII)	New Delhi
Tropical Forest Research Institute (TFRI)	Jabalpur
Institute of Forest Genetic and Tree Breeding (IFGTB)	Coimbatore

Temperate Forest Research Centre (TFRC)	Shimla
Centre for Forest Productivity (CFP)	Ranchi
Centre for Social Forestry and Environment (CSFE)	Allahabad
International Rice Research Institute (IRRI)	Manila (Philippines)

Important Days

Ist January	World Peace Day
2nd February	World Wetland Day (Ramsar Convention on Wetlands was held on this day).
8th March	United Nations Day for Women's Rights (International Women's Day).
21st March	World Forestry Day and International Day of Racial Discrimination.
22nd March	World Water Day (UNDP)
23rd March	World Meteorology Day (WMO)
7th April	World Health Day (WHO was constituted on this day).
22nd April	Earth Day
Ist May	Labour Day
3rd May	World Press Freedom Day
15th May	International Day of Families
31st May	World No Tobacco Day
5th June	World Environment Day (Stockholm Conference on Human Environment was held)
17th June	World Combat Day on Desertification
20th June	World Refugee Day
21th June	World Yoga Day
11th July	World Population Day
28th July	World Nature Conservation Day
6th August	Hiroshima Day
9th August	International day of World's Indigenous People
8th September	International Literacy Day
16th September	World Ozone Preservation Day
Ist October	World Elders' Day
Ist Monday of October	UNESCO Day
Ist–7th October	Wildlife Week
13th October	International Reduction on Natural Disaster Day
16th October	World Food Day
17th October	International Day for Eradication of Poverty
Ist December	World AIDs Day
2nd December	International Day of Abolition of Slavery
3rd December	International Day for Disabled Persons
10th December	Human Rights Day
12th December	C. Darwin's Day
29th December	International Biodiversity Day

U.N. Years

2004	International Year to Commemorate the Struggle against Slavery and its Abolition; and International Year of Rice.
2005	International Year of Microcredit: and International Year for Sports and Physical Education
2006	International Year of Deserts and Desertification
2008	International Year of Potato and International Year of Planet Earth
2009	International Year of Human Rights and International Year of Astronomy
2010	International Year of Biodiversity
2011	International Year of Forests.
2011-2020	The United Nations Decade on Biodiversity, Deserts and to combat Desertification.

2012	International Year of Sustainable Energy for all
2013	International Year of Water Cooperation
2014	International Year of Family Farming
2015	International Year of Soil
2016	International Year of Pulse
2017	International Year of Sustainable Tourism & development
2018-28	International Decade for action Water For Sustainable development
2019-28	United Nations Decade of Family Farming

Extreme Atmospheric Events and their Duration

Event	Mean Duration
Lightning	Milliseconds
Tornadoes	Minutes
Hailstorms	Minutes
Thunderstorms	Minutes
Blizzards	Hours
Flash floods	Hours
Heat waves	Days
Tropical cyclones	Days
Cold waves	Days
Regional floods	Days
Drought	Months

Main Commercial Fishing Areas (% of world catch)

Ocean	Percentage of world catch
Pacific Ocean	71.0 %
Atlantic Ocean	20.3 %
Indian Ocean	8.6 %
Southern Ocean (Antarctic Ocean)	0.1 %

Natural Disasters in India (1980–2010)

No. of Events	431
No. of people killed	143,039
Average killed per year	4614
No. of people affected	1,521,7261
Average affected per year	49,087,940
Economic damage (US $1000):	48,063,830
Economic Damage per year (US $ × 1000	1,550,446

Source: Preventionweb

Major Crops of the World

Crop	Geographical Conditions Required	Leading Producers
Rice	Temp. 15°–27°C; rainfall minimum 100 cm; Clayey soil	China, India, Indonesia, Bangladesh, Thailand, Japan, Myanmar, Vietnam, Malaysia. Leading exporter in the world: Thailand
Wheat	Temp. 12°C to 25°C; rainfall 25–75 cm; Loamy well drained soil.	China, India, USA, Russia, Australia, Canada, France, Turkey. Leading exporter in the world: USA.
Barley	Temp. 10° to 25°C; rainfall 50 to 75 cm; Well drained loamy soil.	Russia, China, Canada, USA, France, U.K., Germany, Turkey. Leading exporter in the world: Russia
Maize	Temp. 15°C to 27°C; rainfall 65–125 cm; Well drained loamy soil.	USA, China, Brazil, Mexico, Russia, Romania, India, South Africa. Leading exporter in the world: USA
Millet	Temp. 20° to 27°C; rainfall 25–75 cm; Well drained loamy soil.	China, USA, India, Nigeria, Ukraine, Thailand, Russia, Turkey. Leading exporter in the world: USA
Soybean	Temp. 25° to 27°C; rainfall 25 to 60 cm; Well drained loamy soil.	China, USA, Brazil, Argentina, Ukraine, Japan, Russia, Columbia. Leading exporter in the world: USA
Sugarcane	Temp. 20° to 27°C; rainfall 100 to 150 cm; Well drained loamy soil.	Brazil, India, China, Pakistan, Thailand, Mexico, Cuba, Colombia. Leading exporter: Brazil
Sugarbeet	10°C to 25°C; rainfall 25 to 50 cm; Well drained loamy soil.	France, USA, Germany, Russia, China, Ukraine, Poland, Turkey. Leading exporter in the world: France
Cotton	Temp. 18°C to 25°C; rainfall 50 to 75 cm; Frost-free days 180.	China, USA, India, Brazil, Pakistan, Uzbekistan, Egypt, Turkey. Leading exporter in the world: USA
Rubber (Natural)	Temp. 22°C to 27°C; rainfall 150 to 200 cm; Well drained alluvial soil.	Thailand, Indonesia, Malaysia, India, China, Sri Lanka, Liberia, Brazil. Leading exporter in the world: Thailand
Tea	Temp. 15°C to 25°C; rainfall 100 to 150 cm; Well drained soil on the hilly slopes.	India, China, Sri Lanka, Japan, Kenya, Indonesia, Bangladesh, Turkey. Leading exporter: India
Coffee	Temp. 20°C to 25°C; rainfall 100 to 150 cm; Well drained alluvial soil.	Brazil, Colombia, Indonesia, Vietnam, Ivory Coast, Mexico, Ghana, Cameroon, India. Leading exporter in the world: Brazil
Cocao	Temp. 20°C to 27°C; rainfall 100 to 200 cm; Well drained alluvial soil.	Ivory-Coast, Ghana, Indonesia, Brazil, Cameroon, Nigeria, Ecuador, Costa-Rica. Leading exporter in the world: Ivory-coast
Tobacco	Temp. 18° to 25°C; rainfall 75 to 100 cm; Well drained alluvial soil.	China, USA, India, Brazil, Turkey, Japan, Bulgaria, South Korea. Leading exporter in the world: USA

(*Contd.*)

(*Contd.*)

Crop	Geographical Conditions Required	Leading Producers
Groundnut	Temp. 20°C to 25°C; rainfall 50 to 75 cm; Well drained loam to sandy loam.	India, China, USA, Sudan, Senegal, Indonesia, Argentina, Myanmar. Leading exporter in the world: USA
Apple	Temp. 15°C to 20°C; rainfall 50 to 100 cm; Well drained alluvial soil.	USA, France, Italy, Spain, Mexico, India, Argentina, Turkey, Russia, Greece. Leading exporter in the world: USA
Banana	Temp. 15°C to 20°C; rainfall 50 to 100 cm; Well draimed alluvial soil.	Brazil, Costa Rica, India, Mexico, Honduras, Leading exporter in the world: Costa Rica
Grapes	Temp. 15° to 20°C; rainfall 60 cm; Well drained alluvial soil.	Spain, France, Russia, Italy, USA, Chile, Argentina, Algeria, Greece. Leading exporter in the world: France

Pesticides Banned for Manufacture, Import Use

1.	Aldicarb
2.	Aldrin
3.	BHC
4.	Calcium cyanide
5.	Captofol powder (80%)
6.	Carbofuran (50% wp)
7.	Chlordane
8.	Chlorobenzilate
9.	Chlorobromopropane
10.	Copper acetoarsenite
11.	Dieldrin
12.	Endrin
13.	Maleic hydrazide
14.	Menazone
15.	Methomyl (12.5%)
16.	Methomyl (24%)
17.	Nicotin sulphate
18.	Nitrofen
19.	Paraquat dimethyl sulphate
20.	Penatachloro nitrobenzene
21.	Pentachlorophenol
22.	Phenyl mercuric acetate
23.	Phosphamidon (85% SL)
24.	Sodium methane arsonate

Major Fruits, Vegetables and Plants of India

Fruit Crops of India

Almond, Aonla, Apple, Apricot, Avocada, Bael, Banana, Ber, Bread-fruit, Carambola, Cherry, Date-palm, Egg-fruit, Fig, Grape, Guava, Jackfruit, Jamun, Karonda, Kiwi, Limes and lemons, Litchi, Loquat, Mahua, Mandarin-orange, Mango, Olive, Papaya, Peach, Pear, Pecan-nut, Persimmon, Pineapple, Plum, Pomgranate, Sapota, Strawberry, Sweet-orange, Walnut, and minor tropical fruits.

Vegetable Crops

Agathi, Ash-gourd, Beet-root, Bitter-gourd, Bottle=gourd, Brinjal, Broccoli, Cabbage, Capsicum, Carrot, Cauliflower, Celery, Chilli, Cowpea, Cucumber, Curry-leaf, Drumstick, French-bean, Garlic, Kale, Knol-Khol, Lablab-bean, Lettuce, Muskmelon, Okra, Onion, *Palak* or Indian-spinach, Parsley, Pea, Pointed-gourd, Pumpkin, Radish, Ridge-gourd, Round-melon, Snake-gourd, Soinach, Sponge-gourd, Tomato, Turnip, and Watermelon.

Tropical Tuber Crops

Arrow-root, Cassava, Coleus or Chinese-potato, Elephant-foot yam, Sweet potato, Tannia, Yambean, Yam.

Mushrooms

Mushroom.

Ornamental Plants

Annual-flower, Anthurium, Carnation, Chrysanthemum, Gladiolus, Jasmine, Orchids, Rose

Medicinal Plants

Asgand, Dill, Guggal, Henbane, Isabgol, Khasi-kateri, Liquorice, Opium-poppy, Periwinkle, Pipali, Rauvolfia, Senna.

Aromatic Plants

Ambrette-seed or muskdana, Celery, Chamomile, Davana, French -jasmine, Indian-basil, Javacitronella, Kewada, Lemon-grass, Mint, Palmarosa oil-grass, Patchouli, Rose-geranium, Scented-rose, Vetiver.

Plantation Crops

Arecanut, Cashew, Cocao, Coconut, Coffee, Oil-palm, Rubber, Tea.

Spices

Betelvine, Black-pepper, Cardamom (small), Cardamom (large), Cinnamon, Clove, Coriander, Cumin, Fennel, Fenugreek, Ginger, Nutmeg, Tamarind, Turmeric.

Environmental Laws of India

The laws regarding environmental protection in India include acts, rules and notification. All aspects of environmental laws in India are now included under Environmental Protection Act which was enacted in 1986 after the Bhopal Gas Tragedy. The three policies are the basic structure for environmental protection as follows:

1. The National Forest Policy, 1988.
2. Policy statement for abatement of pollution, 1992, and
3. National conservation strategy and policy statement on environment and development, 1992.

Table I Main Environmental Laws of India

Environmental Law	Salient Features
1972	The Wildlife (Protection) Act.
1986	The Environmental Protection Act All aspects of environmental laws in India are now included under the Environmental Protection Act which was enacted in 1986 after Bhopal Gas Tragedy.
1989	(i) The hazardous waste (Management) Rules are meant to control the generation, collection, treatment, import, storage and handling of hazardous waste. (ii) The Manufacture, Storage, Import of Hazardous Chemical Rules, 1989. (iii) The Manufacture, Use, Import, Export and Storage of Hazardous Micro-organism/Genetically Engineered Organisms or Cells Rules, 1989.
1992	The Public Liability Insurance Act and Rules Amendment, 1992.
1995	The National Environmental Tribunal Act, 1995, to award compensation for damages to persons, property, and the environment arising from any activity involving hazardous substances.
1997	The National Appellate Authority Act, 1997, to hear appeals with respect to restrictions of areas where industries are set up or prescribed subject to certain safeguards under the Environmental Protection Act (EPA), 1986.
1998	The Biomedical Waste (Management and Handling) Rules, 1998.
2000	(i)The Municipal Solid Waste (Management and Handling) Rules 2000. (ii)The Ozone Depleting Substances (Regulation and Control) Rules 2000, for the regulation and consumption of ozone depleting substances (such as CFCs)
2002	The Biological Diversity Act.
Water-Pollution Laws	
1974	The Water (Prevention and Control of Pollution) Act, 1974.
1991	The Coastal Regulation Zone Notification, 1991.
Air Pollution Laws	
1923	The Indian Boiler Act, 1923
1948	The Factories Act
1951	The Industries (Development and Regulation) Act.
1991	The Air (Prevention and Control of Pollution) Act
Radiation Laws	
1962	The Atomic Energy Act,1962
1971	Radiation Protection Rules, 1971
1986	The Environmental Protection Act,1986
1994	Environment Impact Assessment Notification, 1994, as further amended in 1994.
State Laws Water Pollution	
1953	Orissa River Pollution (Prevention) Act The U.P.
1954	Agricultural Disease and Pests Act.

(Contd.)

(*Contd.*)

Environmental Law	Salient Features
1958	The Kerala Agricultural Pests and Disease Act.
1963	The Gujarat Smoke Nuisance, Act.
Wildlife Act	
2006	Wildlife (Protection) Act. This Act provides provision for the creation of Tiger Conservation Authority and the Tiger and other Endangered Species Crime Control Bureau (Wild Life Control Bureau). The offenders shall be punished for not less than 3 years which may extend up to 7 years, and also with fine not less than Rs.50,000/- which may extend up to Rs.200,000/-

Table II Chronological Development of Technology

Chronological Phase	Major Technological Development
The New Stone Age	Earliest communities, the Neolithic Revolution-8000 B.C.
The Urban Revolution	Crafts, use of copper and bronze, irrigation, urban manufacturing, building and transmitting knowledge.
Greek Civilization (500 B.C. – 500 A.D.)	Mastery of iron, mechanical contrivances, and building.
Middle Ages (500-1500 A.D.)	Power sources, agriculture and crafts, architecture, military technology, transport and communications.
Emergence of European Technology (1500-1750 A.D.)	The Renaissance, steam-engine, metallurgy and mining, new commodities, agriculture, construction, transport, communications and chemistry.
Industrial Revolution (1779-1900 AD)	Wind-mills, steam-engines, electricity, internal combustion engine, petroleum, metallurgy, civil engineering, transport, communications and military technology.
Period of Modernization in Europe(1900-1945)	Fuel and power, industry, food and agriculture, civil engineering, transportation, communications, military technology, aeroplanes, helicopters and electronics.
Post Second World War Period (1945-2000)	Power, new raw materials, automation, computers, information technology, space technology, food-production, bio-technology, transport, highways, communications, military technology, nuclear technology, remote-sensing and GPS, population control, environmental technology and consumerism.

Table III Pharmaceutical Plants, Drugs and Use

Drug	Plant Source	Use
Atropine	Belladonna	Anti-cholinergic, reduces intestinal pain in diarrhea
Bromelain	Pineapple	Controls tissue inflammation due to infection
Caffeine	Tea, Coffee	Stimulant of the central nervous system
Camphor	Camphor tree	Rubefacient; increases local blood supply.
Cocaine	Cocoa	Analgesic and local anesthetic; reduces pain and prevents pain during surgery.

(*Contd.*)

(*Contd.*)

Drug	Plant Source	Use
Codeine	Opium puppy	Analgesic and local anesthetic; reduces pain.
Colchicines	Autumn crocus	Anticancer agent
Digitoxin	Common foxglove	Cardiac stimulant used in heart diseases
Diosgenin	Wild yams	Source of female contraceptive; prevents pregnancy
Ergotamine	Smut-of-rye or regot	Control of hemorrhage and migraine headaches
Glaziovine	Ocotea glaziovii	Antidepressant
Gossypol	Cotton	Male contraceptive
Indicine N-oxide	Heliotropium Indicum Mint	Anticancer agent
L-Dopa	Velvet bean	Controls Parkinson which leads to jerky movements of the hands
Menthol	Mint	Rubefacient; increases local blood supply and reduces pain on local applications
Monocrotaline	Cotolaria sessiliflora	Anticancer agent
Papain	Papaya	Dissolves excess protein and mucus, during digestion
Penicillin	Penicillium fungi	General antibiotic, kills bacteria and controls infection by various microorganisms
Quinine	Yellow cinchona	Antimalarial
Reserpine	Indian snakeroot	Reduces high blood pressure
Scopolamine	Thorn apple	Sedative
Taxol	Pacific yew	Anticancer (ovarian)
Vinblastine	Rosy periwinkle	Anticancer agent; controls cancer in children
Vincristine	(Vinca rosea) (Sadaphali)	Anticancer agent; controls cancer in children

Source: Wilson, E.O., 1993, *The Diversity of Life,* Harvard University Press.

Table IV Major Fruits Producing Countries of the world

Country	Area in Ha	Production in MT
1. China	11,042,621	107,837,629
2. India	6,100,900	68,465,530
3. Brazil	2,455,867	38,988,300
4. USA	1,160,595	28,202,514
5. Italy	1,243,225	17,653,457
6. Mexico	1,201,897	16,122,211
7. Indonesia	720,260	15,917,953
8. Spain	1,895,782	15,835,000
9. Philippines	1,118,530	15,420,664
10. Iran	1,354,381	13,604,303

Table V Villages having the highest Population in India

Village	District	State	2011
1. Mandoli	North East	Delhi	145,942
2. Khora	Ghaziabad	Uttar Pradesh	122,381
3. Dabgram (P)	Jalpiguri	West Bengal	83202
4. Kannan Devan Hills	Idukki	Kerala	73,965
5. Goura	Begusarai	Bihar	66.589
6. Dhone (Dronachalam)	Kurnool	Andhra Pradesh	63,810
7. Kharia (P)	Jalpaiguri	West Bengal	58,173
8. Edakkara	Malappuram	Kerala	57,979
9. Gola Range	Nainital	Uttarakhand	57,979
10. Pallichal	Thiruvananthapuram	Kerala	57,851

Table VI Estimate of Wasteland (Saline and alkaline, water-eroded, wind-eroded, non-forest degraded and forest degraded areas

State	Million hectares
1. Madhya Pradesh	20.142
2. Rajasthan	19.934
3. Maharashtra	14.401
4. Andhra Pradesh	11.416
5. Karnataka	9.165
6. Uttar Pradesh	8.061
7. Gujarat	7.836
8. Odisha	6.384
9. Bihar	5.458
10. Tamil Nadu	4.401
11. West Bengal	2.536
12. Haryana	2.478
13. Himachal Pradesh	1.958
14. Meghalaya	1.918
15. Assam	1.730
16. Jammu & Kashmir	1.565
17. Manipur	1.438
18. Nagaland	1.386
19. Kerala	1.279
20. Punjab	1.230
21. Tripura	0.973
22. Sikkim	0.281
23. Union Territory	3.604
Total	**129.580**

Table VII States with Largest Barren and Un-cultivable Land Area in India

State	Area in thousand hectares
1. Gujarat	2607
2. Rajasthan	2427
3. Andhra Pradesh	2098
4. Maharashtra	1719
5. Assam	1447
6. Madhya Pradesh	1406
7. Odisha	0843
8. Karnataka	0788
9. Himachal Pradesh	0672
10. Jharkhand	0573
India	**17438**

Table VIII States with Largest Cultivable Wasteland Area in India

State	Area in thousand Hectares
1. Rajasthan	4611
2. Gujarat	1877
3. Madhya Pradesh	1177
4. Maharashtra	0914
5. Andhra Pradesh	0695
6. Meghalaya	0450
7. Uttar Pradesh	0439
8. Karnataka	0416
9. Odisha	0392
10. Uttarakhand	0384
India	**13,239**

Table IX Three Largest Producing States of India of the Major Crops

Crop	State	Percentage share of production to all India production
Rice	1. West Bengal 2. Punjab 3. Uttar Pradesh	20.0 12.25 11.15
Wheat	1. Uttar Pradesh 2. Punjab 3. Haryana	36.27 21.80 14.10

(*Contd.*)

(*Contd.*)

Crop	State	Percentage share of production to all India production
Maize	1. Madhya Pradesh 2. Andhra Pradesh 3. Karnataka	14.56 14.45 13.40
Total coarse grains	1. Maharashtra 2. Rajasthan 3. Karnataka	23.48 18.46 14.35
Total Pulses	1. Madhya Pradesh 2. Uttar Pradesh 3. Maharashtra	19.84 18.49 18.40
Total Food-grains	1. Uttar Pradesh 2. Punjab 3. West Bengal	20.84 13.49 08.91
Oilseeds		
Groundnut	1. Gujarat 2. Tamil Nadu 3. Andhra Pradesh	25.0 22.50 18.81
Mustard & Rapeseed	1. Rajasthan 2. Uttar Pradesh 3. Haryana	33.67 19.39 17.60
Soybean	1. Madhya Pradesh 2. Maharashtra 3. Rajasthan	56.58 34.65 05.25
Sunflower	1. Madhya Pradesh 2. Andhra Pradesh 3. Maharashtra	45.05 30.77 16.48
Total oilseeds	1. Madhya Pradesh 2. Maharashtra 3. Rajasthan	19.92 15.47 11.62
Sugarcane	1. Uttar Pradesh 2. Maharashtra 3. Tamil Nadu	41.31 13.15 11.55
Cotton	1. Maharashtra 2. Gujarat 3. Andhra Pradesh	29.85 19.27 12.50
Jute and Mesta	1. West Bengal 2. Bihar 3. Assam	75.50 10.00 06.30
Tea	1. Assam 2. West Bengal 3. Tamil Nadu	53.00 24.00 11.00

(*Contd.*)

(*Contd.*)

Crop	State	Percentage share of production to all India production
Coffee	1. Karnataka 2. Kerala 3. Tamil Nadu	56.00 25.00 09.00
Rubber	1. Kerala 2. Tamil Nadu 3. Karnataka	
Tobacco	1. Andhra Pradesh 2. Maharashtra 3. Gujarat	
Potato	1. Uttar Pradesh 2. West Bengal 3. Bihar	43.88 29.80 06.22
Onion	1. Maharashtra 2. Gujarat 3. Karnataka	29.10 17.00 10.60
Black Pepper/ Cardamom/ Clove	1. Kerala 2. Karnataka 3. Tamil Nadu	60.00 31.00 09.00

Table X India's rank in world agriculture

	India	World	India's share	India's rank in the world	Next to
1. Total area	329	13425	2.5	Seventh	Russian Federation, Canada, USA, China, Brazil, Australia
2. Land Area	297	13062	2.3	Seventh	Russian Federation, China, Canada, USA, Brazil, Australia
3. Arable Land	162	1364	11.9	Second	U.S.A.
4. Irrigated area	55	272	20.2	First	-
Total cereals	231	2086	11.1	Third	China and USA
Total Pulses	11	52	21.2	First	-

Table XI Source-wise Irrigated Area

Source	Area in million hectares	Percentage
Govt. Canals	15.79	28.88
Private Canals	00.20	00.37
Tube wells	21.73	39.74
Other wells	11.55	21.12
Tanks	02.52	04.61
Other sources	02.89	05.28
Net irrigated area	54.68	100.00

Table XII States with Largest Cropped Area in India

State	Area in thousand hectares
1. Uttar Pradesh	25800
2. Maharashtra	22571
3. Rajasthan	21534
4. Madhya Pradesh	20113
5. Andhra Pradesh	12811
6. Karnataka	12438
7. Gujarat	12202
8. West Bengal	09635
9. Odisha	08677
10. Punjab	07983
India	193,723

Table XIII States with Largest Cultivable Area in India

State	Area in thousand hectares
1. Maharashtra	18800
2. Rajasthan	18703
3. Uttar Pradesh	17903
4. Madhya Pradesh	15504
5. Andhra Pradesh	13313
6. Karnataka	11670
7. Gujarat	11670
8. Bihar	06222
9. Odisha	06165
10. Tamil Nadu	06033
India	155535

Table XIV States with the Largest Net Irrigated Area in India

State	Area in thousand hectares
1. Uttar Pradesh	18939
2. Rajasthan	07958
3. Punjab	07722
4. Madhya Pradesh	06543
5. Andhra Pradesh	06070
6. Bihar	04325
7. Karnataka	03603
8. Tamil Nadu	03309
9. Chhattisgarh	01486
10. Uttarakhand	00549

(Contd.)

Table XV States with the Largest Net Irrigated Area by Canals in India

State	In thousand hectares
1. Uttar Pradesh	4030
2. Rajasthan	2370
3. Andhra Pradesh	2298
4. Punjab	1909
5. Karnataka	1377
6. Madhya Pradesh	1137
7. Bihar	1061
8. Chhattisgarh	0982
9. Tamil Nadu	0944
10. Jammu & Kashmir	0412

Table XVI States with the Largest Net Irrigated Area by Tube-wells

State	Area in thousand hectares
1. Uttar Pradesh	13651
2. Punjab	05799
3. Bihar	02895
4. Rajasthan	02400
5. Andhra Pradesh	02020
6. Madhya Pradesh	01838
7. Karnataka	01149
8. Tamil Nadu	00461
9. Chhattisgarh	00316
10. Uttarakhand	00293

Table XVII States with the Largest Net Irrigated Area by Water Tanks

State	Area in thousand hectares
1. Andhra Pradesh	696
2. Tamil Nadu	569
3. Karnataka	212
4. Bihar	183
5. Madhya Pradesh	153
6. Uttar Pradesh	152
7. Rajasthan	137
8. Chhattisgarh	055
9. Jammu & Kashmir	005
10. Punjab	001

Table XVIII Crop-wise Irrigated Area

Crop	Area in thousand Hectares	Percentage of the cropped area
1. Wheat	22.67	88.10
2. Rice	23.96	53.96
3. Total oil-seeds	5.24	12.55
4. Coarse-cereals	3.78	12.50
5. Total pulses	2.54	12.50

Glossary

Abiotic: Nonliving.

Abyssal plain: Flat, cold, sediment-covered ocean floor between the continental rise and the oceanic ridge at a depth of 3700 to 5500 metres. Abyssal plains are more extensive in the Atlantic and Indian oceans than in the Pacific Ocean.

Acid precipitation: Precipitation that is more acidic than natural precipitation, which has an average pH of about 5.5.

Acid rain: Rain containing acids and acid forming compounds such as sulphur dioxide and oxides of nitrogen.

Actual Evapotranspiration: Actual amount of evaporation and transpiration that occurs; derived in the water-balance equation by subtracting the deficit from potential evapotranspiration.

Adaptation: An inheritable structural or behavioural modification. A favourable adaptation gives a species an advantage in survival and reproduction. An unfavourable adaptation lessens a species ability to survive and reproduce.

Advection fog: Active condensation formed hen warm, moist air moves laterally over cooler water or land surfaces, causing the lower layers of the overlying air to be chilled to the deq-point temperature.

Aeolian: Wind-blown.

Aerology: The study of the free atmosphere through its vertical extent.

Aeroplankton: Spores and other microscopic organic particles and organisms that drift in the air because they weigh so little that they fall only slowly and are likely to be carried aloft again by raising air currents before settling on a surface.

Aerosol: A substance consisting of small particles, typically having diameters that range from 1/100 micrometer to 1 micrometer.

Afforestation: It is a type of social forestry. If the trees are planted on a piece of land which was formerly not under plant cover for commercial or any other purpose is known as afforestation.

Agro-biodiversity: This is subset of biodiversity related to agriculture. It could be defined as diversity of agricultural systems, all agricultural related species and individuals within species.

Agroclimatology: The scientific study of the effects of climate upon crops.

Agroforestry: This is a system of land use where woody perennials are deliberately used on the same land management units as annual agriculture crops.

Albedo: The reflective quality of a surface, expressed as the relationship of incoming to reflected insolation and stated as percentage; a function of surface colour, angle of incidence, and surface texture.

Algae: Collective term for nonvascular plants processing chlorophyll and capable of photosynthesis (singular, alga).

Algal bloom: The rapid and excessive growth of algae. It may deoxygenate the water leading to the loss of wildlife.

Alien species: When plants and animals get introduced in new areas crossing their own physical boundaries on land and sea, these are known as alien species. Alien species could either get introduced accidentally or deliberately. Their deliberate introduction could be for the sake of food, fodder, raw material, sports, aesthetics or any other necessity.

Alkaline: Basic. See base.

Alluvial fan: Fan shaped fluvial landform at the mouth of a canyon, generally occurs in arid landscapes where streams are intermittent.

Alluvium: General descriptive term for clay, silt, and sand, transported by running water and deposited in sorted or semi-sorted sediment on a floodplain, delta or stream bed.

Alpine Glacier: A glacier confined in a mountain valley or walled basin, consisting of three subtypes: valley glacier (within a valley), piedmont glacier (coalesced at the base of mountain, spreading freely over nearby lowlands), and outlet glacier (flowing outward from a continental glacier).

Alternation of generation: A reproductive cycle in which plant alternates between sexual and asexual stages.

Anemometer: A device to measure wind velocity.

Angiosperm: A flowering vascular plant that reproduces by means of a seed-bearing fruit. Examples are sea grasses and mangroves.

Angle of incidence: In meteorology, the angle of Sun above the horizon.

Animal: A multicellular organism unable to synthesise its own food often capable of movement.

Aneroid barometer: A device to measure air pressure using a partially emptied, sealed cell.

Antarctic bottom water: The densest ocean water (1.0279 g/cm^3), formed primarily in Antarctica's Weddell Sea during Southern Hemisphere winters.

Antarctic Convergence: Convergence zone encircling Antarctica between about 50° and 60°, marking the boundary between Antarctic Convergence and the south by Antarctica.

Anticyclone: A dynamically or thermally caused area of high atmospheric pressure with descending and diverging air flows.

Aphelion: The most distant point in Earth's elliptical orbit about the Sun; reached on July 4 at a distance of 152,083,000 km (94.5 million miles), variable over a 100,000-year cycle.

Aphotic zone: The dark ocean below the depth to which light can penetrate.

Aquaculture: The growing or farming of plants and animals in a water environment under controlled conditions.

Aquatic ecosystem: These are the ecosystems that occur in water and are also known as marine ecosystems.

Aquifer: Rock strata permeable to groundwater flow. Aquifer recharge area: The surface area where water enters an aquifer to recharge the water-bearing strata in a groundwater system.

Arboreal: The tropical rainforest animals live on trees are known as arboreals.

Arctic Circle: The imaginary line around the Earth, parallel to the equator at 66°33′N marking the northernmost limit of sunlight at the December solstice. The Arctic Circle marks the southern limit of the area within which, for one day or more each year, the Sun does not set (around 21st June) or rise (around 21st December).

Arctic hurricanes: An intense low pressure system that develops along the edge of the pack ice in the Arctic. Arctic hurricanes produce high winds and heavy precipitation and represent a major hazard to shipping along their path.

Arctic Ocean: An ice-covered ocean north of the continents of North America and Eurasia.

Arctic Tundra: A biome in the northern-most portion of North America, Europe and Russia, featuring low ground level herbaceous plants as well as some woody plants.

Artesian water: Pressurised groundwater that rises in a well or rock structure above the local water table; may flow out onto the ground.

Asthenosphere: Regions of the upper mantle just below the lithosphere known as plastic layer; the least rigid portion of Earth's interior; shattered if struck yet flows under extreme heat and pressure.

Astronomical twilight: The period after sunset or before sunrise ending or beginning when the Sun is 18° below the horizon.

Atmosphere: The thin veil of gases surrounding Earth, that forms a protective boundary between outer space and the biosphere, generally considered to be below 480 km (300 miles).

Atmospheric circulation cell: Large circuit of air driven by uneven solar heating and the Coriolis effect. Three circulation cells form in each hemisphere (Hadley cell, Ferrel cell and Polar cell).

Atoll: A ring-shaped island of coral reefs and coral debris enclosing, or almost enclosing, a shallow lagoon from which on land protrudes. Atolls often form over sinking, inactive volcanoes.

Atom: The smallest particle of an element that exhibits the characteristics of that element.

Atomic nucleus: A small positive central portion of the atom that contains its protons and neutrons.

Autecology: It is concerned with the study of ecological relations of individual species in a given ecosystem.

Autotroph: An organism that makes its own food by photosynthesis or chemosynthesis.

Aurora: A display of coloured light seen in the polar skies; called *Aurora borealis* in the Northern Hemisphere and *Aurora Australis* in the Southern Hemisphere.

Australian biome: Eucalyptus dominates the landscape in the Australian biome. Karri is the tallest species of eucalyptus. The height of Australian eucalyptus reaches 70 metres or more.

Authogenic succession: When a set of habitats paves way for another, it is known as authogenic succession.

Automorphic succession: It refers to the biotic changes on a predominantly inorganic site.

Autotrophs: The primary producers (plants) are known as autotrophs.

Autumnal (September) equinox: The time around September 22–23 when the Sun's declination crosses the equatorial parallel; all places on Earth experience days and nights of equal length. The Sun rises at the South Pole and sets at the North Pole.

Aves: A class of birds.

Backwash: Water returning to the ocean from waves washing on to a beach.

Barrier island: A long, narrow, wave-built island lying parallel to the mainland and separated from it by a lagoon or bay.

Barrier reef: A coral reef surrounding an island or lying parallel to the shore of a continent, separated from land by deep lagoon. Coral debris islands may form along the reef.

Base: A substance that combine with a hydrogen ion (H) in solution.

Bathyal zone: The ocean between about 200 and 4000 metres deep.

Beach: A zone of unconsolidated (loose) particles extending from below water level to the edge of the coastal zone.

Beaufort wind scale: A system for estimating wind velocity (named for its inventor).

Beej-Bachao Andolan: This movement was started in the Garhwal Region of Uttarakhand in the 1970s. During the movement the local collected seeds of diverse staple and non-staple crops of Garhwal. In fact, the seeds of rice varieties. *Rajmah* (Kidney beans), pulses, millets, maize, vegetables, spices and medicinal herbs were collected with the set objective to conserve and grow the indigenous seeds.

Benthic zone: The zone of the ocean bottom (pelagic zone).

Benthic organism: A plant or animal that lives at or near the bottom of a body of water/ocean.

Benthos: Aquatic life living on, in or at the bottom of a water body like oceans, seas, lakes, rivers, etc.

Biochemical Cycle: The various circuits of flowing elements and materials (carbon, Oxygen, phosphorus, water) that combine Earth's biotic and abiotic systems; the cycling of materials is continuous and renewed through the biosphere and the life processes.

Biodegradable: Able to be broken by natural processes into simpler compounds.

Biodiversity: An abbreviation of 'biological diversity' and usually taken to mean the total number of species presently living on Earth.

Biodiversity decline: The reduction in the species of plants and animals. It is estimated that about 20,000 species became extinct every year indicating a rapid decline in biodiversity.

Biodiversity hotspots: A small area of land that contains an exceptional number of endemic species and are at high risk from human activities.

Biogas: Methane produced by fermentation of organic waste.

Biogeography: The study of the distribution of plants and animals and related ecosystems, the geographical relationships with related environment over time.

Biological clock: It is basically a rhythm of daily activities and bodily processes.

Biological control: The control of pest population without using chemical pesticides, most commonly by stimulating parasites and predators of the pest.

Biological factors: A biologically generated aspect of the environment, such as predation or metabolic waste products, that affects living organisms. Biological factors usually operate in association with purely physical factors such as light and temperature.

Biological resource: A living animal or plant collected for human use. Also called a living resource.

Bioluminescence: Biologically produced light.

Biomass: The total mass of living organisms on Earth or per unit area of a landscape; also, the weight of the living organisms in an ecosystem.

Biomass energy: Biomass fuel are produced from plants and animals waste and residues.

Biome: A large terrestrial ecosystem characterised by specific plant communities and formations; usually named after the predominant vegetation in the region. In other words, it is a well-demarcated environment that contains a complex of organism defining the ecology of the region. Tundra and rain forest are examples.

Biosphere: That area where the atmosphere, lithosphere, and hydrosphere function together to form the context within which life exists; an intricate web that connects all organisms with their physical environment.

Biosynthesis: The initial formation of life on the Earth.

Biota: The total flora and fauna of a region.

Biotic: Living

Biotic continuam: The vegetation undergoes gradual continuous changes and cannot be differentiated into different communities. This continuity in biotic system is known as biotic continuity.

Biotic succession: Biotic communities are not static but these keep on changing continuously with time, so much so that with time some communities get replaced by others. Such an orderly and progressive replacement of one community by another, until a relatively stable community called the 'climax community' occupies the area, is known as ecosystem development or biotic succession.

Biotope: Sub-division of habitat where an area, in which all the faunal and floral elements (Biota) are uniformly adapted to the environment in which they occur.

Black smoker: A hydrothermal vent on the ocean floor emitting fluid containing iron, manganese, and copper. These tend to be black and resemble smoke. Vent fluids containing zinc and arsenic are usually white, and known as 'white smokers'.

Blizzard: High winds accompanied by blowing snow; usually associated with winter cold fronts in mid-latitudes.

Bloom: A rapid and often unpredictable growth of a single species in an ecosystem.

Brackish: Describing water intermediate in salinity between seawater and fresh water.

Calcification: In a soil, calcification takes place when evaporation exceeds precipitation. In this case the material moves upward due to capillary action, bringing calcium rich compounds upwards.

Calorie: The amount of heat needed to raise the temperature of 1 gram of pure water by 1°C.

Canopy: The leafy part of a shrub or a tree.

Carbonation: A process of chemical weathering by a weak carbonic acid (water and carbon dioxide) that reacts with many minerals, especially limestone, containing calcium, magnesium, potassium, and sodium transforming them into carbonate.

Carbon monoxide: An odourless, colourless, tasteless combination of carbon and oxygen produced by the incomplete combustion of fossil fuels or other carbon-containing substances, CO.

Calcification: Calcification in a soil takes place when evaporation exceeds precipitation. In this case the material moves upward due to capillary action, bringing calcium rich compounds upward.

California biome: The topmost layer of natural vegetation in this type of biome is dominated by oak canopy, chaparral, is located at the middle layer and small grasses lie at the bottom layer.

Carbon credit: A way of reducing the impact of greenhouse gases emission. It allows an agent to benefit financially from emission reduction. It represents one tone of carbon dioxide either removed from the atmosphere or saved from being emitted. It is also known as emission permit.

Carnivora: The order of mammals that includes seals, sea lions, walruses, and sea otters.

Carnivore: A secondary consumer that principally eats meat for sustenance. Top carnivores in a food chain is considered a tertiary consumer.

Carrying capacity: The size at which a particular population in a particular environment will stabilise when its supply of resources – including nutrients, energy, and living space – remain constant.

Cell: The basic organisational unit of life on this planet.

Chaparral: Dominant shrub formations of Mediterranean dry summer climates; characterised by (sclerophyllous) scrub and short, stunted, and tough forests; derived from the Spanish chapparo, specific to California. It has short-leaved evergreen shrubs and small trees.

Chemical energy: The energy that is absorbed when chemical bonds are broken or released when they are formed.

Chemical weathering: Decomposition and decay of the constituent minerals in rock through chemical alteration of those minerals. Water is essential, with rates keyed to temperature and precipitation values. Processes include hydrolysis, oxidation, carbonation, and solution.

Chemosynthesis: The synthesis of organic compounds from inorganic compounds using energy stored in inorganic substances such as sulphur, ammonia, and hydrogen. Energy is released when these substances are oxidised by certain organisms.

Chemotroph: Organisms that obtain energy by the oxidation of electron-donating molecules in their environment.

Chinook: A warm, dry wind blowing down off the Rocky Mountains of western North America.

Chipko movement: Started in 1970s, it was a people's movement to counter deforestation in Garhwal (Uttarakhand). The large scale felling of trees was stopped by the local women supported by Sundar Lal Bahuguna and Chandi Prasad Bhat.

Chlorofluorocarbon Compounds (CFCs): Large manufactured molecules (polymers) containing chlorine, fluorine, and carbon; inert and processing remarkable heat properties; also known as halogens. After slow transport to the stratosphere ozone layer CFCs react with ultraviolet radiation freeing chlorine atoms that act as a catalyst to produce reactions that destroys ozone.

Chlorophyll: A light-sensitive pigment that resides within the chloroplast bodies of plants in leaf cells, the basis of photosynthesis.

Cirque: A scooped-out, amphitheatre-shaped basin at the head of an alpine glacier valley; an erosional landform.

Cirrus: Wispy filaments of ice-crystal clouds that occur above 6000 m; appear in a variety of forms, from feathery hair-like fibres to veils of fused sheets.

Climate: The consistent, long-term behaviour of weather over time, including its variability, in contrast to weather, which is the condition of the atmosphere at any given place and time. In other words, all types of weather that occur at a given place over time.

Climatic regions: Area of similar climate, which contain characteristic regional weather and air mass patterns.

Climax: The stable, enduring plant community that is the final result of a succession of communities (sere). The succession begins with the colonisation of bare or water that sustains no plant life.

Climatology: A scientific study of climate and climatic patterns and the consistent behaviour of weather and weather variability and extremes over time in one place or region; including the effects of climate change on human society and culture.

Closed System: A system that is shut off from the surrounding environment so that it is entirely self contained in terms of energy and materials; Earth is a closed material system (See open system).

Cloud: An aggregation of moisture droplets and icy crystals that are suspended in air and are great enough in volume and density to be visible; basic forms include stratiform, cumuliform, and cirroform.

Coal: A biochemical rock, rich in carbon; including lignite, bituminous, and anthracite forms.

Composite volcano: A volcano formed by a sequence of explosive volcanic eruptions; steep sided, conical in shape; sometimes referred to as a strato-volcano, although composite is the preferred term.

Codensation: The change of state from a gas to a liquid.

Community: IT is a collection of species population, e.g., in a stand of pine-trees, there may be many species of insects, birds, animals, each being a separate breeding unit, yet each being dependent upon others for its own existence.

Components of environment: There are three basic components of environment. These include (i) abiotic (physical or inorganic) components; (ii) biotic (organic components); and (iii) the energy component.

Conduction: The slow molecule-to-molecule transfer of heat through a medium, from warmer to cooler portions.

Consumer: Organisms in an ecosystem that depends on producers (autotrophs), organisms capable of using carbon dioxide as their sole source of carbon for their source of nutrients.

Continental glacier: A continuous mass of unconfined ice, covering at least 50,000 sq km; most extensive as ice sheets covering Antarctica and Greenland.

Continentality: A qualitative designation applied to regions that lack the temperature-moderating effects of the sea and that exhibit a greater range between minimum and maximum temperatures, both daily and annually.

Contour Line: Isolines on a topographic map that connect all points at the same elevation relative to a reference elevation called vertical datum.

Convection: Vertical transfer of heat from one place to another through the actual physical movement of air; involves a strong vertical motion.

Coordinated Universal Time (UTC): The official reference time in all countries, formerly known as Greenwich Mean Time; now measured by six primary standard atomic clocks whose time calculations are collected in Paris (France), by the Bureau International de l'Heure.

Coral: A simple, cylindrical marine animal with a saclike body that secretes calcium carbonate to form a hard external skeleton; lives symbiotically with nutrient-producing algae.

Core: The deepest inner portion of Earth, representing one-third of its entire mass; differentiated into two zones – a solid iron inner core surrounded by a dense, molten, fluid metallic-iron outer core.

Chorley, R.J. 1969, *Water, Earth and Man*, ed., London, Methuen.

Coriolis Force: The apparent deflection of moving objects on Earth from a straight path, in relationship to the differential speed of rotation at varying latitudes. Deflection is to the right in the Northern Hemisphere and to the left in the Southern Hemisphere; it produces a maximum effect at the poles and zero effect along the equator.

Crater: A circular surface or pipe; can be at the summit or on the flank of a volcano.

Crust: Earth's outer shell of crystalline surface rock, ranging from 5 to 60 km in thickness from oceanic crust to mountain ranges.

Cybernatics: It is the science of systems of control in an ecosystem.

Cyclone: A dynamically or thermally caused low-pressure area of converging and ascending air-flow (see wave cyclone and tropical cyclone).

Daylength: Duration of exposure to insolation, varying during the year depending on latitude, an important aspect of seasonality.

Daylight saving time: Time is set ahead one hour in the spring and set back one hour in the fall in the Northern Hemisphere. Time is set a head on the first Sunday in April and setback on the last Sunday in October – only Hawaii, Arizona, portions of Indiana, and Saskatchewan exempt themselves.

Debris avalanche: A mass of falling and tumbling rock, debris, and soil; can be dangerous because of the tremendous velocities achieved by the onrushing materials.

Decomposers: Microorganisms that digest and recycle organic debris and waste in the environment; includes bacteria, fungi, insects, and worms.

Deflation: A process of wind erosion that removes and lifts individual particles, literally blowing away unconsolidated, dry, or non-cohesive sediments.

Deforestation: It refers to the forest loss. Once the degradation of forest becomes serious, the reversal of the process is very difficult. Through the process of deforestation, the forest area is converted into arable land, pastures, or wasteland.

Delta: A depositional plain formed where a river enters a lake or an ocean; named after the triangular shape of the Greek letter delta.

Denudation: A general term that refers to all processes that cause degradation of the landscape: weathering, mass movement, erosion and transport.

Deposition: The process whereby weathered, wasted, and transported sediments are laid down; deposited by air, water, or ice.

Desert Biome: Arid landscape of unique adapted dry climate plants and animals.

Desertification: The spread of desert like conditions in a given location.

Detritus Food Chain: Food chain that starts from dead and decayed organisms, to the mocro-organisms, to the detrivores or saprovores and these predators form a chain called detritus food-chain.

Detrivores or decomposers: The decomposer organisms are known as detrivores. All energy finally passes to decomposer organisms.

Dew point temperature: The temperature at which a given mass of air becomes saturated, holding all the water it can hold. Any further cooling or addition of water vapour results in active condensation.

Diatom: The Earth's most abundant, successful, and efficient single-celled phytoplankton. Diatoms possess two interlocking valves made primarily of silica. The valves contribute to biogenous sediments.

Diffuse radiation: The downward component of scattered incoming insolation from clouds and the atmosphere.

Disasters: Disaster are sudden adverse unfortunate extreme events or hazards which cause great damage to human beings as well as plants and animals. Disaster may be natural or arthropogenic.

Dissolved load: Materials carried in chemical solution in a stream derived from minerals such as limestone and dolomite, or from soluble salts.

Diurnal: Occurring in the daytime or having a daily cycle.

Divergent evolution: Evolutionary radiation of different species from a common ancestor.

Diversity: A principle of ecology: the more diverse the species population (both in number of species and quantity of members in each species), the more risks are spread over the entire community, which results in greater overall stability.

Doldrums: The zone of rising air near the equator known for sultry air and variable breeze. Also known as the inter-tropical convergence zone.

Drainage Pattern: A geometric arrangement of streams in a region; determined by slope, differing rock resistance to weathering and erosion, climatic and hydrological variability, and structural controls of the landscape.

Drought: A time of unusually low water supply, due to reduced rainfall, reduced snowmelt, or low levels of streams.

Dune: A depositional feature of sand grains deposited in transient mounds, ridges, and hills, extensive areas of sand dunes are called sand seas.

Earth Summit: As a follow up of stockholm UN sponsored environmental conference of 1972, the Second Earth Summit was held at Rio-de-Janeiro (Brazil) on June 3-14, 1992. The world community deliberated upon Agenda 21, i.e. biodiversity, climate change and sustainable development.

Earthquake: A sudden motion of the Earth's crust resulting from waves in the Earth caused by faulting of the rocks or by volcanic activity. Earthquake magnitude is estimated by the Richter Scale, intensity is described by the Mercalli Scale.

Ecological balance: In a natural state, there exists perfect harmony between various cycles and flow of energy, establishing a dynamic and fluctuating equilibrium in any ecosystem. This is known as ecological balance.

Ecological efficiency: The percentage of energy transformed from one level to the next higher level of the trophic structure is called ecological efficiency.

Ecological niche: The role that an organism takes in the ecosystem is known as ecological niche.

Ecological Succession: The process whereby different and usually more complex assemblages of plants and animals replace older and usually simpler communities. Changes apparently move toward a more stable and mature condition.

Ecology: The science that studies the interrelationships among organisms and their environment and among various ecosystems.

Ecosystem: A self regulating association of living plants, animals, and their non-living physical and chemical environment.

Ecotone: A boundary transition zone between adjoining ecosystems that may vary in width and represent areas of tension as similar species of plants and animals compete for the resources.

Effusive eruption: An eruption characterised by low viscosity, basaltic magma, with low-gas content readily escaping. Lava pours forth onto the surface with relatively small explosions and little tephra; tends to form shield volcanoes.

EIA (Environmental Impact Assessment): It is the analysis of any possible alteration of environmental conditions, adverse or beneficial, caused by the project under consideration.

El Nino and La Nina: A southward-flowing nutrient-poor current of warm water off the coast of western South America, caused by a breakdown of trade wind circulation. The return of the cold water along the Peru coast and warm water back to western Pacific Ocean is known as La Nina.

Eluviation: The downward removal of finer particles and minerals from the upper horizons of soil.

Endangered species: The species that face a very high risk of extinction in near future.

Endemic species: The native or local species that are not found anywhere else in the world. Endemic species have very restricted distribution due to the ecological requirements.

Endemism: In general, it means native to or characteristic of a particular geographical area.

Endozoochory: The carrying of plant seeds by an animal on the outside of its body (e.g. in its coat or feathers).

Energy: It is one of the components of environment. Energy is vital for the generation as well as sustenance of organic life. It includes both solar as well as geothermal energy, though the main source of energy in the environment remains the Sun.

ENSO: Acronym for the coupled phenomenon of El Nino and the Southern Oscillation.

Entropy: A measure of the disorder in a system.

Environmental equilibrium: When man is in nature not creating too much waste while fulfilling his basic needs is known as environmental equilibrium.

Epiphyte: A unit of geologic time equivalent to a series, a division of a period.

Environmental ethics: It is the field of applied ethics that consider the moral basis of environmental responsibility. It also considers how humans should relate to the natural environment.

Environmental pollution: Environmental pollution means adding to the environment a potentially hazardous substance or source of energy faster than the rate at which the environment can accommodate it. Environmental pollution is an undesirable change in physical, chemical or biological characteristics of air, water and land that may be or will be harmful to human life and other living organisms, living conditions, industrial progress and cultural assets and will deteriorate raw material resources.

Epicentre: The surface area directly above the subsurface focus where movement along the fault plane was initiated. Shock waves radiate outward from the epicentre area.

Equatorial and tropical rain forest: A lush biome of tall broadleaf evergreen trees and diverse plants and animals. The dense canopy of leaves is usually arranged in three levels.

Equilibrium: The status of a balanced energy and material system; maintains the system's general structure and character; a balance between form and process.

Environmental resistance: All the limiting factors that act together to regulate the maximum allowable size, or carrying capacity of a population.

Environmental temperature lapse rate: The rate of temperature decrease upward through the troposphere, standard value is 6.4°C per km.

Equilibrium line: The area of a glacier where accumulation (gain) and ablation (loss) are balanced.

Erg desert: Sandy desert, or areas where sand is so extensive that it constitutes a sand sea.

Erosion: A process of being gradually worn away. Denudation by wind, water, and ice, which dislodges, dissolves, or removes surface material.

Estuary: The point at which the mouth of a river enters the sea and freshwater and seawater are mixed; a place where tides ebb and flow.

Ethology: An approach to study the animal behaviour in the natural environment. It examines the causes of evolution of behaviour.

Euphotic zone: The upper region of a lake or sea within which light intensity is sufficient for photosynthesis.

Eustasy: Refers to worldwide changes in sea level that are not related to movements of land but rather to a rise and fall in the volume of water in the oceans.

Euphotic zone: The surface volume of water in the ocean or a deep lake that receives sufficient light to support photosynthesis.

Eutrophic: Fertile, productive, usually of lakes.

Eutrophication: A natural process in which lakes receive nutrients and sediment and become enriched; the gradual filling and natural aging of water bodies.

Evapotranspiration: The merging of evaporation and transpiration water loss into one term (see potential and actual evapotranspiration).

Evolution: Change. The maintenance of life under constantly changing conditions by continuous adaptation of successive generations of a species to its environment.

Exosphere: It is an exteremly rarefied outer atmospheric halo beyond the thermopause at an altitude of 480 km (300 miles); probably composed of hydrogen and helium atoms, with some oxygen atoms and nitrogen molecules present near the thermopause.

Exotic: A term normally used to describe a plant or animal which is kept, usually in a semi-natural or artificial manner, in a region outside its natural habitat. A wide range of garden plants and aviary birds are exotic, having been introduced by horticulturists and bird fanciers from widely differing regions of the world.

Exotic stream: A river that rises in a humid region and flows through an arid region, with discharge decreasing toward the mouth; for example, the Nile River and the Colorado.

Explosive eruption: A violent and unpredictable eruption, the result of magma that is thicker, stickier (more viscous), and higher in gas content and silica, than that of an effusive eruption; tends to form blockages within a volcano; produces composite volcanic landforms.

Ex-situ conservation: It is practised outside the habitats of genetic resources by conserving sample population of the species in zoos, genetic resources centres, botanical gardens, etc. The role of gene banks, seed banks, germplasm bank, genetic engineer is vital for ex-situ conservation of species of plants and animals.

Famine: The scarcity of food over a large region, resulting in malnutrition or starvation for very large numbers of people.

Fauna: The sum of all animal life of any particular region or time.

Fire climax: A condition in which the continuance of a given ecosystem is maintained by fire.

Fire ecology: Recognises fire as a dynamic ingredient in community succession. Controlled fires secure plant production and prevent the accumulation of forest litter and brush; widely regarded as a wise forest management practice.

Flood: A high water level that overflows the natural (or artificial) banks along any portion of a stream.

Flood Frequency: Flood frequency in a particular area may vary over time, especially as a result of human activity, and in some areas damage produced by floods has increased despite expenditure on flood protection simply because there is a tendency to assume that flood protection measures have completely eliminated the flood hazards. Some of the steps which may go a long way in the control of floods are given below.

Floodplain: A low-lying area near a stream channel, subject to recurrent flooding; alluvial deposit generally mask underlying rock.

Flora: All the plants found in a region.

Fluvial: Stream related processes, from the Latin fluvius for 'river' or 'running water'.

Fog: A cloud, generally stratiform, in contact with the ground, with visibility usually restricted to less than 1 km.

Food chain: The circuit along which energy flows from producers, who manufacture their own food, to consumers; a one directional flow of chemical energy, ending with decomposers.

Food web: A complex network of interconnected food chains.

Forb: Any broadleaf herbaceous plant growing in grassland.

Fresh water: Bodies of water such as ponds, lakes, rivers, and streams containing low concentrations of dissolved salts and other total dissolved solids.

Gaia: The ancient Greek goddess of the earth. This word has recently been used to describe the biosphere and to emphasize the interdependence of the earth's ecosystems by linking the entire biosphere to a single living organism.

Gene pool: The total number of genes possessed by all those members of a sexually reproducing species or population that are capable of reproduction (i.e. in the reproductive phase of their lives).

Genetic classification: A type of classification that uses causative factors to determine climatic regions; for example, an analysis of the effect of interacting air masses.

Genetic control: The genetic control of pests involving releasing sterilised pests into the affected area. When these pests made with the female of their species, there are no offspring, leading to a decline in the number of such pests.

Genetic engineering: The process of artificially removing specific genes from one organism and replacing them with genetic information from another.

Geography: The science that studies the interdependence among geographic areas, natural systems, processes, society, and cultural activities over space – a spatial science. The five themes of geographic education include: location, place, movement, regions, and human–Earth relationships.

Geologic cycle: A general term characterising the vast cycling (hydrology, tectonic and rock) in and on the lithosphere.

Geologic time scale: A listing of eras, periods, and epoch that span Earth's history; reflects the relative relationship of various layers of rock strata and the absolute dates as determined by scientific methods such as radioactive isotopic dating.

Geomorphology: The science that analyse and describe the origin, evolution, form, classification, and spatial distribution of landforms.

Geosphere: It is a term refers strictly to inorganic state of the Earth. It consists of lithosphere, hydrosphere and atmosphere.

Geothermal energy: Energy derived from the heat of the earth's interior.

Geostrophic wind: A wind aloft flowing parallel to the pressure gradient, with the pressure gradient and the Coriolis force in balance.

Glacier: A large mass of perennial ice resting on land or floating shelf-like in the sea adjacent to the land; formed from the accumulation and recrystallisation of snow.

Global warming: It refers to gradual rise of temperature in the atmosphere and the consequent change in global radiation balance mainly due to human activities that cause climate changes at local, regional and global levels.

Grazing Food Chain: It starts from green plants and through carnivores, it reaches the decomposers for final breakdown of the complex elements into simpler one.

Greenhouse effect: The process whereby radiatively active gases absorb and delay the oss of heat to space, thus keeping the lower troposphere moderately warmed through the radiation and re-radiation of infrared wavelengths.

Greenhouse gas: A gas that absorbs infrared radiation, carbon dioxide, methane, nitrous oxide, chlorofluorocarbon and troposphere ozone are greenhouse gases.

Green Party: A political party of Germany launched in 1981, with a manifesto to conserve ecology and environment.

Groundwater: Water below the Earth's surface. It generally occurs in pore spaces of rocks and soils.

Gully erosion: Gullies are deeper incisions into land in comparision to rills.

Habitat: That physical location in which an organism is biologically suited to live. Most species have habitat parameters or limits.

Hazard: Hazard is an extreme event which may become disaster only when it strikes the inhabited area.

Herbivores: The primary consumers in a food chain, which eats plant material formed by a producer that has synthesised organic molecules.

Heteromorphic succession: It refers to biotic changes on a predominantly organic site.

Heterotroph: An organism that obtain the organic substances it needs for nourishment by consuming other organisms.

Heterosphere: A zone of the atmosphere above the mesopause, 80 km in altitude; composed of rarified layers of oxygen atoms and nitrogen molecules, includes the ionosphere.

Heterotroph (Consumers): An organism that derives nourishment from other organisms because it is unable to synthesise its own food molecule.

Holozoics: These are those animals who take their food through their mouth.

Home range: The area in which an animal travels and gathers its food.

Homosphere: A zone of atmosphere from the surface up to 80 km, composed of an even mixture of gases including nitrogen, oxygen, argon, carbon dioxide, and trace gases.

Hot spot: An individual point of upwelling material originating in the asthenosphere; tend to remain fixed relative to migrating plates; some 100 are identified worldwide; exemplified by Yellowstone National Park, Hawaii, and Iceland.

Human–Earth relationship: One of the oldest themes of geography (the human–land relationship); includes the spatial analysis of settlement patterns, resource utilisation, and exploitation, hazard perception and planning, and the impact of environmental modification and artificial landscape creation.

Humification: The process of humus development is known as humification. It consists of slow oxidation or burning of vegetative matter. Acids, known as organic acids, are formed during humification. These help in decomposing the minerals of parent rock material of the soil.

Humus: A mixture of organic debris in the soil, worked by consumers and decomposers in the humification processes; characteristically formed from plant and animal litter laid down at the surface.

Hurricane: A tropical cyclone that is fully organised and intensified in inward-spiralling rainbands; ranges from 160 to 960 km in diameter, with wind speeds in excess of 119 kilometre per hour; a name used specifically in the Atlantic and eastern Pacific.

Hydrocarbons: These are released mainly by automobiles as industries. The hydrocarbons cause some health hazards.

Hydrograph: A graph of stream discharge over a period of time at a specific place on a stream. The relationship between stream discharge and precipitation input illustrated on the graph.

Hydrological cycle: A simplified model of the flow of water and water vapour from place to place as energy powers system operations. Water flows through the atmosphere, across the land where it is also stored as ice, and within groundwater.

Hydrosere: A sere (ecological succession) that begins in water.

Hydrosphere: A abiotic open system that includes all of Earth's water.

Hygroscopic water: Water held by surface forces of soil particles.

Ice age: cold episode, with accompanying alpine and continental ice accumulations, that has repeated roughly every 200 to 300 million years since the late Precambrian era (1.25 billion years ago); includes most recent episode of during the Pleistocene Ice Age, which began 1.65 million years ago.

Ice cap: A dome shaped glacier, less extensive than an ice sheet (<50,000 sq km), although it buries mountain peaks visible above the ice.

Ice field: An extensive form of land ice, with mountain ridges and peaks visible above the ice.

Ice sheet: An enormous continuous continental glacier. The bulk of glacial ice on Earth covers Antarctica and Greenland in two ice sheets.

Ice wedge: Formed when water enters a thermal contraction crack in permafrost and freezes. Repeated seasonal freezing and melting progressively expand the wedge.

Iceberg: Floating ice created by calving ice or large pieces breaking off and floating adrift; a hazard to shipping because the ice is 91 per cent submerged.

Illuviation: A depositional soil process as differentiated from eluviations; usually in the B horizon, where accumulations of clays, aluminium, iron, and more humus occur.

In-situ conservation: The genetic resources are conserved by maintaining them within a natural or artificial man-made ecosystem to which they belong. Nature reserves, cultural landscapes, biosphere reserves, national parks, sanctuaries, natural monuments, are included in in-situ conservation.

Insolation: Solar radiation that is intercepted by Earth.

Isotopes: Atoms of the same element that have different mass number.

International Date Line: The 180° meridian; an important corollary to the Prime Meridian at 0°, Greenwich, London (England); established by the Treaty of 1884.

Ionosphere: A layer in the atmosphere above 80 km where gamma, X-ray, and some ultraviolet radiation is absorbed and converted into infrared, or heat energy, and where the solar wind stimulate the auroras.

Isobar: An isoline connecting all points of equal pressure.

Isotherm: An isoline connecting all points of equal temperature.

Jet stream: The most prominent movement in upper level westerly wind flows; irregular, concentrated, sinuous bands of geostrophic wind, travelling at 300 kmph (190 mph).

Joule: A fundamental unit of energy, 4.184 joules = 1 calorie.

Keystone species: When conservation efforts are focused on a single species, it is called 'keystone species'.

Kinetic energy: Energy of motion.

Landslide: Landslide is a general term for relatively rapid types of mass movement, such as debris flow, debris-slide, rockslides, and slumps. It is a sudden, rapid, down-slope movement of a cohesive mass of regolith and/or bedrock in a variety of mass movement forms under the influence of gravity.

Land reclamation: Restoring a saline affected area or waste land for agriculture or pastures.

Langmuir precipitation: A type of precipitation in which drops of rain fuse together to create large drops as they fall quickly. This happen often in cloudburst.

La Nina: A strengthening of the normal circulation over the southern Pacific Ocean.

Lapse rate: The rate at which air temperature changes with altitude. This depends on local conditions, especially in humidity.

Laterisation: A pedogenic process operating in well-drained soil that are found in warm and humid regions; typical of oxisols. High precipitation values leach soluble minerals and soil constituents usually reddish or yellowish in colour.

Leaching: It is process by which water while percolating downward through a soil, removes humus in solution, soluble substances, sesquioxides, etc. form the upper horizon A and deposits the same in the underlying illuvial horizon B.

Life zone: An altitudinal zonation of plants and animals that form distinctive communities. Each life zone processes its own temperature and precipitation relationship.

Lithosphere: Earth's crust and that portion of the uppermost mantle directly below the crust that extends down to 70 km. Some use this term to refer to the entire Earth.

Little Ice Age: A period when average temperatures were lower than they are today throughout middle latitudes in the Northern Hemisphere. It lasted from about 1550 to 1860, with an especially severe episode in the early 1660s.

Littoral: The coast of an ocean or sea, or the banks of a river, lake or estuary.

Loess: Large quantities of fine grained clays and silts left as glacial outwash deposits; subsequently blown by the wind great distances and deposited as a generally unstratified, homogeneous blanket of material covering existing landscape. In China loess originated from desert land.

Mangrove: Large flowering shrub or tree that grows in dense thickets or forests along muddy or silty tropical coasts.

Mangrove swamp: Wetland ecosystems between 30° N or S and the equator; tend to form a distinctive community of mangrove plants.

Mariculture: The farming of marine organisms, usually in estuaries, bays, or nearshore environments or in specially designed structures using circulating seawater.

Marine: Regions that are dominated by the moderating effects of the ocean and that exhibit a smaller minimum and maximum temperature range than continental stations.

Marine pollution: The introduction by humans of substances or energy into the ocean that change the quality of the water or affect the physical and biological environment.

Marshland: Treeless land, covered with grasses, reeds, sedges wherein either on the surface or close to the surface.

Mean sea level: The average of tidal levels recorded hourly at a given site over a long period of time, which must be at least a full lunar tidal cycle.

Mediterranean shrubland: A major biome dominated by Mediterranean dry summer climates and is characterised by scrub and short, stunted, tough (sclerophyllous) forests.

Meridional circulation: Air flowing in a circulation pattern that is essentially aligned parallel to meridians of longitude.

Mesocyclone: A large rotating circulation initiated within a parent cumulonimbus cloud at the mid-troposhere level; generally produces heavy rain, large hail, blustery winds, and lightning; may lead to tornado activity.

Mesosphere: The upper region of the homosphere from 50 to 80 km above the ground; designated by temperature criteria and very low pressures.

Metamorphic rock: Existing rock, both igneous and sedimentary, that goes through profound physical and chemical changes under increased pressure and temperature. Constituent mineral structures may exhibit foliated or non-foliated textures.

Meteorology: The scientific study of atmosphere that includes a study of the atmosphere's physical characteristics and motions, related chemical, physical, and geological processes, the complex linkages of atmospheric systems, and weather forecasting.

Methane: A radiatively active gas that participates in the greenhouse effect; derived from the organic processes of burning, digesting, and rotting in the presence of oxygen; CH_4.

Microclimatology: The study of climates at or near Earth's surface.

Microhabitat: A defined part of a habitat within which a particular species or community is most likely to occur.

Midlatitude broadleaf and mixed forest: A biome in moist continental climates in areas of warm-to-hot summers and cool-to-cold winters; relatively lush stands of broadleaf forests trend northward into needle-leaf evergreen stands.

Mid-latitude grassland: The major biome most modified by human activity; so named because of the predominance of grass-like plants, although deciduous broadleafs appear along streams and other limited sites; location of the world's breadbaskets of grain and livestock production.

Mineral reserves: The estimated supply of ore in the ground.

Monsoon: From the Arabic word *Mausam,* meaning 'season'; refers to an annual cycle of dryness and wetness, with seasonally shifting winds produced by changing atmospheric pressure systems; affects India, South-east Asia, Indonesia, northern Australia, and portions of Africa.

Natural selection: A mechanism of evolution that results in the continuation of only those forms of life best adapted to survive and reproduce in their environment.

Natural system of classification: A method of classifying an organism based on its ancestry or origin.

Nautical mile: The length of 1 minute of latitude, 6076 feet, 1.15 statute mile, or 1.85 kilometres.

Net Primary Productivity: The net photosynthesis (photosynthesis minus respiration) for a given community; considers all growth and all reduction factors that affect the amount of useful chemical energy (biomass) fixed (chemically bound) in an ecosystem.

Niche: The basic function, or occupation, of a life form within a given community; the way an organism obtains its food, air, and water.

Nitrogen dioxide: A reddish brown choking gas produced in high temperature combustion engines; can be damaging to human respiratory tracts and to plants; participates in photochemical reactions and acid deposition.

Nitrogen fixation: One of the functions of soil bacteria and algae is to take gaseous nitrogen from the air and convert it into a chemical form that can be used by plants. This process is known as nitrogen fixation.

Nonextractive resources: Any use of the ocean in place, such as transportation of people and commodities by sea, recreation, or waste disposal.

Nonrenewable resources: Any resource that is present on Earth in fixed amounts and cannot be replenished.

Nonvascular plant: Plant having no obvious vessels for the transport of fluid and lacking leaves, stems, and roots. Examples are algae.

Nor'easter: A large low-pressure system in the atmosphere that travels north along the east coast of the United States. It may result in heavy precipitation and flooding along the coast. In winter, nor'easters produce large amounts of snowfall.

Northern needle-leaf forest: Forests of pine, spruce, fir, and larch, stretching from the east coast of Canada westward to Alaska and continuing from Siberia westward across the entire extent of Russia to the European Plain; called the *taiga* (a Russian word) or the *boreal* forests.

Nuclear winter hypothesis: An increase in Earth's albedo and upper atmospheric absorption of insolation resulting in surface cooling; associated with the detonation of a relatively small number of nuclear warheads within the biosphere. Now encompasses a whole range of ecological, biological, and climatic impacts.

Nutrient cycling: It refers to various cycles that keep the nutrients cycling so as to support life on the earth. Such nutrient cycles include the carbon cycle, the nitrogen cycle, the sulphur cycle, the phosphorus cycle and the hydrogen cycle.

Ocean: The great body of saline water that covers 70.78% of the surface of the Earth. One of its primary subdivisions, bounded by continents, the equator, and other imaginary line.

Oligotrophic: Deficient in nutrient. An ecosystem with very little nutrient level and thus offers very little to sustain life.

Omnivores: A consumer that feeds on both producers (plants) and consumers (meat) – a role occupied by humans, among other animals.

Open system: A system with inputs and outputs crossing back and forth between the system and the surrounding environment. Earth is an open system in terms of energy.

Organic farming: A type of agriculture in which biotic manures are used. There is no application of chemical fertilizers or insecticides and pesticides.

Orographic precipitation: Precipitation that results from the lifting of air over some topographic barrier such as a coastline, hills, or mountains.

Outwash plain: Glaciofluvial deposits of stratified drift from meltwater-fed, braided, and overloaded streams; beyond a glacier's morainal deposits.

Ox-bow lake: A lake that was formerly part of the channel of a meandering stream; isolated when a stream eroded its outer bank forming a cutoff through the neck of a looping meander.

Oxidation: A chemical weathering process whereby oxygen oxidises (combines with) certain metallic elements to form oxides; most familiar as the 'rusting' of iron in a rock or soil that produces a reddish-brown stain of iron-oxide.

Ozone: Oxygen in the triatomic form (O_3); highly corrosive and poisonous.

Ozone layer: See Ozonosphere.

Ozonosphere: A layer of ozone (O_3) occupying the full extent of the Stratosphere (20 to 50 km) above the surface; the region of the atmosphere where ultraviolet wavelengths are principally absorbed and converted into heat.

Paleoclimatology: The science that studies the climates of past ages.

Pangaea: The supercontinent formed by the collision of all continental masses approximately 225 million years ago; named by Wegener (1912) in his continental drift theory.

Pedalfers: Such soils are rich in aluminium and iron. These are formed in regions where evapotranspiration is less than precipitation.

Pedocals: Such soils are rich in calcium. These are formed in regions where evapotranspiration exceeds the precipitation.

Pedology: The scientific study of soils.

Pedon: A soil profile extending from the surface to the lowest extent of plant roots or to the depth where regolith or bedrock is encountered; imagined as a hexagonal column; the basic soil sampling unit.

Periglacial: Cold-climate processes, landforms and topographic features along the margins of glaciers, past and present, that occupy over 20 per cent of Earth's land surface; including permafrost, frost action, and ground ice.

Perihelion: That point in Earth's elliptical orbit about the Sun where Earth is closest to the Sun; occurs on January 3 at 147,255,000 km; variable over a 100,000 year cycle.

Permafrost: Forms when soil or rock temperatures remain below 0°C for at least two years in areas considered periglacial; criterion is based on temperature and not on wheather water is present.

Permeable: The ability of water to flow through soil or rock; a function of texture and structure of the medium.

Photochemical smog: Air pollution produced by the interaction of ultraviolet light, nitrogen dioxide, and hydrocarbons, produces ozone and PAN through a series of complex photochemical reactions. Automobiles are the major source of contributive gases.

Photoperiod: The duration of daylight experienced at a given location.

Photosynthesis: The joining of carbon dioxide and oxygen in plants, under the influence of certain wavelengths of visible light; releases oxygen and produces energy rich organic material (sugars and starches).

Physical Geography: A science that studies the spatial aspects of the physical elements and processes that make up the environment: energy, air, water, weather, climate, landforms, soils, animals, plants, and Earth.

Physical weathering: The breaking and disintegrating of rock without any chemical alteration; sometimes referred to as mechanical or fragmentation weathering.

Phytoplankton: Planktons comprising plants, most of them single-celled algae.

Place: A major theme in geography focused on the tangible and intangible characteristics that make each location unique.

Planimetric map: A basic map showing the horizontal position of boundaries, land-use activities, and political, economic, and social outlines.

Plankton: Small organisms, including the juvenile stages of many larger organisms, that drift near the surface water.

Plant kingdom: It consists of macroflora (trees, shrubs, herbs) and micro flora (bacteria and fungi).

Plate tectonics: The conceptual model that encompasses continental drift, sea-floor spreading, and related aspects of crustal movement; accepted as the foundation of crustal tectonic processes.

Playa: An area of salt crust left behind by evaporation on a desert floor usually in the middle of a bolson or valley; intermittently wet and dry.

Plinthite: An ironstone hardpane structure formed in oxisol subsurfaces or surface horizons that are exposed to repeated wetting and drying sequences; quarried in some areas for building materials.

Pluvial: Pertaining to precipitation; referring to a period in the past, principally during the Pleistocene, when there was greater moisture availability or efficiency; resulted in increased lake levels and seasonally arid regions-*paleolakes*.

Podzols: These soils occur in cool humid areas where the bacterial activity is low.

Podolization: A pedogenic process in cool, moist climates, forms a highly leached soil with strong surface acidity because of humus from acid-rich trees.

Polar front: A significant zone of contrast between cold and warm air masses; roughly situated between 50° and 60° latitude.

Polar high pressure cell: A weak, anticyclonic, thermally produced pressure system positioned roughly above each pole.

Polar stratospheric clouds: Very high, thin clouds that form in the stratosphere, particularly over the Antarctic continent.

Polypedon: The identifiable soil in an area, with distinctive characteristics differentiating it from surrounding polypedons forming the basic soil mapping unit; composed of many pedons.

Population: A group of individuals of the same species occupying the same area.

Population ecology: The branch of ecology dealing with the size, growth and distribution of population of organism.

Porosity: The total volume of available pore spaces in soil; a result of texture and structure of the soil.

Positive feedback: Feedback that amplifies or encourages responses in a system.

Potential evapotranspiration: The amount of moisture that would evaporate and transpire if adequate moisture were available; the amount lost under optimum moisture conditions – the moisture demand (POTET).

Precipitation: Rain, Snow, sleet, and hail – the moisture supply.

Predation: An interaction in which some individuals eats other animals.

Pressure gradient force: Causes air to move from areas of higher barometric pressure to areas of lower barometric pressure due to pressure differences.

Prey: An organism consumed by a predator.

Primary consumer: Initial consumer of primary producer. The consumers of autotrophs; the second level in food webs.

Primary producer: An organism capable of using energy from light or energy-rich chemicals in the environment to produce energy-rich organic compounds, an autotroph.

Primary succession: The process of species colonisation and replacement on sites not occupied previously by any other communities of plants and animals is known as primary succession. Such pioneer sites may include sand-beach, sand-dune, fresh lava-flows, volcanic ash plain etc.

Prime meridian: An arbitrary meridian designated as 0° longitude, the point from which longitude is measured east or west; agreed to in an 1884 treaty.

Producer: Organisms that are capable of using carbon dioxide as their sole source of carbon, which they chemically fix through photosynthesis to provide their own nourishment; also called autotroph.

Protected Forest: An area notified under the supervision of Indian Forest Act or the State Forest Acts having limited degree of protection. In Protected Forests, all activities are permitted unless prohibited.

Pyrophytic: Fire resistant vegetation.

Radiation fog: Formed by radiative cooling of the surface, especially on clear nights in areas of moist ground; occurs when the air layer directly above the surface is chilled to the dew-point temperature, thereby producing saturated conditions.

Rain forest: A forest ecosystem that develops in regions with high rates of precipitation year round. Rain forests consist mainly evergreen vegetation, with trees dominant.

Rain shadow: The area on the leeward slopes of mountain range; in the shadow of the mountains, where precipitation receipt is greatly reduced compared to windward slopes.

Red tide: A red, orange or brown coloration of water caused by a bloom or population explosion of algae; red tides cause serious environmental harm and threaten the health of humans and animals.

Reflection: The portion of arriving energy that returns directly back to space without being converted into heat or performing any work (see albedo).

Reforestation: If the trees are planted on a piece of land which had once been under forest but which had been deforested due to some reason, it is known as reforestation.

Refraction: The bending effect that occurs when insolation enters the atmosphere or another medium; the same process by which crystal, or prism, disperses the component colours of light passing through it.

Region: A geographic theme that focuses on areas that displays unity and internal homogeneity of traits; includes the study of how a region forms, evolves, and interrelates with other regions.

Regolith: Partially weathered rock overlying bedrock, whether residual or transported.

Relative humidity: The ratio of water vapour actually in the air (content) compared to the maximum water vapour the air is able to hold (capacity) by at that temperature; expressed as a percentage.

Relief: Elevation differences in a local landscape; an expression of unevenness, height, and slope variation.

Renewable resources: Any resource that is naturally replaced on a seasonal basis by the growth of living organisms or by other natural processes.

Reserved Forest: An area notified under the provisions of Indian Forest Act or the State Forest Acts having full degree of protection. In reserved forests, all activities are prohibited unless permitted.

Respiration: The process by which plants derive energy for their operations; essentially, the reverse of the photosynthesis process; releases carbon dioxide, water, and heat into the environment.

Revolution: The annual orbital movement of the Earth about the Sun; determines year length and the length of seasons.

Richter scale: An open ended, logarithmic scale that estimates earthquake magnitude; designed by Charles Richter in 1935.

Rock: An assemblage of minerals bound together (like granite), or may be a mass of single mineral (like rock salt).

Rock cycle: A model representing the interrelationships among the three rock-forming processes: igneous, sedimentary and metamorphic.

Rockfall: Free-falling movement of debris from a cliff or steep slope, generally falling straight down or bounding downslope.

Rossby waves: Undulating horizontal motions in the upper-air westerly circulation at middle and high altitudes.

Rotation: The turning of Earth on its axis' averages 24 hours in duration; determines day–night relationship.

Run-off: The combination of surface runoff and interflow.

'S' wave: Secondary wave. A transverse wave associated with an earthquake and which cannot move through liquid.

Salinity: The concentration of natural elements and compounds dissolved in solution, as solutes, measured by weight in parts per thousand (o/oo) in seawater.

Salinisation: A pedogenic regime that results from high potential evapotranspiration rates in deserts and semi-desert regions. Soil water is drawn to surface horizons, and dissolved salts are deposited as the water evaporates.

Salt marsh: Wetland ecosystems characteristic of latitudes poleward of the 30th parallel.

Sand drift: The movement of sand over an area of dunes in a desert. Sand drift is due to the heating of the sand by the Sun and is primarily a daytime phenomenon. The sand moves along the surface and is responsible for a large part of the movement of the dunes.

Sand sea: An extensive area of sand and dunes; characteristic of Earth's *erg deserts*.

Savannah: A type of tropical or subtropical grassland, savannah are common in Central Africa.

Scattering: Deflection and redirection of insolation by atmospheric gases, dust, ice, and water vapour; the shorter the wavelength, the greater the scattering.

Sea: Simultaneous wind waves of many wavelengths forming a chaotic ocean surface. Sea is common in an area of wind wave origin.

Sea floor spreading: As proposed by Hess and Dietz, the mechanism driving the movement of the continents; associated with upwelling flows of magma along the worldwide system of mid-ocean ridges.

Seagrass: Any of several marine angiosperms. Examples are Zostera (eelgrass) and phyllospadix (surfgrass). Sea grasses are not seaweeds.

Seaweed: Informal term for large marine multicellular algae.

Secondary consumer: Consumer of primary consumers.

Secondary succession: Ecological succession after a disturbance that did not eliminate all the organisms originally living in the site.

Seismic waves: The shock waves sent through the planet by an earthquake or underground nuclear test. Transmission varies according to temperature and the density of various layers within the planet.

Seismograph: A device that measures seismic waves of energy transmitted throughout Earth's interior.

Sere: The succession of distinct plant communities that follow one another and lead from the community of primary colonisers to the climax community.

Sewage: Mainly liquid waste containing some solids produced by humans. For example, faeces, urine, laundry waste and other garbage materials which go down drains and toilets from households and industries.

Sheet flow: Water that moves down-slope in a thin film as overland flow, not concentrated in channels larger than rills.

Sheeting: A form of weathering associated with fracturing or fragmentation of rock by pressure release; often related to exfoliation processes.

Shield volcano: A symmetrical mountain landform effusive eruptions; gently sloped, gradually rising from the surrounding landscape to a summit crater; typical of the Hawaiian Islands.

Silent valley: It is a unique valley of tropical biodiversity in W. Ghats, Kerala (South India). This valley was declared a National Park in 1984. The proposed hydel project at silent valley was stopped. This was achieved by several dedicated individuals, groups and organisations lobbying to save the area from being submerged under water with the set objective to protect its rich biodiversity.

Slopes: Curved, inclined surfaces that bound landforms.

Soil: The dynamic natural body made up of fine materials covering Earth's surface in which plants grow; composed of both mineral and organic matter.

Soil creep: A persistent mass movement of surface soil where individual soil particles are lifted and disturbed by the expansion of soil moisture as it freezes, or even by grazing livestock or digging animals.

Soil fertility: The ability of soil to support plant productivity when it contains organic substances and clay minerals that absorb water and certain elemental ions needed by plants.

Soil horizon: The various layers exposed in a pedon; roughly parallel to the surface and identified as O, A, E, B, and C.

Soil taxonomy: A soil classification system based on observable soil properties actually seen in the field; published in 1975 by the U.S. Soil Conservation Service.

Solar constant: The amount of insolation intercepted by Earth on a surface perpendicular to the Sun's rays when Earth is at its average distance from the Sun; a value of 1370 watts per m^2; averaged over the entire globe at the thermopause; or 1.98 calories per cm^2 per minute.

Solar energy: Energy derived from the Sun.

Solar wind: Clouds of ionised (charged) gases emitted by the Sun and travelling in all directions from the Sun's surface. Effects on Earth include auroras, disturbance of radio signals, and possible influences on weather.

Solifluction: Gentle down-slope movement of a saturated surface material (soil and regolith), in various climatic regimes, where temperatures are above freezing.

Solum: A true soil profile in the pedon, ideally, a combination of A and B horizons.

Solution: The dissolved load of a stream.

Specific humidity: The mass of water vapour (in grams) per unit mass of air (in kilograms) at any specified temperature. The maximum mass of water vapour that a kilogram of air can hold at any specified temperature is termed its maximum specific humidity.

Species: Any group of actually or potentially interbreeding organisms reproductivity isolated from all other groups and capable of producing fertile offspring. The word species is both singular and plural.

Species diversity: The number of species present in a particular area or community.

Speed of light: Specifically, 299,792 km per second (186,282 mile per second), covering more than 9.4 trillion km per hour – a distance known as a light year.

Stability: A condition of a parcel, whether it remains where it is or changes its initial position. The parcel is stable if it resists displacement upwards, unstable if it continues to rise.

Stomata: Small openings on the underside of leaves, through which water and gases pass.

Storm surge: Large quantities of sea water pushed inland by the strong winds associated with a tropical cyclone.

Stratosphere: That portion of the homosphere that ranges from 20 to 50 km above Earth's surface; temperature ranges from –57°C at the tropopause to 0°C at the stratopause. The functional ozonosphere is within the stratosphere.

Stratus: A stratiform (flat, horizontal) cloud generally below 2000 m.

Subduction zone: An area where two plates of crust colloid and the denser oceanic crust dives beneath the less dense continental plate, forming deep oceanic trenches and seismically active regions.

Sublimation: A process in which ice evaporates directly to water vapour or water vapour freezes to ice (deposition).

Subtropical high pressure cell: Dynamic high pressure areas covering roughly the region from 20° to 35° N and S latitudes; responsible for the hot, dry areas of Earth's arid and semi-arid deserts.

Succession: The changes in species composition that lead to a climax community.

Sulphur dioxide: A colourless gas detected by its pungent odour; produced by the combustion of fossil fuels that contain sulphur as an impurity; can react in the atmosphere to form sulphuric acid, a component of acid deposition.

Summer (June) solstice: The time when the Sun's declination is at the Tropic of Cancer, at 23.5° N latitude; June 20–21 each year.

Sunspots: Magnetic disturbances on the surface of the Sun; occurring on an average 11 year cycle; related flares, prominences, and outbreaks produce surges in solar wind.

Surface creep: A form of eolian transport that involves particles too large for saltation; a process whereby individual grains are impacted by moving grains and slide and roll.

Surplus: The amount of moisture that exceeds potential evapotranspiration; moisture oversupply when soil moisture storage is at field capacity.

Suspended load: Fine particles held in suspension in a stream. The finest particles are not deposited until the stream velocity near zero.

Sustainable development: The development that meets the needs of the present generation without compromising the ability of future generations to meet their own needs.

Swamp: A wetland that features temporary or permanent inundation of large areas of land by shallow bodies of water and covered by aquatic vegetation.

Swell: Regular patterns of smooth, rounded waves in open water; can range from small ripples to very large waves.

Symbiont: An organism that lives in symbiotic association with another.

Symbiosis: A situation in which two organisms of different species live together and are closely associated. The term generally implies some benefit to both, but is sometimes used to include parasitism.

Synecology: It is the study of plant communities in relation to their habitats of a given ecosystem.

System: Any ordered, interrelated set of materials or items existing separate from the environment, or within a boundary; energy transformations and energy and matter storage and retrieved occur within a system.

Taiga: See northern needleleaf forest.

Temperate rain forest: A major biome of lush forests at middle and high latitudes; occurs along narrow margins of the Pacific Northwest in North America, among other locations; includes the tallest trees (Duglus-fir) in the world.

Temperature inversion: A reversal of the normal decrease of temperature with increasing altitude; can occur anywhere from ground up to several thousand metres.

Tephra: Pulverised rock and clastic materials ejected violently during a volcanic eruption – all pyroclastics from a volcano.

Terrestrial ecosystem: A self regulating association characterised by specific plant formations; usually named for the predominant vegetation and known as a biome when large and stable.

Thermal equator: A line on an isothermal map that connects all points of highest mean temperature.

Thermopause: A zone approximately 480 km in altitude that serves conceptually as the top of the atmosphere; an altitude used for the determination of the solar constant.

Thermosphere: A region of the heterosphere extending 80 to 480 km in altitude; contains the functional ionosphere layer.

Thunder: A violent expansion of suddenly heated air, created by lightning discharges, sending out shock waves as an audible sonic bang.

Tidal energy: Energy derived from the movement of the tides.

Tide: Patterns of daily oscillation in sea level produced by astronomical relationships among the Sun, the Moon, and the Earth; experienced in varying degrees around the world.

Till: Direct ice deposits that appear unstratified and unsorted; a specific form of glacial drift.

Top consumer: An organism at the apex of a tropic pyramid, usually a carnivore.

Topographic map: A map that portrays physical relief through the use of elevation contour lines that connect all points at the same elevation above or below a vertical datum, such as mean sea-level.

Topography: The undulations and configurations that give Earth's surface its texture; the heights and depths of local relief including both natural and human made features.

Tornado: An intense, destructive cyclonic rotation, developed in response to extremely low pressure; associated with mesocyclone formation.

Total runoff: Surplus water that flows across a surface toward stream channels; formed by sheet flow, combined with precipitation and subsurface flows into those channels.

Trade wind: Northeast and southeast winds that converge in the equatorial low pressure trough, forming the inter-tropical convergence zone.

Transpiration: The movement, as water vapour, out through the pores in leaves of water drawn by plant roots from the soil moisture storage.

Trophic pyramid: If the numbers at each trophic level are represented by horizontal bars (as in the age-pyramids), the numers taper off rapidly giving it a shape of a pyramid known as trophic pyramid.

Tropical cyclone: A cyclonic circulation originating in the tropics, with winds between 30 and 64 knots (39 to 73 mph); characterised by closed isobars, circular organisation, and heavy rains (see hurricanes and typhoon).

Tropical savanna: A major biome containing large expanses of grassland interrupted by trees and shrubs; a transitional area between the humid rain forests and tropical seasonal forests and the drier, semi-arid tropical steppes and deserts.

Tropical seasonal forest and scrub: A variable biome on the margin of the rain forests, occupying regions of lesser and more erratic rainfall; the site of transitional communities between the rain forests and tropical grasslands.

Tropic of Cancer: The northernmost point of the Sun's declination during the year; 23.5° N latitude.

Tropic of Capricorn: The southernmost point of the Sun's declination during the year; 23.5° S latitude.

Troposphere: The home of biosphere, the lowest layer of the homosphere, containing approximately 90% of the total mass of the atmosphere, extends up to the tropopause, defined by the temperature of –57°; occurring at an altitude of 18 km at the equator, 13 km in the middle latitudes, and at lower altitudes near the poles.

Tsunami: A seismic sea wave, travelling at high speeds across the ocean, formed by sudden and sharp motions in the seafloor, such as sea-floor earthquakes, submarine landslides, or eruptions from undersea volcanoes.

Tundra: A treeless plains of the Arctic, a climatic region exhibiting tundra vegetation.

Typhoon: A tropical cyclone in excess of 65 knots (74 mph) that occurs in the western Pacific.

Unclassed Forest: An area recorded as forest but not included in reserved or protected forest category. Ownership status of such forests varies from state to state.

Upwelling current: Ocean currents that cause surface waters to be swept away from the coast by surface divergence or offshore winds. Cool, deep waters, which are generally nutrient rich, rise to replace the vacating water.

Urban heat island: Urban microclimates, which are warmer on the average than areas surrounding countryside because of various surface characteristics.

Valley fog: The settling of cooler, more dense air in lowlying areas, produces saturated conditions and fog.

Valley glacier: A type of alpine, or mountain, glacier within the confines of a valley; can range from 100 m to 100 km in length.

Vascular plant: Plant having vessels for transport of fluid through leaves, stems, and roots. Examples are sea-grasses, mangroves, and maple trees.

Vernal (March) equinox: The time when the Sun's declination crosses the equatorial parallel and all places on Earth experience days and nights of equal length; around March 20–21 each year. The Sun rises at the North Pole and sets at the South Pole.

Virga: A thin veil of rain seen hanging from a thunderstorm, but not reaching to the ground. The droplets are evaporated before they reach the ground.

Volcano: A landform at the end of a conduit or pipe which rises from below the crust and vents to the surface. Magma rises and collects in magma chamber deep below, resulting in eruptions that are effusive or explosive forming the mountain landform.

Vulnerable species: A species which is likely to become endangered unless the circumstances threatening its survival and reproduction improve.

Walker circulation: The atmospheric circulation over the southern Pacific ocean. The Walker circulation follows the general model of the Hadley cell, with westward drift of the trade winds along the surface near the equator and counter-flow aloft.

Watershed: The catchment area of a drainage basin; delimited by divides.

Waterspout: An elongated, funnel-shaped circulation formed when a tornado takes place over water.

Water table: The upper limit of ground water; that contact point between zones of saturation and aeration in an unconfined aquifer.

Wave cyclone: An organised area of low pressure, with converging and ascending air flow producing an interaction of air masses; migrates along some tracks. Such lows of depressions form the dominant weather pattern in the middle and higher latitudes of both hemispheres.

Weather: The short-term condition of the atmosphere, as compared to climate, which reflects long-term atmospheric conditions and extremes. Temperature, air pressure, relative humidity, wind speed and direction, and Sun angle are important measurable elements that contribute to the weather.

Weathering: The related processes by which surface and subsurface rock disintegrate, or dissolve, or are otherwise broken down. Rocks at or near Earth's surface are exposed to physical, organic, and chemical weathering processes.

Westerlies: The predominant wind flow pattern from the subtropics to high latitudes in both hemispheres.

Western intensification: The piling up of ocean water along the western margin of each ocean basin, to a height of about 15 cm produced by trade winds that drive the oceans westward in a concentrated channel.

Wetland: Wetlands are the areas where during a large part of the year, water stands at 2.5 cm to around 300 cm. Wetlands include swamps, bogs, fresh-water lakes and marshes, estuaries and deltas, salt marshes, mangroves, rivers and streams, rice-fields, fish ponds, reservoirs, etc.

Wilting point: That point in the soil moisture balance when only hygroscopic water and some bound capillary water remains. Plants wilt and eventually die after prolonged stress from long lack of available water.

Wind: The horizontal movement of air relative to Earth's surface; produced essentially by air pressure differences from place to place; also influenced by the coriolis force and surface friction.

Wind chill factor: An indication of the enhanced rate at which body heat is lost to the air. As wind speed increases, heat loss from the skin also increases.

Xerophytes: are adopted to drought conditions, ephemerals shorten their life cycle, holophytes are plants growing in saline condition. Even desert animals avoid hottest and driest season by becoming in-active. This process is known as *aestivating*.

Xerosere: A sere (ecological succession) that begins in arid conditions.

Zenith: A point in space directly above a person's head; a point on a line passing through the zenith.

Zonal soils: On the basis of climate soils are classified into seven types of zonal soils namely Tundra soils, Podozol (soils of cool and humid regions), Brown Forest Soils (occur in milder climate), Lateritic Soils (Soils of tropical and sub-tropical areas), Chernozen Prairie Soils (occur in grasslands of moderate rainfall, and desert soils.

Zone of aeration: A groundwater zone above the water table, which may or may not hold water in pore spaces.

Zone of saturation: A groundwater zone below the water table, in which all pores spaces are filled with water.

Zoogeography: The science of the distribution of animals, linking the subject matter of the discipline of zoology with the viewpoint of geography.

Zooplankton: Animal members of the plankton community.

References

Agarwal, S.K. 2005. *Environmental Management*, APH, Pub. Co. New Delhi.

Alexander, D.E., 2000, *Confronting Catastrophe*, *New Perspective on Natural Disasters*, Terra, Harpenden.

Alexander, J.W. and T.A. Hartshorn,2002, *Economic Geography*, 3rd ed., Prentice Hall of India.

Allaby, M. 2002. *Basics of Environmental Science*, Routledge, London.

Allbay, M., 1988, *Basics of Environmental Science*, 2nd ed. London, Routledge.

Barrow, C.J., 1999, *Environmental Management: Principles and Practice*, Routledge, London.

Barrow, C.J., 2005, *Environmental Management and Development*, London, Routledge.

Basak, A.,2009, *Environmental Studies*, Delhi, Pearson.

Bennett, H.H., 1938, *Soil Conservation*, New York, McGraw-Hill.

Bennett, J.W., 1976, *The Ecological Transition, Cultural Anthropology and Human Adaptation*, Oxford, Pergamon.

Bennett, K.D., 1997, *Evolution and Ecology: the Pace of Life*, Cambridge, Cambridge University Press.

Bharucha, E., 2003, *Biodiversity in India*, the Mapin Publishing.

Bharucha, E., 2011, *Textbook of Environmental Studies*, New Delhi, UGC-Universities Press.

Bhattacharaya, P. and Ajitava Chaudhuri Roy,, (ed.), 2000, *Globalisation and India : A Multidimensional Perspective*, New Delhi, Lancers Books.

Brawdshaw, M.J., 1979, *Earth, the Living Planet, ELBS*, Hodder and Stoughton.

Brewer, R., 1979, *Principles of Ecology*, Philadelphia and London.

Brundtland, H., 1987, *Our Common Future,* (Report), World Commission Environment and Development, Oxford, Oxford University Press.

Bryant, R.H., 1976, *Physical Geography*, New Delhi, Rupa Co.

Bryant, Richard, H., 2002, *Physical Geography*: *Make Simple Books*, Rupa Co.

Callenbach, E., 1999, *A Pocket Guide*, University Press.

Canter, L. W., 1996, *Environmental Impact Assessment*, MacGraw Hill, Inc.

Chadha, K.L. 2012, *Handbook of Horticulture*, Indian Council of Agricultural Research.

Chandna, R.C., 2002, *Environmental Geography*, Ludhiana, Kalyani Publishers.

Chatterjee, B.N. and S.K.De Datta, 1984, *Cropping System-Theory and Practice*, New Delhi, Oxford University Press and I.B.H. Pub. Co.

Choeley, R.J., ed., 1969, *Water, Earth and Man: A Synthesis of Hydrology, Geomorphology and Socio-Economic Geography*, London, Methuen.

Christopherson, R.W., 1995, *Elemental Geosystem: A Foundation in Physical Geography*, Englewood Cliffs, New Jersey, Prentice Hall.

Crutzen, P.J., and M.O. Andreae, 1990, Biomass Burning in the Tropics: Impact on Atmospheric Chemistry and Biogeochemical Cycles, *Science* 250.

Cuningham, W.P. and Cooper, T.H., 2001, *Environmental Encyclopedia*, Jaico Publishing House.

Dandekar, V.M. and Nilkantha Rath, 1971, Poverty in India, EPW, Bombay, p.17.

Darlington, P.J., 1957, *Zoogeography*, New York, John Wiley.

Detwyler, T.R., 1971, *Man's Impact on Environment*, New York, McGraw Hills.

Dhar, P.K., 2013, *Indian Economy: Its Growing Dimensions*, New Delhi, Kalyani Publishers.

Dhar, P.K., *Indian Economy: Its Growing Dimensions*, 2013, New Delhi, Kalyani Publishers, In brief, it is the borderless world. p.749.

Dwyer, E., J.M. Gregoire, and J.P. Malingreau, 1998, A global Analysis of Vegetation Fires using Satellite Images: Spatial and Temporal Dynamics. *Ambio 27*, pp.175–181.

Ehrenfeld, D.W. 1970, *Biological Conservation*, Hold, Rinehart and Winston, New York.

Ehrlich, P., and Ehrlich, M. 1970, *Population, Resources, Environment*, San Francisco, Freeman.

Francis, P.W., 1976, *Volcanoes*, Harmondsworth: Penguin.

Garrison, T., 1994, *Essentials of Oceanography*, London, Wadsworth Publishing Company.

Golley, F.B., Lieth, H. and Werger, M.J.A. eds. 1982: *Tropical Rain Forest Ecosystems*, Amsterdam, Elsevier.

Goudie, A.S., 1993, *The Human Impact on Environment*, Oxford, Blackwell.

Gould, P. and White, R., 1974, *Mental Maps*, London, Penguin.

Gubbi, S., 2003, *Fire, Fire Burning Bright! Deccan Herald*, Bangalore India, available from http:/ wildlifefirst.info/images/worldfiles/fire.doc. (accessed January, 2004).

Guilcher, A., 1988, *Coral Reef Geomorphology*, Chichester: Wiley.

Hare, W.L. et al., 1990, *Ecologically Sustainable Development*, Australian Conservation Foundation, Fitzory, Victoria.

Hawkins, R.E., 1989, *Encylopadia of Indian Natural History*, Oxford University Press.

Hazel, Henderson, 1999, *Beyond Globalisation: Shaping A Sustainable Global Economy*, West Hartford.

Heyward, V., 1995, *Global Biodiversity Assessment*, Cambridge. Cambridge University Press.

Holdgate, M.W., 1979, *A Perspective of Environmental Pollution*, Cambridge, Cambridge University Press.

Houghton, J.T., Meira Filho, L.G., Callander, B.A., Harris, N., Kattenberg, A., and Maskell, K., 1996, *Climate Change1945*, *The Science of Climate Change*, Cambridge: Cambridge University Press.

Hudson, N., 1971, *Soil Conservation*, London, Batsford.

Husain, M. 2013, *Geography of India,* 5th ed. New Delhi, Tata McGraw Hill.

Husain, M., 2009, *Fundamentals of Physical Geography*, Jaipur, Rawat Publications.

Husain, M., 2011, *Human Geography*, Jaipur, Rawat Publications.

Husain, M., 2012, *Geography – Terms and Concepts*, Delhi, Tata McGraw Hill's Series.

Husain, M., 2012, *Models in Geography*, Jaipur, Rawat Publications.

Husain, M., 2014, Indian and World Geography, 2nd ed. McGraw-Hill.

ICAR, 2012, *Handbook of Agriculture*, 6th ed. published by the Directorate of Knowledge Management in Agriculture, Indian Council of Agricultural Research, New Delhi 110012.

Issacs, J.D., 'The Nature of Oceanic Life', *Scientific American*, 221, 1969, pp.147–162.

Johstons, R.J. et al., 1995, *The Dictionary of Human Geography,* 3rd edition, Oxford, Blackwell.

Joshi, P.C., *Land Reforms Implementation and Role of Administrator,* EPW, September

Kakde, J.R., 1985, *Agricultural Climatology*, New Delhi, Metropolitan Book.

Katyayan, A.,2012, *Ecology and Environment-Plant Physiology*, Plant Pathology, Varanasi, Kushal Publications and Distributors.

Katyayan,A., 2012,*Kaushal Publications and Distributors*, Varanasi.

Kemp, D.D., 1990, *Global Environmental Issues: A Climatological Approach*, London, Routledge.

Khor, Martin, 2001, *Rethinking Globalisation: Critical Issues and Policies*, Banglore, Books for Change.

Khullar, D.R., 2005, India: *Comprehensive Geography*, New Delhi, Kalyani Publishers.

Khusro, A.M., *Economies of Land Reforms and Farm Size in India*, 1973, p. xiii

Kidwai, Z., 2002, *Environmental Education*, New Delhi, Institute of Advanced Studies, Jamia Millia Islamia.

Mahajan, P., *Contemporary Geography and Environment,* Jammu, Knowracle Publications.

Mallanby, K., 1972, *The Biology of Pollution*, London, Edward Arnold.

Mather, J.R., 1974, *Climatology-Fundamentals and Application*, New York, McGraw Hill Book Co.

Mayhew, S., 1997, *Oxford Dictionary of Geography*, Indian edition, Oxford University Press.

Milani, B., *Designing the Green Economy*, 2000, Rowman & Littlefield.

Miller, T.G. (Jr), 1997, *Environmental Science*, Wadsworth Publishing. 30, 1948, p.A.82.

Morgan, G.C. and G.C., Leong, 1982, *Human and Economic Geography*, Oxford University Press.

Naik, S.C. and T.N. Tiwari, 2005, *Society and Environment*, New Delhi, Oxford & IBH Publishing Co. Pvt. Ltd.

Newson, M., 1992, The Geography of Pollution, in M. Newson, ed., *Managing the Human Impact on the Natural Environment: Patterns and Processes*, London, and New York, Belhaven Press, pp. 14–36.

Odum, E.P., 1969, *Principles of Ecology*, London, Croom Helm.

Odum, E.P., 1971, *Fundamentals of Ecology*, Philadelphia, W.B. Saunders.

Oliver, J.E. and J.J. Hidore, 2002, *Climatology – An Atmospheric Science*, 2nd ed. Delhi, Pearson Education.

Ollier, C.D., 1988, *Volcanoes*, Oxford, Blackwell.

Park, C.C., 1980, *Ecology and Environmental Management*, London, Butterworths.

Pearce, F., 1987, *Acid Rain*, New York, Penguin Book.

Planning Commission and *Economic Survey*, 2011-p.310.

Pugh, D.T., 1987, *Tides, Surges and Mean Sea Level*, Chichester, Wiley.

Rajaram, K., 2009, *Geography*, Spectrum Books Pvt. Ltd.

Ramadas, L.A. 1964, *Crop and Weather in India*, ICAR, New Delhi.

Reddy, G.H.S. and T.Y. Reddy,1992, *Principles of Agronomy*, Kalyani Publishers.Sen, A., 1977, '*Poverty and Economic Development*' in Charan D. Wadhva (ed.) Some Problems of India's Economic Policy, New Delhi, pp.246-247.

Savage, J.M., 1971, *Evolution*, London, Holt, Reinhart and Winston.

Saxena, H.M., 2010, *Environmental Geography*, 2nd ed. Jaipur, Rawat Publications.

Seddon, B., 1971, *Introduction to Biogeography*, London, Duckworth.

Sen, A, and Dreze, J., 1989, *Hunger and Public Action*, Oxford: Clarendon Press.

Sen, A.,1981, *Poverty and Famine*, Oxford: Clarendon Press.

Sen, A.K., and A. Rudra, 1982, *Indian Agricultural Economics*, New Delhi.

Shankar IAS Academy, 2014, Environment, Chennai.

Simmons, I.G. 1974, The Ecology of Natural Resources, London, Edward Arnold.

Singh, Satvinder, 1991, *Environmental Geography*, Allahabad, Prayag Pustak Bhandar.

Smith, K., 1992, *Environmental Hazards*, London, Routledge.

Stoddart, D.R., 1990: 'Coral Reefs and Islands and Predicted Sea-level Rise' *Progress in Physical Geography*, 14, pp. 521–36.

Strahler, A. and A. Strahler,1996, *Physical Geography: Science and Systems of the Human Environment*, New York, John Wiley & Sons, Inc.

Strahler, A., and A. Strahler,1997, *Physical Geography*, New York, John Wiley & Sons, Inc.

Tansley, A.G., 1946, *Introduction to Plant Ecology, London*, Allen & Unwin.

Tarachand, et al., 2013, *General Science*, Tata McGraw-Hill.

The World Guide: Global Reference Country by Country, 2007, 11th edition, Oxford, New Internationalist Publications Ltd.

Thomas, D.S.G. and A. Goudie, 2004, *Physical Geography*, Balckwell Publishing.

Thomas, D.S.G. and Middleton, N.J., 1994, *Desertification : Exploding the Myth*, Chichester, Wiley.

Tivy, J., 1982, *Biogeography*, Harlow, Longman.

Tomlinson, P.B., 1986, *The Botany of Mangroves*, Cambridge, Cambridge University Press.

UNDP, 2012, *Human Development Report India*, Oxford University Press, New Delhi.

UNESCO, 1981, MAB Information System: Biosphere Reserves< Compilation No. 2, p.313.

United Nations, 1993, *Earth Summit, Agenda 21, The United Nations Programme for Action from Rio*, United Nations Publication, E.931.11.

UNO, *World Resources*, 1988–89, New York.

Vyas, A.K., *Introduction to Agriculture*, 5th ed. New Delhi, Jain Brothers.

Walter, H., 1979, *Vegetation of the`Earth*, 2nd edn. Berlin: Springer-Verlag.

Ward, R.C., 1978, *Floods: A Geographical Perspective*, London, Macmillan.

Watts, M., 1983, *Silent Violence : Food, Famine and Peasantry in Northern Nigeria*, Berkeley, CA: University of California Press.

Wheeler J. O. and Peter O., Muller, 1986, *Economic Geography*, 2nd ed. New York, Wiley.

Yegnanarayana Aiyer, A.K.1975, *Principles of Crop Husbandry in India*, 5th ed. Banglore, The Banglore Printing and Publishing Company.

White, J., 1974, *Natural Hazards*, London, Oxford University Press.

Wilson, E.O. ed. 1988, *Biodiversity*, Washington, D.C., National Academy Press.

Wislon, J.T. ed. 1976, '*Continents Drift and Continents Aground*'San Francisco, W.H. Freeman.

Zaruba, Q. and Mench, V. 1069; *Landslides and their Control*, Prague: Academic and Elsevier.